LETTERS OF
HENRY ADAMS
1858–1891

Henry Adams

From a sketch made by Samuel Laurence, 1868,
in the possession of Mr. Evelyn Milnes Gaskell

LETTERS OF HENRY ADAMS

(1858–1891)

EDITED BY

WORTHINGTON CHAUNCEY FORD

BOSTON AND NEW YORK

HOUGHTON MIFFLIN COMPANY

1930

The Riverside Press
CAMBRIDGE · MASSACHUSETTS
PRINTED IN THE U.S.A.

NOTE

HENRY ADAMS gave his version of his career in a volume which is, in form and matter, unique in American literature. "The Education of Henry Adams" is as remarkable for its reticences as for its frank admissions — confessions, he would have called them. Measuring his capacity by his own standards, in which inheritance formed an important factor; outlining a part of his ambitions in the more modest form of aims or purpose of life; estimating his performance in terms of "failure"; and seeking to discover a law which could explain, if not control, social growth and tendencies, he gave a review of the period in which he lived that was as brilliant as it was partial. Above all, he was unjust to himself. No one familiar with his writings in history would apply the word "failure." No one of the students falling under his teaching in his short service as professor in Harvard University would deny the influence he exerted upon them. Familiarity with the political history of the United States since 1865 only emphasizes the fact that his aims were of the highest and that he and his fellow independents in politics were unable to effect their ends because of the irresistible tendencies, economic, political, and social, against their proposed reforms. He possessed the political instincts of his Adams forebears, a leaning towards public life; but like them, his views were not of party but were national, involving a radical change in party methods, in the hope of bringing into the public service moral standards which no party was then willing to accept or capable of applying. The "failure" in his ambitions was laid upon him by circumstances, and it turned his endeavors from a public career to the writing of history. Even that "failure" brought its greater compensation.

Because of the partial narrative of "The Education of Henry Adams" I gathered such letters as I could locate and I give a selection in this volume, covering the years of promise, growth, and fruition. Beginning with his studies in Germany, after graduating from Harvard University, the series closes with the publication of the last volume of his "History of the United States, 1801-1816." The letters speak for themselves and require no comment. They tell the story, still in his own terms, of a youth of exceptional ability, inherited and acquired, who passed through the inevitable years of early hopes and wishes, disappointed ambition, and domestic tragedies more or less common to all. Disillusioned in many directions, he enjoyed life and savored its best. If these letters result in making Henry Adams better and more humanly known than he can be from the detached examination of himself in the "Education," my purpose will be accomplished. The indiscretions are wholly the Editor's. Frank comment on men and things only carries on the tradition of the Adams family, and to suppress or correct that frankness would deprive the letters of their chief value, both as records of the man and as history.

About 1885 Henry Adams destroyed all his diaries, notes, and correspondence. He also recalled, from time to time, his letters from his correspondents and destroyed them. The impulse leading to that act is easily understood, however much the loss of record may be deplored. It is fortunate that what escaped his attention tells so connected a story.

To the Adams family I owe the greatest debt, and especially to Mrs. Charles Francis Adams, of South Lincoln, who permitted the free use of the letters to Mr. Charles Francis Adams.

The family of Mr. Charles Milnes Gaskell readily acceded to my request for the letters to that almost life-long friend of Mr. Adams.

The late Senator Henry Cabot Lodge not only gave me such letters as he had, but added notes explaining references in the text.

Mrs. J. Don Cameron (Elizabeth Sherman Cameron) generously contributed the remarkable series of letters in this volume under her name.

The family of Hon. Carl Schurz, through the friendly intervention of Mr. Frederic Bancroft, supplied copies of interesting political letters.

To these and to others unnamed I express my thanks.

WORTHINGTON CHAUNCEY FORD

PARIS, *February* 16, 1930

CONTENTS

THE LETTERS OF
HENRY ADAMS

I
GERMANY
1858–1860

To Charles Francis Adams, Jr.

BERLIN, Wednesday, November 3, 1858.

MY DEAR FELLOW: — With that energy of expression and originality of thought for which you are so justly celebrated, you have remarked in your last that the pleasures and pains of life are pretty equally divided. Permit me in the particular instance before us to doubt the fact. In the long run it may be so, but as between you in Boston and me in Europe I deny it in toto and without hesitation.

I humbly apologize to you for the remarks in my last letter, which were written under the supposition that you had forgotten me. Your letter was satisfaction itself. I already knew the main points, but I can ask nothing more complete than your particulars. As to the nomination I am delighted with the manner of it.[1] The election took place yesterday and a fortnight from to-day I shall certainly know all about it, if not from you at any rate from Governor Wright[2] at the American Legation.

Here I am, then, in Berlin. It is now night; I am writing in my room, which is about ten or twelve by eighteen or twenty feet; by the light of a lamp for which I paid yesterday two dollars; independent; unknown and unknowing; hating the language and yet grubbing into it. I have passed the day since one o'clock with Loo,[3] who is now here and remains till Friday, and with whom I go about to Galleries and Museums, and then dine at her hotel. As you say, I am not rich and

[1] Of Charles Francis Adams to Congress.
[2] Joseph Albert Wright, of Indiana (1810–1867).
[3] Louisa Catherine Adams (1831–1870), married Charles Kuhn.

am trying to institute a rigid economy in all my expenses. There is one advantage in this place; if forced to it, one can live for almost nothing. Today I was extravagant. I ordered a quantity of clothes; an inside suit and an overcoat of expensive stuffs. The overcoat is a peculiar beaver-cloth, a sort of velvety stuff; and its inside is thick fur, like sealskin, I suppose; so thick that I can't have it lined. The suit is very strong, fine cloth, as good, I fancy, as the man had. But then I had to pay dear. Altogether it cost me fifty-one American dollars. Now in Boston perhaps this is not so much, but here it is a great deal.

Then this frightful German! I have had the most amusing times with my landlady who's a jolly Dutch woman and who has a power of clack that is marvellous. If I have her called in and she once gets agoing I can no more hope to make her understand what I want than if she talked Hebrew. So I have recourse to my Dutch teacher, whom I pay very high even for America, and get him to mediate between us and look over my bills and see that I am not cheated. He comes every morning at ten and I read and talk with him and he corrects my exercises.

What shall I say of this city? Why, Lord bless my soul, I have got things enough to see and study in this city alone to take me two years even if I knew the language and only came for pleasure. The Museums, picture Galleries, Theatres, Gardens; there are enough to occupy one's time for the next six months. Then do the same with the half-million or so engravings. Lord! Such engravings!

The truth is, in the soberest earnest, I am quite as pleasantly situated as I ever expected to be. Sometimes, of course, I feel a little lonely and shall feel more so, I suppose, when Loo goes away and I have no one to think of as near me. Sometimes too I get angry at the excessive difficulty of this very repulsive language, and wearied to death at the continual and fatiguing learning by rote which is necessary for almost every phrase. But on the whole, life here is exceedingly pleasant; there is no relaxation from continual occupation; no excuse for the blues, which always with me come from ennui. Here one is surrounded by art, and I defy any one but a fool to feel ennuyéed while he can look at the works of these old masters.

Here you have my life then. It will be for the next two months a continual dig at the language varied occasionally by a moment or so of Art. The evenings at the Theatres, concerts or balls, perhaps, such as they have here, queer affairs, I imagine, and the day in hard study.

(*Saturday eve*. Nov. 6.) I resume my letter where it was broken off, and hope to send it tomorrow. I have just left Loo, who is still here but expects to go to Dresden tomorrow night. She is suffering tonight under one of her fearful headaches, or I should be with her. She has been very kind to me indeed; very kind; we have been together all the time, going from Gallery to Gallery, and I have almost been living at her expense these two days, for she would not allow me to pay for my own dinners. I sat with her till ten o'clock last night, and have passed all the afternoons with her (that is, from eleven till six) every day. In consequence I have had to sit up till twelve o'clock to write my exercises.

I have received my clothes, and on the whole they are the best I ever wore. The great coat is a miracle. I look in it like a veteran. German cloth is, if anything, even better than English. However, they ought to be good. They cost enough.

My friends here are all right. I received a letter today from Crowninshield[1] in Hannover in answer to one of mine, in which he represents himself as pretty well except for the fleas. I was very bad that way myself on my arrival here and had a very funny scene with my landlady on the subject, which reached so involved a point at last that an interpreter was called in and as he pretended to speak English but didn't, I'm inclined to think the poor woman to this day doesn't understand. However, I instituted vigorous measures and have not been troubled lately. Anderson[2] is settled here. I went to see him once, but he is a long way off, and I've heard nothing from him for some time. Plenty of Americans are here; one in the next house; but I have had nothing to do with them though I met half-a-dozen at the American Legation last Wednesday. They are of all kinds; some, not attractive. As soon as possible I shall make German acquaintances and in a couple of months I hope to be well enough on in the language, to join the University and make acquaintances there among the donkeys who walk around with absurd caps on their heads; rather more offensive than the soldiers.

Apropos to this, you ask me what my plans are, here and in life. I hardly know how to follow a plan here, for the way is not at all clear. When I left America my intention was first to accustom myself to the language, then to join the University and systematically attend lectures on the Civil Law, at the same time taking a Latin tutor and translating Latin into German; and to continue this course in Heidelberg or in Paris or in both. The plan was simple enough; useful

[1] Benjamin William Crowninshield (1837–1892).
[2] Nicholas Longworth Anderson (1838–1892).

enough; and comprehensive enough. But now I see difficulties. I must join the University here in the middle of its term; I certainly can not join to any advantage before January. Shall I be likely to learn much law by breaking in on a course of lectures in this manner? To be a student of civil law I must be an absolute master of written and ordinary Latin; though I need not speak it or write it myself. Now, is it well to study law, Latin and German all at once? Can I have time enough to do all this, or ought I to resign the Law and devote myself to Latin? But supposing I were to do this, devote myself to Latin; I may as well give up the University for it would be mere waste time to attend lectures like Corny Felton's[1] at Cambridge, and, as Carlyle says, these Germans are the worst Dryasdusts on the face of the earth.

These objections will, as I advance further and see clearer, either vanish entirely, or gain strength and finally force me into some new course. I hope it will be the former. I already see very clearly that the two years which are allotted to me here, are not nearly enough to do all that I had hoped to do, or a quarter part of it, and I tell you now fairly that if I return to America without doing more than learn German and French, I shall have done well, and these two years will be the best employed of my life. I am satisfied of this, and though I shall not work any the less hard because I believe it, still I shall feel less disappointed when I return without universal knowledge. At present I adhere to my original plan; and this plan, as you see, involves the necessity of my omitting Greek entirely. I am sorry enough to do it, but I became convinced that to attempt the study of Greek now and here, would be hopeless unless I gave up Latin. One or the other I must sacrifice. If I were to include this fourth language in my plan, I should never do anything. Two years will not teach one everything. You may think that as a scholar I should have preferred to sacrifice Latin. As a scholar I should, but as a lawyer I must have only one choice. I take it. And this brings me to the other branch of your question.

As for my plan of life, it is simple, and if health and the usual goods of life are continued to me, I see no reason why it should not be carried out in the regular course of events. Two years in Europe; two years studying law in Boston; and then I propose to emigrate and practice at Saint Louis. What I can do there, God knows; but I have a theory that an educated and reasonably able man can make his mark if he chooses, and if I fail to make mine, why, then — I fail and that's all.

[1] Cornelius Conway Felton (1807–1862), Eliot professor of Greek literature.

I should do it anywhere else as well. But if I know myself, I can't fail. I must, if only I behave like a gentleman and a man of sense, take a position to a certain degree creditable and influential, and as yet my ambition cannot see clearly enough to look further.

In a conversation I had with Mr. Dana a few days before I left home, I said all this to him, and the latter part of it he treated with a little contempt. He insisted that I was looking towards politics; and perhaps he was right. There are two things that seem to be at the bottom of our constitutions; one is a continual tendency towards politics; the other is family pride; and it is strange how these two feelings run through all of us. For my own ideas of my future, I have not admitted politics into them. It is as a lawyer that I would emigrate and I've seen altogether too much harm done in this way, to allow myself to quit law for politics without irresistible reasons.

So here you have a few of my thoughts about what I am going to do. Here in Europe, away from home, from care and ambition and the fretting of monotony, I must say that I often feel as I often used to feel in College, as if the whole thing didn't pay, and if I were my own master, it would need more inducements than the law could offer, to drag me out of Europe these ten years yet. I always had an inclination for the Epicurean philosophy, and here in Europe I might gratify it until I was gorged. Give me my thousand a year and free leave and a good conscience, and I'd pass as happy a life here as I'm afraid I never shall in St. Louis. But now I am hurried; I must work, work, work; my very pleasures are hurried, and after all, I shall get most pleasure and (I believe) advantage, from what never entered into my calculations; Art.

However, there is no use talking. The magd has just come in to prepare my room for the night, and her "Gute Nacht" tells me that it is nine o'clock, and I want still to write to John. There will be time enough to despond hereafter. Just now I am sure is the pleasantest time I shall ever see, for there is entire independence, no cares, and endless and inexhaustible pleasures. As for my expenses I cannot yet calculate them, but when I square my accounts at the end of the month I shall be able to talk with some degree of certainty how I am to come out. Incidentally you might remark in the hearing of the family circle, that an Englishman the other day said in my hearing that Berlin was an expensive place; nothing was cheap in Berlin.

So farewell. I shall not close this letter on the whole till Sunday night, so I may say if Loo goes.

(*Sunday night.*) I have just seen Loo off. She had a bad night, but to-day recovered and I dined with them as usual. Tonight at seven o'clock they went off for Dresden. They wanted me to go with them and you may imagine I should have liked to have done so. I am now alone here and shall study hard. I shall write to Hollis[1] next week but probably not home as there will be little to say. Nick came to see me today. He is all right but I shall see very little of him. This letter will reach you about Thanksgiving, when I am to dine at Magdeburg with Crowninshield and the rest. Five of us. Good-bye.

To Charles Francis Adams, Jr.

BERLIN, December 17-18, 1858.

MY DEAR FELLOW, — Your letter dated Thanksgiving day arrived yesterday, and I give you my word that though I have been having a delightful time here and have enjoyed life to the hubs, still I have never felt quite so glad of being out of Boston as I felt after reading that epistle. There was in it a sort of contented despair, an unfathomable depth of quiet misery that gave me a placid feeling of thankfulness at being where I am. If Boston hadn't been to me what you describe it; if I hadn't felt society to be a bore even while I was yet on the threshold; if I had found one single young woman who had salt enough in her to keep her from stagnating; I believe I never should have thought of leaving home. John and I have already talked on this subject and I know his ideas. For myself, I believe that I can find more interesting women among the very dregs of society here, than Papanti's Hall can turn out. However, at present I can dispense with both....

I tell you what, my boy, you don't crow over political successes at home more than I do here. The old Free Soilers, sir, are about the winning hosses, I reckon, just now. What the devil has become of your Seward's speeches[2] I can't imagine. I've heard so much of them that I'd like to read them, but I can borrow the paper here. The *Courier's* howl I glanced at. It *was* funny, very. As for Mr. Sumner I've heard no more about him since he left. He's not written, and Loo has not mentioned him in her letter.

So much for these things. And now for personal matters. You repeat in your letter the kind offer you made before I left, to help me if I needed help. The Governor, too, in his letter which I received with

[1] Hollis Hunnewell (1836–1884).

[2] Seward's "irrepressible conflict" speech at Rochester, N.Y., October 25, and a second, at Rome, N.Y., October 29, 1858.

yours, has rather a queer passage to the effect, that he is afraid I shall spend here in Europe much more money than my brothers did and that it will be necessary after my return to make arrangements about it. Meanwhile he will keep me supplied, as I send notice. Now this is very well, it is true. I am exceedingly obliged to you, and also to the Governor, who seems all of a sudden to have forgotten his original remarks about a thousand a year. But nevertheless I am determined for various reasons to abide by the original sum. If necessary I can live on half of it, even here in Berlin, though not a very pleasant life. I have been making, and am now making steady efforts to reduce my expenses at least two hundred dollars within my income, but that cursed journey from Liverpool and the necessary expenses of living here, for the first month, have, I'm afraid, brought me hard onto the thousand this year. Meanwhile I am now, for the present at least, pretty well at ease about European expenses. ... Apropos, perhaps if you'd like to buy some German books, I can knock off a little of my debt to you so. I can get you what is I believe the best edition of Goethe for twenty-five or thirty dollars, thirty volumes, bound, but forty or more, unbound. Lessing and Schiller I shall buy for myself soon. The books here are nicely bound, and very cheap. The Goethe and Lessing higher than the others, though I can get you editions of both for almost nothing. As for engravings, etc., I mean to pick some up, but not here. Everything is dear in Berlin. There is nothing that I have heard of, here, that is worth the expense of buying to take home, and I shall only get a few engravings of the pictures in the Galleries, and photographs of the city.

I wrote in my last that I was going to leave these rooms. They are too dear and too many Americans are round. I have taken others quite as good, or rather decidedly better than these, but one story higher, and at least half an hour's walk from the University. They cost with my coffee and bread for breakfast, service, heating, etc., about ten dollars a month. My present ones cost about $16.50. The difference itself is not great, but you will know, if you ever have occasion to live economically, that where one's rooms cost much, everything else costs proportionably. It is not however this expense that will hurt me. But you see, a single bat, a single evening passed as is sometimes done, from six in the afternoon till three in the morning, at the theatre and concerts and wine-shops and bier-locals and balls; a single evening may make necessary a week's economy. And in my new rooms I can economize more easily than here, I think.

Meanwhile I live a quiet life here, occasionally about once a week looking in at a ball, and going pretty regularly once a week to a classical concert and the Theatre. This week I've been three times to the theatre; twice to the Opera House to see the Zauberflöte and Fidelio, great German operas which I can't appreciate; and once to the Schauspielhaus to see Hamlet. It was well done; remarkably well done. Setting aside the scenery, which is always perfect here, it was an exceedingly well acted piece. But Dessoir [1] was not equal in stage effects to Booth and I've seen Mrs. Barrow (?) do Ophelia much better than the little Fräulein Fuhr, who didn't at all satisfy me. Then the German spoils it to an Englishman. The speech "'Tis not alone my inky cloak, good mother" begins in the German "Gnädige Frau." The whole thing sounds flat to me in German. Othello was given the other night but I could get no seat; I fancy however it was not better. They have good actors here, but no wonders; and as for the singers, I've heard no particularly good one. But the orchestra, the scenery and the ballet in the Opera House are glorious.

As I said, I live a quiet life, usually ending the day with a beef-steak, or some sausage and a glass of bier and a pipe, though this evening I'm on the economical, having dissipated yesterday in taking dancing lessons. Nick Anderson and I took a lesson of two hours. I usually write as much German as possible in the daytime, and read in the evening, but it is desperately slow work, and I expect to be occupied by little else but the language all the winter. The University will be of little use to me, but I may take a private Tutor in Latin. At present I am still at the rudiments. I can't once in a dozen times speak a grammatical sentence, and understand what is said only when very slowly spoken. As for a continued lecture, I can't catch anything at all, and at the theatre very little. But there is certainly a regular advance, and I am desperate in my attempts to talk it.

The great drawback to one's enjoyment here is the weather. Today is the first day for four weeks that the sun has been out, and that we've not had a heavy, muggy fog. Today has been clear and cool and very enjoyable.

And so, my poor boy, condemned to labor in that happy city of Boston, don't you wish you were here? Perhaps Berlin may not be so pleasant as Vienna or Paris, but I think you wouldn't object to be here notwithstanding. Christmas comes off soon and if the fellows from Hannover come on, there'll probably be a pretty loud time, and the masked-balls, etc., will hear of it. At present, however, I'm draw-ing back from most of my American acquaintances, but I have not yet

[1] Louis Dessoir (1810–1875) or his son Ferdinand (b, 1835).

succeeded in supplying their places with German. There seems to be no place here where German students meet much. Very little student life in Berlin, and what I've seen of that is dirty and fleay.

I have however made one philosophical discovery here; and that is that it doesn't matter where I live or what I do, there will come occasionally fits of crossness and disagreeable feelings. The advantage of living here is however that when one gets bored and cross, there are so many means of driving it away. I myself usually prefer a beef-steak and a bottle of Rhine wine, with a companion, or "vielleicht" two bottles, but I have known a ball to be tried with success, or in fact almost any change of action. One is always doing something new here, if it's only discovering a new bier-local, or going to a new concert-room. I mean some evening to set out on a tour of exploration and visit two or three dozen concert-rooms and balls. As yet I know comparatively few.

As for the inhabitants of Boston, I can't say that I feel any very absorbing interest in their affairs, and though it is rather amusing to hear what is going on, still I can't say that I should care much if I didn't hear a word except from the family, while I am away. I am however always very glad to hear from home. Since I began to prepare to wander, I have thought a good deal more of home than I ever did before. I assure you, my dear fellow, one doesn't appreciate home properly, at home. Especially before I started, I had my attention drawn to one thing, to which it ought to have been drawn long ago; how excessively selfish and exacting we children always were toward mamma, and still more, how much she felt it. Before I came away, I had two or three long talks with her, and I came out of them feeling more like a selfish, low-minded fool than I ever did before in my life. I determined then that I would at least try not only to show more respect and affection for her in my manner towards her, but also try to get you and John to do so. I spoke to John about it, and he took it as I hoped he would, and as I meant he should. I write now to put the same thing before you, if John has not already done it, not, of course, intending to find fault or interfere, but only to represent that we are now men, grown up and independent or nearly so; that we owe a certain amount of respect and affection to our mother, and that it is not enough to merely *have* this affection; we ought to *show* it more in those little matters that a woman feels most. I do believe that a reasonable amount of delicate attention and *respect* from her sons, would make mamma perfectly proud and happy.

She felt too very deeply the way we treated Brooks, and I think myself that we ought to try our hardest to tolerate the child, who is really a first-rate little fellow, apart from his questions, and we ought not to snub him so much. It will break his spirit, or at all events, can have no good effect. That boy's disposition will either make something of him or kill him. Perhaps our influence, well applied, might give him a start and keep him straight. At all events it will be very bad to make home disagreeable to him, and drive him off to learn all sorts of low things from his companions. That is the very worst that can happen.

As for Mary, I don't know what will become of her. It seems to me that she'll be a great strapping girl, with as little consciousness of what God made her for, or of what she wants to do besides getting a husband, as any of our other friends. Her manners too will never be good I'm afraid. She has too many brothers.

I am sure that you'll take as I mean, all that I have written. To me, the first one of us that has left home, the real feelings that existed there were probably shown clearer than often happens. I felt more strongly than ever before that it was an entire mistake for me to suppose that I had only myself in the world to care for; and I appreciated for the first time that there were those who would feel much more for my death or misfortune than I should myself. It made a strong impression on me at the time, and I am not likely to forget it in Europe, where the tone that I hear is so low, so selfish and so irreligious, that it compels me more and more to a love for what is pure and good. I should become a fanatic, I believe, and go into the pulpit if I remained here long.

With this letter I send a list of the letters I have written and the letters and papers I have received. I'm inclined to think some must have missed. Either with this letter or by the next steamer will come a letter for papa, but I shall mail this first, though I've no idea how soon it will go. I'm much obliged to you for your offer about the paper but I don't much care for one. They're at the Legation. Pray send the *Atlantic Monthly* though, as I wrote papa, and if there's anything in the papers, like Seward's speeches, for instance, I'd like to see them. These had better be sent by Bremen.

I've sat up till one o'clock to write this, and shall close it here as I have a lot more to do before bed-time. I turn night into day a good deal. Yours, etc.

To Charles Francis Adams, Jr.

BERLIN, January 18, 1859.

MY DEAR FELLOW: — Don't crow too quick about the pleasures and pains of life. To prove to you that I am not inclined to change my position, I will merely remark that I should decline for the present any offer of increasing my allowance, if any such offer were made. The deficit must be made up if, or when, it comes, but that is all. I received a short enclosure from the Governor on this subject in a letter dated the 13th December. He says that he means to send a hundred pounds more, after New Year's, and his concluding passage was incomprehensible to me till I received your last. He says: "On the general subject" (that of money affairs) "I shall have some ideas to suggest hereafter which may have the effect of arranging the affair more satisfactorily." Meanwhile he seems to think that I'm "putting up with privations of all kinds," and he's right too, but I'm happy and what's the odds. All the privations I see won't hurt me, except going without a good breakfast in the morning and having to run to school so fast that I can't enjoy my cigar.

It's rather a good joke that you should blame *me* for not acknowledging what I've received, when to this minute I don't know how many of my letters have reached home. If you'd put off your reproaches till my next letter to you arrived (dat. Decem. 18) you would have received the whole list. Also the directions about newspapers, all of which I have received, that you sent, but want no more except in case something remarkable happens. I'm exceedingly obliged to you for both your letters and papers. You are altogether the most valuable correspondent I have, and I can tell you, I always gloat over your letters and do them the especial honor of reading them twice; a distinction granted to no others, except perhaps the Governor's — when they come.

Your news too I acknowledge. Bear my greetings to the hub of creation and its society. If any remarkably attractive young woman who is marriageable and has a large property at her own disposal enquires after me, give her my love. Perhaps you might induce her to enter into a correspondence which may produce the best results. My own female friends haven't, so far as my present information extends, put their affection for me to so great a test as to show it by letter, and so far as I know, there are very few whom I should think would shine in such a demonstration. So much the better. I wish nothing more than to be wholly forgotten by them all.

Your new set are strangers to me. Miss Crowninshield I never spoke to; Susy Amory I knew very little. Georgy Blake, however, I did know, and rather wonder how she has managed to break down the wall of exclusiveness. For my sake treat her tenderly. Add, too, in your next, if convenient, who my successor is with the fair Caroline. I have vacated the place by her side which I held with some obstinacy for two or three years, and now I am curious to know what new Telemachus that truly innocent Syren has caught, for indeed I'll do her the justice to say that she is as innocent a Syren as ever was growed, and never fished for any one while I knew her. I wish she had. In that case there'd have been more life and spirit in the acquaintanceship.

If there is any message that I ought to send to any one, just be kind enough to make it for me. I give you carte-blanche to say what you will to everyone, and will acknowledge any speech or message that you put into my mouth short of an offer of marriage.

I watch American politics with much interest, and feel disgraced when a German asks about them. By Jove, it is humiliating to have to acknowledge the condition of our statesmanship. I am often ashamed to be known as an American here. Sumner can't return and won't resign, I'm afraid. I received a letter from him and wrote one to him, hinting that I wished and hoped that he would give up all idea of returning until he was really recovered, and rather resign his seat than return to relapse again. I wrote as delicately as I knew how, but of course I could not help implying a wish that he would resign. He has not answered it as yet. Perhaps not received it; perhaps he will not write again though I asked him to.

But how of greater literary works? Could I write a history, do you think, or a novel, or anything that would be likely to make it worth while for me to try? This too is not adapted to me, and yet, rather queerly, this is the only one of the branches of your idea that has struck me as practicable. I don't know whether you had it in your mind or not when you wrote, but it seems probable that the duty of editing our grandfather's works and writing his life, may fall on one of us, and if it does, that alone is enough for a man, and enough to shape his whole course. I don't think this occurred to you, however, and it is too far off to found any plausible argument on.

Now, my dear fellow, my mind may be pretty but it's not original and never will be, and I shall never get any good out of it if I allow it to sprinkle all its little vigor away in newspapers and magazines. Adams the scholar prefers to live, but Adams the scholar would rather disconsolately die, and let Adams the lawyer do as he can, than make one of that butterfly party which New Yorkers seem to consider their literary world. To become more, the law must be my ladder; without it, you might as well at once press me out into so many pages of the *Atlantic Monthly*.

My dear fellow, we must make some income; that is necessary. To do it by literature is less to my taste than to do it by law. Behind the law, and with it as a support to fall back on if necessary, I can do as every other man in the same circumstances has done. Without some firm footing we shall go to the devil. With it, God knows what we may be able to do. I hold still by my plan. I hope that you will not succeed in shaking it, for then I shall lose myself entirely, and there will be an end to me. In it I see an object worth fighting for, and one to which I am trying to direct all my resources. Without it I lose my whole life and gain nothing. Stick by the law. Ten years hence we will see how things look, and use our best weapons; not now.

Meanwhile, nevertheless, I acknowledge gratefully your offer to negotiate for me about any article I may care to write. It has occurred to me that as I am here at school, it would not be impossible to write an article on the Prussian schools, which, if thrown into a sufficiently conversational form, and hashed up with an intermixture of my own personal experiences, might be made as they say, at once readable and instructive. There is no hurry about this, however. I shall remain three months here, and you can give me your opinion of this plan in your next. You see, the subject, as I would treat it, offers a pretty wide surface for anything that I should care to say, whether political, metaphysical, educational, practical, or any other "cal." If you like the plan pray give me any ideas developing it that happen to come into your head, and I will send you my own to criticise.

I have no more to say just now till receipt of your next. If we don't find out what we want in life, why the devil must be in it, that's all....

I shall write to Mary as soon as I have time, so I hope she won't be impatient. As I am a school-boy again I am not responsible for delays. By the by, I've not given you my reasons wholly for becoming a school-boy and changing my plans again. Never mind! If you find fault I'll justify myself in my next letter. I shall expect to hear in my next whether I shall send you any books or not. They are very cheap here and sometimes very good. Yrs. etc.

To Charles Francis Adams, Jr.

BERLIN, February 9, 1859.

DEAR CHARLES — I will pay your last letter the compliment to say that it had effect enough over me to make me feel unpleasantly for two days. Not that I found fault with it. I do not do so, and hope that you will continue to write just so. But it bothered me damnably. For what you say as to my remarks on the Boston young ladies, though your criticisms are rather hard on me, I acknowledge that you are wholly in the right. What one writes is considerably influenced by the accidental state of his mind at the instant of writing, and it is not strange if, among so many letters, when I am hurrying to put down the first thing that comes into my head, and fill out a sentence as quickly as possible, it is not strange, I say, if I say many silly things. Your remark about care in writing what the Governor is to see, surprised me much more than your criticisms, for possessing as I do a *mens conscia recti*, I would be perfectly willing to have him see all my thoughts in reference to my country and believe he would approve them all. If he has expressed unfavorable opinions I wonder that his letters say nothing about them. They, on the contrary, have been very kind and mild, and his last, on finances, the contents of which you seemed to know, was even very liberal, so that I have not a single word to say against his mode of treating me. It is true I shall do my best to make no use of this liberality, but am none the less obliged to him, on that account. It is a satisfaction to feel that I *can* spend, and have an ample margin....

Money matters are now very easy with me. I have about six hundred dollars on hand, counting the Governor's late remittance as only five hundred; and this here is equal to eight hundred. I owe not a cent except to you and Hill. This latter I should like to see off my hands, and I'd pay him myself devilish quick if he were here, but as I can't do that nor get the money to him, I'm afraid that I shall have to ask you to see to him. For God's sake, though, don't do it if it will inconvenience you. I feel now that I am perfectly well in condition to pay him myself if I could only send the money, but it is so small a sum that it is hardly worth while to send it by the Barings....

In politics you can judge better than I, but I myself believe that Douglas will win. He is playing a devilish hard game; in fact he is repeating in the nation the operation which was so successful in his own state. We shall see.

About myself I have hardly anything to say beyond what I have said in my last letters. I cannot say that my present life is wildly exciting, nor that the capital of Prussia has as yet shown itself to me in any violently attractive light. But at least if I have not had an exciting time, I have at all events not had an unpleasant one, and if the last month has been particularly quiet, there is at least the satisfaction of knowing that it has been a particularly instructive one. My school is perfectly satisfactory, and I am better satisfied of the wisdom of the step than of anything else I have done. I go a good deal to the Opera, which is a great temptation; to the Theatres not so often for the playing is almost poor and the plays, except when Schiller, Goethe, or Shakespeare is produced, not much. I've not been on a real bat for ever so long, being in a very quiet and economical set, and though often indulging after the theatre in a steak and glass of bier or bottle of Rhine wine, this never leads to anything worse. As I have to get up six mornings in the week at either seven or eight o'clock, I have also to go to bed early and not drink too much. I'm virtuous as St. Antony and resist temptation with the strength of a martyr. I've not been to a disrespectable ball for a month or nearly a month, but can't say how long this will last. The way the virtue of the purest is corrupted here is wonderful.

You can imagine that my school lessons don't take up much of my time out of school, though the poor little devils of boys have to work all the time. The master inquires if I can recite, and I say yes or no as it happens. My German is slowly advancing under this pressure, but I must say that I never expect to master it as I once expected. It is terribly long and tedious and my advance can be measured not by days but by months. I read very little German, for most of my time for reading is occupied by my Latin. It may seem to you that this sort of life is not exactly what we usually connect with our ideas of life in Europe, but my experience and observation to the slight extent of four months, goes to show that the American idea of life in Europe, as given by such men as Gus Perkins, the Hammonds, etc., etc., etc., is an absurd one and just worthy of them. I've not seen Paris yet, but it's my impression that to a sensible person who has no particular object in staying there and is not in French society, it's just as slow as any other city, and except in its Galleries and Palaces, no better than New York. Indeed I've heard sensible fellows who had lived in both places assert, that in its means of enjoyment New York was ahead of any city in Europe that they had seen. I don't undertake to indorse this, but it shows how differently people think on this point, and for my own part I never feel thoroughly jolly anywhere till my whole time is employed.

Lately, it is true, I've been rather more out of my room in the evenings than usually, but I hope not to do so much of this after this week. Consult John's sheet for information as to my sights and dissipations.

I will now proceed, my amiable brother, to discuss the last philosophical propositions of yours, and the plan which you propose for my course in life. I confess that it filled me with wonder and general bewilderment. I think in my last I said that you paid me a left-handed compliment, in your idea of my mind. Permit me to retract; humbly apologize. I never made so great a mistake in all my life. I have usually considered myself a conceited fellow. Every one told me so, and I believed 'em. I *had* thought that I set about as high a price on my mental capacities as most other people; perhaps a peg higher. I was mistaken; I've put its market value up at least twice as high again since your last.

Were you intoxicated when you wrote that I am to "combine in myself the qualities of Seward, Greeley and Everett"? Mein lieber Gott, what do you take me for? Donnerwetter! do you suppose I'm a statesman like Seward, or that my amiable play-philosophy would ever set me up to guiding a nation; do you imagine that I have a tithe of Greeley's vigor, originality and enterprise; are you so blinded by the tenderness of your fraternal affection as to imagine that the mantle of Cicero has fallen upon my shoulders, or that I inherit the pride and ample pinion that the Grecian sophist bore? Nimmermehr! What would be the result if I were to return home and gravely and coolly set myself to doing what you propose? Bah! mine brother, you seem to have written under the idea that I am a genius. Give that idea up, once and forever! I never did anything that I should be treated like this. I know what I can do, and I know what a devilish short way my tether goes, and the evening before I received your letter, I had, in my daily lesson in Ovid, read the fable of Phaethon, whose interesting and suggestive story you'll find at the end of the first and beginning of the second Book of Metamorphoses.

Now a word as to my own condition, and then for our discussion. You know by my last that I have joined a Gymnasium, like our Latin School, only much larger and thorougher. Here I go every day from three to six hours. It is not very good fun; that is of course. But it admirably answers my purposes. Here I pursue my original design of studying Latin and Greek. Here is tremendous practice in hearing and talking and learning German. Here it is very cheap. Here I am free enough and yet must obey the rules where they are not excepted in my favor. I go four mornings in the week at eight o'clock. Three afternoons there is no school and the others are no trouble to me. The boys received me with open arms and my proceeding caused some noise in Berlin, for every one of the four hundred and odd told it at home, and I became quite famous. One or two of the little fellows I am quite fond of, and you would split if you could see me walking away from school with a small boy under each arm, to whom I have to bend down to talk to. None of them know English, so of course I speak only German, and am familiar enough with it to get along very well. I am stared at as a sort of wild beast by the rest of the school, who only see me when I come and go, for there is no recess, and no outdoor playing, so that I know only the boys in my own room. As yet I only see the boys at school, where they treat me with a certain sort of respect, and yet as one of themselves. They never push me or trouble me in any way, nor play tricks on me. Perhaps they think that I know how to box, and it's as well to let me alone, but anyway, they are many of them first-rate fellows, and two especially I cherish with paternal affection. I've not as yet recited in Latin or Greek, but soon shall begin; to translate, that is, into German. I *can* study all the time, or not at all, but I *must* go to school, and that is study enough to satisfy my conscience.

I am also busied during my leisure odd minutes or hours in studying art, and reading and studying theoretically painting. Music occupies me too, during certain hours every week, and more than these certain ones, if there is any that I wish to hear. So you see that I have enough work (or play-work if you prefer to call it so) to occupy me all my time. I seldom do nothing. In my new rooms I seldom see Americans, but know very few Germans indeed. In short I am busy, contented, and only once in a while cross....

So the world wags on here, quietly as possible. The weather is detestable. Formerly it was always bad. For a month we didn't see the sun. Now we have one fine day, and two bad ones. It grows cold and clears, then thaws and clouds up. Still, when one passes nearly all his daytime in school, it doesn't matter much what the weather is.

In money matters I have to be very careful, and this month have rather overstepped my bound as I have bought several expensive books, but I hope to need no more money from home till the first of March, and unless next summer ruins me, I shall get through. It isn't pleasant to have to calculate every cent one spends, but independence is a great thing, and I shall do my best to hold to it. I keep my accounts most rigidly; have no debts except my monthly accounts with my landlady; and always know where I am. As I have always had to be very careful, it is not so hard now. I economize as much as I can, but sometimes can't resist spending too much.

And now as to the last part of your letter, over which I have thought a good deal, and been a little troubled. I acknowledge the force of what you say, and yet I disagree with your conclusions. Let me proceed systematically if possible.

You try to put me on the horns of a dilemma. You attribute to me a certain kind of mind, and argue that if I am to be a lawyer, or in other words, follow my own plan which I have followed for several years, then what I learn in Europe is worse than thrown away. Hence, to be a lawyer I must cease to be what I am. If I acknowledge that my mind is not adapted to my plan, I must give my plan up. If on the other hand I assert that my mind *is* adapted to my plan, I must give Europe up. This I take to be the ground of your letter. I disagree with it, and think that you are mistaken not only in your judgement of my mind, but also in your idea of the necessary result of two years in Europe. But I shall not go into this subject now. Perhaps in another letter I may give you some reasons for believing that what I am learning here in Europe is not in opposition to what I propose to do hereafter. Just now I prefer to attack your position rather than to defend my own. It's easier and there's more fun in it.

I don't deny the truth of what you say, that law is not a pleasant study, and that we are not adapted to make great lawyers. But beyond this I think you lose yourself and run aground. You say that I am not made for a lawyer; but hardly hint at what I am made for. The same things that you say of me, you also apply to yourself. Now let me see if I can carry out your idea to any result that will give a fellow a minute's firm footing.

The law is bad, you say. Wohlan! what then? Why then, you continue, take something that suits you better. And what would be likely to suit me better? What is this kind of mind that you give me? I must say that you pay me a very left-handed kind of compliment in your estimation of me. You seem to think that I am adapted to nothing but the sugar-plums of intellect and had better not try to digest anything stronger. You would make me a sort of George Curtis or Ik. Marvel, better or worse, a writer of popular sketches in magazines; a lecturer before Lyceums and College societies; a dabbler in metaphysics, poetry, and art, than which I would rather die, for if it has come to that, alas! verily, as you say, mediocrity has fallen on the name of Adams.

But, I suppose, you will deny that your letter leads to this and assert that such men as Mr. Everett, Mr. Sumner, the Governor, Mr. Palfrey and the like, are a wholly different class. I would just suggest that all these began either as lawyers or clergymen; and I merely propose to do the same. But now let's go back to generalities, and see whether something can't be fished up.

In the most general terms then; you would say, I take it, that my mind if not adapted to law, at least *is* adapted to literary pursuits, in the most extensive meaning of the term; and to nothing else. I couldn't be a physician or a merchant, or a shopkeeper or anything of that kind, so well as I could a lawyer. Literary pursuits are very extensive, but I *must* make some money to support me, so we must say, "literary pursuits that produce money." Now literary pursuits that produce money and that I am eligible for, are very few.

To begin with, perhaps, if I were a better man, I might feel inclined to become a clergyman. But as I'm very much a worser man, we'll count that out.

Then you once proposed to me to go into the newspaper line and become an editor. The objections to this are as many and as strong as to the law, but if you don't see them, will reserve the subject for further discussion.

Of *Atlantic Monthly* and *Putnam* and *Harper* and the men who write for money in them, my opinion is short. Rather than do nothing but that, or make that an object in life, I'd die here in Europe.

No, mein Liebster, this is one of these propositions which would kill any man's chances in America, even though he had all the training of Gorgias (if that was the beggar's name), and all the philosophy of Frank Bacon; (I refer to the Viscount Verulam and not to the young Bostonian of the same name). Yet after all, your idea is not so very distinct from mine, except that it throws out into the strongest relief the object that I proposed to make dependent on circumstances and success in other respects. We are considerably in the same box, brother mine, and what applies to me, applies also, with slight alterations, to yourself. As you say, there are differences between us, and my character isn't yours; in fact, I know many respects in which I wish it were; but still we have grown up in the same school and have, until now, drawn our mental nutriment from the breasts, metaphorically speaking, of the same wet-nurse; indeed we may consider ourselves a case of modern Romulus and Remus, only omitting their murderous propensities. What is still more, we are beautifully adapted to work together; that is, *you* are. I stand in continual need of some one to kick me, and you use cow-hides for that purpose. So much the better.

Continue to do so. In other words, I need you. Whether there's any corresponding necessity on your side, is your affair. But it's a case of "versteht sich" that we can work better together than apart. Under these circumstances, let us be very careful how we take a step that will probably knock one of us in the head forever, or so separate us that our objects would become different. I shall hesitate a very long time indeed before I decide to earn my living by writing for magazines and newspapers, for I believe it to be one of the most dangerous beginnings that a man can make. Recollect that thread-bare old Arabian Nights magnetic mountain *that drew all the metal out of the ships* and then sunk them.

I say that our ideas are not far different. The real difference is this: Yours begins by assuming as your ground plank and corner stone that I am capable of teaching the people and of becoming a light to the nations. Mine on the contrary begins by leaving that to develop itself in the future or to remain proved on the other side, without suffering a public disgrace from slumping as I infallibly should do under your idea. I said in my last what I wanted of the law; that I considered it the best grounding in the world for anything that we wish or are likely to do; that is the strongest point to fall back upon and the best position to advance from; at once offensive and defensive, it gives one a position as literary as if he did nothing but write for periodicals and a good deal more respectable; as a profession it offers many inducements; as merely an occupation it offers still more, and there is much more chance both for you and me to work *up* from it, than there is doubt in my mind that I at least should drop like a stuck monkey from the perch on which you want me to place myself. Perhaps it is my wish and hope that we may do something of the sort you propose, but I do not wish for so large a scale of action, because I know my own weakness; I do not wish to go to work in the way you propose, because in the first place I believe it to be a wrong way, tending to fritter away the little power of steady and long-continued exertion I have, and in the second, it seems to me not to offer that firm and lasting ground work that the law does. I do wish to adhere to my original plan because, though even that is more, I am afraid, than my powers are up to, yet it seems to me as feasible as any that has yet come before me, and if I can do nothing in that, why let me go to the devil at once, for there's no use staying here. Gott bewahr mich from funny Lyceum lectures and rainbow articles in *Atlantic Monthlys* with a proof of scholarship as exhibited by a line here and there from "the charming old Epicurean Horace" or "the grand thunderbursts of superhuman strength " from God knows what old Greek trotted out for the occasion. If I was born to be the admiration of girls and Tupperian philosophers, I'll cheat fate and quietly do nothing all my life.

So here I will lay aside this subject and wait for your next. As this letter has been written partly in school, partly here, and is the work of some six or eight different sittings, I'll excuse you for finding fault with it, as with my former one, but you must also excuse the faults. On your theory of my proper plan of life, however, I ought never to say any foolish things, but my lips should drool wisdom and my paths should be by the side of Socrates, and Isocrates; (by the way were these two men related and why have they so similar names?) I hope your next will take a more practical view of life.

Meanwhile this last week I've been exceedingly dissipated; out every night in one way or another, and able to do very little real work. The last two days too, the weather has been charming. Yesterday Jim Higginson [1] and I took Mr. Apthorp [2] out on a spree. He has had us there to dine and gave us some of the best champagne I ever tasted; perhaps the very best; I've dined twice with him and got talking very fast both times. The ladies retired to their room and left us to our wine, and as Mr. A. doesn't stint the supply and I make it a rule never to refuse a good glass when it's offered, the inevitable consequence is very clear. A bottle of wine is the outside of what I can carry, and in both cases I drank devilish close onto the limit. Yesterday we returned the hospitality by taking Mr. A. out for a day of it, to show him the style of our ordinary life. Higginson and I went for him at two o'clock and carried him off to our dirty little restauration, and there dined him and gave him a glass of beer. You know the style of our dinners from my letters, I think. Then we went to a concert till six, and leaving the concert before it was over, we walked down to a little theatre called Wallner's, a devil of a way off, and saw a drama called "Berlin wie es weint und lacht"; a thing very popular in Berlin, and has run 137 nights. It's by far the best drama of the sort that I've seen, too. Thence we walked back and sat till twelve o'clock in a wine-cellar, or Wein-Stube as they call it which was crowded with exceedingly respectable old people, but which, though very clean, yet hasn't the vestige of a table-cloth on ary a table, and was hot as hell and filled with clouds of tobacco smoke. Here we eat and drank and talked and Hig and I smoked, and passed a very jolly evening, drinking two bottles and a half of Rhine wine, really better than I've often tasted at home, for which two bottles and a half we paid something less than an

[1] James Jackson Higginson (1836–1911).   [2] Robert East Apthorp (d. 1882).

American dollar. This is a dear place for wines too. On the Rhine, I am told, they cost much less. I very often come in here after the theatre and drink a bottle, commonly with Higginson, or if I'm on the heavy cheap, go to a cellar and get a couple of boiled sausages and a mug of beer. The sausages I tell you are good. My supper commonly costs quarter of a dollar or less. My dinner the same. As for cigars, I consider myself extravagant when I smoke really good ones which cost me $15.00 the thousand. They're not proud like yours, but curse me if they don't taste as good as any I used to pay at the rate of $50 and $60 for.

So I will now wind up this letter, which though not so long as yours, has yet the excuse that I've more letters to write than you. I will now proceed immediately, as you say, to put on my paint and feathers (devilish dirty paint in the shape of my old dress suit) for a grand ball in the Opera House, at which I suppose all the Court will be, and which I shall try to tell about in my letter to John. I go from a sense of duty, though it costs me three thalers, and I'd rather stay at home, but one ought to see these things and I presume it will be handsome and stupid as double-distilled damnation. I don't know any one except Americans there and if I did, it wouldn't make any difference. Meanwhile, allerhöchstgeborner Herr, accept the assurances of my deep respect. If I knew enough of this cursed language I'd write you a letter in German, but I don't and never shall, curse it.

Give the tokens of my highest consideration to the family at large. My last letter home was February 5th to mamma; before that, January 29th to the Congressman. No letters as yet received this week. Yrs.

To Charles Francis Adams, Jr.

BERLIN, March 13, 1859.

MY DEAR FELLOW: Yours of the 14th came to hand on the day I expected, just after I had sent off a letter to mamma. I received a letter from mamma on the 24th and one from papa on the 21st. I sent an answer to papa on the 23d, and to mamma's on the 2d. Papa's letter contained as I expected from what you said before, indications of trouble, which were expressed in a manner that irritated me a good deal, and I sat down on the spot and wrote rather an impertinent reply, which may settle the question or may only make him angry, I don't know which. I hope an end will be put to all this stuff. I'm doing my best to do well here, God knows, and it's excessively unpleasant to be told without any why or wherefore that I'm becoming a damned fool.

Your warnings and advice I've taken readily, and been very glad to take, but you don't deal in enigmas. What the deuce does the Governor mean by a perfectly Delphian vaticination in his last, from which all that I could understand was that some one (of the Apthorps I suppose) had been abusing me, and I'd better be careful? Confound it, a fellow must know a little more than this before he can work straight. Understand, I don't want to be told that I'm a good boy and deserve a sugar-plum in the shape of encouragement, but I do want to know the why and wherefore of things in a sensible manner.

I'm glad that you approve my Gymnasium course, and still think myself that it's the best thing I could have done. You estimate the effect of school too highly however. It has enabled me to give method and concentration to my studies, but I have found here that it is impossible to go back ten years in one's life, or graft on to one system the growth of a very different one. I am a man among boys here. They sit on my knee and pull my whiskers and ride on my back and listen to my marvellous tales of home, and yet know five times as much as I do on many things. I too cannot feel their rewards or punishments, nor study except what I please. The mill in which they are placed is forming their minds, but my mind is already formed in a very different way, and the process has very little influence on me. However if it teaches me a little German, I'll thank God and be satisfied....

My life here in Berlin is in no way changed. I cannot stagnate simply because new ideas are pouring into my mind so fast that I have always something to think of. My only trouble is want of time, and I economize in it as much as I care to. School every day; more or less music, opera or concert every week; study in the evening, or sometimes a call or a blow-out of some sort which occasionally keeps me up very late. I'm anything but dissipated. Indeed the little tendency I ever had that way has almost wholly disappeared. I can't say that life is unpleasant, and it isn't certainly exciting, but I hope that I'm learning something, and am waiting patiently till the time comes for me to go down to Dresden. Nothing could tempt me to remain in Berlin later than May, if I could get away.

It seems probable that we shall have war next summer, but no one knows except Napoleon and he won't tell. His behavior is very strange and contradictory. His latest declarations look towards peace, but very soon war will be inevitable unless he declares himself plainly and honestly. All Europe except Italy is against it, and yet every one says that all Europe will take part in it; probably France, Russia and Sardinia against Austria, England, and the German Confederacy. Italy is in a confoundedly hard position it is true, and so far as Austria is concerned I'd like to see that nation wiped out, but the good that war may possibly do to the Italians is almost sure to be more than counterbalanced by the evil it will do to the Germans.

War however will not change my plans. It isn't probable that any Austrian will shoot me in the valleys of the Tyrol, nor that any Frenchman will chase me up to the top of Mont Blanc. Italy will be the seat of war, and I doubt if the Tyrol feels it, at least in the first campaign. However, after all, it seems to me contrary to reason to suppose that Napoleon is going to do so crazy a thing. Every one here is so perplexed, the papers so full of contradictory rumors; all nations arming; ambassadors rushing from Court to Court in hot haste; stocks rising and falling at every breath; and no one knowing anything about the matter except Napoleon himself; that no fair and cool judgment can be made. We must wait and see, but meanwhile I shall do as I intended. If they chase me I'll run to Turkey like Charles the twelfth.

For our discussion I have little more to say. Our ideas are really not very widely separated, and if I didn't feel my own weakness so much, I might perhaps try to change a very little. But I am tired of trying to direct what I have no power over. It's been a great consolation to me to know that these things will work themselves out for us, and that they will come right of their own accord if they come right at all. I shall stick to my present course, which up to a certain point is identical with your plan. When that point comes, I'll be ready to decide.

You have already come to the point and must either decide or leave time to unravel the twist. Even a decision will not necessarily settle the matter if it's against your tastes and wishes. For my own part I feel as certain that I shall never be a lawyer, as you are that I'm not fit for it. If you are cut out for one, why go in, and God help you. I believe myself however that you'll not get far, and I hope you'll not stay long. Yet what else to do just now I have no idea, unless you beguile the time which your absent clients leave you, by the pursuits of writing, etc., which you recommend to me.

As for the family papers I know only one thing; that it is not *in* me to do them justice. I am actually becoming afraid to look at the future, and feel only utterly weak about it. This is no new feeling; it only increases as the dangers come nearer.

I am collecting materials to write an article on the schools. How soon I can do it, or whether I can do it so as to satisfy myself at all, I can't say. I shall adopt the first person in it, and write just as I always did and do. It will interfere somewhat with my studies, but six weeks

I hope will change my present arrangement and Dresden will give me more time.

This warm weather and a glimpse or two of clear sky lately, are so extraordinary that it almost makes me homesick, for it seems as if there was no fine weather in Berlin. For nearly five months I have seen very little but clouds, or rather a dead dull sandy sky, and dark, rainy or damp days. The thermometer has only twice fallen below thirty since I've been here. I hardly ever wear a great coat, day or night, yet have never had so little trouble from colds or sickness. The Americans are beginning to leave Berlin. A number went down to Vienna this last week. Nick Anderson goes in a fortnight to Dresden and in June to England probably, to meet his father. Crowninshield leaves Hannover and we expect him here very soon, to abide with us a few weeks before also going to Dresden....

Now that my time's nearly up at my school, only three weeks more to run before the examinations, I am beginning to find myself in rather a disagreeable position there. Within the last two or three days I have seen indications, very slight to be sure, but still awkward for me, that the masters don't like me. My own master behaves with the most perfect regularity, and they are all very polite, but naturally they find it very hard to know how to treat me. Tomorrow evening I am to call on Schwarz, the Ordinarius of my Class, to get some information from him about the schools (of course I've said nothing to any one about writing of them) and I mean to find out what the difficulty is. Of course, you know, if I find I am giving trouble, I shall withdraw at once, and perhaps now that my three months are nearly over, it will be as good a thing as remaining, for, you see, by doing this in a polite manner, I can get some claim on Schwarz's gratitude, and make him a friend instead of a master. Now, I want to visit several of the schools here, and also to obtain a large amount of information that I should perhaps not be able to get except through him. So, if I find tomorrow evening that my suspicions are right, I shall strike while the iron's hot and do my best to turn the trouble to my advantage. On the other hand, if I am mistaken, and have imagined all this, I shall hold on at the school, which really is quite pleasant, till the term's over and try to get what I want gradually. More than the three months I cannot remain, for many reasons, a part of which you will see of course in what I said at first about the general result of the experiment. But more directly than that is the fact that after the warm weather sets in I should not dare go there. It would give me the typhus fever or something horrible in a fortnight. So soon therefore as

I can get things wound up here, I shall go on to Dresden, taking my same course of study with me.

I was at the Legation last evening talking with Governor Wright, returned Californians, young medical students, etc., etc. I see that my visit to Humboldt has got into the papers as I supposed it would, confound 'em. Nick was also at the Legation. He leaves Berlin on the 24th not to return. We expect Crowninshield very soon, perhaps this evening, but he may not come for a week. I hear that Billy Howe[1] is at Vienna, Secretary of Legation, I was told. It is possible, if I feel rich, I may go down the Danube to Vienna before going into the Tyrol in July or August. If so I shall look for William....

To Charles Francis Adams, Jr.

BERLIN, 6 April, 1859.

Verily, my beloved Brother, thy last gave me pleasure. Thy wit is well-favored though coarse withal, and i' good faith pleases me. For my own part I imagine that my letters for the last few months can hardly have caused much delight, inasmuch as they have neither been written in good spirits, nor always in good temper. I received at the same time with your last, one from the head of the family in answer to a particularly cross effusion of mine. The paternal rejoinder was good-natured, though with a not unhappy strain of sarcasm, which for a person of his time of life was really not so bad. You know the usual run of the article in elderly individuals. We can only gently pity the weakness and forget it. I answered the letter (omitting the satire) in a dignified manner and hope it will rest there. Really these liberties must be discouraged. We cannot allow Congressmen to address us in this familiar way.

Thy own letter, mine Brother, needs an answer in extenso. Our discussion I will let drop. The truth seems to be that your idea is on a large scale and mine on a smaller one. I'm drifting that way and have been all my life. On the other hand you've struck on a snag, but I'm in hopes the Governor's political life will give you something to think of and to do. My path is clear to me for five years yet, and, I think, for any number of years.

As for your "hitting me," though one is softer in this atmosphere than anywhere else, yet I don't beg off. Hit away, my boy, as hard as you please and if you're always as right as you were in that matter, I'll stick it out. We're all mortal and all liable to feel cross and blue;

[1] William Edward Howe (d. 1875). He was not secretary of legation.

especially when one doesn't see a clear sky or a bracing atmosphere more than three days in six months. So peg away as much as you like. I'm expecting a sisserara all round from home in consequence of my last letters, but as I'm a good way off I shall bear it philosophically. There *is* a comfort in getting a blow-up a month old. Independence is a mighty pleasure.

I tell you what, young man, Boston's a little place, but damn me if it isn't preferable to this cursed hole. I don't think I've ever heard more promiscuous swearing than I have from all sorts of fellows within these three months about this sort of life. Such a cussin' and a damnin' from religious individuals, such a consumption of steaks and Pisporter of evenings to raise one's spirits, such an amount of study from disgust at everything else, is unparalleled in history. Society! Good God, a man might as well try to get into the society of the twelve Apostles as any society worth having here. They're as proud as damnation and as mean as the vile climate. I never saw a flirtation going on, though they've got some jolly places for it. I've no idea where the balls are, that is the fashionable balls, for their palaces aren't any too good for one, and the private lodgings utterly incompetent. The aristocracy all belong to the Court and hate everything that smells of America. They seem to have no hospitality, as we do, and as for "making a house one's home," no one but a Prince of the Blood dares to invite any one to dinner. I really believe that there is no society in Germany that would give me any great pleasure, it seems to be so different from all I ever met before. The idea of every one's living in suites of rooms, cursed holes that at home no man with two hundred and fifty dollars a year would be willing to look at. Then this keeping mistresses is all very well, but from what I've seen of it, I'd rather have one respectably bright girl to talk to if she was as ugly as my German shoes.

Now, my good youth, don't air your sarcasm on me for running into extremes in this way. The truth is I've pent up my wrath till I'm tired, and now that I'm on the point of leaving Berlin for six months, I'll just abuse it as much as I damn please. Not that it's worse than other places. Paris is just as bad if I can believe dozens of different fellows' reports. Dresden is infinitely worse and Hannover just ten times worse. Munich may be better, but I don't believe it; and so with Wien. But I've eaten German dishes till I'm nearly run to pieces. I've lived in this air till I'm all used up. I've studied the damned language till I'm utterly lost in it, and finally despair of ever becoming a German. For the last fortnight I've been afraid to eat any more of their vile compounds, and have lived on a beefsteak a day.

My pleasantest reading has been Cicero de Officiis and v. Rönne,[1] das prussische Schulwesen; my only polite society the Apthorps; my greatest amusement Sinfonie Concerts, Mozart's Operas and Rhine wine, and now, by God, I'm going. So there you have it summed up nice.

I'm in a jolly good humor tonight, or I should calumniate this city. But as it is, I am rather lenient towards it. I only say the world is wide; manners are different; and German customs don't suit my ideas. It's got brutally played out. Fellows who can live on music or art or women are all very well here. I've done as well as I could at all three. The two first are good. The last is a damned humbug. But I need something more yet, even if Law is thrown into the bargain....

You ask my plans for the summer. They're not formed yet further than I've described in my last letters home. One thing is determined. I leave this city on the 12th April. Higginson wants to go off to Weimar for a few days and as my school is up now, I may as well go off with him. Thence to Dresden. Ain't I glad, though the weather is no better than it was last November, December, January, February and March.

My article or articles on the schools is going on to an enormous length. At Weimar and Dresden I'm going to re-write it and throw it into the form of letters; three or four; but I long ago gave up any idea of printing them; I write only to keep my hand in, and for future use, after I get home. Don't suppose that this is affectation on my part, and that I want to be urged. I merely don't care to write for publication now.

Crowninshield is pottering round here without apparently any object, and also Cabot.[2] Ben talks unendingly about Hannover which if I hadn't seen it, I should imagine from his account to be a sort of a sixteenth Heaven. He hates it bad though; much worse than I do Berlin. Joe Bradlee[3] is perfectly happy there with his music and the young Unger.

I'm a philosopher, and eat beef-steaks, the only things, actually and truly, that are cooked here so that any nutriment remains in them. My God, I wish I could make you eat "erbsen, sauer-kohl and pökelfleisch," or "kartoffelnklos," and if you didn't blaspheme, I'm mistaken.

April 9.... I'm now busy in packing and taking leave, and as it is always well to provide for contingencies, I will just notify you that in

[1] Ludwig Moritz Pehr von Rönne (1804–1891).
[2] Louis Cabot (1837–1914).   [3] Josiah Bradlee (1838–1902).

a large box which Higginson and I leave at Anhalt & Wageners, filled with books, etc., is a package addressed to you. In case I should come a Frank Howe game, you must take care that that package does come to you and to no one else, for it contains my journal for five years, and some of my own letters, yours, John's, Hunnewell's, etc., etc., etc. There is also a short letter of directions in it. This providing for un-pleasant contingencies seems queer, but can't be helped. I'm sure one has warnings enough that he set his house in order, from the way that fellows drop off.

You needn't show the first part of this letter to the parients nor tell them how I blow up. The great difficulties here are really only three; one that the weather is so bad; the second that the city and country is so flat and unpleasant; the last that one cannot get nutritious and healthy food. Otherwise the place is pleasant and attractive.

You can however tell the Congressman that I have just come in from a P.P.C. visit to Baron v. Rönne. He gave me a card of admit-tance to a debate of the Landtag a little while ago, for which I wished to thank him. He was exceedingly kind. He and I had a quite long conversation, extending over a number of subjects, from the schools, in which I am interested, to the war which he says will surely come, though Prussia wants bad to dodge it. Such is fate. Among other things he invited me to call on him at Bonn if I was there, and advises me next winter to be presented at Court. The Baron looks dreadfully unwell, but I sincerely hope I shall find him here next winter, for he might be of great assistance. I shall call on him at Bonn where I shall be for some time in the fall.

I've bid good bye to my school, the semestre of which ends the day I am to leave Berlin. The boys have always been very polite to me, and I've had not a shade of trouble with any one, scholar or master. It has taught me a good deal, but the two chief things are 1st. to understand what is said; 2d. to talk with confidence, and not to think I mustn't speak because I can't speak like a German. Lord, you ought now to hear me coolly wind myself up in German conversation. The people laugh, but they understand. At Dresden I am going into a family to try that experiment. The arrangement is all made and my trunks go right on, while I stop a day or two round in spots, Witten-berg, Leipsic, Weimar, etc., etc.

Don't imagine because I blow up at Berlin that it's so intolerable as all that. The truth is I've had a great deal of low spirits here, and am only now getting really the better of them, permanently, I hope. (Don't think I've got the pox or am in love; neither is true.) Still the winter as I look back on it has been by no means so bad, though I'm devilish glad it's over. At all events it's changed my ideas and course of life immensely. But one of your balls would have been a God-send to me any time last month.

You have my Dresden address. H. G. Bassenge & Co. How long I shall stay there I've no idea; perhaps a month, perhaps two. Puchta and the Institutes [1] and Cicero will satisfy my cravings for literature. You don't know Puchta. Well, he's a cussed old jurist....

To Charles Francis Adams, Jr.

DRESDEN, April 22, 1859.

MY DEAR FELLOW: — Your letter of the 3d arrived to-day. I owe three to the family; one to mamma which I'm afraid must go unanswered except for what you can read for the common benefit in this; one to John, which I shall enclose with this; and one to you. Taking your letter through in order, in the first place if it's all right about the paternal "hints" and my "explosions," I am contented and let it remain so.... You find fault with my wishing that you may not remain long in the law, and if your three alternatives are right, I acknowledge I'm wrong. I wrote however under the idea that there were other branches of development open to you. Society I'll leave for John. Yet I will say incidentally that I agree with you in your ideas about your position in it, and I wouldn't be sorry to see one or both of you married....

I know nothing about public and newspaper matters with you. Sickles's [2] trial I had not heard a whisper about. I hope he'll hang though. Whoever told you that an Atlantic voyage salts a letter, never said a truer thing. It gives a most rare and delicate flavor, and you never made a greater mistake if you imagine that your letters don't repay the trouble they give. If all your effusions are read by the public with as much interest as your letters are by me, you'll be a devilish lucky fellow.

Your letter needs so much answering. On the other hand I shall have no difficulty in filling up my sheets this time, for I've been off on a lark and I've more than enough to say.

Well, Gott sei Dank, I've seen the last of Berlin for a considerable time, and here I am in the good city of Dresden among the Saxons, and also a heap of Americans, to all of whom except two or three I've

---

[1] Georg Friedrich Puchta and his Cursus der Institutionen [of Justinian].

[2] Daniel Edgar Sickles (b. 1823), who shot Philip Barton Key, and was acquitted.

shown and shall show a very cold shoulder. On the twelfth, at seven o'clock in the morning I left Berlin in company with Crowninshield, Higginson, and Mr. Apthorp with his wife, mother-in-law and small son Willy, who went along with us so far as Wittenberg to perform a pilgrimage to the shades of Luther and partly to bid us adieu. Never mind the particulars. Wittenberg is a dirty, stupid little place, and one's elevated sensations turn into extreme weariness after a couple of hours in it. Mr. Apthorp's crowd here turned back, and we, after two hours of slightly stupid waiting at the little depot, took tickets on to Halle. To Halle we should have gone, if some restless devil hadn't inspired us with an admiration for the appearance of Dessau from the car-window, and induced us at forty seconds warning to step out of the car and sacrifice our tickets to Halle. As we had no baggage except our carpet bags, shawl-strap-contents and travelling pouches, this was easy. The inhabitants of the charmingly neat little Dessau, however, who don't see a stranger more than once in a life-time, must have been somewhat bewildered at seeing our procession march through their silent streets. For throughout our trip we insisted on carrying our own baggage and were usually accompanied to and from the hotels by from two to six large men who seemed to think we were madmen over whom it was their part to exercise a careful surveillance. We used to try all sorts of experiments on them to see what their ideas were; stopping short, to see if they also would stop too; walking fast, walking slow; but they never left us at any price. I suppose in Germany no gentleman carries his own carpet bag. Luckily there were enough of us not to care whether they did or not.

So we landed at Dessau and rambled round the town till we found a hotel. Never mind Dessau, however. I'm not going to copy Murray nor Baedeker, the German Murray, which we always carry. It's a nice, funny little Pumpernickel. Read Fitzboodle for the best idea of these one-horse principalities. We left it the next morning in the same order of march, and went on to Weimar, which is much such another, only they bore you to death there with Goethe and Schiller. Vide Murray for sights, all of which we saw, the funniest sight however being ourselves. Here unexpectedly John Bancroft [1] joined us, as he was removing from Dresden to Düsseldorf. He was a great addition to our party. Modest, agreeable, good-natured and both able and cultivated, he is a remarkably pleasant companion, and as he talks better German than any of us, was usually our spokesman. We never put up at the best hotels if there was a cheaper one, and I can tell you,

[1] John Chandler Bancroft (1835–1901), son of George Bancroft.

if it isn't always so comfortable, it is in the long run a great deal pleasanter. If you were as tired of great hotels as I am, you'd see why this is so, and why I, exclusive of money considerations, prefer to sacrifice a little comfort and get a little something new. We travelled cheaply sometimes, but when we chose we spent as much as we liked. It wasn't much though.

The next day we went on to Eisenach (my plans of work at Weimar were knocked in the head). Eisenach is delightful. The old Wartburg above it is covered with romance and with history until it's as rich as a wedding-cake. The walks and views are charming and I would willingly have remained two or three days, but the next morning we packed every shred of extra baggage off to Dresden; made a grand immolation of our beavers (except Higginson who clung to his with a love that was more than love, and left it with the baggage master, "to be called for") and taking an open carriage rode through a heavy rain down to Waltershausen, a little place south of Gotha, where we proposed to begin — what! Why a walk in April through the Thuringian Wood.

We carried only our great coats and Ben and I a night shirt. A tooth-brush in one pocket; some collars in another, and some handkerchiefs in a third. I strapped the coat over my shoulders with a shawl strap; the others tied theirs *à la militaire*. We never wore them while walking and though mine is very thick and heavy I never felt it disagreeably. We started from Waltershausen that afternoon and walked some three hours, stopping once only to drink a glass of bier and smoke a cigar. The scenery was very pretty and, perhaps, three centuries ago, wild. The sky reasonably clear, and the weather cool so that we were not too warm. That night we arrived at a little place called Georgenthal where we got a jolly supper and slept in two most romantically large, rickety, cold and ghostly chambers, with the wind outside blowing like fits and creaking the dismal old sign in the most pleasing manner. Up the next morning at about eight and had a delectable breakfast of which honey was the great delicacy, and I never before appreciated how good honey was. Set out under the care of a man who pretended he would guide us through the woods, but he was consummately stupid and we soon found ourselves on the highroad again. So we dismissed the guide and pegged ahead through heavy snow showers which we didn't mind in the least, stopping once at a little dorf where we had a glass of bier and smoked a cigar and Bancroft sketched a dog. Bier is a first-rate thing to walk on and we marched along for an hour up a charming valley with a clear sky and the best of spirits. Crowninshield and Higginson were geese enough to tire themselves by running up a tremendous hill on time, against bets of a bottle of wine, which they won and which like other bets we made, haven't been paid. By and by we began to get deuced tired. The road wound up and up and up and it seemed as if it would never end. We first got into mud, then into slush, then into snow two inches deep, and at last I for one was pretty much used up, and the others not much better. Oberhof appeared however after a tramp of near five hours; a little village perched on the top of the hills, where it was yet dead winter with more snow than I'd seen for a year. It snowed heavily all the afternoon, and as I declared I walked for pleasure and not to get over ground, and wouldn't stir another step that day, Higginson who urged going ahead, was forced to give in and we passed the afternoon as well as we could, finishing by a round talk and a couple of bowls of a compound known as Glühwein; claret punch, hot, with spices and things. The next morning we set off again at eight o'clock in a snow-storm, with from two to eight inches snow on the ground, over a mountainous country. You may think this wasn't much fun, and indeed I believe I was the only one who really enjoyed it, but the glow, the feeling of adventure and the novelty; above all, the freedom and some wildness after six months in Berlin, made it really delightful to me. I haven't felt so well and fresh for ever-so-long. After two hours we reached the Schmücke, a couple of houses on the other side of the hills, and here, sir, we indulged ourselves in a real American tipple. We procured the materials and under Ben Crowninshield's skilled direction, we brewed ourselves a real ten-horse-power Tom and Jerry, which had a perfectly miraculous effect on our spirits and set Ben to walking down that hill with the speed of a locomotive. Bancroft and I took it more gently and fell behind. The day cleared; the snow gradually disappeared as we descended and we got to Ilmenau to dinner at about two o'clock. Rode on in an open wagon from Ilmenau two hours to Königsee through mostly uninteresting country, and at Königsee slept. The next morning, in the most curious manner and without previous concert we all caved in and agreed nem. con. to ride the remaining day's journey. So we did ride it, whiling away the time in an intellectual and highly instructive series of free fights to keep us warm, which commonly ended in a grand state of déshabille all round. The scenery was pretty; one view quite charming, but the day was mostly cloudy and cold and for my part I was so exhausted with fighting and laughing that I hardly cared for anything. We dined at Rudolstadt, the capital of the little Principality of Schwarzenburg-Rudolstadt or something of the sort. It had as usual an enormous palace, and the Prince I believe is as poor as a rat. Hence we pressed on, hiring a lumbering old travelling-wagon, and after six hours of going up interminable hills and going down interminable hills, we jolted down by the statue of old Wieland into little Weimar and put up zum goldnen Adler as before. So our journey was over. It had been made wholly without plan. None of us knew six hours ahead what we were going to do. It was jolly as could be and the fellows were all pleasant and indifferent to everything except what was pleasant, so that we had a jovial time. Still I did not object to getting through with it. We none of us cared to lose more time. Düsseldorf and drawing were calling Bancroft. Bonn and the Pandects were yawning for Higginson. Dresden and Puchta shouting for me, and whatever Ben's plans are, it was time he should begin some application in earnest. So we were not sorry to find ourselves in Weimar again.

So with the exception of a few hours stay in Leipzig, here I am comfortably settled in Dresden, thanks to Higginson who got me my room. Bancroft is already in Düsseldorf. Higginson sets out in a day or two for Bonn. Ben is here seeking a family, but I doubt if he gets what he wants. Anderson is here, but unless he changes his set, he'll not see me much. Many other Americans are here, but if possible I shall not go near them. A Mr. Stockton [1] is consul and does the hospitalities, but except under compulsion I shall not go within a mile of him. I mean to leave Arthur Dexter's letter on his brother if he's here, though I don't expect that it will do me much good. Until I get tired, there's no need of seeking this society which, I imagine is confined to the Americans and English whose name is legion.

Puchta arrives on Monday, by which time I hope all my arrears will be done up and I shall set to work to try and make something out of old Herr Justinian's Institutions, which it is quite time I was at. Dresden is a pretty place with much more attractive points than Berlin; as good a theatre and the best Gallery north of the Alps. It's shut now but reopens again soon, when I shall go and learn it by heart. Weather of course bad as usual; the worst ever known, say the Germans. But as yet I don't mind that and have got plenty to do even though in this Holy week every place of amusement is closed and not even a concert to be heard, thanks to their idiot of a King's being Catholic. The change of residence has done me good and I feel better in every way than I did in that damned hole of a Berlin.

[1] P. A. Stockton, consul at Leipzig.

So you may count on my remaining here for two months and I imagine that they'll be pleasant ones, although after my Berlin experience I've become confoundedly skeptical about all places, unless there's some absorbing mental application. It's delightful to live a little while in a new city but when the fun is exhausted, it gets played out.

I've received a letter from Loo at Rome in fits about the Dying Gladiator. What she means to do this summer I've no idea. I wrote to her that if she'd settle anywhere in Switzerland I'd bring my books down and walk with her husband. This blasted war which will probably break out within a week if they're not at it already, knocks the Tyrol in the head. Then there will also probably be fighting on the Rhine so that God only knows where a fellow can go, except to Norway, which indeed I would like to visit. Extras are out to-night which indicate that the Austrian troops are preparing to cross the Rubicon, and then all Europe's ablaze; Austria, Prussia, Bavaria, Hannover and Saxony, to say nothing of the various other "Bundesgenossen" who contribute ten men and a drummer apiece to the "Reichs armee."

You'll be out in the country when this reaches you, and can philosophize in peace over it there. But I recommend you if you mean to travel, to do it first in America. You speak of astonishing the relatives, I suppose by trotting off somewhere, but it don't pay to come to Europe and rush over it, and that's just what does pay at home. Go out into the wilds, boy; pass a month round among the Mormons and then come back with a clear head and a little practical knowledge. I don't know how Loo can stand her travels and be in raptures still at everything. I get so bored by all these sights that I only want to get out of their way. A Gallery ought to be visited once a week an hour each time, to really enjoy it; otherwise one loses his power of appreciation....

To Charles Francis Adams, Jr.

DRESDEN, May 15–17, 1859.

MY DEAR CHARLES, — I suppose by this time you've received my letters all square. I've answered every one of yours most religiously; one arrived April 1st, and was answered April 10th. Another received April 22d was answered April 25th with John's. The present one arrived two days ago.

I wish I could write as long as you, and I admire your last exceedingly. You've made a first-rate letter out of common-place materials. But the truth is, though I have probably a thousand things to your one to say, I get so tired of writing them that it comes hard. However I'll do my worst and let her go....

For my school article, I've already written to you about my change of plan. It's now finished in the form of two letters, about the same length, very poorly written and excessively stupid. Don't imagine I'm modest. If you ever see them you'll appreciate that my remarks are not at all unjust. At present they are lying in my trunk, and are likely to remain undisturbed until when years are over, I shall have occasion perhaps to use them. They are now in a wholly unpublishable state, and of no use except as a series of notes and references. The last *Atlantic* was remarkably good. I passed a whole rainy morning reading it, and my laughter over parts of the Review of Wilson's Mexico aroused the Fräuleins in the next room to the belief that my reason was yielding.... In other words, I'm really obliged to you for your offers but, as I felt here just as soon as I began to write, I can't do anything to satisfy myself or anyone else, and as I have here a very positive objection to making myself uncomfortable, I think I shall let the matter remain in its "trunk-ated" state.

I feel precious little like working very hard here, I can tell you. With the exception of a few pages of Roman law every day, I don't do much labor, unless you call long walks on fine afternoons, and talking nonsense with the Fräuleins labor. This place is a most decided improvement on Berlin and my position here is much pleasanter in every way. In the first place I'm far enough along in the language to be able to feel at my ease among the people. Then it's summer and we occasionally have a real American day. Then the country round Dresden is delightful. In fifteen minutes one can walk out on any side to very pretty scenery and get a glass of beer in thousands of pretty little restaurations. Then I'm in a family and don't feel lonely. And finally and perhaps the greatest reason of all, it's still new and I haven't yet got tired of it.

You think I suppose of course that one must be happy as pie under such circumstances, and I confess that I do enjoy myself exceedingly and can imagine that it will be tough to come home into an amiable lawyer's office. But the deuce of it all is that one gets so used to it, and doesn't at all appreciate his position. It's only when I think of you and your daily routine and your necessary confinement in Boston that I feel the contrast and see in what a pleasant place my lines have fallen. Still, the longer I remain here and the more I wander about, the firmer my conviction is that old Milton was right when he talked about the mind's being its own place, etc., etc., and sich. I believe I enjoyed myself just as much at home as I do here, though of course there were times when it was infernally slow. The difference is that the whole ground is changed. My pleasures and my troubles are all different from what they were at home, and I shall have really to get home and at work before I shall appreciate how much I really have enjoyed myself here.

Society with you is over. With me it is just begun. Perhaps too ended at the same time. Last Wednesday, one of the brothers of my establishment, a Lieutenant, was married and I was invited to the feast. So at five o'clock I came to my room and costumed myself in that same old dress coat which has seen so many experiences on both sides of the ocean; and then taking one of those nondescript one-horse carryalls which are known through Germany as droschkes, I rode over the bridge and arrived at the Hotel known as the Stadt Wien, or Hôtel de Vienne. Here I was shown upstairs and had taken off my coat and was calmly drawing on a pair of gloves, when the servant opened the folding-door and I was horrified at seeing before me an army of white dresses and sternly fixed countenances arranged in order, and all staring, gravely, as if it were a funeral, at me as if I was the coffin. With that grace and suavity of manner for which I am famous, I marched up and stormed the phalanx by a series of bows. I did attempt one speech at a person whom I supposed to be the father of the bride, but he looked so alarmed and seemed so thoroughly over-whelmed with his white cravat, that I backed off and took to flight without an answer. Probably I should have remained smirking in the middle of the floor all the evening if I hadn't caught sight of one of my Fräuleins grinning at me. I bolted to her and began chattering non-sense fluently. Admired the bride's dress as in duty bound. She wore all white, as is necessary, and a myrtle wreath on her head, fastening her veil and a bouquet of white flowers in her hand. The bridegroom who had just that day received his promotion as Ober Lieutenant or First Lieutenant, was very polite to me, probably because I had pre-sented to my four Fräuleins, his sisters, bouquets all round just before they set off to the church; a piece of extravagance which I had in-tended should cost me six dollars but which through a stupid blunder of the gardener who didn't understand my German and sent smaller bouquets than I ordered, only did cost one American dollar and a half. So here I ensconced myself, behind the muslin, and talked idiocy till all the officers and guests had arrived. It is true I found myself alone among the female portion; all the males standing in a corner and talking together. However it wasn't my business. I did know some of the women and didn't know any of the men and they didn't seem to care to trouble me or make my acquaintance, so I didn't trouble them. At last a movement was visible. The alarmed old party in the white cravat paired off with a stiff old lady who had made a bow when I was presented to her. The officers bolted for their partners and I was notified to take the Fräulein Emmeline Strauss into the supper room the which I did. Here we

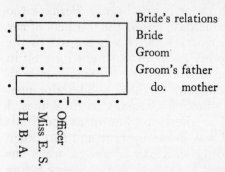

Bride's relations
Bride
Groom
Groom's father
do.   mother

H. B. A.
Miss E. S.
Officer

were arranged at table as per diagram. I was placed in a seat which I imagine was not *the* seat of honor and had my partner on my right and a small boy on my left who eat and drank largely and didn't answer my only observation to him. Other small boys opposite who drank too much and eat quite enough. Dinner began (seven o'clock) with soup; then meat, game, all sorts of German dishes, wine (sherry, claret and Rhine). I talked at intervals and the Lieutenant next my partner also talked largely and we had rather an amusing time, making a good deal of noise so that the papa came down and reproved Fräul. E. Strauss.

Presently after the first course one of the numerous officers arose and recited a piece of poetry which I couldn't understand very well and which he himself hadn't committed very well. However it passed and ended with a call for a grand "hoch" or hurra, so we all "hoched" and marched round and touched our glasses with the bride and bridegroom. Then another course, another speech, another "hoch" and drinking. And so on till the program was at last varied by quite a pretty ceremony. The sister and brother of the bride came up behind her and took off from her head the myrtle wreath, which only maidens can wear, replacing it with a simple little band of flowers, and at the same time the sister reciting another piece of poetry applicable to the occasion. This again ended with a "hoch" and more touching of glasses, and then another course. In the next interval one of the young ladies appeared as a market woman in costume, with a great basket strapped on her shoulders as the common women wear them here; and standing behind the bride she made her another poetical address producing from her basket the emblems of her household

duties, such as a lot of eggs, flour, butter, etc., etc. I couldn't understand the poetry very well. It was none of it original, but as I was
told made for the occasion by poets whose business it is and whose
advertisements are to be seen in the papers.

After this the supper ended. The company left the rooms for a
while, and when the tables had been removed we came back and the
dancing began. We had had music on and off all the evening. As I
was talking with one of the young ladies, the bridegroom came up and
asked me if I wouldn't come and take a glass of wine, so I went with
him into a smaller room which looked into the supper room and
where most of the gentlemen were smoking and drinking. Not to be
peculiar I also took a cigar and a glass of wine and made an effort to
talk with one of the officers. The conversation naturally fell on the
war, and I expressed a regret (which the Lord knows I don't feel) that
the Austrians should have let their two days start be lost by negotia-
tions. My very modest remark was taken in such dudgeon that I
dropped the whole affair and walked off into the dancing room where
I took a turn or two in the polka. They dance very fairly here indeed,
though I don't like it so well as our own style at home. So the evening passed in variations of dancing and cigar, but I confess that what
with the fish, etc., at supper, I was fearfully and overpoweringly
sleepy towards twelve o'clock. It was all very quiet though. I didn't
see any overdrinking as I'd expected. There was no noise nor indeed
any very large amount of liveliness that I saw, and at about half after
twelve (the married couple having disappeared) we separated and I
conducted my large flock over the quiet old bridge in the moonlight,
home; for the father is sick and had to retire early and I had the keys.

There may have been about forty or fifty people there. Almost all
the men were Lieutenants. The women were as German women
usually are, but dressed I think in less bad taste than the Berlinese.
German women don't please me; at least those of this class, which is
second or third rate. I've not met any of the nobles or first society and
probably never shall, but these that I have met, all look too coarse
complexioned and dowdy; remind me too much of their diet and want
of soap and water. None that I've seen have any ideas beyond their
households and little general information. They are good-natured
and polite, but evidently an American is not the thing here. America
is much disliked now in Europe and no one will believe anything good
of it. I never allow myself, or very seldom to get into a discussion on
the subject for they are wholly incapable as a rule of understanding
our ideas on these points. They live in another atmosphere.

This is a good place for engravings if you want me to get some for you. I myself have thoughts of being extravagant in this connection and I want you to do a small commission for me. I want you to go down to your engraving man, I forget his name, and ask him whether he has a good engraving of the Madonna di San Sisto, by Müller, and how much he charges for it. You can also if you will, find out what he calls his best engravings of this picture and send me the engraver's name and prices annexed. I saw last winter at his store a number of these engravings and I want to find out whether the difference in price is enough to warrant my buying one here. Müller's engravings of this picture have the highest reputation here; so I wish you particularly to ask about the prices of the same man's works in Boston.

The world goes on here quietly enough. I know very few persons in this city, Ben Crowninshield being the only American I see much of. We walk together a good deal, if the weather suits, which happens about once a week. I wonder whether they ever have good weather in Europe. I've seen just four days, I think, really clear and bright straight through.

I remain in Dresden pretty certainly till the 1st of July. Not having heard from Loo for ever-so-long, I sent off last week a laconical note to her which I think will bring an answer, if she's received it. Of course I can't settle any plans till I hear from her and this cursed war, which has already reduced Austrian paper money fifty per cent, and makes me give nearly five per cent discount on my drafts on London, they say, though I've drawn none since the war began.

My God, my boy, what a bad affair that Sickles trial was. What cursed fool made that "Sunday morning" opening for the prosecution? How can the people act so like idiots as to treat such a man so? It horrifies these German idiots here and makes me damn mad, for I can't defend it. Yours, H.

To Charles Francis Adams, Jr.

DRESDEN, June 7, 1859.

MY DEAR CHARLES, — You're unlucky. You say in your last that you never took so little pleasure in going out to Quincy as this year. In your first letter from Boston last fall you said you had never been so sorry to leave Quincy as then. Get your mind into a right state again.... John, I see, will be a farmer yet. If he wishes, I'll write a series of "Farmer Letters from Europe" for his benefit, to tell how things are *not* done here. Take the stupidest way possible and you'll know how they *are*....

For the philosophy of your letter, I'm now in such a jovially pleasant and lazy condition that I can't for the life of me discuss it. Work is really out of the question. I've looked for Gibbon but can't find him. Try again next winter in Berlin. Really now the weather is too fine, the country too pretty and the life too lazy to allow of energy.

Why, this life is regal. I don't recollect to have done a great deal since we began our fine weather, but I lounged lots.

Just this instant the Herr Secretär bolted into my room in his shirt sleeves with a telegram that the French had entered Milan. Luckily the Herr Secretär is himself no friend of Austria, and as I always affirm that "Frankreich und Oesterreich sind mir ganz einerlei," I don't get into arguments. Still it's deuced hard to avoid cheering and kicking somebody when the good news comes. For some time Ben and I tried to remain neutral but 'twas no go, Sir. I thank God that as yet I've met no Austrian in Dresden who doesn't side with Sardinia. In conversations with Germans I never mention the subject, not because I'm afraid of the police, for there is little danger of that here, but because it's a disagreeable subject. Just once though I'd like to open my mouth and express to assembled Saxony that I, H. B. Adams, consider them a pack of cowardly, stupid idiots. Ben has once or twice let out his opinion roundly and quite eloquently, of course not in public nor to everybody, but quietly at home. His host is a republican, as are very many people here, but they are all so scared about France that they've lost all presence of mind. Prussia alone keeps cool and knows what she's about. Ben and I have regular old hallelujerums together every night when a fresh battle's won. If Milan's taken, citadel and all, before July first, I lose a dinner to him at Munich.

You mustn't complain if we talk a good deal about the war. It occupies a very large angle in our thoughts and talk here, and gives zest to our life.

I tell you what, old fellow, I begin to appreciate what the beauty of European life is. In Berlin I had no idea. This is considerably a different thing. The weather is somewhat ahead of everything yet. The city is full of strangers and occasionally a pretty face. One hears Russian on one side, French on the other, English everywhere, German occasionally and samples of every other tongue at intervals. From five o'clock in the afternoon till nine we are usually walking or at concerts. Sun doesn't set till after eight and I tell you that a sunset concert on the Brülsche Terrasse at Dresden, sitting under the trees and smoking with a view down the Elbe at the sunset, and a view up the Elbe to the pine hills above, is something jolly. I don't deny it, I enjoy this life.

We have enough excursions planned to keep us going every day of a stay here. Last Sunday I walked out to a village named Kesselsdorf (where Napoleon fought; one of his greatest battle grounds is almost under my window) with two of the Fräuleins and the father, to visit that couple whose marriage I described in one of my last letters. They are established there; a battery of artillery quartered on the town. We passed the morning here and dined with them, driving down to a Brewery in the afternoon and remaining here till sunset. Just imagine a father and two young ladies and a German boarder setting out from Boston on foot at eight o'clock Sunday morning to walk to Quincy and visit a friend. This was a good two hours' walk and none of us noticed it in the least, or felt tired after it. Indeed from eleven o'clock in the morning till I went to bed at night I was in a state of continual boozyness from repeated seidels (or töppfchens as they're called here) of bier which I had to drink and which quite opened my heart.

One afternoon Sauren (who is now gone) and I took the steamer and went up the Elbe to a famous fortress called the Königstein, to which, in case of a war the king of this great land always packs off the Madonna and some other great pictures, the contents of what is known as the Grünes Gewölbe, including the regalia, and finally his family and himself. I believe the various Royal Majesties have several times had opportunities to see their armies surrender, and yet had the satisfaction to know that there was no getting at their own royal persons. Neither Frederic the Great nor Napoleon could take this place. We didn't bother about the fortress, for which see Murray, but the river was deuced pretty and parts of what they call the Sachsen Switzerland were quite fine.

As for social position it's much as usual. The Fräuleins are well apparently and I am on the best of terms with them all. I strive with giant resolution to do the pretty, but don't effect much on that score. Luckily there's no danger of my affections being made away with, though I like the girls and try always to be polite.

As for sights and all that I've tried to see them, but except the gallery it was rather a bore. Goodish collection of armor and weapons; best in the world I believe in some respects. Grünes Gewölbe, lot of old knick-knacks, precious stones and all that; decided bore. Palace, frescoes, rather good but no great. In short sight-seeing is an infernal nuisance and I now cut it down as short as possible.

My German is I believe really profiting by my stay here and has got on quite a step. It is poor enough, Lord knows, but it serves and improves. Ben and I talk it a good deal together and I've worked quite hard on it this last week, writing and committing it. However it's a beastly matter and I never expect to speak it really well. Such a hobbly, hopeless matter I never saw. Only occasionally I feel consoled, as the other day on the steamer for instance when I stepped in to help an Englishman who couldn't even ask for anything to eat. It's the set conversations that knock me, especially when I get excited and can't recall words.

No one is here or has been here that I know of. I doubt if I should trouble them if they did come. I read the stranger list every morning and always see more or less Americans' names, but as I've not yet troubled the Consul, it does not seem very probable that extra-society will trouble me. One evening at the theatre I sat next to a young fellow whose bill I borrowed and who was polite enough to offer me his glass. Thereupon I made sundry remarks to him in German, sir, that were worthy of a double-distilled native. He didn't answer. Says I to myself he's a foreigner and isn't up to Deutsch. Then I racked my brains to invent a French sentence but all my small stock of French was long since driven out of my head by German. So finally I addressed him in English. It turned out that he was an American, a young fellow named Storrs, from near Worcester in Massachusetts, come abroad for his health, been in Italy, and left Milan in the last train that came through. Since then he has left his card on me and I shall call on him. He seems to be a very quiet, gentlemanly "boy," perhaps nineteen years old, and further I know nothing about him....

To Charles Francis Adams, Jr.

NÜRNBERG, July 3, 1859.

DEAR CHARLES: — I've just come in from a walk in the dusk alone through this exquisite old city. Ben has gone to bed....

This week has been a tremendously busy one and at the same time hot as tophet. Last Tuesday afternoon Ben and I visited Tharandt, a pretty little town some nine miles from Dresden. The next morning at seven we took the cars and went up the Elbe and came to Königstein, a great fortification perched on a high rock. From here we crossed the river to a place below which is pretty and commands a beautiful view. This country is called the Saxon Switzerland. I tell you what, this seeing sights on a flaming July day is tough. However,

I found it very pleasant, for when at about three o'clock we came down to take the steamer, we fell in with a gentleman and two ladies, one of whom was young and quite pretty. Naturally we entered into conversation with the gentleman who was pretty well on in life. He was a Russian-Swede; spoke six languages but not English; "my daughter speaks English, however." Ja wohl! I made a note of that. We continued our conversation, steamer was late; ladies sat a little way off and were unapproachable; steamer at last came and I manœuvred so as to get a seat by the pretty girl and under the apology of bad German entered into an English conversation with her. She was clever, highly cultivated and interesting. Had just come from Italy and was strong Italian. Spoke pretty English. Was a little taller than I in figure; slim; light eyes; distingué. We talked of travelling, of poetry, of art, of Italy and of many other things. I passed a pleasant summer afternoon and liked my friend very much. We arrived at Dresden; left the boat; touched our hats; I never shall see the pretty Swede again, but that's a traveller's luck and God forbid that I ever see enough of a woman in Europe to care for her. That would make a fuss. Ten chances to one it makes a fellow unhappy. But now my pretty Swede's in Hamburg, I'm in Nürnberg; we never shall meet again, but I have a pleasant recollection and count myself richer than before by some agreeable hours.

That evening I ordered down some ice-cream and wine and treated my assembled family to an abschiedsfest. We all got tight, played Schwarzen Peter or old maid at cards and as the Frl. Camilla lost, I corked a pair of moustaches on her face. This Frl. is quite nice; we abuse each other and call each other names, but I rather like her; she's bright and not bad looking. What the family think of me I can't say. They seem to think that I'm lazy and selfish. The first I plead guilty to, but the last not. They wanted my photograph but I told them I was far too handsome to give away my likeness in that way and they must wait till all other prior claims are settled. Finally so far as this family goes I've nothing more to say than that they were aways kind, good-natured, and obliging; I have learned here twice as much German as I knew when I came here and my recollections of this place are all pleasant.

On Thursday morning began packing up in earnest. Ben left a trunk here in which I deposited ten shirts and other articles in that way and a number of books which will all go on to Boston. I visited too the Gallery for the last time and the Madonna, the most exquisite of all exquisiteness. After dinner I just managed to get my trunk packed as the time for departure came, and waited for the droschke which ought to have come at quarter past two. It knew better and nary appeared. Waited till the last instant, then rushed off with a carpet bag and travelling pouch and great coat in a shawl strap. Since then I've had no handkerchiefs, nor drawers nor stockings nor linen shirts nor anything else. Rushed like a mad bull to a droschke station; ordered the coachman to drive as fast as possible to the depot; arrived as the door shut but bolted for a ticket "to Nürnberg." On tearing out my purse to pay I discovered I had only four thalers and the ticket cost eight. My money had gone beyond all idea and I had relied on Mr. Ben, who was already in the cars. I said that I had not enough money and wished a ticket to Leipsic instead. No! I had ordered Nürnberg; it was stamped and I must take that or none. With a tempest of choice English and German execrations I bolted towards the glass door to get in without a ticket. No go. Guard forced me back. At this instant as I turned round in despair to leave the whole concern, Ben's host who was there and had learned my position hurried up with Ben's purse which held just enough. I got on board the train which had probably waited for me, and in a state of pure heat I indulged in a general curse to the whole affair, continuing steadily fifteen minutes till I got cool. Then we set to work to calculate our resources. Ben's position was the same as mine and we could raise only four thalers between us. Both of us had however Baring's letters in our pockets and our tickets were already paid to Nürnberg.

So we went on to Leipzig in a heat that made us gasp for air, and amused ourselves by reading, talking with a couple of Cadets, and also by smoking, as I do, but Ben doesn't indulge in the flagrant Bremen. At Leipzig we stopped an hour and attempted to raise money but the fool of a banker wouldn't do it and we had no time to enquire further. Baring has no agent here. At seven or so we started again. In our wagon was a traveller's real set. A Russian with wonderful hair and beard parted across his chin; three Poles who spoke their native language, which is a mixture of French, German, Italian and Greek; one German who said Ja and Nein and no more; and ourselves. We fraternised with the hairy Russer and the Poles and had quite a jolly time and lively talk till the night came on and towards twelve o'clock at a place called Plauen, the Poles departed. We then had each a seat and it was cooler. We stretched ourselves out and slumbered as well as we could. So we went on all night, changing cars at the Bavarian frontier, till towards five o'clock I woke up feeling dirty as you please, and sticking my head out of the window got some cool morning air and watched the pretty fields of Franconia with their old road-side saints, crucifixes and Madonnas. At six or so we came to Bamberg and Ben and I here got out; we wanted to see the city and the Cathedral. Cleaned ourselves; breakfasted on milk, hard boiled eggs, bread and butter and then rambled up and saw the Cathedral which is peculiar and remarkably pretty. Here again we applied for money, but as they said we could certainly get it at Nürnberg we didn't insist on drawing here. We bought a large quantity of cherries instead and went back to our hotel, eat, drank and slept till the cars came at two and we had to go out again into the burning heat.

Two hours on to Nürnberg. A jolly Nürnberger was our only companion, and we were dead of heat. At three we arrived here and came straight to this house, the Hotel Zum Strauss. So there are our travels!

Monday, 4*th*. Our grand American spread eagle has been remembered by us today but not celebrated. We drank a glass of wine and water to him and let him swim.

Ben hurries me on. I would stay here a week but we go tomorrow morning. My amiable brother, what do you want me to say of this city. I hardly know how to express it at all. Think me spooney if you will, but last evening as I wandered round in the dusk smoking a cigar in these delightful old peaked, tiled, crooked, narrow, stinking lanes I thought that if ever again I enjoy as much happiness as here in Europe, and the months pass over bringing always new fascinations and no troubles, why then philosophers lie and earth's a paradise. Ben and I have passed the day in a couple of great churches, lying on the altar steps and looking at the glorious stained glass windows five hundred years old, with their magnificent colors and quaint Biblical stories. So fascinating these things are!... There's no use talking about it. Let it go! Nürnberg is Nürnberg. If I go on I shall be silly, even if I've not been already.

So tomorrow we bid good-bye to Dürer and old Peter Vischer, the churches and the streets; the glorious old windows and the charming fountains and all the other fascinations of this city, and march on to Munich. The weather bids fair to last forever; we roast and broil in this absolutely cloudless sky, but sleep well and enjoy life. How long München will take us is a problem, but not more than a week. Ben wants to get through. As I'm determined at any price not to return to Berlin before the November semester begins, and hate the very idea of seeing that city, I'm in no hurry.

I've not got your letter by me. As to the lecture you administer in regard to writing and money, I'm obliged but just now can't undertake to discuss it. As for my studying, although I still assert the principle that it is well to work I must confess that any slight efforts I've made in that direction have ludicrously failed. Since I left Berlin I've not done a thing except pretend to read a page of law a day, an effort which unhappily never succeeded. In fact I've acted precisely as you recommended, and am quite well satisfied that so far as real work goes I shall do little in Europe. At the same time I do not think that the time could be better employed and believe that what I'm picking up now is of more use than my two years of Blackstone and Carry Bigelow, etc., would have been at home. Nevertheless you need not scare the Governor by this reflection. Next winter in self-defense I must peg away and probably hard. But as for the law I learn in that way making me a jurist, I doubt it. That it may help to make me a strong man is more possible; that it may be a mere extra accomplishment kept for show is most likely of all....

To Charles Francis Adams, Jr.

THUN, August 6, 1859.

DEAR CHARLES, — I received your letter of the 2d–9 July the day before yesterday together with a splendid batch of others, including one from papa and one from John who seems like the ancient Phœnix to have become young again and this time so thoroughly that I can't begin to keep along with him. When my unhappy conscience will be relieved from this weight of letters Heaven only knows. Some time ago I wrote a line to mama from Zürich and since then have had every moment taken up, what with mountains and general accelerated motion. Loo however still writes I suppose à la steam engine and she supplies all gaps.

Here I am as you see in Switzerland and have seen this lion or a part of him at last. Very fine he is too, but Englishmen have rather injured the primitiveness of the beast. Here in Thun we have been for several days leading a delightfully primitive and lazy life; Kuhn, Theodore Chase,[1] Ben Crowninshield, Loo and I; all economising, and I in particular looking forward to that £100 that should be here in a week, with a firm consciousness that if it doesn't arrive I shall have my movements rather stopped off. Travelling is perfectly frightful. A pound a day is the lowest a man can calculate on. You can see about where I shall be at the 1st of November.

[1] Theodore Chase (1832–1894).

Tomorrow I'm off for Mt. Blanc, shall see Fred Hauteville [1] at Vevay, be back here on the 15th and set off immediately with Kuhn, Loo and Theodore over the St. Gothard into Italy where we shall visit Turin and Milan and I shall again leave them at Como and come over the Splügen onto the Rhine. This is an innovation on my original plan, but Loo wants me to do it and it will only take about two days. Then I shall rejoin Ben at Baden and we shall do the Rhine together.

This is the program. Hope they wont find fault with it at home. It will all be done before you receive this letter.

My own conscience smites me at times when I think of what a big plum-cake I've got hold of and what an indigestion it may give me. I wish to God I was not the first of the family who had done all this, for it renders necessary all sorts of carefulness and puts me as it were under obligations and bonds for future conduct. Travel as modestly, yes, as meanly as I will, it is wholly impossible to keep independent of the Governor's assistance and that will bring its discount, I suppose, with it, if not in one way, then in another. But what can't be cured must be endured....

To his Mother

DRESDEN, November 8, 1859.

At No. 4, Kleine Schiessgasse we're getting on as well as could be expected. Frightful kindness overwhelms me from all sides, and I am put to my trumps to be polite. I daren't even joke except in my letters, and ever have a benign smile on my face. Certainly if I don't become as stiff as a German it's not because I don't try. You would scream to see me contest with the Herr Hofrath [2] which of us shall enter a room first. I open the door and stand back with a bow; he says with a gesture towards the room: "bitte recht sehr; après vous;" to which I smile deprecatingly and remark: "bitte, Herr Hofrath, wollen Sie so gut sein;" if he still insists, I yield and precede; if not, he enters and I close the door after him with the highest respect. He is frightfully learned and buried in science, so that he seldom comes out, but is a good old soul and very kind. This afternoon he has been showing me all over the royal natural history collection, of which he has the care. He wants a stuffed swordfish and a lot of American sea-weeds. I should like to help him, but hardly know who to apply to.

The Frau Mutter is benign as ever. Yesterday afternoon we all

---

[1] Frederic Sears Grand d'Hauteville (1838–1918).

[2] Heinrich Gottlieb Ludwig Reichenbach (1793–1879), botanist and geologist.

went to a concert; that is the Professor, the Mother, the Augusta and I. There *we* met two of *our* friends, a Countess Rodolorowowski or something that sounds like that, and her mother. Goodness gracious, the formalities, the bowing and scraping and hopping up and down, the air of majesty with which those corpulent ladies swelled about and visited their acquaintances at the other tables. My eye, wasn't it rum. Meanwhile I sat next the amiable Fräulein (who looked deuced pretty and all the Lieutenants envied me) and I think, take the four hours through, I may have spoken about ten words an hour; in the interval sitting still and looking at my kid gloves. The Countess, too, was particularly gracious and addressed several remarks to me. Only think!

As for the Fräulein, ain't she a one-er, that's all. She reminds me all the time of Nelly Lowe; in fact I call her "Miss Nelly" now. She's a will of her own and gives me the most immense delight. A perfect little Tartar, and smooth as a cat. I'll do her the justice to say however, she doesn't seem to have any designs on my person, and it's only within a few days that she has begun to recognize my presence at all, for I don't talk a great deal and haven't paid her any profuse attention, seein' as the German girls never know what to make of it when a person takes any notice of them. So I laugh at her nonsense and avoid personal contact.

With the brother, Theodor, about twenty-four or five years old, I'm better acquainted. He has a large collection of coins and is passionately fond of all sorts of antiquarian rubbish. If papa wants any particular German coins I might perhaps be able to get them through young Reichenbach. The other day we went off on a foot-excursion and from nine o'clock till nearly four we hardly stopped. Visited a lot of villages, old churches, graveyards, and pretty walks and views. The neighborhood of Dresden is, as you know, remarkably pretty, and as the Theodor knows every foot of it and its history, and the local legends in which Saxony abounds, it is very pleasant to wander about, though I was pretty tired when I returned. Just now I am in hopes of getting up a still more interesting excursion. You must know Saxony has lots of ghosts, ruined castles, haunted churchyards and the like. Madame Reichenbach is superstitious and in her heart, if she only dared say it, believes them all. Indeed I believe every man in Germany, high or low, has more or less of this, and they gravely assert that the White Lady who is said to haunt half the royal places in Germany, and announce by her appearance the death of the King or the birth of an heir to the throne, has been seen so often and the fact so clearly authenticated that it is impossible to doubt it, and they tell a lot of ordinary ghost stories to prove it.

When sensible people talk this way, I can only make a face, shrug my shoulders and politely smile. Of course I believe that it's all stuff and nonsense, and wish I could see one of their white ladies. But as this is impossible, I have set to work to see if we couldn't hunt up a ghost, and just as sure as I can find a promising one, I am going after him; and we propose (to Madame's horror) to select some haunted ruin and sleep there a night to see if the spectre will be hospitable. Of course it must be really romantic; otherwise it will only be a bore.

I'm pretty well settled now for the winter. Three mornings in the week at nine o'clock I go down and take riding lessons; three others my fencing master comes and teaches me how to use a rapier. This secures a tolerable amount of exercise and regularity. At eight o'clock in the evening I am summoned to tea and we talk till past nine, but then usually to bed. At one we dine. Madame is horrified that I don't eat anything. She's accustomed to German appetites and seems to think that a man must starve if he doesn't swill sauerkraut and pickled potatoes. Still I will say she does spare me the sauerkraut as much as possible, and her table is the best I have yet seen....

To Charles Francis Adams, Jr.

DRESDEN, 23 November, 1859.

MY DEAR CHARLES, — Your letter arrived this morning and I will try to answer it at once though I can't make my answer as long as yours. I've too many letters to write for that. But I do what I can.

To condense then. As you seem to begin by wishing to force me to eat my own words I will grant you that pleasure without an argument. I'm not the first nor likely to be the last whose ideas on subjects of which he is ignorant have turned out to be silly. I acknowledge therefore as broadly as you wish, that so far as my plan went, I have failed and done little or nothing. At the same time I feel for myself convinced that this last year has been no failure, but on the contrary is worth to me a great deal; how much depends on the use I make of it; but the worth is there. You say you think I'm a humbug. That implies that you once believed I was something. I don't pretend to know how far you're right or wrong, but I protest against your judging about the advantages of a few years in Europe from my case. The problem is in fact just this. I have acquired here great advantages; if I am a humbug, they wont help me; but I shouldn't have done any better if I'd remained in Boston; if I am not a humbug, we shall see; but in either case the advantages are there, and the failure, if failure it is, will be in me and not in the European experiment which may be of immense use to a capable man.

As to my occupation for the next year, I am now going on in a general course of German reading mostly in the constitutional history of various countries and desultory light reading, but the German is still the main object. This means you see in point of fact that I'm doing nothing. So far as learning a trade goes, idle I'm likely to remain until I return home. So far as education goes, I consider these two years as the most valuable of my life. Indefinite, you will say. But so far as I can see, it is what you yourself recommend.

You recommend me to write. My dear boy, if I write, I must write as I think. Amusing, witty, and clever I am not, and to affect the style would disgust me and bore you. If I write at all in my life out of the professional line, it will probably be when I have something to say, and when I feel that my subject has got me as well as I the subject. Just now this is anything but true, for I can't seem to master any of the matters that interest me. So don't ask me to be sprightly and amusing for that is what I never was, am not, never shall be....

Your suggestion about rouge et noir is therefore a mistake, though not uningenious. The money I won paid my hotel bills several days and I have never seen a gambling table since. As the Governor has been kind enough to leave me here without money I've had to write to London to ask an extension of credit which I got and the Governor may send when he chooses.

This contest of purpose; this argument about aims, you began against, or if you will, for me. You blame me very fairly no doubt, and try to protect yourself from retaliation by pleading guilty; a sort of Yankee Sullivan tactics, hitting a lick and going down. Face the music yourself. I acknowledge I've failed but I believe I've discovered a treasure if I can but use it. But you; why do you plead guilty to the "tu quoque" before I'd said it. Why do you recommend writing to me who has been hurrying around Europe like a steam engine and am so busy with learning that I can't spare a second for teaching; why recommend this to me when you yourself are smouldering worse than I, when you have never published a word so far as I know. Busy you are, no doubt, and have worked and studied hard; I believe it; but physician, heal thyself. Nearly three years older than I, plead guilty to a "tu quoque" and pass the $5 + x$th winter dancing with little girls just out of the nursery. The Governor's last letter warned me against writing magazine articles on the ground that they are ephemeral. Is that your objection too? Or why have you, who urge it so on me when I'm busy with another language and haven't properly any right to talk, think or write English, why have you in those three years of law not broken the path yourself? You haven't even used the chances you have. Of the society of Boston outside of Beacon Street, I don't believe you know a soul. Of the distinguished men there who could aid you a little and change your course of thought, I doubt whether it ever occurred to you to make the acquaintance of one. There is a very good literary society whom it would be well worth while to know, beginning with Waldo Emerson and going down, and it's from able men that one learns; not from talking old woman nonsense with girls, however good fun that may be. You talk about being stifled in Boston and I don't believe you know anything of Boston except half a dozen drawing rooms and bar ditto. You haven't or hadn't a friend in it, worth having. You try to be a society man and yet want to do work that would necessarily cut you off from that society.

Do as Frank Palfrey[1] does, according to Mr. Hillard.[2] "Oh, he's very well; getting along quite encouragingly. Works hard. Only he is *such* a favorite in society that he has to go out more than he ought. It distracts him, but among the young ladies he is *so* liked that the temptation is too much."

You mention the position I shall have to take when I come back as if you expected me to return a complete lawyer or a Professor or something. Of course I shall stand to all appearances as you stood on entering an office. I don't see how *you* can expect anything else, though I am fully prepared to hear the Governor lay the fault of every failure and every error in my life to Europe. God Almighty could not get an idea out of his head that had once got in. I shall return and study law; when that's done I shall call my preparations finished, and shall toss up for luck. What I have learned here is a part of my capital and will probably show itself slowly and radically.

I have dived into your letter and hauled out these few points to answer. If it pleases you to criticise the answers, do so. No doubt it's good practice, this fencing with each other, and I certainly, as it concerns me, am the very last to find fault. If I had more time and could dilate more, I should like to do it, but home letters come round so fast that I have to hurry them off as fast as I can.

You mention politics. It's my own opinion, believing as I do in an

[1] Francis Winthrop Palfrey (1831–1889).   [2] George Stillman Hillard (1808–1879).

"irrepressible conflict," that I shall come home just in time to find America in a considerable pickle. The day that I hear that Seward is quietly elected President of the United States, will be a great relief to me, for I honestly believe that that and only that can carry us through, even if that can. We've set our hands to the plough and wouldn't look back if we could, but I would thank God heartily to know that comparatively conservative men were to conduct this movement and could control it. If the Governor weathers this storm he has a good chance of living in the White House some day. All depends on the ability he shows as a leader now.

But if things go wrong as they easily may; if a few more Sumner affairs and Harper's Ferry undertakings come up, then adieu my country. I wouldn't give a bad grosschen for the United States debt. We shall have made a brilliant failure with our glorious Republic and the prophet can't say what'll turn up. If our constitution stands this strain, she's a stunner, that's all.

What effect all this may have on our lives, we can't calculate in any way. I mean to come home prepared as well as I know how for luck or unluck, and not be frightened if I can help it. In America the man that can't guide had better sit still and look on. I recommend to you to look on, and if things don't change within a year then I'll eat my head. If all goes right, the house of Adams may get its lease of life renewed — if, as I've various times remarked, it has the requisite ability still. Till then we needn't compromise ourselves and will watch what comes.

So much for philosophy and that sort of thing. In reference to life here I have a good deal that I *could* say, but this letter would then be the size of yours and that I can't allow myself who write a letter a day almost. So I'll digest.

My family satisfies me and gives me all I want. They are kind and very German, poor, as you say, and proud in proportion. I think Frank Brooks needn't have been so delicate in his ideas about writing to them; on the contrary I think a short letter on the occasion of introducing me, would have pleased them if written diplomatically enough. Luckily I never mentioned having asked him for a letter, so his refusal didn't embarrass me at all.

They rather spoil me here. German politeness is a cumbrous affair consisting chiefly in elephantine compliments and profuse lies. The Frau Hogräthin is master of the art, but I have learned to watch the countenances of her son and daughter as indexes, and can now nearly tell when there's a deviation from truth. The daughter, the Fräulein

Augusta, is a brick. She might be dangerous if — well, if it only weren't that to me she isn't. I don't know why. One can't explain these things.

Billy Howe is in great feather here. He got disgusted with Vienna; you ought to hear him cut up Glancy Jones;[1] and is now living here waiting Sidney's [2] arrival. A few evenings ago he gave a stunning little card and supper party in his rooms. Governor Lawrence, two daughters and that amiable son [3] who was your friend and messmate in College and who has just arrived here; Mr. and Mrs. Stockton, the Consul, and myself. Just enough for two whist-tables and a pleasant sit-down supper. Of course it was stylish and very jolly; I didn't get home till three o'clock. The next night there was a little blow at the Biddles', son of old Nick Biddle, at least so says Billy. This was rather slow, but Billy, the Miss Lawrences and I had our whist and heard an Italian woman sing. Afterwards we smoked and drank punch in his room and I got home at two.

On the 22d Shep Brooks [4] walked into my room. He was from Paris for Vienna and leaves on the 25th he says. I kept him that day to dine with me, and family and all went out to a concert in the Grosser Garten in the afternoon, at which he seemed to be pleased. I did what I could to make his stay agreeable; introduced, or rather got him acquainted with Billy Howe and the Lawrences and we all went under Bill's care to the Biddles.

Mr. Robert C. Winthrop and his family has also arrived and we three Bostonians sent our cards into him yesterday, as we happened to be all dining at the hotel. This morning his courier brought his card to my house, so he lost no time about it. It's queer how the Americans are piling in here now just when the season's over. The Gans's are here; I believe either you or John knew Miss Bertha at Sharon; I don't care to be introduced to her; in the first place I should feel as if I were flirting with my aunt, to follow in your elderly footsteps; and then Madame objects to my talking so much English and I don't go out more than is absolutely necessary. I myself prefer a quiet life at home with a fight about once a week and a flirtation now and then, but lately I've talked more English than German.

Wiggins' catalogue as I have already twice written reached me in

---

[1] John Glancy Jones (1811–1877), United States Minister to Austria.

[2] Henry Sidney Everett (1834–1898), son of Edward Everett.

[3] Albert Gallatin Lawrence (1834–1887). The father was William Beach Lawrence (1800–1881).

[4] Shepherd Brooks (1837–1922).

Münich and I've had no time to attend to it as I wanted to. As my own expenses will be this year larger than last, I shall probably spend as little money for myself as possible though I have no objection to paying off my debt to you in this way. I mean to devote a few hours to engravings this winter and shall get the Hograth to introduce me to the overseer of the royal collection. If I see any good heads in the shops, I shall buy a few, though not without advice as to their state, for I know nothing about these things as yet.

Beecher's sermon has not yet arrived.

Yesterday was Thanksgiving I suppose. Shep, Billy and I drank to the health of those at home. Last night we saw Dawison,[1] a famous German, as Hamlet. It was a very remarkable rendering, something entirely new and very striking, but repulsive and painful. I don't want to see it again and yet it showed more genius than any I ever saw. Yours affectly.

November 25.

To his Mother

DRESDEN, March 4, 1860.

Tonight, or last night, for it's now six o'clock and the day breaking, I've not been to bed, having just received a new book which interested me exceedingly. It is a volume of Humboldt's letters to a friend of his in Berlin, and from distinguished characters to him, and it is making a great talk in the world. They say it's to be suppressed by the Government, but the cat is already out of the bag. The letters are personal to the tip-top, and there's hardly a public man or interest that doesn't come in for a notice. Half the Princes in Germany are ridiculed in it, and Prince Albert of England comes in for a scorcher. All Berlin is ridiculed and abused, to say nothing of the very strong political opinions and religious ideas which will set the stupids into a howl. And yet it does more honor to Humboldt and shows more what he was than fifty biographies, for this is all in short, formless, scribbled notes without connection and hardly to be understood by a non-Berliner. I can't understand half of it. How it ever came to be published is a wonder to me, for it certainly cuts dreadful close and the letters reach to within two years....

March 6. It's aggravating to have to sacrifice the carnival and even the Easter week at Rome, which I regret more than all the rest. But it will be worse if war comes, and Napoleon is playing Villa Franca

[1] Bogumil Dawison (1818–1872).

over again. People say there'll be no war. I think they are crazy. War or revolution, or both, and it's my belief that if Napoleon hopes to turn conservatist now, it'll only make the troubles worse and the success less. I should think the statesmen and premiers in these days would go crazy with the responsibility and more than that, with this uncertainty and swaying to and fro. To us who stand so far on the extreme left that all European parties and party fights seem matters of the last century, this doubt about the present is irritating to a degree.

Humboldt's[1] book or letters are suppressed in Berlin and also here. Apropos, American slavery comes in for its notice; a letter of Baron Gerolt's is in it, anti-slavery, but not up to our points; Humboldt's own ideas were ours. A letter of "the great American Historian Presscott" is in it — not political.

To his Mother

DRESDEN, March 10, 1860.

Billy Howe has just given me a Boston *Advertiser*,[2] which contains a letter from Washington partly filled with papa and his action in the matter of the House Printer. My opinion one way or the other is of course of no account, but as I can imagine how disagreeable and vexatious the affair is, and how many hard words it must have cost, and as I see how very cautiously and treacherously the *Advertiser's* correspondent expresses himself, I think I can allow myself a little word about it. Papa may not be much encouraged by knowing that his son ever so far off, and without much acquaintance with the matter, thinks as he does, and enters with all his heart into his view of what are his duties; but at least it will spare him the doubt as to whether I can appreciate the position he has taken. I am too far away to know how public opinion stands on the matter, but I feel sure that whatever the momentary impression may be, his action can in the long run only give him strength and position; and as for me myself, if that can be of interest to him, I'm ready and willing, in perfect and common sense, to lay all my hope and ambition for the future, on the same stake. I have not an instant's doubt that every one whose opinion we value, feels as I do about it; and as for his constituents, if there isn't enough honor left in the Third District to back up such a position as this, then so

---

[1] Friedrich Heinrich Alexander von Humboldt. *Briefe . . . an Varnhagen von Ense* [ed. by Ludmilla Assing]. Leipzig, 1860. English and French translations appeared in the same year.

[2] *Boston Daily Advertiser*, February 25, 1860.

much the worse for the Third District. Thank God, we're not reduced so far as to truck and dicker off our principles in that way, even though much more depended on it than a seat in Congress. But in spite of the hint of the *Advertiser*, I have enough faith in morality still to believe that this affair, far from weakening papa's strength in Massachusetts, will increase it tenfold; and if he can maintain himself on the floor of Congress, and hold to this beginning, he'll soon be the most popular man in the State, as his father was before him. So far as I can judge from the various papers I've seen, the spectacle of an honest man in Congress seems to be something wonderful and beyond all calculation. No one seems to know what to say to it; whether to praise or blame; and I think I can imagine the various newspaper articles as clearly as if I had them here. Luckily it's not the first time we've been in a minority of one, and if the campaign of '48 hasn't broken us in to sneers and abuse, it's time something else did it. Sneers and abuse have got to be taken; there is no help for that; we must only get callous to it; but at least there's one comfort, and that is that we needn't be afraid of it. There's no "spot on our scutcheon" that I know of, where anything can take hold.

We must all feel the importance of this start. It's the first declaration of the colors we sail under, and whether successful in its immediate object or not, it cannot fail to have a good result and make an impression on the honest part of the people. I know it's a hard trial for you and papa; even at this distance I feel it; but it must have come sooner or later, and on this matter as well as another. We young ones don't count much now, but it may at least please papa to know that those who are nearest and dearest to him, go heart and soul after him in this path.

To Charles Francis Adams, Jr.

DRESDEN, March 26, 1860.

.   .   .   .

Your letter is healthier than usual. It doesn't smell of Boston Common and State Street and I was devilish glad to get it. I'm glad you had a good time in society. There is no society in Europe as we understand it, so I can't imitate you. Your first letter about the printing-affair I happened to see through Billy Howe; without knowing who wrote it; I executed a *pas seul* with variations and warwhoop accompaniment in my apartment on reading it. Then I sat down and wrote a florid letter to mamma in which I honored your epistle with the epithet "treacherous." A few days afterwards I was rather taken aback by receiving a package of papers with your initials as "Pemberton." [1] The game is a risky one; take care of your incognito or else it may react and people think it was a political trick of the Governor's to help himself. Putting this aside, it was a great success. Indeed I'm inclined to believe that papa's "coup" owed a very considerable part of its success to that letter, and not a small part to its low tone. Even the *Courier's* "Giant among Pigmies" [2] was quite as much a hit at the *Advertiser* as a bonbon for papa. The *Courier* fell into that trap beautifully. Anyway I congratulate you on your success which is in its way quite as decided as papa's. As none of my home letters have mentioned all these letters as your work, I've said nothing about it either, nor to any one here, and shan't till I hear that you've avowed them.

Seward's speech [3] is a great thing. I think there are as few assailable points in that speech and yet as broad a position, as is possible. Even the *New York Herald* will blunt its dirty teeth on that. As a statesmanlike production too I'm proud of it, and we shall do well to take a lesson from it. The Senate in its best days never heard anything better done....

You come down in your political philosophy to the principle of education; from different grounds I did the same here some time ago. It's the main idea of all progressists; it's what gives New England its moral power; Horace Mann lived in this idea, and died in it. Goethe always said that his task was to educate his countrymen; and that all the Constitutions in the world wouldn't help, if the people weren't raised; and he and Schiller did more for it than anyone else. Our people are educated enough intellectually but its damned superficial and only makes them more wilful; our task so far as we attempt a public work, is to blow up sophistry and jam hard down on morality, and there are as many ways of doing this as there are men in the country. This idea was at the bottom of my letter of the 21st January, and it's only the manner in which we can invest our strength to the most advantage in prosecuting this idea, that can trouble us. For I for one haven't the courage of Horace Mann. As for the union, our field of action remains about the same, whether it stands or falls.

However because we are virtuous we'll not banish cakes and ale.

[1] A second letter of Pemberton appeared in the *Boston Daily Advertiser*, February 28, 1860.

[2] An editorial under that title, praising the course of Mr. Adams, appeared in the *Courier*, February 22, 1860.

[3] In United States Senate, February 29, 1860.

I've been trying this winter to make my path clear to myself but haven't quite succeeded. I still waver between two and shall leave fate to decide. In the meanwhile I mean to have as good a time as under the circumstances will do, and shan't interfere with others....

Your Washington letters have stirred me up. As you know, I propose to leave Dresden on the 1st of April for Italy. It has occurred to me that this trip may perhaps furnish material for a pleasant series of letters, not written to be published but publishable in case they were worth it. This is my programme. You may therefore expect to receive from week to week letters from me, beginning at Vienna and continuing so long as I don't get tired of it. What the letters will be about depends of course on circumstances. Now, you will understand, I do *not* propose to write with the wish to publish at all hazards; on the contrary I mean to write private letters to you, as an exercise for myself, and it would be of all things my last wish to force myself into newspapers with a failure for my first attempt. On the other hand if you like the letters and think it would be in my interest to print them, I'm all ready. In any case you can do just what you choose with them so long as you stick by your own judgment. But if, under any absurd idea that I wish to print, you dodge the responsibility of a decision, and a possible hurting of my feelings; by showing me up to the public amusement without any guarantee against my making a slump, you'll make a very great mistake. I could do that without your help. But it needs a critic to decide what's copper and what silver and I suppose you have courage enough not to be afraid to tell me in case my coinage should turn out copper or copper-gilt. So gird on your sword and don't be idiotic enough to bother yourself with family affection or brotherly sympathies.[1]

The life here doesn't change a hair. I feel like a snake thawing out after being frozen in all winter. My family here bores me. Once or twice I've sat up all night playing cards with the Howes. That was my only excitement. I never make calls for they're slow. My books are now all sent off so I've nothing to do but write. The Howes leave this week; the gambling shop in the Prager Strasse is to be closed, and there will be another winter a closed book. In the whole of it I've not had one good-time. I've digged like a Freshman; hardly once has my pulse beaten faster than usual except at news from home or over plans and thoughts of my own. On the other hand my health has been excel-

[1] Letters were printed in the *Courier* as follows: April 30, May 9, June 1, July 10 and 13, 1860, dated: Vienna, April 5; Venice, April 11; Bologna, April 16; Palermo, June 9; and Naples, June 15.

lent; my spirits uniform; I've never been unhappy; hardly felt the blues; not been discontented; and usually been more or less amused. So there's pro and contra. The life has been a pleasant life enough and very useful and such as it is, I'm satisfied with it.

Billy and I presented a letter on a Mr. de Cramer of the Russian Legation which the Mogul (Uncle Sidney[1]) sent me. At my request he included Billy's name. What on earth induces the Mogul to notice me for the first time in his life? Very kind indeed; very; but quite a new trait. He doesn't intend to remember me in his will, does he? No such luck. That's all for his namesakes....

To his Mother

ROME, May 6, 1860.

. . . .

You mention Charles's *Advertiser* letter about the printing affair. When I wrote to you I called it "treacherous" without knowing that it was his, till a copy from him arrived a few days afterwards. That changed the case entirely. As the matter stands, I think it couldn't have been better, and papa owes to that letter a good half of the credit he has got from his action. It was an admirably clear and even partial statement of the case, and the more effective on account of its lowness of tone, and appearance of impartiality. You would see that from the noise it made, and the way it was quoted and attacked. There was a force in the statement independent from the force of papa's position. I am watching from here with a sort of sickness at heart, the course of American politics. These Connecticut and Rhode Island elections and the contemptible tone politics take with us, are no pleasant forerunners to an election like next Fall's. Not that I feel discouraged; but that each postponement of the final victory confuses matters so dreadfully. However I hope we shall do better as we go on and as long as there's no dodging or begging the question on our side, I'm not afraid....

To his Mother

PARIS, 1 July, 1860.

. . . .

I'm waiting patiently for papa's speech to arrive. The sketch I've seen of it and the papers which Charles sent me, gave me the general

[1] Sidney Brooks.

idea, which was precisely what we would expect. It's all right. This session has gone off admirably for him, and couldn't be better. As for you, I know that in many ways you must feel homesick; but have there never been times at home when you felt homesick and unhappy too? For my own part, I'm getting dreadfully old and cautious. I find that people are unhappy everywhere and happy everywhere. Charles writes me a plan according to which I should study law in Washington and stay with you always. I never knew before this how I liked Quincy and Boston, and how sorry I should be to cut loose of them altogether; but this course, which certainly is the one I should choose and follow, if it will go, finishes setting me afloat. I shall make up my bed in Washington, and no doubt it will be just as pleasant as anywhere else. At all events, whether it is or not, it's the place that my education has fitted me best for, and where I could be of most use. So if papa and you approve this course and it's found easy to carry out, you can have at least one of your sons always with you. For my own part, it's the only idea I've met with as to my own course that satisfies me entirely....

II

WASHINGTON

1860–1861

To Charles Francis Adams, Jr.

[WASHINGTON], December 9, 1860.

DEAR CHARLES: — I propose to write you this winter a series of private letters to show how things look. I fairly confess that I want to have a record of this winter on file, and though I have no ambition nor hope to become a Horace Walpole, I still would like to think that a century or two hence when everything else about it is forgotten, my letters might still be read and quoted as a memorial of manners and habits at the time of the great secession of 1860. At the same time you will be glad to hear all the gossip and to me it will supply the place of a Journal.

The first week is now over and I feel more at home, though I've not made many acquaintances. It's a great life; just what I wanted; and as I always feel that I am of real use here and can take an active part in it all, it never tires. Politically there is a terrible panic. The weak brethren weep and tear their hair and imagine that life is to become a burden and the Capitol an owl-nest and fox-hole. The Massachusetts men and the Wisconsin men and scatterers in other states are the only ones who are really firm. Seward is great; a perfect giant in all this howling. Our father is firmer than Mt. Ararat. I never saw a more precious old flint. As yet there has been no open defection, but the pressure is immense and you need not swear too much if something gives at last.

Of course your first question would be about Seward. He came up here last Tuesday evening and I heard him talk for the first time. Wednesday he came up to dinner and was absolutely grand. No one was there but the family, and he had all the talking to himself. I sat and watched the old fellow with his big nose and his wire hair and grizzly eyebrows and miserable dress, and listened to him rolling out his grand, broad ideas that would inspire a cow with statesmanship if she understood our language. There's no shake in him. He talks square up to the mark and something beyond it.

He invited us down to dine with him on Friday. His wife[1] hasn't

[1] Frances Adeline Miller, daughter of Elijah Miller.

come here this winter, so he has persuaded Mr. and Mrs. Israel Washburn [1] to put up with him till they go off. We six had a dinner, at which the Governor caused a superior champagne to be brought out; not his usual tap. Israel was as usual; ugly as the very devil, but good-humored and nervous and kindhearted as ever. The Governor was chipper as a lark and swore by yea and by nay that everything was going on admirably. The state of society here worries mamma very much and she was sorrowing over the bitterness of feeling and change of bearing in her acquaintances, but the Governor was implacable. He swore he was glad of it and delighted to see 'em down. He'd been through all that and come out on the other side. They had been all graciousness to him as a Whig while they tabooed Hale [2] and Sumner and Giddings. [3] They had tried to taboo him too, later, but then it was too late, and now he was glad they did feel cut up and meant they should.

He is the very most glorious original. It delights me out of my skin to see the wiry old scare-crow insinuate advice. He talks so slowly and watches one so hard under those grey eye-brows of his. After our dinner we went into the parlor and played whist. Gradually a whole crowd of visitors came in, mostly staunch men such as Potter [4] and Cad. Washburne, Sedgwick [5] and Alley [6] and Eliot, [7] etc. Among others who should turn up but the two Rhode Island Senators, Anthony and Simmons, [8] both very fishy and weak-kneed. Anthony is the man whom mamma gave a tremendous hiding to last spring, for a remark he made more than usually treacherous, but he called on us the other evening notwithstanding. The whole company knew all about it, however, and Seward knew they did. I was sitting somewhat back, just behind Anthony and Seward and watched them both carefully. Anthony remarked deprecatingly: Well, things look pretty bad, Governor, don't you think so? No, growled Seward, I don't see why they look bad. Well, said Anthony still more timidly, these financial troubles coming so with the political ones. Why, answered Seward, you can't run a financial and a political panic together, the first will

[1] Israel Washburn, Jr., brother of Elihu Benjamin Washburne and Cadwallader Colden Washburn, a representative from Maine. He married Mary Maud Webster.

[2] John Parker Hale (1806–1873), of New Hampshire.

[3] Joshua Reed Giddings (1795–1864), of Ohio.

[4] John Fox Potter (1817–1899), of Wisconsin.

[5] Charles Baldwin Sedgwick (1815–1883), of New York.

[6] John Bassett Alley (1817–1896), of Massachusetts.

[7] Thomas Dawes Eliot (1808–1870), of Massachusetts.

[8] James Fowler Simmons (1795–1864), and Henry Bowen Anthony (1815–1884).

regulate itself. Poor Anthony fairly broke down and acquiesced. The manner in which Seward spoke fairly bluffed him. But Seward was unmerciful. The first thing we knew he dragged mamma out; wanted to put her against some of these Carolinians; she was the person to take care of them; put 'em in a dark room and let 'em fight it out, etc., etc.; to all which mamma of course answered laughingly while everyone in the room was on the broad grin. I thought he'd never leave off this talk. He wouldn't stop, but rubbed it in and in till Anthony looked blue. At the very first pause and change of topic he got up and took leave. Of course it did not please mamma too well to be used as a sort of a false target in this way, but the Governor only smiled grimly and neither apologised nor confessed his intentions.

December 13. This letter is still waiting to be finished and this week I've been regularly jammed up for time. What with the duties of secretary, of schoolmaster, of reporter for the papers, and of society-man, I have more than I can do well.

Frank Parker arrived here day before yesterday and will be with you nearly or quite as soon as this. To me fell the duty of guiding his steps and I think he imbibed good republican doctrine and lots of it. All day yesterday we were up at the Senate talking in the cloak-room and today I left him in the House where he was well looked to. Last evening I took him down to Seward's, and today Seward and Mr. and Mrs. Israel Washburne came up to dine with us and him. By the way W. H. S. was urgent on me to tell you that he had lately received a letter from his wife in which she said that a letter dated last October I believe, and addressed "Auburn, Mass.," had arrived from you after going to its direction. With various complimentary remarks the Governor said that as he was epistolarily exhausted, he wanted me to acknowledge the receipt of this letter, etc., etc., etc. Mrs. S. sent him on the letter I believe, saying that it was too good to be lost.

We had an interesting time today. As you of course see, all the mean material we've got is coming out now. Dixon of Connecticut [1] flattened out, and so has Sherman; [2] so will Anthony, Foster, [3] Collamer [4] I believe, and a heap in the lower House. The Thirty-Three committee is sitting now every day and all day, and they'll be reporting some damned nonsense or other soon. Today we were all waiting for our good father before dinner, when in he popped in a state of con-

---

[1] James Dixon (1814–1873), Senator from Connecticut.
[2] John Sherman (1823–1900), Representative from Ohio.
[3] Lafayette Sabine Foster (1806–1880), Senator from Connecticut.
[4] Jacob Collamer (1792–1865), Senator from Vermont.

siderable friction and reported that his committee had sprung a resolution on them yielding everything, which had passed in spite of him with only eight negatives; New England, New York and Wisconsin. Seward looked blue and little Washburne was disgusted. However, as it's not to be submitted to the House, but only intended for effect on South Carolina, there's no immediate danger, though it embroils things badly and will inevitably break the Republican line. So we went to dinner and Seward almost killed me by telling some stories and laughing over them. He goes home tomorrow to be gone a week and Mr. and Mrs. Blatchford who are coming to stay with him will be received by John and entertained by the Washburnes. Why he goes home I don't know. *He* says it's not politics that drives him, but W. H. S. is not to be sounded by ordinary lines.

I shall write for the Monday's *Advertiser* setting some things forth.[1] You may be aware that our good papa bears up the opposition in the Thirty-Three. I have therefore reserved my fire so far as he is concerned, but now he will have to be sustained. My communications will perhaps be on the crescendo principle and if the battle waxes hot and Charles Hale does not rise to it, you must thumb-screw him a little. Send Dana and Horace Gray [2] round. I shall write to Hildreth too, probably. My theoretical letter of last Monday was good. I say it because I have my doubts. It takes forty-eight hours for a letter to go and be published so I didn't send one this evening as it would wait till Monday.

We're chipper as can be here and I try to keep a general look-out over things. Our men are not afraid, but you must prepare for *any* compromise that the South chooses. Our only hope is that they'll kick us out and refuse everything. This is not improbable, but nothing is sure.

I am only making acquaintances so I can't give you much outside news. There is little or no society as yet and will be very little all winter unless the Southerners accept the olive-branch. As I am very busy, I don't care much, for there is so much life here as to allow one

1 The *Boston Daily Advertiser* does not appear to have had a regular correspondent in Washington, and in its issue of December 3, 1860, appeared a letter from that city, signed "Nimrod," as "Correspondence of the Boston Daily Advertiser." A second communication thus signed appeared December 5, but beginning with the third, December 7, the signature was dropped and "From our own Correspondent" was adopted. Communications with that caption appeared in the *Advertiser* on December 10, 13, 20, and 27; January 1, 11, 15, 16, 17, 22, 24, 26; February 2, 6, 8, 11. After that Charles Hale himself went to Washington and took over the correspondence, signing his communications "Carolus."

2 Horace Gray (1828–1902).

to dispense with balls. Sidney Everett I've seen twice but as yet not to make any treaty with him, so to speak, and I am the less anxious to do so, as he seems wholly taken up with his Carrolls and I see no hurry to get in with them....

We are all well and happy. Our mother allows herself to be distressed somewhat by disunion, but in action she is straight and has a reputation such that the fishes are afraid of her. Parker will enlighten you verbatim as to matters here, as he has seen all our side and has gone deep into the state of affairs. I'm afraid however I only speak exact truth when I tell you to prepare yourself for a complete disorganization of our party. If the South show any liberal spirit, the reaction will sweep us out dreadfully and thin our ranks to a skeleton. Luckily we have our President and can hold on till the next flood tide. How many there will be faithful unto the end, I cannot say, but I fear me much, not a third of the House. But the Governor will be great: *our* Governor I mean.

Hints of any sort are welcome.

To Charles Francis Adams, Jr.

[WASHINGTON,] Tuesday, December 18, 1860.

DEAR CHARLES: — I'm a confoundedly unenterprising beggar. It's an outrageous bore to make calls and as society is all at odds and ends here, I make no acquaintances except those of the family. Even political matters are slow. There are no fights. Every one is good-natured except those who are naturally misanthropic and even those who are so frightened that they can't breathe in more than a whisper, still keep their temper.

This makes it almost slow work. Then we dine at five and after that I don't feel as if I wanted to run much, especially as there are no parties nor receptions. The President divides his time between crying and praying; the Cabinet has resigned or else is occupied in committing treason. Some of them have done both. The people of Washington are firmly convinced that there is to be an attack on Washington by the Southerners or else a slave insurrection, and in either case or in any contingency they feel sure of being ruined and murdered. There is no money nor much prospect of any and all sources of income are dry, so that no one can entertain. You see from this that there's no great chance for any violent gaiety.

Every one takes to politics for an occupation, but do you know to me this whole matter is beginning to get stale. It does not rise to the

sublime at all. It is merely the last convulsion of the slave-power, and
only makes me glad that the beast is so near his end. I have no fear
for the result at all. It must come out right. But what a piece of mean-
ness and rascality, of braggadocio and nonsense the whole affair is.
What insolence in the South and what cowardice and vileness at the
North. The other day in that precious Committee of Thirty-Three
where our good father is doing his best to do nothing, in stalked the
secessionists with Reuben Davis [1] of Mississippi at their head, and
flung down a paper which was to be their ultimatum. That was to be
taken up at once or the South would secede. The committee declined
to take it up till they had discussed the Fugitive Slave Law. So out
stalked the secessionists but not wholly away. They only seceded into
the next room where they sat in dignity, smoking and watching the
remaining members through the folding doors, while Davis returned
to say that he did not wish to be misunderstood; they seceded only
while the other proposition should be under discussion. Is that not a
specimen of those men? Their whole game is bare bluff.

The heroism of this struggle is over. That belonged to us when we
were a minority; when Webster was pulled down and afterwards in
the Kansas battle and the Sumner troubles. But now these men are
struggling for power and they kick so hard that our men hardly dare
say they'll take the prize they've won. In Massachusetts all are sound
except Rice,[2] but we've some pretty tight screws on him, and I think
he'll hold. Thayer [3] I count out. Of course he's gone. But Pennsylvania is rotten to the core just as she was in the revolution when John
Adams had such a battle with Dickinson. There is some sound principle in the western counties but Philadelphia is all about our ears.
Ohio is not all she should be, and Indiana is all she should not be, just
as that mean state always was. Illinois is tolerably well in some respects and Wisconsin is a new Vermont, but there's too low a tone
everywhere. They don't seem to see their way.

December 20. Mr. Appleton [4] and Mr. Amory [5] have been on here
the last four or five days engaged in saving the Union. Mr. Appleton
has buried himself among his southern friends so as not to encourage
much any politeness on our side. After passing two whole days in the
senate chamber with Mason [6] and his other attachments, he tapped

[1] Reuben Davis (1873–1890), Representative from Mississippi.
[2] Alexander Hamilton Rice (1818–1895), Representative from Massachusetts.
[3] Eli Thayer (1819–1899), Representative from Massachusetts.
[4] William Appleton (1786–1861).   [5] William Amory (1804–1888).
[6] James Murray Mason (1798–1871), Senator from Virginia.

Sumner on the shoulder and pretended to be very glad to see him. Sumner had not taken any notice of him of course till then, but on this notice he turned round and they shook hands. The conversation however was not very brotherly, as Sumner in answer to some remark on the state of affairs, immediately began to haul the Boston *Courier* and Caleb Cushing over the coals as the great causes of the present misrepresentation, which Appleton of course couldn't quite agree in. However, it was all friendly enough, I believe. Appleton called here when he knew that our father must be at the House, without asking for mamma, and never has called on Sumner at all.

Mr. Amory dined here today. Mr. Etheridge[1] was invited to meet him but didn't come. Anthony of Rhode Island was also invited and did come. We had a very pleasant dinner. Mr. Amory was amusing and told us his experiences in saving the country, which don't seem to have been very successful. He had talked with Douglas a long time and Douglas had been moral, demonstrating from the examples of Wellington and Peel, that a change of sentiments in cases of urgency was the duty of good citizens. Mr. Amory seemed to think that Douglas was the very dirtiest beast he had yet met. He is, by the way, by his present course, destroying the power he has left. Pugh's[2] speech today was disgusting. Those men are trying to build the Democratic party up again.

That blessed committee is still at work all the time and tomorrow a vote will be taken on the territorial question. Our father's course will be such as not to need much active support since Winter Davis[3] is assuming the decided course of breaking with the South and he will bear the brunt of the battle. It seems likely that no minority report of any consequence will be needed. Tomorrow will decide and I have a letter all ready for next Monday's *Advertiser* in case the vote should go right. As to last Monday's letter, which has not appeared, I am not sorry for it, as it was written when everything looked fishy. You can tell Hale this and mark what he says or looks, for I do much mistrust me that he suppressed that letter. One ought to have appeared this morning and I shall look with curiosity tomorrow to see.

I am not sorry that affairs have taken such a turn as to relieve our father. He will be strongly pushed for the Treasury and I don't care to have him expose himself now. Lincoln is all right. You can rely on that. He has exercised a strong influence through several sources on

[1] Emerson Etheridge (1819–1902), Representative from Tennessee.
[2] George Ellis Pugh (1822–1876), Senator from Ohio.
[3] Henry Winter Davis (1817–1865), Representative from Maryland.

this committee and always right, but as yet there is no lisp of a Cabinet. Not even Seward had been consulted a week ago, though perhaps this visit of his to New York may have something to do with it.

As for my *Advertiser* letters it will take a little time for me to make headway enough here to do much. But I do not wish to hurry matters. As yet there has been no great demand; that is, no active fighting, and I doubt if there will be. But these things will arrange themselves so soon as I begin to take a position here.

Johnson's [1] speech yesterday was a great relief to us and it cut the secessionists dreadfully hard. Jeff. Davis was in a fever all through it and they all but lost their temper. Sumner dined here yesterday and was grand as usual, full of the diplomatic corps. He told Alley a little while ago that of course if he went into the Cabinet it could be only as Secretary of State, and Alley recommended him to give up all idea of it. I think he'd better.

To Charles Francis Adams, Jr.

WASHINGTON, December 22, 1860.

MY DEAR BOY: — I sent you off a letter last night, but begin another at once as events pass quick here. I sent off a letter this evening to Hale which is important: the most so of any yet, and perhaps a little indiscreet, but as I don't know how much the world knows, I can't judge exactly how much I ought to say. I hoped yesterday that our M. C. for the 3d. would get through quietly, without rubbing, but it may not be so. They've been discussing the Territorial business in the Thirty, and Winter Davis has fairly cut himself loose and declared his intention to vote against the Missouri-Compromise line as an amendment to the Constitution. He did this yesterday in a speech which followed one from C. F. A., and this speech of C. F. A.'s may cause some kicking. Our men are now tolerably firm and face the music. Those who voted for the resolution a week ago, offering concession, "whether just cause of complaint existed or not," have been so dreadfully pulled over the coals for it by their constituents that they're now stiff. The President elect has signified too in more ways than one, what the Committee had better do and what leave undone. Now our good father in considering this ultimatum of the South declared that rather than consent at this day, before the eyes of the whole civilized world, to see a constitution which did not countenance slavery

[1] Andrew Johnson (1808–1875), Senator from Tennessee.

and was made for freemen, turned into an instrument discountenancing freedom and protecting slavery, he would see the Union dissolved and endure the consequences whatever they might be.

Now if the *Post* or *Courier* get hold of this and misrepresent it, you must see that the case is rightly stated. Don't dodge the issue. Proclaim that sentiment as loud as you please. We shall stand by that. But recollect to state, in case of attack, that this sentiment was not an ultimatum of Mr. A[dams]'s. The ultimatum came from the other side, and it was an answer to a demand from the South. New England will mostly stand up to this mark, but it is not wished to force it on the Republicans, as a majority cannot be got up to it in Congress and there would infallibly be a disastrous split. However, it looks pretty well here now. After papa's speech, Winter Davis came out with his declaration, which had the effect of utterly discomfiting the Southerners and of combining the North. So they did not take a vote, seeing that their ultimatum would be rejected by three or four majority, and today, finding that it was no use, they concluded to adjourn the committee over to next Thursday, so that we have a week's respite to draw breath and get ready for the next round.

The tone of the Republicans improves. Even Corwin [1] is kept down, and some of the fishy ones are wholly converted. Tappan [2] of New Hampshire and Washburne [3] of Wisconsin swear they won't move a hair nor concede a bad cent's worth. Dunn [4] of Indiana is all right and Kellogg [5] of Illinois will keep. You will see by my *Advertiser* letter our ideas about compromise, and will understand that we would yield a good deal to avoid a split now which would be very bad. C. F. A. is decided to vote for Winter Davis' proposition, but this is private. It may never come up. Davis says that Maryland is all right; he has seen Governor Hicks and is sure that there's no secession about her.

That cursed Senate will make trouble if it can. Douglas recants all his heresies; his past life is to be wiped out, and he inscribes the slave power as his deity on the first page of the new book. I'll bet my head to his old whiskey bottle that this step will lay him out cold in Illinois.

The Pacific railroad bill has been pressed as a bribe to the Pacific states. But it's not a good bill and at any other time our friends would all have voted against it.

[1] Thomas Corwin (1794–1865), Representative from Ohio.
[2] Mason Weare Tappan (1817–1886), Representative from New Hampshire.
[3] Cadwallader Colden Washburn (1818–1882), Representative from Wisconsin.
[4] William McKee Dunn (1814–1887), Representative from Indiana.
[5] William Kellogg (1814–1872), Representative from Illinois.

There's nothing more to say. We are in a state of anarchy so far as the President goes, but I doubt the story of his allowing Fort Moultrie to be given up. It can't be true even of him. Mr. Amory told us the other day of a letter he had seen from a New York stock merchant, which ran like this: "The market today much affected by political rumors of disturbing tendency. Towards the close of the day a report was circulated that President Buchanan had gone insane, and stocks rose." Pretty commentary on the popular opinion of the President of these Disunited States. But General Scott is reported as saying that Mr. Lincoln is a man of power. Several letters have passed between them.

Old Cass, after having been kicked by all his colleagues for three years and ten months, has brilliantly invested the remaining two by resigning. He never made such good use of any other two months in his life.

Weed [1] is said to be coming here and if so, there will be trouble perhaps. He has behaved too badly. It may come to a struggle to get Seward to give him up. If he urges concession, C. F. A. will perhaps have to step in. Yours ever.

To Charles Francis Adams, Jr.

WASHINGTON, 26 December, 1860.

MY DEAR CHARLES: — I received a letter from you last night, almost wholly occupied with criticisms on my *Advertiser* letters. What you say is perfectly true and I am and have been as sensible to it as you. Naturally it is hard at first for a beginner as I am to strike the key note; still I think I can manage it in time; and meanwhile criticise away just as much as you please. I've had the deuce's own luck, though, for my last letter, intended for Monday's paper, seems to have missed too, and as my next was to have been a pendant to it, I wouldn't write it till I had seen the first in print. I wanted in them to explain the position that Winter Davis and papa are taking on a proposed measure of settlement to be offered by the Republicans on the committee through papa. So I shall have to begin again and do it all over, I suppose. I can't imagine what has happened to the letter, for I'm sure Hale would have published it if he had received it.

I have been rather busy this week in the recess in making calls and getting into a little society, though nothing has begun in that way yet. The only great political excitement has been about the de-

[1] Thurlow Weed (1797–1882).

falcations which I'm not in a way of knowing much about. Governor
Andrew has been on here and I had some talk with him which didn't
lead to much. But his visit here will have a good deal of effect on his
course. He saw all the people, and there is, I believe, no great difference of opinion among the leaders as to the course to be pursued. He
told us of a curious conversation he had had with Senator Mason, who
is one of that class of secessionists who want to use secession as a means
of forcing the North ultimately into yielding everything. They have
even a plan by which all the states except New England, New York
and Wisconsin and perhaps Michigan should secede and reconstruct
the Union without those states. Mason said that he knew of no possible compromise; that slavery and freedom were in conflict and must
be; but that if all the northern states would repeal all their laws prohibiting slavery, perhaps something might be done. But, says Andrew,
Massachusetts never passed a law prohibiting slavery. Her courts
held that slavery was abolished in Massachusetts by the adoption of
the Bill of Rights. Well, rejoins Mason, the bill of rights is of the nature of a law. Andrew repeated this conversation to us one morning
when he came in to breakfast, and papa, who is posted up, immediately broke out: George Mason, this man's great-grandfather, was virtually the author of that Bill of Rights. John Adams merely adopted
his idea.

So, you see, we are to be towed out to sea, up there in Massachusetts,
and left to ourselves. Bon Voyage!

Seward has come back but I've not yet seen him. The position of
the Republicans is getting stronger every day, thanks to these defal-
cations and the treason of the Administration. I rather think they'll
have to impeach Buchanan in the end. Tomorrow I expect to hear
of this settlement measure of the Republicans on the Committee. It
will be based on Winter Davis' proposition to admit New Mexico as a
state, but I don't know the particulars. Papa will be made to father
the thing, being, as Corwin says, the Archbishop of antislavery.
Davis will support it, I suppose. Andrew accepts it, but the Massachusetts men look very doubtful when they first hear it. With a few
exceptions it will however have the support of all the Republicans and
the South will have to take the responsibility of its rejection, which
they will do.

Our good father stands in a position of great power. Crittenden
says that he is the greatest block in the way of conciliation, and some
one else says that his speech on the territorial question in the Committee will prevent his confirmation as *Secretary of State*, which is rather

a wild remark in more ways than one. Now he will have to bear the brunt of all attacks from the ultra men. But he can stand that well enough, and it may even do him good.

Cushing is said to be encouraged. On the one hand he labors under the delusion that there's a great popular reaction in Massachusetts. On the other, the feud between the Douglas and Breckinridge wings of the Democracy is healed, and they hope that the southern states may be brought back, in which case we should be in a devil of a fix. Still, it is hardly probable that they should be such miserable idiots as to come back before the 4th of March, and once the Cabinet confirmed, it's only a question of time anyway.

You see we feel much better here than usual. What may happen, God knows, but if we can drag on to the 4th of March, it's all right. I've written a long letter to Hildreth and shall probably write tomorrow to the *Advertiser*, but nothing can appear till Monday....

To Charles Francis Adams, Jr.

WASHINGTON, 29 December, 1860.

MY DEAR BOY: — I'm sorry to see that you've worried yourself so badly about the "back-down," but as I've written a long letter to Hale about it and as you can obtain from Andrew all the information you want, I can't undertake to discuss it. Just wait till the matter is aired, as it must soon be, for the Committees, after having consumed much time and leaving matters precisely as they stood at first, have adjourned in disgust, and must very soon report. In which case the speaking will begin.

As you up North begin to get mad, we here are getting cool. Sizzle away. Perhaps when the North has been kicked enough, people will stop saving the Union. When the northern Democrats have had their noses sufficiently ground down by South Carolina, perhaps they'll get tired and resist. It's coming hot and heavy and in a month you'll be cool again, as we are, and the Union-savers will be howling for war.

We had a funny dinner here yesterday which would have done you much good. Seward was here with Buffinton [1] and the messenger with the electoral votes, I've forgotten his name. As usual, Seward was great. He kept all the talking to himself and was as chipper as could be. He assents to the "back-down" as you see by the vote on a similar proposition in his committee. We talked away on all the matters of interest and he cussed and swore as usual. I said incident-

[1] James Buffinton (1817–1875), Representative from Massachusetts.

ally that if Major Anderson were disavowed and cashiered it would be a most unfortunate thing. Why so, says he? Why because it would make the North wild, said I, and provoke an outbreak of violence. And what harm would that do? rejoined he in his gruff way. I hope they'll cashier Anderson and make Scott resign. I *want* the North to be mad. So long as the Democrats up there, and the great cities, stick to the South, they'll bully us. If they can only be kicked hard enough to make 'em hit out, there's some chance of settling this matter. Screw 'em up to the war pitch and the South will learn manners. But so long as New York city has it in its power to cut me off from New York state, we can't settle this matter.

The old file has taken a great shine to my cigars and we smoke our good papa perfectly dry after dinner. He submits like a Christian however, and the Governor always finishes two and pockets a third for the way home. He gave us last night a dissertation on dress which was magnificent considering his style of raiment.

After he left, old Pennington [1] came in and sat a couple of hours. He delighted me to a degree inexpressible. I never had seen him before and had a precious tough piece of work to keep my countenance. He rambled ahead in his usual "bonhommy" style, gave his opinions on politics, told how his barn had been burned down at Newark with his horses and carriages; what a splendid run he had made in his District, nearly three thousand ahead of Lincoln and only two hundred behind his opponent, and how his defeat had all come about; what a piece of work he'd had in forming the Committee of Thirty-Three, and how Eli Thayer expected to represent Massachusetts; how the Southerners were overrated and what a set they were, etc., etc., etc., till we all were tired to death. He seems to be a good-natured soul, with a great deal of shrewdness, and weak on the side of his self-esteem. He and Seward are two remarkable specimens of the men one meets here. Pennington is a big man and his legs sprawl out over the room and his boots are very prominent and he keeps his knife in his hand opening and shutting it while he talks. Seward sprawls about too, and snorts and belches and does all sorts of outrageous things, but Pennington's talk is feeble and Seward's, though he says the same things, is brilliant from his manner of putting them. He is by far the roughest diamond I've ever seen, and the originality makes half of the attraction....

The Cabinet is in another row as the telegraph will tell you. Poor old Buchanan! I don't see but what he'll have to be impeached. The

---

[1] William Pennington (1796–1862), Representative from New Jersey and Speaker of the House.

terror here among the inhabitants is something wonderful to witness. At least the half of them believe that Washington is to be destroyed by fire and sword. Some are providing for a retreat for their families.

To Charles Francis Adams, Jr.

WASHINGTON, 2 January, 1861.

. . . .

As to my letters, your remarks are very just. I shall try to work on them. I see that the *Times* of this morning reprints one of my letters with copious italics. I don't like this. Can they suspect or have they been told whence they come?...

Towards night I got over to Mrs. Douglas, where I sat a little while and told Mr. Rust [1] of Arkansas that I was very glad to see with how much moderation and forbearance gentlemen acted now, for that I thought if all bitterness of manner could be done away with, it would end three-quarters of the trouble. Mr. Rust is the only man in the Committee who is rude and overbearing.

People are in the dumps here; vide my *Advertiser* letter on Friday or Saturday. But the battle is over, I believe, with Floyd's resignation. Meanwhile our good father is becoming a very Jove in his committee. He has now pretty much the entire control of it, and has fairly driven the extremists out of the field, as vide my *Advertiser* letter Saturday. He is making himself a great reputation here and on the whole he is sustained at home. He has an immense hold on Massachusetts. No other man could have done what he has done, for he has changed the whole course of the State and is throwing her whole influence, and more than her due influence into the scale now. I consider that the unity of the Republicans is due in a very great measure to him, as well as the unity in the entire North, and I believe that his action alone may turn the scale in the border states.

Wilson [2] was in here tonight and gave us some news about the Cabinet. He says that Seward will be Premier, or rather that he is it already. This is good. Cameron's appointment to the Treasury is thought very bad. People fear jobbing. Bates is good; he will be Attorney General, says Wilson. From New England we shall have Mr. Gideon F. Welles, which is also good. Of course our father remains where he is — to be Premier, I expect, in '64. He prefers his present position, which is certainly one of great power, and I don't

[1] Albert Rust (d. 1870), Representative from Arkansas.
[2] Henry Wilson (1812–1875), Senator from Massachusetts.

know that he's not right for the present. He's a growing man and will soon have a national fame and power inferior to no one unless it be Seward.

His position on the present difficulties will, I think, be sustained in the country, and if it is, as I hope, made the means of uniting the whole North and securing the border states, our good father will be invincible in Massachusetts. His strong point is in not being a mere Massachusetts politician, nor confined to one idea. This is the second time he has kicked over the traces in Congress and I think it will be a great thing.

South Carolina has got to eat dirt; yea, and repent in sackcloth and ashes. I doubt if any other State goes so far, but all the cotton states may go and welcome, if we can keep the border ones. You've no idea how deep the treason is. Joe Lane [1] is said to be at the head of it; that is, when Washington is seized, he will be declared President. Caleb Cushing knows about it too. Couldn't you hang him? I tell you we have just escaped a cursed dangerous plot, and if we have indeed wholly escaped it, it is by God's grace, not for want of traitors.

Seward is well and speaks of you. He's a precious foxy old man, and tells no one his secrets. I'm inclined to think that he has arranged or is arranging everything with Lincoln through Thurlow Weed.

It's one o'clock at night and I've been writing all day. So I must stop off. What did the New York merchant reply to the order of a Charleston house for flour? "Eat your cotton, God damn ye." Yours ever.

To Charles Francis Adams, Jr.

WASHINGTON, 8 January, 1861.

I think we do not feel so confident here as usual. Seward is evidently very low-spirited, though that is owing partly to the labor of preparing his speech. But I have noticed a marked change in the tone of our excellent father, consequent on information which he has received but has not yet confided in me. Until now he has steadily believed that the border states would not go, and his measures were intended to influence them. But now I think he gives it up. His theory is that all depends on Virginia and that Virginia is lost. If this turns out to be the case, it increases our difficulties very badly. It makes war inevitable; war before the 4th of March.

[1] Joseph Lane (1801–1881), Senator from Oregon.

God forbid that I should croak or foresee what is not to come. You and I are young enough to be sanguine where others despair. For one, I intend to remain in this city. If there is war I intend to take such part in it as is necessary or useful. It would be a comfort if such times come, to know that the Massachusetts regiments are ready, and if one can be formed on the Cromwell type, I will enroll myself. Of course we can not doubt the result; but I must confess that I had hoped to avoid a real battle. If Virginia and Maryland secede, they will strike at this city, and we shall have to give them such an extermination that it were better we had not been born. I do not want to fight them. Is thy servant a South Carolinian that he should do this thing? They are mad, mere maniacs, and I want to lock them up till they become sane; not to kill them. I want to educate, humanize and refine them, not send fire and sword among them. Let those that will howl for war. I claim to be sufficiently philanthropic to dread it, and sufficiently Christian to wish to avoid it and to determine to avoid it, except in self-defence. Tell your warlike friends in Massachusetts that we want no blood-thirsty men here. If the time comes when men are wanted it will be men who fight because there is no other way; not because they are angry; men who will come with their bibles as well as their rifles and who will pray God to forgive them for every life they take.

I am confident that if an actual conflict could be kept off for a few months, there could be none. The South are too weak to sustain such a delay. There would be a reaction among themselves from mere starvation and ruin. But if Virginia goes out, I do not see how it is to be avoided.

This is solemn, but I have enough self-respect to keep me from joining with any body of men who act from mere passion and the sense of wrong. Don't trust yourself to that set, for they will desert you when you need their support. They don't know what they're after. Support any honorable means of conciliation. Our position will be immensely strengthened by it. We cannot be too much in the right. It is time for us who claim to lead this movement to become cool and to do nothing without the fear of God before our eyes....

My letters have, I think, done some good in sustaining papa at home and it was a relief to see the *Advertiser* of yesterday declare itself at last. I am convinced that his course is the only true and great one, and that it will ultimately meet the wishes of the whole North. You need not fear a compromise. The worst that is to be feared is, in my opinion, a division in the party. No compromise would, I think, call back the South. We are beyond that stage where a compromise can prevent the struggle. Let them pass their measures if they can; the contest is on us and all the rotten twine that ever was spun can't tie up this breach. Yours ever.

To Charles Francis Adams, Jr.

WASHINGTON, 11 January, 1861.

Edward Pierce's [1] step in attacking papa in the *Atlas and Bee* surprises me. I wish to God he would publish papa's letter to him in answer to one to papa; that would I think end him; not that it was severe, for it was not, as his own letter was very polite; but I think the State would prefer our lead. *Du reste*, what he says is easily demolished and amounts to a misrepresentation and gross ignorance of his subject. It is not that which troubles me. It is the fellow's treason. He thinks papa will go into the Cabinet and he wants his place, but in such a case I hope Claflin [2] will get it.

Apropos of the Cabinet, things are going all round the lot. Lincoln offered Cameron the Treasury without Seward's knowledge. Seward was utterly taken aback and would have preferred any other man. He sent Thurlow Weed on to Springfield to urge C. F. A. for the Treasury, but the New England man selected was Welles and Lincoln seems jealous of C. F. A., as too Sewardish. He wants some one to balance Seward's influence. Meanwhile Cameron's appointment has raised a tremendous storm round Lincoln. Every one is violent against it, and Cameron has actually been forced out. He told Alley lately that he was for C. F. A. for the Treasury, which is queer. He will probably keep the War Department for himself, as he can job there too. The Massachusetts delegation were raving that Massachusetts was left out in the cold and all united in a memorial recommending C. F. A. as the New England member. Lincoln as yet has resisted all this influence and what will be the end, he knows, I do not. At all events it is not so sure that C. F. A. may not come in after all. He rather dreads the place as the hardest in the whole Government.

We had a very pleasant dinner of nineteen yesterday. General Scott, Winter Davis and his wife,[3] the two Connecticut Senators [4] and wives, with Pennington and his three women,[5] etc., etc., etc. Winter Davis wanted to be remembered to you. Scott was pompous as usual. He seemed to hint that the President was vacillating again, but we

---

[1] Edward Lillie Pierce (1829–1897).   [2] William Claflin (1818–1905).
[3] Nancy (Morris) Davis.   [4] Lafayette S. Foster and James Dixon.
[5] Caroline (Burnet) Pennington.

have him under the screws now so that I think he must go right. His Adjutant Keyes [1] wants Major Anderson to bombard Charleston in case they fire on his reinforcements. I am utterly delighted with the course of things down there, if only they've hurt some one on the Star of the West. It puts them so in the wrong that they never will recover from it. Then it will raise the North to fever heat and perhaps secure Kentucky. My own wish is to keep cool. No man is fit to take hold now who is not cool as death. I feel in a continual intoxication in this life. It is magnificent to feel strong and quiet in all this row, and see one's own path clear through all the chaos.

Many remonstrating and many impertinent letters come from the North about papa's propositions, but all either from Garrisonians or men without weight and generally both. Meanwhile his name is kept before the country, which is the great balance to any loss on that side. As a measure of statesmanship, I will stake my head on it. As a mere measure of low political policy I think it will help him too....

To Charles Francis Adams, Jr.

WASHINGTON, January 17, 1861.

. . . .

I tell you we have been watching the political weathercock hard here for the last six weeks. Hard driven on this lee-shore, as we have been, and forced to sail so close on the wind that the sails keep a continual flapping, we have watched and prayed for a lull in the storm and some sign of a break in the sky. It is hard to say whether it has come now or not, but we think it has. Seward's speech [2] has done great good. As you must see, it sustains and relieves our father on one side, and cuts the ground right from under the feet of the agitators in the border states as well as the northern Democrats and Whigs on the other. It is next to impossible now to get Maryland out of the Union before the sixth of March whatever may happen, and I think Kentucky and Tennessee are all right, so that we may sail through it all yet.

As you might suppose, our people are a good deal divided. In Massachusetts, only Rice and perhaps Wilson will support Seward openly; the others have not the courage though several would be glad to. I was present at a funny little scene last Sunday, when Sumner and Preston King [3] came up to dine here. You know what sort of a

[1] Erasmus Darwin Keyes (1810–1895).
[2] In United States Senate, January 12, 1861.
[3] Preston King (1806–1865), Senator from New York.

man King is; the most amiable, fat old fanatic that ever existed. Sumner is always offensive to his opponents; he can't help it; but he can no more argue than a cat. He states his proposition and sticks to it, but the commonest special-pleader can knock him into splinters in five minutes. King is never offensive and is always so good-natured as to be pleasant, even when saying things that in Sumner's mouth would be unpardonable.

After dinner, when mamma and Loo and Mary had gone up, and King had got his cigar and decanter of wine, we got into conversation on the settlement measures of the Committee of Thirty-Three and the New Mexican proposition and King attacked them in his genial way and Sumner sustained King in those round, oratorical periods that you know so well. I have noticed for some time past that our good father has been getting restive at Sumner. That speech last winter was against his advice, but then Sumner always acts with his eye on his personal figure before posterity and our father with his eye on the national future; which, as you see, are two different ends. This evening I foresaw fun, and sucked my cigar and kept still. Soon it began. After a little good-natured preliminary sparring King hit out rather harder than usual with something about compromise, and papa parried the blow with some energy. Then Sumner struck in on the other side, with a re-assertion of our being right, and that the South must be made to bend. Egad, it would have done you good to see how papa faced round on him and hit in, one, two, three, quick as lightning. "Sumner, you don't know what you're talking about. Yours is the very kind of stiff-necked obstinacy that will break you down if you persevere," etc., etc. All which Sumner took mildly as a lamb and hardly attempted an answer. Still he did make some remark about the unreasonableness of the southern troubles and the want of dignity in our descending to quiet them, whereupon I got out Lord Bacon and read him a few lines of the Essay on Seditions and Troubles which seemed to trouble him badly. The battle went on between King and papa after Sumner had been thus squelched and King maintained himself very well till they talked themselves out and agreed on the points where they should agree to differ. It amounted to this, that King thought that coercion was the only satisfactory end, and that papa declared coercion out of the question if the fifteen slave states go out together.

Sumner was up here again yesterday when papa rapped him again over the knuckles. Ultra as he is, he is the most frightened man round; not personally that I know of, but in believing and repeating all the reports and rumors round town.

Yesterday we had the funniest little party. Seward once invited us all down to dinner, but we insisted that not more than one of our younger set should go at a time with the parent birds. So finding that he couldn't manage it any other way, he invited us four children to dine with him yesterday; Loo, Mary, Brooks and I. Loo had to leave her bed to do it, as she was just under one of her head-aches, but do it we did in grand style. The Governor was grand. No one but his secretary Mr. Harrington was at table with us, but he had up some Moselle wine that Baron Gerolt [1] had sent him and we managed to be pretty jolly. He is now, as perhaps you do not know, virtual ruler of this country. Whether he is ever made President or not, he never will be in a more responsible position than he is in now, nor ever have more influence. Since the eighth of December he has been virtually Secretary of State and has been playing a game of chess with the southern men and beaten them too. To-night he was full of the criticisms on his speech, and the *Courier's* delighted him. If the *Courier* said that, he knew he must have said exactly the right thing.

After dinner, the instant we got back into the parlor, out came the cards and he made Loo and Mary sit down and play whist in spite of all resistance on their part. He will have his own way and treats us all as his children. The other evening at our house, after taking off his boots to dry his feet, in the parlor, he patted mamma on the head like a little girl, and told her that she might come down after dinner and pass the evening with us, if she felt lonely without her children. From any other man this would make our dear mother furious, but he is so hopelessly lawless that she submits and feels rather flattered, I think. I have excited immense delight among some young ladies here by a very brilliant proposition which I made, to dye the old sinner's hair bright crimson, paint his face the most brilliant green and his nose yellow, and then to make an exhibition of him as the sage parrot; a bird he wonderfully resembles in manner and profile. If I had a knack at drawing, I would make some such sketch for *Vanity Fair*.

Today my friend Mr. Lars Anderson dined here; the major's brother. He has been in Charleston, has seen his brother and had all the talk with him he wants. The Governor of South Carolina allowed him to do so. He says they are all crazy down there, but polite and chivalrous. Every one is a soldier, but no one holds any rank lower than that of a Colonel, of whom there are five thousand. He says that his brother can hold out two or three months, though not with comfort, and yesterday when I called and had a talk with him about his

[1] Friedrich von Gerolt.

brother, he had to wipe his eyes several times in speaking of him and the pride he took in his behavior. He has seen the President and General Scott and had interviews with them, and the result will be one of two things. Either the rebels will allow the Major to have his letters and to get fresh provisions from day to day, or else supplies will be put in at any price and at all hazards. Mr. Anderson did not say this, but I infer it. He is hopeful for the Union, and only asks time and line, to let the fit exhaust itself.

The truth is a good deal depends for us on a little bit of a fight. Unless this had seemed inevitable, I doubt whether Seward would have made just that speech, or papa his propositions. If that does not happen, I'm afraid that the North may not fully appreciate the concessions of those two gentlemen. But the North ought to be worsted in the fight, in order to put the South in the wrong. If Major Anderson and his whole command were all murdered in cold blood, it would be an excellent thing for the country, much as I should regret it on the part of those individuals.

As for an elaborate paper on things in general here, it's no use. Papa will speak soon; Seward has spoken; I regard the critical point as passed and think that every day will strengthen those two gentlemen. Edward Pierce has dished himself, I believe, and what little temptation I once had to try to serve him up, has passed. The *Atlas and Bee* is a venomous little sheet and will do papa all the harm it can, which, thank God, is not much. I would like however to have the columns of the *Springfield Republican* open to me. It's the best paper in the State and carries most weight. Hale amuses me in his arrangement of my letters....

I am easier about fighting. It is possible that there may be a war, but if I understand Seward, it's more likely to be a siege. We shall blockade and starve them out. They can be tired out in a year, I think, even if they all go; in two years certainly. The cotton states can be finished in nine months or I'm a beggar. It's a mere question how much money they've got, and South Carolina has spent $1,400,-000 in sixty days. That can't last long.

To Charles Francis Adams, Jr.

WASHINGTON, January 24, 1861.

I begin a letter to you though I've little to say, as no new developments have lately come out. We are waiting here. Our father is preparing his speech, the rough draft of which I have quietly read, and which I foresee will raise considerable hesitations in your Hotspurs of the North. I hardly know what to think of the condition of the North now. There are strong signs of a sweeping reaction there. You see our friend Washburne has lost his senatorial election in Wisconsin to a conservative man,[1] and that in the face of his minority report of the Committee of Thirty-Three. Pennsylvania is all gone, headed by Cameron, it is hinted, in revenge for having been kicked out of the Cabinet. Lincoln's position is not known, but his course up to this time has shown his utter ignorance of the right way to act, so far as his appointments go. It is said, too, here, that he is not a strong man. I'm afraid they'll manage to compromise us, and for my own part, believing as I do that the game is ours anyway, unless we're forced into a war, I don't care much what they do, except that it splits the party.

January 26, 1861. It's a curious state of things here. I am trying hard to comprehend it, but as I only see one side and am so hard at work that I don't have much chance to see the other, it is rather hard to follow events with a proper appreciation. At all events I think disunion has run its length. With or without compromise it will end, and the states come back. All we have got to do is to see that the rebound doesn't knock us Republicans over.

The speaking has been good this week and the South Americans have come out bravely. Virginia will go, however, I rather think. Still, there's no knowing. I've seen no big men lately to speak of, except Seward, who dined here yesterday. He puzzles me more and more. I can't see how he works at all. Now, I'm inclined to believe that all Weed's motions, compromises and all, have been feelers on Seward's part. He will not compromise, himself, but he'll let others believe he will, and anyway, this disunion matter must be stopped, is his theory. He is in communication with pretty much everybody; says he receives as many letters from Virginia as he ever did from New York. Scott and he rule the country and Scott's share in the rule is but small.

January 28, 1861. I am so crowded with work that I have no time to write much on my own account. I have been busy all day copying papa's speech for Hale to publish in advance of the ordinary course. I hope to get it done tomorrow and he will probably speak Thursday. You can judge of it when it appears. As I have not yet read it all in its last form, I can't express an opinion.

The last rumor is a resurrection of the old danger of an attack on

[1] Timothy O. Howe.

Washington. Scott is said to have demanded ten thousand volunteers and Buchanan is unwilling to give them on account of a fear of irritating Virginia. These men are mad if they have such a plan, but madmen are sometimes dangerous. *Nous verrons.*

I have written a letter to the *Advertiser* chaffing the five wise men of Boston, which Hale will not publish I suppose. As he always cuts out the spicy parts of my letters, I don't expect it. Still I thought I would make the attempt....

To Charles Francis Adams, Jr.

WASHINGTON, January 31, 1861.

Papa has just spoken. The House listened with a perfectly intense attention, and you could have heard them breathe, I believe, if you'd tried. They were evidently with him and every word told. The galleries, which were pretty full, applauded him several times. His hour out, an extension was granted which is rather rare now, and he finished, applauded at the close. As usual he held them with a regular grip, and when he ended, every one got up and a poor devil who wanted to speak got mad because no one would listen. I didn't see Sumner there, but old Winthrop and Everett were on the floor and seemed rather less well pleased than I should have thought they would have been. After it was over I saw nearly all the delegation come up to congratulate him very heartily, and a perfect host of others.

In my opinion it's a great speech and one that will tell effectively. It's the best stroke the old gentleman ever made yet. It's what the republicans have got to stand on, and you'll see that everyone will ultimately settle on it except the abolitionists and the disunionists.

Papa has been perfectly overwhelmed with congratulations, the delegation being delighted. Winthrop did not speak to him. Everett shook hands and said he agreed with *nearly* everything he said.

I've never seen papa more affected than by the reception he met. Buffington got it in, inducing Corwin and Sherman to let him have the floor on the Pacific rail-road bill. This is a *very* rare thing. The *Herald* man says he's going to telegraph the whole speech on to New York tonight. Fifteen or twenty thousand copies are already ordered for Maryland....

On the whole, *c'est une grande victoire. Voilà tout.*

To Charles Francis Adams, Jr.

WASHINGTON, February 5, 1861.

Yours of the 17 duly arrived. You find fault with me for not writing more, but as I generally have to sit into the morning hours to write what I do, I can only say I am sorry. As for my *Advertiser* letters, Hale does not encourage brilliancy. Chaff seems to be his horror and he promptly expunges all that I write of an unfavorable personal character. The consequence is that I lose all interest in what I'm saying, as I'm never sure he will print it. So it is with all our Boston papers. Indeed the *Journal* has cut Poore's[1] letters so that he pretty much stopped writing at one time I believe. I never see the *Journal*, so I can't say. That was the story here.

Thirty-odd letters arrived this morning full of the most enthusiastic praise of our speech. Personally I am more than satisfied with it and its reception, but so far as its influence on the South goes, I believe it might as well not have been spoken. I'm afraid the game is up and that we shall have to make a new Capital on the Mississippi, for a new Northern Union.

Virginia has decided our fate today. If she has gone, the trouble and violence will begin at once and I have little doubt there will be actual war before the 4th of March. Still, do not repeat this to anyone. It will be known soon enough before there will be any need of getting into a funk over it.

I have little that is new to tell you. Yesterday I went in to see Sumner and found that old beast Gurowski[2] there. I'm afraid Sumner is going to make a fool of himself. His vanity has been hurt and that is enough for him. The difficulty was a miserably small one and not worth the noise it has made. It seems he was consulted as to this appointment of Commissioners to come here.[3] He wrote a letter against it without consulting any of his friends, as any man, asked such a question, of no great importance, might do. The next day John P. Hale, who had managed New Hampshire, wanting to be supported, came to C. F. A. and urged him to recommend the measure to Andrew. Accordingly C. F. A. wrote a short form which was signed by all the delegation until he came to Sumner, who then told him that he had written against it the night before. Sumner is said to be hurt with Hale's behavior, which was certainly not open, for though Hale says he did not know that Sumner would oppose it, he probably believed

---

[1] Benjamin Perley Poore (1820–1887).   [2] Adam Gurowski (1805–1886).
[3] To the Peace Convention. Mass. Hist. Soc., *Proceedings*, LX, 225.

he would, and ought at any rate to have consulted him. But meanwhile, Sumner was put in opposition to the delegation, and the Legislature in Massachusetts telegraphed forward and back, making a mountain out of a potato-hill, till it was almost a trial of strength between the two sides. When I saw Sumner, nothing was said, of course, and he told me he expected to dine with us, but he didn't come and I fear he means to make a personal matter of it. He thinks that C. F. A. has ruined himself, and no doubt the whole Garrison wing are doing their best to widen the breach.

Seward on the other hand received the speech with the most generous praise, calling it what he had tried to say and had not said so well. A majority of the delegation are with us, I believe, and at all events I have no fear that they will hurt us. But Sumner is no great mind in these things. His vanity, or modesty, or what you will, is sensitive as a woman's.

I have seen no one lately except Colonel Keyes, Scott's aid, who was here yesterday and full of war. He says that there is undoubtedly a plot against the Capital, and to put down every doubt and make us all right and as we should be, we need ten thousand men here. If Virginia goes we must have them instanter.

Of the Cabinet I know nothing. It is said that Fogg went to Springfield some time since with letters of introduction from various Senators, and told Lincoln that Cameron was not an honest man. Cameron heard it and says he shall hold those Senators to account for it. Cameron's a mean rascal and will do harm if he can.

You need not be surprised if a joint resolution is sprung on Congress and the votes counted and the election declared before the usual day. It is talked of, but I'm not sure that it can be done. I've not looked up the laws nor heard them discussed....

To Charles Francis Adams, Jr.

WASHINGTON, February 8, 1861.

You counsel boldness at the very time when a bold slip might close my mouth permanently. It was but this morning that C. F. A. cautioned me against writing too freely. The *New York Times*, which has always shown particular respect towards my letters, gave to one of them the other day an official character, reprinting it as a leader, with comments. This makes it very necessary that I should be exceedingly cautious in what I say, unless I want to be closed up altogether. Besides, in the present state of the delegation, when there are but three or at most four who will follow our lead, I can't be very bold without bringing Pangborn on my back, and getting not only myself (which I would rather like) but Papa into hot water.

As for Sumner, the utmost that can be expected is to keep him silent. To bring him round is impossible. God Almighty couldn't do it. He has not made his appearance here for more than a week, though there is as yet, so far as I know, no further change in the position of matters between him and C. F. A. As usual I suppose he will stand on his damned dignity. Once Governor Seward and he had a quarrel. The Governor wanted him to vote for an Atlantic steamship bill, and after exhausting all other arguments, tried to act on his feelings and urged him to vote for it as a personal favor in order to aid his re-election. Sumner replied that he wasn't sent to the Senate to get Mr. Seward's re-election. On which the Governor, losing his philosophical self-command, said, "Sumner you're a damned fool," and they didn't speak again for six months. I'm of Seward's opinion. Let Sumner get the idea that his dignity is hurt, and he *is* a damned fool. However, you can rely upon it, we shall do all we can to prevent his bolting, and I mean to flatter him all to pieces if I have a chance.

The Convention is in secret session. Like most meetings of this sort, I suppose they will potter ahead until no one feels any more interest in them, and then they may die. I have not yet seen any of our Massachusetts men.

This temporizing policy is hard work. I'm sick of it, but the 4th of March is coming and we shall soon be afloat again. These cursed Virginians are so in-grain conceited that it's a perfect nuisance to have anything to do with them. Let the 4th March pass and unless I'm much mistaken they will be allowed to send their secession ordinance to the people, and have it rejected too. Just now however there is nothing for it but to delay. Our measures will pass the House, and perhaps the Senate; at least I think so, but we shall see. Forty or fifty on our side will oppose them, but not violently....

The ancient Seward is in high spirits and chuckles himself hoarse with his stories. He says it's all right. We shall keep the border states, and in three months or thereabouts, if we hold off, the Unionists and Disunionists will have their hands on each other's throats in the cotton states. The storm is weathered.

To Charles Francis Adams, Jr.

WASHINGTON, February 13, 1861.

The family have gone up to the Capitol to see the counting of the votes. As I don't anticipate any show, and am no longer a reporter and wanted a little leisure to write to you, I've remained at home.

Charles Hale has come on and means to stay over the 4th. I have of course stopped writing for the *Advertiser*, and left it to him. He evidently had no objection, though complimentary in his remarks generally. On looking back over my letters this winter, I am on the whole tolerably well satisfied with them and their effect. They have had some good influence in shaping the course of opinion in Boston, and the *Advertiser* and the *New York Times* have both profited by them. Now that I'm out of the traces I'm not sorry for it on some accounts. I'm no longer at home, and living out of the house destroys my evenings. Then our house is so full, and there are so many people here and so much society that it's next to impossible to do anything. And finally, the Convention has assumed the whole affair and I should have to take a world of trouble to find out what was going on, and probably couldn't do it at all. At any rate Charles Hale can do it better than I, and wants to, so I am willing.

I don't think much of the Convention. I don't see much ability in it, nor much life. I don't believe any great good can come from it, except to gain time. I think the battle is won. I'm beginning to lose my interest in it since the Tennessee election. In my belief everything is going to simmer down, and wise men will keep quiet. The next administration will give us trouble enough, and I for one am going upon the business or the pleasure that shall suit me, for every man hath business or desire such as it is, and for my own poor part — look you — I will go write an article for the *Atlantic Monthly*, intituled "The Great Secession Winter of 1860–61." [1]

Mrs. Douglas [2] gave a crush ball last night. Her little beast of a husband was there as usual; God pardon me for abusing my host, whose bread and salt it is true I had no chance to touch, but a very little of whose champagne I drank, diluted with water, the common property of the human race. Mamma and Fanny went first to the President's reception and afterwards to the ball, and I assure you, the young Crowninshield was some astonished with the sights she saw. It was without any exception the wildest collection of people I ever

[1] Printed in 1910, in Mass. Hist. Soc., *Proceedings*, XLIII, 656.
[2] Adele (Cutts) Douglas.

saw. Next to the President's receptions, the company was beyond all description promiscuous. Mrs. Douglas, who is said to be much depressed by the general condition of things, received and looked as usual, handsome — "Splendidly null." Poor girl! what the deuce does she look forward to! Her husband is a brute — not to her that I know of — but gross, vulgar, demagogic; a drunkard, ruined as a politician; ruined as a private man; over head and ears, indeed drowned lower than soundings reaching in debt; with no mental or literary resources; without a future; with a past worse than none at all; on the whole I'd rather not be Mrs. Douglas. Still, there she stood and shook hands with all her guests, and smiled — and smiled.

A crowd of admiring devotees surrounded the ancient buffer Tyler; [1] another crowd surrounded that other ancient buffer Crittenden. Ye gods, what are we, when mortals no bigger — no, not so big as — ourselves, are looked up to as though their thunder spoke from the real original Olympus. Here is an old Virginia politician, of whom by good rights, no one ought ever to have heard, re-appearing in the ancient cerements of his forgotten grave — political and social and men look up at him as they would at Solomon, if he could be made the subject of a resurrection. I nearly got into several fights with various men and women, in the attempt to get through the crowd....

I have little to tell you in politics. I am so taken up with work and play that I've no time to hunt secrets. Sumner still holds out and has not been near us, though he is very cordial when we meet. The trouble there was greater than I supposed. Our irascible papa got into a passion with him for attempting to call Alley to account in his (C. F. A.'s) presence. Perhaps Sumner might have forgiven this, but then Massachusetts has preferred C. F. A.'s lead, and that finished him. However, all quarrels and secessions must be healed soon. It's the order of the day.

I've not seen Seward very lately and don't know much about him. He is hard at work I suppose, and I don't like to go down and interrupt him. I can't get over my modesty about those things. The last time he was here he was very jolly indeed and sanguine as could be. Between Lincoln and the secessionists he must have a hard time.... Dana's step is a great thing. It raps those confounded Rump Whigs who are doing their worst to hurt us. As its ground is more than usually distinct and independent it will support us the more.

[1] Ex-President John Tyler, who presided over the Peace Convention.

III

LONDON

1861–1868

To Charles Francis Adams, Jr.

We are planted here in London, as no doubt other people's letters have told you, in a way that is to me anything but pleasant. Our hotel is poor, our quarters confined, our eating to my overeducated mind miserable. I feel in poor health myself and am easily tired and irritable. London is a great unpleasant body, and my freedom seems to me now of more worth than this sort of existence, where one has Earls' cards on one's table but can't stir a step for fear of violating etiquette. As yet I have no acquaintances. No one has asked me to dinner; nor have I found that my reputation has crossed the Atlantic before me. I pass my time in doing errands and am not sure that this will not be my duty and only duty always. I can assure you, my own share in matters in general will be very small. The Governor was presented today and the Queen was gracious, but made no remark further than to say she believed he had been in England before. Mr. Dallas[2] goes off tomorrow and leaves the Legation today in our hands. Papa and Wilson[3] have been informally introduced and now we have pretty much got going, except that we've not yet found a house. I've been to see several and there's one in Grosvenor Square that would do for six months, but the rent is five hundred dollars a month for three months and it's doubtful whether we could get it for six, even putting aside the rent question. As for taking one for the whole term, I am rather opposed to it now, until we've had time to look about.

The Governor is in the hands of all the usual crowd of old buffers and will begin his dinings out at once, I suppose. Mamma is in good hands and laboring hard with etiquette. Of course we have each

---

[1] A good part of Henry Adams' letters from London to his brother Charles, 1861–1865, was printed in *A Cycle of Adams Letters*.

[2] George Mifflin Dallas (1792–1864).

[3] Charles Lush Wilson, of Chicago (d. 1878), Secretary of Legation. He had been editor of the Chicago *Daily Journal*.

day's lesson rehearsed four or five times for our benefit and that of visitors and friends, till there is no danger of any one's forgetting it. A hen with a brood of ducklings is a joke to it. Madam Bates and her daughter, Mrs. Van de Weyer,[1] give us law, and their names are inscribed in high places in our household Gods. Altogether I feel pretty sick and tired of the whole thing, though I am no more than a listener.

To Charles Francis Adams, Jr.

LONDON, June 10, 1861.

The expences in this city are enormous and if the Ambassador's private income fails we must cut our establishment down to a very low figure, as one can do little here with less than forty thousand, and nothing with less than twenty-five thousand dollars. People must occasionally live on less, but if so, they must have assistance from the public charities. The scale of living and the prices are curious examples of the beauties of a high civilization.

As for myself, I have only the same old story to sing which I have chanted many times, especially in my letters to you. I have done nothing whatever in the way of entering society, nor do I mean to take the plunge until after my presentation on the 19th. Getting into society is a repulsive piece of work here. Supposing you are invited to a ball. You arrive at eleven o'clock. A footman in powder asks your name and announces you. The lady or ladies of the house receive you and shake hands. You pass on and there you are. You know not a soul. No one offers to introduce you. No one even looks at you with curiosity. London society is so vast that the oldest habitués know only their own sets, and never trouble themselves even to look at anyone else. No one knows that you're a stranger. You see numbers of men and women just as silent and just as strange as yourself. You may go from house to house and from rout to rout and never see a face twice. You may labor for weeks at making acquaintances and yet go again and again to balls where you can't discover a face you ever saw before. And supposing you are in society, what does it amount to. The state dinners are dull, heavy, lifeless affairs. The balls are solemn stupid crushes without a scintilla of the gayety of our balls. No one enjoys them so far as I can hear. They are matters of necessity, of

[1] Joshua Bates (1788–1864), of the house of Baring Brothers, married Lucretia Augustus Sturgis. Their daughter married Silvain Van de Weyer, Minister of Belgium at London.

position. People have to entertain. They were born to it and it is one of the duties of life. My own wish is quietly to slide into the literary set and leave the heavy society, which without dancing is a frightful and irredeemable bore to me, all on one side....

You want to be posted up politically. If the *Times* has published my letters without mutilation, you will see what I think about it. We arrived here just as the Queen's Proclamation was issued. Of course the question arose what course to take. Papa's instructions and especially a later despatch would have justified him in breaking off at once all diplomatic relations with this Government, and we felt no doubt that, as you say, the Americans would have upheld him. But I must confess such a policy appeared to me to be the extreme of shallowness and folly. In the first place it would have been a tremendous load for the country. In the second place it would have been a mere wanton, mad, windmill-hitting, for the sympathies and the policy of England are undoubtedly with us, as has been already shown. In the third place it would have been ruin in a merely private point of view. Two such wars would grind us all into rags in America. One is already enough to cut down incomes to a dreadful extent.

Papa took the course that seems to me to have been the correct one. He had an interview with Lord John and told him, without bravado or brag, how the matter was regarded in America, or was likely to be regarded, and announced plainly what course he should be compelled to take if the Government really entertained any idea of encouraging the insurgents, and demanded a categorical answer as to the course the Government meant to pursue. Lord John promised to send this answer by Lord Lyons, protesting at the same time the unreasonableness of the American feeling, and the perfect good-faith of his Government. Since that time no opportunity has escaped the Government of proving their good-will towards us and unless you in America are run mad, and are determined to run your heads right against a stone-wall there need be no more difficulty whatever.

Feeling as I did in the matter, of course I did my best in my letters to the *Times* to quiet rather than inflame. If you choose you can suggest to the *Advertiser* a leader developing the view which I take, and pointing out the good sense of our worthy Ambassador in maintaining the dignity of the country, and yet avoiding a rupture, as contrasted with those noisy jackasses Clay and Burlingame, who have done more harm here than their weak heads were worth a thousand times over. I believe it to be essential to our interests now that Europe should be held on our side. Our troubles have gone too far to be closed by foreign jealousies. The cotton states would rather annex themselves to England or Spain than come back to us.

I have tried to get some influence over the press here but as yet have only succeeded in one case which has, however, been of some use. That is the *Morning Herald*, whose American editor, a young man named Edge,[1] came to call on the Ambassador. He is going to America to correspond for his paper; at least he says so. If he brings you a letter, let him be asked out to dine and give him what assistance in the way of introductions he wants. He is withal of passing self-conceit and his large acquaintance is fudge, for he is no more than an adventurer in the press; but his manners are good, and so long as he asks nothing in return, it's better to have him an ally than an enemy....

Tuesday, 11th. To return to politics, and this in absolute secrecy, for I let you know what I've no business to. A despatch arrived yesterday from Seward, so arrogant in tone and so extraordinary and unparalleled in its demands that it leaves no doubt in my mind that our Government wishes to face a war with all Europe. That is the inevitable result of any attempt to carry out the spirit or the letter of these directions, and such a war is regarded in the despatch itself as the probable result. I have said already that I thought such a policy shallow madness, whether it comes from Seward or from any one else. It is not only a crime; it's a blunder. I have done my best to counteract it; I only wish I could really do anything. I urged papa this morning, as the only man who could by any chance stop the thing, to make an energetic effort and induce the British Government to put us so much in the wrong that we couldn't go further. I think he has made up his mind to some effect of the sort and I hope it will succeed with all my soul.

Does Seward count on the support of France? It is not likely, for this despatch applies as much to her as to England. But if he does he is just as much mistaken as he ever was in his life. Any one who knows Napoleon knows that he means to stick with England. I cannot tell you how I am shocked and horrified by supposing Seward, a man I've admired and respected beyond most men, guilty of what seems to me so wicked and criminal a course as this.

I do not think I exaggerate the danger. I believe that our Government means to have a war with England; I believe that England knows it and is preparing for it; and I believe it will come within two months —if at all. If you have any property liable to be affected by it, change the investment. Don't go into the army yet. Wait for a Canadian

[1] Frederick Milnes Edge.

campaign and meanwhile live if you can on hay. Our incomes will soon have to go to pay our taxes. There's only one comfort that I see in the whole matter and that is that within a year we shall all be utterly ruined and our Government broken down; in other words, the war on that scale must be short and we of the commercial interests shall be the first to go under. If I have any marine insurance stock, sell it and invest in Dick Fay's woollen manufacturing arrangement if you can; if not, in anything reasonably safe; Massachusetts or Boston city stocks.

I'm in a panic you see.

To Charles Francis Adams, Jr.

LONDON, 20 February, 1863.

I wish you were out of your "long siege in mud and rain," which is likely to be as unpleasantly famous as any in Flanders. Hilton Head, I should have thought, would have been a Paradise compared with this.

Bad as your report is about the army of the Potomac, and bad as I fully expect the news to be of the attack on Charleston and Vicksburg, still I have derived a grain of comfort from what I think looks like a gleam of improvement in the political look of things at home. Of all results, a restoration of the Union on a pro-slavery basis would be most unfortunate. Yet I dread almost equally a conquest that would leave us with a new and aggravated Poland on our hands. If we could only fight a peace that would give us Virginia, Tennessee and Mississippi river, then we might easily allow slavery to gather to a head in the cotton states, and crush it out at our leisure on the first good opportunity; but such a vision is reserved for the just made perfect.

As to your avowal of belligerent intentions for life, if you expect me to quarrel with you on that account, you will be disappointed. As the Chief always says, when his lady complains of my follies: "My dear, Henry is of age and can do what he likes." You are of age, and even if you choose to become a Methodist minister, I don't propose to forbid the consecration. Perhaps I am prejudiced against your career from my observations on military men in Europe, where so far as I can judge, they are the greatest curse and nuisance in existence. The life of a soldier in time of peace seems here to have had a very bad effect indeed upon the mass of the officers. If I know it, our country has had about as much war as she wants for the present, and if we don't have peace and long peace, our game is up. You and I look at things from different points. My view is that peace and small armaments will be our salvation as a united and solvent nation. You prefer to speculate on the chances of war or convulsions, and throw your net in troubled waters.

Though I don't propose to bother you with useless remonstrances, I must decline *in toto* to have anything to do with opening the subject in the family. My belief is that it had better not be mentioned till the time comes. Whenever the war does end and you then do become obliged to inform your relatives of your intention to cool your heels for life in some fortified swamp in Louisiana or Arkansas, I shall take a month's vacation and visit you till your said relatives come to the earth again. We can then discuss this and other matters over a pipe of peace, if you can provide mild tobacco. Otherwise I prefer a cigar....

We are beginning to be gay here. By the way, Monckton Milnes,[1] who is the only man in England that ever did me a kindness, I believe, has had me invited to a literary club here, for a time, where I have a great chance to meet the curiosities of the place. Tom Hughes[2] has been of great use to me and has introduced me to a number of very pleasant acquaintances; few young men there, however. The season is beginning again too, and I am nerving myself to all the torture that invariably follows and accompanies all my attempts in this line. I have serious thoughts of quitting my old projects of a career, like you. My promised land of occupation, however; my burial place of ambition and law, is geology and science. I wish I could send you Sir Charles Lyell's new book on the *Antiquity of Man*, but it wouldn't do very well for camp-reading.

To Charles Francis Adams, Jr.

LONDON, 6 March, 1863.

. . . .

Such a bother and a fuss as all the world keeps up about this unhappy Prince of Wales, who would give his best pair of new breeches to be a very humble private individual for the next week. He is quite popular here, for he is thoughtful of others and kind, and hates ceremony. So it seems as though a temporary bee had lodged in the bonnet of this good people, who have set to work with a sort of determined, ponderous and massive hilarity, to do him honor. I suppose you will get from first hand a correct account of the events of last

[1] Richard Monckton Milnes, Baron Houghton (1809–1885).
[2] Thomas Hughes (1822–1896).

Saturday at Court. Also you will receive a photograph of our sister as she appeared. She is now fairly launched. Pretty, attractive, sympathetic and well-informed; but time and contact with the world will have to do much to develop her. To my mind, London fashionable society (routs, receptions, dances, I mean) is intolerably stupid. I've not the genius to find anything in it worthy of tasting, to one who has drunk the hot draughts of our flirtatious style of youthful amusement. If she can learn to prefer the heavy patronage of stupid elder sons, to a gayer style of thing, she will learn, no doubt, to have a good time.

As to public affairs I have nothing to tell you, as we are going on excellently well. We have done our work in England, and if you military heroes would only give us a little encouragement, we should be the cocks of the walk in England. But diplomacy has certainly had no aid from the sword to help a solution of its difficulties. Couldn't some of you give us just one leetle sugar-plum? We are shocking dry.

Of course, there is plenty to do. I am busy writing, recording, filing and collating letters and documents four or five hours every day, and my books and files for the last two years are beginning to assume a portentous size. Still it is very easy and mechanical work and doesn't prevent me from another sort of application which is more on my own account. But it's precious hard to work on one's own account in these times, when the chances are indefinitely against one's ever succeeding in bringing the results into action.

Tomorrow is to be the entrance of the Princess Alexandra, and all the world is going to see it. Next Tuesday is the wedding and an illumination. Ye Gods! what an infernal row it is!...

To Charles Francis Adams, Jr.

LONDON, 20 March, 1863.

. . . .

We are in a shocking bad way here. I don't know what we are ever going to do with this damned old country. Some day it will wake up and find itself at war with us, and then what a squealing there'll be. By the Lord, I would almost be willing to submit to our sufferings, just to have the pleasure of seeing our privateers make ducks and drakes of their commerce. I'll tell you what I mean to do....

But meanwhile, as I say, we are in a worse mess here than we have known since the *Trent* affair, and the devil of it is that I am in despair of our getting any military success that would at all counterbalance our weight. Where our armies try to do anything they are invariably beaten, and now they seem to be tired of trying. I'll bet a sovereign to a southern shin-plaster that we don't take Charleston; either that we don't try or are beaten. I'll bet five golden pounds to a diminutive greenback that we don't clear the Mississippi, and that we don't hurt Richmond. My only consolation is that the Southerners are suffering dreadfully under the tension we keep them at, and as I prefer this to having fresh disasters of our own, I am in no hurry to see anyone move. But meanwhile we are in a tangle with England that can only be cleared with our excellent good navy cannon. If I weren't so brutally seasick, I would go into the navy and have a lick at these fat English turkey-buzzards.

At the same time, individually, I haven't at all the same dislike to the English. They are very like ourselves and are very pleasant people. And then they are quite as ready to blackguard themselves as anyone could wish, if they're only let alone. There are all the elements of a great, reforming, liberal party at work here, and a few years will lay in peace that old vindictive rogue who now rules England and weighs like an incubus on all advance.[1] Then you will see the new generation, with which it is my only satisfaction here to have some acquaintance, take up the march again and press the country into shape.

Thanks to Monckton Milnes, Tom Hughes and a few other good friends, I am tolerably well known now in the literary and progressive set. I was amused the other day to hear that I was put up for a Club in St. James's Street, by Mr. Milnes, and seconded by Lawrence Olifaunt,[2] a thorough anti-American; and better still, I am endorsed by your friend, Frederick Cavendish,[3] as he is commonly called here; the brother of Lord Hartington; the son of the Duke of Devonshire. Several other names are on the paper, I believe, but I don't know what they are. I'm thinking my character would not be raised in America if I were known to keep such malignant company. Certainly, however, aristocracy is not my strong point. My most sought acquaintances are men like Hughes, and his associates, the cultivated radicals of England.

How long I shall remain in contact with this sort of thing, who can say? Verily, the future is black and the ocean looks as though it were yawning for us on our approaching passage.

[1] Palmerston.

[2] Lawrence Oliphant (1829–1888).

[3] (1836–1882). He was second son of William Cavendish, seventh Duke of Devonshire and was murdered in the Phenix Park, Dublin, on the afternoon of the day on which he had taken the oath as chief secretary to the Lord-Lieutenant of Ireland.

To Charles Francis Adams, Jr.

LONDON, 23 April, 1863.

. . . .

I sympathize with you in your blueness. Not that I am blue now. I like excitement at times and I enjoy all this row and confusion immensely, on my own account, as a spectacle and study, though of course, in a national point of view it is a cause of anxiety to us all. But your position is by no means a pleasant one, and I don't wonder that you are down in the mouth. The camp as you now have it, must be a very unpleasant place....

I see that you and everyone speak of Fitzhugh Lee as commanding against you. Surely this can't be my friend Rooney.[1] It must be his brother, I suppose. I doubt whether Rooney would make a good cavalry colonel, though he might do well as a major or captain. I wonder what's become of Jim May[2] and Ben Jones. I suppose that they too have been "gobbled" by this voracious cotton-demon. And Julius Alston![3] do you ever hear of him? If we can keep these foreign countries off some three months more, I rather think we shall hear of trouble down south. This long steady pressure must be terrible to them; worse than fighting; and if their rail-roads are worn out and their food eaten up; riots in their cities; laziness or worse among their slaves, and strange corruption in all branches of their Richmond Government, it seems to me that their cause is, I do not say, desperate, but liable to be overturned at what would seem a small thing. Davis now alone unites them. Would Lee do so? or Johnson? We hear of an attack on Charleston, but as you know, I have no faith in its success.

To Charles Francis Adams, Jr.

LONDON, 25 June, 1863.

. . . .

We are dragging our weary carcasses to balls and entertainments of every description. I had occasion to go last night to a reception over in Kensington, about three miles from us, and as it was a soft moonlight night, I walked part of the way. Accustomed as I am to London, and after seeing three seasons in it, I could not help feeling impressed by the extraordinary scene. I passed through Grosvenor Square and round Hyde Park to Apsley House, and the streets seemed alive with

[1] William Henry Fitzhugh Lee (1837–1891). *Education*, 57.
[2] James May (1837–1876).   [3] John Julius Pringle Alston (1837–1863).

carriages in every direction. Gentlemen in white cravats were scuttling about, like myself; cabs were rushing furiously in all quarters, hundreds of carriages were waiting, or setting down or taking up their people before great houses, as I passed from street to square, and from square to street. There was a rush and roar all through the West End, that one can see only in London. Six weeks hence, if I go through the same streets again at midnight, there will not be a soul there except a policeman. Acres and miles of houses will be as silent as a Virginia forest. And so they will remain until next April.

There is no doubt about it — every one, except children in their first season and a few peculiarly constituted people, feel all this riot to be a bore. Every one looks intensely bored. Nobody enjoys it and nobody can enjoy it. These great routs are a sort of canonization of mediocrity. No one attempts to have a good time, and if they did, they would be voted vulgar. In the whole system I see nothing to admire and sincerely believe that it hurts everyone who gets into it.

Lothrop Motley, however, says it's the perfection of human society. If his remark applies merely to a few dinners and a few visits to country houses with clever people, I shouldn't quarrel with it. But as for fashionable society here, I say clearly that in my opinion it is a vast social nuisance and evil....

To Charles Francis Adams, Jr.

LONDON, 3 July, 1863.

·   ·   ·   ·   ·   ·   ·   ·   ·   ·   ·   ·

The rush and fuss of society is still going on and will last another week. We have been here and there, knocking about at dinners, balls, breakfasts, from Rotten Row to Regent's Park, and entertaining at home in the intervals. We had a tremendous ball at a neighbor's on Tuesday and the dawn looked in on us while we were still at it. We watched the gathering light from the conservatories, and looked faded and pale. But the ball-room was the most magnificent I ever saw, and I really had a very tolerable time, for once, though only enough to remind me of the want of that happy absurdity which I feel in American society. Sleep in these times is scarce. One rides in the Park two hours in the morning, dines out in the evening, and goes to a ball; rises to a breakfast the next day; goes to a dance in the afternoon, and has a large dinner at home, from which he goes to another ball at half after eleven. Luckily this only comes by fits and starts, for two or three days together, and leaves the intervals tolerably clear....

To Charles Francis Adams, Jr.

London, 10 July, 1863.

Our news brings us down to the 27th of June, and leaves us without the slightest conception of what is really going on. Of course we are extremely anxious, and though various and innumerable idiots about me are croaking hoarse notes and putting on that "I told you so" expression of complacent misfortune which always irritates me beyond bearing, I find it needs an effort even on my part to sustain the appearance of placid confidence which we always make it a rule to bear, and which alone has any effect in shaming the sparrows. I wish people at home in respectable positions would at least hold their tongues, and not maunder over misfortunes before they come.... Our people would do well to recollect that ancient maxim of Frederick the Great, or some one, that it's best to wash one's dirty linen at home. They have a way of putting it all out to wash, and the dirtier it is, the louder they call foreign nations to look at it....

In these days I have very little work to do except in a domestic way, and of course I am becoming more and more uneasy and discontented. It hardly seems consistent with self-respect in a man to turn his back upon all his friends and all his ambitions, during such a crisis as this, only for the sake of conducting his mother and sister to the opera, and a ride in Rotten Row. I cannot tell you how much I am disgusted at this situation. If it were not for the Chief, I would not stay here a moment, but at least I hope my presence here is necessary for him, since I feel as though it were simple suicide for myself. My consolation is that we are approaching the end of our stay, and if things get worse we shall be recalled, while if they get better at home, the Chief will probably resign so soon as he can without appearing to shirk his duty....

I met your friend Sir Edward Cust,[1] some time ago, who expressed great interest in you, and envied you your position, picket duty being according to him, the liveliest and pleasantest part of a military life and a light mounted regiment being the pleasantest branch of the service. He told me various stories of his adventures in Spain, while engaged on similar duty, and I tried to learn from him what the best manual of cavalry tactics was that I could send you. On this subject he said he was not well posted. The German books were the best, and the Germans were better cavalry than the English. They took more care of

---

[1] (1794–1878), who had served in the Peninsular campaign, and had written military histories, acceptable in their day.

their horses. If they were to march at five o'clock in the morning, they would up at three, groom their horses, and give them a feed, so that they would be all awake and fresh for the start. Whereas an English trooper would turn out and kick up his horse at the very last moment, and hurry him off without any sort of care. Sir Edward likes the German soldiers, though they will steal, he says. They don't get drunk like the English, and they are careful and soldierlike....

To Charles Milnes Gaskell[1]

INVERGARRY, FORT AUGUSTUS, N.B.,
Tuesday, 18 August, [1863].

MY DEAR GASKELL,

I had supposed you were in Persia or Astrachan by this time, for your ancestral majestie whom I cross-questioned in Stratton Place (if that's right) was profoundly ignorant as to your whereabouts. As I left with a sigh of happiness all the delights of Rotten Row and Portland Place, a fortnight ago, I failed to get your letter till today. But having at last turned up in a Christian spot again, I take a spare moment to give you what little light I can. Consider that I have been, according to the pious writer, where I could read my title clear to mansions in the Skye, but as yet am far from bidding farewell to any tear or wiping my weeping eye on that account. *Bref*, I've just passed five days on the isle of Skye, of which the rain descended and the floods came during three, with a vehemence that would have done justice to the tropics. I have fed on nothing but oatmeal porridge and hard boiled eggs, and short allowance too, and my opinion of Skye, its inhabitants, climate, and "umliegende Ortschaften" (to use a phrase which I know you can't understand, for it's bad German) is one which I will have a regard for your feelings as an Englishman and a Britisher and not expatiate upon.

I have a letter from William [Everett] which you may peruse I suppose, taking care to forget the somewhat too characteristic allusions to his surroundings. I know nothing more of him than that. It is possible that he may try a little soldiering, as many do, but probably on some officer's staff, if anywhere.

Apropos to Octave Feuillet! You say you have read him through. Have you done so with his last work, *Sybille*?[2] I have read it since

---

[1] Charles George Milnes Gaskell was son of James Milnes Gaskell, Member for Wenlock. The story of the meeting of Adams and young Gaskell, which resulted in a lifelong friendship, is told in *Education*, 204.

[2] *Histoire de Sybille* had appeared in *Revue des Deux Mondes*, Aug.–Oct., 1862.

starting. As one can't quite think that everything depends on belief in the efficacy of prayer, I am sorry to say that Octave looks very like a dependent of the Faubourg, writing what he knows to be decayed matter (*vulgo*, rot) for an earthly reward at its hands.

To Charles Francis Adams, Jr.

LOWOOD HOTEL, WINDERMERE,
Thursday, 3 Sept., 1863.

. . . .

From Banavie, where we slept, our road lay for several miles along the head of Loch Eil. Then it rose among the mountains, wild and desolate scenery, where hardly even a miserable cabin is to be seen for miles together. At intervals it rained, and at times we caught a little sunshine, which had a wonderful effect in lighting up a scene so sad and dark without it that even our spirits could only counteract the impression by attempts to learn Gaelic phrases from our driver, a *divertissement* which kept us roaring for miles. At length, after some twelve miles of this work, we suddenly came upon a marshy plain at the head of a long loch [Shiel], where a solitary stone column rose in a way that impressed me curiously with the dreary nature of the place. Of all things in the world a monument of that size seemed to be the thing one least expected there. I asked the driver what it was, and he told me it commemorated the spot where Prince Charles the Pretender was killed. I could not conceive what the blockhead meant, being aware that the Pretender had not gratified his enemies by getting himself put an end to. But as the dogcart came to a halt for an hour to rest, a short distance further on, Brooks and I walked back, and after much wading and jumping and wetting, we reached the spot and found a long inscription in English, Latin and Gaelic, stating that it was here Prince Charlie raised his standard in 1745. A more desolate, repelling spot I have seldom seen, and I appreciated for the first time the courage of that young fellow, who could drag himself from Paris and sunlight, in order to lead a desperate venture of filthy barbarians and to plant his standard on a spot like this.

In long reaches of Scotch mist, diversified by gleams of gray sunshine, we climbed mountain after mountain, all barren as your saddle, except for heath and waterfalls, and all stamped with the same character of stern and melancholy savageness. The roads however are excellent and as there is never much snow or great cold, they keep in good order. We changed our horse some ten miles further on, and then began descending towards the sea. As our miserable horse, urged on by steady and vigorous chastisement, slowly worried forwards, the weather began to improve, and to my surprise, the country began to take on a civilised aspect. When at last we reached the sea-shore, we found a lovely landscape — wide woods, and green pastures, cattle and even deer, a mild air and a pleasant sun beaming upon us, as though there had never been a Scotch mist (a phrase which means a heavy rain). This is the peninsula of Arisaig; a sort of Wood's Hole, only much larger. A little hamlet lies on a pretty harbor, silent and deserted in the afternoon sun, and at an inn, the only one, we descended and dismissed our vehicle. Two cares oppressed my mind. The first was to order some dinner, for it was five o'clock. The second to procure a boat to take us over to Skye. The first was soon eased. We had our dinner, if a dish of burnt steaks and potatoes deserves that honored title. The second was also relieved, but as it takes every Highlander two hours to do what should occupy fifteen minutes, and as our men had to be summoned from the plough and the anvil, it was seven o'clock before we were on board. Three men made our crew, and a boat like a man of war, and in this form, in consideration of the sum of five dollars, we were to be conveyed to the nearest public house in Skye, a distance of ten or twelve miles.

The evening was calm, hardly a breath of air helping us, but it was fine. A gentle roll swelled against our quarter, and yielding to its influence, I lay down on the seat across the boat, and watched our course.... The long mountainous coast of Scotland, lighted by the sunset and twilight, looked very grand in the distance, and on our left were the mountains of Skye covered with heavy folds of mist. For three hours or more we went on in this manner, the men relieving each other at the oars, for they had to pull the whole way. I enjoyed immensely this evening sail on the Hebridean seas. Civil wars, disgust and egoism, social fuss and worry, responsibility and worry, were as far at least as the moon. They left me free on the Sound of Sleat. I felt as peaceful and as quiet as a giant, and saw the evening shades darken into night, and phosphorus waves of light swell in the air and under the boat, with a joyful sense of caring not a penny when I had my breakfast.

Arrive we did at last, though Brooks thought we never should, but this part was rather embarrassing. The little hamlet near Armadale Castle boasts a landing place only at high tide, whereas the tide was now low. We had therefore to land on the rocks and paddle in the dark over the bogs to firm land. As we stepped along, our shoes, crushing the wet seaweed, called out at every movement bright, flashing phosphoric flames, so that we seemed to be walking on liquid fire. Pretty thoroughly wet, we did at last reach a road and made our way to a wayside inn, from which much merriment and singing proceeded. The maid who appeared at our call, was innocent of the tongue of Shakespeare and Milton. She owned allegiance only to her native Gaelic. A man, however, was at length produced, who seemed mortified to have no better to offer us, but the nearest town was fifteen miles and more, and there were no vehicles. If there had been, we shouldn't have used them. There we were and there we meant to sleep, so we took possession of two rooms, which were new and therefore reasonably clean. Our sheets were clean but ragged, and the other bed-clothes! Well they were rough! After nearly being assaulted by one of the band of minstrels, who were salmon fishers, drinking and howling a monotonous song, which they accompanied by stamping their feet, I got some supper, tea, toast, boiled eggs, etc., and Brooks and I having sleepily supped, and waited long for the salmon fishers' drunken dirge to cease, turned in towards midnight and so slept in peace.

The sun was bright on our first morning in the Hebrides. I looked out at about nine o'clock, shuddered at the sight of my resting-place, and dressed with a cheerfulness and a light heart. Poor Brooks, however, came into my room, looking very fishy, and complained of a sick headache. We had breakfast, and I swallowed much porridge, a dish that is in itself neither savory nor rich, but which is far superior to tough ham drowned in bowls of oil, or even to hard boiled eggs. I then desired a conveyance to the next town, seventeen miles, but to my alarm (on Brooks' account) learned that no conveyance was to be had except one, which I proceeded to examine and which proved to be a heavy farm cart, which might have been drawn by oxen, but which in fact was conducted by a horse. *Que faire!* Seventeen miles in an ox cart with a sick headache! Still, our baggage must go and my mind resigned itself. The sluggish cart was drawn before the door, and my pipe being lighted, I sounded boot and saddle. Before we departed, however, the Gaelic damsel persuaded me through an interpreter to buy a pair of woollen socks knit by her fair hands, which I may send to you, and in case their proportions be too elephantine, you can make them over to some deserving foot.

I can't tell you how I enjoyed this morning. England boasts of few days in her year. For ten miles I walked along the shore of the Sound, and a more splendid scene I couldn't put my finger on. The west coast of Scotland is rugged and wild, with deep scorings or indentations that form salt water lochs. Towards this shore I was looking, across a sound some five miles broad, which gradually was lost in the lands towards the north. Mountains were all around, but they were so softened by the sun that again and again I fancied myself in Italy. This corner of Skye is quite civilized too. There are trees, hedges and green pastures towards the sea-shore, and it was only as I advanced and at length turned away from the east, that we reached a desolate region, where heather and peat-bogs are the sole articles of production. I shall always remember my morning between Armadale and Broadford as a day *comme il y en a peu.*

Poor Brooks was far from enjoying it. Between the effort of walking and the jolting of the cart, he was put to it to make a choice, but after trying each, he subsided in moody silence into the cart. I was anxious about him, but could only press on, and one by one the slow milestones crept by. Resting myself at the tenth, having walked about two hours and three quarters, I too took a turn in the cart, and so at last we reached our aim, both coming in on foot. Here we again struck the sea, but this time on the northern coast of the island, and opposite to us was another part of the Scotch shore, while the ocean lay nearly open towards the northwest. As yet we had crossed no mountains, the land being only rolling and peaky.

At Broadford I wished to stay, but Brooks said no! So I ordered a dog-cart and dinner. The dinner even to my appetite was barely touchable. Brooks cursed it and lay on a sofa. We were glad to be off again at four, leaving the small village and dirty inn behind.

If the morning's walk from Armadale was lovely and made me think of Italy, the afternoon's drive to Sligachan was enormous and belonged to no country on God's earth except Skye alone. Between smooth conical mountains, whose sides were tinged with a doubtful green where the gaunt skeleton did not break out, and the blue sea, our road drove on, round silent lochs and through a howling wilderness strewn with the débris of ancient glaciers, and offering not one blade of grass or grain, except on a narrow strip along the sea-shore. The mountains of Skye are peculiar, but more of that hereafter. Not only was our ride delightful on account of the beauty of the scenery, the exquisite evening and all that, but Brooks showed signs of returning peckishness, and from the rapid fire of questions which he, *à la* Charles Kuhn, began to open on the driver, I knew he felt better. Several miles of the distance we walked, and when we rounded the last headland and had but two miles more, I sent them ahead, and in a solitude and deadly silence walked up the long loch at the head of which stands the solitary inn of Glen Sligachan, where I arrived just as the purple mountain tops were changing to a dark, cold, and solemn gray. It reminded me of my voyage with Ben Crowninshield up the Furca Pass in Switzerland. Solitude of utter barrenness on every side.

A supper of broiled salmon made up for our dinner, and Brooks had at last found his appetite. The inn was not a paradise, being like all highland inns, of an ugly, mouldy and throat-cutting appearance. But you will have no great sympathy for me on this reckoning.

The next morning was cloudy, and I felt that a storm was brewing. As I have no fancy for early rising, and am quite ready to leave to you the benefits of that habit, I ordered breakfast at our usual hour of nine o'clock and ponies for ten. As Brooks and I were seating ourselves at breakfast, contemplating the broil with pleasure, in comes a new arrival, seats himself at the table and coolly asks me to help him to some of the salmon; *my* salmon, by the Lord, and he poached it as coolly as though he were proprietor of fish in general. This man is a sucker, thought I to myself, and we will avoid him. Consequently, when we mounted our ponies and I saw that the person had also ordered a pony and joined himself to us and our guide, I was very short and sharp, and ignored him entirely, treating with silence his mild hints as to the route. So our caravan of three ponies and a guide moved slowly off, up Glen Sligachan.

We were to see the one great sight in the island. About mid-way on the southern coast, a cluster of mountains, called the Cuchullin or Coolin Hills, rises abruptly, and encloses a small lake called Loch Coruisk. To reach it, one has to cross the island by a very rough bridle-path, and at last to climb a tough hill, from the top of which one looks down upon the lake and the sea. Glen Sligachan is itself a specimen of desolation. Along the whole seven miles there is no human habitation, no cultivation, not a tree or a shrub, and at best only a few highland cattle and sheep try to support life on the heather and tufts of grass that partly cover the base of bleak mountain ridges. The path winds over the chaotic mounds of earth and loose rocks, that are called moraines, and that are the invariable indication of former glaciers. I walked much of the way, and climbed on foot the steep hill at its end. Beyond this there was no path at all. Our guide told us that we must walk down to the lake, and so we did, if scrambling down a precipitous mountain and over bogs can be called walking. It was only a mile to the shore of the lake, but it took us a long time and was precious tough work.

Quietly and between ourselves, I am no admirer of the Scotch mountain scenery. It is too uniform in its repulsive bareness. I like another sort of thing. Grand mountain peaks covered with glittering snow, whose base descends towards Italian plains and is green with olive trees and vineyards; that is my ideal of the sublime and beautiful. Yet certain it is that the scenery of Loch Coruisk made an impression on me that few things can, and like all great master-pieces, the more I think of it, the more extraordinary it seems to be. Evidently it was formerly the bed of an enormous glacier. A vast volume of ice, creeping down year after year, to the sea, carried with it every trace of soil, and scored and polished the rocks over which it passed. When the glacier yielded to some unexplained change of temperature, it left behind it nothing but this lake among the rocks close to the sea, and in a semi-circle around it, a series of sharp mountain peaks, jagged and excoriated, whose summits seem to have raised a barrier against the outside world. I might give you a good-sized volume of epithets without conveying the least idea of the really awful isolation and silence of this spot. There is as yet nothing human within miles of it, nor any trace of man's action. Even in Switzerland I recollect nothing like it, nor can there ever be, unless the ocean is brought to the foot of the Alps. Should you ever come to England, by all means go and see Coruisk. I would like to have a chance to go with you, and even to pitch my tent there and pass a few days in examining this melancholy district.

For about an hour we lay on a point of rising ground above the lake, and looked about us. Then, feeling rather bothered by the idea of our return climb, we turned back, and dug our way with a tremendous amount of labor and some doubts as to our road, back to our ponies. It was just as well that we did not delay, for the rain began before we reached our inn at five o'clock, and a drenching storm set in that evening with tremendous force.

My original idea had been to go on to Portree and the extremity of the island, but as I found there was little or nothing to see there, and as the weather was so unpromising, I concluded to turn back and make my way to a civilised land. So the next morning we set out on our return. The salmon poacher asked to join us in a carriage, and we departed in an open wagon. Before we had gone five miles, the rain descended and the flood came. Tremendous gusts of wind from the mountains drove down regular waves of water on us, and coats and umbrellas were wet through like sieves. The fifteen miles were long as the road to Heaven, and the scenery was, ah! *quantum mutatus ab illo!* When we arrived at Broadford I determined to go no further, and incontinently ordered a lunch of broiled herrings, which were indeed savory.

The storm, which was furious, showed no signs of slackening that evening, and the next day, which was Sunday, it continued with the same violence. As the passage to the mainland was an unknown road to me, and as there are no inns near the ferry, I did not venture to leave my quarters. It was not gay. Brooks tried going to church, but having entered in the middle of service at about one o'clock, and listened some time to the Gaelic parson, he asked his neighbor how long it would last and on hearing that it would be over at five, he precipitately fled. I made no such venture. The only satisfactory thing I did was to have a long talk with a man who had some reason to be acquainted with the island, as to the people. You must know that I have been greatly disgusted with the appearance of the brave highlanders. They strike me as stupid, dirty, ignorant and barbarous. Their mode of life is not different from that of African negroes. Their huts are floorless except for earth; they live all together in them like pigs; there are no chimneys, hardly a window; no conveniences of life of any sort. Dirty, ragged, starved and imbruted, they struggle to cultivate patches of rocky ground where nothing can mature, and in wretched superstition and prejudice they are as deep sunk as their ancestors ever were. One of the best things in Scott's novel of the *Pirate*, which indeed apart from its absurd story, I rate higher than most men do, is a character of the people of Zetland put into the mouth of Triptolemus Yellowley. It would do tolerably well for the Hebrides as well. The character of such out-of-the-way people must always be narrow and ungenerous. Everything tends to crystallize and remain stationary. They are envious, jealous and prejudiced. Any population is too much for such barren regions, and the numbers of the people always tend to undue increase, for they pup like rabbits. Hence a continual struggle for existence, and eternal misery and degradation.

Monday morning, it did not rain. We had some difficulty in getting away, and had to share a dog-cart with a lunatic-inspector as far as Kyle Rhea ferry. As the lunatic was slow, we walked ahead, intending to be caught about five miles out. When we had gone the five miles, it began to rain again, and as no lunatic made his appearance we trudged on the whole eleven miles, to the wretched inn at the ferry. Here we waited and eat oatmeal porridge, Brooks amusing himself by feeding a small dog with it, till, as he expressed it, he "burst"; that is, became very ill. At last the lunatic appeared and we got across the strait, which is here hardly a mile wide, to Glenelg, where after much highland delay we had to take a carriage and went on, cold and wet, to Shiel Inn, where we got a dog-cart and pressed forward ten miles more to Clunie Inn. Imagination had painted here a luxurious supper and snowy beds. Reality showed squalidity and starvation. Unable to stomach it, we took another dog-cart and drove on another ten miles across the mountains to Tomdown Inn. From its neat appearance we imagined wealth and plenty, as we came to it at ten o'clock at night, but our supper consisted of broiled ham and two eggs, all they had, which we eat ferociously.

The next day our family picked our baggage up as they passed from Mr. Ellice's to Invergarry, and Brooks and I walked the eleven miles, and went to stay several days with Mr. Peabody and Mr. Lampson....

To Henry Lee Higginson

London, 10 September, 1863.

My Dear Major: Your letter, after slumbering in my brother's pocket for an indefinite period, did at last manage to cross the Atlantic and, not finding me in London, had to take another long journey and follow me to Scotland. There at last I received it, and as I was at that time on my vacation travels, and not able to attend to labors, I had to put off all action till my return a few days ago. It was then so long since your directions as to the garments that I had some doubt whether I ought not to refer it back to you for confirmation and new directions, but concluded on reflection that military men are well known to be ferocious, and that as they like to be implicitly obeyed, if I were to fail to carry out orders, I might get my ears cut off with such a ferocious sabre as I forwarded to Ben Crowninshield. Accordingly, I hurried straightaway to Poole's and the articles are now in process of making and will be sent on in due course. May they be pleasing to your eyes and soften your wrath against your slave.

I remain in no little trouble about Jim [Higginson]. As yet I have had no account of how he was taken or when he is likely to escape. So soon as he does get again into the land of the free, I hope he will write me a letter, especially as I wrote the last to him. Give him my energetic sympathy whenever you can, and tell him that I exalt in the punishment of Rooney Lee (not his hanging, however) as a make-weight on our side of the account.

You are more fortunate than I. After your work you will enjoy your fun, and when you do again come abroad what a good time you will have. Whereas I, who now for so long have been living as a Sybarite, am no longer able to enjoy America or Europe. I want to come home badly, and when I do come, I shall expect an invitation to reside with your regiment as a volunteer, until I have had some experience in military life and duties, and can make interest to get an appointment on some cuss's staff. As for the army as a profession, *video meliora, proboque*; but can you expect a vile diplomat who has a profound contempt for Courts and a still profounder disbelief in the virtues of camps, to follow so illustrious an example? I fear that the experience of an amateur will be all that I can swallow, long custom having given me tasks which are decidedly inconsistent with dirt, routine and salt pork, but who knows! Perhaps we shall have a war with France or England, and in that case we may all hope for honor.

News I have none, not even of Berlin, Vienna or Paris. It is now more than a year since I was at the latter spot, but I trust to run over there again soon. Joe Bradlee has gone home, and no one except Fez Richardson [1] is left at Paris, and he is politically on the fence. New friends I have none, and the old ones don't seem to turn up. Why doesn't John Bancroft come back? I hope he doesn't mean to become soldier. Floods of people are perpetually passing and repassing, but as we have to dine them all, and as I don't meet any pretty girls among them, our acquaintance stops there. We feel tollable well just now, and talk up pretty plain to the Britishers, only I hope you will manage to give the rebs another gentle suasion before the year's out, as a quiet hint to hurry. A good dose once in three months keeps the Britishers quiet.

The particulars as to your garments shall be sent hereafter. How to get them over I don't know, but they shall come. Ever yours.

P.S. I have omitted to offer sympathies for your wounds, especially because I am brilliantly in the dark as to their nature and extent. Hoping they were only enough to get you a pleasant vacation, I trust you'll be spared any more.

To Charles Francis Adams, Jr.

LONDON, 13 Nov., 1863.

As the Lord liveth, I have not one word to say to you this week. Positively there has nothing happened under the light of the sun and moon that I can tell you about, except it be our friend Napoleon's

[1] Henry Hobson Richardson (1838–1886), the architect. He was from Louisiana.

Congress and speech to the Chambers; but I suppose the Cuisinier will give you the benefit of his solemn judgment on that affair. I came up to town the day before yesterday as usual, and have been busied with a heap of things, none of which are epistolary. It is astonishing, even to me, how long I may remain in a place without growing to it. Friends! I have none, and my temper is now too bad ever to make another. Society! I know it not. Laziness, stupidity and self-distrust have shut its doors to me. It is wonderful, stupendous to consider, how a man who in his own mind is cool, witty, unaffected and high-toned, will disgust and mortify himself by every word he utters or act he does, when he steps out of his skin defences. Thus it has happened that now, after five years of uninterrupted travel and mixing with the world, and after a steady residence of half that time in this place, surrounded by the thickest of the rush of society and fashion, I now find myself in London alone, without a house I care to go to, or a face I would ask to see. Melancholy, is it not! And yet I never was so contented since the last time I was in love and fancied, like an idiot, that man was a social animal.

Apropos to the Congress, you may perhaps be pleased to know that I am as ignorant on the matter as an Irishman. Of course my Club is a turmoil of excitement on the subject, and there I should learn the daily news — war or peace — Congress or none — and so on. But although I believe I did once know an attaché, such is not the case now. My circle of acquaintance does not include any of the sources of information, and is restricted to a few English fellows, the farthest removed from political connection that I can find. You, my dear Brother Imperator, will probably sneer at me for this neglect of opportunities. To skulk away like this, when I might make myself so necessary, so useful and so well known! Truly such were my ideas two years ago.... But my present course is not entirely without system and justification. Your military experience has probably cured you of much of that lechery for publicity which always marks our young men. Here of all places in the world a man must guard himself from exposure, and must mind his own business. Moreover the European powers are all socially connected and there is a bond of union among their representatives. We, on the other hand, are democrats, and you may be sure that in Europe a democrat is never and never can be really received into the circle of monarchists. In purposely keeping aloof therefore, and forestalling the people I meet, in maintaining a mysterious reserve on public affairs, I believe I can best maintain our own dignity and alone retain any good position....

To Charles Francis Adams, Jr.

LONDON, 18 Decr., 1863.

Nothing, I imagine, could be emptier than the ordinary run of letters you receive from here in these days. What indeed is there to tell you? We do nothing. Life is merely a habit, so far as we are concerned, and it is the toughest of all work to describe or enliven a habit. I don't want to talk about the war, yet what else is there to mention? The Chief, I know, is at this instant describing to you at his table over there, the Westminster play that we went to last night together, where he and the Archbishop of Canterbury were seated side by side in the front row, the dignitaries of the occasion. I was amused with the performance and came to the conclusion that the Greeks and Romans knew precious little about play-writing, however clever they were in other matters. In many respects, however, the piece shows a state of society quite ahead of our own. I could wish that we could return to the excellence of their primitive views respecting the relations between the sexes, for instance. But our age is hopelessly lost.

The letter of Mr. Lawley,[1] which I inclose to you, will probably have been published in the American papers before you receive this. The truth is, it tells us more than I had ever hoped. Mr. Lawley is demoralized. On the question of Meade's fighting, he is, as you perceive, of our opinion, and I was therefore the more pleased to see that the General had saved us from another Fredericksburg. I suppose Meade will be removed. Nothing indeed can surprise me since the removal of Rosecrans, and I fully expect that our eastern army will in the end be utterly disorganized by this repeated interference of the War Department. In the end Stanton must be turned out, but he has been probably as bad a Secretary of War as circumstances allowed him to be, and if he can deprive us of success, he will. Lawley says distinctly that it takes weeks to transfer a single corps to the West, and that co-operation does not exist between the armies. This being the case I had hoped to hear that we had brought half Grant's army to Virginia to cut between Lee and Richmond while Meade held him on the flank. But I fear, the opportunity is gone. From Lawley's intimations, I have no doubt that we could put two armies into Virginia, each nearly double Lee's force, before he could get a division from the South.

Meade, whether removed or not, has my sympathies, and I believe him to have done us more good by avoiding a great battle than if he had done as Burnside did and fought against his judgment....[2]

[1] Francis Charles Lawley, correspondent of the London *Times*. [2] Referring to Fredericksburg.

Life flows on here in such an equable, peaceful way that I really believe we shall go ahead till we wake up some morning and find ourselves quietly dead in a green old age. We are rooted here thoroughly. Your mamma has found a new set of friends who insist upon kissing her just as the women used to do in Boston, and the Chief, if he has no set of intimates like the immortal trio of Boston, is still contented and placable. As for me, my old tendencies grow on me more and more. If we lived a thousand years ago instead of now, I should have become a monk and would have got hold as Abbot of one of those lovely little monasteries which I used to admire so much among the hills in Italy. Those who choose to play the Luther may try it for all me. They had better let it alone in my opinion, for the universe is rather too big to be so precisely gauged by their yardstick. I prefer the character of Luther's friend, Melanchthon wasn't it, for my own part, and the difficulties that can't be conquered by plain reason had better be left to that weapon till they can.

All which is written to fill up a page in want of anything else to say, as well as because you being a man purely of action are bound to call it all damned nonsense.

To Henry Lee Higginson

LONDON, 18 Dec., 1863.

You wrote me last May asking me to order some clothes. My brother Charles kept your letter three months in his pocket and it reached me in August when I was in Scotland. So soon as I came back to town I ordered the garments and at the same time wrote a letter to you on the 11th of September explaining the delay. But before either the clothes or the letter could have reached you, I received a second epistle from you, from which I infer that you think my dignity damaged by being asked to do a commission. Keineswegs, mein Feld Mareschal! But as I hoped you would in the interim receive my letter of Sept. 11th (sent through Charles), I delayed answering yours of September in the hope of again hearing from you.

Not having had that pleasure, I resume my letter-paper. And first of all, let me say one word as to your announcement to me. As a general principle and in the most offensive sense of the word, I consider him who marries to be an unmitigated and immitigable ignoramus and ruffian. In your particular case, however, I incline to the opinion that there are palliating circumstances. I have not the honor of knowing Miss Agassiz,[1] though I have an indistinct recollection of

[1] Ida, daughter of Louis Agassiz.

once seeing her somewhere. But I have heard a great deal about her, from an early youth, and this has induced me to believe that she is a person whom weak-minded men like you and me instantaneously, profoundly and irredeemably adore. Probably I shall have some occasion to tell her so some day if ever a misguided Providence permits me to go home. Meanwhile I only hope that your life won't be such an eternal swindle as most life is, and that having succeeded in getting a wife so much above the common run, you will succeed in leading an existence worth having. If I knew your fiancée, I should congratulate her upon getting for a husband one of the curiously small number of men whom I have ever seen, for whom I have morally a certain degree of respect. This perhaps wouldn't be quite so enthusiastic praise as one might give, but it's more than I ever said of any one else. The truth is, a good many of my acquaintances have been getting engaged lately, and I believe yours is the only case that has made me really, sincerely glad to hear about.

Under these circumstances I have a favor to beg of you, or her, if necessary. It is that you will give me photographs of you both. I do not know what latitude is now allowed in America to photograph-giving, but if you choose, the likenesses shall go into my sister's book and be called hers. They will do us honor and shall be pointed out to Dukes and democrats. I shall be greatly pleased and flattered if you will do me this kindness.

Colonel Ritchie [1] gave me the first real information I had about your wound, for Charles's letters are few and short in campaigning, and as for Boston correspondents, I doubt whether in the whole city a single person ever takes the trouble to remember the existence of a five-year absentee. To this day I never have heard what has become of Jim since his capture at Aldie, nor have I the least idea whether he has yet been exchanged or not. Now, my long residence in England has not increased the very small number of friends I ever had, and it would be gratifying to hear occasionally what has become of the old ones. I see no reason why you shouldn't be heard from unless your wound is still too bad. Do try and send me a little news.

Your first informed me that your home was in future to be with the regiment and that you hoped after the war to run over here again for a visit. Your last announced your engagement and countermanded the clothes you had ordered. Am I to understand that you have changed your mind as to a military life? As the clothes had already gone, I couldn't countermand them and can only hope they arrived all right.

[1] Harrison Ritchie (1825–1894).

The war progresses. I'm glad Meade didn't fight. Let's have no more battles north of the James. We stand here with our noses pretty high in the air now. Ever yours.

To Charles Francis Adams, Jr.

LONDON, 10 June, 1864.

As I sat last Sunday at our Club window (by the by, we've built out a bow and made it the best in the street) reading the weekly papers, a brute of a man running along outside, shouting "Great Federal Defeat" and brandishing his vile *Observers*. My face was of iron! Quite so. But my stomach collapsed and stopped working. I rose presently with a frown, and lounged with an indifferent air out of the door and round the corner, at which point I pursued with vindictive animosity the wretch, who began now to cry "Great Federal Victory." When caught, he sold me a paper, from which I learned that Lee had retired to the No. Anna. Naturally the revulsion in my mind was not a little pleasing. At the same time there is no danger of my becoming very sanguine. In fact, so far as I can see, our turning Spottsylvania is only a proof that we have failed to defeat Lee there, which I presume was Grant's purpose. Nevertheless, to go forward is an immense gain and as the war seems now destined to assume more than ever its peculiar pulverizing character, I can only hope that each step gained is something added to us and lost to them....

To Charles Milnes Gaskell

SORRENTO, 3 March, 1865.

MY DEAR GASK: — Since I last saw you, I have made a ponderous march across Europe. It took precisely four weeks to reach this place, never sleeping more than three nights in the same house. I took a vettura at Nice and we did the Cornice, coming down to Spezia in that way. Our whole journey was a success, but that part of it was a triumph, and I consider myself to have earned the laurels of high Generalship in my skilful direction of this arduous campaign in mid-winter. We had weather fit for Gods to travel in, and not a mishap nor a difficulty.

At present behold me installed at the Tasso, surrounded by my amiable and interesting family, over whom I exercise a mild and paternal sway. My prime minister is my Italian courier, and my form of Government is constitutional, not absolute. Like other kings I reign but do not govern, and my premier, though gentle and protecting, is my master. As I do not travel for my own amusement, this state of affairs is not burdensome.

Sorrento is empty or nearly so, except for a stray American or two whom we do not know. Amalfi would be better, with equally good hotels. But the air is soft and the orange and lemon groves full of fruit. I can contrive to drag on a burdensome existence, even though it does rain today; especially as the cuisine is good. I could wish that the weather was a little steadier and that there was some medium between a rainy Sirocco, and a howling Tramontana, but if one must be a victim to weather, one suffers as little at Sorrento as at most places. I can still smoke my Italian cabbages under the oranges, and cultivate philosophy in the shade of the olives, with one eye on Naples and the other on Vesuvius. My courier could do it better than myself, for he squints like a colossus.

At Pisa I saw Sir Robert Cunliffe's [1] name on the board, as occupying a room in our hotel, and I took the occasion of sending you a message, to make his acquaintance. As he said he should write to you, he probably has, or will inform you that he came in to make us an evening visit, and to make himself very agreeable. The next morning we went on to Leghorn to suffer miserably on the sea, and he went on to Florence, so that I saw him no more.

I asked him to inform you that our plans forced us to leave Rome aside, so that your letter and commission would be a trifle stale if it waited my arrival at the holy city. It is to be hoped that you contemplated this possibility in writing it. Otherwise you can write a new one, once a month; codicils, so to speak; and I will deliver them all, with proper directions for reading. I say "once a month," for I have not the most distant idea when I shall turn my face northwards, or when it will please my father to order me to some new occupation. If I am to remain here abroad to enact the honorable and active part of sheep-dog, I shall certainly do my best to keep the sheep quiet, and to keep them here, as I do not delight in moving my flock when it has found good pasturage.

We have met one or two acquaintances at different places. The last was Edward Ellice, who was here when we arrived. I have no wish to meet any more. My sheep are always made more or less restless by them, especially since the middle-aged traveller is always a confirmed grumbler. All the plagues of Egypt are loose in the land,

[1] Sir Robert Alfred Cunliffe, fifth Bart. (1839–1905); married (1) Eleanor Sophia Egerton, and (2) Hon. Cecilia Victoria Sackville-West.

according to the way-side rambler, who has nothing to do but to find them out. We are innocent and we are happy. It is the true doctrine of the true Church.

I trust that as I have nothing whatever to tell you, the equilibrium of correspondence may be kept up by your sending me a quantity of news. I understand that Her Majesty has at last invited me to Court, and that I have respectfully regretted being a thousand miles away, more or less. As it has taken four years for my existence to be recognised by authority, I'm in hopes it will be kept in mind should I return. But I can't say that I mean to come back this time, for the pleasure of again showing H. M. my legs in pink silk stockings....

To Charles Milnes Gaskell

Rome, 23 April, 1865.

Caro amico mio: — Your letter reached me duly at Naples, for which receive my thanks. Meanwhile I have transferred the family quarters to Rome, coming up here on the 8th for the functions of Holy Week, and meditating a contingent remainder till May. Thus far my expedition has not met any mishaps, but I am still in the dark as to our future movements.

Your letter and book have been duly delivered and cards duly exchanged. But I am told that the Marchesa has been very ill this winter, and not able to go into society nor entertain as usual. Before I go away I shall make an effort to see her, and to take any return message she may have to confide to me. Meanwhile my society relations are quite limited and the care of a family as *exigeante* as mine takes up all my time. But happening to be at a reception of Mrs. Story's the other evening, and looking about me in that distrait manner acquired from long practice in London drawing-rooms, I saw quite a pretty blonde in blue enter the Barberini halls, and I at once inquired her name, supposing her a fellow-citizen of the Republic one and indivisible. "Miss Macallister," was the response. Vague recollections of her name as associated with you, entered my mind. Not remembering however, what you had said about her, I thought it would be easiest to ask herself, what it probably had been, and I accordingly requested Mrs. Story to introduce me, which she at once did. No sooner was I in her august presence than I suggested your existence as a fact possibly productive of topics of conversation. Not having ever had the pleasure of meeting the gentle female before, I can't say whether she was embarrassed or blushed, or was natural as usual, but I am quite confident that her powers of conversation appeared remarkably limited, and though she certainly did acknowledge the general fact of your existence as possible, and perhaps even probable, it was all she seemed prepared to grant. I was therefore rapidly driven from the field and was soon glad to escape from the monosyllabic Hebe, much discomfited. This is all I can tell you of your Roman friends.

Rome, however, in spite of the cantankerous men and women in it, is as enjoyable as ever. That is to say, whatever power is still left for enjoyment in a miserable and worn-out ruin like myself, is as available here as elsewhere. I am in no hurry to leave it, for the summer has come, and the Borghese is not a bad place to lie at the feet of damsels in blue, and to smoke cigars at one *scudo e mezzo* the hundred.

[FLORENCE, 10 *May*.] I should begin a new letter, but the above is a sort of guaranty that my intentions were better than my performance. In fact I delayed finishing this epistle at Rome for two reasons. The first was that I might get from Story two MSS. which were from the unpublished correspondence of my cousin William, and which were said to be most extraordinary productions of his pen. Story had lost them, so that I was deprived of the amusement of reading them, and you also must go without it. If you see or write to Will do not ask for them nor mention them....

My second reason for waiting was to see your friend the Marchesa, who was ill of bronchitis and whose husband was in Naples. I did succeed in my object, but except to tell you that she has been very ill and is now, I suppose, on her way to England, I have little to say. She told me that I might tell you that the serene Anglo-Roman society had been extremely quarrelsome apropos to the races, which everyone had wished to manage in his own way. I might say the same of the Americans who are slandering each other like angels.

I remained in Rome until the 3d of May. It was full summer, hot, green and fascinating, but the charge of a family has made me prematurely grey and bald, and Heaven forgive me if I was glad to make a new step towards London. I was absolutely glad when we rolled under the Porta del Popolo with our faces northwards. I dragged my party round by Terni and Perugia, and came down to Siena, before reaching Florence, where we arrived on the evening of the 8th. We stay here till the 17th or so; then go through Bologna to Venice, Milan; and (if I can manage it) into Switzerland by June 1st; but not stay there. If alive, I mean to be in London before the 1st July. I am rabid to get back there. You can imagine my reasons in public matters without baptising me with any new-born adoration for that city.

Lady Francis Gordon desired me to get her some stones of turquoise-blue. Did she say for a necklace or a bracelet? I have racked my brains to recollect which, but without success, and finally I got a half dozen stones which she can do what she likes with. Between you and me, in your secret ear, *she* said *lava* of turquoise-blue. I find that the thing does not exist. What she had is a composition made in Rome, and moulded, not cut. Altogether it gave me more trouble than Lady F. is ever likely to deserve at my hands. But if you mention it, you will surely perish.

We have been nearly broiled to death on our way from Rome. We have not had a drop of rain since April 1st. This city is going into fits over the Dante festival, which I wish was in Dante's Inferno. Such is my news.

I received today a letter from Ralph Palmer all about the President's assassination. He seems (forgive the equivoque) rather proud that Englishmen are disgusted by it. To us the assassination of the President is a matter of personal feeling, the result of his qualities as a man. If other people don't feel as we do about it, we might be disgusted, but that they should is so much a matter of course that I should never have doubted it. But as for the nation, pity is wasted. I am much too strong an American to have thought for a moment that we are going to be shaken by a murder. I shall answer Ralph's letter soon.

If you know Miss Montgomery (the blonde) tell her that she looks like the Venus of Medici. I am coming back to write a new work on art, which is to smash the Greeks. You shall get the *Westminster* [*Review*] to publish my introduction. If you answer this, send it to the Legation.

To Charles Francis Adams, Jr.

FLORENCE, 10 May, 1865.

I can't help a feeling of amusement at looking back on my letters and thinking how curiously inapt they must have been to the state of things about you. Victories and assassinations, joys, triumphs, sorrows and gloom; all at fever point, with you; while I prate about art and draw out letters from the sunniest and most placid of subjects. I have already buried Mr. Lincoln under the ruins of the Capitol, along with Cæsar, and this I don't mean merely as a phrase. We must have our wars, it appears, and our crimes, as well as other countries. I think Abraham Lincoln is rather to be envied in his death, as in his life somewhat; and if he wasn't as great as Cæsar, he shows the same sort of tomb. History repeats itself, and if we are to imitate the atrocities of Rome, I find a certain amusement in conducting my private funeral service over the victims, on the ground that is most suitable for such associations, of any in the world.

But the King being dead, what then? Are we to cry "Live the King" again? To me this great change looks like a step downward to our generation. New men have come. Will the old set hold their ground, or is Seward and the long-lived race about him, to make way for a young America which we do not know? You may guess how I have smiled sweetly on the chains that held me here at such a time, and swore polyglot oaths at Italy and everything else that keeps me here. I have looked towards London as earnestly as What's-her-name looked from Bluebeard's tower, for the signs of the coming era, but no sign is given. The Minister is waiting also apparently. I have written to him that *of course* now he must remain where he is, but whether he agrees to the of course or not, I can't say. It is clear to me that if Seward lives, he must stay; and if Seward retires, he should leave upon the new Secretary the responsibility of making a change. To throw up his office would be unpatriotic; it would be a blunder. Do you assent to my doctrine? To be away from my place at such a time is enough to enrage a tadpole. And I can't be back before the end of June....

To Charles Francis Adams, Jr.

LONDON, 14 July, 1865.

We reached London only at the very end of the season, but I had time to find it changed since I went away. America is a subject dropped out of sight now, except by those who have been our friends. Society avoids it as a disagreeable topic. They feel that they went too far, and they feel that we know their feelings. The only question now upon which they venture to be aggressive, is the fate of Davis. They take the keenest interest in him, and talk very impertinently about our executing him. Even our best friends here are very earnest in begging to have him spared.

We are in the middle of a general election, the only feature in which is the return of John Stuart Mill; a creditable thing to do. Tom Hughes also comes in. In fact our friends everywhere show very strong, and so far as America is concerned we have nothing to do but to restore peace and arrange our finances, and our influence on England will be strong enough to carry a new reform through within ten years. Circumstances might hurry it, but naturally and peacefully it will come in about ten years, I think. Then there will be another long step forward here. Piece by piece the only feudal and middle-age harness will drop off, that still remains. I look to see in Europe during the next quarter of a century, the public acknowledgment of a heap of changes that are now simmering quietly in the minds of society without much expression. You have no idea how thoughtful society is in Europe; even more so in some respects than in America, because there are practical hooks to hang thought on, like the church, education, poverty and the suffrage, which are points all forgotten with us, but very much alive here and lead men far, when they once begin....

Politics seem queerly confused in America. Sumner, Dana and the rest are in an amusing provincial hurry to get into opposition. Why so fast? We have done with slavery. Free opinion, education and law have now entrance into the south. Why assume that they are powerless, and precipitate hopeless confusion? Let us give time; it doesn't matter much how long. I doubt about black states. I fancy white is better breeding stock.

To Charles Francis Adams, Jr.

LONDON, 20 October, 1865.

Before this letter reaches you, the American papers will have republished our passage at arms with Earl Russell. These notes made here a very deep sensation, and have created a very uneasy feeling. The newspapers have treated our portion of the documents with great respect, for them, and hammer away, day after day, with long leaders, trying to overthrow our positions. All this is, of course, a great personal triumph, and I think that your papa's reputation as a public man is scarcely inferior now in England, to that of any of their own men. In point of fact these notes of his are, in my humble opinion, not surpassed. I do not know whether America will notice them. Others as good have lain and will be buried forever in Seward's hopeless volumes of Pub. Docs. It is possible, however, that so unusual an English endorsement may persuade the Americans that some good writing may come out of their own country, and induce them to honor us with their notice. At present your papa's English reputation is greater than his American. I flatter myself that the dictum of this

Legation now is listened to with a respect and reflected upon with an earnestness not usual in the English mind, nor ever before felt in such a degree. We hold at this moment the whole foreign policy of England in our hands. She can't express even an opinion. If she tells Count Bismarck that he'd better mind his eye, the Count winks at us, and puts on his heaviest cowhides, and administers to her a licking that excoriates her figure. She can't resent it, because our Legation, while she meditates revenge, comes forward with profound bows and presents a few more items of our little bill. This process has already lasted two years, and Lord Russell is aware of it even to a degree of lively sensibility. We have already checkmated them against Russia and Prussia, and if I could suggest an idea secretly to the Emperor of Russia, it would be to strike now for Turkey. We wield a prodigious influence on European politics now, and the time is coming when the world will see it with a painful clearness. At the same time we have never touched an intrigue and have not even a single secret source of information, or a single channel of communication other than those that are regular and legitimate, with any Court or party in Europe.

A system more directly opposite than this to the old practice of European diplomacy, could not be invented. Lord Palmerston and Lord Russell have belonged both to the old school of secret and intriguing diplomacy, though the former was much deeper in it than the latter. We have got the better of both of them. How much better, time will show. Lord Palmerston was a man without any fixed opinions. If a clear and decided majority of the people had by some perverseness decided to turn back upon its track and re-enact all the abuses that flourished under Lord Castlereagh, Palmerston would have undone the work he had helped to accomplish, with perfect good nature, and maintained that he merely went with his time, forward or backward, it mattered little. But for all this, our friend who is dead, had one really active antipathy, and that antipathy was America. He would have worked with her, or flattered or conciliated her, if necessary, for he was as callous as a rhinoceros, and to get a useful instrument would swallow his strongest attachment or his strongest dislike with an equally cheerful face. But he would much have preferred to do her a harm, and he did what he could for that purpose. We not only survived his attempts, but we have survived him, though he lived long enough to see us assume our offensive, and throw England on her back. What is to be the result of his disappearance? I think it will weaken England and strengthen us. Lord Russell is no match for us, as has been long evident, and Lord Clarendon would certainly not be an advance on Lord Russell. Palmerston gave the Government great internal strength. A new Ministry must inevitably devote itself to internal affairs and face serious questions at home. Our attitude, therefore, will become more than ever embarrassing to them, and our action or abstinence from action may in future preserve or ruin Ministries.

Under these circumstances I must confess that I doubt whether Mr. Seward will care to change our representation abroad or would be wise to do so. I have much doubt whether we shall be released next spring, as your papa still pretends to expect. Seward as yet has given us not even the ghost of a sign, although the resignation has been for three months in his hands, and Mr. Evarts, to whom I wrote on the subject, after seeing Mr. Seward, could not give me any reason to suppose that a change was practicable. If the change of Ministry, coming as it will on the published correspondence on our claims, does not give Mr. Seward a good reason for compelling us to remain here, if he really wants us to do so, I am much mistaken. For my own part, I should not object. I am doing as much for myself here as I should be likely to do anywhere...

To Charles Milnes Gaskell

54, PORTLAND PLACE.
Wednesday, 2 May, [1866.]

DEAR CARLO: — Many blessings light upon the wig! I too once hoped to reach the proud distinction you have gained, but now that this hope has been permanently crushed, I hereby make over to you to have and to hold in fee simple or by any other tenure you prefer, all my right and title in any glory, gain, or emolument whatsoever, which might have become mine in the pursuit of a legal career.

You are either so early or so late that your note found me still in bed this morning. I studied it for ten minutes before comprehending its meaning. Five minutes before, my mind had been crossing the Isthmus of Panama, and was greatly exercised at having left its boots at Aspinwall in the hurry of departure. On returning to 54 P. P., it was still hazy in its vision. I sent a verbal 'Yes' at last in reply, and to-morrow evening will appear in my war-paint and feathers at quarter to eight.

Where think you that I go tonight? To swell the noble Houghton's train, I dine for the Literary Fund and if you were the man I took you for, you would go there too. But the world grows dull and duller. Lady Cranborne has not asked me. But Mrs. Gladstone remains.

To Charles Francis Adams, Jr.

LONDON, 1 March, 1867.

Do you know things look awfully black to me at home. I begin seriously to doubt whether the country can ever get out of it. The whole South must be soon like Greece and Asia Minor, a society dissolved, and brigandage universal. Eliot's and Stevens' bills [1] ought to produce that effect, if any, and though it is now law that the negro is better than the white man, I doubt whether even the negro can restore order to the South. The issue presented to the President in answer to his advance, is sharp. He has no alternative but to meet it, for these bills are monstrous. The impeachment, therefore, seems to my mind to have come a long stride nearer....

To Charles Milnes Gaskell

LONDON, 26 March, 1867.

MY DEAR BARRISTER, — I am nearly at the point of death from pure curiosity to hear your travels. Reflect however, that if you publish, you will at once be known, and therefore moderate the personalities. I think you might entitle your work: "Journey etc: By various hands;" and include a chapter by H. E. L. J——m; and another by Lord P——n. I am going to ask Sir C. Lyell whether there are any investigations *now going on* near Liège; if not, there's no chance of our seeing anything. If there are, I shall be able to get the proper directions. It is easy enough to write on the subject without any acquaintance with it, but a dash of truth would add a certain base to the dish. Could you not hammer out a few couplets in the style of Heine or some other fellow, on the *Bos primigenius*? Or any other subject? There is nothing like an experiment. Catch an idea, and then hammer out the rhymes. Or omit the rhymes and do it in classic style; Horace, Catullus, Tibullus, Propertius, or some other blessed antique. You send me one verse and I will try to cap it.

Palgrave, by the way, is scoring my *North American* [2] wildly. I've not read his comments yet, but I saw the thing at his house, and the

---

[1] Thomas Dawes Eliot, of Massachusetts (1808–1870), and Thaddeus Stevens, of Pennsylvania (1792–1868). See New York *Nation*, February 21, 1867.

[2] His essay on Captain John Smith appeared in the *North American Review*, January, 1867.

marginal notes made it look like a variorum edition of Plato. He has instigated me into going to an auction sale and giving £12.0. for a Cuyp. He swears it's dirt cheap at the price. You shall see it when you come up. I've sent it to be framed and shall hang it in my room. I fully expect to be ruined by him ultimately, for drawings are my mortal point and I can't resist....

I have literally nothing on hand but Belpertia. You may imagine that I find it a trifle dull. To amuse myself I study currency.

Bye-bye! Let me know how the travels come on, and *do* hunt up one or two good Latin quotations, with a sting in their tail, out of some imaginary middle-age poet. Ever yours,

H. B. RAMPHO.

To Charles Francis Adams, Jr.

LONDON, 3 April, 1867.

.   .   .   .

It is curious how rapidly the tides shift at home. You recollect last autumn how quickly it rose between your leaving England and reaching America. Only a month or six weeks has passed since my last letter, and the change has been equally decided.

In February I overestimated the radical strength. I tested it by the passage of Eliot's Louisiana Bill in the House, and by the known energy and determination of Stevens and his associates. I knew that the impeachment alone would give them success, and I thought their party could see at least that to stop was ruin. But the event has proved that the party was little better than a mob of political gamblers and timid time-servers. They funked the whole issue. They saw a turn of public opinion in the air, and they knuckled down on the spot.

The crisis is over, with the month of March, and I breathe free again. The New Hampshire election satisfied me, and that in Connecticut I felt too sure of to doubt....

You are quite wrong, I believe, in thinking that the American people are disposed to abrogate or alter the Constitution, or that they can do so. The last month proves it to me. The truth to my mind is that the duty of guarding the Constitution was put by the people in the hands of the Republican party; that party has betrayed its trust, and the Democratic party has succeeded to it, since the people had no other choice. And now your friend Dana, and Andrew, and Palfrey and the rest, see the false position they are in when the Democrats turn upon them and ask what they have done with the Constitution. John[1] alone has acted the part of a man. I care mighty little who gets the offices or the popular applause, but I admire John all the more for what he has done, in proportion as I feel how in his place I should have fallen.

I tell you frankly that when I think of the legislation since last year, my blood boils and I feel my lazy temper ready to break out in any sort of expression that could signify direct and personal hatred of every man in that Congress. Depend upon it that what affects me so violently will affect the average man at last. The Connecticut election is a sign. As for the President, he may be an object of supreme contempt, and he may do all the harm he can; but for all that it may not be impossible that the Democrats should renominate him next year and elect him too. Popular fluctuations are queer things. Remember Lincoln's case. It is sacrilege now to name the two together: but four years ago!...

To Charles Milnes Gaskell

54, PORTLAND PLACE, LONDON,
4 April, 1867.

MY DEAR CARLO, — Since receiving your note I have seen your mother, who leans to the idea that we shall start on Wednesday morning by the early mail. For my own part, I assent to this arrangement. I find that I have a ball on Tuesday evening at Mrs. Ewing Curwen's, and that house is very convenient to the Victoria Station. Though why we should go by Victoria I can't see. Charing Cross is nearer and nicer.

Let me have your opinion on this point. If you decidedly prefer it, I am willing to go down to Dover on Tuesday night, and if it's calm, to cross and sleep at Calais. If stormy, take the chance of better weather by the morning boat.

I dined out twice in succession this week, which always does for my stomach. In consequence I have been seedy. The truth is, we eat too many sweet things, and drink too many wines — not too *much*, you understand. That I should deny.

I have a suggestion to make to you. Will you tell me the most disagreeable thing you ever heard said of me? Without giving its author of course. I will in return set the conversation with all my acquaintances running upon you, and when anything sufficiently ill-natured has been said, you shall have it hot.

[1] John Quincy Adams.

Lord have mercy upon us, miserable sinners! I would do anything to experience new sensations, even disagreeable ones, and a good, spiteful, vicious attack is such a tonic!

I met Lady William and the two Sweet Williams, at Mrs. Baillie's, as well as Miss Wortley, and a number of other young women who looked all manner of dislike at me for not dancing. It was a nice ball, I should think, although I am not very learned in such matters. I stayed till half after one, and talked incessantly — gabbled, in fact.

Since your departure I have got me Owen's *Palæontology*, which has a list of all the Greek names at the end, and their meanings. I am trying to look over the book, but one idea in ten pages is the best I can collect. Geology is low comedy in comparison.

If this devilish wind continues to blow, we shall have a *mauvais quart d'heure* on the channel.

To Charles Francis Adams, Jr.

LONDON, April 30, 1867.

The *North American* improves... I shall have one more article in the October number, on the Bank of England Restriction, 1797–1821. Then I shall stop....

I wish you would subscribe for me to the New York weekly, the *Nation*, isn't it? There seems to be merit about it. I wish also that you would send out to me anything that appears to you worth noticing in American literature, anything new, I mean, which seems to you to be capable of standing criticism. If I write here, I shall write what I think, and not be soft on people's corns. And as I shall write merely for practice and not for reputation, it matters little what I say. Therefore if you hear of anything that owns a voice and not an echo; that talks itself, and not Dante or Tennyson, send it me, and add your own comments on the margin....

Since my last letter I have been to Luxemburg, Treves, down the Moselle, up the Rhine, round by Saarbrück. Saarlouis, Saarburg r. [Rhine] and back by way of Spa. You see it was a military and strategic excursion. I come back inclining to France. We all hate cant, I suppose. I hate, for instance, your cant of submitting to all that is because it is; as much as you hate mine of objecting to it for the same reason. Among other cant, I detest the German rot about nationality. Luxemburg is really French more than Prussian, and as to its military value to Prussia except as a menace to France, it's utter fallacy.

Luckily both nations are now so equal in strength that they hesitate before fighting. Otherwise we should have had a war long ago. But sooner or later they will fight, and it is just as well to remember that fact. If you speculate, remember that well-informed people here expect war....

To Charles Francis Adams, Jr.

LONDON, 8 May, 1867.

I said, and I say it again, that your theory of "fighting it out within the party" is a piece of self-delusion which you use to cover your own intellect from seeing and confessing what is really fear of public opinion. I said that Dana and all his friends and the whole conservative Liberalism of New England had been whipped and kicked like a mangy spaniel by Sumner and his party, and had cowered under the flogging without a growl or even a whine. *Did* they ever try to "fight it out within the party"? Was ever a voice raised within the party? If so, it didn't reach us. Dana is a sucking M. C. and at nurse. He couldn't risk popularity. Andrew was better, but he too had too much to lose by open rebellion. John alone said that his soul was his own....

Practically, however, we are tolerably agreed. The epithet "monstrous" which seems to have weighed on your mind, was applied by me to Eliot, the other man's Louisiana Bill and the tariff bill, not to Sherman's measure, which I then supposed to be a general application of Eliot's. We all consider, I suppose, that the Southern states had better try to do something with the existing law. As to the Constitutional question, it will in such a case merely lie in abeyance. I don't believe you will find it very easily settled, however.

As for the Republican party, the future will have to decide what our relations to it are to be. Next year, I expect that party lines will be pretty much rubbed out, unless the Republicans try to nominate some other candidate than Grant. After that we shall have a new division of parties, I hope. You and John and I are likely to be found together in such a case, and I suspect, not in Republican ranks. But we shall have first to wait and see what the issues are to be.

Dana meanwhile writes an elaborate letter which it would amuse you to read, I am sure. Dana seems to have become as thorough a politician as Sumner, and to have lost far more than he the faculty of looking at things from an "objective point" of view, if you will forgive my using the term. He is or seems to be tormented by the fear that our chief is going over to the Democrats. His fear of Democracy is very like an English Bishop's hatred of dissent.

You can quiet his mind on that point. I believe nothing is further from the mind of the party in question. The time for such a change, when it could have done good, is passed for the present, and no occasion whatever exists for changing the position hitherto occupied.

This brings me to the last part of my reflections. I think another effort will be made to get out of our present situation, and I think that the close of this year will see us free. In that case our return would not take place, however, till August 1868. Many reasons combine to make me think it desirable that this arrangement should be carried out. What say you? Do not write to the family as though the idea came to you from me.

To Charles Milnes Gaskell

54, PORTLAND PLACE,
Saturday, 11 May, '67.

DEAR KARL, Your departure was a surprise to me. Hervey, Lady William, and the Sweet Williams, were all expecting you at Lady Waldegrave's ball; and when I called the next day in Stratford Place to see what had become of you, behold you were gone. For your sake I was glad. You know I have always preached change of air and no medicine. Turn over a new leaf. Scour the Edge and dig Nummulites or some other fellah out of the limestone. Grow fat. But don't take drugs. I live on pepsine and cod-liver oil, but then I don't call those drugs.

Of course you want to know about Lady W[aldegrave]'s blow-out on Wednesday evening. By the way, I went to Lady Goldsmid's first, and I assure you I have never seen so superb a display as her rooms made, in any private house. It was actually royal. But I had to escape through the conservatory in order to go down to Lord Stanley's; and thence to Lady W.'s.

The best thing I did at Lady W.'s was to march up and talk to the Comte de Paris, who didn't know me in the least. I had to patronise him a good deal before he remembered me.

I have made such violent love to Lady William that the consequences will be disastrous to me, as the young ladies will consider me a bore. The whole Hervey clan was on parade at Lady W.'s, jewels and all.

On the whole I enjoyed the ball. I admired John Hervey who danced like a sylphide. There was a very swell tribe of people, whom I did not admire so much. Two or three dozen Duchesses who looked awful. By the way I did the Argyll girl, and rather liked her. She has a pretty complexion; and is very fresh and unaffected; at least, so I thought, after ninety seconds conversation.

Console yourself on your absence. I have on my engagement book just three names — three and no more — and what do you think they are. No. 1, the best, is a dinner at my friend Forster's. No. 2, Mrs. Darby Griffith!! No. 3, The Lady Mayoress!!!

What have I done to suffer humiliation like this? And what are we to do, if it goes on?

I've not seen your mother since her return, in spite of my efforts, but I shall try again tomorrow.

I am regularly done by those brutes of tailors. I ordered my spring clothes on the 23d and have not been able even to try them on yet. What to do!

P.S. My termination, as above, would satisfy Hubert.

To Charles Milnes Gaskell

BADEN-BADEN, 25 August, '67.

MY DEAR KARL, — Life has been a burden to me for the last fortnight so that I have not been able to put pen to paper since I left England. We crossed to Paris on the tenth and in that infernal city we remained till the twentieth, waiting for ladies' dresses and the milliners' bills. You should run over to Paris by all means. Otherwise you will be deprived of the precious privilege of abusing it; a privilege which I value so highly that I have done little else but exercise it since I arrived there. I do not hesitate to say that at present it is a God-forsaken hole, and my party unanimously agreed that their greatest pleasure since arriving was in quitting it; and as we are all more or less familiar with the town, our opinion is entitled to weight. I never imagined the city so thoroughly used up, and given over to hordes of low Germans, English, Italians, Spaniards and Americans, who stare and gawk and smell, and crowd every shop and street. I did not detect a single refined-looking being among them, but there may have been one or two who like ourselves had drifted there by accident or necessity, and were lost in the ocean of humanity that stagnates there in spite of its restlessness. As for the Exhibition, I advise you to go to see it, but go at eight o'clock in the morning and come away at ten, and don't go too often. Plaster temples of Karnac, and canvas Mexi-can structures, and eastern palaces in slightly worn-out stucco may be seen once. The pictures are worth a good deal of study to fully appreciate that they are not worth it. For the rest, I recollect a chaos confounded. The devil only knows what is in it. I did not go there as a sensible being ought, in the reserved hours from eight to ten, and the consequence was that I was disgusted. I went five times, and hate it in consequence.

You will be delighted to hear that I got into a row which came very near being serious to us. We went to Versailles on the 15th, the *fête Napoléon*. Coming back, our train was overfilled and at a station about half way a great crowd of *ouvriers* in blouses could not get seats. About twenty were at our door trying to get in, so I stood up in the doorway to stop them till the guard came. A big devil tried to force his way in, so I put my shoulder against him and pitched him out into his friends' arms. Upon this the crowd flared up into a regular French passion. We pulled the door to; the foremost of them tried to force it open, or struck in through the window at my brother and me; my big friend I saw howling in the middle of the mob, shaking his fist at me and shrieking at *cet homme-là*; while I, expecting to be dragged out by the legs, was preparing to hurt as much as I could the first fellow that got in, sure of getting no mercy from the rest. Luckily the crowd got in each other's way, so that although the door was several times partly opened, no one could enter. It must have been nearly a minute before the guard came and just then the train started. One blouse did then come in, but the rest, my *vengeur* among them, were left on the platform howling.

In short our ten days in Paris were horribly expensive — hotel bill frs. 2,500 — and far from agreeable. We threw up our hats on reaching this place, not that there is not a shocking crowd here too, but at least we have fresh air and some one decent — or indecent — to look at. Everyone who is usually at Paris, seems to have taken refuge here. Such a swarm of our country-people! The twang of my native land is echoed in every direction by the British burr. The two nations glare contempt at each other in the correct fashion. I have found no English acquaintances here, but we are already in three days overrun with American, and knowing well the national jealousies I am quite willing not to have to combine the two. It is hopeless to try the management of a double team.

Morally Baden is delicious. The females one sees, are enough to make one's hair stand out in all directions. The men are mostly vulgar, but whether Germans, French, English or Americans are most vulgar, is a serious question about which I am led to reflect much. The styles are different, but the result reached is identical. Play runs high. A brother of the Viceroy of Egypt, after losing £6000 at Homburg, has come here, where he plays day and night, but whether he has won or lost I do not know, though I saw him lose nineteen thousand francs in half an hour. Modern version of the Egyptian Sphinx. A beast he is to look at, but very like his brother. I occasionally try a five franc piece at roulette, but as yet have lost nothing.

We stay here a fortnight or so longer. If you write, address care of F. S. Meyer, Banker. Remember me to your father and mother. I hope you keep on writing, but after all, writing is only one half the art; the other being erasure. No one can make real progress that doesn't practice the latter as vigorously as the first. I have done it so effectually as to have expunged all my last thing.

To Charles Francis Adams, Jr.

BADEN, 4 September, 1867.

We passed two days in Paris while on our way here, and there I saw Hunt's[1] picture of the Minister, which he completed while we were there. As you and John no doubt feel an interest in it, I want to say a few words about it.

The picture is not a full-length; it comes only to the knees. The ground on which the figure is painted is perfectly simple; a warm foxy color, which age will darken to black. There is no background other than this. The figure itself stands out boldly; the face slightly turned to the left; the black frock coat buttoned up, a scarf covering the shirt, and only the collar showing any bit of white. There is no color anywhere. One hand is thrust into the coat front; the other hangs down with a roll of paper. The expression of the face is marked, but not excessively so, and I think you and I have seen him rise to speak in public, when he had almost precisely the same air and manner.

You can understand from the description that Hunt has dealt with his subject in the most honest and straight-forward way. There are no tricks nor devices in the picture. It is in the severest and truest style; so severe that most people will think it commonplace. I imagine that you and everyone else, except a few professional men, will look at it with a sense of disappointment, and feel that something is wanting; a

[1] William Morris Hunt (1824–1879).

bolder or freer touch; a more expressive attitude; more animated features; a less subdued background, or a dash of color in the dress. There is nothing for the eye to fasten upon and to drag away from the whole effect. In your language, as applied to literature, it is dull.

You know by this time my canons of art pretty well, and you know that what pleases the crowd would have a poor chance of pleasing me. Whoever is right, the majority is wrong. I consider Hunt's picture to be just what a portrait of our papa should be; quiet, sober, refined, dignified, a picture so unassuming that thousands of people will overlook it; but so faithful and honest that *we* shall never look at it without feeling it rise higher in our estimation. I need to see it among other portraits in order to get at its relative merit, but at any rate I don't hesitate to say that I think we have a first-rate likeness of the Governor....

To Charles Milnes Gaskell

BADEN, 22 September, 1867.

CARO CARLISSIMO, — What the deuce is Frank Doyle's[1] rank, regiment and address? I am afraid I've got it wrong and so I send it to you to correct. If you will forward it, I will pay you the postage by cheque or otherwise as you prefer. The youth must have his letter after I've taken the trouble to write it.

To my astonishment who turned up here the other day but Pollington *mit Gattin und Bedienung*; also mit papa-in-law and other sister. I went at once to see him and we chatted a while. He swore you were a humbug for not writing to him, so I read him your letter to me. Since then I've not heard of him, whence I infer that he is still swallowed up in the arms of the Gattin. He has not gone however, for I saw him in the distance last night, hedged in by Erringtons. As I am occupied all the time by my woman-kind, I infer that he is ditto (to use his own elegant style). She was very chatty however, the moment I saw her.

The Houghtons also appeared on the same day, and went on to Berne. They said they were in better health and to winter at Nice or elsewhere.

As you can imagine from seeing us still here, we find Baden too pleasant to care for leaving it. We pass almost the whole day in the woods, among the hills, and trouble ourselves very little about the

[1] Francis Grenville Doyle, who died in 1882 from the effects of the Egyptian campaign.

world. Fashionable people have gone away. Lord Houghton arrived too late to give another breakfast to Cora Pearl. I suppose we shall have to move our quarters also this week, but whether up or down the Rhine I can't say; probably towards Switzerland, and then some of these days back to London, but when or wherefore I know not, inasmuch as everything is in a muddle and mankind a humbug.

One thing however seems certain. I shall not get up to the latitude of Yorkshire this year — perhaps not even the next; so I want you to give all sorts of the prettiest messages to your mother and say that the weight of several nations on my shoulders all at once could alone prevent my coming up to see her. I had meditated a letter to her, but on the whole thought she would be more bored than pleased by it, so abandoned the idea.

I was shocked at one passage in yours. You say that the hero in Gerald Estcourt entreats the heroine to distinguish between "*l'infidélité du corps et l'infidélité du cœur*," and that this is new. Now, it is many years since I read Tom Jones, but if you will turn to Chapter something of that work, I am sure you will find this very speech; and Sophy's reply is that she will never marry a man to whom the infidelity is not in each case the same. At which Thomas, the town bull, as one of my literary friends called him, was disgusted.

I have amused myself here for the last fortnight by drinking a bottle of water every morning and walking about five hours every day, so that I am now in good condition. Moreover I had a rapid run (not on foot) down to Cologne, and was sorry not to be able to take Trèves on my way as you would wish to have the last news from the Rothes Haus and Doctor Staub. As it is I shall scarcely be able to bring you any at all.

A sigh of regret passed through my soul when I read of your party at Wenlock, but when fate takes me by the coat-tails I am only too well contented to be dragged to as pleasant a place as this. The gallant Baronet [Alderson] and my noble friend, I am sure did no harm to the partridges.

54, PORTLAND PLACE,
Friday, 19 October, '67.

BRUTE, — Your offer is most liberal, but I should think you might put yourself down for something and not leave it all for your guests. I appreciate deeply Miss Alderson's generosity. As for the Baronet, it is only what I expected.

I am at my desk nine hours a day, doing up awful arrears of work.

Dogs, or red hot tweezers applied to the toe-nails might draw me away. Nothing less; not even Thornes.

This devotion to duty is all on the supposition that we are going to Rome and I must then get leave of absence; it will come easier if I am laborious now; but I am beginning to fear that things look bad for Rome; there's the deuce to pay there, and a grand continental war and day-of-judgment on the cards. If there is a war, I suppose Rome will be hard to get to and uncomfortable when reached. Nevertheless, *justum et tenacem*, etc. I stand firm though the skies fall.

Though in person I am compelled to absent myself, yet remind your interesting guests that in spirit I am with you even when agitated Fenians require most letters. That long-promised sight of Wentworth will never come off; but it's not of the least consequence, as poor Mr. Toots used to say; I've no doubt it's a humbug; everything is; — except you and your family, and the Baronet and Lady Alderson and the Misses Alderson (2) and Thornes and Wenlock. Shall I also except Palgrave? He and his wife[1] dine with us tonight along with the Froudes and Browning.

I saw the sweet Williams last Sunday; mamma and daughter. They were cordial, with the usual dash of satire; what do they say of us within their happy domestic circle? I suspect we catch it, but we can bear much, and after all we have faults; few and slight, it is true, but *enfin* we are not perfect.

Oblige me by not consuming more of the *old* port than is absolutely required. In regard to the rest of the wine I will not restrict the company.

Remember me to your mother. If I did not know what a pleasant party she had, I should come merely to be of use to her; as it is, there are no stupid young ladies for me to talk to; besides, the Baronet is there. Bye-bye. Fenians call.

To Charles Francis Adams, Jr.

LONDON, 16 November, 1867.

• • • • • • • • •

We have received this morning the election returns. Curious! It takes, as you see, only one year for a nation to follow the lead of its most sagacious men; a fact which in my opinion is worth noting. It is almost equivalent to a vessel's turning on its own length; at least, it

---

[1] Palgrave married, December, 1862, Cecil Grenville, daughter of James Milnes Gaskell and sister of Charles Milnes Gaskell.

does obey its rudder. As for our brother John, I kotow before him. Tell him that I should write a letter of wisdom to him, if I weren't afraid of being suspected of worshipping a rising son and brother. The only aspect in which I derive the honest satisfaction from his brilliant debut, apart from the fact that he is a S. & B. as above, arises from the confident belief that Messrs. Sumner and Wilson have received a distinct and dignified reprimand for the insult they thought proper to put upon us last summer in respect to the custom house. I confess that rankled. I have not forgotten it, nor shall I. There is too a certain genial pleasure in thinking that after all, our family and our names command sympathy and some support at home. We grow in a dry and rocky soil, but we grow. We are a power, if not a very strong one. The 65,000 have my thanks. We don't care for the damned old Governorship, but we are pleased by 65,000 compliments to our youngest. You will say so, please — from me.

The death of Gov. Andrew troubled me principally on your account, for my own relations with him were, as you know, limited to having seen him. But my second thought was one of deeper regret. I had hoped that he would run Sumner out of the Senate next year. In his absence who can our conservative friends concentrate upon? Our Governor Senior? And if so, are we to fight the Senatorship *and* the Governorship next year? Isn't this cutting it a trifle too fat?...

Charles Norton's wit improves, in fact, its value has nearly doubled since last January. But the triumph of earning $240 in paper in one year does not satisfy my ambition. John is a political genius; let him follow the family bent. You are a lawyer, and with a few years' patience will be the richest and the most respectable of us all. I claim my right to part company with you both. I never will make a speech, never run for an office, never belong to a party. I am going to plunge under the stream. For years you will hear nothing of any publication of mine — perhaps never, who knows. I do not mean to tie myself to anything, but I do mean to make it impossible for myself to follow the family go-cart.... I shall probably remain under water a long time. If you see me come up, it will be with an oyster and a pearl inside. If not, why — so!...

To Charles Milnes Gaskell

LONDON, 26 November, 1867.

MY DEAR CARLO, — I have waited for something decisive from Ireland until I am ashamed to wait any longer. Nothing comes, at least down to this moment nothing has come to me, which makes me at all wiser than I was last Saturday. So I think it best to write at once and proceed on the supposition that you are coming along *tant bien que mal* but still hopefully. A letter is all that I can offer you and it may keep up your spirits a little which Cork alone would depress sufficiently, and which must be completely used up between Cork on one side and your brother's illness on the other. I can't write about unpleasant things, for that wretch Palgrave, who on Friday promised solemnly to keep me informed, has never sent me a sign, and I only know what I can learn at your door.

Your sudden departure was a thunderbolt in our various camps. Within an hour after getting your letter, I received a note from Lady Alderson asking me to fill your place at dinner on Saturday, which I naturally promised to do. You will be curious to have a report of the dinner; I will satisfy your wishes. There were about a dozen people there; I took the lovely one to dinner and we were, I am obliged to confess, somewhat gay. You can measure it by the fact that we became sentimental and poetical before we rose from table. I gave a short discursive sketch in about fifteen minutes, of the nature and objects of love. She blushed and listened. Of course I spoke only as your representative. The elder sister flirted abominably with that old Hindu idol, that cross-legged Buddha, Brahma, Vishnu, Siva, and the rest of them — I mean the *Saturday Review*.[1] Remembering the wrongs of humanity, I avoided this Juggernaut. I glared at him across the table. He told stories after dinner, and I went to sleep in his face; I was in my right, for the stories were stupid. That was all I had to do with him. Not having received from you authority to act, I could not make him disgorge the brains he has swallowed. He did not show a proper appreciation of me, by requesting articles for his wretched newspaper. My dinner — I beg pardon! *your* dinner — amused me and I hope I acted your part with feeling and propriety.

Sunday afternoon I sat one hour and twenty minutes in Cadogan Place; a feat which shows that I make progress even as I approach thirty. We passed the time in abusing you. I told them I should repeat all that was said, but unfortunately I have forgotten it, all except my concluding touch, which was to invite the eldest girl to go down to Thornes with me on the first of January; a carriage to be reserved for us at Euston Square or King's Cross — wherever it is — and I to be allowed to smoke. This arrangement delighted me. There was a calm

---

[1] Meredith White Townsend (1831–1911) and Richard Holt Hutton (1826–1897) were the editors of the *Spectator* at this time. The reference is probably to Townsend.

impudence about it in the touch of my asking her to your house, which is equal to our best. She accepted the invitation. We are also all going together to Rome, with your mother to matronise.

Sunday I dined with Mrs. Russell Sturgis. Yesterday I dined at a new house, out in Bayswater, an American girl who married an Englishman. I admired her as a girl; she was fast but handsome and lively. I had a dinner there last night which carried me off my legs. I talked all the time, eat all the time, drank all the time. In short, I was *en train*. I drank a great deal too much and fell desperately in love with my hostess and told her so. There are oases in the desert of life. Such a one was Inverness Terrace last night. My only regret was that you were probably not finding such an oasis at Cork.

Tonight I dine at the United University with Ralph Palmer and young Malcolm. My family is rejoicing at Rondcomb, where the party remains till Thursday. I have a note from my father giving me good advice and a list of guests; the Heads; old Mrs. Mildmay; Admiral and Mrs. Stopford (?); Mrs. Goldsmid, and "three or four young men" making eighteen at table. Which do you think preferable, Cork or country-houses? I don't know myself. After Cork one would certainly relish the country-houses, but after the country-houses one might relish Cork.

Work comes forward very slowly. My progress is not only far from rapid but very unsatisfactory. I pass most of my time every day in erasing what I had written the day before. I have read your chapters I, II, III. They are not so good as I have read of your work; all the religion will have to come out, as you remarked, I think; but vigorous compression is all it wants. I've no doubt they will do, with a little filing, and come out like new-laid eggs, warm and fresh.

Of course all this is for your eye exclusively. I wish I could have seen your poor mother before all her trouble came. It seems now so long since I came near her, that I feel a stranger. I shall go to Lady Doyle's funeral if allowed. If Palgrave doesn't appear soon, I must hunt him up for instructions.

To Charles Milnes Gaskell

54, PORTLAND PLACE,
Monday, 30 December, 1867.

Your note arrived this morning. Many thanks for the historical information it contains. I have no immediate use to make of it, but will put it aside and make it come into something one of these days.

I am led to infer that your hopes were disappointed. My poor boy, this world is a disappointment altogether. Let us quit it punctually next Sunday.

My impression on the whole is one of relief at not having shared your adventures. Now that a new sun is beginning to shine upon me from beyond the Atlantic, I am beginning — yes, decidedly I have begun to be tired of having stupid people with titles sit upon me habitually. William the Conqueror was good once, as our view of *Punch* was; but in the long run he is a bore. You and I have done our best to resist the attempt to subdue us. We have carried the war at times into the enemies' country and harried their young women. But we are but two, and dulness is omnipotent, omnipresent, eternal. I am going to run away from it, and you had better give up resistance at once. Sooner or later you will be its victim and why prolong the struggle? "Ancient associations and a prejudice in favor of" the Athanasian creed will get the better of your immortal longings ultimately. Mammas and brothers and William Rufus put together are irresistible — when they're not one's own. On the whole, if you are driven to accept the English creed and swear that you believe in one Duke the master etc. and one mother-in-law who corresponds to the Roman idea of the *sainte vierge*, I hope you will get your own mother to make the selection. I've no faith in any of those that we have chosen.

If I were to go to a big place now, so strong is the spirit of the devil in me since your departure, I know I should do something shocking. Rebellion is good! I like to rebel against everything. Poor Lady William! if she knew my feelings she would think you certainly lost and destroyed in such company.

I have seen no one — not a living being. I mean to make no calls. Certain rheumatic twinges, or some unpleasant pains, warn me that we had better start at once. If the Baronet arrives on Thursday, when shall you come? He suggests starting on Saturday. In hopes of a certain remeeting.

P.S. Your letter is not burnt. Nor do I understand whether Lady M. says she's not a negative or is a positive, or is not positively negative; or whether it is that she has not a better appetite after the Athan: Cr: or finally whether it is that she has not grown. Grown or not she is too tall for you! beware.

To Charles Milnes Gaskell

54, PORTLAND PLACE,
Wednesday, 1 January, 1868.

What the deuce do you mean by talking about being lame and going
to Suffolk again? I rather think you had better be here by Saturday
at latest. If not, ——! Never mind! I shall go, even if you and Cunliffe both fail and the eternal skies tumble. Next Sunday *I* mean to
be on my way to France. If I am in my bed I can't go, but if destiny hasn't got some better way of balking a fellow than by the exercise of mere brute force, destiny may go hang. If allowed a fair
field I mean to leave London next Sunday at latest. Come! — or
beware!

The Palgraves called here this morning! I told a lie to your sister.
She asked where you had been since Christmas and I said you had
told me you were going to Cambridge. Let that sit heavy on thy soul
tomorrow. I don't see but that you must keep the thing secret now
on my account if not on your own.

I have no news, having seen no one. London is beastly. The
weather brutal. I hope we shall be at Vaucluse this day week, out of
the reach of snow and ice. I don't want to be caught by the impending
storm on this side Lyons.

Nothing more from the Baronet from which I augur well. He should
report at headquarters tomorrow evening.

Letters from my brother-in-law and sister [Kuhn] at Florence
expect our arrival. They are very gay — *tant soit peu* fast I suspect,
but agreeable.

Hoo Hoo! mauvais soldat! according to the *Grande Duchesse*. I
recognise the Bretton party. I hope you gave an eloquent message on
my part to Lady Comet; you can't pitch it too strong now that I am
going away. Intimate a long but hopeless and suppressed passion, and
that my nervousness won't allow me to meet her again. How is it that
Lyvedy isn't there? I suppose he is, by this time. Ah, well! another
Christmas I shall not have the pleasure of losing the charms of Bretton. You will be there, and I hope you will be caught like poor mute
inglorious Milton, and yoked to a Beaumont or a Lascelles or some
such cattle. Then indeed you will have earned your reward like dear
Wayland.

I intend to write to your mother before our departure. May I
mention the engagement? As things look now I shall not be in London
or in England much more than two months after we return; three at

the outside; perhaps only a few weeks. So in real truth, this departure is my breakup. I only return to pack and toddle.

Alas for Blacky![1] Never mind! We will cook up something for him among us and you shall put it on paper. If he fails to print that, he's a Dutchman.

By the way, I read nearly all the second volume of Piebald. It certainly does read itself. It is natural, simple, easy; there is a vein of sentiment in it which seems to me quite "tender," as F. T. P. would say. I am not criticising Balzac or Walter Scott or Thackeray, but *enfin* Boyle. And I was agreeably disappointed.

Sunday, 1.40 P.M. Through.

To Charles Milnes Gaskell

LONDON, 30 March, 1868.

Got your note — your peripatetic note — this morning, after so long a silence that I was almost persuaded to believe Miss Hervey who declares we have quarreled. Glad you are coming, and hope you will like London better than I do. I have been regularly to Cadogan Place for the last three Sundays to learn news of you — to very little effect; but was smiled upon. The Sheriff has come to town but is rusty; his dignity has turned his head. When he can spare time from his aristocratic acquaintance he means to come here to dinner — though we no longer give dinners. It's so kind of him! He has promised to come on Wednesday (my Governor is out that night) and if you come by way of Calais you will have time to come in too — and there we shall be, the three heroes! I don't go anywhere now, being already forgotten by London, not having left cards; but I expect to go somewhere — the Lord knows where — out of England, after Easter. I pass my days in packing-cases like big baths and have almost finished with them. Books, drawings, bronzes and all, will soon be hermetically sealed. Dined last night with the Goldsmids, and a good dinner with true feeling in the Boudins Richelieu which were not like Roman ones; and a divine discovery in the cheese way. You should have been there; the others were incapable of taste. Tonight I do Tom Baring! I shall be a rude critic, and Thomas may well quail before my eye. No other good dinners, only political ones. Had an invitation for you the other night to go to Mrs. Benzon's to hear Clara Schumann and Joachim play. Frank Palgrave has given me three of his drawings, to my great delight. Called yesterday at the A[lderso]ns' and sat an hour

[1] John Blackwood (1818–1879), publisher and editor of *Blackwood's Magazine*.

alone with Flo! Nothing came of it. Sir Ivor Guest is engaged to Lady C. Churchill! What do I care? The opposition is to have twenty-three majority on the Irish Church; if you doubt it, wait till Friday. Gladstone's Latin makes me shiver — what is exantlatis[1] — I've no Lexicon and never saw the word. Bye-bye! Oh yet remember me! Ever.

To Charles Milnes Gaskell

FLORENCE, Thursday, 5 March, [1868.]

I ought to have written yesterday and did not — *pour cause*. I ought also to have started for London today, but did not — also *pour cause*. My reason for not going as I intended was that my sister made a point of my staying to a little dance of hers on Friday night, so that I shall have to start Saturday morning and travel through without stopping even in Paris. After all, I shall reach London Monday evening, and that is soon enough.

My second reason is a corallary from the first (a devilish word — the fourth letter is *o* — *d'ailleurs* it is spelt right, or I'm a Dutchman). You will easily infer that I preferred to wait if I could, till I had something to say; which I have accordingly done.

Hence (let us be logical — otherwise why read J. S. M[ill], not to mention Aristotle, whom, as in fact you know, I never did read) hence, I say, you may rashly infer again that I have now something to say. Under all ordinary rules this apparently legitimate deduction would be incorrect. I never have anything to say when I write. In this exact case, you happen however to be exceptionally right. I have something to communicate.

For two days I hunted hotels in vain. This morning I began at the Ponte Vecchio and went down the street knocking at every door, and at the last house before the Caseine (I mean the Hôtel de la Paix) I discovered the names I sought. Disregarding the mendacious assertions of the porter that they were sortiti, I grasped the trembling caitiff of a courier and sent him up with my card. Need I say that I was at once admitted?

My lady was very gracious and told her tale. They had remained three days in Genoa which they left yesterday morning coming through by our route in one day. Her Ladyship was astonished at my having found them so quickly. I explained that I had come to the hotel intending to call on an acquaintance, and very much by accident

[1] More commonly *exanclo*, to draw or bring out as a servant.

seeing their names, thought etc., etc., etc. Her Ladyship goes to Rome on Monday and has secured rooms at the Europe.

I was the recipient of various inquiries about you, which I answered according to my instructions. Finally with a pleasing air of embarrassment her Ladyship asked whether you had ever received a letter from her. Cynic that I am, I thought to myself that I had heard people ask that question before, and I looked stolid. — No, I thought you could have received no letter. At least you might have done so, but you had not told me of it. In fact, perhaps you had, but in short I knew nothing about it.

I was then informed that such a letter had been written late in January, requesting you to look out for rooms, and with mixed sensations of alarm and horror they had in vain awaited an answer. On inquiry I ascertained that it had been addressed to the poste-restante at Rome. Hasten there, my friend, and obtain the valuable autograph.

Other conversation I had, but it was of a general nature. I will only add that I saw my Lady Mary also, and as she had her visor down, ready to go out walking, I could not tell how she was looking. I sat fifteen or twenty minutes and then took my leave for an indefinite future, though she says she will be in London late in April.

Such, oh my *Geliebter*, is my story. Further I have nought to tell. I go to a dance tonight and dance again tomorrow night; what awful riot! Saturday, Sunday and Monday I travel. Rest! oh rest!

I have found no books to buy, except an Aldus Dante of 1502; forty francs; very pretty, but how about the price!

Addio, caro mio! Remember me in your days of amusement.

To Charles Milnes Gaskell

46 Rue Neuve St. Augustin,
Hôtel d'Orient, 3 May, 1868.

The world runs devilish *à travers*. (I have *not* forgotten English, but prefer to write so.) Instead of my being back in London today as I hoped a week ago, I am as far or further from it than ever. Those imbeciles at Washington don't do anything, and are as likely as not to let the President off, after all. In which case I shall be in a nice way. I have clothes with me for one week, which is now up. I abhor Paris and am profane beyond belief in my desire to get back to London and begin work. But I see *no* chance of returning before next Saturday and perhaps not even then.

Thus far I have passed my days and nights in my room geologising.

I have seen no one. Your friends the Bristols passed me on the channel, as you have no doubt guessed. The Paran Stevens tribe I have not yet called upon, not caring to provoke an extra visit to my mother at a time when she does not want to visit at all. If there is anyone in Paris whom I know, I have not heard of it, and I shall not stop the individual in the street.

You may tell our friends in Cadogan Place that I have executed their commissions, but do not know when I shall be able to bring the plunder over to them.

I have been twice to the theatre. Once I saw Paul Forestier.[1] I thought it very poor; the last act even worse than poor. And once to the Gymnase where little Pierson,[2] who becomes very fat, came out as a much better actress than I ever supposed she could be. But hélas! I grow old, for I know that eight years ago the women on the stage here were the freshest young girls in life. And now they are coarse and big. Even Schneider[3] was younger then, though she has always been coarse and fat since I've known her.

Monday morning. I kept this document back in order to obtain the information you wanted about the surgeon. But as it may be another day or two before I can satisfy myself, I decide to send.

My father is at the Brunswick House Hotel, Hanover Square. If you ever want information about my probable movements, apply to him.

---

[1] By Guillaume Victor Émile Augier.

[2] Blanche Adeline Pierson (b. 1842), who was at this time passing from the rôles of an ingénue and coquette to more serious parts, gaining in reputation by the change.

[3] Catherine Jeanne Hortense Schneider (b. 1838).

IV

QUINCY AND WASHINGTON

1868–1870

To Charles Milnes Gaskell

QUINCY, 25 September, 1868.

Your letter of August 30th arrived here the other day safely. Many thanks for it. Write me what the canvass looks like from time to time in case anything new turns up, and especially what is the result, when the election comes. Of course I am equally interested to hear, no matter whether you succeed or not. My own theory is that patience carries the day, and that in politics there is no such thing as failure to a young man unless he fails to support himself.

In return I have only to tell you that I am still here, waiting till the first frosts shall have made Washington habitable. We have already had our first frost in this region and the woods are now dotted with scarlet and purple, but in Washington the cold weather comes nearly a month later than it does in this polar climate, and I do not care to arrive there before the middle of October. Accordingly I remain here doing nothing for a fortnight longer and then go on to New York where I must devote several days to seeing different people, and shall arrive in Washington about the fifteenth. Then there will be rooms to get, and a thousand difficulties to meet before I shall be comfortable and able to begin work in earnest. In fact I expect very little enjoyment from my first winter.

So far, life has been really pleasant. After finishing up my article on Lyell which occupied me till near the end of August, I went down to Newport which is a very gay sort of Torquay, and there I performed the butterfly with great applause, for a week. Everyone was cordial and the young women mostly smiled upon me more beamingly than I had been accustomed to, during my residence among the frigid damsels of London. In fact I must acknowledge to what Robert used to chaff me about: the simple savage never was nor could have been entirely tamed. I get along better on my native heath, with tomahawk and feathers, than I did in sword and breeches at Buckingham Palace. The life here would not suit you, and in the long run it may disgust me too, but at the first start I breathe freer.

My father and mother have settled down to as quiet an existence as the world has to show, and as for my sister she has been flying about the country, visiting her friends, and has scarcely been at home these six weeks. I fancy the change is more agreeable to her than to the rest of us, for England is a dull place for young girls who have no family connection. I used to ask our friend Miss Warren why she had no friends of her own age and sex, and she indignantly replied that she had *one* — Miss Tollmache. In America young women are as intimate and generally acquainted among each other as young men are among themselves, and of course they are made more independent of male society. The system may be bad, but they like it.

My mother wanted me to send a message about your father's orange-brandy. I believe she very nearly lived upon it while on board ship, and I know it was all drunk up, and without my ever getting a drop. The doctor insisted on her taking stimulants while she was seasick, and the brandy suited her better than anything else she could find.

Will you do a little favor for me? The next time you are in town, ask Bumpus whether he can get for you the *second* volume of the English translation of Mommsen's *History of Rome*. I want it to replace a lost one. If he can, will you send it to me here by post? And if you will show this note to Mr. Russell Sturgis, he will pay you for the book and postage and charge it to me.

Remember me especially to your father and mother. I shall soon write to the latter. To Robert I sent a letter not long ago. Ever yours.

To Edward Atkinson

QUINCY, 5 October, 1868.

If you can spare time from brother Butler,[1] will you write me a short line of introduction to Mr. Godkin of the *Nation*? I want to talk with him when I am in New York next week.

I watch — and shall continue to watch — your contest in the Essex District with the keenest interest. The General is playing for high stakes. Think for a moment what a place he will hold if he wins now! He has got Dana and you and all other respectable men in the State in such a position that if he goes back to Washington at all, he will carry your scalps in his belt. You must crush him now, or he will grind your faces in the dirt.

[1] Butler had just been renominated for Congress on a policy of paying the United States bonds in greenbacks.

If I can assist you from Washington, I will do so cordially. I hope measures have already been taken to bring out from their pigeon-holes those reports about Mr. Butler of which so much has been said.

To Charles Milnes Gaskell

158 G STREET, WASHINGTON, D.C.,
5 November, 1868.

Eccolà! If you can master the idea of streets named after letters of the alphabet, know that the above is my address. Moreover, "D. C." stands for District of Columbia, though you mightn't guess it. The great step is taken, and here I am, settled for years, and perhaps for life. Your last letter was sent on to me a few days ago.

My experiences so far have not been disagreeable, and yet I think and hope they have been the least agreeable part of my experiences past or to come. I left Boston on the 12th of October and stopped several days in New York, intending to come on here and stay at a hotel until I could move into rooms. But one day I met Mr. Evarts on the street. You recollect his visit to Cambridge with me in 1863, since which he has become a great man, saving the President in the Impeachment by his skill as Counsel, and in consequence of his services then, appointed a member of the Cabinet as Attorney General not long afterwards. He stopped me to urge that I should stay at his house in Washington until I settled myself. Naturally I assented and we came on together. His family was all away, and he and I kept house for ten days. He took me to call on the President, who was grave and cordial, and gave me a little lecture on constitutional law. The Secretary of State, as we call the Foreign Secretary, Mr. Seward, was also cordial, and his major-domo selected rooms for me. With the Secretary of the Treasury,[1] I am on the best of terms and he pats me on the back, not figuratively but in the flesh. Finally the Secretary of War[2] and I are companions. The account so far is a good one, is it not? Unfortunately this whole Cabinet goes out on the fourth of March, and in the next one I shall probably be without a friend. Politics makes a bad trade.

I staid ten days with the Attorney General and then I moved to the house of an aunt I have here, where I still remain while my rooms get into shape. If you come over, I can give you a bed and you can stay as long as you will. You will find all my old books in my cases, my drawings (and memorials of Cannes) on the walls, and my lion and

[1] Hugh McCulloch (1808-1895).   [2] John McAllister Schofield (1831-1906).

ostrich magnificent and beautiful for ever. My establishment is modest, for my means are exiguous, but it has more civilisation in it than the rest of Washington all together. Come and see.

In fact this is the drollest place in Christian lands. Such a thin veil of varnish over so very rough a material, one can see nowhere else. But for all that, there are strong points about it. From the window of my room I can as I sit see for miles down the Potomac, and I know of no other capital in the world which stands on so wide and splendid a river. But the people and the mode of life are enough to take your hair off. I think I see you trying to live here. You couldn't stand it four-and-twenty hours. Alas! I fear I never shall eat another good dinner.

My geological article was published a month ago, after I left Boston and I have heard nothing of it (the best news I could hear), except that it has paid me £20. I am now beginning Finance again, and you will probably read as much as the title of my next production. In about five years I expect to have conquered a reputation. But what it may be worth when got, is more than I can tell. The sad truth is that I want nothing and life seems to have no purpose.

Our elections as you see, have passed off as everyone expected and we are approaching a new reign. Personally we have nothing to expect from it. My father is not in sympathy with the party in power, and my brother [John] is a prominent opponent of it. I am too insignificant a cuss to have my opinion asked, but my eyes and ears are wide open, and we mean to be seen and be heard as well as see and hear. I wait now with great interest for your election. Write soon about it. Give my best love to everyone. I shall write again soon.

To Charles Francis Adams, Jr.

158 G STREET, WASHINGTON,
Monday, 23 Nov., 1868.

·   ·   ·   ·   ·   ·   ·   ·   ·   ·   ·   ·   ·   ·

My mind is more occupied now about politics than about literature, but I have my next article sketched out in my head and expect that it will be good, an improvement on my "British Finance," and on the same model. Politics are gaining interest and I am studying the science in a devilish clever school. If I can hold my own in it, I shall think well of my capacity. Should you see Gurney [1] you may tell him that I have a very handsome letter from Sir Charles [Lyell] about my

[1] Ephraim Whitman Gurney (1829-1886), editor of the *North American Review*.

article, which he called "the most original he has yet seen on his new edition, and the only one which has called due attention to what is new in it."

13 Dec., 1868.

Things are beginning to move. I expect Wells [1] here tomorrow or next day, and then I am in for six weeks of hard work, which will be over the 1st Feby. and I shall have time for a little intrigue. I mean to block the movement to put the Governor into the Cabinet. I don't want him there. He would be in my way. Besides, this first Cabinet will be a failure.

To Charles Francis Adams, Jr.

Washington, 8th Jany., 1869.

I have not thought it worth while to answer your remarks about my judgment in the Governor's case, because you and I are wider apart than the poles. I have not changed my opinions, however, as to the wisdom of his course in retiring, and everything I have seen here encourages me to think that his position is now far higher and more unassailable than if he had remained in London.

I am working very hard and yet it is work absolutely thrown away. It amuses me, however. Q. E. D.

To Charles Francis Adams, Jr.

Washington, 18 January, 1869.

I will send you Butler's speech as soon as I can get a copy. If our Congress were not the trash it is, such a speech ought to be the end of Butler. But Garfield, [2] Wells, Walker [3] and I have held his inquest, and Garfield will score him in the House.

These booksellers haven't the *North American*, but I shall get it in a day or two and will write you about it. [4] As for style, I am rather surprised at your criticism. You find fault with us for doing precisely what I wrote in such despair of ever correcting. Polish be damned. I never tried to polish in the sense of smoothing. All I ever wanted was to polish away my stilts and get down to firm ground, and that is

---

[1] David Ames Wells (1828–1889), the economist.

[2] James Abram Garfield (1831–1881).   [3] Francis Amasa Walker (1840–1897).

[4] The *North American Review* for January, 1869, contains an article by Charles Francis Adams, Jr., on railroad deflation. Possibly the unsigned paper on "A Look Before and After" was by Henry Adams.

precisely what I despair of doing. If you glance your eye over my last things as compared with the *Harvard Magazine* you will see how bald I have become, thinking that that first step should be to unlearn a vicious habit before hoping to start again. That is all I have ever said of your style. Get rid of your tricks. What will then come, is according to the will of God and your own good sense.

If the Governor does not hear this week of his appointment as Secretary, I think the moment has passed. I suspect it has already passed week before last. I guess this from Seward's manner of talk to me. But I grope in the dark.

To Charles Francis Adams, Jr.

WASHINGTON, 22 Jany., 1869.

. . . .

There is no news here. Every one is in the dark. I am very hard at work and care very little for the new administration, as I find I can get on without it. What do you say to this? Our labored work does not gain us all it ought. I want to be advertised and the easiest way is to do something obnoxious and do it well. I can work up an article on "rings" which, if *published in England*, would, I think, create excitement and react through political feeling on America in such a way as to cover me with odium. Wells says, don't disgrace us abroad. I say, Rot! The truth is open to expression anywhere. No home publication will act on America like foreign opinion. I am not afraid of unpopularity and I will do it.

To Charles Francis Adams, Jr.

WASHINGTON, 27 Jany., 1869.

I can't do my "Rings" in short time. I am going to make it monumental, a piece of history and a blow at democracy. I mean to put into it all I've got in matter, thought and style, so that I may be a year or two in working it up, but the return in public horror and disgust will, I hope, make me a "degenerate son," and a "traitor," a "cynical sceptic," and a "person whose career is closed before it has begun."

So go on with your article, for I shall be very slow about mine, and you will help me rather than otherwise. I have, however, another idea, which is to write a popular article showing the practical expedients by which traders make a profit out of the currency. These fields are gloriously rich and stink like hell, if we were only of the force to distil their flowers.

As for disgust at oneself, I feel it every time I steal an idea from Evarts, who produces them naturally. My article on Lyell humiliated me. It was so neatly put together and not an original idea in it. But don't be cast down. We are small enough creatures absolutely, but relatively to the mass of fools who make mankind, we are at the top of the ladder. After all, even Stuart Mill has only added to, and not created, his sciences, and I think he is sometimes superficial. Men measure people's knowledge usually by their own ignorance....

To Edward Atkinson

158 G STREET, WASHINGTON, 1 February, 1869.

I have already a dozen ideas in my head which if elaborated would occupy me years. I shall note the suggestion you make and work it up, if I get time, but from what I see here I suspect that our people may be properly divided into two classes, one which steals, the other which is stolen from; and we have got to take the matter up with a high hand and drag it into politics if we are to hope for success. If I am right, it follows that our time and labor will be most usefully spent in a regular hand-to-hand fight with corruption here under our eyes. To follow the protectionists over to England is to go off on a false scent. I could rather scarify a few of them personally as they stand. The whole root of the evil is in *political* corruption; theory has really not much to do with it.

You in Massachusetts are not really in the Union. Butler is the only man who understands his countrymen and even he does not quite represent the dishonesty of our system. The more I study its working, the more dread I feel at the future. Our coming struggle is going to be harder than the anti-slavery fight, and though we may carry free-trade, I fear we shall be beaten on the wider field.

Are our Boston people mad that they petition against the Alabama Convention? [1] If ever Boston was interested in any matter of Government, she is interested in adopting this Convention. Its rejection means a determination on our part to have, sooner or later, a war with England, and I fear it will be rejected. If our friends are wise they will make all the Eastern Senators support the Treaty, for the West will try to shove us into a struggle in which we alone can be the sufferers.

[1] The Clarendon-Johnson convention, providing machinery for the settlement of the Alabama and similar questions between the United States and Great Britain.

To Charles Francis Adams, Jr.

WASHINGTON, 3 Feby., 1869.

. . . .

I have no news for you and am pretty indifferent to news. Following my rule, I have avoided the Capitol till I have ceased to think of it. The politicians, I am told, are furious at not being consulted by Grant. To an insignificant cuss like me, the reflection that I am at last under a silent despotism where the many headed monster is muzzled, has its charm. At any rate I know as much as any fellow, and that is, they say, the highest wisdom....

To Charles Francis Adams, Jr.

Tuesday, 23 Feby., 1869.

No news yet, but look out for it soon. The knowing ones tell me that this week will settle it. The Congressional slate contains the following names — you can shuffle them as you like and leave out to choice.

Wilson of Iowa [1]	Schofield
Williams of Oregon [2]	Evarts — Pierpont [4]
Holt of Tenn. [3]	Fessenden — [5] Boutwell [6]
	Wells

I pity the man that goes into that Cabinet. You are more hopeful than I am, if you expect to be pleased by it. We here look for a reign of western mediocrity, but one appreciates least the success of the steamer, when one lives in the engine-room. I swear I feel as though I ought to give my soul a thorough washing....

To Charles Francis Adams, Jr.

WASHINGTON, 11 March, [1869.]

The last turn of the cards is not altogether satisfactory. Boutwell is not a Wells man. Meanwhile Grant has made Congress madder than the devil. Between ourselves, the home appointments are not what we want. I am afraid there is more favoritism than public good in them. It's the old game with fresh cards. But we are in the boat and have got to stay there.

[1] James Wilson (1835–1920).   [2] George Henry Williams (1823–1910).
[3] Joseph Holt (1807–1894).   [4] Edwards Pierrepont (1817–1892).
[5] William Pitt Fessenden (1806–1869).   [6] George Sewell Boutwell (1818–1905).

Nothing from you this long time. I have been awfully worked this week; ten hours a day for four days, and politics on top of it. The *Edinburgh Review* will have an article of mine in April. Reeve [1] says it is the best article on American affairs ever printed in an English periodical and that he attaches the greatest importance to it. I don't see its astonishing merits, nor will you. But I hope it will make me unpopular. Q. E. D. I send an article today [2] to Gurney which will help. If it embarrasses the Governor, stand by to whitewash him of all responsibility.

To Charles Francis Adams, Jr.

WASHINGTON, 29 March, [1869.]

After a good deal of difficulty I have succeeded in getting a copy of the report on election frauds, and must now try to get a frank for it. As it contains a thousand pages, postage comes heavy. Few copies of the evidence were printed, and at the document-room they refused me one, but I got round them by corrupt influence. The report, however, is not valuable, in fact, the minority report, which is included, suggests more ideas to me than all the rest. I care little whether one or fifty thousand fraudulent votes were cast, but I would give much to be inside Tammany Hall.

I have nothing new to say. We are all grumbling here, but you perhaps may see some cause for confidence that we do not. I go from Wells to Evarts, and from Evarts to Sumner, and so round the list, and find them all disgusted in their own branches. *Coelum non animam mutant qui novum Presidentem eligunt.* It is the old régime, and Grant is, between ourselves, less capable than Johnson. I am astonished by his behavior, but I am even more puzzled than astonished, for I can read it only in one sense. Well! at the end of the end, we shall succeed if we have one single element in Gen. Grant — that of intelligence. But what I see and hear makes me often think with a horrible shudder of John's remark, which you quoted to me, that Grant's mind was of the same order, if not of the same degree, as Ward Frothingham's.

I propose to return to Quincy on the first of June. In the interval I dawdle here. The life is pleasant, rather than otherwise, and I am more contented here than I could be elsewhere. Besides, I want to see what is going to happen. I assure you the Government in all its

[1] Henry Reeve (1813–1895), for forty years editor of the *Edinburgh Review*.
[2] The Session, in *North American Review*, April, 1869.

branches is now a mere bundle of sticks held together by old rags. I am curious to see when it will strike root again and sprout.

To Charles Milnes Gaskell

WASHINGTON, 30 March, 1869.

Yours of the tenth from Nevers reached this misbegotten spot some days since, curiously enough, arm in arm with one from Palgrave. Your journey interested me; journeys always do interest me; I have done nothing this fortnight but read books of travels. I wish you would send me better news of your family, and in fact of everyone, but so long as you are yourself well, I glide over the rest. Poor Lady de Tabley! I never see an English paper nor get English news, so all I have heard about her is through you. As for Robert, I despise him. What the dickens does he mean by giving a ball and not asking me to it! I pardon him — since I can't help it — for never writing, but I hate to be left out of a party.

Upon the honor of a gentleman I have not a single thing to say, for my last was written so short a time ago that nothing has happened since from which I could make a paragraph. That I am politically dissatisfied is unquestionable, but then I have yet to find anyone who is not in the same situation, though the newspapers lie in chorus and make me laugh, for I know how their editors talk in private. Fortunately I can't take office, for I care too much for my precious health to tie myself to a post; and I won't do it, for I despise the whole calabash and prefer to say so publicly. Motley wants to be our Minister in England, and no doubt I might go with him if he goes, but you can imagine that I don't care for such a position. I shall however try to put a good fellow into it, if the chance occurs. I have no great faith in its occurring, however, for our foreign appointments are queer. Probably no New England man has much chance.

Meanwhile I am quietly waiting for the explosion of my two fire-crackers on the 1st April, and between then and the 1st June I have no special plans or projects though I've no doubt there will be plenty of work offered if I care to undertake it. On the 1st June I return to Quincy where a laborious piece of literary work in the line of biography, waits my arrival and will occupy the whole summer except a few weeks which I mean to give to nature, geology and Canada. Then in October I return again to my residence here and start fresh — or rather, stale. In the meanwhile I devote four hours every day — when there's no deluge — to rambling over the country here and

picking up a sort of familiarity with nature which is the only satisfactory companion I have. I live comfortably and rather cheaply on
the whole; at least, well within my means, and as there are few men
here who have any means, and the members of Congress and the
Cabinet have only about twice my income or less, I get along very
well and am thought a Crœsus. It is a prodigious relief to escape the
oppressive contact of young men who keep a stable and are "gentle-
men-riders" at the steeple-chase. I detest swell young men who talk
horse, and here there are none. On the other hand, life is certainly
common-place. My despondent fit has passed away again and been
succeeded by cheerfulness and contentment, thanks, I believe, to my
long walks and careful life, without medical interference, but I am
thin and bearded and very — very bald.

I hope you picked up a French play or two or a novel for me, miserable mendicant that I am. I can get English books through Bumpus,
but France is beyond my reach. I have received Browning's poem
and am at it. If you hear of anything nice in English poetry, tell
Bumpus to send it. I enclose you a letter for your uncle. Please read
it, and if it's all right, close and deliver it; so you will obtain my thanks.

I presume all is well with my family though I seldom hear except
from my father whose letters are mostly political. Society is extinct
and I see no one but a few intimates. So write as often as you can, for
your letters are my sole tie to mankind — the European part of it. As
for the American, Robert has discovered the prehensile tail to be tie
sufficient.

To Charles Milnes Gaskell

WASHINGTON, 19 April, 1869.

Yours of April 2d arrived this morning. You can imagine the impression it made upon me. But I would rather not write about the
gloomy side of life. At this distance I can neither assist nor even express any sympathy worth hearing. Keep me well-informed as to your
mother's state.

Your London gossip proves that I have not lost much by my absence, so far as the old tread-mill is concerned. Let it grind! We have
here a few of these butterflies who belong properly to the circle of
Lady Sebright and the Gallo-Anglican set, and it would amuse you
to see how utterly unsaddled they are. Their only resource is to invent
here a little bastard set, and play being in a great society. As you
know, this city does not answer all the proudest desires of my own

heart, but at any rate, what with politics, literature, geology, botany, and society, I am on the whole happy except when my liver is disordered. I have to walk from two to three hours every day to correct my liver, but as the country and charming scenery is within a mile of my door, I find the walks a great pleasure. But these poor French and Germans tear their hair and are fit to die, or even to get married. This winter they have had peculiarly hard luck. By the bye, our friend Schlözer[1] passed through here on his way to Mexico. I called just too late.

What a thing it is to have a good liver! My walks have cured all my ails. Everything otherwise has gone wrong. My hopes of the new Administration have all been disappointed; it is far inferior to the last. My friends have almost all lost ground instead of gaining it as I hoped. My family is buried politically beyond recovery for years. I am becoming more and more isolated so far as allies go. I even doubt whether I can find an independent organ to publish my articles, so strong is the current against us. But I rather like all this, for no one can touch me and I have asked nothing of any living person. I express pretty energetically opinions all round, and I wait till the cards are played out. I can afford to wait. We have won our rubber on the old game.

That I should figure at the Royal Academy is an alarming event. I hope the Motleys will overlook it. These successors of ours will be in London in June. You know them and my relations with them. Pray keep me informed as to their goings-on. General Grant's historiograph Badeau goes with them. He is a sociable little man with a red face and spectacles. I shall give him some letters, but won't bore you, although if you meet him you will find him amusing. As I am not in sympathy with the foreign policy of my friend Charles Sumner who is grand Panjandrum here, little button and all, and who appoints Motley to England, I have avoided the whole caravan.

Of my family I know almost as little as you do. My father writes me every week, the others very seldom, having nothing to say. My father is deeply engaged in heavy building operations, his real estate having run to ruin in his absence and never having been in good condition. I suppose he feels poor, in consequence, but he has utterly abandoned politics, and is devoted to his home projects. My sister's last epistle was filled with English gossip out of her letters. My mother has not written for a month. You may judge from this that their existence is not exciting. I am myself preparing a volume of

[1] Kurd von Schlözer (1822–1894).

Memoirs which may grow to be three volumes if I have patience to toil. It is not an autobiography — *n'ayez pas peur!* An ancient lady of our house has left material for a pleasant story. As for my vagabond April articles, Heaven only knows where they are; at least the *North American* has not yet appeared, and if the *Edinburgh* is out,[1] I am none the wiser. Nor do I much expect that either article will be printed as I wrote it. To hope this would display infantile ignorance of editorial nature.

Robert's letter never has arrived. I don't believe it was ever sent. Never mind! I shall pretty certainly come over in June, 1870, and then I will punch his head, Baronet though he be. I have however a long letter from John Bright, one from Ralph Palmer and one from Thomson Hankey on my table, and sent off one for F. T. P. this morning. Give my best love to your mother.

To Charles Francis Adams, Jr.

WASHINGTON, 29 April, 1869.

I can't get you an office. The only members of this Government that I have met are mere acquaintances, not friends, and I fancy no request of mine would be likely to call out a gush of sympathy. Wells has just about as much influence as I have. He can't even protect his own clerks. Judge Hoar has his hands full, and does not interfere with his colleagues....

Thank God, all this business is over now and I am left here solitary but happy, and busy with an entirely different sort of subjects....

Senator Sprague[2] has kindly advertised me, as you see. I sent you my letter in order that you might not imagine I had been mixed in his affairs, the letter being written a month before he made his speeches, and Atkinson being responsible for it. Do you notice T. Chase's effusion?... Washington is almost empty, and the country perfectly lovely. All the trees are in leaf, even the oaks. Such a place for wildflowers I never saw. I pass my days in the woods.

To Charles Francis Adams, Jr.

WASHINGTON, 17 May, 1869.

I have received a letter from Reeve calling for another article "some months hence" on the "changes of the American Constitution which

---

[1] The Session, in *North American Review*, April, 1869. An article on American Finance appeared in the *Edinburg Review*, April, 1869.

[2] William Sprague (1830–1915).

have resulted from the war." As I am not a constitutional lawyer and furthermore believe that the essential and fatal changes in our Constitution were not the results of the war, but of deeper social causes, which each need a volume to discuss, I shall decline the invitation. The Governor likes that sort of thing and I wish he, or G. T. Curtis, or Evarts, had time for it. At all events, I shall not attempt it, and I write to tell you that I am ready to offer Reeve your Erie article in place of what he wants, if you like. I find that I have unexpectedly jumped into notoriety enough for the first go-off, through my two April balloons, and mean to hold my tongue carefully till I have more to say. If the future goes straight, I will make my annual "Session" an institution and a power in the land. But there is time enough and patience conquers. I may add for your further consideration that Reeve's check was for £30. Make a little sum of it: £30 (gold) = $200 (paper) or thereabouts. The *N. A. R.* pays $75. 200:75:1:375, or in other words, the *N. A. R.* pays about $\frac{1}{3}$ what the *Edin.* gives for a first article of an untried and unknown foreigner. At any rate, there is your standard. Insist on at least $5 (gold) a page, or offer your article to England. I don't notice that British gold is dirtier than our paper....

To Charles Milnes Gaskell

WASHINGTON, 17 May, 1869.

I have just received a letter from Thomson Hankey in which he announces the death of your aunt [1] as a thing I should no doubt have seen mentioned. As I did not think it likely you would have much time to write, I decided not to wait for your next letter, but to send you a line at once, not to condole, but to amuse you if possible. Your poor aunt! What a charming, sympathetic woman she was, and how naturally one became attached to her! In one sense I wish I were in England, and could be of use to you, so that you could have some kind of change of atmosphere and throw off occasionally this perpetual sense of gloom which is round you. On my own account, the distance is a relief, for all our life in England seems now like a novel, except when letters come, and you can imagine that I am glad to escape the pain of thinking about your poor aunt and mother whenever I can. Of course the real suffering with me was a year ago when I came away, for we all knew then that we should never see each other again, and the hardest trial in my life, in the way of parting, was when I bade your mother

---

[1] Charlotte Williams-Wynn, sister of Gaskell's mother, died April 26, 1869. A volume, *Memorials of C. W. W.*, edited by her sister Harriet Hester Lindesay, appeared in 1877.

good-bye. Your letter of April 19th was therefore a shock without being a surprise. I knew what was in it almost when I saw it, as I had not expected anything from you so soon.

I hope soon to hear from you what your plans for the future now are, and after this long strain on your spirits, I hope you will feel a sort of relief at last as you turn from the past to the future. Luckily for you, you can't, like me, become a Bohemian. You must look ahead and build up a new family in place of the one destroyed, and make a new centre for the branches to lean upon. No doubt you will write me about these matters as they happen to come up. If you do, I shall always express my own ideas about your affairs without any reserve.

Now let's drop this dreadful subject which always brings the tears into my eyes. You need a little amusement, and I have a magnificent story for you. In the first place, my *coup d'essai* has proved an unexpected success. My article on "The Session" in the 'North British' (as you call it) or the 'North Atlantic' (as the Secretary of Legation here calls it) or the *North American* as it calls itself, has been read. For once I have smashed things generally and really exercised a distinct influence on public opinion by acting on the limited number of cultivated minds. As evidence of this in a small way, I enclose to you a long slip from a Massachusetts newspaper, probably the most widely circulated of all these Massachusetts papers, in which I am treated in a way that will, I think, delight you. Of course it is all nonsense. I am neither a journalist nor one of the three best dancers in Washington, nor have I a profound knowledge of the cotillon, though I confess to having danced it pretty actively. But you see I am posed as a sort of American Pelham or Vivian Gray. This amused me, for you and I both have always had a foolish weakness for combining social and literary success, but the part of the joke which pleased me less, was to come.

This leader was condensed into a single paragraph of half a dozen lines by a western paper, and copied among the items of the column "personal" all over the country. In this form it came back to New York. Hitherto my skill as a dancer was kept a mere artistic touch to heighten the effect of my "brilliant" essay. Now however the paragraph is compressed to two lines. "H. B. A. is the author of article etc., etc., etc. He is one of the three best dancers in W." The next step will be to drop the literary half, and preserve the last line, and I am in an agony of terror for fear of seeing myself posted bluntly: "H. B. A. is the best dancer in W." This would be fame with a vengeance.

My *Edinburgh* article has attracted no notice so far as I know, though I see no English newspapers. Reeve has behaved very well about it, praising it highly, printing it too accurately even to clerical blunders (the proofs were lost), and paying me £30. He now wants more, but I am busy elsewhere on a work that will amuse you one of these days.

I hope to hear from you this week. Give my warm regards to your father, and believe me ever yours.

To Charles Francis Adams, Jr.

Friday, 21 May, 1869.

I see you are getting back to your old dispute with me on the purpose of life, by means of an attack on my self-esteem. You are quite right in the point you make. I do think too much about my own productions and myself generally. Stick to that and you may kick me all day long. I will not go down into the rough-and-tumble, nor mix with the crowd, nor write anonymously, except for mere literary practice. My path is a different one; and was never chosen in order to suit other people's tastes, but my own. Of course a man can't do this without appearing to think a great deal about himself, and perhaps doing so in fact. The very line he draws requires care to observe, and is invidious to everyone else. In America there is no such class, and the tendency is incessant to draw everyone into the main current. I have told you before that I mean to be unpopular, and do it because I must do it, or do as other people do and give up the path I chose for myself years ago. Your ideas and mine don't agree, but they never have agreed. You like the strife of the world. I detest it and despise it. You work for power. I work for my own satisfaction. You like roughness and strength; I like taste and dexterity. For God's sake, let us go our ways and not try to be like each other.

To Charles Milnes Gaskell

Washington, 20 June, 1869.

Yours of the 14th May arrived in due course, but as I had already answered it before it arrived, I rather preferred to wait in hopes of receiving another letter written under more cheerful circumstances. The best of all would be that you should run over here yourself for a few months, but I suppose you can scarcely get away. I hope to get a letter from you this coming week.

Meanwhile the great Robert has actually succeeded in sending me his semi-annual despatch which I answered at once by way of encouraging the young man, though perhaps such promptness might be rather *dis*couraging. Palgrave, however, has abandoned me, and I hear nought of his doings. If you see him, convey my regards.

I also received a newspaper from you containing allusions to dead and forgotten articles written by my humbleness. I have yet to learn how this Yorkshire luminary happened to light on my production, and can only guess that some London news-sheet had previously picked my bones. May the meal prove fattening!

As you see, I am still hanging about the Capital although the world has long ago deserted it, and only a handful of people are still here. One finds so many last things requiring attention and so many preparations requiring to be made, that time gets ahead and the weather becomes hotter and hotter until flesh and blood can't stand it. I shall hang on yet another ten days before dropping down upon Quincy where my family expect me, and I shall take to salt water. The different members of my paternal abode are well, so far as I know, but the female portion honors me with extremely few letters, and I have not the least idea what is their manner of life. They have been making their house habitable, I believe, and the Lord knows the house needed it. Also they are building or to build a fire-proof affair for the library and the family papers, but what species of thing, I know not.

As for me, I glide along quietly through life, and enjoy it at times a good deal. But my opinions and dislike for things in general will probably make my career a failure; so far as any public distinction goes, and I am contented to have it so. There are no very clever men here, but some very fair ones, and as things are generally going to the devil, I don't much care who is uppermost and am well-pleased to have no strong personal friends in power. I am looking forward with great rejoicing to my visit to England next year. Meanwhile work pours in on me, and I can't do half what men urge me to do. But I am sorry to say that in a pecuniary point of view, the profit is inconsiderable, not to say devilish small. Why is it that the deserving never get their deserts? My deserts are about £10,000 a year, but how far below my receipts!

Fortunately society here pays little attention to one's pecuniary means, and as there are few people in Washington even among the highest officials, who are relatively richer than I, there is no difficulty in getting along. I am tolerably intimate with some members of the Cabinet, and have no enemies that I know of, and as there are so few cultivated people here, one's social value is out of all proportion to what it would be in London. But I don't expect that anything except perhaps literary reputation will ever come of it. The pressure for office from every part of the country is so tremendous that unless one is backed by strong party support and personally worries the Government, there is no chance of obtaining anything.

I see so few English papers that I know little of what goes on with you, and my letters are few and far between. New books I never see, unless I write to Bumpus for them, but there does not seem to be any extensive supply even in London. I read much Political Economy and am deep in the currency and the foreign exchanges. Our foreign relations too are interesting and I keep as well posted on them as I can. But all is vanity!

After the terrible experience you have had this year, I am anxious to hear that your health has not suffered, and I hope that you are still busy with literary and political projects. Stick to it, for even though one fails, the occupation is an amusement. I regret bitterly that I could not have been with you at Wenlock at the funeral. Sad as it was, I would have liked to pay this last sign of respect to your mother's memory, but I hope to go down there with you next year, and trust that by that time your life will have settled itself in a new course with more cheerful associations so that the pilgrimage will not be a painful one to either of us. Give my best respect to your father and Mrs. Lindesay and believe me as ever.

To Charles Francis Adams, Jr.

WASHINGTON, 22 June, 1869.

I congratulate you heartily on Wendell's attack. Besides being a perfect gentleman he is a good thermometer. One's value is fairly measured by his abuse. I confess always to a desire to do to him what we used to do to our dogs that misbehaved themselves in the house — "rub his nose in it" — but reason tells me that this modern Thersites is useful for our objects and that we could ill spare the advertisement. Give him my love, and send him my articles with the promise of a $10 note if he will mention them with "good ordinary," or $25, for superfine best abuse. By no means leave out the fine old hit at the Adamses; it always tells....

Wells and Garfield are coming to Boston. I have invited them to Quincy. We will have Atkinson too, and Greenough, and cut out our work. Garfield will talk about a railway-schedule with you, for his census — which is a bore. So get ready to help him, for he may help you some day. We may never come up, but he probably will swim pretty strong.

To Charles Milnes Gaskell

QUINCY, 11 July, 1869.

My wrath at the baronet is considerable for having dared to write me a long letter five days before his engagement was announced, and never hinting at it to me, nor holding back the letter till he could add a post-script.[1] I also confess to no little doubt whether I can ever succeed in winning the good-will of the young woman whose face I never saw and whose character no one knows. However! let us hope that we shall sail through. In fact I rather wish you would follow the example and show me a mistress to Wenlock next June. My visit would not perhaps be better for it, but Wenlock would certainly be improved. Only don't attempt the old experiment again. Imitate Robert and take a new start.

Your two last letters are both on my table unanswered. My last days in Washington were very busy and disturbed, so that I postponed all work I was not obliged to do, and now that I am here my first week has already passed without giving me a single day to spare. This is alarming, for I have a whole desk-full of stuff which must be attended to and no end of visits to make. See what it is to be a busy man!

Mr. Robarts was sent to me by two gentlemen, one of whom wrote that he was a bore, and the other, Sir F. Doyle, hinted it less openly. I suppose this is the person whom you declined to introduce. He appeared in Washington one morning; and left a letter at my house with a message that he should leave Washington the same evening. I do not know whether he means to turn up again or not, but if he passes only one day at a time in the principal cities here, he is not likely to catch me.

I find my family unchanged and looking very well and contented. They are trying to make their house habitable, but Wenlock is a joke to it in this particular. I never was in such a wretched old trap, for it hasn't even the merit of being well-built. In fact I am not enthusiastic about the homes of my ancestors, and only wish their taste had been better. Nevertheless I am enticing everyone out here to stay, in order

[1] Sir Robert Cunliffe married August 5, 1869, Eleanor Sophia Egerton, daughter of Col. Egerton Leigh, M.P., of West Hall, High Leigh, and Jodrell Hall, Cheshire.

that my father and mother may not absolutely go to sleep, as they seem bent on doing whenever the outside world stops pushing them.

Meanwhile I am meditating a series of prodigious efforts next winter, both political and literary, which will produce astonishing results. What they are to be, I don't know, but if you could see the gravity with which I attend the private meetings of discussion which are to settle our coming policy, you would roar with delight. What a humbug one is! Nevertheless, I must keep up the illusion, or be trodden upon, and at present my hands are full. By-the-way, can you tell me, or find out for me a little piece of English family history. About a century ago there was a Lady Tyrconnel [1] of whom I know nothing except that she had a mysterious hand or wrist. I want to learn what was the matter with her hand, and what there was in it that was supernatural. This is apropos to literature, not to politics. The two are rather mixed up in my mind. As for finance, I carry buckets of it about with me, and duck it over the head of everyone I meet. I read acres of books on it and know just as little as the rest of mankind. What more does anyone want? I should be better pleased if I could only find out what I myself want. Certainly not office, for except very high office I would take none. What then? I wish some one would tell me.

I must send Robert a wedding-present, but the Lord knows what or how. I have not yet had time to think of the matter, but shall do so rapidly. Nor have I written yet to the wretch, but you can tell him that I forgive him. Would to God that I too could find a mate, but I despair of that. So, as it is good that there should always be a few unmarried men to maintain society and the social bond, I devote myself to this noble task. Apropos to your offer of one of your mother's drawings as a memento, I should be greatly pleased by it, and in fact I meant to ask for some little characteristic thing, something that might remind me of her and of you all. If you find anything of the sort, and can put it into small compass, not larger than a good-sized volume, you can send it to the Secretary of our Legation, Mr. Moran, [2] and he will forward it.

I feel at times a little bewildered to think that the first year has gone since we all parted, though enough has occurred in it to make it seem long. If the great object of life is to experience all the sensations it has to offer, this year has put us a long step ahead. I hope better on your account from the next.

[1] The Tyrone Ghost Story is in *Diaries of a Lady of Quality* [Frances Williams-Wynn], edited by Abraham Hayward, 43.

[2] Benjamin Moran (b. 1820).

To Charles Milnes Gaskell

QUINCY, MASSACHUSETTS,
27 August, 1869.

Your account of Robert's wedding amused and even touched me. Not that there was anything pathetic in your humor, but that I recalled to mind Lord Houghton's letter to Odo Russell, and doubted which of the two to choose, Jodrell or death. Let us hope for the best. At the same time I have my doubts.

Your Tyrone ghost-story is evidently the one I wanted although my authority, I believe, said Tyrconnel. I suppose I ought to have Hayward's book. Tell Bumpus to send it to me whenever you happen to be in town. Meanwhile many thanks.

Yet another thing. After much despair I have got a present for the Baronet. It is silver, for I did not know what else to find in this land where arts are in their cradle. So I got him a little piece of American workmanship, a cheese-dish in fact, and on the lower rim of it I have had a line from Ovid inscribed, intimating that not only cheese but friendship is good at all seasons of the year. I shall send this *objet* to you by the venerable Hooker who will pass through London on his way to Rome sometime about the 25th September. Will you see that Robert eats his cheese out of it *always*, since cheese is surely part of every Cheshire meal, and there can be no excuse for stuffing so useful a dish into a silver-chest. And more. My Latin verse will, I suppose, not run entirely round the base. If therefore you can cap my motto by another more apposite, embracing not only friendship and cheese, but mice also (since two mice look over the edge and serve as handles) let some silver-smith put it on, before you send it to Robert, whose address I don't know. Thus shall the offering unite our minds and supply to the future port and cheese of the bucolic baronet a subject of winey reflection and boosey tears.

In short, select out of your vast stores of learning in various languages and of every period, some apt quotation displaying at once your wit and your taste, and with it add to the value of my gift which will thus become the owner of eternal fame as a monument to us all.

After near three months hard labor I am just *accouché* of another ponderous article which is now I hope in the printer's hands. You can form an estimate of my impudence when I tell you that I mean to circulate this as a pamphlet and send copies to all members of the Government and of the legislature. It is very bitter and abusive of the Administration. I expect to get into hot water, but have nothing to lose. Meanwhile I have projects which may affect my mode of life a little and of which I shall write to you if anything comes of them. My two brothers and I are up to the ears in politics and public affairs, and in time we shall perhaps make our little mark.

Since my arrival from Washington, life has been so quiet and so steadily occupied that I have seen no society and gone scarcely anywhere. I am now beginning to look forward to my return to Washington only about six weeks hence. Meanwhile I have seen no one whom I have been compelled to fall in love with, and the Bohemian existence is more firmly fixed than ever. How can one marry a woman one does not love? I am afraid that if I try this I shall never be blessed with heirs.

To return to Robert and his sheep. He sent me a photograph of his Audrey, which was very kind of him though I could tell better from it what she was not than what she was. You seem not to have lavished on her those *petits soins* which were the means of attracting her fancy. If I see her I want to have plenty of sugar-plums to please her with, so you must find out what she is like, and what particular class of flattery is most to her taste. All is the same to me, but it saves time to know beforehand.

You have had our college crew over there and I offer you my congratulations on beating them. I had hoped otherwise, but apparently Oxford is too much for us. Two of the crew are, I believe, gentlemen and good fellows; the others are rather of the unpolished style.

It is a long time since I have written to Palgrave though I have had a letter of his on my table for six weeks, but I mean to rub up my correspondence now. I hear of parties at the Salisburys', but, alas, you and I are not there, and the lovely Blossett mourns for us I hope. Sir Henry Holland threatens us with a visit in October. I hear of no other Englishmen about. If you have any to send, trot them out. Hooker gave me the latest gossip from Rome which was small.

To Charles Milnes Gaskell

QUINCY, 13 September, 1869.

I enclose you a note to Robert as I don't know his address. Almost as soon as you receive it, the great Hooker will have left in Stratford Place a box for you which contains my wedding present to Robert. As he is, I presume, on the continent, you will have to keep it till he returns in the Spring, but you can forward my letter. Meanwhile rub up your classics and cover my dish with quotations.

I have nothing on earth to tell you. Never was there a calmer season. But the leaves are turning yellow and the nights are growing long, warning me that I must soon fly south again. My summer has been wasted. I have done little, and enjoyed less. Drat the whole concern! I scarcely know what to make of life or of myself, but so we go.

I had a sort of idea that I should get an epistle from you about this time, but I suppose you have no more to write than I. The next time you epistolise tell me what Palgrave says about Peabody's statue. Has our friend Story raised or lowered his reputation? What is it good for?

My family rejoices in prosperity, so far as I know. Life here is on too small a scale for man to sustain it without idiocy, but the idiocy is harmless. This year's experiment, however, is too much for me. Next year I shall go abroad. The year after, I shall go to the Pacific. In fact, nothing but sheer poverty shall ever reduce me to passing a whole season here again. It is pleasant enough, but it is dead. There is no spring in it, no novelty or freshness, and in this particular I am a finished *débauché*, and must have excitement.

I go to Washington about the 20th of October or earlier if the weather is cold. Until then you had best address to me here. I have work that ought to keep me but I neglect it.

To Charles Milnes Gaskell

QUINCY, MASSACHUSETTS,
5 October, 1869.

Yours of 12th September having reached me, I disinterred your last three letters to discover what it was I had failed to answer, but am still left in the dark. My disquisition on American literature was, I think, exhaustive, to use a newspaper expression. I called your attention to all that was worth it. You asked about Jefferson and I recommended his famous Declaration of Independence as the best specimen of his style. You can quote a few paragraphs with effect. There is nothing in Everett. Webster's best things were legal arguments and you don't care for got-up eloquence. By all means quote the whole of Lincoln's little speech at Gettysburg and a sentence or two from his second Inaugural to show the biblical influence on American minds. In poetry you might extract from Bryant the last few lines of Thanatopsis, or the lines to a water-fowl, or the "melancholy days have come;" from Longfellow a stanza or two of the Wreck of the Hesperus or the Skeleton in Armor, both pretty ballads well adapted to a popu-

lar audience; from Lowell a stanza or two from the first series of Big-
low Papers, the one signed "Bird o' Freedom Sawin" would be best
for your purpose and would make your audience laugh, or in another
poem the "Vision of Sir Launfal" there is a pretty description of June
and winter as an example of Lowell's other style; from Whittier a
ballad, say Maud Muller, or two or three verses about scenery, "nowhere fairer, sweeter, rarer," in the Ranger. If you want a specimen of
style from Hawthorne, take the description of old Pynchon sitting
dead in his chair, in the *Seven Gables*, or the discovery of Zenobia's
body, in the *Blithedale Romance*. Your audience will listen hard to
either. Mrs. Stowe's scenes with Topsy in *Uncle Tom* are about as
good as anything she has done — always excepting her *Byron*. It is a
pity you can't quote some choice lines from Walt Whitman. In the
way of letters there is nothing but my old great-grandmother Abigail
Adams's that are worth reading, and I don't remember anything to
your purpose in them. You don't want to be didactic and you do
want to amuse your audience, so I advise you not to dwell long on historians, essayists or critics, except in the case of Washington Irving
whose account of Bracebridge Hall might amuse, and is a good specimen of his style. A few sentences or half a page of it would do for you
to point the customary allusion to Addison upon. Cooper's novels are
no great.

But if you want really to run over the old ground there is a sort of
Cyclopædia of American literature, full of biographical notices and elegant extracts, like the English one of Chambers. If you are in London
you will find it at some of the libraries. There is nothing very new.
We have no writers now.

Since my last, we have been invaded by Englishmen. Old Sir H.
Holland has been with us, as much of a bore as ever. Your friend
Robarts too has turned up and passed a night here. We were agreeably
disappointed in him. He is perhaps a bore, but not very radical, and
decidedly a gentleman in manners and talk. In fact, my boy, if you
could see the Britishers we do groan under in this country, you
would think Robarts a model of everything attractive. He returns
to England tomorrow with Sir H. H. Another individual named
Lawrence has also been here from Wimbledon way. I know no more
of him.

A letter from Robert at Cologne reached me with yours, bringing
me the pleasant suggestion of honeymoons, the Rhine, Venice and
Sorrento. I suppose the youth is lost to us, but don't, for the Lord's
sake, allow yourself to be lost too. The only condition on which exist-

ence is tolerable for solitary fowl like you and me, is that of living in the thickest of the world. Once fall and let it go over us, and we had better die.

Why not a motto for mice? Homer offers you a battle. Theocritus ought to yield curds and whey. I never asked you to specify the beasts, but to make a triple application. Go to! You have all winter. At least I hope the sagacious Hooker has arrived by this time, and Robert is not likely to return.

I have no special news for you. I believe I told you that I am just *accouché* of another article in the *N. A. R.* which will appear in a fort-night.[1] It is rather bitter, rather slashing, very personal, and the editor and my brother speak highly of it. No one else has seen it. I expect to get into hot water, and shall be disappointed if no one retaliates on me. Three weeks hence I return to Washington to start again, and expect to have work to do. Meanwhile I am reading Gibbon and wasting time.

All the members of my family are well and lively. They are sur-rounded by visitors and chatter all day. Give my regards to everyone, especially to your father.

To Charles Francis Adams, Jr.

WASHINGTON, 2 Novr., 1869

I dined at S. Barlow's[2] Sunday evening — Evarts and I and old Judkins. Barlow told some instructive stories about Erie, Atlantic and Great Western, etc., including McHenry,[3] whose counsel he is. He remarked that he understood both Gould and Barnard had expressed the intention of taking hold of you if ever you came to New York. Alas! the chance is gone.... I came on yesterday and as yet have seen no one.

To Charles Milnes Gaskell

158 G STREET, WASHINGTON,
Sunday, 7 November, 1869.

Your folio of the 15th October was forwarded to me here, where I found also your great-aunt, on my arrival. For the letter accept my respectful thanks. How you ever filled it, I can't conceive, but as you

---

[1] Civil Service Reform, in *North American Review*, October, 1869.

[2] Samuel Latham Mitchell Barlow (1826–1889), connected with the struggle for the control of the Erie Railroad.

[3] James McHenry (b. 1817).

hadn't written for an age I cut in halves and called it two, the first half being long overdue....

Confound your majesty's laziness! Aren't you a some-class-or-other in classics, and can't you bother me enough with Greek when I don't want it? And now you deny me a verse which you can invent if you like. Who says there's no analogy between cheese and Leighs! The rhyme alone is worth a permanent monument *ære perennius*. As for mice, I firmly believe the Baronet has married a country-mus, who will convert him to her destiny. The analogy is astonishing. But my amiable one, you *baisse*, evidently. You are not what you were when your polish was fresh. Look out for a *de te fabula*. I shall pass the rustic mouse as your portrait and have your name in Gothic capitals carved under it, unless you provide my inscription.

So I have happily quitted the home of my ancestors, and am once more in winter quarters, planning a winter campaign *autour de ma chambre*. I left all well at Quincy, where they are still freezing, but move to Boston next week. On my way hither I passed some days in New York, and saw many editors; some thieves; and many more fools. The editors were just then very familiar with my name, apropos to a certain article of mine of which I wrote you, and which called the wasps about me. I will send it to you in pamphlet one of these days, and expect you to admire my impudence.

As yet there is nothing here to instruct or amuse. Except for Cabinet officers I am alone in the city, and have nothing to do but to set my springes for future woodcock. I notice that you say little of your mental condition, your contentment or spleen. For my own part I suffer just wretchedness enough at times to make me conscious of the sun when the clouds go. Life is more thoroughly enjoyable than ever, after a few days when death seems a happy relief. Dyspepsia and a guilty conscience, my friend! Beware of champagne, but as you love your God (if you have a God) fly from the Rhenish vintage at all times! at least, such is my case.

I will say that your Legation here, considering its size, contains the queerest lot of Britishers it was ever my bad luck to meet. When I left England I thought I had some vague idea of English society — not the fashionable part of it, for that I never did know nor care for — but of society as a whole, good and bad, dull and clever, swells and snobs, mixed up and taken at bedtime. You have six or seven men, and four or five women here, who are too much for this vile world, and should be translated to a better. I will tell you stories about them one of these days which will amuse you. All the women are a little mad.

All the men (those that don't drink) are apparently fools. A state of things I regret. How is it that people always appear so unfavorably out of their own country!

I can't possibly be in London till [afte]r the first of June, so you can take your spring stroll quietly and meet me on your return. My principal object in going over is to see my few friends, get some clothes, wash my mind out a little, do a few politicians, and come home. The shorter such trips are made, the better, and however short they are made, half the time is always wasted in wondering what the deuce one has come for. Nothing but permanence wears well. Of all the horrors I know, a Sunday at York in 1860, combined, I think, the widest range, unless it was the succeeding Sunday in the Tavistock Hotel, Covent Garden. I wouldn't repeat it for the fee simple of that celebrated estate.

Addio! don't imagine me as having any chance of promotion. My last attack on the administration would have ended that, had it ever existed, as it never did.

To Charles Milnes Gaskell

Washington, 23 November, 1869.

I sit down to begin you a letter, not because I have received one since my last, but because it is one of the dankest, foggiest, and dismalest of November nights, and, as usual when the sun does not shine, I am as out of sorts as a man may haply be, and yet live through it. Do you remember how, on such evenings we have taken our melancholy tea together in your room in Stratford Place? My heart would rejoice to do it now, but solitude is my lot. This season of the year grinds the very soul out of me. My nerves lose their tone; my teeth ache, and my courage falls to the bottomless bottom of infinitude. Death stalks about me, and the whole of Gray's grisly train, and I am afraid of them, not because life is an object, but because my nerves are upset. I would give up all my pleasures willingly if I could only be a mouse, and sleep three months at a time. Well! one can't have life as one would, but if ever I take too much laudanum, the coroner's jury may bring in a verdict of wilful murder against the month of November. Bah! I never felt it half so keenly when I was in England where there is never any sun.

Now then, where may we sometimes meet and by the fire help waste a sullen day, what time we can from the sad season gaining? And to think that the brute Robert is happy and gay in the sunshine of Rome! I am as lonely as a cat here. Acquaintances without number I have, but no companion. And what avails it to be intimate with all men if one comes home at five o'clock and abhors life! Send a decent Britisher here, do!

Do you know I have taken up the ever youthful Horace Walpole again, and make him my dinner companion. What surprises me most is that he is so extremely like ourselves; not so clever of course, but otherwise he might be a letter-writer of today. I perpetually catch myself thinking of it all as of something I have myself known, until I trip over a sword, or discover there were no railways then, or reflect that Lord Salisbury and not Lord Carteret lives over the way. But all seems astonishingly natural to me; strangely in contrast to what it once seemed. If we didn't know those people — Primo-ministerio Palmerstonis — then we knew some one for all the world like them. Florence too! *Peste!* how little the world has changed in a century. Hanbury-Williams and Watkin-Wynn, Hervey; Arlington Street; I know I shall find Lady Sebright further on, and Lady Salisbury will come in for a wipe.

What! shall I imitate H. W. and tell you about this Court; a pack of boobies and scoundrels who have all the vices of H. W.'s time, with none of its wit or refinement? Or force either, for the matter of that! For where to find a Walpole or a Pitt here, I am at a loss to know. We are all Pelhams, and our President is as narrow, as ignorant, and as prejudiced as ever a George among you. Your friend — *que voici* — alone, and a few others, have any brain. But what of that! The world goes on, and I send you herewith my last political pamphlet which, I have reason to know, represents the opinions of a minority, and, I think, of a majority of the Cabinet. The violent attack on the Treasury has done me no harm.

I am writing, writing, writing. You must take the *New York Nation* if you want to read me. I have written that animal Reeve a letter, offering him an article — such an article! — and he does not even answer it! I have written to Palgrave to make advances to the *Quarterly,* and I will make my article *SUPERB* to disgust Reeve. I enclose you a puff — from my own paper. But it is written by a Britisher.

To Charles Milnes Gaskell

WASHINGTON, 7 December, 1869.

Yours of the 24th which is excellent besides being in a manner encyclopedical, arrived today, and I start an answer in the ante-dinner hour for fear I may be too busy later in the week. Your items of news affected me in various manners. My sympathies are strong for Lady Rich, and not less so for your sister. The Kenlis-Pollington story, however, alarmed me. Is one to expect that kind of thing usually now-a-days? Would you and I do it to Robert for example at Wenlock? Of course if it's the custom, I'll do it, but let me know in time. How stands the Mordaunt scandal now? I never have heard the upshot of the story, and would like well to hear about the letters. You see, I have no scandal here. We are vulgar but correct. As for my acting as scape-goat for Robert's sins, I am glad to be able to serve him so well. It doesn't hurt me and it helps people to hope for him. I never have been told that I was answerable for you also, but no doubt Lady B. would have said so if she has thought it worth while. Congratulate yourself that you are not classed with me in the ranks of sinners and re-publicans. The deuce of it is that here, all my sins are laid to you.

So, you are at the old tread-mill again. I am glad of it, and hope it bores you. To be sure it does. A good, healthy, downright, old-fashioned bore, in the shape of a country-house, is an excellent thing, and one should take it habitually, like weak tea, in small quantities. I should imagine Wynnstay a trifle worse, but Bretton will do. To be sure you are now a swell and shoot, which is wise, but it would be wiser still to hunt. Riding is always pleasant, though I confess following the hounds is as great bore as walking with the ladies. I know all about it. I did it at Rome. You may remember the occasion.

Does Florence want my love? Don't allow her to go without so slight an ornament. Tell her to say like Mme. Delaunay: *Je me trouve parée de tout ce qui me manque!*

What do you care to know about my goings on? If I thought you really felt the remotest interest in the people who are about me, I would tell you who and what they are. I would also tell you of the manner in which I am actually winding myself up in a coil of political intrigue and getting the reputation of a regular conspirator. My progress in a year has alarmed me, for it is too rapid to be sound. I am already deeper in the confidence of the present Government than I was with the last, although that was friendly and this a little hostile.

It seems a little strange that after the violent attack I made on it in the pamphlet I sent you, there should be no soreness, but the fact is, nearly every member of the Cabinet is in perfect sympathy with me in abusing themselves. You see there is a line of division in the Cabinet, and I am on the side which has the strongest men, and Reform is always a sure card. All this means nothing, however. I am only a very small fly on the wheel. But it amuses me as a play would, and so, though I have no power whatever and am held up solely by social position and a sharp tongue, yet I float — till later advices.

I must now stop to dine. I am fashionable tonight. The Foreign Secretary[1] feeds me. Last night it was his sub., the Assistant Secretary for Foreign Affairs.[2] Sunday night I had the Secretary of the Interior[3] to dine with me and a very small party at which very important conversation took place! *Voilà mon cher!* We fishes do swim! we eagles do soar! we donkeys do bray! don't show this letter, however. I am afraid a third person would not see the joke, and think me a — well! whatever you like.

10*th*. I thought so. I have never had a minute's leisure since I broke off above. I have had to write a violent personal attack impugning the pecuniary honesty of a highly respectable gentleman who is a friend of mine, and after sending it to a New York paper I have had to sit down and write another long article abusing everybody for another paper, besides a variety of other occupations too numerous to mention.

Let me tell you a story, which has some mysterious and portentous connection with my future fate. You will I am sure be impressed by it.

A week ago as I was walking through a street, little frequented, in the suburbs of this city, I was suddenly conscious of a rushing noise behind me, and before I knew what was the matter, I was struck violently by a soft substance on the back of the head, and flung to the ground so quickly that I did not even make an effort to save myself. I was somewhat stunned and a good deal hurt, but I jumped up mechanically, with the desire one always has to escape ridicule and appear as though one's internal anguish were a pleasure and quite the sort of thing one likes. Bewildered by the blow from behind and the equally severe fall; covered with sand from beard to boots; my gloves torn; one finger flayed; two others nearly dislocated, and a painful swelling raised over my knee, I staggered to my hat, and picked it up. Perhaps in my foggy condition I should have hurried on without ever

[1] Hamilton Fish (1808–1893).   [2] John Chandler Bancroft Davis (1822–1907).
[3] Jacob Dolson Cox (1828–1900).

stopping to search the cause of my disaster, had the cause not been too evident. There, on the ground half a rod in front, flapping painfully, and gazing at me with eyes to the full as amazed and bewildered as my own, was a huge, white, tame goose.

What does this portend? Will you not write some Latin verses describing how I came to my end, not like the poetic bird, by one of my own feathers, but by the entire carcass of the beast whose feathers had made my wings? Daedalus was nothing in comparison. He melted at the rays of the sun. But I was floored by the stupidest, dirtiest and coarsest of domestic dung-hill fowl. Here is a moral! Aesop, relate!

The worst of it is that I am not yet recovered from the blow. My knee is still stiff, and I came very near calling a physician to examine it today, as one's knees are sensitive points. I hope, however, it will pass away, and that goose will have no such disaster to regret.

Gen. Badeau, who was Motley's Secretary of Legation last season, and has since returned, has taken the vacant suite of rooms below me, and we now keep house together in a magnificent manner. We dine every day in state, and full dress, including white cravats, and we entertain freely, or mean to. Between us we know everybody, and those we don't know, know us. We are quite independent in other respects, like an old-fashioned nobleman and his wife, but we combine for society. I must now break off again to dress and dine with him and go to a reception at the Secretary's in the evening.

13th. At length I expect to conclude this species of autobiography which is becoming a volume. I have no news to give you of my family except that all were well last week, and actively employed in beginning their fashionable season. They seem to be very happy and contented as usual. My father is hard at work arranging family papers for publication, and is likely to do nothing else for years to come. My mother is doing nothing but fuss over her household, which is now quite a small one, as my younger brother [Brooks] is at College and I am away.

You talk of "celebrating" my arrival next year. Ah, my child, hold thyself far from it! Let us be quiet and sober lest the Gods should again be wrathful! We will silently eat our chop (with sauce Soubise; my weakness when well made) and drink a very little really dry champagne (which, alas, does not exist in this hemisphere) and when we talk just an old hour afterwards, we will talk soberly, allowing ourselves to sink out of our weary minds, and drawing mild hope and consolation from literature, art, society, if you will, but not from that society where our calmness is ruffled by obnoxious people. I go to

England for a moral bath. I want to wash out the dirty creases which life is making in the corners of my soul's eyes. I want to forget myself if I can, and enjoy what is outside of me. Let us get rid, therefore, so far as may be, of the vanities of life and of its social trials, and become serene Epicureans for a month, at least. Find me a place in London where we can be contented with a little, but let that little be so good that it will reconcile us with the fatigue of living, and strengthen our faith in Providence!

Don't show this at Pantyochin! The old ladies might not quite see that my influence is good in the main.

What is your uncle's (Sir F. Doyle) address? I want to send him a copy of my pamphlet in acknowledgment of his lectures[1] last year. I would send one to Lady Salisbury if they weren't such bitter America-phobists in that house. As my production would flatter their pride and encourage their contempt, I prefer to wash my dirty linen quietly at home. I would like to show you some of the attacks I have met in the press here. They are usually based on my great-grandfather, but occasionally on my extreme youth, and I expect to catch it hotter than ever in the course of the winter when the subject comes up in Congress. Before long I expect to be quite crushed, and then, please God, I will retaliate with a Dunciad.

Last evening I went with General Badeau to call for the first time on the President and his wife. We were admitted to the room where General Grant and half a dozen of his intimates sat in a circle, the General smoking as usual. There was some round conversation, rather dull. At last Mrs. Grant strolled in. She squints like an isosceles triangle, but is not much more vulgar than some Duchesses. Her sense of dignity did not allow her to talk to me, but occasionally she condescended to throw me a constrained remark. I chattered, however, with that blandness for which I am so justly distinguished, and I flatter myself it was I who showed them how they ought to behave. One feels such an irresistible desire, as you know, to tell this kind of individual to put themselves at their ease and talk just as though they were at home. I restrained it, however, and performed the part of guest, though you can imagine with what an effort.

Won't you be glad to find this letter has an end! And nothing to talk about either! Well! addio! sleep well after it.

[1] Lectures before the University of Oxford, London, 1869. He had succeeded Matthew Arnold as professor of poetry in the University.

To Charles Milnes Gaskell

2017 G St., Washington,
13 January, 1870.

Which is not a new address, but only a new number, and means that I live on G Street, in the 17th house beyond 20th Street. There's arithmetic for you! What a thing it is to live in a new country!

I received your note from Farming Woods, and was duly frightened about Robert! drat the boy! I hope your next will announce his return home, or at least his departure from Rome. I shall be uneasy till I hear.

There! my letter is at an end. I have no more to say; at least nothing that pertains to England. Our season has begun here, and I am prancing and flirting every night more or less, and every morning I am lazily political. The life amuses me as you can imagine it would. It is in fact a brilliant sort of butterfly existence, which cannot last very long, but may pass for some years still. I am gradually tending more and more towards journalism, which gives me a little money to buy gloves with, and a certain power to make myself felt. The world is kind to me. Society accepts all sorts of impertinences from me, without showing its teeth. Married women are friendly. Girls are confiding, and feel just a little flattered by attentions. The only real trouble is that one is here eaten up in one's self-conceit, and wants that taking-down which is so necessary for one's good. If one only heard the abuse as well as the flattery, it might restore the balance, but one can only hope for that. Meanwhile, let us bask in the sun if it shines. I mean to get out of life all the pleasure I can, and as little pain as may be.

You would have been amused to see me the other day acting as groomsman at a great wedding here. Eight bridesmaids were selected from the prettiest and most fashionable girls here, and we had a most distinguished show. Your humble servant is supposed to be attentive to one of these young women, just on the threshold of twenty, and in fact not without fine eyes and no figure. Perhaps in your vulgar mercenary eyes her chief attraction would be £200,000. In mine her only attraction is that I can flirt with the poor girl in safety, as I firmly believe she is in a deep consumption and will die of it. I like peculiar amusements of all sorts, and there is certainly a delicious thrill of horror, much in the manner of Alfred de Musset, in thus pushing one's amusements into the future world. Shudder! oh, my friend, why not! You may disbelieve it if you like, but I assure you it is true that every

sentimental speech or touching quotation I make to her, derives its
amusement from the belief that her eyes and ears will soon be inappre-
ciative. Is not this delightfully morbid? I have marked it for a point
in my novel, which is to appear in 1880. Meanwhile my attentions are
not limited to this, or any other, individual. I sometimes wonder how
I ever cared for anyone. My heart is now as immoveable as a stone,
and I sometimes doubt whether marriage is possible except as a matter of convenience.

The fact is, I think it would answer all our purposes if you would
come over here next May and pass your summer with us instead of my
going to England. You could bring me some clothes which I want
damnably! Think about it! You may marry all the fortunes here, so
far as I can help you, and set up for a Duke. What do you say?

To Charles Milnes Gaskell

2017 G STREET, WASHINGTON, D.C.,
30 January, 1870.

Your verses do honor to me and to yourself. I am highly honored
by such a display of your poetic genius. If there were anyone here to
understand them, I should spread your fame through society. As it is,
I must confine them to myself.

We have had your third Prince [1] here for a week. As I don't fancy
Princes, I was not eager to have him come, nor sorry to have him go,
nor have I been presented to him, nor do I care much about him except
that his surroundings made me lose my temper a little, as I thought,
at just this time, the less he was put above society, the better. The
fact is, his visit has not been entirely lovely, and it is difficult to say
whether your people or ours are least pleased.

You see, here is the trouble. Your people considered him to be
royalty, shut him up with the diplomatic corps and state officials, and
even acted as though he were the President's superior. Your Minister [2]
wanted the President to meet him at dinner, and actually persuaded
him to go to the Prince's ball. The Prince assumed to write to the
President only through Elphinstone, [3] his equerry. As regarded society, he acted just as he would have done in London, sending for his
partners, and, what ground my soul most, allowing his suite to tell my
special favorites that they were on no account to speak to the Prince
unless they were spoken to.

[1] Arthur William Patrick Albert, Duke of Connaught and Strathearn (b. 1850).
[2] Sir Edward Thornton (1817–1906).   [3] Sir Howard Crawford Elphinstone (1829–1890)

Our view of the matter was very different. The Cabinet, after consideration, decided that every civility should be paid to the Prince which would be paid by the Queen to the third son of our President, or of any other potentate not related by blood. Had this been strictly adhered to, the Prince would have been ignored, for you know how much notice the Queen takes of such people. Precedent however required that the Prince should be asked to dinner, and he was asked. Every civility was shown him by all the Government officials, but the President very rightly and properly refused to treat him as an equal, and the consequence was that your people, who can't get into their heads the fact that our President ranks with the Queen and the Emperor, were furious, and I myself, who thought it bad taste in the Prince to come at all except as a private gentleman and subject of the Queen, was quite unable to keep my temper in discussing the subject with them. I went to the ball given to him by your Minister, and it was very pretty, but an exact imitation of a Court ball at Buckingham Palace, all the forms included. The Prince himself made a pleasant impression on every one, and is a decided favorite. He did a great deal to redeem the blunders of the people about him, but it would have been better if he had not come.

All this is not whispered in public, and I write only because your people here are writing their accounts home, which are bitter enough against our manners. My opinion of their manners is of no consequence, but whenever the Queen sets an example of civility to us, our President will no doubt be happy to follow. She can begin by going to a ball at the Motleys'. I won't require her to go back and ask my father or me to dinner or to Windsor. She can start fresh, and if the Viceroy of Egypt visits England again, perhaps she will not rest satisfied with asking him to lunch at Windsor.

If you hear any attacks made on this score, I hope you will repeat what I say; viz: that the snobbishness of the whole affair was disgusting.

I have a long letter from Robert. My poor friend Hartman Kuhn has broken his neck hunting on the Campagna, which throws my sister at Florence into mourning. We are in our full season here, and I hard run between writing lampoons and waltzing.

To Charles Milnes Gaskell

WASHINGTON, 20 February, 1870.

Yours of the 2d has arrived and is grateful. I am busy as a flea on a clean baby, and open my eyes at your suggestion of travels. I shall come over in all probability just three months hence, and come back three months later. I ought not to go at all, but shall do it all the same. As for other travels; *que nenni!*

And let me stop here to say what I shall otherwise forget: Imprimis: I know nought of Pruyn: Secundo: Canvas-backs had flown before your letter arrived. They were costly, too, this winter; about a guinea a pair; so don't order recklessly. I believe you can get them regularly in Liverpool and Southampton, but next year I will see if I can manage it from Baltimore. There is the capital of ducks! but, after all, canvas-backs are not unlike other ducks and unless cooked by an experienced hand taste not unlike the animal of domestic horse-ponds.

If you see John Hervey, tell him that I have seen his friend Coore[1] and tried to make his stay agreeable. Dinners are rare with us, as we have no club and no men to ask. I never dine anyone except for political intrigues when there is something to be gained. But I tried to introduce him everywhere and to set him going. He was set going, and went—south! He and his companion, a youth named Jackson, also of Eton and the Cam, remained here a week, and departed. You know Coore well enough, I suppose, to — know all there is of him. Why these men travel, I don't know. The pleasure must be slight and the gain infinitesimal. They amused me, however. Their criticisms and remarks were full of humor which they were scarcely aware of. They were gentlemen, too, and made a pleasant impression, though sublimity of patronage could hardly be carried further except by you and me who do it intentionally and not with the same naïveté as these young ones command.

For the love of God, send me Pollington's book[2] when it appears! I bind him up.

News! bother me if I know any! yes, but I do though. Lyulph Stanley is on his way to Yeddo or Cochin China, or to the devil I hope, and *en route* is boring my poor family at Boston, and will bore me here next week. I am ready to jump into, or over, the Potomac with dread of him. And I, busier than a dozen clerks and writing day and night! I shouldn't mind if people ever seemed grateful for civilities, or if they ever by any accident amused me; but all the bores on this miserable earth seem to travel, and in time one ceases even to enjoy having one's country and people patronised by bores. I prefer to patronise others, but to have Lyulph patronise me is a trifle too

[1] Alfred Thomas Coore.

[2] In 1870 appeared a translation of Fernandez y Gonzalez's *Margarita*, made by John Horace Savile, Viscount Pollington.

strong an emetic. This is bore No. 5 who has afflicted me in a month. Can't you for once send me a good fellow and redeem your countrymen? You have sent me no one yet. At the same time I should feel much hurt if any friend of anyone's came here without bringing a letter to me, even if he were a bore, and for this reason I would not have you hint my remarks to anyone, least of all to John Hervey.

Battle is a place I should like to visit. I have seen it, but no more, though familiar with the neighborhood where my sister and I used to ride a great deal in old days. Your list of guests, however, made me shiver. I am so used to incessant excitement here and the rough-and-tumble of bohemianism, that my soul sinks at the thought of respectability. Our season is now nearly over, and my goose has not yet made good her portent. Politics are soon to become sharp again. My side is undermost, but precious wicked and pretty strong. There is soon to be a very lively fight, and I dodge about with my pen in my hand, lampooning the other side. One of my newspaper attacks irritated a member of Congress so much, the other day, that he denounced it before the House at great length. I did not declare the authorship.

Addio! My regards to everyone.

To Charles Milnes Gaskell

WASHINGTON, 7 March, 1870.

In a sort of kind of a half way, I thought there might be a letter from you this morning, as my last was dated the 2d February, but if there is one on the way, it is stuck in the snow which was falling all day yesterday. Our winter comes in the spring. As usual, I have nothing to say except that I am well and have gone through a pleasant season and am now going to church every day, that is to the church door as the young women come from afternoon service. You know me better than to expect more. I have been busy as a Roman flea in May, and have written a piece of intolerably impudent political abuse for the *North American* for April — but it is finance and you needn't read it — where I am to say that never since the days of Cleon and Aristophanes was a great nation managed by such incompetent men as our leaders in Congress during the rebellion — *bien entendu* that I am Aristophanes. The editor has not acknowledged it yet, but begged for it piteously. By the way, did you ever receive my pamphlet? I sent you a second copy, but the devil is in the posts. At the same time I write about two articles a month in the *Nation*, and if I want to be very vituperative, I have a New York daily paper to trust. So I come on and the people here are beginning to acknowledge me as some one to be considered. In my review of the Session next July, I am going to make an example or two *in terrorem* and go to England to escape retaliation. There! this is all there is about myself, and as for my surroundings I can only say that now Lent has come, society is at an end, and I am left alone, or to the resource of evening visits which may or may not be pleasant. The winter has been very agreeable to me because no other men have been here who could at all interfere with me, and I have had it all to suit myself. As for the other people, many of them are decidedly agreeable and there has actually been no scandal nor quarrelling nor even much ill-nature. For all that amusement, I rely on England. I have read the first day's proceedings in the Mordaunt case, and was delighted with it. As I happen to be in a good humor today, I will say that I am glad to feel satisfied that the girl was really insane. But it's hard on Mordaunt to have — I was going to use a word of Swift's and Defoe's — himself as he has, since he has not proved that he's not cuckolded, and has made himself very ridiculous. And shouts of demoniac laughter must welcome Sir F. Johnstone through this world and the next. What an introduction to society! Who is the man? Do you know him? and in whose set is he?

I was wrong about Coore and Jackson. They had not gone when I last wrote. My letter to you was just finished and still on my table, sealed and stamped, when they came in to take leave. So they are now gone for good and all, and I have no more to say about them, except that they were well-behaved and very-very-very English. Lyulph Stanley has not appeared and I hope by this time he is in China or any place he likes that is further away. The members of your Legation tell me that there are some other strolling Britishers in town, but they disturb me not.

You must remember poor Hartman Kuhn in Rome! He was a good fellow, though he had too much of the Philadelphian in him, and his wife was a very attractive little woman. I suppose you must have heard of his death at Rome by his horse falling back on him. It was a terrible affair, but I have not heard the details, and am too sorry for him to wish to hear anything so painful. My sister, however, in Florence, has been much distressed about it.

Since my last I have not had a line from any of you. Even Palgrave has not written, and I am waiting to ask him to introduce me — absent — to the editor of the *Quarterly*, if the *Quarterly* has an editor. *Ecco perché!* if that is good Italian. I am about to write an article on a very curious and melodramatic gold speculation that took place in New

York last September. It involves a good deal of libellous language which I can't well publish here. I wrote to Reeve offering it to him. He, after three months' delay, has just replied that he wants nothing controversial about currency. If this is a pretence, or if he really thinks I am ass enough to open a currency discussion instead of telling a story which has no parallel, I am equally contented to be done with him, but I mean to write the article all the same, and I will offer it to the *Quarterly* if I can get an introduction to the editor. So I want Palgrave to introduce me. *Voilà tout!* He need take no further responsibility, and if the *Quarterly* doesn't want it, I will on coming over find some editor who does. *J'y tiens* to make Reeve sorry to have lost the best thing his rotten old *Review* has had a chance to get into its July number. As I have been pulling wires behind the Congressional Committee of Investigation, and have been up to my neck in the whole thing, I know all that is known.

Aweel! aweel!! I have no more to say at this moment, so I will lay this by, and see if anything comes from you tomorrow.

Tuesday. Nothing at all. So I will close you up and put you into the letter box. I must now go to settle up my income tax, — which amounts to one pound, — to talk with the Special Commissioner of the Revenue [Wells] about politics, and to lunch with Jephtha's daughter (Chase, C. J.) whose remarks I told her the other day were "twaddle and cant," and I must reconcile.

To Charles Milnes Gaskell

Washington, 28 March, 1870.

A letter from you of March 2d! Bravo! I began to think you had retired to Wenlock permanently, or eloped with Mrs. Thingamy your housekeeper *ibidem*. Though why the deuce you should write — or I either — or any one — surpasses my comprehension. Were it not better done as Robert does, to sport with Lady Cunliffe in the shade? If one had but a Lady C. to sport with! Well, go to! as soon as I get some money I am going to take my passage for the 18th May, which will bring me to Southampton on or about the 30th of that same month, and if these blessed politics will offer me no corrupt hopes — as hitherto I have enjoyed none — I shall experience three months of civilisation again, and wash the dirty linen of my mind. As yet I have not made a single project for my movements after reaching London. I do not know whether I shall go further, or not. I do not know, nor do

I care to know, nor do I mean to decide anything, for if I move on to Paris or the Rhine or to Switzerland, it will only be to see my sister, and for the shortest time, and it will not prevent my doing society in London, nor my immolating those happy pea-chicks under the abbey walls. Considering how I hate a sea-voyage and the forlorn misery I suffer on that cursed element, I mean to enjoy all I can in recompense, and my freedom from projects or plans. I will wander with you to every old house in Shropshire if you like, and swing on all the styles in the midland counties wherever there's a church with a tomb or good Gothic. We will rail in set terms at anyone we choose. Only I wish you would discover a new man somewhere to admit to our society. We need larger sympathies with the race, and I fear that Robert can't be trusted.

Meanwhile the time flies away so fast that here is the Spring again, and my favorite flowers are all coming out, while the work which last winter was all done before now, is not even begun, and must somehow or other, be crowded into the next six weeks. I have wasted the winter writing for newspapers and dabbling in politics, and am only deeper and deeper in them as time goes on, but except for the experience there is little satisfaction in it, though it suits my black-guard tastes. Such a coil as there is here now! Confusion beyond idea! a universal free fight, with everyone abusing everyone else, and tripping each other up wherever they can. The President and his Cabinet and the Senators and the Congressmen are all squabbling together, and if the ill-temper goes on increasing as rapidly as it has done for three months past, we shall have an earth-quake again as we did four years ago. All this concerns me in no way. I am *lié* with another set of men, strong in the press, but weak in power. We despise all the people in control, and all we can do is only to make a little more noise. So we are going into the elections next November, and next winter perhaps the weather will be more settled. At any rate, we are more likely to gain than to lose by the passage of time. Personally I am still at a loss to know what the devil I want, or can possibly get, that would be an object, in case my friends came into power. So far as I know, however, my hands are still clean. I want nothing and fight only for the amusement of fighting.

3 *April.* Lo! how time flies! one cannot put down one's pen without a week's slipping in between paragraphs. I can't help it. I've been bothered and cross. This eternal whirl of politics is a kind of dirty whirlpool; one is sucked into it and goes round and round, all the time

hoping to reach something, and never clean. We are now in the middle of a battle over revenue reform, free trade and what not; and I, as lieutenant of a government official who heads the movement, have been helping him to organise our forces, which is difficult because it involves the splitting of the majority and the practical formation of a new party on this issue. However, we seem to have succeeded. At least I had a dozen of the leaders at a meeting in my rooms the other night, and we effected a close alliance. The next week will prove whether we can control Congress. Meanwhile I am busy on my last literary efforts for the season, and have no end of things to think about. We hold a secret but weighty political caucus on the 18th to which our friends — the small number of high panjandrums — from all quarters, are to come. And I have a wedding on the 21st at which I am again to officiate as second fiddle. No sign yet of my own appearance as *premier amant*. The young maidens no doubt adore me, but I am obdurate. I wish you would do better and have some one nice to flirt with me at Wenlock.

Not a line from anyone for an age. England has forgotten me and even Palgrave has stopped writing. As for Robert I never seriously expect the beggar to write a letter. It isn't in his lazy nature. But Ralph Palmer's spasmodic epistles have now ceased, and Mrs. Sturgis has not written for many months. Such is the frailty of human memory that it can't survive eighteen months' absence.

Auf wiedersehen! Ever.

To Charles Milnes Gaskell

WASHINGTON, 29 April, 1870.

Oh my beloved, I haven't written since the 4th because why? I have been too busy to live. Yesterday I sent off to Palgrave a big manuscript for the *Quarterly*, which I hope may arrive safely, and be favorably received, as it is of interest to more persons than myself. Tomorrow I must set to work on a new political article for the *North American* for which I have only a fortnight. I sail on the 18th. My passage is paid for, and my ticket on my table before my eyes. I have been up to the roots of my hair in politics and our winter has been highly successful, and our summer will, I hope, show the effects of it. On me personally its effects will be nothing, except so far as they give me wider range of audience. I have been offered the editorship of the *North American Review*, but have declined it, and may become its official editor for politics if we can make an arrangement. *Enfin!* we are all merrily boiling like lobsters in a pot, and it amuses after a fashion. I have had a political convention of half the greatest newspaper editors in the country at my rooms, where the world was staked out to each of us and the fulness thereof, and the foundations of Hell were shaken. All which has created great curiosity in man, to know what the deuce the mal-contents are brewing. This done, and my writing concluded, I shall be glad to get over to you and out of the dust and dirt of politics. By-the-bye! I have brought all the respectable old fools of the country down on me by a mighty impudent article published in the April *North American* under my name though I was only half-author.[1] Well! it certainly was savage!

I am coming over along with half Washington. Such an exodus to Europe was never known. Among others my colocataire Badeau goes over to be Consul General, and half your British Legation clears out in the course of the summer. Next winter will bring an entirely new tribe, and I am becoming one of the oldest inhabitants.

Do you know my old tailor Skinner of Jermyn Street? If so I wish you would do me a favor. Go to him and tell him to cut out for me a morning suit, dark blue coat and waistcoat, and light, greyish trousers, to be ready for me to try on the moment I arrive. If I wait till then before ordering it, he will keep me a month. I shall want lots of clothes, so he had best look sharp.

Did you find a horse? I think I shall have to take one for the season in order to feel respectable and ride with you. Get me an invitation to the St. James's Club for June. I will get one to the Travellers' through Hankey if I can.

Do you think of anything else by way of preparation? I am going to brush up my visiting list so as to leave cards everywhere at once. I want to meet everybody, talk with everybody, and know everybody. I propose to be as tender as an angel to all the young women. I propose — God have mercy on my soul — to talk with all the rising young men. And I propose that you shall carry me about everywhere and do the same things, else how can we laugh at them together.

The unhappy Robert, as I supposed, will be lost to us. It was his fate. I hope her Ladyship will have a pleasant confinement and that the new heir to Ravenswood will be all that we, his uncles — or is it second cousins — could wish. That generation is treading so hard on my heels that I have to run away from them, but at any rate I am already a bald and bearded old man and shall not look so very much older at fifty.

[1] Chapter on Erie, signed Charles F. Adams, Jr.

You will not be able to answer this letter, as I am to sail before an answer could reach me. I will therefore only add that I expect to reach Southampton about the 30th May, and to be in London as soon as the railway will take me there. I don't know the exact length of passage made by these boats, but if I do not arrive by the 1st or 2d, it will be because I can't.

My people are all well and meditating a removal to what they call their country quarters which are about as much country as Putney or Twickenham. My father is on the point of going west on a journey. My elder brother has been here on a visit to me. My younger brother is going to California, he says. My mother and sister stay at home, quiet and solitary.

Give my regards to everyone and tell them I'm coming. They may send me invitations for anything, everything, beforehand. You can accept them all for me. Five hundred thousand invitations showered on me at my arrival! They needn't be bashful because it's I!

Farewell! I shall write once more a note the week before I start and expect to receive one more from you.

WASHINGTON, 11 May, 1870.

CARO CARLAZZONUCCIO, — I write a line to say that I still expect to start this day week. You may expect to hear of my vessel about a week after you receive this. She will arrive two or three days after the Scotia which leaves New York on the same day. If you want to get at me at once, write a note to me at the post-office in Southampton. I will call as I land. As I come over largely to see you and yours, I will seek you in Stratford Place or elsewhere, and as for my subsequent movements they will be so mere a matter of chance that I won't even discuss them.

I am struggling with a mound of manuscript and fearful parting visits. I expect to be driven to the very last moment, and to get aboard my steamer in a state of exhaustion. At the most critical instant of my work I have been dragged into a violent public controversy with a man whose scalp I took in the April number of the *North American*, and who is trying to take mine in return. We call each other fool and idiot in the papers, and carry on a very friendly private correspondence meanwhile. I have no news for you, and as I shall not go north to see my family before I sail, and as in fact I don't precisely know where my family is, or will be, a week hence, I can't send much news of them. Let us now prepare for our June campaign, and let us make it a smasher.

V

SUMMER IN EUROPE

1870

To Charles Milnes Gaskell

Hôtel d'Amérique,[1]
Bagni di Lucca, 8 July, 1870.

Had I been able to write anything satisfactory I should have written a week ago. As it was, I preferred to wait for your letter which arrived this morning. Many thanks for it. In return I will give you an account of my adventures which have not been gay.

On quitting you I travelled through to Paris where I had four hours for breakfast and bath, and went on to Mâcon where I was delayed nine hours and went to bed. Crossed the Cenis Wednesday, and reached this place at four o'clock Thursday afternoon, without adventure or incident of any sort.

I found the hotel turned into a sort of camp, and a dozen of my sister's friends regularly keeping guard. Italians, English and Americans, a motley but rather agreeable crew, surrounded her bedside, and acted in regular relays as nurses, night and day. I found that my sudden summons was owing to the fact that lock-jaw had set in, and for a week my poor sister had been struggling in the very jaws of death, which were by no means locked against her.

It is hardly worth while to describe to you the details of the eight days that have since passed. They have been in many ways the most trying and terrible days I ever had. The struggle has been awful. We have had a series of ups and downs which would test the courage of Hercules. We have swum in chloroform, morphine, opium, and every kind of most violent counteragent and poison, like nicotine and Calabar bean. At times we have abandoned all hope. One night my sister, reduced to the last extremity, gasped farewell to us all, gave all her dying orders, and for two hours we thought every gasp was to be the end. Her breath stopped, her pulse ceased beating, her struggles ended, a dozen people at her bedside went down on their knees, and my brother-in-law and I dropped our hands and drew a long breath of relief to think that the poor child's agony was over even at the cost of suffocation. But after nearly half a minute of absolute silence, the pulse started again, the rattling in the throat recommenced, and presently she waved her arm as though she were ordering death away, and to our utter astonishment commanded us to bring her some nourishment. It has been the same thing ever since. Such a struggle for life is almost worth seeing. She never loses courage nor head. She knows what is the matter, and her own danger, but in the middle of her most awful convulsions, so long as she can articulate at all, she gives her own orders and comes out with sallies of fun and humorous comments which set us all laughing in spite of our terror at the most awful crises. Of course her talking is only a growl between her teeth and even this often quite inarticulate, but we have learned to understand it pretty well, and habit has made even so horrible a disease as this, so familiar that we stroke and joke it. Indeed the situation, desperate as it is, has its amusing side. Our friends come out in strong colors under such a test as this. They show qualities which go far to redeem human nature. Such kindness I never had seen in mere friends of society, and I can overlook a deal of faults if they are backed up by such courage and patient devotion. As for me, I was at first a wretched coward, but now I am hardened to the impressions and face a convulsion, with death behind it, as coolly as my sister herself.

I can't tell you what will be the end. I haven't a notion how long it will last. I can see no essential difference between the situation now and a week since. As she is still alive and strong after fifteen days of incessant struggle and after swallowing more deadly poison than would have killed all of us about her, who are well, I hope she may pull through. But I ask no questions and make no plans. I am with her about fifteen hours a day, and seldom leave the house at all. I am writing this letter while I attend her, so its style is a trifle eccentric, but you must put up with it for the occasion. Enough for the present. My regards to every one. Give Mrs. Sturgis news of me if you can.

To Charles Milnes Gaskell

BAGNI DI LUCCA,
Wednesday, 13 July, 1870.

It is all over. My poor sister died this morning. I will tell you about it some day or other, but now I am fairly out of condition to write details. The last fortnight has been fearfully trying and the last few days terribly so. I long to get back to you and be quiet again, somewhere away from society and condolence.

I shall start north again next week but I do not yet know the precise day. Nor can I yet tell how I shall come. I must stop a day or two in

Paris, and may not reach London much before the 1st August. But I will let you know my movements.

If you could drop in and tell Mrs. Hankey what has happened, I should be greatly obliged. I don't want to have to tell the story more frequently than is necessary.

To Charles Milnes Gaskell

OUCHY NEAR LAUSANNE,
Monday, 25 July, 1870.

Your letter of the 16th followed me from place to place and caught me yesterday here. I left Florence last Monday night and came up to Stresa on the Lago Maggiore with my brother-in-law and an American family who were with us at Lucca. We passed two days at Stresa and then crossed the Simplon and arrived here Saturday afternoon. The weather has been hotter than it ever was in the earth's condition of primitive incandescence, but I have been so happy to get a few days in the wilderness where there was no society and nothing to think about, that I was very sorry to arrive here where I am deep among Americans whom I least care to see. I am waiting for my brother-in-law who has gone on to Geneva on business, and we shall go up to Paris tomorrow or the day after. A week hence I expect to go back to London. He will be with me and we shall probably go to some hotel. I shall have to stay about a week in London to finish my purchases and commissions. After that I shall have three weeks free to occupy as I choose. My brother-in-law goes back to America before I do, and will not stay more than a week or ten days in London. If you are at Wenlock I will join you there some day after the eighth.

This devilish war upsets all my calculations. My single hope is that France will get so far thrashed as to make her mind her own business in future, and that Germany will have the same fate. How both can be beaten at once, I don't know, but I hope it may turn out so. As yet I can see no other good likely to come out of it, and of course it puts an end everywhere to any chance of carrying out a regular course of politics. I am rather amused, however, to see how little Europe is really changed by what we call progress. Louis XIV himself never did anything more arbitrary, and certainly nothing in so dishonest a form. What a fine thing universal suffrage is!

If Italians ever publish anything, I have not found it out, but I have read very little since I came, and have seen nothing of literary people. The Italian novel at best is an utterly hopeless and Godforsaken pro-

duct of intellectual impotence, and I firmly believe that the newspapers now contain all there is of literary life in Italy. The rest is mere
imitation so far as I have seen anything. But I've had no means of
pushing my knowledge much further than the backs of books.

I suppose I shall find the political people still in London. I want to
talk with a few of them and shall hunt them up. Everyone else may go
if they like. As I can't go to routs I don't care who can. But I can go
and talk politics and I mean to do it.

As I suppose you to be out of town I won't send my regards to
anyone. Indeed I shall probably be in town before you can answer this
letter. Of course I shall have to go at once to your house to see about
my traps, and you can write to me there. Or if you want anything in
Paris and will write to me there in care of Messrs. Hottinguer & Cie,
bankers, I will perform your commissions provided I get the letter by
Saturday.

A rivederci! I am now going to swim in the lake, an amusement I
much affect.

To Charles Milnes Gaskell

Grove Farm, Leatherhead,
Thursday, 4 August, 1870.

I received your note successfully, but can't yet fix my day for coming down. When does Warren come? I will call there and ask. There
are so many last things that need attention in London and so many
orders to be executed that I fear I shall have to come up again in about
three weeks and start from here. I have seen scarcely anyone but
Palgrave and as you can imagine I did not find him in very cheerful
circumstances. My brother-in-law returns to Paris Saturday evening,
which will leave me a little freer, as I am now obliged to keep him in
company, but as yet I find myself likely to be left a species of solitary
pilgrim on his departure. I haven't even a club, and the question of
dining is a serious one. What is worse, I am so busy that I've had no
time to look up friends. We came down here yesterday afternoon to
pass a night quietly at the Sturgis's. Tomorrow evening I am going to
dine with Palgrave, not a festive occasion but rather the contrary.
I hope to see your sister for a moment. Sunday I may beg a dinner at
the Motleys', who are also companions enjoying a state of mind anything but cheerful. So you can conceive without difficulty that I
should be ready to quit London at the earliest opportunity. It is not
gay....

To Charles Milnes Gaskell

Friday, 5 P.M. [August 12 or 19, 1870.]

A hitch in my movements, and a change of base for strategic purposes. They had given me a bad stateroom for the 30th, so I made a row, and am transferred to the Cuba which sails on the 3d for *New York*. So I have four more days. Perhaps if you are good, I'll pass Thursday with you at Wenlock. I go to the Langham tonight to be with Wells. Tomorrow I go to Leatherhead and stay till I leave London.

I've seen your father. He is quite alone and gives a rather poor account of himself. Mrs. Lindesay is at Norwood. I don't know with certainty, but I should say your father was a little uneasy about himself. At any rate he expects a long affair.

This by way of posting you as to our concerns, but I am in a hurry and must stop.

To Charles Milnes Gaskell

STRATFORD PLACE,
Tuesday, 30 August, 1870.

DEAR REPTILE, — As you have left my last note unnoticed and have declined to encourage me to pass one night at Wenlock, I shall punish you by coming to stay two. I shall arrive tomorrow evening at eight o'clock, and shall remain till such hour on Friday as I see fit. You will do well to be civil. So have my bed aired. You may shoot as much as you like. Only mind that I shall follow this note within twelve hours of its reaching you. I shall have things to say.

Ever, my dear Batrachian, yours.

VI

HARVARD COLLEGE

1870–1872

To Charles Milnes Gaskell

WASHINGTON, 29 September, 1870.

I wish you had seen me sailing out of the harbor at Queenstown. It blew hard from the southwest, dead ahead, and I, who had been ashore all day, went incontinently to bed, and remained there much the better part of forty-eight hours, during which the water slopped over us as though we were a tin pan. The voyage on the whole, however, was passable. I made Miss Nilsson's acquaintance, and found a number of friends on board. Mr. Mundella, M.P., was also with us. I do not know Mr. M., but once happening to go near the spot where he was lecturing an admiring audience, I heard him burst into an eloquent panegyric on John Bright's oratory; "The first orator in the world," said he; "Talk of your Demosthenes and your Euripides, they're nothing to him." I retired in silence. Who knows but that Mr. Mundella was right! Euripides might have been surprised at the company he was in, but I was not.

I passed the custom-house safely, unshorn, and reached home without any accident. I found my family as well and as cheerful as I could have expected, only one of my aunts with whom I was very intimate here, had suddenly died in the interval. I found myself growing in consequence. My last article had not only been reprinted entire by several newspapers, but the party press had thought it necessary to answer it, and I cut out some of their notices to send over to you, but forgot to bring them with me. What is more, I am told that the democratic national committee reprinted it in pamphlet form and mean to circulate two hundred and fifty thousand copies of it. If I get a copy I will send it to you as a curiosity. You see I have a tolerably large audience at least.

But what is much more interesting is that on my return home I found the question of the professorship sprung upon me again in a very troublesome way. Not only the President of the College and the Dean made a very strong personal appeal to me, but my brothers were earnest about it and my father leaned the same way. I hesitated a week, and then I yielded. Now I am, I believe, assistant professor of history at Harvard College with a salary of £400 a year, and two hundred students, the oldest in the college, to whom I am to teach mediæval history, of which, as you are aware, I am utterly and grossly ignorant. Do you imagine I am appalled at this prospect? Not a bit of it! *Impavidum ferient!* I gave the college fair warning of my ignorance, and the answer was that I knew just as much as anyone else in America knew on the subject, and I could teach better than anyone that could be had. So there I am. My duties begin in a fortnight and I am on here to break up my establishment and transfer my goods to Cambridge where I am fitting up rooms regardless of expense. For I should add that what with one thing and another my income is about doubled, and I have about £1200 a year. With the professorship I take the *North American Review* and become its avowed editor. So if you care to write thirty pages of abuse of people and houses in England, including Sir Roger, the Sketch-book, and country squires in general, send the manuscript to me and if you are abusive enough you shall have £20.

At the same time Will Everett accepts a tutorship either in Greek or Latin, I forget which. I am glad he has at last gained his chance of success, and if he succeeds he will no doubt be made professor. I have not yet seen him, but am told he is pleased. He has taken a house in Cambridge and will live there.

I think I have now written you news enough and you can reflect upon it at your leisure. My engagement is for five years, but I don't expect to remain so long, and my great wish is to get hold of the students' imaginations for my peculiar ideas. The worst of the matter is that I shall be tied tight to the college from the 1st December to the last of June, which will seriously interfere with my freedom of movement when you come over. This, however, must be managed as we best can. I get three months' long vacation in summer, but this is all, except a fortnight at Christmas. I have nine hours a week in the lecture room, and am absolutely free to teach what I please within the dates 800–1649. I am responsible only to the college Government, and I am brought in to strengthen the reforming party in the University, so that I am sure of strong backing from above. You can fancy that my influence on the youthful mind is likely to be peculiar to say the least. And yet my predecessor was turned out because he was a Comtist!!!

I came on here yesterday, and am very hot, very lonely, and very hard run. I passed an hour today with Secretary Fish, who was very talkative, but there are few of my political friends left in power now, and these few will soon go out. This reconciles me to going away, though I hate Boston and am very fond of Washington. By-the-way, I see John Hervey's name in the papers as having arrived, and Tom Hughes is flying about.

We have an awful drought. At Quincy everything is literally burned and nothing like it ever known. Since coming home I have been roasted.

To Henry Lee Higginson

HARVARD COLLEGE, CAMBRIDGE, MASS.
24 October, 1870.

MY DEAR HENRY: — Thanks for your very kind letter. It is pleasant to be remembered and to think that there is any one who sympathizes in one's destiny. The truth is, I have come back here not so much to teach as to learn. I am working harder than I ever worked as an undergraduate, and I hope in time to know something. If I succeed — so! If not, then one only remains as poor a cuss as one was intended to be. I am writing this at a faculty meeting, and there is not a student here who would feel less at home in the company than I do. I want to grant all the petitions, and excuse all the students for everything. Am I not one of them myself? But no one asks my opinion and I am bored to death.

Whenever, or if ever, you come out here, come to see me at No. 1 Wadsworth Hall, once Mrs. Humphrey's, and still longer ago the old President's house. There I renew my youth. Send my love to Jim and believe me ever yours.

To Charles Milnes Gaskell

HARVARD COLLEGE, CAMBRIDGE, MASS.
Tuesday, 25 October, 1870.

Here I am, fairly established, and frightfully hard at work. After a struggle such as you can imagine, I broke up my camp at Washington and pitched it again here. I lose by the change. The winter climate is damnable. The country is to my mind hideous. And the society is three miles away in Boston. In return I have only the satisfaction of hoping that I may be of use, and it is little more than a hope, as I don't believe in the system in which I am made a part, and thoroughly dislike and despise the ruling theories of education in the university. So I have undertaken to carry on my department on my own bottom, without reference to the Faculty or anyone, and unless I am interfered with, which is improbable unless I make great blunders, I shall quietly substitute my own notions for those of the College, and teach in my own way. There will be some lively history taught, I can tell you. I hardly know how I am getting on with the students, but I think we shall be on good terms. I have about a hundred, all more or less advanced, as to age at least, though as a rule they are supernaturally lazy and ignorant. I pound at them in vain nine hours every week. If it weren't that I am always learning, I should soon grow fearfully tired of teaching. Add to this that I am much bothered in mind about the *North American*, and you will feel that I have not come back to sleep on so quiet a bed as I hoped.

Will Everett is very grand. He has the Freshmen in Latin and has taken a house in which three of his youths are quartered besides four more who take their meals with him. I have not yet visited him and his Freshmen in his quarters, but I reserve that pleasure for a future day. Meanwhile I see him occasionally at the Faculty meetings.

On some accounts I am not sorry to have left Washington as things have taken a political turn there which is by no means favorable to me. All my friends have been or are on the point of being driven out of the government and I should have been left without any allies or sources of information. As it is, I only retire with the rest and leave our opponents to upset themselves, which they will do in time, I think, and when I go back there, it will be to study a new situation.

My family muddle on in a stupid way out at Quincy, and I go over there every Saturday and pass Sunday with them. My sister drives about the country in a little basket wagon, and my father arranges his books in a new library he has just built. They are not gay, but luckily the autumn has been very warm and fine so that there has been no unnecessary discomfort, and in a fortnight they will come to town and see something of their friends. I hope to pick up a few new acquaintances whom I like, for my old friends don't amuse me much and as the novelty of my work wears off, I am likely to be bored unless some new excitement can be invented.

What rubbish you talk about presents. As though I hadn't been living on you the better part of three months, and had no debts of acknowledgment. For God's sake don't carry out your idea of sending me anything, for I can find nothing here to reciprocate with, and I don't want to feel my debts increased or I shall never dare visit you **again**. But why doesn't Frank send the photographs? Please express my deep regret to the Warrens at being unable to accept their invitation, and say everything pretty on my account to anyone you meet, except those we detest. I expect a letter from you daily, and am anxious to know how your father comes on. Give my best regards to him.

To Carl Schurz

Harvard College, Mass.
27 October, 1870.

Dear Sir, — I came to you last spring on the part of the *North American Review* to ask a political article from your hand. You were then too busy, and I know how busy you still are. Yet, having assumed the charge of the *Review*, I venture again to write to you to renew my request. I do this, not because I am an editor, but because I would like to support your course, and make known to the eastern people the true nature of the contest you are engaged in. I want an article on the political condition of Missouri and the West, with an energetic account of the present campaign there. I want the public to know, if possible, how far you and your party represent principles which are of national interest; how far free-trade and reform are involved in the result; and what influences have been at work to counteract success. We in the east know little of what takes place in the west, and feeling so strong a sympathy as I do in your political career since you took your seat in the Senate, I would be glad to extend the range of your influence so far as is in my power.

Hoping that you may find time to carry out my wish without inconvenience, I remain very truly yours.

To Charles Milnes Gaskell

Harvard College, Cambridge, Mass.
19 November, 1870.

Besides a letter from Frank Doyle, with his photographs, I have lately received a letter from Robert, yours of October 28, and this morning one from Palgrave, so that I am now deep in debt. As it happens that I am fearfully hard worked, my chances for letter-writing are fewer than I could wish, but then you will no doubt be recompensed by your appreciation of my great importance, which lends so much more value to my remarks. My reputation for deep historical research is awful. I have, however, unearthed only one important fact on which I propose to dwell at great length to my classes, which is that your Norman ancestors were principally distinguished as a class for one peculiar vice which modern prejudice has absurdly condemned as unnatural, and thus that Messrs. B——, P—— and Lord A—— C—— are evidently descended from William the Conqueror and proudly justify their claim to be considered among your best and oldest families. Unfortunately I have to devote so much time to the mere work of my lectures that I cannot go so deeply into this interesting subject as I should.

Between my history and my *Review* I have all I can manage. The retirement from Washington has by no means thrown me out of politics. On the contrary, as editor I am deeper in them than ever, and my party is growing so rapidly that I look forward to the day when we shall be in power again as not far distant. Two or three years ought to do it. Meanwhile I am smashing things here, and have declared war against the old system of teaching, in a manner which is not respectful to the University though my students like it. All this is very grand of course. Equally of course it is probably unmitigated rot. But who cares? So long as I am amused, I mean to go on with it, and to be very busy is a sort of amusement. At any rate I have no time to think of disagreeable subjects, and if our climate were less of a nuisance I should feel fairly satisfied.

I see that the last *Westminster* contains my article,[1] about which I had so much difficulty while with you. I sent it to the editor just as I was coming away, as a last experiment, and heard no more of it till I saw it in print. The editor has not written to me on the subject, and I have not written to him.

Your English gossip interests me in my western banishment. I am sorry for the Motleys, especially as he has now received his *coup de grâce* in peremptory dismissal. For skill in insulting people commend me to our excellent President. I suspect he will get us into trouble with you before long, and if you go to war with Russia as you seem bent on doing, you will certainly have us on your backs. It is not very creditable to us to pursue a policy of this sort, but I have no doubt we shall do it, as we have made no secret of our intentions. In case of a war, I shall wait till it is over before I next visit England, for I don't mean to fight and I shall not be found in the ranks of the army that sacks Wenlock. I presume you will not cross the ocean to attack Quincy, but if you are the destined man to plunder my ancestral halls, I prefer your doing it to another. You'll find little to loot. Save the spoons. They will serve for Wenlock when I next come.

[1] The New York Gold Conspiracy, in the July number.

I am sorry for the Warrens, all the more as I wanted you to marry Margaret. As it is, I suppose I shall return some day to find a stranger presiding in the dining-hall, who will think it an infernal shame to have me on her hands for a month at a time when she wants her brother the Captain just home from New Zealand. Well! I shall take lodgings in Marylebone Lane and you will come to see me quietly after breakfast.

My people seem to be tolerably well. They are now in Boston and I go in occasionally and dine with them. As yet I have seen no society. I am too busy and have to read every evening as my young men are disgustingly clever at upsetting me with questions. Luckily I have a little general knowledge which comes in. I gave them the other day a poetical account of Wenlock in relation to Gregory VII and Cluny. You see how everything can be made to answer a purpose.

Next week I go on to New York to a political gathering of members of the press on my side; quite a demonstration, which will make a noise in the newspapers. I go to press the interests of my *Review*. Meanwhile my flock must wait for their historical fodder till I return.

Frank's photographs are very pleasant little reminders of our summer. I shall stick them in a book with — F. Doyle, Maj. Gen. fecit — under them. Give my love to Robert. I shall write to him soon. Also to his wife. I suppose things look lively in politics now, and I hope your turn is coming.

To Charles Milnes Gaskell

Harvard College, 19 December, 1870.

It's an age since I wrote, but if you will credit the alarming fact, I am now driven to use the official time of the College to give to you. Here I sit, at the regular meeting of the College Faculty, while some thirty twaddlers are discussing questions of discipline around me, and I have to hear what they say, while I indulge you in the charms and fascinations of my style. This is what it is to be a Professor, not to say an editor. I have not had a clear hour of time for a month. I have read more heavy German books and passed more time in the printing-office; I have written more letters on business, and read more manuscripts of authors; I have delivered more lectures about matters I knew nothing of, to men who cared nothing about them; and I have had my nose ground down more closely to my double grindstone, than ever a cruel Providence can have considered possible. My happy carelessness of life for the last ten years has departed, and I am a

regular old carthorse of the heaviest sort. As for society, I have not
seen the hem of a female garment since I came out here. Life has
resolved itself into editing and professing. I always swore I never
would descend to work, but it is done. Lo! the poor fallen one!

The curious part of it all is that I don't dislike it so much as I expected. I am so busy that I have not had the time to think whether
I enjoyed myself or not, and now the Christmas holidays are nearly
here, and I am so nearly half through the year, at least in labor, that
it quite bewilders me to think how time goes. I wish you would try
a few months of good hard work, when you have to count your
minutes to keep abreast of the team, and then tell me how you like it.
I believe it would do you good. But how these old buffers do bore me!
They talk! talk! talk! Ugh!! I wish I could scalp 'em.

Have I sent you my circular? No? I will!! It is grand, and involves the deepest interests of literature. I am sending it to all mankind, and of course mankind rushes to see it. Apropos! I have never
sent you the reply which Senator Howe [1] of Wisconsin made to my
"Session." He blackguards me and all my family to the remotest
generation. He calls me a begonia! a plant, I am told. To be abused
by a Senator is my highest ambition, and I am now quite happy. My
only regret is that I cannot afford to hire a Senator to abuse me
permanently. That, however, might pall in time, like plum-pudding
or ——.

At the end of this week, just as soon as I have got my January
Review off my shoulders I shall go on to Washington for the holidays.
This is the only recess I get for six months, and I want to make the
most of it. What do I do after getting there? I go to my dentist's,
oh, my friend! Yes! I pass a fortnight with my dentist. At any rate
he will stop my talking for a time.

Will Everett is here in the room. Shall I ask him whether he has
any message to send you? I will ——

He says he is going to write to you himself and send you some of his
publications.

By the way, I am told that his children's books are not at all bad.
Perhaps your mind, after Siluria, will be ready to unbend to them. I
see poor old Murchison [2] has gone up. He ought to, after such a work.
Will is now making a speech — Heaven bless him! Lord, how dull
they all are!

What a droll idea it is that you should be running about England,

[1] Timothy Otis Howe (1816–1883). Education, 292.
[2] Sir Roderick Impey Murchison (1792–1871), geologist.

visiting people, and I shut up in this Botany Bay, working like a scavenger. Lord bless me! Do those people really exist, or did I dream it all, after reading Horace Walpole and eating a heavy dinner? I doubt your existence at times, and am not altogether certain about my own. Give my tender love to Gretchen — I mean Lady Margaret. What dress does she wear now? How are the Marguerites?

By the bye! Do you know that I hope to appear soon at the bar of the Old Bailey, or whichever of your Courts has the jurisdiction? James McHenry wants to sue me for a libel. I have written over that this is precisely what would suit me, and that he may try it if he likes. You will, I doubt not, hear of it, if the *Westminster Review* is brought into Court. Perhaps it would bring me over to England again, as I mean to hurt him if he gives me a chance.

I went to New York a month ago to a political meeting, and we laid vast and ambitious projects for the future.

But the Meeting is breaking up, and I must break up too! Thank the Lord! The clack is passed for one week, and a week hence I shall be in Washington.

24 *December.* I have been too busy to finish the above, and now I start for Washington in an hour, for my holidays. Nothing new from anyone. I am just *done!* Run to death by printers and students. But my work is finished and time is up. I am going to have some fun.

To Charles Milnes Gaskell

HARVARD COLLEGE, 13 February, 1871.

Your letter of the 18th arrived just after my last was despatched. I at once rushed to the club and read your article in the *Saturday Review*, and was inspired with the wish of getting you to write something for me. Why can't you write me a book-notice now and then? If you meet a promising book, why not write me a notice of it? These notices are always read and a good one is a difficult thing to get. They are not signed, therefore, if you notice a book of English memoirs and rake up a heap of old family scandals, no one will know who did it. I want someone in England who can do this, for no one here is up to such work. We do not even get the English books unless they are reprinted. Now be a good fellow and write me at least one such notice a month. Travels, memoirs, novels, poems, anything, so long as something is to be said about it. Show a surprising familiarity with English affairs, and create a circulation for me there. A book-notice should be about a column, more or less, of the *Saturday Review*; more if the book is worth it; less if it isn't. You can make a sensation by a good one.

As for my own affairs, they now go on with a regularity which is beautiful to see. I see the days roll on with a fearful rapidity, and already today my first half-year of professing is over. I have worked like a dog and learned more than I ever expected to do. On the whole I am well pleased with the result though there is no special fame or honor about it. My youths are lazy but not bad fellows, and I seem to get along as well with them as anyone does. At any rate I have found them very civil and have never been obliged to light upon a student for misconduct, though I rather have been watching for a chance. Imagine me sitting in a chair, in a huge lecture room, discoursing day after day to classes of fifty men, and unfolding the true principles of mediæval history. You would be proud to know as much as they do. I don't think the subject is taught in England at all, but by the time I have had my men for two years they will scare you out of your wits by their familiarity with English affairs.

I have no news for you except that my mother has amused herself by falling down stairs and spraining her ankle. It is a pretty severe shock for a person of her age, and she is likely to be kept on her back for six weeks or more. But I hope she will get over it all right. There is always more or less danger of future stiffness in such cases, but I think she will get all straight again by the time summer comes.

1 *March.* This blessed letter has been waiting an interminable time for its quietus. I have been to New York in the interval, and besides a public dinner there, have been concocting our new attack on the men of Erie in the next number of my *Review.* They have now found out that I wrote the *Westminster* article, and New York will soon be too hot for me. Cyrus Field was after me, but I did not see him though he called before I was out of bed. Libel suits are looming ahead. There is going to be a very lively scrimmage in which some one will be hurt. We are in dead earnest on our side and our trains are laid far and near. Pray that we may not go under!

Yours have arrived — the two Reviews and the letter of the tenth. I think your last article the best thing you have done. It shows progress. The training is good, and I hope you will go on. Your batch of news-items is astounding. Let us hope that Miner Hervey will be happy with her Pussy! Also that Augusta will enjoy a Pussy of her own! But I am sorry for the Warrens. Their course shows that the affair must have been very outrageous, and I am not sure that any adult — male or female — is under any obligation to live with a father who behaves like his Lordship. That he is mad is no excuse among a nation of madmen. You should have gone in for ——. Her troubles will improve her.

My mother is coming on, but cannot yet put her foot to the ground. My work lasts till July and begins again October first. While it continues I cannot leave Cambridge except for a day now and then. Come over and join the University.

To Charles Milnes Gaskell

HARVARD COLLEGE, 27 March, 1871.

Nothing from you since I last wrote! Nor have I anything in particular to write about. By the time your next letter arrives, however, I shall perhaps have this despatch ready to go, so I shall begin now and look to hear from you before I get very far, at my present rate of letter-writing.

My labors are drawing to a close for this year. I have brought my youths so far that I can now see the end. My heavy reading is pretty much finished. My April number of the *N. A. R.* will be out on the 30th and my work on it is over. So I am ready to enjoy the Spring and to grumble that I have not enough to do. The fact is, I like being overworked. There is a pleasing excitement in having to lecture tomorrow on a period of history which I have not even heard of till today. I like to read three or four volumes of an evening, and to leave as many more unread, which are absolutely essential to the least knowledge of the subject. How long the excitement will last, I can't say. Probably not more than another year, after which I shall be bored.

In my reading I have only picked up one book which I can recommend to you, and I am only surprised that I did not tumble over it while I was mousing about in England, or that Palgrave did not call my attention to it when I was reading Fergusson and Ruskin. This book is a translation of Viollet le Duc's [1] essay on military architecture in the middle ages. It will give you, if you have not read it, a new interest in architecture and will start you on your travels again with a new object of interest. The original, I believe, is in Viollet le Duc's *Dictionary of Architecture*, and is or may be difficult to get at, but the translation, which is published by Parker, contains all the original illustrations.

I wish I had a good historical collection of cathedrals in photograph.

[1] Eugène Emmanuel Viollet le Duc (1817-1879).

My trouble here is in getting this sort of illustration. You can imagine me giving lectures on mediæval architecture, cribbed bodily out of Fergusson and Viollet le Duc. Precious lucky it is that Palgrave isn't here to snub me for my intolerable impudence. If he could hear me massacre the principles of historical art, he would brandish my ancestral tomahawk over my head and brain me where I sit.

Nothing very lively has turned up since I last wrote. My mother is hobbling about again and will gradually recover her ankle, I suppose, though it will be long before it is quite strong again. Otherwise my family retains its Bostonian stupidity. I go into town nearly every day to dine with them, and come out again after dinner. As for society I am still a barbarian. I have not seen the inside of a house, nor have I even suggested attachment to any young woman. The conversation I hear at home is of the mildest description; nothing more serious than the flabbiest local gossip. Empires are smashed and it is quite true that *impavidum ferient ruinae*, we don't care a cuss.

The next morning. Ho! a letter from you. You walk into my door, or rather through it, arm in arm with Mrs. Sturgis, and naturally I lay myself out for no end of gossip. What do you say to the Harcourt-Ives marriage?[1] And what odds that we don't live to call Mrs. Ives-Vernon-Harcourt "Your Ladyship"? Or perhaps I should say, to hear her footmen address her in that manner? And what better purpose could the lamented Ives, the husband of three weeks, put his money to, than to help support your bloated aristocracy? For my own part, I like the match. To external view Harcourt, I must say, has more the appearance of a murderer and gallows-bird than I should like in a husband, but internally I am confident he is a cleanly sepulchre.

The book has not yet arrived, but I await its coming with impatience. Shall I write a notice of it for the *New York Nation*? Perhaps I will try. At any rate I shall read it with peculiar interest. As for Mr. Horner, I will be as civil to him as my professional or professorial labors permit. Palgrave has not written to me for an age. I want some more bronzes and drawings. Mine have already *poséd* me here as a protector of the fine arts. Please tell F. T. P. for the love of God not to forget me. My reputation rests on him. I have the lowest opinion of you for letting Miss Maggy escape you, but such is human frailty. As for the Baronet, I have just written to him. I hope he won't do himself up with the season.

[1] Sir William George Granville Venables Vernon Harcourt (1827–1904), married, December 2, 1876, Elizabeth, widow of J. P. Ives and daughter of John Lothrop Motley.

How about your visit to us? I am so tied down, between professing and editing as to have no time really free, unless it is July and August, which are abominably hot. You ought to come over and pass a winter with us. Will Everett will be gracious to you. I think him a nuisance, but we have not yet been inside each other's threshold.

The book has just arrived — very fine. I see it is not published. So I suppose you object to publicity. *Quelle luxe!*

To Charles Milnes Gaskell

HARVARD COLLEGE, 18 April, 1871.

Yours of the 3d arrived today. For once I step up promptly, which is due to the fact that today is Monday and that Monday evening is Faculty meeting, when I am obliged to attend some three hours to business discussions, and occupy my time in writing letters. This is the fearfullest bore I have to undergo, and I mitigate it as I best may.

Yours is full of items, to which I have little enough by way of answer. I rather hope you will accept your education, because I think education a good thing for its own sake. To be sure I should lose your visit, but I am now so tied down that your visit would not be half the satisfaction I expected from it. Moreover I shall probably have to run over to Europe for a couple of months a year hence, in order to do some mediæval work in France and Germany. You might perhaps take a run with me on the continent. I shall not be able to get to England before the end of the season, in any case, so that you can do no better, unless you remain quietly at Wenlock, which I confess is better than any travelling at midsummer. In this way, only your visit to us would be lost, or rather, postponed, and I don't think America will run away at present. It will wait till you are ready to come, and in my opinion improves by age.

I would much like a notice of Labouchère's book,[1] which decidedly requires it. I don't know what can be said about it that would have any intrinsic value of its own, but if there is any concealed meaning or secret history to be brought out of its pages, I would like to show it up. Labouchère shows his peculiarities, I suppose, enough to lay him open to gentle roasting. I see the book about, but read nothing this side of 1400. By the bye, I wish I knew your friend Green better. He is a swell I believe on my line, and he might be useful to me now, for I suppose he knows all that is doing in his branch. As it is, I am all be-

---

[1] *Diary of the Besieged Resident in Paris. Reprinted from the "Daily News,"* by Henry Labouchère. The notice appeared in the *North American Review,* July, 1871.

hindhand in the gossip of my trade. I would like, too, to know Stubbs, at Oxford, who seems to be a first-rate man and modest withal. One of my objects in going over next year is to talk with these gentlemen, and meanwhile I read them solemnly. Who does the Church-work for the *Saturday*? I suppose you know your confrères.

You trouble me about poor Mrs. Sankey. But Wenlock is just antique enough for small-pox. I suppose the monks used to have it, and left it in a cup-board. Modern people ought to feel it as quite a favor to have a good old-fashioned disease in an old-fashioned way.

Your aunt's book makes a curious impression on my mind. How she worried her poor head with Kant and Fichte and Schlegel, and how it only made her more melancholy. I never met with so curious an instance of a fine feminine nature turned into pursuits so utterly uncongenial. The more of her letters I read, the more regret I feel that a woman who had such qualities should have found no more congenial a life than the one she led. One can't read a page of her letters without seeing that she had not and never could have had any real sympathy with philosophy and equally little appreciation of philosophic method. The distinction between her nature and that of a philosopher, is radical. The latter delights in studying phenomena, whether of his own mind or of matter, with absolute indifference to the results. His business is to reason about life, thought, the soul, and truth, as though he were reasoning about phosphates and square roots; and to a mind fairly weary of self, there is a marvellous relief and positive delight in getting down to the hard pan of science. He never stops to ask what the result of a theory or demonstration is to be on his own relations to God or to life. His pleasure is to work as though he were a small God and immortal and possibly omniscient.

Now your aunt with all her love for speculation shrank from this sort of pure science by a feminine instinct which I think was much to her credit. And her experience is another evidence to me, if I wanted another, that it is worse than useless for women to study philosophy. The result is to waste the best feminine material, and to make very poor philosophers. Your aunt's strong point continued to be sympathy, not science, just as much as though she had never read a German book, and her happiness would have consisted in a family and children, just as your mother's did. As it was, her mind only fed on itself and was neither happy nor altogether free from morbid self-reflections which always come from isolation in society, as I know to my cost.

I hope you will find out for me something about May Sturgis's lover. Robert ought to know him, if he is a Guardsman. The way you blasted Britishers are marrying Americans is awful, but I hope it isn't true that the youthful Campbell in New York is engaged to Mrs. Paran Stevens's daughter. In that case the Queen, Elizabeth Duchess etc. and Mrs. Paran would form an interesting group of mammas-in-law.

To Carl Schurz

HARVARD COLLEGE, 25 April, [1871.]

MY DEAR SIR, — I have received yours of the 21st and perfectly understand your difficulty. On the whole, however, looking at the matter in as large a way as I can, I am inclined to think that your own objects will be as much advanced by the paper I suggested, as by any other form of activity, and I therefore do not hesitate to urge you to draw it up. In order to relieve you of labor as much as possible, however, I will make a new proposition. If you will send me your rough draft, as elaborate as time will allow, or your notes and general directions, I will put the article into shape and return it to you in manuscript for correction and improvement. In this case I should have the manuscript or the notes at as early a day as possible. If this idea suits you, you will let me know when I may count on receiving the first instalment. Nothing would please me better than to write at your dictation at any time, but my own professional work is not a little exacting of time, and I want as much of yours as you can spare, to help me out.

What between the Force Bill, the Legal Tender Case, San Domingo, and Tammany, I see no constitutional government any longer possible. I hope you will show that I am mistaken, for the public is gravely in want of some such light.

To Carl Schurz

HARV: COLL: 16 May, 1871.

MY DEAR SIR, — Yours of the 11th has duly arrived. I much regret that you cannot carry out the project of reviewing the Session, especially because your other efforts have little or no effect upon the class of readers who can only be reached by more permanent influences than the daily press, while through the daily press anything you say to a small and cultivated audience would at once be spread everywhere over the country. A speech, especially a hustings speech, is the creature of a day. Once made, it is lost and forgotten in the files of a newspaper. The effect of it is weakened by the mere fact that it is a speech and that speeches are like newspaper leaders, ephemeral. The object I have at heart is to obtain from you a bit of political diagnosis that will last, and to which all our friends can appeal as applicable to the condition of the country now and at all times. Such a work is more difficult, but also much more permanent than most speeches. For the same reason I cannot help thinking it much more necessary, especially at a time when we have hardly a man in political life who has the knowledge and the ability to make a respectable generalisation.

I am therefore very unwilling to abandon my purpose, and I still hope that you may find the necessary time. Would it be of any use if I offered to wait till the 15th June before filling the space?

As for the Treaty, I can understand that it is troublesome. It appears to me to be less advantageous to us than the Johnson treaty. But I favored that and I favor this. Of all the crazy acts our friend Sumner ever did, and they are many, I think his speech on that occasion the maddest. How he is going to escape from it now, I am curious to see. If he resists the treaty and fails, he is done for. If he resists and succeeds, he will break himself down here, I think. If he accedes and votes for the treaty, Grant drags him in triumph at his chariot-wheels, as Sumner would say. I trust our friends will not be drawn too far by Sumner, though I foresee that the success of the English treaty will be a long step to the administration towards carrying San Domingo too.

I am very truly yours.

To Charles Milnes Gaskell

HARVARD COLLEGE, 22 May, '71.

Here is summer come again, with the thermometer up above 80° and a new drought, yet I go grinding on in the dust and heat with as much regularity as ever, and have another month of it before me with no prospect of getting away till after the first of July. The worst of it is, however, that I don't know what to do after I am free, and look forward with anything but confidence to the prospect of enjoying myself during my vacation. I must certainly go away to some new pasture, but where it will be I can't say; probably *un peu partout*. Meanwhile I only wish I were on the water again, with Europe before me, and proof-sheets a long way behind.

Have I written since receiving yours announcing your acceptance of the burdens of office? I think not! At any rate I am glad you have so decided. It can hardly do you any harm, and I fancy the habit of steady application is a good one to get, though to people of our habits of life, any habit that is useful is extremely difficult to get, and the source of infinite misery in getting.

Pray give Mrs. Sankey my sympathy. I am very sorry for the poor woman, who began married happiness (supposing it to have been happiness) late in life, and is left alone early. I hope the girl will do well and console her.

I finished your book with much interest and a sad sort of pleasure. I am growing old. To contemplate a finished life depresses me. I try to kick back the advancing years, and to make my falling hairs stick into my head. I shun church-yards and groan when my liver reminds me that I have a body. Had I never met your aunt I should have read her letters with a cooler judgment.

I found but two misprints in the volume; one (p. 274) Charlottenberg for burg; the other (p. 277) Rosenlani, for Rosenlaui. If these are all, you may congratulate yourself. I who do little now except correct proofs, find that everything escapes me. I have long since despaired of approaching accuracy.

Hurry up Labouchère! I want him as soon as possible and would send him to the printer now if I had him here. Thank the Lord, my summer work is now taking shape and I can see the end of it. But I have an awful job on hand for next year in the shape of a course of written lectures on mediæval history; a post-graduate course, as it is called. The labor is tremendous and the effect nil. But I do it because it is almost a part of my work. Poor Will Everett has delivered a course this year, and is said to have threatened to do something decisive when he found that his best lecture had for an audience only two women.

As for Will, I never see him. He threatens to write an article for me, but I shudder at the prospect of having to cut out all his fine writing. My own life is quiet as ever. My family has emigrated again to Quincy where they live merrily or at least soberly in their pig-stye, and I go over once or twice a week to see them. Here in Cambridge there is but one house at which I am intimate; that of Prof. Gurney,[1] Dean of the Faculty, and my predecessor as editor of the *North American*; he married a clever Bostonian of about my own age, and his house is an oasis in this wilderness. Otherwise I never enter a threshold except my own, and nowadays, what with heat, and the annual examinations next month, and a book of essays I am printing, and my July

---

[1] Ephraim Whitman Gurney (1829–1886), professor of history in Harvard University. He married Ellen, daughter of Robert W. Hooper.

Review, and my lectures, I don't much care to throw away time, though I can't resist long walks and spring-flowers. But the region about me is not Wenlock Edge.

I see that Mr. David Dudley Field is after me in the *Westminster* for April. I have smashed that gentleman so awfully in the *North American*, since he wrote his letter to the *Westminster*, that I pity the man and shall respond mildly. Indeed I should say nothing except that Chapman has written two letters about it. He is not accustomed to our way of carrying on controversies and I suppose he is impressed by Field. As for me I am so accustomed to being called a liar and a fool that I miss the excitement if a week or two passes in quiet. The fact is, we are getting ourselves into a tight place. One of these days I expect to find my head cracked by something harder than a newspaper leader.

I want to notice Palgrave's new volume, but hardly know what to say about it.[1] I can't find anything very poetical in it; nothing, I think, so good as his hymns. What do English critics say?

To Carl Schurz

HARV: COLL: 24 May, 1871.

MY DEAR SIR, — On reflection I am inclined to think that it would produce a better effect if you could give me the review for publication in October. Politically speaking, in view of the coming presidential question, you will speak then with more influence than now. Can you offer me a prospect of furnishing it by the middle of August? Your last letter seems to hold out such a hope, and I am so earnest in my wish to bring your influence to bear on our friends here that I can leave nothing untried in order to effect it. I am very truly yours.

To Charles Milnes Gaskell

CAMBRIDGE, 20 June, 1871.

Your letter and manuscript arrived some time ago, but I have been so busy finishing up the year's work, that I have not had a minute to spare. I was glad to hear that you had got into harness, not that I think your enjoyment of the work will be intense, but that, such as it is, it will drive you to new fields and make you think of new subjects. If you are half as bored as I am by thinking of the old ones, you will find the change agreeable.

[1] *Lyrical Poems.*

I write now from among a dozen of my boys who are indulging in the excitement of an "Annual," an institution not unlike your Cambridge "Little go," except that ours come every year. The poor wretches have to pass a week in the examination rooms and I am sorry to say that I am the object of unlimited cursing, owing to the fact that I intentionally gave them papers so difficult that half the youths could do very little with them. I very nearly had a rebellion, but I think they will find out that no one is hurt who doesn't deserve it. Mine is an "elective" department, and I have been obliged to drive the lazy men out of it, which can only be done by putting gentle pressure on them, the "gentleness" consisting in telling them that I will take away their degrees if they ever put themselves in my clutches again. It would be fun to send you some of my examination papers. My rule in making them up is to ask questions which I can't myself answer. It astounds me to see how some of my students answer questions which would play the deuce with me.

After this week I am, I hope, free again, and unless some unexpected difficulty arises I shall at once start on an expedition which will lead me for the next six weeks into paths unknown to European blokes. One of my friends [1] who is engaged on a government survey in the West has asked me to go with his party on an expedition down the cañon of the Green river, an upper branch of the Colorado. If you have a modern atlas you may find the district not far from Salt Lake and the Mormons, a hundred or two miles to the Southeast. Of course it is an absolute wilderness. We carry our camp with us and geologise, shoot, fish, or march, as occasion requires. I shall not be back within reach of mankind before the 1st September, and my next letter to you may perhaps be written from a country wilder than anything in Siberia.

At the same time I shall not feel sure of getting away until I am fairly a day's march from Fort Bridger. As luck will have it my sister has just been taken down with one of her terrible colds, and I may have to remain about here in order to travel with her, as she needs a change. Then, too, I have so many irons in the fire, so much printing going on, and correspondence to look to, that I never feel sure of my own time. My July *Review*, a very dull number, is just going through the press (you will appear in it in due course, not, I hope, to the increase of its dulness,) and my October number has got to be seen to. Meanwhile my lectures are all in arrears, and literally I have no time for reading or study. The last few weeks of the year are mere drudg-

[1] Clarence King (1842–1901).

ery. Luckily the weather has been cool and we have had rain, not before it was needed. Within three months of the time when I wrote you that the thermometer was at 10° below zero, the same thermometer at my window stood at 93° in the shade. I call that a fair range.

Now that my first year is fairly over I am racking my brains to decide whether I ought to consider it successful or not. As things go, and as professors run, I suppose I have done fairly, but from any absolute point of view I am still nowhere. Fortunately I came here with few illusions, and have had all the advantage I counted on. Whether Will Everett is equally self-satisfied I don't know. He has had more difficulties to meet, and two hundred very unruly boys to control. I am told that his eccentricities are growing on him; he is more than ever given to hysterics; but he has held his own better than I expected. As I have managed to get into the "inside ring," as Americans say, the small set of men who control the University, I have things my own way. Will is less lucky. He can't get things to suit him.

So you are fairly in Norfolk Street. I hope you find it swell. I hear nothing of the London season. Are there any new beauties? Are any of our friends going into the Tuileries when rebuilt? And are any Britishers coming over here? I have seen none for an age.

I like the notion of the Scinde rugs, but how to get them over I don't know.

To Charles Milnes Gaskell

Camp of U.S. Survey, 40th Parallel,
FORT BRIDGER, WYOMING TERRITORY,
Sunday, 13 August, 1871.

PECCAVI! I ought to have written long ago, but I have been wandering and letters did not come easy. Just now I am in luxury for a few days. It is a glorious morning and I have the camp all to myself; main camp, where I have a mattress and camp-bedstead, luxuries unknown to me for a month, and a table to myself. I seize the moment as it flies and serve it up for your benefit. Your letter of June 10th is before me. It came out here in my pocket. Since leaving home I have had no letters.

I knocked off editing and professing on the 8th of July and started by rail for this place. Four days and nights of steady travelling carried me as far as the town of Cheyenne where it is customary to go through a railway process called dining, and here I happened to tumble over the leader of the very party I was on my way to join. We had a half hour's consultation at the end of which he went east to New York and

I stopped in the middle of Laramie plain, four hundred miles short of my destination. You see there are twin parties under the same chief, one about four hundred miles from the other, and as the nearer one was just starting on an interesting trip, I decided to take a month with them before going on. So it was done. I went at once into camp and proceeded to spurn tents and sleep in my blankets under the sky, for the purpose of studying sunrises. I was given a big black mule, and got a little rifle which I hung at my saddle-bow. I put on a flannel shirt, leather breeches and big leggins, and having climbed to the top of the mule I proceeded to career across the country mostly at a slow walk, climb mountains where my hair stood on end, and shoot at rabbits and antelope with enthusiasm if not with success. The party was large, some twenty men or more, with wagons and a mule train, and during the month I was with them we did a good deal of country, marching several hundred miles and exploring many mountains and valleys. Certainly the life was hard and the living pretty poor, but we were at an elevation of from six to twelve thousand feet, the air was superb, and my appetite voracious. I was frequently twelve hours a day on the march, in very rough mountainous country, but I stood it well enough though once or twice a temperature of about 100° in the shade made me wish to find a little shade to get into. I did not kill any antelope nor see any elk or bear. The latter I should have passed by unnoticed. Nor was I cornered by rattle-snakes, though plenty of them were rambling about on their summer pleasure trips. Nor was I carried away with enthusiasm by the scenery, though some of it was very beautiful. It does not approach Switzerland. But I enjoyed the life and learned a deal about my own country, and forgot all the history I had studied for a year.

But this country was too civilised. There were no end of farms and cattle in it. I became tired of seeing them, so at last I packed up my blankets, took rail at Cheyenne and came on to this place, in an awful wilderness of alkali desert covered with low sage-brushes, without a spire of grass or a stick of timber except in the river courses. Here everything is wild enough to suit me, and I have no nearer neighbors than the Mormons, about one hundred and fifty miles to the westward. I am resting here luxuriously a few days before joining the party in the field and exploring the Uintah mountains to the south. I fish for trout, which I sometimes though rarely catch, and I sleep in a big tent all to myself. The days are hot still, but the nights make an average. There was about an inch of ice in the water-pails this morning. We are some seven thousand feet up, with snow mountains behind us, and, except the military post, hardly an inhabitant. From here I expect to go out on an excursion of a fortnight or three weeks during which I shall hear nothing of mankind unless I see a bear. There are no mails in those parts and no means of sending letters, so I take the last opportunity of giving you my news. Early in September, however, I must be at home again, and begin grinding for ten months more.

I doubt whether you would be enthusiastic about this existence, and I confess that for a permanence I see drawbacks in it. But here is a wild Indian — a Shoshone — just riding up to the door of my tent and silently watching me as I write, who probably likes the life. You ought to see the long-haired cuss and his get-up which is dirty enough and far from poetical. There are quantities about here, but luckily a friendly tribe. Among the Sioux I should not feel quite comfortable. I wear moccasins in camp of Indian make and they are rather comfortable though they spoil the shape of the feet. Out here the Indians are still a real thing and take scalps when they get a chance. The whites are afraid of them and hate them with a bitter hatred, but the government tries to maintain the peace and this post is for that purpose. On the whole I think I shall leave this country in possession of the noble savage without a pang. He may wander at will in the alkali for all me.

I see by the newspapers that my father is to go to Europe again. I don't know when nor for how long. This will not delight him greatly as he is very rusty, but I am glad of it. Have him down to Wenlock and rub him up. The publishers sent me a check for twelve dollars or thereabouts for your notice of Labouchère, and I send you an order on Baring for it. Sturgis will pay it. Send me more. I suppose there are letters from you at Quincy, but I shall not get them till my return.

To Charles Milnes Gaskell

HARVARD COLLEGE, CAMBRIDGE, MASS.,
2 October, '71.

I am mortified and disgusted to find myself abominably behindhand with my letters. I carry three of yours unanswered in my pocket habitually, which ought to flatter you, for I sit down about once a day to answer them, and as I read them over first, I am generally interrupted before I reach the end, and begin again afresh the day after, so that I am in a fair way of knowing your writings by heart. It is good of you to remember a banished cuss like me, for I have nothing in the way of news or gossip to write back except about myself. And as a topic I find myself a mistake. Colorado and Utah were, I confess, great, and in the character of Robin Hood or Alan A Dale I pleased myself better than usual. To stand on the top of a lofty mountain and survey proudly the surrounding country with a haughty smile at civilisation and a proud consciousness of my own savage freedom, was a gratifying experience. My last trip, in the Uintah mountains was a stunner. I never felt so lively and so much in the humor for enjoyment, and how I did eat! The venison melted away at the very glare of my voracious eyes. But how it was good! I have eaten much in many places, and as you may recollect I enjoyed an occasional meal last year in London, but by my faith I never in London or Paris, nor yet in Florence or Rome eat such meat as came from that fat buck which our Californian trapper brought into camp in the Uintahs. When it was eaten up and we could get no more, then and not till then did I turn my face eastward, but even then I cast many longing lingering looks behind. But the fact is, the season was waning and the morning frosts were becoming uncommon sharp. To sponge in a brook before sunrise with the thermometer at thirty and a bracing breeze blowing, tries the epidermis. I wanted to go out again, but duty called me home, and after all I do like luxury as a steady business, so I came, and here have I been these three weeks, editing reviews, making visits, and generally busier than a young cat, though I can't run after my own tail. My duties have all been neglected and my correspondence all postponed till I could get out here and settle down to work. Lo! here I am! this very morning I came from my father's halls at Quincy and began my valued instruction, feeling much more at home in my Mediæval chair than I did a year ago. The machine has therefore begun its daily revolutions and for nine months to come I am to go on feeding the engines. On the whole I am not unwilling. The work is not so nasty as some, and will be easier this year than last. I am in a hopeful state of mind and look forward with satisfaction upon life in general and my own in especial. About six months of winter will probably take this species of gaiety out of me pretty thoroughly, but why bother about unborn devils!

My book [1] is out, and you will receive a copy in due course. My own share in the volume is as you will see, less than half and nothing new. Of course the thing was not expected to make a noise, being a mere reprint, and although of course few works except possibly some few of

---

[1] *Chapters of Erie and other Essays.* Boston, 1871. It contained three papers by Charles Francis Adams, Jr.

Aristotle and Bacon contain anything to compare with the wisdom of this, still I am aware that it is vain to expect proper appreciation in this world and I have my doubts whether I shall fare much better in any other. You however will support me, I am sure, in my indifference to vulgar opinion.

I don't know much about my papa's movements. No more does anyone else. He expects to arrive in November, I believe, but all depends on future orders. I pity him if he is to pass a whole winter in Geneva. My mother and sister stay at home. My brother Brooks goes as private secretary. If you come across them, extend to them the sunshine of your favor. How long they are to stay I know not, but if they stay over the summer, it would not surprise me if my whole family were over there, and wandered about wildly. My own purpose still holds of going over next June, but I have so many projects in my head and am so much bothered by their interference with each other that I daren't count on anything. Just now the great burden on my mind is the necessity of taking a house and setting up an establishment of my own. My present style of life is too barbarous to endure. So I am looking about for a proper place, and am dreaming of furniture and upholstery. Add to this about a dozen other engrossing subjects of thought and you can conceive my state of mind. Will Everett, who usually has the most disturbed existence of any known mortal, is nothing to me.

I look eagerly for your future contributions to my *Review*. Make them pointed. Nothing but what is particularly sharp will attract attention in a Quarterly. Stand on your head and spit at some one. Give my love to the Baronet and his lady, and remember me to everyone, and write again soon.

To Charles Milnes Gaskell

HARVARD COLLEGE, 23 October, 1871.

I had already, my dear boy, spotted your second article in the *Saturday*, which I scented from afar, as I should probably have recognized the first if I had not passed it over. In return I have ordered my own volume to be forwarded to you; also to Sir F. Doyle and others. I did not send one to your father, because I thought it would bore him to think himself obliged to acknowledge it, but I will do so if you think it would give him the least pleasure.

We have had stray English (young) men about here; Darwins, Longleys, and others; the gentleman and beast mixed more or less in their composition, as usual. But I have seen little of them. They always hunt in couples and carry each other everywhere, a habit which is no doubt conducive to their own amusement, but hardly to the end of breaking the British shell and breathing American atmosphere. Moreover, one letter of introduction is not meant to carry two persons. I protest against any such abuse of mine. Don't allow yourself to be put upon by any fellow who brings a letter from me, and asks if he may bring his friend to Wenlock with him.

I am deep in German again, working up no end of history and thinking of naught besides. This is a working month, as is November too, but I suppose I shall start in society again in about six weeks. Meanwhile my father and younger brother are preparing for their cheerful November voyage. I suppose they will be in London about the 1st of December.

I am greatly exercised in my mind about next year. I mean to take a house and go to housekeeping, and I mean to go to Europe and do some travelling, and the Lord knows how I am to do both, to say nothing of my confounded *Review*, which is always claiming attention at unexpected moments. I had meant, too, to write some lectures, but have pretty nearly given that up as impossible. Three separate courses are all I can manage. Now if you would give me some of your spare time, I could use it to advantage. Lord! wouldn't I like a month in Germany at this moment. By the way, don't forget the book-notices!

This is only a note *passim*, which means *in passing*. Next time I will write you an essay.

To Charles Milnes Gaskell

CAMBRIDGE, 13 November, 1871.

Your brief and very private epistle of October 24th lies before me. The honor of a notice in the *Saturday* is greater than I could aspire to.[1] In fact I have thrown the volume on the world with a greater degree of cold-bloodedness than ten years ago I could have believed possible. Probably I am becoming hardened to seeing my name in the papers and satisfied with the amount of noise I have made in the world. Although I have to go frequently to my publishers I have never condescended to ask how the book sells. I am too swell for such trifles. As for the papers, they have, so far as I have seen them, been highly civil. But I should like to see an English notice. It would be a novel

[1] A notice of *Chapters of Erie*, in *Saturday Review*, December 30, 1871.

sensation. To be sure, when a man is so thoroughly aware of his own merits as I trust we are and always shall be, public applause or criticism must be equally indifferent to us, but still there is a certain prickly sensation about it still, which is not without elements of amusement.

My father and brother sail tomorrow. They will stay a week or two in London, and I give Brooks a note to you. He is a budding law-student, enthusiastic about your Courts and Judges. If you can put him in the way of seeing that Menagerie at Lincoln's Inn and Westminster, you will earn his eternal gratitude. I don't know whether he would like three guineas worth of the St. James's Club or not, but perhaps he might. They hang out at Maurigy's I believe.

As for me I am still hard at work and settled down to the discontented season, with a rough winter ahead. News is as scarce with me as ever. An occasional dinner, or an evening passed with some hospitable and sociable friend is the extent of my dissipation. Fearful German books are my daily bread, and my hair is several shades thinner than it was.

I close up in haste in order to catch the post.

To Charles Milnes Gaskell

HARVARD COLLEGE, 14 December, 1871.

It is an age since I have had a letter from you, and it is a good while since I have written. In fact I believe I have not sent you a line since my father sailed, a month ago. But then I have been worked like a dog, and have barely had time to get my face washed o'mornings. Just this time of year, and this time six months, are my toughest labors, and I have been awfully bothered of late, not by anything very distressing, but by the fact that my staff of contributors suddenly broke down and left me sprawling. Nothing but an unexpected boost from Frank Palgrave, and three weeks of extra work on my own account, have put me on my legs again.

After all, I have only the old story to tell. I have done nothing outside of the old bounds. Since my father went away, I have had to pass rather more time than usual at home. And one of my aunts died a fortnight since, which has for the moment rather put a damper on any wild gaiety. We have had a Russian Grand Duke here, but I kept out of his way, and he did not force me to leave my retirement. If work is the essential to happiness, I ought to be as happy as the angels of light, for I work like a badger.

Palgrave tells me that you have a Sicilian expedition before you, like a new Alcibiades, if he's the one. I congratulate you. Give my love to the lemons and olives. I would that I were going, for the winter promises a lively amount of exercise to the mercury, and I expect soon to see several feet of snow under my windows. I am beginning to hunger and thirst after a green thing of some kind, though the worst of the year is only coming.

By the way! Frank Lawley[1] has taken to puffing my *Review* violently, if not altogether learnedly, in the *Telegraph*. Have you set him up to it, or does it come from his own brilliant imagination? His last describes the *N. A. R.* as having "sprung into existence;" a fact which sounds queerly in this benighted land, where the periodical has been hitherto considered as a species of mediæval relic, handed down as a sacred trust from the times of our remotest ancestors. He selects, too, for especial praise, the two poorest articles in the number. Not that I object. It is a mere matter of taste, and so long as the trumpet is blown, it matters little what the tune is. I have had it reprinted in the papers here, as an excellent advertisement and spread as widely as possible.

21 *December*. Thank the Lord, I can now breathe free again! The Christmas holidays have practically begun; my January number is practically through the press; and I start for New York on the 27th with the agreeable purpose of having my teeth set in order for the year. The thermometer is down below zero again, and ears are freely frozen. Nice weather for a pleasure trip. I sometimes wonder how this intensely dry cold, or cold dry, will suit you when you pass that winter here which is to be the event of your future plans. Better, I suspect, than the awful heat of the summer.

Still no letter from you. I begin to wonder what has happened to you, especially as I hoped you would have sent me your notice of Lady Susan. A somewhat similar experiment is now on the stocks here, with a posthumous publication of Hawthorne's.[2] The first chapter has already appeared, and I think it evident enough why Hawthorne suppressed it.

Palgrave has given me a charming little article[3] for my coming *Review*, just the kind of thing I most wanted. I don't know what the public will say to it, as the public is not deeply trained on *Amourists* and *Lyrists*, but I have for once enjoyed the labor of proof-reading.

I see by our papers that my father has returned to London after his Geneva expedition. If you see him, give him my love, as I have not

---

[1] Francis Charles Lawley (1825-1901).   [2] The unfinished story *Septimius Felton*.
[3] Thomas Watson, the Poet, in the January *Review*.

yet found time to write. I had nothing to say, so it doesn't matter. As one of the overseers of this venerable institution, he may be interested to know that my part of it, which is all I know about, is all right.

The world is still quiet here. Society languishes. I dine about a good deal among friends. And have dodged a meeting of politicians at Washington. I see myself sinking into provincial professordom with anguish, and struggle bitterly, but it is fate, and *Dieu dispose*!

Glance at my notice of Freeman's *Historical Essays* in my next number, if you see it. I think I have caught him out very cleverly, but I would like to know what you say.

To Charles Milnes Gaskell

HARVARD COLLEGE, 22 January, 1872.

I believe I have not yet answered your letter of December 8. At Christmas I went away to New York for ten days, and the trip completely demoralised me. I have lived from hand to mouth ever since, much disgusted with the daily duties of life, and despairing of getting back to any regular course of existence. Since my father's absence I am obliged to live almost entirely in Boston with my mother and sister, and to come out here every day to my work. Of course I am drawn a good deal into society and the consequence is that I never can find time to do anything. If this goes on, I might as well give up pretending to teach, for I shall disgrace myself to my scholars.

Thanks for your laudable efforts in respect to my book. I see they have produced a flattering notice in the *Saturday*, and I suppose that the death of my friend Fisk[1] will be of a certain value to it. At the same time I never expect to see that remarkable volume appreciated at its true value which is of course enormous. How can it be appreciated in an age which is so degraded as ours? Posterity no doubt will print it uniform with Bacon and Montaigne. I only hope posterity will not oblige me to re-read it in a future world.

Of course I shall be glad to print anything that John Warren will send me, and I hope you are going to come to my rescue too, though I have heard nothing of your promised notice of Edward Denison.[2]

Poor Lady William! she had what I call an unfair lot in life and I hope future generations will invent some method of making things

---

[1] James Fisk.

[2] *Letters and other Writings of the late Edward Denison, M.P. for Newark.* Edited by Sir Baldwyn Leighton. *North American Review*, April, 1872.

smoother for women. She must have suffered most from the idea of leaving her daughter alone in the world. Do you ever see John Hervey now? I am always expecting to hear that he is married. He is just the man for domesticity.

If you are like me, you will find general society a trifle monotonous. On making my first appearance at a great ball here the other night, I was bewildered. Fourteen years ago or thereabouts, I left the same people doing the same things, and now I found it necessary to recall features through all the fat and wrinkled mask that fourteen years had stuck on them. It was worse than Hamlet's skull. Where be your jibes now? They gibbered, it is true, but I felt as though I had two legs in the grave and they had come to insult me. This is one reason why I adore new acquaintances. They don't insult me by associations.

Not that I find society unpleasant here. The women especially are bright, pretty, and terribly well-bred. But one is too well known in such a place as this. I am sure that every idiocy I ever committed as a boy, is better remembered here than I remember it myself. I shudder to think that we can't impose on each other. Elsewhere a thin veil is always spread between one's inner life and the outer world, but among one's school-friends one's very soul seems to shiver in nakedness. I wish to the Lord I were wasting life in Italy with my father. To be sure, however, the first quarter of the year is always my discontented season when life seems most nearly rubbish.

Give my love to everyone and tell Robert that I hold him dear. As for Palgrave I do not know whether I owe him a letter or he me.

To Charles Milnes Gaskell

CAMBRIDGE, 8 February, 1872.

I had barely put your or rather my last to you in the post, when one arrived from you of the 7th January, and now I have your note of the 13th, with the *Saturday* adjoined. Your puff of my poor work is judicious and handsome, better than anything else I have seen on it. As for the *Pall Mall*, its man has got the wrong book, and reviewed a little publication of my brother's in 1869.[1] I never saw a stupider performance. He has evolved title and author out of his own imagination or memory. However, it probably answers an equally good purpose as an advertisement, and as for the book itself, it is now an old story and must float the best way it can. I have not yet received your notice of Denison, but expect it daily.

[1] *A Chapter of Erie*. By James [sic] F. Adams, Jr., in *Pall Mall Gazette*, January 10, 1872.

From a retired and dignified Professor I have come out again as a social butterfly and waste most of my time at balls where I no longer dance, and in calls where I have no business to be. I still have a contemptible weakness for women's society and blush at the follies I commit. Only last Saturday I made a sensation by giving a luncheon in my rooms here, at which I had the principal beauty of the season and three other buds, with my sister to preside; a party of eleven, and awfully fashionable and larky. They came out in the middle of a fearful snowstorm, and I administered a mellifluous mixture known as champagne cocktails to the young women before sitting down to lunch. There was a matron to do respectability who had known twenty summers and was married a few months since. They made an uproarious noise and have destroyed forever my character for dignity in the College. I assure you, the young women in this land are lively to go, and the curious thing about it is that, so far as I know, these Boston girls are steady as you like. In this Arcadian society sexual passions seem to be abolished. Whether it is so or not, I can't say, but I suspect both men and women are cold, and love only with great refinement. How they ever reconcile themselves to the brutalities of marriage, I don't know.

Your people appear to be making no end of row about the Geneva Arbitration. I can't for the life of me understand what it's about, but I suppose we shall find out. Only I certainly can't compliment Mr. Gladstone on his diplomacy. A worse position than he puts himself into if he now breaks up the Commission, I can't conceive, but I suspect that he is driven into some folly or other by one of those utterly imaginary alarms which every now and then run away with us poor idiotic nations. I recommend him to have and to teach a little more quiet to the excitable Bull. The utter astonishment which has seized our people at the goings-on of the London press, is very ludicrous. They don't know what the deuce has got into England and are hesitating whether to laugh or swear.

I suppose my father must be in England at about this time, and not very well pleased at the course things have taken. I confess to being a little nervous myself, for a break-up of the Commission would throw our foreign affairs into the control of a pretty dangerous influence. And I want to go to Europe this year and be a swell.

I am about to dine with the President of the University to meet the Governor of the State![1] Hey! Sounds grand, I guess! And to go to a very select ball afterwards! *Quel bonheur d'être professeur!*

[1] William B. Washburn.

To Charles Milnes Gaskell

HARVARD COLLEGE, 26 March, 1872.

Your Roman epistle of the 5th inst. has just reached me. As you are on your wanderings, I rather doubt whether my letter written in a great hurry some four weeks since, with announcement of my engagement, has yet reached you. As the event became public here about the tenth, and created quite a lively sensation in this rural community, I suppose some one will have posted you up about it before you reach England.

Having now had a month to quiet down, I start on another letter to tell you all I did not tell you before. Imprimis and to begin with, the young woman calls herself Marian Hooper and belongs to a sort of clan, as all Bostonians do. Through her mother, who is not living, she is half Sturgis, and Russell Sturgis of the Barings is a fourth cousin or thereabouts. Socially the match is supposed to be unexceptionable. One of my congratulatory letters further describes my "fiancée" to me as "a charming blue." She is certainly not handsome; nor would she be quite called plain, I think. She is twenty-eight years old. She knows her own mind uncommon well. She does not talk *very* American. Her manners are quiet. She reads German — also Latin — also, I fear, a little Greek, but very little. She talks garrulously, but on the whole pretty sensibly. She is very open to instruction. *We* shall improve her. She dresses badly. She decidedly has humor and will appreciate *our* wit. She has enough money to be quite independent. She rules me as only American women rule men, and I cower before her. Lord! how she would lash me if she read the above description of her!

We sail for Liverpool on the 9th July, and are to be married a week or so before sailing. I expect to pass a fortnight or three weeks in England, before going to the continent. And we shall probably pass the season in London next year. I have work to do there and people to meet. We shall probably take a house, and a cook. Will you dine with us? cold roast mutton at seven.

Further information may be deferred till we meet, which will, I suppose, be soon. Of course I shall go to Geneva, if my people are there, but just now, no one knows what is to happen. I expect to see as much of you as you can reconcile yourself to, and if life will only run smooth, I trust to enjoy it still.

Of course all this new complication has thrown a deal more in the way of business onto me than I had before, and what with teaching, editing and marrying, I am a pretty well-occupied man. I have however found time to write to Robert and Palgrave, so that as you are still perambulating the continent, you will hardly have the satisfaction of giving them the first information of this news. Meanwhile, to stop my intended's mouth, who was worrying me to know if I had ever met a very attractive Englishwoman, I have given her your aunt's letters to read, with which she expresses herself greatly delighted and has insisted on making half her friends read the volume.

My father has taken passage for the 24th April and in case the Geneva business is not stopped, he and my mother and sister will be in England early in May. I shall be married very quietly, without any company outside our immediate families, about the 1st July in the country.

I am sorry that Italy seems so dull as your letter suggests. But things change awfully fast, and one is always in danger of being the last at the party. I don't want *you* to marry though. One of us surely should remain single for the good of all.

I must stop to make love.

To Charles Milnes Gaskell

HARVARD COLLEGE, 27 April, 1872.

Your letter from Venice is welcome as possible, though I was sorry that mine did not reach you so as to give you the earliest news. I gave yours to my young woman who was greatly pleased by it, and I hope you will soon find out that she is worthy of our society. I suppose I may now consider myself as comparatively settled and tolerably well able to decide whether I am likely to be contented with her or not. As yet I see no reason to doubt it. Life glides along very smoothly. If it weren't that I am such a sceptical bird, I should say that we two were a perfectly matched pair and that we were sure to paddle along through life with all the fine weather and sunshine there is in it, but perhaps when one is in the lover's stage, it is safest not to look at the future. Our plans still hold. We sail on the 9th July and shall be married in June. You are charming with your suggestions of Wenlock. What do you say to coming down from London on the 20th July and receiving us at Wenlock? As we shall be only a short time in England I am afraid that unless we meet you on our way to London, we may not get a good healthy chance at you. I suppose the Baronet and his wife couldn't be got to join the lark, though it would be fun to see them again there. I shall have been nearly a month married by that time, so that there will be no occasion for blushes, and my young woman is not at all an infant nor afraid of society.

Love, however, though an amusing pastime, and exciting withal, is by no means the only matter of concern to me. My family sailed three days ago for Liverpool and are by this time nearly a thousand miles away. It was quite time, for a new presidential canvass is beginning and all the elements of discontent with the present administration have agreed to meet at Cincinnati next week and strike hands. The gathering will be tremendous and my old political friends are deep in it. We do not know what will be done there, but as yet my father commands much the most powerful support for the nomination, and it is not improbable that all parties may combine on him. If so, there will be the most exasperating election that has taken place for years, and one of which it is impossible to guess the result. Of course I keep out of it with great care, and am glad to be off to Europe. But my father's absence is a perfect blessing and I groaned with pleasure when I saw him fairly on board the *Russia*.

Curiously enough I have found myself comparatively little disturbed by the infernal row which is going on. That one's father should be President is well enough, but it is as much as his life is worth, and I look with great equanimity upon the event of the choice falling on some other man. Meanwhile the fight makes a useful counter-irritant to love. My fiancée, like most women, is desperately ambitious and wants to be daughter-in-law to a President more than I want to be a President's son. So we are altogether in a chaotic condition.

I hope you did not take my remarks in my letter *qua* masculine want of sympathy quite in earnest, as you hint in your concluding paragraph. I do miss and regret your mother very much, but it was only relatively that I questioned masculine friendship. As for losing each other, I doubt it. My future wife is too fond of society to lose her husband's friends.

I am looking for another letter from you. Perhaps I will send you a young artist to teach.

To Charles Milnes Gaskell

BEVERLY FARMS, 30 May, [1872.]

Yours of May 13th came quickly. I handed it over to my fiancée who now appropriates my correspondence, and who is quite as appreciative a reader as I am. As I am now staying with her in her father's cottage on the seashore about twenty miles north of Boston, you will understand the date of this epistle.

What does old Holland mean? He wrote me an impertinent letter about the *N. A. R.* notice,[1] and he cackles like an antediluvian hen. I thought the notice a very complimentary one indeed to him, if not to his book, which is a *very* poor book, though I didn't say so. And now this octogenarian duffer flies into a passion and sputters like a child of five. He *says* he doesn't know who wrote it, but I believe he lies.

I have received £5 on your account for your notice of Denison, the whilk I will pay to you on our meeting. I give up the *N. A. R.* on my marriage. Whether I shall resume it or not on my return, I don't know.

As you saw my people in London, there is not much to tell you. My father narrowly escaped being the next President, but has come out of the fight very sound and strong, while his successful rival is likely to be not only disgraced but beaten. At least this is my present impression. If the Gods insist on making Mr. Greeley our President, I give up. Otherwise all is dark as Erebus. What the matter is with the Treaty no one will tell.

Meanwhile I am happy as ideal lovers should be, and my marriage is to come off four weeks from to-day, Thursday, June 29th. If things go right I shall land at Liverpool on July 20th. I highly approve of Viollet le Duc, by the bye, since you ask me. I meant to get him anyway, and it would be in the best keeping to have a copy from you. *We* had both read your article on this subject and had a proper appreciation of it. The idiosyncrasy of this neighborhood appears to be coffee-spoons. We shall have coffee-spoons enough to run the Grand Hotel. So don't let us have any spoons, please. We can do spooning enough without them.

I shall see you so soon now that I will not discuss your Parliamentary affairs till I can do it in talk. Both you and Robert are on my mind. I hope to see you both leading the House at the same time. I have no such ambition about Congress, but perhaps I may catch it from you.

Robert has written me a charming long letter, which, like the rest of my correspondence, was confiscated by my young woman and much pleased her. By the way, she desires me to say to you that she feels very warmly your kindness in asking us to Wenlock, and that all I said about her accomplishments is a lie. This, I lament to confess, is

---

[1] *Recollections of Past Life.* By Sir Henry Holland, Bart. The notice is in the *North American Review*, April, 1872.

the term she used. In fact it *is* rather droll to examine women's minds. They are a queer mixture of odds and ends, poorly mastered and utterly unconnected. But to a man they are perhaps all the more attractive on that account. My young female has a very active and quick mind and has run over many things, but she really knows nothing well, and laughs at the idea of being thought a blue. She commissions me to tell you that she would add a few lines to this letter, but unfortunately she is unable to spell. I think you will like her, not for beauty, for she is certainly not beautiful, and her features are much too prominent; but for intelligence and sympathy, which are what hold me. She is quite ready to like you indefinitely, and as she is fond of society and amusement, I do not fear her separating me from my friends.

Basta! you will after all be quite able to judge for yourself. I am at present learning to photograph, for we mean to go up the Nile next winter and I want to carry a photographic apparatus with me. Meanwhile if we come to Wenlock on our way up (and both of us will be most delighted to stop there) I want you to take us over to Maw's works to see what he is doing. Further, I shall get you to order me some clothes in London, as I want to be delayed there as short a time as possible. Finally I want to have you gravely consider whether we could find a little house in London at a reasonable rent, for the spring and summer of next year. If anything human could be discovered, within my means, I would like to go in for it. Robert writes that he means to be up also. I am not eager about society, but have work to do, and feel more at home in London than in any other great city.

To Henry Cabot Lodge

CAMBRIDGE, 2 June, 1872.

Your letter of May 16th arrived safely a few days since and gave me the pleasant sensation of thinking that I may after all have done some good at College; if you ever try it, you will know how very doubtful a teacher feels of his own success, and how much a bit of encouragement does for him. Poor Simpson's[1] death, too, seemed utterly disheartening. What is the use of training up the best human material only to die at the start!

[1] Michael Henry Simpson (H.U. 1871). He was one of the first scholars in his class, a young man of great ability, strong character both mentally and morally; much valued by Henry Adams whose course he had taken at Cambridge. He died of typhoid fever at Florence in the spring of 1872. — H. C. L.

There is only one way to look at life, and that is the practical way. Keep clear of mere sentiment whenever you have to decide a practical question. Sentiment is very attractive and I like it as well as most people, but nothing in the way of action is worth much which is not practically sound.

The question is whether the historico-literary line is practically worth following, not whether it will amuse or improve you. Can you make it *pay?* either in money, reputation, or any other solid value.

Now if you will think for a moment of the most respectable and respected products of our town of Boston, I think you will see at once that this profession does pay. No one has done better and won more in any business or pursuit, than has been acquired by men like Prescott, Motley, Frank Parkman, Bancroft, and so on in historical writing; none of them men of extraordinary gifts, or who would have been likely to do very much in the world if they had chosen differently. What they did can be done by others.

Further, there is a great opening here at this time. Boston is running dry of literary authorities. Any one who has the ability can enthrone himself here as a species of literary lion with ease, for there is no rival to contest the throne. With it, comes social dignity, European reputation, and a foreign mission to close.

To do it, requires patient study, long labor, and perseverance that knows no limit. The Germans have these qualities beyond all other races. Learn to appreciate and to use the German historical method, and your style can be elaborated at leisure. I should think you would do this here.

I shall be in London, I hope, on the 1st August, to be heard of at Barings'. If we are there together, we will have a dinner and talk it over. Remember me to your wife.

To Charles Milnes Gaskell

BEVERLY FARMS, 23 June, '72.

One more letter before I am swung off. Here I am, within four days of my execution, gay as a lark and looking forward with the greatest pleasure to seeing you again. I suppose my people told you what manner of ceremony I am to have. For once I am to carry out the idea of my most cherished prejudices, and have a wedding which is absolutely private. It is to be performed here in my bride's house, at noon. The clergyman is a very jolly young fellow of our set, intimate with me and my fiancée, and ready to do all we wish in the way of cutting down the service. Only brothers and sisters are to be present, eight in all, besides the papa, so that the whole party will be only ten or eleven. And I start off at once after the breakfast to go down to a little seaside place called Cotuit, where one of my future uncles has a country house which he has lent to us. Here we remain till we sail on the 9th. Of course nothing could be quieter than all this, and unless we were both of us persons of a certain age and understood to be bent on doing things as we please, we should not have so easy a time of it. Luckily for us, no one dares interfere. Relatives submit like lambs to being left at home, and we are treated beautifully by every one. When you know my young woman, you will understand why the world thinks we must be allowed to do what we think best. From having had no mother to take responsibility off her shoulders, she has grown up to look after herself and has a certain vein of personality which approaches eccentricity. This is very attractive to me, but then I am absurdly in love, and I won't guaranty your liking it. You must judge for yourself. You need not be afraid of her coming between me and my friends, for I believe she likes agreeable men as much as I do.

The world, for all that I know, may think it peculiar that I should calmly come down here and live with my fiancée for a month before our marriage. But my father-in-law,[1] who was educated as a physician and only gave up his profession because he was rich enough not to care for the income, is a sensible man in such matters, and a good deal of a slave to his two daughters, the elder of whom, a few years ago, married a great ally of mine, Professor Gurney, Dean of the University and my predecessor as editor of the *North American Review*. Among us we have a good deal our own way, and the Doctor interferes as little in his children's affairs as I can conceive possible....

I have not yet decided what hotel to go to in London. I wish there were a good one on one of the Parks, but Piccadilly is very noisy and Brook St. not much better, and as for Dover Street and Grafton, they are hopelessly gloomy.

You must write me a note to Liverpool to tell me whether you will be at Wenlock. I expect to arrive in Liverpool Friday night if we have a good passage; Saturday or even Sunday if the passage is bad. If we could get to Wenlock to pass Sunday with you, my wildest wish would be gratified. But this I hardly expect. You had better address your letter to the Adelphi (it is the Adelphi, is it not?) Hotel at Liverpool. If you can't be at Wenlock, I shall come up to London at once.

We are to have a pleasant party on the *Siberia*. My confrère, James

[1] Edward William Hooper.

Russell Lowell and his wife, and Professor Francis Parkman, our best American historian and a very agreeable man, are on board. We are all Professors and friends, and I hope we shall enjoy our voyage. I have taken two staterooms, on deck, with windows and every luxury that the effeminate Sybarite could desire.

As Robert wants to know about our wedding, you can impart this letter to him with my blessing. I fear I shall not see him in England this time if he is down at Scarborough, but I entertain affection for him all the same. Of course you will tell the rest of your family all they want to know about me, and give my tender regards to Major General Field Marshal Frank Doyle.

VII

A EUROPEAN YEAR

1872–1873

To Charles Milnes Gaskell

THOMAS'S HOTEL, August 1, 1872.

MY BELOVED C. G. M. G., — I scribble you a line late at night for fear of not having another chance before marching. We have had a very busy and so far a successful week. Your father sent for us to dine with him on Monday which we did, and he gave us a very excellent dinner, with the Stopford Brookes, Palgraves and Mr. C. Wynne. The latter by the way called at once. I have tried and hope to return it before leaving, but if I am unable to do it, will you tell him that I shall return it at once next Spring when I hope to find him in town. Palgrave being solitary, dined with me the next day. Everyone else is out of town. Your father goes tomorrow. We start on Saturday. We went down to Greenwich yesterday to dine and go to the Sturgis's at Leatherhead tomorrow. Hankey writes to ask me to Tunbridge, but I can't go! These are all our festivities. Of course I have been too busy to run after anyone but shopkeepers.

My wife didn't in the least know Lawrence's portrait of me, which pained your father much. The latter, by the way, looks very well and was particularly agreeable. We were on our way to call on him this afternoon when we met him in the street and took our leave.

No news known to me. Frank Doyle came to see us, and this evening sends me a wedding present which really touched me, for I had not supposed he would dream of such an act. Robert writes a charming letter from his palace by the sea, but without news. My family write pleasantly from Geneva, but also no news. In short, I am in London in August.

Purchases are all now made or in fair way, and I hope to be in Brussels on Sunday. Write to me to the Barings Bros. & Co., 8 Bishopsgate Street Within, for the present, or to Lombard Odier & Co., Geneva, if you don't write for a week or two.

To Charles Milnes Gaskell

BERNE, 29 August, 1872.

Many thanks for your letter which came to me the other day at Geneva where I was doing arbitration. After leaving England I went to Holland and came up the Rhine. At Bonn I received a letter announcing that the arbitration would probably be all over before I arrived unless I were quick about it. So I postponed Berlin and came straight up the Rhine, reaching Geneva just in time to see all there was to look at.

I suppose the results of the arbitration will be known to all mankind by the time this letter reaches you. So far as I can understand, the tribunal has condemned England to pay damages on three ships: the *Alabama*, the *Florida* and the *Shenandoah*. The amount of the actual money damages is not yet fixed. I rather imagine it will not much exceed three millions sterling. As for the legal value of the decisions, I know very little, but I believe the Court was unanimous in almost all its votes, and went by a majority of four to one on the rest.

You can tell better than I how the result is likely to be received in England. I think on the whole you get off cheaply, considering everything, and yet I am inclined to think that we have got nearly, though not quite, all we could lay any reasonable claim to. I am curious to see how my country people will feel about the result, and whether it will affect the Presidential election.

England was not happy in some ways. I think Cockburn[1] turned out rather poorly as a diplomate. His temper is so bad and his character if possible so much worse than his temper, that he played throughout into our hands. He browbeat his colleagues on the bench as if they were counsel in his own court, and got awfully snubbed for it, besides prejudicing his cause. I don't believe that as an actual matter of fact the result would have been different if a better man had been sent in his place, but I've no doubt that he made it much easier for the three arbitrators who were to decide, to go against him.

Sir Roundell[2] has had the gout badly and looks poorly. All the men, young and old, who have been here, have been tremendously worked and swear diabolically. Lady Laura[3] and her two daughters are the only ladies belonging to the British family here. She was very gracious and friendly with me and my wife, but the English had a nasty custom of all living and feeding together in a hotel, so that they can do no entertaining and appear horribly exclusive, which is another diplomatic blunder. What social influence there has been in the matter, has been on our side and its effects were visible enough, I thought, though

[1] Sir Alexander James Edmund Cockburn (1802–1880), lord chief justice of England, who represented the British Government at Geneva under the treaty of Washington.
[2] Sir Roundell Palmer, Earl of Selborne (1812–1895), of counsel for Great Britain.
[3] Lady Laura Waldegrave, daughter of William, eighth Earl Waldegrave.

of course not tangible. I doubt whether Cockburn has a single real friend here, British or foreign. Lord Tenterden[1] on the other hand is popular, and Lady Laura works hard.

Lord Houghton made his appearance of course, looking much as usual, only rather thinner and paler. He dined with us and talked as fast as ever, but seemed to have little to say. I don't think I succeeded in picking anything out of him, except a very funny story that Livingstone was living in the holy bonds of concubinage with the Queen of Ujiji and did not want to have it known, which was the reason why nothing was heard from him.

As I was coming from Basle a fortnight ago, who should enter the train and sit down by my side in mild unconsciousness, but his Lordship of Pollington! I did not at first recognise him, but on his drawing out a copy of the *Times* and a pair of scissors, and proceeding to cut out a leading article on his own election, I ventured to call him by his name and claim acquaintance. He was very gracious and rather madder than ever; so mad, in fact, as to put into my hands a bundle of newspaper extracts on his election, with which I beguiled an hour of time, and gained a very thorough conviction that he had made a terrible display of himself. He seemed rather pleased with himself and his career, and not a bit abashed about his blunders. Houghton told me that Childers[2] claimed to have been very forbearing in reading only one letter, for Polly had written him two more; and Poll himself remarked to me that if they wanted it, he could produce a letter he had written at the same time in an opposite sense, to the conservative whip! He seems to have only a very indistinct notion of what sanity is.

I am now on my way to Berlin where I hope to arrive as soon as the Emperors are gone, for it is useless to try to get in there next week. After this visit is over, I turn resolutely towards Italy and open my winter campaign. We have bought nothing as yet, and I will add that we have seen nothing that we could have bought without ruin. The prices are colossal. Every bit of wood is £20. But I am not anxious to buy things this year as I can do nothing with them. My address is the Barings in London. My wife sends all sorts of pleasant remembrances and encloses a note to forward.

[1] Charles Stuart Aubrey Abbott, third Lord Tenterden (1834–1882), who had assisted in preparing the case of Great Britain.
[2] Hugh Culling Eardley Childers (1827–1896).

To Charles Milnes Gaskell

FLORENCE, 5 November, 1872.

Except a short scrawl from you I have now heard nothing for an age. No one writes to me, and if it weren't that people occasionally write letters to my wife, I should think the world had cast me out. As I am now on the point of starting for the east, I am going to try whether I can send you a reminder of my existence first, especially as I am in despair of hearing from you without it. Robert owes me two letters, but I suppose he is excused from writing by the pressure of his Parliamentary duties. Give him my love.

I have quite forgotten where I last wrote from. Geneva or Berlin? At all events I have pranced over half Europe and have passed more than a month in Italy. At Berlin I had the luck to find our minister, Mr. Bancroft, who is a connection of my wife's and was extremely civil. I met Mommsen and Curtius at dinner at his house, and did the historians very satisfactorily. I succeeded easily in carrying out my other schemes there, and getting a small library of books which I carry about with me like a travelling menagerie. But Berlin was so disagreeable that we hurried away as soon as we could, and after a few days passed at Lucerne, crossed the St. Gotthard to Lugano where we stayed a week and then moved over to Cadenabbia. Then the rains began, and we were jovially amused. For a month it rained pretty much all the time. You have seen the newspapers and know what the results have been. The lake rose till I expected to be floated up to the top of Mt. Blanc like a modern Noah, but I stuck to Cadenabbia vigorously. What could one do? I wanted to go to Venice, but it seemed shameful to take Venice in such a season. We stayed a fortnight at Cadenabbia and then moved to Venice where we remained ten days, three of which were fine. Then we came on here, and the new moon seems to have brought better weather. It is clear and cold and Florence is very pretty.

In all my wanderings I have met scarcely anyone but a few Americans. At Venice indeed we met rather an attractive young couple with whom we became quite intimate, and on parting exchanged names. The youth called himself Lord Kingston; an impecunious Irish Earl, I suppose. With that exception we have seen only bores of the travelling Anglo-Saxon type. Florence is still empty and the swells are at their Villegiatura, but of course one always finds stray acquaintances enough at a place like this. We are not violent sightseers and take things easily, so that I really can't say whether the place has anything new in it, but as I have come to the conclusion that the effort of buying anything is too great for our weak minds, I have given up even looking into shops. The only thing I have done in that way has been to visit Hähnel in Dresden and order some bronzes.

We sail for Alexandria on the 15th and I hope to be fairly afloat for the winter by the first December. What is to come afterwards I do not know, and am utterly in the dark as to the time of our return to London. There is trouble in our house-arrangements for Boston, as our original plan seems likely to break down, which may oblige us to go home early. Or we may be slower than I calculated, on our journey northwards, for it is hard to get clear of Italy and Paris. Altogether I prefer to shut my eyes and trust to chance which is pretty sure to drift us to London sooner or later. But I am obliged to confess that the London house seems very vague.

My wife sends her fond regards. She is wrestling with clothes and thus far gets the worst of it. I am rejoiced to think that on the Nile one can go nearer the costume of our original parents. My love to all yours. Write soon.

To Henry Cabot Lodge

LUXOR, 2 January, 1873.

I received your letter of November 3d just as I was leaving Cairo, and as I have been busily reading myself, I delayed answering till I knew what I had to say. So far as I can see, you are acting on such good advice and working in such good company that I can add very little to your means of getting ahead. Perhaps to a critical eye, the field you have entered may seem rather wide. I doubt whether a man can profitably spread his reading over a very large range unless he has some definite object clearly fixed in his head. My wish is to lead you gradually up to your definite object, but what it must be will depend on the bent of your own tastes. I can only tell you the style of thing that seems to me best.

The first step seems to me to be to familiarise one's mind with thoroughly good work, to master the scientific method, and to adopt the rigid principle of subordinating everything to perfect thoroughness of study. I have therefore advised your learning German, because I think the German method so sound. I am glad you are reading Sohm.[1] But Sohm's work is on too large a scale to imitate. I would like to have you take up some of the smaller works, which have broken the way for

[1] Rudolph Sohm (1841-   ).

him. Read as most kin to your interests, von Maurer's *Einleitung*,[1] Thudichum's *Gau und Markverfassung*,[2] Brunner's *Entstehung der Schwurgerichte*.[3] Study these, not merely for their matter but as literary work. See how the men go at it, and then take an English work, Mayne if you like, or Freeman, and see how they reach their results. I do not mean to set up the Germans as exclusive models at all. But they have the great merit of a very high standard of knowledge. An ignorant, or a superficial work could hardly come from any distinguished German student. I can't say the same for other countries. Great as is Mr. Freeman's parade of knowledge, he has never written anything really solid, and Mr. — or rather Sir Henry — Mayne's book is precisely such a one as I like to give to students to admire and to criticise. I know of no writer who generalises more brilliantly. But everyone of his generalisations requires a lifetime of work to prove it.

I propose no more to the fellows who are kind enough to think my teaching worth their listening to — those of them I mean who take the thing in the spirit I offer it in — than to teach them how to do their work. The College chose to make me Professor of History — I don't know why, for I knew no more history than my neighbors. And it pitchforked me into mediæval history, of which I knew nothing. But it makes little difference what one teaches; the great thing is to train scholars for work, and for that purpose there is no better field than mediæval history to future historians. The mere wish to give a practical turn to my men has almost necessarily led me to give a strong legal bent to the study. Starting from this point, I found that at the outset the Family was the centre of early law. To study the Family therefore in its different relations, was the natural course to follow. From this point we must follow down the different lines of development. The organisation of the Family, the law of inheritance, of testaments, of land tenure, of evidence and legal procedure, the relations of the Family to the community, in its different forms of village, county and state, as well as many other parallel lines of study lay open before me and I have only to indicate them to true students whether of law or of history, and let them go to work and develop them. Of course I don't pretend to have mastered these subjects myself. No one has yet done so. But men like you and Ames[4] can win

---

[1] Georg Ludwig von Maurer (1790–1872), *Einleitung zur Geschichte der Mark-, Hof-, Dorf-, und Stadt-Verfassung.*

[2] Friedrich Wolfgang Karl Thudichum (1831–1881).

[3] Heinrich Brunner (1840–1915).   [4] James Barr Ames (1846–1910).

a reputation by following up any one line of investigation, and the occupation is as good as mathematics for the logical faculty, while it leads ultimately to all the nearer subjects of historical study.

Of course our own law and institutions are what we aim at, and we only take German institutions so far as they throw light on English affairs. I think you would do well to keep this in mind and to take some special line of work so soon as you have become tolerably acquainted with the general bearings of things. Of course you will choose whatever you think best suits your tastes. It does not follow that preliminary legal reading is to make you a historian of law, any more than preliminary grammar reading would result in making you a historian of philology. It matters very little what line you take provided you can catch the tail of an idea to develope with solid reasoning and thorough knowledge. America or Europe, our own century or prehistoric time, are all alike to the historian if he can only find out what men are and have been driving at, consciously or unconsciously. So much is this the case that I myself am now strongly impelled to write an Essay on Egyptian Law, for I have a sort of notion that I could draw out of that queer subject some rather surprising deductions, perhaps I could fix a legal landmark in history, but I have too much on my hands and must let the Cheopses and the Ramses alone.

The Nile is not a bad place for study, and I have run through a library of books here. I want to write to Ames, but until I have got some sort of order into my ideas I shall have nothing to say. But I would be very glad to have a line from him to know how he gets on and whether he has struck any new vein. There are many points I want to discuss with him but they will keep. Meanwhile pray continue to write to me how things are going with you and at Cambridge. Send for a copy of Schmid's *Gesetze der Angel-Sachsen*; it may be useful to you next year, as I want to go hard to early English law. I have got to learn to read Anglo-Saxon, but that is too much to expect from you or anyone not obliged to do it.

Pray give my best regards to your wife.

To Charles Milnes Gaskell

CAIRO, 4 March, 1873.

On going to my banker's yesterday morning for the first time since my return down the river, your telegram of February 19th was put into my hand. The bankers had not been willing to forward it so that apparently I should never have known its existence unless I had happened to go in person to the office. It astonished and perplexed me not a little, but I sent an answer off at once, and it was not until some hours afterwards that my wife, happening to take up a copy of the *Pall Mall Budget*, was instantly struck by the announcement of your father's death.

I cannot say that I was surprised at this sudden blow, for, although your last letter gave no reason to expect it at once, I had long thought your father's health in a very poor condition and his mode of life very far from likely to strengthen it. But though not surprised, and indeed partly prepared for it by the telegram, I felt as much shocked as one must feel at the death of a person whom I not only respected so much as I did your father, but to whom I was under so many personal obligations. After some fifteen years of knocking about the world, in every city and nearly every wilderness between Salt Lake City and the Second Cataract of the Nile, I believe I must frankly confess that among all my experience with human nature, the uniform and extraordinary kindness shown me by your father and mother has been the rarest and the most amiable phenomenon, and that, too, in a world the kindness and cordiality of which is a matter of never-ending surprise to me. To go back to London now, is becoming a rather doubtful pleasure. I tremble to think what it may become in five years more at the same rate. But you and I are extraordinarily unlucky, for our friendship seems to revel in gravestones and terrors. Few persons, I fancy, whose intimacy was only ten years old, could look back over so much common association in death and trial. I shall miss your father greatly. His judgment, his wit, his large experience among men and knowledge of books, were just what were peculiarly valuable and agreeable to me, and I have so few friends of the kind that I can ill afford the loss. I am anxious too to hear from you the particulars of his last illness, for I fear it may have come rather severely on you, and even without it, you would have quite care enough thrown on you by the necessity of attending to the details of business consequent on his death. I suppose these alone will tie you down to England this Spring, otherwise I should hope that you might have run over to the continent for a time so that we could have seen you in Italy or in Paris.

And now to reply to your very kind offer of your house. We could not accept it, tempting as it was, under any circumstances, for the plain and, as I think, final reason that nothing ought to justify anyone, especially married people, in quartering themselves on their friends. I would not do it with my own brothers or father. One cannot be too delicate in such matters. The man who ventures to make an indefinite settlement on a friend, deserves to lose that friend, and in fact is running very rapidly towards that result, at least when he brings wife and maid with him. This alone was enough to decide me at once so far as accepting your offer was concerned. Perhaps other reasons would have been equally decisive if there had been any possibility of hesitating on this one. For our own movements are too uncertain and my objects too special to let me make a hotel of your house in the way you so kindly offer. All this, however, was quite apart from any connection with your mourning, which, when I learned it, only confirmed my opinion.

What we shall in fact end in doing, is still a mystery to me. I do not yet know when I shall get to Paris, and it is pretty certain that I shall not get off with less than a month there, for my wife's wardrobe is in the condition which you can imagine after some nine months of steady traveling. We quit Egypt on the tenth, at the same time, I suppose, with this letter, so that I shall be a thousand miles nearer you by the time you receive it. My address is to the Barings in London.

As for news of our past movements, I will give you all I can. From Thebes we sailed up to Assouan where we arrived about the seventh or eighth of January, and then went up the cataract to Philae where we lay a week. Philae is the spot on earth where winter is a pleasure. But there was a confounded sanitary cordon established just above Philae to keep off the cholera, and we were not allowed to go further. So we lay at the island of Philae a week, and I photographed and wandered about the hills, and lazed, and found the place perfect. Just as we were about to turn, however, and come down the river, Lord Harrowby's [1] boats arrived, and such a pressure was put on the Khedive to let them pass, that the cordon was raised and we at once darted off into Nubia. If I ever come to the Nile again, I shall go as far as Thebes on a steamer or by rail, and pass the winter in Nubia. The climate and the scenery are far away the most perfect we have met, though you would find it rather warm, perhaps, seeing that the thermometer keeps pretty steadily in the seventies and eighties except when it occasionally rises into the nineties. We were a week going up to Aboo Simbel, which is forty miles below the second cataract. I enclose you my photograph of Aboo Simbel, not because it is the best I have taken, but because it is the grandest subject, and none of the professional photographs for sale here have at all caught its spirit. I should not say this if I thought the credit of selecting the point of

[1] Dudley Ryder, second Earl of Harrowby (1798-1882).

view belonged to me, but as this in fact belongs to a Mr. Ward, an American friend of ours with bankerial and artistic tastes, whose dahabieh has been our companion, I do not hesitate to say that my photograph is worth half a dozen of any I have yet met. The colossus is sixty odd feet high. As a sight, there is nothing I have seen in the world equal to this temple, and on coming to it, I sat down mildly and forgave my poor old Ramses all his architectural sins in Egypt.

Then we turned our faces homewards. One sails up the Nile, but one floats down, and though floating is a rather ignominious process, it is quicker than sailing. My boat was a poor sailer, but tremendous on floating, and accordingly we had everything our own way. I agree that for one week, from Luxor to Sioot [Assiût], the weather was diabolic. The wind blew a tempest every day, making me quite seasick, and shutting us up in our cabins. My thermometer fell from 92° at noon on the 15th February, to 40° at sunrise on the 19th, and though the change did us no harm, it was not pleasant to feel to one who hates being "braced," as I do. We reached Cairo again on the evening of March 2d, along with three or four other boats which had been more or less companions on the river, among others the excellent but amusing Monteiths, with their Holy Virgin on one mast and their St. Joseph on the other, their Father Scully with his brogue, and their homeopathic pills. So the next morning everybody came up to Shepheard's Hotel, and began a week of Cairo together.

Egypt, therefore, is, so far as we are concerned, a thing of the past, and I can consider myself a judge in matters concerning it. It is a horribly expensive place. I think I should estimate my expenses, including purchases, at something like two hundred pounds a month, for the four months of our absence from Europe; a sum that Gifford Palgrave would laugh at, but then Gifford Palgrave knows the East, and probably is not so squeamish as women are. On the other hand, I never knew before what could be done in the way of luxury in traveling. And the journey alone is well worth the money.

Since I began this letter I have received a package which went up to Luxor and followed me down again. It contained your two notes, which were the proper precursors of the telegram. It was immensely kind of you to think of me in all your cares, and I can't tell you how much I feel about it. If I don't accept your offer of unlimited hospitality, it isn't because I don't appreciate the kindness, but simply because I am sure you will get more thorough satisfaction out of us if you are not loaded down with the care of our caravan. We hope to tumble across the channel early in May, and we must sail for home about the 20th July, unless Heaven furnishes us a house in Boston without consulting us. So I count on two clear months in England, and a very lively campaign among the shops.

Talking of shops, we have had great fun here among them. Shopping in Cairo is a pursuit by itself. But this is over, and we start tomorrow for Alexandria and Brindisi.

8 March.

NAPLES, 15 March. Here we are all right, after a pleasant voyage. His awkward Grace the Duke of Sutherland[1] was on board, very friendly, and showed me this morning a private telegram just received announcing Gladstone's resignation. I hope you will now get your chance.

To Charles Milnes Gaskell

HOTEL COSTANZI, ROME,
28 March, 1873.

Your letter of the 23d has just arrived and I can't help sitting down to answer it directly. I am sorry for more than one reason not to be in London. Perhaps we could brighten up your low hours a little if we were there. You must find your position solitary as well as melancholy and laborious. I am not at all surprised to hear that you are not well, and in that particular we can sympathise with you, if not in low spirits. The Italian air has let our systems down by the run, and both my wife and I are a great deal nearer a Roman fever than I like to confess. I have called in a doctor and shut off every amusement, so that we are now avowed invalids, confined to our rooms until further orders. And I hope that as I have lost no time, we may escape with the fright. Your neuralgia comes also, I suppose, from a low system. The main difference is that our spirits are gay enough, as we have nothing except indisposition to depress them. Meanwhile the weather is delightful but awfully relaxing, and I long to see the Alps.

Your offer about Norfolk Street is so tempting that I sincerely trust the house is already let, so that I could not take it if I would. To do so would amount simply to taking five or six hundred pounds out of your pocket, in order that I might have a few weeks' lodging, which is hardly my idea of social propriety. Furthermore I can only hope to reach London by the 1st May, and if we are going to break down here the Lord only knows what is before us. So I stick to my opinion about

[1] George Granville Leverson-Gower (1786–1861).

the house and think very modest lodgings will have to serve our turn after all. But we fully appreciate the offer, and if my original plan had not broken down as to the duration of our English visit, I think I should go to your agent and make a quiet offer for the house behind your back. As it is, I think we shall be hardly up to keeping house for two months only.

I am glad you have taken up your father's papers. They should be well worth arranging and publishing within the limits of a not too ponderous book which it would be a pleasure to write, especially as the author would necessarily be brought into contact with a good many prominent persons now living. But perhaps it is still too early to think of such a work.

We have been busy with very different ideas. Naples, barring malaria, was very fascinating — much more so to me than Rome. My wife and I had travelled about Europe last year and turned up our noses rather superciliously at the contents of the shops. But at Naples we came to grief, and were shipwrecked on Greek terra-cottas to begin with, after which we fell into no end of other temptations. I confess that the terra-cotta vases struck me as gems in their way, and quite equal to other Greek work. I will show you ours when we reach London and if your soul is not poisoned by envy, I shall be sorry for it. But we were foolish enough to let an exquisite little porcelain figure, Capo di Monte of Carlo Terzo, escape us, and some Abruzzi porcelain which was very nice. The rest of our plunder, such as it is, you will see. We are on the highroad to ruin. But then I find nothing in Rome worth getting, as we do not go deeply into Castellani's work. Indeed I went the other day to the studio of Fortuni,[1] the youthful Spaniard whose pictures are supposed to have created a new inspiration in Spanish art and to recall the glories of Murillo or Lord knows who. As usual I found that the pictures were not exactly my notion of good painting, but on the other hand Fortuni's studio is famous even among Roman studios, since the young vaurien, for whose pictures on the easels Goupil offered £18,000 not long since, works when he will, but buys without limit. So his studio is crammed with artistic rubbish which I examined without finding much to envy and with no wish to exchange. Possibly, however, Deck may do for me in Paris. Him I dread. But nothing I have yet seen in shops seems to me so well worth buying as a good specimen of Greek terra-cotta. Wait till you see mine.

The truth is that we had a charming week at Naples which was almost — not quite — worth a Naples fever. We burrowed in the

[1] Mariano Fortuny y Carbo (1839-1874).

depths of the place with a good healthy energy of enjoyment such as grows only under the sun of the East. We brought with us from Nubia a little of the real color of life, which fades soon enough in our watery and washy sitz-baths of countries, but is worth feeling while it lasts. I am sorry to have come to the end of it so soon, for Rome this afternoon looks as though I could get a deal of life out of it — not like the gay, warm life of Cairo — but still rich and full. But my legs are weak and between malaria and calomel very little except good spirits is left me to travel on.

You ask about our plans. My present plan is to be in Paris between the 15th April and May 1st and if that time is enough for my wife's requirements there, we shall at once scuttle over to London and begin on our work there; which work consists for me in trying to understand some early English history, and for my wife in furnishing her house. If you can get over to Paris, do come. We will ransack all the bric-à-brac shops and buy nothing unless we like it, and we will dine at all the restaurants and you shall order the dinner. If you dread milliners too much, come over about the 25th when we shall have solved most of the millinerial problems, and try only a week of it. After which we can go back together.

I don't know who is in Rome, and have made no calls, but people as usual are very civil and I suppose we should find ourselves in the ordinary sluiceway of dinners if we could go to them. But the Doctor forbids, and we dine today on chicken-broth and beef-steak on the fourth story of Costanzi's. The fare is mild and the company limited to a tête-à-tête, but you remember the dinner of herbs. This sounds perhaps a little spoony, but is only so in appearance. In reality, you know, there are no herbs. The doctor forbids them. So the comparison fails.

Give my love to Robert. Poor boy! I'm sorry his parliamentary duties wear on him so heavily that he can't write me a line, but I can feel for him. Also my love to all yours. We hope to see them all soon. My wife says my spirits need cheering and you must come over to help her do it.

To Charles Milnes Gaskell

HÔTEL DE LA PLACE DU PALAIS ROYAL,
PARIS, 22 April, 1873.

I have been here a week and very busy, hoping every day to be able to fix the time of our coming to London and write you accordingly.

But as yet I can only say that I hope to get away within a fortnight. We shall probably go to Maurigy's for a few days until we can find apartments.

Yours of the 8th and Robert's of the 12th arrived here in a happy condition. But you are both of you becoming so political that I expect to be obliged to drop you. I am sorry. I am always sorry to cut a friend. But what can I do! To eat with one's knife, to be made a co-respondent, or to talk politics, are acts or misfortunes which society cannot overlook. I should only compromise myself without helping you, if I consented to appear indifferent on a matter which is properly considered to lie at the foundation of sociology.

From Robert's concluding message, I infer that you won't be able to come over here, as we hoped, this week. Till now the labors of shopping have absorbed our souls, but I hope that as time passes we shall open our souls to other influences. I expect my brother Charles in a few days, on his way to Vienna as commissioner.[1] If you can get here for a few days next week, we will end our Paris campaign with a lark. That is, we will try to find some communard plunder, and we will hope to get a good dinner, a thing I have not yet seen. But as I shall be declared bankrupt the week after, I must make the most of my time.

I shall see you so soon that it is sheer extravagance to write a long letter. So, if you don't come over here, I shall not write again till I send you a note to say that we have arrived. We are both well, and I hope you will take care of your own insides. You have had a severe strain and ought to be very careful.

To Charles Milnes Gaskell

Paris, 23 April, 1873.

A couple of hours after sending my note of yesterday to the post, I received yours of Sunday announcing the failing condition of your uncle. I hope you will at least stay no longer in Yorkshire. The country and solitude is a poor place for you, and I hope at any rate to find you in London next week. I am sorry you cannot be here a little while with us. A week passed in bookshops, studios and porcelain fabrics would amuse you, I think. But we will try to employ your leisure in London, for we have much to buy there. My wife sends her warmest regards, and we both look forward to seeing you in ten days or so. I do not offer sympathy for your uncle's death, because in this case I think the

[1] To the international exposition of that year.

living need more thought, and all this trouble and care might well try the strongest of us.

To Charles Milnes Gaskell

PARIS, 8 May, 1873.

Your note of the 5th has just arrived and has thrown us into a state of great perplexity. You remember the old play with the questionable title of "She would and she wouldn't." We were in that condition at the time we received your former letter. Now, however, "She would" has carried the day. In spite of all feelings of delicacy, pecuniary and otherwise, we are strongly disposed to accept your offer. Indeed it is so kind that we hardly know how to refuse it. At the same time, I feel as though it were a very questionable liberty we are taking, and my wife insists that as a first condition, you shall keep your own rooms and be our guest, coming and going as you please, with a plate always laid for you at our table.

We hope to reach London Saturday evening. Send me a note to Maurigy's to say what steps are to be taken in case the house is still vacant. If it has been let in the interval, you need not worry yourself in the least. We shall only go on with our search for apartments as we meant to do on our arrival.

I hardly know how to thank you enough for the kindness of your offer, and my wife insists that I do not say half what she wants me to say about it. If I don't, it is only because I don't know how.

Your uncle is a wonderful old man. I would like to congratulate him on his recovery.

And of course my wife adds her warmest regards.

Everett has, we are told, really had a success in his new rôle.

To Charles Milnes Gaskell

16 SUFFOLK STREET, PALL MALL,
Sunday, 11 May, 1873.

Here we are, but we seem to be about the only people who have not left town for Sunday. The Palgraves are rambling. So are the Cunliffes. You are away. Even Mrs. Russell Sturgis is absent. I am tired of front doorsteps.

I wrote to you at Wenlock, but I suppose you did not get my letter, that we were very strongly inclined to accept your offer about the house. On arriving here and looking about us a little, we still feel as though you were offering us something we could hardly refuse. At the same time I do not know where to look for servants, and we both rather tremble at the idea of facing a scratch household, with no one in it we could trust. We are waiting to talk with you about it and see what can be done.

The hotels are just crammed. We got temporary accommodations here, in default of Maurigy's. This afternoon we applied at Claridge's, Fenton's, Thomas's, the St. James's, Batt's, Fleming's, the Brunswick — no rooms! We were reduced at last to taking the second floor of No. 4 Albemarle Street, a dependance of the Albemarle Hotel. You will find us there.

I am anxious to see you and to find you all right. My wife sends her best regards. Weren't we glad, though, to get out of Paris!

To Charles Milnes Gaskell

NORFOLK STREET, Friday, [1873].

MY DEAR CARLO,

How you must shiver at Wenlock! This wind goes down one's throat like a rat-tail file.

How comforting it is to be comfortable again and how we do say so to ourselves fifty times a day!

We are *lancés* and although as yet we have no footman, we have a cook, and we have china and linen and have been prancing about town all the afternoon in a brougham, leaving cards — mostly on Americans, however, as Madame is proud and will call on no British female who doesn't intimate a wish to that effect.

The Baronet, somewhat exhausted and overwhelmed by the official burdens attached to his eminent position, managed however to stop here "on his way to the 'Ouse" (the quotation is not from him) and was as agreeable as ever. Milady called, but was sent away by your majestic, whose intelligence is, as you say, on only a limited scale of developement. She left, however, a card for dinner on the 7th. The 'Ouse, I presume, is in the way of short invitations. It is very kind in her Ladyship and I am sorry that three visits have now been exchanged without a meeting.

Palgrave came in one morning and talked an hour, but not much to say. He too is very busy. Everybody is so busy that I want to be busy too, but can't, as I have too many things to do, and nobody to tell about it.

Gunn being defunct, I sent for a woman from Douglas's to wash

Madame's hair yesterday. In the evening Douglas sent up some trifles ordered, with the bill, as was proper, plus a note saying that he "would be 'appy to open an account if I would furnish a 'satisfactory reference.'" Cheeky, isn't it? I paid his shop a short visit this morning, returned the articles, and intimated that as I could unhappily furnish no reference that I could expect to prove satisfactory, he need not trouble himself to send the woman again.

You had better come back to town. In this weather life is not safe in the country, and this house is just perfect. We are putting away all your valuables for fear of breakage. If you want to break some, you must hurry.

Madame says she is going to write to you, and meanwhile sends enthusiastic messages.

To Charles Milnes Gaskell

28 NORFOLK STREET, PARK LANE,
Monday, [1873].

I have been to Agnew and Foster, and seen the pictures and discussed the question. After the best examination I could give, I decided that if they were my pictures I should sell them without reserve. You can't hang them, and you don't want them in your attics. I am no judge of market-values, as you know, and have only one principle to go on, which is to make up my mind whether or no I want a given thing at all. If you think that you could do anything with the Bouchers or the Cignani or the Padovanino, if they came back onto your hands, I would put a reserve on them. But I assume that you can't; otherwise you would not have sent them up for sale. So I told Foster that he had better sell them without reserve unless he heard from you to the contrary.

At the same time, Foster says that they will probably sell for very little. So if you prefer keeping the pictures to throwing them away, you had better write or telegraph to him tomorrow. He evidently thinks that it is mere chance whether anyone of them fetches five pounds or fifty. If he is right, a reserve of twenty or thirty pounds on each of the best pictures, would be likely to bring them in, and you can write or telegraph to that effect, tomorrow.

I understand Palgrave to agree with me about it. But I will talk with him again.

He and your sister dine with us today, with Woolner, Stopford Brooke, and J. R. Lowell, who is staying with us until made a Doctor at Oxford.

Our visit is now half over and I have only seen you a couple of hours. I've not seen very much more of Robert, but he, poor lad, is a politician. His hay cold has begun.

If you don't come soon, you will only catch us on the steamer at Liverpool.

To Charles Milnes Gaskell

28 NORFOLK STREET, PARK LANE,
Saturday, [1873].

Your telegram has just arrived. I am glad to be sure of your safe arrival, and doubly glad because you would have found today very trying in London. It is sultry.

Unless you feel distinctly better, I certainly would not risk coming up this week. Much as we want you, and much as we shall miss you if you do not come, I do not like the responsibility of bringing you here. At the same time, it does not matter in the least what you write on Monday. Your seat at table will be kept for you, and the house will be absolutely empty in any case, and you can occupy any room or all the rooms as you like, without notice of any kind. We shall make our arrangements as though you were coming, and shall expect you down to the last minute.

We went to Lady Margaret's last night, and took Lowell there, at Lady Margaret's request. It was pleasant; small, and lively. Her Ladyship quite beaming. But what on earth makes the Alderson tribe so uncommon grouty!

Goodbye! I am just starting for Greenwich with Woolner.

To Charles Milnes Gaskell

28 NORFOLK STREET, PARK LANE,
May 18th, [1873].

I'm afraid if I don't write to the "fairy godfather" that the palace will turn into a pumpkin and Mrs. Sows into a rat. So before the clock strikes twelve I shall sign my name to this. We are very happy tho' Sir R. Cunliffe, who is green with envy at our prosperity, vows that we have reached the summit and must descend steadily the hill of fortune. We enjoy being swells if only for ten weeks and find our pasture very green and sweet. Shall I break in a man servant for you? Heuy has been civil and done nicely, poor Mrs. Sows who is bright and smart remarks, "I think Mum he's a little *vacant;*" but he has worked faithfully and we are most grateful for your kindness in leaving him here and shall hope for his safe arrival at Wenlock tomorrow. Many thanks for your kind Whitsuntide invitation. We accept with great pleasure and will consult with the Cunliffes as to time, etc., — but do make us a visit first and see how nice it is — everyone who comes to call says how pretty the drawing room is. The Lord Chancellor and Dean Stanley smoke in the *drawing room* and borrow your choicest books and dog's-ear them! *You* must do something about it. I cannot consent to take the new off that new brougham. I shall hire an old one. Living in Park Lane is quite enough gorgeousness but thank you all the same. Hoping to hear that you are better and to see you soon, Very cordially yours,

M. ADAMS.

To Charles Milnes Gaskell

28 NORFOLK STREET, PARK LANE,
[1873].

Don't worry about the rent, and above all don't attach my traps, though I confess the temptation would be great if you saw them. We are cramming your house with rugs, linen, glass, silver, porcelain, and bric-à-brac, and hope to be able to swear their value down to a trifle as all second-hand.

I suppose you mean me to bring a servant to the Abbey. I shall not bring a maid. But will bring a cook if you want one. Mine is fond of beer, but cooks well, and I hope she will have the patience to keep partially sober for six weeks.

Nothing new. We go out very little, hardly at all, but have a few lunches and dinners on hand. Nothing much. I have made a few calls, but not many. Everybody is very gracious, uncommonly so, but we are doing too much shopping to do many calls.

I said rather a clever thing about you the other day. Somebody asked what you were doing and I replied I was afraid you were mildoing. But it would have been better if you were only working up your Polit. Econ.

Have you read Mrs. Grote's life of Mr. Grote? Awfully cheeky book to write, but quite the drollest thing going. Also Monographs? I lunched with the Houghtons yesterday. Monsignor Capel was the party baited for the occasion and appeared very well. I sat next pretty Lady Desart and found an old acquaintance in her. Lady Houghton at table, awfully frail. You will be amused to hear that Mrs. Bouverie-

Pusey has found us out and been, oh, but very civil. Pusey is a lively party, but not so bad after all. They want us to come to Pusey.

I have done nothing about the brougham because I understood you to mean to come up before I took it to try it. We job one now from the next street and do very well.

I have given your message to Mrs. Sow. As yet no one has called.

Write to tell me if there is anything we can bring down. Why not commission me to bring the Shah?

To Charles Milnes Gaskell

28 NORFOLK STREET, PARK LANE,
Sunday Evening, [May 29? 1873].

I have been to see Robert and her Ladyship and tried to combine our plans, rather a difficult matter, as we have accepted an invitation to Oxford together and a number of other engagements crowd us not a little. The scheme arranged is as follows:

We are to be at Oxford on Monday, June third [eighth?], to be shown about by Mr. Charles Clifford. As I shall have to see some people there, I shall have to go down earlier, either Friday or Saturday, and devote a few days to exploring. We then come on to you, Monday evening or Tuesday morning, and remain till Saturday if you like.

Does this please you? If not, notify us to that effect. I send this note down by your man, whom I part with regretfully, as I find the task of replacing even his limited capacity, a labor exceeding my modest powers. But I trust to make a temporary arrangement to-morrow.

We go on swimmingly. I could wish that winter would be somewhat less cordial in welcoming us, but thanks to you we are sheltered from its liveliest embraces. Palgrave has not yet dined here. When he comes, I will tell him to bring his pipe for your sake.

There is no news, except Miss Tolemache's wedding. I have been running about all the week, making calls, and the usual roll of dinners is beginning. You should see Robert's wedding present — a teapot — but a love! Come up this week and look at us. As specimens we are entertaining and harmless.

Forgive this dull letter; the truth is we have had some country-people to dinner and I am *very* sleepy.

The cook is good. Try her![1]

---

[1] From Oxford, on a Sunday in June, he wrote to Gaskell: "We dine this evening with Jowett. Lunch with Montague Bernard. I have inspected the early English MSS. in the Bodleian, and

To Charles Milnes Gaskell

28 Norfolk Street, Park Lane,
Tuesday Evening, [June, 1873].

Here we are back in town, and uncommon glad to have such a "back" to come to. I think the house looks more attractive than ever, on returning to it.

We have been very busy at Oxford and were received there uncommon well. I saw all the men I expected to see — Stubbs,[1] Burrows,[2] etc. — and a number I did not expect to see — as Sir H. Mayne [3] and Laing of Corpus.[4] Jowett [5] dined us. Montague Bernard [6] lunched us. Laing tead us. Clifford did all three. Robarts [7] appeared for half an hour on his way, as usual, from one planet to another. In short we had a very successful visit, ending last night with a carouse at All Souls.

This morning Robert started west and soon afterwards we struck eastward, sorry to part company, but more sorry for your anxiety and trouble. At the same time, as I don't know Seymour, even he will forgive my saying that I am glad it is his broken bones which prevent our party, since it might just as well have been yours.

The vicar delivered the letters all right. Please thank him for his kindness.

Somehow or other you must manage to be here on the 27th, our wedding-day, when we shall have a family dinner. It is understood that you must pass at least a week here in the course of the month, and I hope it will be an indefinite stay when we once get you.

My wife sends her kindest regards and wishes you to know that her new cook, as warranted by Lady Rich, is to come next Saturday, after which she expects you as soon as may be.

By the way, I meant to tell you that we called on Mrs. Charles Roundell on her return, and dined with her at the Selbornes' before leaving town. I may be mistaken, but I thought her a trifle Roun-

mean to attack Stubbs tomorrow. But as yet I find little to make me tremble for my own University in the way of men. The English Universities run too much into money and social distinctions. The spirit is better in ours."

[1] William Stubbs (1825–1901), regius professor of history at Oxford University.

[2] Montague Burrows (1819–1905), Chichele professor of modern history.

[3] Henry James Sumner Maine (1822–1888).

[4] Robert Laing, lecturer in law and modern history.

[5] Benjamin Jowett (1817–1893), regius professor of Greek.

[6] Montague Bernard (1820–1882), first holder of a chair of international law and diplomacy at Oxford.

[7] Charles Henry Robarts, librarian.

delled, statisticiannified, or infected with the ponderosity of manner which characterises her spouse. But she was nervous, perhaps.

To Charles Milnes Gaskell

28 NORFOLK STREET, PARK LANE,
Monday, [June, 1873].

Glad to hear that your invalid is coming on right, and that you will come up to town shortly.

Many thanks for your offer of grapes and pines for the 27th. Bring your man by all means, but I don't know what I should do with Hill. As for your brougham, I've not ventured to do anything about it till you came up.

We will discuss the Thornes scheme when you come. Unless something special turns up, I see no reason why we mayn't have our little lark there.

We dined with Robert on Saturday; very pleasant dinner. The Palgraves; Leo Seymour and his wife; Ralph Palmer; Maggy Warren. The latter very agreeable. Last night a family dinner with Lord Romilly. Tonight a dinner *chez nous*. Tomorrow night a dinner at the Bouverie-Puseys'! Wednesday, at the W. E. Forsters'. But by the end of next week all our imaginable friends must have dined us, and then we can begin a few little dinners at home.

My brother Charles is now with us for a couple of days.

Send along your book. I want to see it. Just now I am rather out of the newspaper line, but we will rub up our friends.

I understand the programme to be that you are to come up here in about ten days or a fortnight, and stay till the 7th, when you suggest taking us with you for a run down to Thornes. I will keep my eye on our invitations so as to make things straight.

To Henry Cabot Lodge

LONDON, 11 June, 1873.

Your letter, which I am surprised to find bears the remote date of Feby. 13th, has been an unconscionable time in my pocket, and if an excuse is necessary, I can only put it on the ground of incessant occupation. It reached me somewhere in Italy, and has come with me to London, without ever finding a spare hour of repose. Even here, though we are keeping house and living as regularly as we expect to do in Boston, I find it hard to provide for correspondence.

That you found yourself wallowing in a boundless ocean of history, I can very well imagine. One has a very helpless feeling the first time one plunges into a new existence, no matter what the medium is. Law is as bad as anything else; art should be worse, for art is lower as now practised, than any other profession, and I recollect well that I have found by turn the same sense of helplessness in entering on each new stage of life, both in Europe and at home. Patience is the salvation of men at all such emergencies. I have never found that fail to pull me triumphantly through.

At the same time I do not deny that I thought, and still think you were trying to cover too wide a field of mere fact. For the present I was much less inclined to trouble myself about the amount you learned than about the method you were learning. I have, no doubt, more respect for knowledge, even where knowledge is useless and worthless, than for mere style, even where style is good; but unless one learns beforehand to be logically accurate and habitually thorough, mere knowledge is worth very little. At best it never can be more than relative ignorance, at least in the study of history. So I wanted you only to read a few specimen books, not large ones either, which would give you an idea of historical methods, and I wanted you to learn to use Latin and German with facility, and I suggested Anglo-Saxon, which I am studying myself and which is quite amusing. Nor do I see the necessity for your working very laboriously even at this. You will work hard enough one of these days if you ever get interested in the study; if not, what does it matter? The question for you is not by any means whether you can do a great deal, but whether that which you choose to do, be it much or little, shall be done perfectly, so as to give you credit worth your having.

I am inclined to think that you will find you have reached a point a good deal in advance of most historians—so called — in spite of your discouragement, and that your time has not been ill-spent. At least I hope you could now take up the ordinary historical work of commerce, such as passes for sound even among educated people, and feel at once that it is not what you call history; that it shows neither knowledge nor critical faculty. And I hope too that you are far enough ahead to be able to decipher an Anglo-Saxon or a Latin diploma, or to track a given idea through the labyrinths of law and literature. A year is well spent if it only gets your mind into a properly receptive condition — to use the language of our newspapers.

But I suppose you are pestered by the question which bothers us all when we are at the beginning of a career, especially if, as is usually the case with Americans, we are a little inclined to thinking too much about ourselves. I mean the question of whether a given line of occupation is going to pay, whether you are really ever going to make your scheme work. I am not going to enter into any argument in favor of the course you selected. I don't care to take such a responsibility as that of giving advice to anyone on a matter which involves the occupation of a life-time. If you have seriously become so far discouraged as to think of changing your line of work, and if you have found any other profession or occupation which satisfies you, I have nothing to say against it. But if, in spite of all discouragements you still think a literary life best suited for you, then I hope that we may begin work next term with rather a more definite aim and better defined instruments.

I have this year been engaged in investigating and accumulating notes upon some points of early German law, out of which I expect in time to make a pamphlet or small book. If you like, I will put these notes in your hands next term, and we will proceed to work the subject up together. As I am so much occupied by teaching, I stand much in need of such help. And I think you will find that the work will exercise your powers and claim no little interest. But it will also require your best knowledge of German, French, Latin and Anglo-Saxon, and I hope you will have more facility than I have, at least in the Latin and Saxon.

If you incline to keep on, then, your path is clear. Don't tell any one the proposal I make, for I am not yet ready to talk about a book. But polish up your languages and on the 1st October, if you are ready to begin, establish yourself in my rooms at Wadsworth.

I shall return to America about August 1st. My wife sends her best regards to yours, as I do mine.[1]

---

[1] "John Bright dined with me yesterday and I asked Robert to meet him. We had much gay talk. But John is much changed. Lord Houghton's note is not to be decyphered." — To Gaskell, July 14, 1873.

VIII

BEVERLY FARMS AND BOSTON

1873–1877

To Charles Milnes Gaskell

BEVERLY FARMS, 12 August, 1873.

Here we are again, bobbing up on this side the ocean, like a couple of enthusiastic soap-bubbles, and telling interested groups of friends how we saw the anthropophagi and men whose heads did grow upon their shoulders. The first sense of relief at getting home is prodigious. To be quite sure that the ocean is behind us; to look out over it when one gets up in the morning, and to damn its eyes, with a sweet sense of security, at least for some years, against its insults, is one of the most rapturous pleasures my existence has ever known. Life seems all a garden of flowers — mixed with cabbages — when the ocean is behind one. For the eighth time, writhing in the miseries of sea-sickness, I have sworn by all the saints and all the devils, that nothing, no, *nothing*, shall ever induce me to go on the ocean again. We shall see....

I think we both suffered more from sea-sickness than we naturally should have done if our fellow travellers had been less obnoxious, but the set of bag-men, German Jews, vulgar Americans, and dull Englishmen on board, was inconceivable to anyone who had not an absolute faith in the vileness of human nature. That one hundred and fifty such people could have come together on an ocean steamer is a fact which damns the human race. The usual types were all represented. There was the invariable English Earl going out to kill buffalo; his name was Dunraven and his Countess [1] was with him. He looked like a billiard-marker, but I did not exchange a syllable with him and I don't know what his virtues are, though I obtained a high opinion of them from the fact that it was said he introduced and managed the Opéra Comique at London. Then there were two young English officers also going out to kill buffalo, and whiling away their time by flirting with the New York young woman who is always on board. Then there was the youth fresh from Christ Church, who also wants to kill a buffalo. Poor buffalo! Then there was Dr. Kingsley, the "Earl and the Doctor," going out with the Dunravens, the only

[1] Sir Windham Thomas Wyndham-Quin, fourth Earl of Dunraven (1841–1926), married Florence Elizabeth Kerr.

agreeable man on board. Then there were one hundred or more commercial travellers, German Jews, Scotchmen, Englishmen, Americans, and what not.

I hear no news here that will interest you, unless it is that Will Everett has been made Professor,[1] which will, I hope, please him and improve his temper. My own work will begin in about six weeks, and I am likely this year to have my hands full. But as I am now pretty solidly fixed in my seat, I don't feel very much worried about success....[2]

To Charles Milnes Gaskell

26 October, 1873.

My lectures began about the 1st October and I was obliged to pass at least three days in the week without seeing my modest establishment between nine in the morning and seven at night.... Of course, the greater part of my time has to be passed at Cambridge, where I have more to do than ever and am put to my trumps to hold my own against my hundred students, who think me too severe; a reputation I am glad to foster. I find twelve hours a week in the lecture room too severe for my taste, and therefore, I have one common ground with my students. Happily, I have not yet been obliged to take the *North American* on my shoulders again, so that at any rate I have one worry the less. And as my old students are some of them still hanging about and wanting occupation, I have managed to harness a few of them to the wheels in such a way as to relieve me of a good deal of the work....

To Charles Milnes Gaskell

BOSTON, 8 December, 1873.

I am sorry enough to find you beginning again with another list of deaths. Poor Sidney Doyle! And yet even her death is only far down in list of those I have heard since leaving England. I can't say that Lord Lyveden's affected me much, for I never clung passionately to that old gentleman. But I shall miss Strzelecki if I ever get back to London; and Tom Baring is a real loss, especially as I have no ties to the younger Barings. Then my genial and cordial friend Benzon is gone,

[1] He became assistant professor of Latin in 1873 and held the appointment for four years.
[2] October 20, Adams moved into 91 Marlborough Street, Boston.

and another house closed. Britishers are common as grass about our streets, but they are rarely valuable in a social point of view. Since Brodrick carried his cadaverosity and his nerves back to England, we have had one Rutson here, ex-private Secretary to Bruce in the Home Office. He brought us letters from Lady Rich and Julia Roundell, and has been going the rounds of Boston houses for the last three weeks. He has dined and breakfasted with us once or twice and proposes to go on to Washington and return later to our bosoms. Another Britisher named Rothary is threatening a visit presently. He is at Washington, I believe, on government business. I met him once at Henry Reeve's at dinner. There is also a young Acland scampering about, but I know him not. I confess to liking to see the English furriner; he amuses us and brings us news from other parts of America which one never gets here except through them. Boston is very well up in all things European, but it is no place for American news. So if any Britishers apply to you, send them along. We are not likely to be bored but only amused by their prattle and pretty ways....

My principal amusement is to swear at the weather which has been diabolical; the last week in November the thermometer never once rose above thirty degrees, and at night fell to unknown abysses. Snow and clouds surround us, and the winds are colossal. Happily our house is very attractive, and we have had neither smokey chimneys nor frozen pipes in it yet. Three or four days in the week I go out to Cambridge, and the other days I work at home, busy enough always. The *North American* comes into my hands after the first January only, but I have been writing for the next number another little notice of Freeman,[1] calculated to improve his temper as I guess....

I am glad to hear of Palgrave's promotion and am meaning to write him a letter one of these days. But letter-writing comes hard to a man who has three courses of lectures to keep up, and a Review to run. My father is busy bringing out the first volumes of my grandfather's Diary; a book you must have at Thornes. I will send you the volumes as long as I live, but there will be a dozen or fifteen, and the Lord knows when they will all be out.

To Charles Milnes Gaskell

WASHINGTON, 13 February, 1874.

The happy students celebrate this period of the year by what they call their semi-annual examinations, and as my presence at these ex-

[1] Vol. cxviii, 176.

aminations is not a necessity, I have a fortnight of vacation.... So here we are, and I find myself again with my foot upon my native asphalt, rejoicing in delivery for a time from the ways of Boston. It is no end of fun to come back here. And though our politics just now are very deep in the mud, and our politicians are a feeble kind of forcibles, still it is fun to see them wriggle and it gives one a lofty sense of one's own importance to be able to smile contemptuously on men in high place. But the more I see of official life here, the less I am inclined to wish to enter it. This was always my feeling, and it always grows stronger. To be a free lance, and to have the press to work in, is my ideal of perfect happiness, at least so far as perfect happiness is to be found in a career. So far as I can see, the life of an official is made wretched by its insecurity. These moral reflections are partially inspired by the thought of your elections, the results of which have not yet reached us except in a rough way by telegraph. It would be rather fun to be a conservative just now and I am waiting with great curiosity to hear what new cards have turned up.

As for my old political associates, they are in a very bad way. No one seems to have any idea what is to happen here, but my own notion is that our next elections will throw a crowd of new men into office, and that no improvement in quality is to be immediately expected. I delight in the barbaric simplicity of our native legislators. They do really offer new types of study. They are far more amusing than your effete members. I always feel a certain vague sense of personal fear when in close proximity to one of our south-western congressmen, as I do when I meet a Sioux warrior on the plains. Now your members never inspire this sensation. I feel it nowhere in Europe, and only among the Bedouins in Africa. Hence, how much more amusing our politicians are than yours. Q. E. D....

To Charles Milnes Gaskell

91 MARLBOROUGH STREET, BOSTON,
26 March, 1874.

Since my last letter, which was written from Washington, I have been waiting for the *North American* for April to appear, so that I could send you a copy of your notice of the Princess.[1] I like it much, and hope you will do me more. But I've not put your signature to it because I want the credit of having written it myself.... Why will you

[1] A notice of Princess Marie Liechtenstein's *Holland House*. *North American Review*, CXVIII, 428.

not send me more? Somebody's memoirs are always appearing and social history is a delightful study. I think you might derive pleasure from reviewing Hayward's Essays, especially if you did it viciously....

Politics are a very unsatisfactory game. Yours are bad enough, but ours are worse. I am becoming a little alarmed about ours, for our people seem to be not alarmed at all. We are more absolutely insane and hopelessly mad than any other branch of mankind, except the Spaniards and perhaps the French. But I cling to the faith that present calm will last my time, and after that I care little for what happens. Philosophy is great and I am one of its prophets. Just now poor Sumner has died and pitched us into one of those nasty little fights which are the meanest part of politics. Among others stirred from their long repose by the commotion thus excited, is my father. A certain number of well-meaning people wish to choose him for Sumner's successor. He has no wish to oblige them, and there are not enough of them, I fancy, to make the scheme very possible, but meanwhile three different parties are fighting for the place, and the wrath of the contestants fills the newspapers and invades our domestic hearth. As my side is commonly beaten in politics, I prefer not to take sides at all; but to laugh at the whole concern. But it is harder to laugh at the badness of our government which is desperate; not so much corrupt as incompetent, enough to make one a howling dervish for life....

To Henry Cabot Lodge

BEVERLY FARMS, MASS.
Saturday. June, 1874.

The printers have now some eighty pages of copy. I consider that from the time the manuscript leaves my hands, it is in yours. That was our division of labor. So I leave the printers to your tender mercies and you can do what you please with them if they are not prompt.

I shall try to leave copy enough to last them in my absence. But if any new matter comes to you while I am away, you had better use your own discretion about sending it to the printers. If it comes from Simon, Pierce, or any other responsible man, have it put in type at once and send the proof to the author. If the writer is not first class, you might keep it for consultation.

You will have to correct the proof of Art. I yourself. I would like to see the second proof. Art. II is Newcomb's and the proof will go to him. Of the critical notices, 1 and 2 must be corrected by you. No. 3

(Marquardt) may be sent to Prof. Allen who is, I believe at Newbury-port, as you know. No. 4 (Wallace's *Heel*) may come to Mr. J. Eliot Cabot here at Beverly Farms.[1]

This is all that is yet in. I will notify you of the rest as I forward it to the printer.

About the Year Books, I know that the great mass of cases are modern law. You must exercise your own critical acumen to find out what will throw light on Saxon law. You are now on a new field of investigation with your spurs to win, and must trust to your own powers. I have only glanced over the volumes enough to see that here and there are some very pretty hints.

I can't tell yet how much we are short of copy, if at all. But good book-notices are desirable in any case.

To Charles Milnes Gaskell

BEVERLY FARMS, 22 June, 1874.

The labor of an instructor at our Universities is really very consider-able, for we are instructors and examiners at once and I am an editor and writer too.... I have got this week to take charge of the freshmen in their history. Then I am reading hard for a new course in American colonial history which I am to undertake next year, and in which I am to expose British tyranny and cruelty with a degree of patriotic fervor which, I flatter myself, has rarely been equalled. Altogether, I feel as though I had not full credit for the work done. Somehow or other, no credit is ever given for industry to any man who is not working for money.

Yours of June 5th followed by your notice of Constable,[2] has at length found me in a week of reasonable leisure. The Constable must go over till October. The July number is already printed and will be out in a few days. I hope you will do Trevelyan's book for me. It will be rather fun to touch him up, and the advantage of knowing an author or editor personally is immense in such cases, as Ste. Beuve witnesses, to say nothing of the delicious pleasure of sticking pins into a human pincushion....

I have myself devoted ten pages in my July number to a notice of Prof. Stubbs's unconscionably dull *Constitutional History*.[3] And I have

---

[1] The articles appear in the October *Review*, cxix.

[2] *Archibald Constable and his Literary Correspondents*, in the *North American Review*, October, 1874.

[3] The first volume of the *Constitutional History of England*, by William Stubbs.

ventured to assert some opinions there which I fear that dignified Professor will frown upon. Luckily for me, a good, heavy-bottomed English University Don rarely condescends to notice criticism, and never American criticism. Even Mr. Freeman now ignores my poor comments. Luckily I am kept up by continental affiliations....

To Henry Cabot Lodge

BEVERLY FARMS, MASS.
Thursday, 25 June, [1874.]

I return the Spencer. It has disappointed me. If his other works are not better thought out, they must have very little sound method to recommend them.

I cannot conceive how any rule of prose can be made that shall not require the subject to stand first. This is a general law, and is equivalent to saying that one ought to begin at the beginning. "Jack loves Joan" is right. "Joan loves Jack" is not the forcible way of saying that Jack loves Joan. "Diana is great" is the ordinary, correct and regular mode of stating the fact. "Great is Diana" requires an interjection mark after it. You may test this rule in practice to any extent. I am satisfied that the first canon of good narrative or argumentative prose requires the subject to precede the predicate.

But as an equally important rule I should insist on the law of variety. The two canons go together and ought to be studied together. The thought should not flow in monotonous forms. And why? The law of economy does not explain this. Poetic rhythm would seem to contradict it. I believe the reason to be that in poetry or prose, monotony ultimately wearies the nerves, just as lying in one position does.

When we come to applying this second canon, the difficulties begin. And these difficulties are essentially the same in verse and prose. To vary your regular construction you may put the predicate first. But clearly this must be done with discretion. Hence we get Canon III: where accentuation is wanted, begin with the word or idea to be accented, whether subject or predicate.

"*I* only lived; *I* only drew
The accursed air of dungeon dew."

Would Byron have made this more forcible if he had put the predicate first?

"The Senator walks off under the States-rights banner; let him go; *I* remain."

"Then Seymour arose," says Macaulay. "Then arose Seymour" is feeble in comparison, as one reads it in the story.

Or as an example in regard to the position of the adjective, which is part and parcel of the same question, take Shelley's famous touch in his Dream of the Unknown:

> "And in the warm hedge grew lush eglantine,
>   Green cow-bind and the moonlight colored May,
>   *And wild roses*, and ivy serpentine."

There is a delicious flavor in those *wild roses*, and why? Simply because the rhythm requires *roses wild*. It is the variety which pleases, not the mere relative position of the words.

So my Canon III would absolutely disregard every rule except one's ear. Canon III requires that in narrative, where the rule is to construct sentences according to Canon I, accentuation is to be gained by putting the accentuated word or idea first. The ear alone can decide what that word or idea had best be.

Another rule, however, which seems to me essential to good prose, is that the reader ought to be as little conscious of the style as may be. It should fit the matter so closely that one should never be quite able to say that the style is above the matter — nor below it. But great effects are best produced by lowering the general tone. Follow Canon I as a rule, and it becomes easy to make a sensation with Canon III. The higher you pitch the key, the harder it is to sing up to it, and the effect no greater.

This is not Spencer's way of putting it. He starts from the idea of variety. To me the simple idea precedent is uniformity. He thinks Ossian's is "the theoretically best arrangement." I think the very absurdity refutes itself. Ossian's uniformity is worse than ordinary uniformity because it applies a wrong rule badly. In short Spencer's essay seems to me to be neither philosophical nor accurate. I am not encouraged to read his larger works.

If you ever feel like it, and want a talk, bring your carpet-bag over here and pass the night.

To Henry Cabot Lodge

BEVERLY FARMS, MASS.
Thursday [Sept. (?), 1874.]

I suppose they mean one sheet I sent to my brother. I returned the rest at once. I shall go over to Cambridge tomorrow morning and will settle everything up....

I want you to keep your eye on one point for me, in your legal studies. Manors, at least in some cases, had gallows. I believe these gallows were appendant to the old right of the special mallus (Lex Gal.) to put to death on the spot the thief caught in the act. Whether the manorial jurisdiction was infang or outfang, I think the thief must be taken in the act, if he was hangable. So I understand the Prior's case, XXXI Edw. I, 500. And as a matter of historical law, the point is very pretty, connecting as it does the whole development of capital jurisdiction.

I want you therefore to watch sharply to discover facts bearing on this point, and to work out the exact procedure both manorial and royal in cases of theft charged as committed in time past. The manorial procedure ought to be by oath or battle if at all. The royal would be ordinary felony. But I want to know whether a manorial lord ever got the right (which the old mallus had not) of executing a man on such a charge. Please collect references on the point.

To Henry Cabot Lodge

Beverly Farms,
20 Sept., 1874.

I am glad you caught Wheeler in a blunder. I detest the man cordially. He insists on writing like a counter-jumper.

I believe all the matter is now provided and all the proofsheets except the last, corrected. I sent back No. 30 on Saturday. No. 31 ought to be ready by Thursday. Diman's notice is admirable. Gray's very nicely written. He improves.... I have not been able to use yours, and reserve it for the future. We will hold a diet on its style for mutual improvement. On the whole, the number will pass muster, especially the book-notices.

I go to Newport on Friday to stay over Sunday, so keep an eye on that last sheet and get us out punctually. I told them to send you a duplicate proof of it anyway, so if I am away, jam it through, though I ought perhaps to correct the proof of Thévenin myself. Yet you are up in the subject.

What's your idea?

To Henry Cabot Lodge

BEVERLY FARMS, MASS.
Sunday, 26 Sept., 1874.

I think your notes very satisfactory, especially in connection with XXII, Edw. I, 466. I took the ground in my notice of Stubbs, that manorial jurisdiction in England was always a mere continuation of hundred jurisdiction. In France the *haute justice* embraced felonies and the *inquisitio*. The constitutional character of English and French feudalism is nicely expressed in this contrast. So we must collect all the evidence, especially in the reign of Henry II, who as succeeding the lawless reign of Stephen must have found manorial power stronger than ever it was again unless under Henry III. I think I see the way to a good monograph by you on this point.

Keep a sharp eye too for all other points of procedure, and especially for all forms of writs and actions. They serve to connect the machinery of the state as well as to illustrate law.

I hope the proofs are all in at last. If you are at Osgood's, pray send me down a copy of the new number. When do you move up?

To Henry Cabot Lodge

BEVERLY FARMS, MASS.
15 October, 1874.

Your paylist arrived safely. I made a few small alterations in it, and sent it to Osgood.

I shall have to do Parkman myself,[1] I fear. As for Froude, I would write a note to Godkin of the *Nation* and ask him to do it. You might ask Harry, or (better, if he would) Willy James to do Bayard Taylor's *Prophet*.[2]

I forgot your question about the *Biographie*. I have never used Michaud, so can't express an opinion. The *Biographie Universelle* is invaluable to an editor.

Channing's letters ought to be noticed. Do you think of anyone to do it?

Please write to Prof. Perry of Amherst (?)[3] for a notice of Nordhoff's new book on *American Communistic Societies*. I enclose a letter for your information.

I have just received a letter from Prof. Whitney, an extract from

---

[1] In the *North American Review*, January, 1875.   [2] *Ib.*
[3] Arthur Latham Perry (1830–1905), of Williams College. The note is in the January number.

which will please you, especially as you come in for a good share of the credit, at least *qua* book-notices:

There have come notes to me from several distinguished English scholars (one from Darwin himself) expressing much satisfaction with the criticism of Müller in the July number.[1] The recent number is an excellent one and its book-notices seem to me rather beyond what one sees anywhere else; the whole tone of the *Review* is much improved upon what it was during your absence.

Laughlin [2] of '73 proposes to join our Ph.D. class.
I am not yet quite healed. But go up regularly to lectures. We come to town about the first week in Nov.

To Henry Cabot Lodge

Beverly Farms, Mass.
31 Oct., 1874.

You had better send Charlton Lewis's book to me. Cairnes goes to Prof. Dunbar. If Weir Mitchell refuses Clarke, don't write to Dalton or anyone else till further notice. Damn C. C. Everett. Tell him (very civilly) that the pressure for space &c., &c., we can't promise publication within any given time. You were quite right to ask Dr. Palfrey. I reckon Anderson may be the man.

I am not registered and so can't vote. Some one has sent me my poll-tax bill, but it's not paid, and I'm not going to town to pay it.

The *Nation's* notice is improved. I wish if you go to Osgood's, you would look up in the drawer the *Christian Register's* notices of the October and July number and send both to me. Tell Osgood I am concocting an advertisement.

You had better write to J. M. Pierce to correct your previous letter on the Ph.D. course: instead of *dropping* your Div. 3, you wish to *change* it for a course of special study on the early English law as exhibited in Anglo-Saxon and Norman sources, with a view to ascertaining and fixing the share that Germanic law had in forming the Common Law.

[1] Darwinism and Language.
[2] James Laurence Laughlin (1850-   ), later professor of political economy in Harvard University.

To Henry Cabot Lodge

91 MARLBORO ST., 30 December, 1874.

Private and Conf.

We are negotiating for the *Advertiser*. Tomorrow morning I shall know whether we can have it. You must of course join us. How much money will you put in? Each share is $5000 and we must buy 18. I shall count on you for one. Please telegraph assent.

To Carl Schurz

91 MARLBOROUGH ST.
12 April, 1875.

MY DEAR MR. SCHURZ, — The danger was over by the time you wrote. Following out the programme, I had entirely withdrawn from all share in the movement, and did not stir till it became clear that something must be done immediately or the whole thing would fall through. Then Sam Bowles, my brother Charles, Cabot Lodge and I, concocted a letter and issued it on Thursday and Friday last (the 8th and 9th) to such gentlemen as were on your lists. Lodge sent it, with the list, to you, and then handed over the whole correspondence to Arthur Sedgwick. He has got a New York committee now raised, and the matter is fairly under way. As you were of opinion that it was best not to give the demonstration the look of an eastern concern, we have not put New England men on the list. Of course we can have any number, but I presume the really important matter is who will come to the gathering, *prepared to accept ulterior results* and form if necessary an organisation, not who will sign the invitation, for everyone will do this. I don't myself care to see you smothered with a mere crowd that does not mean business.

I suppose it will be well for you to send to the New York committee a reply to the invitation to be ready for publication so soon as a suitable list of names has been made out. The day ought to be published as soon as possible. But as the whole management has now gone to New York, I leave it to New York wisdom to regulate the affair.

I sincerely trust our friends will go to New York with definite notions of a policy to be pursued and practical measures to be carried into execution. You know already that I want organisation and consider the New York meeting only valuable as it leads to and facilitates organisation. Would it not be well to arrange beforehand for a small interior meeting, the day after the dinner, to discuss a policy? The word Convention need not be suggested, but the *thing* Co-operation must be made flesh.

To Henry Cabot Lodge

BEVERLY FARMS, MASS.
19 May, 1875.

Please gratify Mr. Reed of Washington by "doing execution upon him with all convenient despatch."

I shall take up your notice so soon as I can get a moment's time. My Cambridge work fills my hands.

Who is the best military critic in the United States? I want an article from him on Sherman's *Memoirs*. But I must have a man of national reputation.

I think of making you edit the October number altogether. By the way, will it be the last of our venerable periodical? My concluding interview with Houghton disinclined me to act with him. He wants to give up paying contributors, at least on the present scale. I think we had better let it die at once and bury it with decency.

You will I suppose attend the sale of the Webster library. When you get a catalogue I should be greatly obliged by your getting one for me. I hope there may be good things in it.

The country is glorious. We are monarchs of all and our reign is undisputed by mosquitoes. *The house is beginning, and such a house.*

To Henry Cabot Lodge

BEVERLY FARMS, 26 May, '75.

I don't see that I have anything to say to Osgood. I don't care to go into the publishing business at all. Of that I am satisfied, and not likely to change my mind again. As for Norton, I sincerely wish he would take the *Review*. My terror is lest it should die on my hands or go to some Jew. If Osgood can shove it off on Norton, I advise him to do so, and will negotiate myself with Norton for the purpose. He is not my enemy, but if he were, I would like no better than to shove him into such a trap and jump out myself on his shoulders. Meanwhile I intend to remain passive.

I advise you to be marshal. It is a bore no doubt, but anything that brings you in contact with men and extends your acquaintance is worth doing. Anything which takes a man morally out of Beacon St.,

Nahant, and Beverly Farms, Harvard College and the Boston press, must be in itself a good.

I am so overrun with work myself that I envy you your leisure deeply. At this season my drudgeries double. I have not been able to look into my English law for a fortnight, and a dreary waste of examination books and Division Returns lies before me. But I wish you would keep yourself and me and all of us posted about our political movement. There is a mass of correspondence, including the raising of money, all of which ought to be conducted and controlled entirely by you, and extended to all the branches of our corresponding committee. To do this with method, brains and success, would put you in a very commanding position if we succeed, and give you a wide range of acquaintance and influence in and out of this mouldy little community even if we fail. I suppose my brother Charles has notified you of the letter of Clarke of St. Louis. I think we shall set that spring working and it is very important we should. I care little whether we succeed or not in getting into power, but I care a great deal to prevent myself from becoming what of all things I despise, a Boston prig (the intellectual prig is the most odious of all), and so I yearn, at every instant, to get out of Massachusetts and come in contact with the wider life I always have found so much more to my taste.

Frank Palfrey has written to offer to do Sherman's *Memoirs*.[1] I can't refuse.

I hardly know anything about the July number. My contributors are all behaving like the devil and would exasperate me if I weren't hardened to it. But I suppose the number will bring itself out. If you can hear of any good articles, you had better secure them. Even for the October number, if you are to be responsible for it, you should begin by June 1st, especially as I fear I shall leave nothing for you; and Gam. Bradford wants to print an article on the City Charter.

P.S. We shall be glad to see you here whenever you feel like a jaunt.

To Henry Cabot Lodge

BEVERLY FARMS, 10 June, [1875.]

Your last two notes are on hand. I only saw the President yesterday and he told me that the courses were so far advanced and the electives for next year have been for the most part handed in, so that he feared it would be impossible to interpolate a new course this year. I ac-

---

[1] A paper on the *Memoirs* of General Sherman is in the *North American Review*, October, 1875. It was written by Palfrey.

quiesced, and he seemed much disposed to press it as a decided affair for next year, to be announced, that is, in April next, for the year 1876–7, which I declined to do, on the ground that you might prefer other occupations. But if you care to go to work on it, with my Syllabus for your outline, and prepare yourself this year, I think we can manage it easily next year if you like.

I am now groaning under examination books and marks. Thanks for your kind offers. I fear I must bear that burden alone.

Mrs. Wister is to appear in July. I have read her and rather like her. She has real *go*, and is readable if sometimes unequal.

Chauncey Wright will be No. 5.[1] The book-notices are not yet all in, but I think all but twenty pages or so are now in the printers' hands.

Did I tell you that Gam. Bradford wants to write an article for October on the new charter, and I told him that we would let him know if we had space?

I don't quite agree with you about the Webster library. I have bid for about a dozen books, and shall be sorry not to get them. I was surprised that you didn't try for Trumbull's *Connecticut*. I hesitated but left it. The books are in good condition too. I went in to look at them. Left my orders with Lunt.

To Henry Cabot Lodge

BEVERLY FARMS,
15 June, 1875.

Your notice of Chatterton[2] has no book-title prefixed. I return it for the purpose. You had better send it to the printers direct.

I recommend you to try going over your manuscript always and strike out every superfluous word. You will find it pays also to try to condense your sentences and recast them for the purpose.

I have roughly scratched your MS. as you will see, as an experiment in condensation. I have also modified and lowered your praises of the poet. But do you think it quite fair to say that a generation which had Gray and Collins for models, and produced Burns, was wholly dust and ashes?

[1] On Isaac Todhunter's *Conflict of Studies*.
[2] Printed in the *North American Review*, July, 1875.

To Henry Cabot Lodge

BEVERLY FARMS, MASS.
Monday, [June (?), 1875.]

I expected you to-day and was horrified by your not coming, as it reminded me that I had not answered your notes. I had to go up Friday, and Saturday all day, and in the bother of work, forgot to reply to you. Indeed I expected you anyway, and perhaps I dismissed reply as unnecessary. Anyway I let it slip my mind, and am specially sorry as I wanted to see you today rather than later as I go to Cambridge tomorrow for the last time, I hope, and could have arranged to meet you there. The fact is, I hardly know what has become of the carpet. It was so full of moths that no one would let it stay in his room, and it was cast into outer darkness. If you receive this note in time and can be at Cambridge tomorrow, you shall take seisin of all there is.

I will resume the "dust and ashes" argument hereafter. I am sorry you think so poorly of Gray, whom I rank very high indeed. But if you insist on having only the naturals classed as poets, why not count in Cowper? I feel a little awkward about literary judgment. Everyone now snubs the last century and I see that Stephen considers Scott to be poor stuff. I confess I do think Pope a poet, and Gray, too, and Cowper, and Goldsmith. But this may be youthful prejudice, or rather prejudice contracted in youth.

I modified your expressions about Chatterton, not so much because they were too laudatory; that was your affair; but rather because it seemed to me that if his verses were trite, affected, impossible and absurd (I forget your exact words) it was well to modify the praise; and if the praise were correct, the blame ought to be modified, or the balance ought to be more exactly drawn. It was easiest to modify the praise, so I suggested that course.

We were thinking of making our descent on you and your wife one day next week. Will that do?

Forgive my not answering your note. I am much mortified at the bad manners, but I really assumed that you would come of course and only wanted an answer in case I was not to be at home.

To Henry Cabot Lodge

BEVERLY FARMS, MASS.
24 July, 1875.

You must first get an act of Congress authorizing the publication and appropriating monies thereto; then you must bring influence enough to bear on the State Department to get yourself appointed editor. I am at a loss to know how to effect either of these objects. At all events some years of active lobbying would seem to be necessary as a preliminary, and with this administration and a centennial presidential election at hand, I should feel rather hopeless of effecting anything. But if you go to Washington you had better see Mr. Fish about it.

I am no great hand at poetical criticism, but if you will send me Queen Mary I will see what I can do with it. At least I can write as good a notice as the *Nation's*.[1]

To Henry Cabot Lodge

BEVERLY FARMS, MASS.
Friday, 6 Aug. 1875.

My eyes are still sufficiently troublesome to make me avoid much use of them, so that I have not yet looked up the charters you ask about. I will do so as soon as may be. I have just read the notice of Digby and forward it to the printers today.[2] It is very good and the only criticism I will make is that your sentences are formed too much alike, so that your style needs variety.

I enclose you a letter from some fellow unknown. Please settle him.

With our best regards to your wife and guests, if these are still with you.

To Charles Milnes Gaskell

BEVERLY FARMS, 4 October, 1875.

... It would bore you to extinction to follow me through my daily struggle to find out how boys who have no minds can be made to understand that they had better be contented without the education of a Newton, and how boys who have minds can be made to understand that all knowledge has not yet been exhausted by Newton and

[1] Printed in *North American Review*, October, 1875.

[2] *History of the Law of Real Property*, by Kenelm Edward Digby, in *North American Review*, October, 1875.

such. This effort to get rid of rubbish and to utilise good material is one of my labors. I am preaching a crusade against Culture with a big C. I hope to excite the hatred of my entire community, every soul of whom adores that big C. I mean to irritate every one about me to frenzy by ridiculing all the idols of the University and declaring a university education to be a swindle. I have hopes of being turned out of my place in consequence, in which case I shall become a reformer and my fortune is made. But this would not amuse you greatly, though I always hold up the English University as the one colossal instance of the mischievous consequences of Culture with a big C. Nor would my editorial duties fail to bore you. I have shoved off the greater part of them upon a junior editor, and confine myself now to direction....

Our politics are getting lively. As yet we independent liberals hold the balance of power and gain strength. But before this letter reaches you, we may be smashed to flinders. We called Schurz back from Germany to fight the Democrats in Ohio. If he succeeds in beating them there, my friends will pretty surely control the next presidential election. Tilden may be our man, or some other. If we are beaten in Ohio, everything will be chaotic, and no man can foresee what will turn up. A new division of parties and a new assortment of party leaders will become inevitable....

Oct. 15. The election mentioned in the last paragraph has come off, and after an awful strain on the nerves we feel at last sure of having effected our object. The Democrats are beaten by about five thousand majority in a total vote of about five hundred thousand. Narrow enough, but every man in that five thousand is one of us. You will hear more of this next year. We will play for high stakes and have nothing to lose....

To Charles Milnes Gaskell

91 MARLBOROUGH STREET, BOSTON.
9 February, 1876.

· · · · · · · · · · · · · · · · ·

Your uncle's death will, I suppose, make you more than ever free of ties. You are getting to the age, however, when perfect freedom becomes the most objectionable form of slavery. I do not know what it is that makes man so base an animal, but true it is that his own good requires him to be bridled and saddled, moderately worked, and his mind carefully filled with details, if he is to be contented. He is not made for unlimited freedom. His mind when it has no daily chopped food set before it, begins to eat itself and to refuse to eat at all. The moral of which is that you must provide some regular occupation if you want to escape hypochondria....

Politics too are miserably out of joint. Our organization has been secretly effected and is ready to act, but is in doubt what it ought to do, and although we have unquestionably the power to say that any given man shall not be President, we are not able to say that any given man shall be President. Our first scheme was to force my father on the parties. This is now abandoned, and we have descended to the more modest plan of pushing one of the regular candidates, or splitting the parties by taking one of their leaders. I am no longer confident of doing good and am looking with anxiety to the future. But things are getting beyond my capacity to influence or even to measure. The worst sign is the general lethargy about everything. The newspapers will probably give you information enough before long, for you to follow our course intelligibly. Only remember that we mean to support the present Secretary of the Treasury, Bristow, for the Presidency, provided he will give us any sort of assurance that he will, if necessary, accept an independent nomination from us....

I have read two chapters of *Daniel Deronda*, but it makes me miserable to see that wicked woman, George Eliot, scratch and claw her poor heroines with a cruelty as fiendish as Mrs. What's-her-name tortured her apprentices with....

To Carl Schurz

BOSTON, 14 Feby, 1876.

MY DEAR MR. SCHURZ, — Now that we are again thrown back upon the wide question of general policy, I suppose there is no impropriety in my venturing to express an opinion again, in regard to our wisest course. My poor brother Charles, to whom I generally leave the duty of declaring our joint opinion, has been very ill and still is too weak and sensitive even to be consulted on the subject. What I have to say, will therefore count for one only.

It is clear that your original scheme must be abandoned. I am not sorry for it. I do not like *coups de main*. I have no taste for political or any other kind of betting, and for us to attempt forcing one of ourselves on a party convention, necessarily entails the jockeying of some-body. It would be the experience of '72 in a new shape, and successful or not it would do no permanent good but rather permanent harm. The caucus system is the rottenest, most odious and most vulnerable part of our body politic. It is the caucus system we want to attack. By making use of it, we lose our own footing.

To attack the caucus system is therefore the end and aim of all my political desires. To that object and to that object only do I care to contribute. Apart from that object, I believe all your political schemes to be mere make-shifts. You wanted to elect my father President. I would prefer to sacrifice him as the candidate of a hopeless minority if I could gain a point in that way against party organisations. Nay, if he were elected, my only ground for giving him support, apart from personal considerations, would be my conviction that he would proceed systematically to purify party machinery by depriving it of the means of corruption.

The present question with me is, then, how to go to work. You have satisfied yourself and me that we are not strong nor united enough to attack in face. The public is not ready to support us. You have therefore, I hope, abandoned that scheme.

The next alternative was to attack in flank. If we could not set up our own man, to support the man who comes nearest to our standard. This is Mr. Bristow.[1] He has a strong popular following. He deserves our support. He would make a good President and would probably in time work round to our opinions. We are therefore safe in supporting him.

Unluckily Mr. Bristow does not now share in our views. He is a firm believer in party loyalty. He will not accept an independent nomination before the party convention meets. He will refuse to run against the party candidate in any case. He would look with unutterable disgust upon any proposition to force a candidate on a party organisation whose candidacy meant to himself the rebellion against that same party organisation. Our support of Mr. Bristow must therefore be avowedly on grounds of policy, not of principle.

Further, nothing is more certain than that Mr. Bristow cannot be nominated. We must not let our hands be tied by any delusion as to his strength in the convention.

Here then are the propositions:

1. We must support Mr. Bristow.
2. We cannot nominate him as an independent candidate.
3. We cannot let our hands be tied by the support we give him.

The essential part of any policy must be to hold our friends together. Whatever support is given to Mr. Bristow or to anyone

[1] Benjamin Helm Bristow (1832–1896).

else, it is all important that we should act ultimately as a unit, and that the certainty of this ultimate action should be the cardinal point of our tactics.

It is now necessary to decide upon these tactics, and after the preceding review of the ground, I will tell you what seems to me the only clear way out of our difficulties.

To effect the essential object of holding our organisation together, it will be necessary to make a demonstration. That demonstration cannot now include a nomination for the Presidency because: 1st, It is our best policy to ally ourselves with Bristow, and his friends. 2nd, Mr. Bristow will not accept our nomination. 3d, If we nominate him without consulting him, and he is beaten (as is probable) in Convention, he will refuse to run as our candidate, and we shall be left hopeless.

The question then rises as to the nature of this demonstration.

My recommendation is that you and half a dozen other gentlemen should write a circular letter addressed to about two hundred of the most weighty and reliable of our friends, inviting them to meet you, say at Cleveland, or Pittsburg, one week after the Republican Convention meets, there to decide whether we will support the Republican candidate or nominate a candidate of our own. I enclose my notion of the draft of the letter.

This letter or address will of course be published. I should suppose it would have all the effect that any demonstration could have, both to unite our friends and to alarm the Convention at Cincinnati. By keeping in your own hands the nominations to our own meeting, you will be able to exclude the most dangerous elements. This is, no doubt, carrying the junto system far. But I have no real fear of juntoes. They are too objectionable in themselves ever to become dangerous like the caucus. And I know no other way of fighting the caucus than with the junto. Together they may not work so badly.

Down to the time of the Convention, let us, within the range of this declaration, work earnestly for Bristow. By establishing close relations with Bristow's friends, we shall probably carry a portion of them with us. If the Convention makes a very bad nomination we may carry nearly all. And Mr. Bristow's friends include all the virtue left in the Republican party.

If the Convention nominates Mr. Bristow, well and good! Our meeting will merely confirm their action. If not, the serious responsibility will fall upon us of placing a candidate before the people. Our meeting must consist of men who will not shirk that responsibility, and there can be but one ground to rest our action upon; namely, resistance to caucus dictation. We cannot vote the Democratic ticket, for that would involve us in the support of a party organisation which it is a hopeless task to reform. But we can found a new party, and are content to bring the Democrats into power as the only means of re-organising parties. As I said before, I am willing to sacrifice my father for such an object, if necessary. He used Van Buren for a similar purpose in '48. But I would rather choose some one else if we could find any one. Our action however must depend to some degree on public feeling.

I suppose you are more than any one else alive to the fact that a blunder now would make us helpless for the whole campaign. We must in the nature of things act cautiously for the simple reason that there is no sufficient popular feeling yet to support us in acting boldly. I see no chance of good to result from our making a premature nomination. The public is fairly determined to wait for the action of the parties. But if we can make the public at large feel in advance that they are certain of having an alternative in case the party conventions are unsatisfactory, we shall sap the foundations of party discipline beforehand without exposing ourselves to any possible attack.

I hope these tactics will coincide with your views. Otherwise I shall wait with great anxiety the decision you shall make. But in any case believe me very sincerely yours.

[Draft of circular letter.]

——, March, 1876.

SIR, The present condition of political affairs is such as to create grave concern in the minds of all reflecting men.

The great party conventions are soon to meet. As yet there is no indication that the choice of these conventions will fall upon persons in whom independent voters can place confidence. All the indications of the time point to the possibility that, in the conflict between personal interests, the interests of the nation may be overlooked, and either a combination of corrupt influences may control the result, or, as has so often happened, the difficulty of harmonising personal claims may lead to the nomination of candidates whom you cannot support with self-respect.

Against such a possibility it is our duty to take every precaution.

The Republican Convention will meet on the —— of June. We have the honor, therefore, respectfully to invite your attendance at a conference of gentlemen independent of party ties, to meet at the city of —— on the —— day of June, to decide whether we can support the nominations made by the Republican Convention, and if not, to place before the people candidates of our own selection. We have the honor, etc., etc.

To Henry Cabot Lodge

91 MARLBOROUGH ST.
15 Feby., 1876.

Yours of yesterday has just arrived. You had better engage the article from Boynton.[1] But you must explain to him our resources and have the question of pay fairly understood. Further you had better stipulate with him that the language shall be moderate. You can add that the editor (he does not know me) in chief reserves to himself in all cases, and rigidly exercises, the right to strike out or modify expressions which he deems too strong. You will find it convenient to make me the partner to be consulted in such cases as in the novel which I can't now recollect. Put all that is disagreeable on my shoulders.

You are now plunged up to the ears in Washington intrigue. Go in for Bristow with all your energy. But remember that the chances are a thousand to one against the nomination of any man who has made so many enemies as he. And bear in mind that it must be the object of Bristow's friends to get our support, but that they will never consent to pledge him to us. If you doubt this, try to urge such a pledge. They will evade you and must do so, because Bristow is a Kentucky Republican and has all the old traditions of party fealty. His friends would no doubt like to have us go into convention to support him, but they can get no promise from him of support to us if we are beaten in convention. If you want practice as a diplomate, try your hands on satisfying yourself whether or not they think their chief will support, or at least not oppose, the party nomination. If they encourage you to think he will bolt the nomination, they are either deceiving themselves or deceiving you, or else I am much misinformed. The game is not unlike that with Blaine last winter, except that Bristow is a more honorable man, and will not intentionally deceive us. Keep

[1] Henry Van Ness Boynton (1835–1905), whose article on the "Whiskey Ring" appeared in the *North American Review*, October, 1876.

your eyes about you and do your best to secure them ultimately for us instead of securing us ultimately to them.

There is nothing new here. Give my regards to your wife and believe me.

P.S. Please get for me a copy of Bristow's Annual Report.

To Henry Cabot Lodge

91 MARLBOROUGH ST.
17 February, 1876.

Yours of the 15th arrived this morning. I think there can be no doubt that Mr. Bristow would make a great mistake by resigning. Most men who have resigned have made mistakes. Always excepting our great hero Jefferson, and if he had been an honester man, he too would have fought out his victory in the Cabinet.

But nevertheless I expect the resignation of Mr. Bristow. I expect it because he and his friends are Kentuckians, and will act on motive of personal dignity. He will do as Clay did to Tyler, and with, I suppose, the same result.

Nevertheless, without imagining that you can exercise much control over the movements of Mr. Bristow and his friends, I hope you will identify yourself as much as possible with his interests, and accept his lead, for the time at least. We shall soon learn whether he has the faculty to lead us, or whether he too is to fall into powerlessness with his loss of office.

Our object is clear enough. We want to break down party organisations which are the source of all our worst corruption. Does Mr. Bristow recognise this necessity? If not, can he be brought to do so?

You ask whether he ought to write a letter or not. It seems to me immaterial. What we want to know is whether he will bolt the nomination of Washburne or Hayes.[1] Will he fight? Will he make one of us? Will he lead? We cannot consent to go blindfold. We can't follow a leader who is going to quit us if a convention tells him to do so. We can't exhaust our strength in fighting for Bristow and then have Bristow vote for Washburne.

You think he is ready to join us. If so his policy seems to me obvious. He should give us the most vigorous lead he can. If he means to break things, he should break all he can. He should issue an indictment against the party that will show the people what we

[1] Elihu Benjamin Washburne and Rutherford Birchard Hayes.

mean. If he is under the delusion that all this horrible corruption can be dealt with by any moderate language or with any blunt weapons, he is useless as a leader. We must have a man who cares nothing for party or he will betray us.

To Henry Cabot Lodge

91 MARLBOROUGH ST.
Sunday, 20 Feby., 1876.

Your letters are extremely interesting and become from day to day more essential to me here. I have, however, spoken of them to no one except my father, whom, for obvious reasons, it is now important to carry along with us. But the time of action is now at hand and I may have to take your place here in our organisation till you return. So continue to write every day if you can. In case you want to telegraph, you will have to use some caution in mentioning names. Schurz and Bristow had better figure as Smith and Brown. I have done nothing about the *Post*,[1] but am willing to put $5000 into it if Bristow is our candidate. What did you do about it before leaving? And how much money do you feel disposed to put into it?

I presume that the verdict in Babcock's case, whichever way it goes, will at once let loose the elements. There are one or two points of immediate importance in regard to this. Much depends on the man selected by the President to succeed Bristow. If a good man is appointed, we may still be embarrassed. Our friends had better keep quiet till that appointment is made or they may go off at half-cock. I don't mean that we are to abandon Bristow, but that we are to give his enemies full swing. My life on it, they will hang themselves.

The second point is that we should know at the very earliest possible moment what is decided in regard to Bristow's nomination by us. We want to move quickly now. The purchase of the *Post*, so far as I am concerned, is conditional on Bristow's candidacy. The organisation of our party here should be effected by the establishment of the organ; the two steps go together. I hope therefore you will try to get Bristow and Schurz into positive coöperation as soon after the former quits office as possible. Let us know what is decided as soon as may be. Bristow's name will be essential to our raising money. Our control of the organ is essential to our management of the canvass.

I shall send for Brooks today and impart to him the contents of your epistles.

[1] *N.Y. Evening Post*, I think. — H. C. L.

Just now it seems as though the Gods were kinder to us than we deserve, and were going to rescue us from our dilemma. I need not say with what extreme anxiety I look forward to the coming week.

You will be pleased to hear that Poole's article makes 35 pages, and Morgan's 43.[1] Your arithmetic seems a little weak. I am going over your Essay and to say that I have launched more imprecations at your head than would sink an archangel, is a mild statement. If you don't get a printing machine, I'll take away your degree. I don't understand more than quarter of your article but hope it's all right. At any rate, I know no better. But surely the king's income from his own land was rent rather than tax. My own MS. is all in type and yours goes to the printer this week.

I went to your house yesterday and stole some book. Wells has not arrived.

With my best regards to your wife, the Admiral and his family, I am.

To Henry Cabot Lodge

91 MARLBOROUGH ST.
23 Feby., 1876.

Your letters of the 21st and 22nd arrived today and are very agreeable. We have little to do now but to prepare ourselves for the struggle and to follow the wishes of Mr. Bristow's friends.

There is, however, one remark of Solicitor Wilson, twice repeated in your letters, to which I think I am bound to take exception. He said that in case Mr. Bristow should be defeated in convention, he would then be in our hands for the second place on a ticket of Adams and Bristow, if we chose. To this I cannot assent. There is in it a suggestion of bargaining, which appears to me inadmissible. I must protest against Schurz entering into any such trade. It is destructive of honorable dealing. If Schurz and our friends consider Mr. Bristow to be the proper candidate to support for the Presidency before the convention, they are bound to hold the same opinion after the convention. We can have but one candidate. I am myself ready to use all my little energies to bring about the election of Mr. Bristow, but only on the understanding that the candidacy of Mr. Bristow is a thing entirely apart, and unaffected by the result of the convention. I do not doubt that Schurz will take the same view, but at any rate I for one protest against any half-measures or trades, and wish you

---

[1] William Frederick Poole's article on "Dr. Cutler and the Ordinance of 1787" and Lewis H. Morgan's on "Montezuma's Dinner" appeared in the *North American Review*, April, 1876.

would distinctly repudiate it to Mr. Wilson as entering in any way into the motives of our action. Our support of Mr. Bristow must rest on higher grounds.

Meanwhile I have been diligently employed all day in the matter of the *Post*. Whether anything will come of it or not, I cannot yet say. But we shall do our utmost, and I have various schemes in my head to effect it. You will know soon.

I have finished reading your article [1] which is indeed profound. If it were mine, I think I should give it more concentration by omitting some portions and connecting the rest so as to be more intelligible to the profane. But this is not my affair and I shall send it to the printer praying that he may be great enough to decypher it.

Redfield's article ends, I think, on page 356.[2] Wells's has not come. I shall write for it.[3]

Please don't forget to send or bring me Mr. Bristow's Report. Also please send me Schurz's address which I do not know. Also please ask Boynton, or Wilson, or both, if they know Horace White's present address, and send it to me if they have it.

I envy you at Washington, not the politics but the climate. We are here all barking like puppies.

I didn't steal *Review* books. I stole your books.

With best regards to your wife, believe me.

To Henry Cabot Lodge

91 MARLBOROUGH ST.
27 February, 1876.

Yours of the 24th arrived last evening, as well as your telegram. I can't come to New York to meet you. My lectures begin on Tuesday, and I am sorry that you are coming away from Washington, for I was on the point of asking you to do something else for us. But one never gets all that life has to offer.

You will present my profoundest compliments to your wife for what I am convinced is the very just appreciation she has of my wisdom. If she would however lend me just a little of her own, so as to let me see my way clear out of the present dilemma, I should be even more satisfied than I am of the perfect superiority of my intellect.

There is but one idea to which I cling as my ark of salvation: that

---

[1] "Land Law of the Anglo-Saxons."   [2] Isaac F. Redfield on "Chief Justice Chase."

[3] David Ames Wells, on "The Reform of Local Taxation," both in the *North American Review* for April, 1876.

is, the objective point of attack; the caucus system. The problem to me is, how most to wound that.

My political education has taught me in this connection only one corollary. Even that is negative. This is, that an attack on the caucus system, if it miscarries, strengthens that system. Schurz proved this terribly in 1872 when he was made the slave of the monster he was fighting.

Now then!

1. We want to crush the caucus.
2. If we go into it, or fail in our attack, the caucus will crush us.
3. ? ? ? ? ? ? ? ? ? ? ? ?

Schurz fills up this third term of the proposition by writing to me on the 24th:

"We shall be utterly powerless if we put off our demonstration until after the convention, unless that convention...renominates Grant. My present intention is to issue invitations to a free conference" in April "to be governed in its action by the circumstances of the times."

Schurz knows better than I, and if he decides to do this, I acquiesce (provisionally) in his better judgment.

At the same time, I would suggest some reasons against its wisdom:

1. Such a conference, not to injure ourselves, must be very weighty in character and influence. Can we now get such an one?

2. It must be united in policy. Any sign of disagreement would weaken us. Are we united in policy?

3. A decision not to act at once, would be an acknowledgment of weakness. *Pro tanto*, it would hurt us.

4. A nomination would be desperate. We all know it. Why do a desperate act before being compelled?

5. A separation in disagreement would be nearly if not quite fatal.

My own diagnosis is a different one. I start from the assumption that we are too weak to do more than profit by our enemy's blunders. Is this an unfair assumption? Even Schurz concedes that the movement started on the other theory was a failure. He only urges that there is still one unknown element, the people. But we have no right to count on an unknown element.

My next step is that if the enemy make no blunders, we are powerless and should do nothing. What is the use of exhibiting our feebleness?

My next conclusion is that we should offer every inducement to the enemy to make blunders. Clear the field for them. One such is to avoid alarming them into caution. If they (the Republicans) nominate Blaine, we are nowhere. Don't deceive yourself by the idea that a presidential nominee can be broken down by charges.

Finally, if all we can hope for is to profit by the enemy's blunders, is it not in the highest degree wise to use such caution as is practicable in order that the enemy may not be able to profit by any blunders of ours? And no one can deny that any public action at all on our part, exposes us to the risk of blundering.

There is one condition and one only on which I can give my adhesion to the proposed conference. This is that Mr. Bristow and his friends should advise and consent to it; that Mr. Bristow's acceptance of its nomination should be secured in advance; and that the meeting should nominate Bristow without discussion, by acclamation, and go home.

In short, I adhere to my previous letter to Schurz. And if you can influence him in any way, I am sure you will impress upon him to the utmost this policy of coöperation with Bristow's friends. If the time shall come, as it soon must, when they shall despair of a regular nomination and shall accede to an independent one, we can call a convention for that purpose at ten days' notice.

One thing more. Lose no opportunity of putting your foot on any revival of the Adams scheme. We are well rid of it. Keep it out of sight. We can do better by other tactics.

When you see Schurz, please ask particularly after his wife on my behalf (as well as your own). I said nothing about her in my letter to him, nor about his father, and you will have to make up for my omission.

Please also make some enquiry about Nordhoff. Is he again in Washington on the *Herald*? What is his address? If White refuses and our negotiation continues for the *Post*, we may settle on Nordhoff if he will come. I know no one else so good.

I am meditating an excursion to California for my wife's cough. If so you will have to take one of my courses.

My best regards to your wife.

To Carl Schurz

6 March, 1876.

MY DEAR MR. SCHURZ, Should you feel disposed to consider the offer of the position of managing editor of one of our chief daily papers here, with a fixed salary of say $5,000 a year, and a percentage on the profits over and above a certain sum?

We are meditating the purchase of such a paper, but our action is entirely conditional on finding an editor. Of course this is very private. I have no authority to make any offer, but I must have some manager to offer to the investors in the stock, and I think with your name I should have little difficulty.

Time is very short and I must decide by Thursday next whether the scheme is to be abandoned or not. Of course I have had to make inquiries in several directions, for I have no confidence in securing you. Yet the prospect for you here, in such a position, would be far from indifferent.

To Henry Cabot Lodge

April, 1876.

Certainly! Come whenever you like. I shall be at home this evening, and tomorrow too unless I have to go to Quincy. Come as usual. My wife will be here if I am not.

You will find no little of the nervousness and wretchedness of the last week, worked off into criticisms of your essay. Don't be alarmed at it.

To Henry Cabot Lodge

BEVERLY FARMS.
15 May, 1876.

I have read your MS.[1] and think it will do you credit. Of course I have made many alterations, not in the sense, but in the words. I have cut out all the "we's" I could get at, and tried to make it less objectionably patronising toward Morse.... Probably much further labor may be profitably expended on it in proof.

You do not of course expect me to acquiesce entirely in your view of A. H. I can hardly explain the reasons of my own *kind* of aversion to him. That it is inherited is no explanation, for I inherit feelings of a very different sort towards Jefferson, Pickering, Jackson, and the legion of other life-long enemies whom my contentious precursors made. I dislike Hamilton because I always feel the adventurer in him. The very cause of your admiration is the cause of my distrust; he was equally ready to support a system he utterly disbelieved in as one that he liked. From the first to the last words he wrote, I read always the same Napoleonic kind of adventuredom, nor do I know any more

[1] On "Alexander Hamilton," printed in *North American Review*, July, 1876.

curious and startling illustration of this than the conclusion of that strange paper explaining his motives for accepting Burr's challenge. I *abhor*, says he, the practice of duelling, but "the ability to be in future useful in those crises of our public affairs which seem likely to happen, would probably be inseparable from a conformity with prejudice in this particular." What should you or I say if our great-grandfathers had left us those words as a deathbed legacy? I think we should not have so high a moral standard as I thank those gentlemen for leaving us. And I confess I think those words alone justify all John Adams's distrust of Hamilton. Future political crises all through Hamilton's life were always in his mind about to make him commander-in-chief, and his first and last written words show the same innate theory of life.

But you will not be able to assent to this.

To Henry Cabot Lodge

BEVERLY FARMS, Sunday, 4 June, 1876.

Your Marblehead friend has sent his notice of Landor.[1] As far as I have read, it strikes me as clerical. But I hand it over to you.

Blaine's nomination would now be a stroke of luck for us. But we have lost our chance. Had this exposure been delayed a fortnight until after the nomination was made, we should have had a clean sweep. As it is we may still be pestered with Washburne or Hayes. I suppose that all the old calculations are now worthless, and I wait the result of the Convention with a sort of perfunctory interest such as I feel at seeing the mosquitoes, now here. They are a nuisance, like the Convention; blood-suckers — like its members; buzzing, stinging, lean and hungry insects which can't be exterminated. We must endure them, but by the prophet — Bristow — we will roast them if we can. Our bonfire, I presume, is ready.

The *Tribune* is a good deal upset. I suspect Reid is at his wit's end for a candidate and a policy. We can now afford to throw him over.

[1] An unsigned review of Forster's *Works and Life of Walter Savage Landor* is in the *North American Review*, January, 1877.

To Henry Cabot Lodge

BEVERLY FARMS.
Wednesday, 7 June, '76.

I send your last sheet of proof. You will find no want of criticism in it. I think, however, that the article, besides irritating all your friends and exasperating all Morse's, will do you no harm. Your abuse of Jefferson is a trifle crude and wants delicacy of touch, but it is always safe to abuse Jefferson and much easier than to defend him. The tone, apart from a rather youthful tendency (which I am myself apt to indulge) to sweeping and extreme statements, is candid, and the criticism just. The weak point is still style. But it is rather above than below the *N. A. R.* average even there.

You see I don't mean absolutely to turn your head by flattery.

I hope to have five or six pages of Ticknor ready by Monday or Tuesday.

Would not W. James write us at short notice something on Howells' story, for the gap if there is one? You might try him.

I am going to write to F. T. Palgrave for a notice of Macaulay. If he won't, I will do it myself.

Gryzanowski will write two articles, both good subjects, the first for October.[1]

Your *order* of men agrees very nearly with mine, but I shall probably raise the scale. The books have arrived. Much obliged.

Our bill for *corrections* on our book[2] is now about $500; as much as the composition itself. It will make the volume cost $1500. I have already paid $750.

Poor Blaine squeals louder than all the other pigs. Schenck, Colfax, Belknap, were all nothing to him. Beecher alone can match him. I think Blaine's speech of Monday matches for impudence and far exceeds in insolence anything that Beecher ever did. We *air* a great people. But disgust has now filled my mind for the whole subject, and I am slowly contemplating the figures of Hayes and Washburne. What a mess it all is! And how glad I am that I have not got to go to Cincinnati. Bullock is sensible.

[1] E. Gryzanowski, "Wagner's Theories of Music," appeared in the *North American Review*, January, 1877.

[2] *Anglo-Saxon Law.*

To Henry Cabot Lodge

BEVERLY FARMS, MASS.
Wednesday, 12 June, [1876.]

The library notifies me that the *third* volume of the Krit-Ueber has not been returned. Do you recollect what became of it?

We miss your visits. I see no one now to keep me posted.

The July *N. A. R.* is very good. I read your article over again and thought it read very well indeed. I fancy it will give you reputation.

I think my three pictures very successful.

When you make up the list of payments, please insert for Thévenin [1] (they have his address) a draft for 150 francs. Let a check for $20 for the notice of Ticknor,[2] be made out and sent to *me*.

The October number will be very political. Besides Boynton's article (would not Wilson have written it now?), Hazen [3] is to send one of twenty pages on the Belknap business; and finally my brother Charles and I mean to concoct a political article together.[4]

I suppose Lowell will not do Transcendentalism. I shall ask Mrs. P. to do it.[5]

With our best regards to Mrs. Lodge.

To Charles Milnes Gaskell

BEVERLY FARMS, 14 June, 1876.

I was rejoiced to see your hand again the other day, and to hear a little of your news. Our correspondence, for the first time has flagged of late, and indeed it is a wonder to me that it does not expire, for I have literally nothing to write that can possibly be of more than a very vague interest to you. If the world in London grows old and wanes towards its dotage, the world here stands still. Boston is a curious place. Its business in life is to breed and to educate. The parent lives for his children; the child, when educated himself, becomes a parent, or becomes an educator, or is both. But no further result is ever reached. Just as at twenty the parent reproduces himself in a

[1] Marcel Thévenin, whose review of Heinrich Gottfried Gengler's *Germanische Rechtsdenkmalen* was printed in the *North American Review*, July, 1876.

[2] In the July number.

[3] William Babcock Hazen (1830–1887), who had brought charges of fraud against post-traders which involved Belknap.

[4] "The 'Independents' in the Canvass."

[5] An unsigned review of Octavius Brooks Frothingham's *Transcendentalism in New England* appeared in the October number.

child, so the teacher reproduces himself in his scholar. But neither as child nor as scholar does the new generation do more than devote itself to become in its turn parent and teacher. Nothing ever comes of it all. There is no society worth the name, no wit, no intellectual energy or competition, no clash of minds or of schools, no interests, no masculine self-assertion or ambition. Everything is respectable, and nothing amusing. There are no outlaws. There are not only no convictions but no strong wants. Dr. Holmes, who does the wit for the city of three hundred thousand people, is allowed to talk as he will — wild atheism commonly — and no one objects. I am allowed to sit in my chair at Harvard College and rail at everything which the College respects, and no one cares. Apparently the view of life fairly adopted here is that the business of each generation shall be to generate and educate a succeeding generation. English women would open their eyes to see the elaboration of our nurseries. Englishmen would be utterly bewildered at the slavery of the parents to their children. As an educator and not as a parent, I am exasperated by the practical working of the system at college, where the teacher assumes that teaching is his end in life, and that he has no time to work for original results. But when a society has reached this point, it acquires a self-complacency which is wildly exasperating. My fingers itch to puncture it; to do something which will sting it into impropriety.

The year's work draws to its end. My lectures are over and my classes dispersed. My book will be out, I hope, in about a month.... The book is fearfully learned. You cannot read it, and I advise you not to open it. But I shall send you a copy. It will cost me about four hundred pounds, very little of which I expect to get back except in my three students, whose work fills three-fourths of the volume. Their success is mine, and I make the investment for them, expecting to draw my profit from their success. My own position will only bring your friend Freeman about my ears. I have contradicted every English author, high and low....

I recollect that my last letters have dealt largely with politics. We organized our party, and as usual have been beaten. After our utmost efforts we have only succeeded in barring the road to our opponents and forcing them to nominate as candidate for the Presidency one Hayes of Ohio, a third rate nonentity, whose only recommendation is that he is obnoxious to no one. I hope to enjoy the satisfaction of voting against him. The only good result of all the past eighteen months of work has been the savage hunting-down of powerful scoundrels and the display of the awful corruption of our system in root and branch. But our people as yet seem quite callous. If any storm of popular disgust is impending, no sign of it as yet darkens the air. We shall keep at it, and good will come in time. I hope only mildly, but croaking is little better than confessing to be a bore....

To Henry Cabot Lodge

Monday, 19 June, [1876.]

Of course we are *joués* by the Hayes nomination. Our organs, perhaps wisely, are trying to capture him, I see, and make him one of us. Organised resistance is impossible and you will have a quiet summer.

It is barely possible that the man may turn out right. I shall wait to get the most exact information I can as to his character. If there is any solid reason to suppose him a capable man, likely to understand and perform his duties, we should do wrong not to support him.

As at present advised, however, I shall vote for the Democrat.

To Henry Cabot Lodge

21 June, 1876.

Pray Heaven I get some of the $60. But I know the College too well.

I passed half an hour today at the printing office trying to make the number come out straight. At last I gave it up in despair. I told them to ask Osgood to give us half a sheet more. If he refused, then to make it come out right anyhow.

I am glad to hear about the books. I had almost given them up. The check shall be sent when they arrive.

Brooks is superb.[1] I shall read that oration.

My mind is made up to shut my mouth on politics. I can't see what we ought to do and I fear doing mischief. But try and preserve the organisation.

E. W. H.[2] is quite right about the College.

To Henry Cabot Lodge

BEVERLY FARMS, MASS.
24 June, 1876.

I presume you saw on the MS. that the printers were ordered to send that proof and MS. to *me*. I am preparing a letter to them — not civil.

---

[1] Brooks Adams delivered an oration on July 4th.

[2] Edward William Hooper (1839-1901), treasurer of Harvard University, 1876-1898.

Meanwhile please bear in mind that the author of that notice made it a condition that *no* one, not even you, should know the authorship. Therefore please send me the MS. and never hint that you know anything.

I am sorry to bother the printers, and still more sorry that you should have had the trouble to write an extra page. Unluckily I have already prepared a notice of Thévenin's to fill the gap (which the printers notified me of when I was at the office), and as we must pay for it anyway, I prefer to utilise it.

Moreover I wish the printers to understand that my orders are to be taken notice of and obeyed. I shall therefore stop everything, and oblige them to send me the Ticknor as well as the Thévenin in proof, with a sharp intimation to them to be more exact next time.

I don't greatly care for Millet's [1] comments on the Centennial. He is a protégé of Charles's, and his experience is not extensive. I would rather get some one whose name carries more weight.

I have taken your corrections of the plates from Young [2] and brought them down here, but have not yet had time to look at them. There is no hurry. Laughlin can hardly go on for another week.

Politics have ceased to interest me. I am satisfied that the machine can't be smashed this time. As I feared, we have ourselves saved it by a foolish attempt to run it, which we never shall succeed in. The Caucus and the machine will outlive me, and that being the case, I prefer to leave this greatest of American problems to shrewder heads than mine. When the day comes on which it will be considered as disgraceful to be seen in a caucus as to be seen in a gambling house or brothel, then my interest will wake up again and legitimate politics will get a new birth.

With best regards to your wife.

To Henry Cabot Lodge

BEVERLY FARMS.
Sunday, 25 June, 1876.

I have been spending a day over your Essay [3] trying to make the corrections fit. As they stand, you would have to break up all the plates and change all the paging. On pages 93–94 you have scratched out 426 letters or letter spaces, and inserted 612, or about three lines

[1] Francis Davis Millet (1846–1912).
[2] Ernest Young, then instructor in History and Roman Law (1852–1888).
[3] The references are to Lodge's *Essays in Anglo-Saxon Law*.

more than there is room for. If the printers can find room, well and good, but as you insert another extra line on page 96, I fear their arithmetic might be stumped.

I found that in order to do the job intelligently I must understand the text, and much to my humiliation that my mind was as much puzzled by it as by Emerson. I had to sit down and write out for myself what you seemed to mean. I accordingly inclose to you my paraphrase of about a page. If this is what you mean, I think with a little condensation you can squeeze yourself into the space. If not, I would like to have my intelligence rubbed up by a more exact statement.

This assumes that 44 lines of 60 letters each, are to be recast. The difficulty on p. 96 can, I think, get itself more easily arranged. I should suggest:

"Duke Alfred in his will prays the kind to give his son the folc-land, in opposition to the boc-land which he devised as of right." Or some such shorter phrase.

Forgive my stupidity. I can *not* understand things that to other men are plain as a poker, and above all I cannot understand law.

P.S. I can't get my books from Leonard's.

To Henry Cabot Lodge

Beverly Farms, Mass.
Saturday — 27/6. '76.

Ah-h-h-h-h-h-h-h-h-h-h-h!!!
I think I see your confusion! You blushed and your limbs shook. Well! I am glad, for I hunted through all my own papers for it yesterday morning in Boston, and had begun to feel shaken in my own methodicality. I regret to say that the list is useless as it is. We must have the exact titles and editions. Moreover, we want none but works actually cited or referred to.[1] Are all these in that category?

By all means get the index ready. Young and I are at work on ours.

Young comes down here Wednesday to pass the night. If you could come either for Wednesday night or Thursday morning, and *bring a copy of your Essay*, we might settle everything. Your Essay is already in Torrey's [2] hands.

I feel little anxiety about Conkling. It would be too much luck for

[1] Probably the "Titles of Works Cited," prefixed to *Essays in Anglo-Saxon Law.*

[2] Henry Warren Torrey (1814–1893), McLean professor of ancient and modern history in Harvard University.

us. But I do fear Blaine, because the Convention will see that we cannot deal with him so easily. He will divide us. I feel *no* real hope about Bristow. But things look to me as though the Democrats might yet help us through.

P.S. I spoke to Charles Eliot about Schurz's LL.D. He expressed some doubts owing to there being two on the stocks. But a little pressure will do something perhaps. Set Brimmer or Harry Lee or my father on him. And see that Frank Parkman and Ned Hooper are posted.[1]

To Henry Cabot Lodge

BEVERLY FARMS,
30 June, 1876.

Your note of yesterday has just arrived and was very pleasing to my feelings. You will one day feel the advantage of my not having spoiled you by flattery. Take care that you do not feel the evil of adopting a different course towards me.

Nothing since I came to Cambridge has given me so much and so unalloyed satisfaction as the completion of our baking this batch of doctors of philosophy.[2] I am pleased with my scholars and proud of them. They have shown qualities which I believe to be of the first order. It is true that the highest quality of the mind — imagination — is utterly wanting in our American character and of course in the best of our students; but so it is now-a-days everywhere else, and the fault is probably in the age. Setting this aside, I believe that my scholars will compare favorably with any others, English, German, French or Italian. I look with more hope on the future of the world as I see how good our material is.

I am gratified at your warm praise of Young's appearance at commencement. His paper read well, better than I had expected; so well that I had no suggestions to offer, which seemed to disappoint him a little. There is a natural neatness about his work which stamps it as quite peculiar. Even in College his mind was almost singular in its clearness. Simpson had a similar mental quality, but I do not know that I have ever met it elsewhere. Young owes nothing to me but opportunity.

[1] The degree of LL.D. was conferred by the University in June on Alexander Hamilton Rice, Carl Schurz, and William Dwight Whitney.

[2] Young, Laughlin and I received the degree of Ph.D. for our Thesis on Anglo-Saxon Law embodied in this book. — H. C. L.

For once I have been in a state of absolute satisfaction for a whole day. I am not only as pleased as Punch about my Ph.D.'s, but highly delighted to have carried our point about Schurz, and to crown all comes Tilden. Before the result, I thought I should be perplexed between Tilden and Hayes, but to my great amusement I found that my mind decided the matter without any need of calling on the will. I have no ill-will to Hayes. If he is elected I shall support him loyally. But I can no more resist the pleasure of voting for Tilden than I could turn my back on a friend. I too fought with Erie! And shall I now reject the leader who then led me to triumph! Schurz may do what he will. I advise him to do nothing. As for me, I have no hesitation.

I would have liked to see G. B.[1] He is an entertaining man, and is the great authority on American history, at least for facts. I am glad he praised your Hamilton, and I wish the latter were out, but they have not yet sent me the last sheet in proof. This morning I get sheet 14 (pp. 209–224) marked as gone to press. The A[nglo] S[axon] Essays are still stationary, but Laughlin and his wife pass Sunday with us, and I hope to set things going again. Brooks is coming down, also, to-day or tomorrow, I hope, to discuss oration with me.

The books arrived, a very useful and interesting lot. I send the check to Leonard at once. Thanks for your trouble. The binding of Niles's Register is a choice sample of American art fifty years ago. I have read Marbury *vs.* Madison with care, and talked with Wendell Holmes on the theory of the constitution.

Give our love to Will Big.[2] He must come and see us again before he goes back.

To Henry Cabot Lodge

BEVERLY FARMS.
Sunday, 16 July, 1876.

I would answer your friend civilly; say that you will be happy to print his productions from time to time; that we are however rather crowded and cannot promise publication; and that you hope he is quite well; and his wife!

I am glad Brooks wrote to you and I would like to see his letter.

I am giving your A.-S. Essay a final revise, and will have the corrections ready for you to see when you next come down. Perhaps it would be better for you and Mr. James to come down next week

---

[1] George Bancroft. *See* Mass. Hist. Socy., *Proceedings*, LX, 305.
[2] Dr. William Sturgis Bigelow.

rather than this; that is, after *next* Sunday. If you come sooner, you may find us occupied; and anyway I shall rather want to see you about a week hence.

To Henry Cabot Lodge

BEVERLY FARMS
31 July, 1876.

I have your two notes, and accept your amendment in substituting *lazy* for *loose*. I didn't mean to say you *couldn't* think closely. If I thought that, I shouldn't blackguard you so steadily for not doing it. But for men like you and me, Buffon's aphorism is the only safe guide: *Le génie, c'est une longue patience!* Keep at it, and never think anything finished while you have time to improve it.

I am very glad my father wrote to you, the more so as I never heard of his volunteering such a compliment to anyone before. He never wrote to me nor even spoke to me in his life about any production of mine. He grows younger with years. His letter will counterbalance mine.

We howled with delight over the Sunday *Herald's* puff [1] of you. Some men, you know, achieve greatness, and some have it thrust upon them. Haskell must have his little joke, but some jokes become earnest in time. We shall come up some day, if not into office, at least into authority.

Bristow's "equanimity" is the result, I suppose, of his conviction that the Republican party is too corrupt for reform, at least in Hayes's hands. My own conviction is that whichever course we take, we shall wish we had taken the other. I see that Sam Bowles represents the Adams family as "solid" for Tilden. Isn't he premature? I had supposed that Tilden's letter was an important element in the case.

I do not see the defect in my statement about Puritan intolerance. The Puritans rose between 1600 and 1630 when the Massachusetts colony came over. I never have understood or been able to explain to my own satisfaction the causes which produced them. I have never seen a satisfactory explanation of them. If you study carefully the court history of James 1st, you will, I think, find no reason for asserting that the court opinions were bigoted — very far from it. That Charles 1st and Laud were bigots has nothing to do with the matter. They were resisting a Puritan movement already full-grown.

[1] A little paragraph suggesting me (as a joke) for Senator from Massachusetts. — H. C. L.

I advise you to read Gardiner's books.[1] They are not written like Macaulay's but they are fairer. And even Macaulay modified his admiration for the Puritans in later life. I admire them as much as ever, but I shall not deny that they were intolerant even according to the age in which they lived.

You say not a word of your wife. Please give her our best regards.

To Henry Cabot Lodge

BEVERLY FARMS, MASS.
2 August, 1876.

Your second Roger Williams has come.[2] It is much improved.

I shall get Read's article on Monday and send it to the printers if nothing else turns up within a week. We can't wait any longer. Our political manifesto must go in last. We shall want to have all the information possible on the course of the canvass. I think we shall have to cut down to four articles this time, for Boynton will need space. Then we shall have Read, Hazen, Boynton and ourselves.

To Henry Cabot Lodge

BEVERLY FARMS, MASS.
August 5, 1876.

We are very glad to get yours of yesterday.

I too have just finished von Holst, and will make you a proposition. If you will write one notice of it, I will write another, and then we will take what is best out of each and roll them into one. I do not propose this merely for the sake of the notice, but because I think it will give us both a spur of emulation, so that we shall do the most perfect work we can. I am by no means unsusceptible to such incitements, and to you they are the best possible tutors. Perhaps we could make an article for October in place of Reed's.[3]

Whitney wrote to me that his MS. had accidentally been held back and would come on soon.

What say you to Tilden's letter? I am curious to see the Republican and soft-money comments. It is obviously directed to Democrats and to the soft-shell wing. I wonder what comfort they will draw from it.

---

[1] Samuel Rawson Gardiner (1829–1902).

[2] A note on Henry Martyn Dexter's *As to Roger Williams and his Banishment from the Massachusetts Plantation* in the *Review* for October, 1876.

[3] The joint review, signed, appeared in the October *Review*.

I am clearly of opinion that Tilden offers us the best chance of currency reform. *Per contra*, Hayes would save us the shock of another cleaning out of all the existing officials, for Tilden avows his determination to do this. Tilden's election would seem to promise best for revenue reform and free-trade. *Per contra*, Hayes offers the best guaranty for good-behavior in the South. Tilden offers however one inducement which to me seems very great. He will give the Democratic party again some principles and some brains, and so force the Republicans to a higher level. On the whole I still incline towards Tilden, without giving up the right to see better light hereafter. My real object is of course to increase the independent power, and to that object all others are in my mind subordinate. Whether the election of Tilden or Hayes will do most towards this, is a point which depends on many accidents and is incapable of solution. Others therefore may rush into the fray. I shall read history....

To Henry Cabot Lodge

BEVERLY FARMS.
23 August, 1876.

I enclose you the review of v. Holst into which I have tried to work all the material. I like it, and think the criticism is sharp enough in places to suit even Brooks. The last two pages are *my* centennial oration. If you are satisfied with it, send it to the printers as Article II.

Trescot's article arrived and has gone to the printers as Article one.[1] It will do to complete the political unity of the number and for a Southerner is in pretty good tone.

If Boynton's article suits, we shall be well provided. But I hear nothing from Hazen. We may have difficulty in filling the gap.

Haskell is a low intriguer. Tell him from me that there is only one matter of political interest. The *Herald* should formally announce that no independent votes will be cast for either Abbot or Frost, but that it is determined to throw away their votes on Martin Brimmer.

To Henry Cabot Lodge

BEVERLY FARMS
25 August, 1876.

Boynton's article is good and well written for a newspaper man. I long to add a page on the political moral, but perhaps it is better for

[1] William Henry Trescot, "The Southern Question."

you to ask him to do so. Will you write to him to say that I have read the paper with delight; that the proofs will be sent to him just as soon as we can get it into type; and that meanwhile I would be glad, as aiming at the general purpose of our whole number, if he would add another page in order to accent *in the strongest possible language* the political moral of the whiskey ring, which I conceive to be that in the struggle for reform the country must expect to have both party organisations against it, and can never be more than temporarily successful until it has struck at the root of party organisations themselves and cut off *all* their sources of political corruption. This is in order to make this article tally with the tone of the number.

Truly we are working a good work. Let us stay blandly on the fence. Perhaps the Democrats will go the Republicans one better, and offer us Evarts. I am ready now to believe that our howling is useful, and, since it works so well, I think we had better go on talking Tilden. I am unwilling to check latent virtue.

Isn't Gen. Banks good on my father? The General is certainly a wonderful creature.

To Henry Cabot Lodge

BEVERLY FARMS
31 August, 1876.

The political field is amusing though somewhat saddening to the believer in human perfectibility. I imagine that the elections in our original volkmotes were better illustrations of self-government, so that we have not got far as yet. I am interested in seeing how very few of our so-called independents have been able to keep their heads clear and to resist the torrent of partisanship. And I have been still more interested to see how with every day the strength of the party organisations has asserted itself more and more, until on each side the old issues and the old forces stand without pretence of reform and idiotically pound at each other and at every one who does not get out of their way. This has some good results. The best of these to me will be the prevention of my father's candidacy by the Democrats, to which I am most earnestly and emphatically opposed, not because Kelly endorses or Banks opposes (I care as little for one as the other), but because it is a thoroughly false position for him to stand in. The Democratic caucuses last night, I hope, have finished this scheme.

The question who to vote for is one which every man will settle for himself. I care very little one way or the other. There are good grounds for voting either way. And whichever side we vote on, we must have either Ben Butler or Ben Allen as a companion. I do not propose to get into this mêlée at all, and if you prefer to halloo for Hayes, and Gen. Bartlett for Tilden, why! go ahead! and proceed to crack your heads reciprocally. Only leave mine alone. The tendency to blackguard the Adamses generally is, however, irresistible to the average American politician and as we shall catch it equally whether we vote for Hayes or Tilden or not at all, we can afford to grin at it.

I did read "Republican Sectionalism" with approval. Haskell's course is still admirable. The only thing in the campaign that really delights me is Butler's candidacy which I hope may be successful. If he and Banks and Frost and so on, go to Washington as representatives of the Republican party, while H. L. Pierce and Seelye[1] drop out, Massachusetts republicanism will be truly virtuous.

Mrs. Lodge's criticism on the terms used in characterizing French and English works on America, is very just, and a *caveat* shall be inserted. I am still buried in avalanches of State Papers and such gay reading, which leave me little confidence in a future life. No life could be long enough for such work.

To Henry Cabot Lodge

BEVERLY FARMS
4 Sept. 1876.

Our last galley of the *Essays* is now about to be made up into pages, and there remains only the index. If you have any further corrections to make, send them in at once.

Thanks for your extract from Tim. Pickering. It is, as you say, very characteristic. What a queer result we should reach if we were always to be precluded from accepting the conclusions of a majority!

I have read all Timothy's diplomatic papers lately. What a man to deal with *tête-montés* Frenchmen! Washington certainly felt the absurd incongruity of this, and Adams still more so. The surly contempt, varied by ingenuity of insult, with which he treated the insanely sensitive Frenchman of that day, is entertaining to see. But I am wholly of my great-grandfather's opinion as to his fitness for his post. There would hardly have been a worse selection for it. At a time when by Jay's treaty we were really doing France a scurvy trick and abandoning ground which she had a right to expect us to maintain, such a man was the very person to add insult to injury. The X.Y.Z. papers

[1] Julius Hawley Seelye (1824–1895), at the time a member of Congress from Massachusetts.

are curiously interesting, and Gerry appears in them to much greater advantage than I supposed. Talleyrand's humiliation before him is very striking and dramatic.

Console yourself about politics. You are indeed the one who has the best right to complain, for you had the most trouble in forming that rope of sand, the Independent party. I cannot help laughing to think how, after all our labor and after we had by main force created a party for Schurz to lead, he himself, without a word or a single effort to keep his party together, kicked us over in his haste to jump back to the Republicans. If he had taken the least pains to hold his friends together, I feel sure we would have spoken with effect. I, for one, would have been glad to join in any combined action, whichever way the majority decided. And in that case, Schurz's voice would not now be isolated and shrill. Well! We knew what he was! I am not angry with him, but of course his leadership is at an end. The leader who treats his followers in that way, is a mere will-o'-the-wisp. I hope he will get his Cabinet office, and I hope he will forget that we ever worked to make him our leader, independent of party. He can hereafter buy power only by devotion to party, and further connection with us would not help us and would be fatal to him.

Don't be disheartened by the excesses of party spirit. It was our interest to have Blaine nominated. It is our interest to have Butler and Banks and all the other scalawags elected. I earnestly wish it. Only so can we expect a strong reaction in our favor two years hence.

To Charles Milnes Gaskell

Beverly Farms, 8 Sept., 1876.

• • • • • • • • •

The worst of home is that one is condemned to listen to all the old hand-organ tunes. The worst of these is the Presidential election. My party, which I labored so devotedly to organise, as I have written you from time to time, got so far as to hold a meeting at New York and issue an address. That was the last of it. The two parties made their offers for us, and we dissolved like a summer cloud. I am left smiling at the ruins. Our principal leader has returned to his party traces. My father has been set up by one party that hates him, as a candidate for the very insignificant post of Governor of Massachusetts, and he will be knocked over by the other party which hates him equally. Both parties are impossibly corrupt and the public thoroughly indifferent.

Of course I must have my little say, and I have devoted the whole October number of the *North American* to a review of the field. The result is sickening. But I consider my October number a historical monument, and am going to avail myself of a trifling disagreement with the publishers to throw off that load also and get rid of my editorial duties, leaving my monument behind me.[1]

My volume of Anglo-Saxon Law will be out next week. This has been a really satisfactory piece of work. I shall be curious to learn whether your universities think they can do better. If so, they have hitherto hidden their powers very carefully.

I am just beginning my grind at the university wheel, and for my sins I am becoming popular in my old age. My classes are very large, one of them is near seventy in number. As I detest large classes, I am much disgusted at this, and have become foul and abusive in my language to them, hoping to drive them away. But I think it more likely I shall be driven away myself. If the new Secretary of State is a friend of mine, I shall try the experiment of passing a winter in Washington, searching archives. I regard my university work as essentially done. All the influence I can exercise has been exercised. The end of it is mere railing at the idiocies of a university education....

To Charles Milnes Gaskell

NEW YORK, 14 April, 1877.

. . . .

I am again in New York, devoting all my energies to the arrangement of a great mass of papers [2] which have accidentally come under my hands, and which may give me some years' work and exercise a good deal of influence on my future movements.... The future is very vague to me. My political friends, or one wing of them, have come into power, but under circumstances which prevent me from giving them more than a silent and temporary sympathy. This is an illustration of the way politics work; always unsatisfactorily. Meanwhile I hob-nob with the leaders of both parties, and am very contented under my cloak of historian. I am satisfied that literature offers higher prizes than politics, and I am willing to look on at my friends who differ from

[1] The October issue contained a notice by the publishers to the effect that the editors having retired from the management of the *Review* "on account of a difference of opinion with the proprietors as to the political character of this number, the proprietors, rather than cause an indefinite delay in publication, have allowed the number to retain the form which had been given to it, without, however, committing the *Review* to the opinions expressed therein."

[2] Papers of Albert Gallatin.

me on that point of theory. Naturally we are not unhappy about your European mêlée....

To Henry Cabot Lodge

BEVERLY FARMS,
12 June, 1877.

Thanks for your translation and invitation. Mrs. Adams has responded to the latter and I will only add that I am sorry we can't come, for I should enjoy a chat. Yet I am just now rather overworked and until I can get things in running order I shall have hardly time to go off except for necessity. Gallatin is unwieldy.

As for the Latin, how was I to know what it meant? A much better translation would be: "What a shame it would be to regret an Essex Junto head."

I don't know but what my late marginal notes are becoming offensively personal. If so, rub 'em out.

To Charles Milnes Gaskell

BEVERLY FARMS, 22 June, 1877.

.   .   .   .

I really wanted to "do" your uncle's book, which has amused and even instructed me and induced me to buy a complete set of Wordsworth, Prelude, Excursion and all, for the first time. But my connection with the press is now at an end. I have no papers to write in. I told him so, but please say something kind to him as from me when you meet him. The truth is, he has humor, and that is worth pretty much everything else in the world; but dull people can't quite pardon it....

To Henry Cabot Lodge

29 June, 1877.

My notice is gone to Godkin to be published next week.[1] It is ingeniously calculated to make everyone, yourself included, furious with indignation. But I think it will excite interest in the book and sell the edition.

My wife tells me you think of going to the Social Science Congress. I hope you will. To know and be known widely is one of the elements of success. Look wise and say nothing. The highest results flow from silence.

[1] Review of Lodge's *Life and Letters of George Cabot*, in *The Nation*, July 5, 1877.

IX

WASHINGTON

1877–1879

To Charles Milnes Gaskell

1501 H Street, Washington,
25 November, 1877.

We have made a great leap in the world; cut loose at once from all that has occupied us since our return from Europe, and caught new ties and occupations here. The fact is I gravitate to a capital by a primary law of nature. This is the only place in America where society amuses me, or where life offers variety. Here, too, I can fancy that we are of use in the world, for we distinctly occupy niches which ought to be filled. We have taken a large house in which we seem lost. Our water-colors and drawings go with us wherever we go, and here are our great evidence of individuality, and our title to authority. As I am intimate with many of the people in power and out of power, I am readily allowed or aided to do all the historical work I please; and as I am avowedly out of politics, there will, it is to be hoped, be no animosities to meet. Literary and non-partisan people are rare here, and highly appreciated. And yet society in its way is fairly complete, almost as choice, if not as large, as in London or Rome.

One of these days this will be a very great city if nothing happens to it. Even now it is a beautiful one, and its situation is superb. As I belong to the class of people who have great faith in this country and who believe that in another century it will be saying in its turn the last word of civilisation, I enjoy the expectation of the coming day, and try to imagine that I am myself, with my fellow *gelehrte* here, the first faint rays of that great light which is to dazzle and set the world on fire hereafter. Our duties are perhaps only those of twinkling, and many people here, like little Alice, wonder what we're at. But twinkle for twinkle, I prefer our kind to that of the small politician....

To Henry Cabot Lodge

1501 H Street
Washington. 2 Dec'r, 1877.

My volume is now in print, all but the index, and I will send you a set of the proofs in a few days.[1] It should be out before Christmas.

---

[1] *New England Federalism.*

You will find that I have used a large proportion of the letters you have printed, but I have tried to do it in such a way as should advertise you. The two volumes ought to sell each other.

We are muchly amusing ourselves here. I find a mass of new Gallatin matter in the Jefferson papers and am burrowing in rich soil. The winter's work is under my eyes. Of course Boston is much preferable to this place, but we manage to get on.

Of politics I keep quite clear, but hear a good deal of it. Schurz is *accouché*, at last, of his report, and is gay again. He dined here with Hewitt,[1] Nordhoff[2] and William Story last week, and the charming Agatha dines here tonight. We met him again on Friday evening at the White House, and he insisted on our going home with him to smoke a cigar, which we did, my wife and I. The Evarts's are very cordial and civil, and the State Department magnificently hospitable.

Politics are a good deal mixed. Republicanism seems gone up. I take little account of it anyway. The condition of the Democrats is more important, and the question when their leaders will take hold again is one of great interest. As for the administration, it is Andrew Johnson over again, with more respectability and a better balance of parties.

Schurz says he has a letter from you which he means now to answer. Lumber and Indians are his sole mental food just at present.

To Henry Cabot Lodge

1501 H Street,
3 Jany, 1878.

I have just read your notice of N.E. Federalism and congratulate you on the judicial elevation you are attaining. The notice is really excellent and leaves nothing to be desired.

Our best regards to you and yours. Nothing new here.

To Henry Cabot Lodge

1501 H Street, Washington,
Sunday, 6 Jan., 1878.

Yours of the 4th arrived yesterday. I had already written to you about the notice and I suppose you received my note on Friday. I will only add that as I kept myself out of the book, so far as possible, I think it just as well that I should keep out of the notices. I have even

[1] Abram Stevens Hewitt (1822–1903).   [2] Charles Nordhoff (1830–1901).

had the binding altered so as to take my name off the back where it was put, contrary to my express order, in imitation, I suppose, of your volume. As there is nothing of mine in it but the preface and the index, it is ridiculous to put my name on the back like an author's.

I do not see newspapers, and except the highly intelligent notices you enclosed to me, I have met with nothing except a paragraph in the *Washington Union* evidently founded on your *Nation* article and pointing a moral for the South. Our books are not for newspapers. We only go for students. I gave Lamar a copy, however, and doubtless you and I will some day be heartily cursed by the New England Congressman.

Gallatin goes bravely on. I have just finished the whiskey rebellion.

As for the silver bill, Nordhoff's letters will tell you all we know. Here we think it will pass in its worst form, and that the President will veto it on the ground that it makes no reserve for the national debt or the import duties. Then will follow an attempt to pass it over the veto. As yet we cannot judge the result. If this fails and the bill is then amended to provide for the bonds and imports in gold, Lamar and others think the President will sign it; Schurz has not spoken to me lately about it, but did believe the President would veto. It will probably pass over his veto.

The consequences belong to the region of mixed influences. I doubt whether they can be very immediate or violent. But doubtless our capitalists will protect themselves. They are warned and are wiser than these children of light.

You can easily hedge by putting up a margin of any required sum on gold, which is better than buying exchange. If gold falls, it is simply a charge to insurance. Otherwise you are all right.

I have doubted whether to write to Ned Hooper on the subject, but decided not. He must judge for himself.

The Bulletin came and I was glad to see it. The College is worth working for in spite of its ponderosity.

To Henry Cabot Lodge

WASHINGTON, 1 Feby., 1878.

I know of no evidence in regard to Jefferson's attitude towards the Chase impeachment except the vote in Senate. By examining that, and ascertaining which way his confidential friends voted, you can form some conclusion as to his own attitude. Of course it would be absurd to suppose that he interfered in the matter otherwise than by holding himself aloof. He was too good a party leader to oppose directly a party measure.

I made an attempt on Nordhoff with a view of sassing Gail,[1] but apparently the *Herald* does not care to mix in the fray. As that episode is now over, I think it too late to ring in. She hurts herself and Blaine more than we can hurt them, and, as a criticism of you, her papers are only absurd. She has missed all the true points. Your danger is a very simple one, and no one can hurt you but yourself. It is that of adopting the view of one side of a question. No man whose mind will not work on its own independent pivot, can escape being drawn into the whirlpool of party prejudices. Unless you can find some basis of faith in general principles, some theory of the progress of civilization which is outside and above all temporary questions of policy, you must infallibly think and act under the control of the man or men whose thought, in the times you deal with, coincides most nearly with your prejudices. This is the fault with almost every English historian. Very few of them have had scientific minds, and still fewer have honestly tried to keep themselves clear of personal feeling.

Your syllabus seems clear and comprehensive. If you can only manage with your large diversion, to make your men work for themselves, you are all right.

I am getting on tolerably well and have finished a first draft of my biography of Gallatin down to 1801. Meanwhile my scribe works away on the Jefferson papers.

Alice Hooper is expected here on the 9th to pass two days with us on her way south. After that, we shall look for you.

Politics have taken a queer turn. Parties are broken up for the time, and the administration is enjoying unexpected repose. As usual the pessimists talk of the end of the world. I confess to being more interested in the practical working out of the situation.

To Henry Cabot Lodge

WASHINGTON, 28 April, 1878.

The winter's work is over and we are soon to start home again. It has quite answered my expectations and I return with much new material and a large part of Gallatin completed. Another year will I hope see this job accomplished.

I have been so busy since you left us that I have been unwilling to

---

[1] Gail Hamilton (Mary Abigail Dodge), whose letters hostile to Civil Service Reform were appearing in the *New York Tribune*.

spare time for correspondence. But we have now fixed the 9th for leaving Washington. As we expect first to go down to Virginia and then to Western Pennsylvania I hardly know when we shall reach home.

There is little to tell you that is new here. Congress is on its appropriation bills and will hardly get the time to play games any more. It has the tariff to deal with. The administration gains ground. This is not saying much, for it certainly had little ground to lose, but I see no reason to regret it. The fact is that the public interests are better off under the present arrangement than they are likely to be under any that promised to succeed it. Mr. Hayes, if he can worry through the rest of this session, has nothing to fear and everything to hope. We shall do well not to bother him, but to mind our own business, and make money if we can.

I hear from the newspapers that you are entered for another year's run at the College. I do not believe you can do better; but keep hard at work. Otherwise you will feel as though it didn't pay. In true light, nothing pays; but nothing certainly pays better than your kind of work if well done. Laughlin too comes into the College I see, and rejoice at. Young has never written to me. How does he get on? Give him my regards if you see him.

We are delighted with our cousin Bell's engagement, but we don't know much about Mr. Balfour. Can you enlighten us? The British Legation can do little towards it.

Give our kindest regards to your wife. I keep your Law Magazine to return at Beverly.

To Charles Milnes Gaskell

BEVERLY FARMS, 30 May, 1878.

. . . .

Of ourselves I can, thank Heaven, give you only pleasant news. We have had a very cheerful winter at Washington. I have worked hard and with good effect. My wife has helped me and has had a house always amusing and interesting. We have had all the society we wished and have found everyone friendly and ready to amuse us and to be amused. Our little dinners of six and eight were as pleasant as any I ever was at, even in London. And Washington has one advantage over other capitals, that a single house counts for more than half a dozen elsewhere; there are so few of them. Among my set of friends this winter has been our old Roman acquaintance Schlözer, who is great fun, eccentric as an Englishman and riotous as a wild Highlander. We lament together over our Roman hostess and her *boudins Richelieu*. But you should just try Schlözer's *Gänsebrust* if you want to experience sudden death. Not many of your compatriots have been in Washington, besides Lord Dufferin [1] who was a success and developed uncommon social tact. The young Britishers who are *on the make*, as they call their search for rich wives, do not come to Washington....

To Henry Cabot Lodge

BEVERLY FARMS,
7 August, 1878.

I should tell Wilson [2] squarely that more harm than good will be done by stirring now. Even Bristow would be injured by trotting him out so early. We are all sick of elections and glad to repose under Mr. Hayes's respectable nullity.

I myself am a Grant man. But I don't say so publicly. The only thing I care about is the Democratic nomination. But I have carefully arranged to be abroad that summer. Presidential elections make me sick.

To Charles Milnes Gaskell

BEVERLY FARMS, 21 August, 1878.

.   .   .   .

I expect that we shall ourselves be coming out again about a year hence, with a view to passing a winter in Spain and Paris, and a spring in London, where we shall probably take a house for the season. I much fear, however, that my diplomacy will get me ashore, for the whole object of my journey is to study the diplomatic correspondence of the three governments, in regard to America, during the time of Napoleon, from 1800 to 1812. Unless I can get this object, I shall throw away my trouble, and so I am straining every nerve to open in advance the doors of three Foreign Offices. I shall come with an official letter of introduction from this Department of State, and shall ask Sir Edward Thornton to give me another. But if you ever see the Salisburys, you might facilitate my movements by sounding for me there.

[1] Frederick Temple Hamilton-Temple Blackwood, first Marquis of Dufferin and Ava (1826–1902).

[2] James Harrison Wilson (1837–1925).

I am afraid that Salisbury has such a suspicious temperament that he will hardly grant such a favor, and I would rather have applied to Derby; but since the great and glorious success which Disraeli has won over Turkey — or was it Russia? — I suppose that Ministry is likely to hold on. Your government is, I believe, very close about its papers and has not thrown them open to anyone later than the close of last century.

If you come across, too, any little box of a house in May Fair which seems suitable for us, please keep your eye on it. I expect to arrive in Liverpool in September or October, and to go on at once to Paris and Madrid, so that I shall hardly get back to London before April. My hope is to pass Christmas in Granada, and making love to Señoritas in Seville and Cadiz. Perhaps we can make a party and bottle a little Andalusian sunshine for our old age. How would your wife like to try the quality of a December moon in the Alhambra? I am now forty and the grave is yawning for me, but I would do my best to smile as I sat on its edge, and to talk as though I were still as young as when you and I first met. Every now and then, in my bourgeois ease and uniformity, my soul rebels against it all, and I want to be on my wanderings again, in the Rocky Mountains, on the Nile, the Lord knows where. But I humbly confess that it is vanity and foolishness. I really prefer comfort and repose. I should not now be meditating the passage of that miserable ocean, if it were not for my literary necessities. I am ashamed to seem restless. It is ludicrous to play Ulysses. There is not in this wide continent of respectable mediocrity a greasier citizen, or one more contented in his oily ooze, than myself....

Of your politics I try to keep some little run, and you can imagine that Tancred has considerable amused me. The truth is, your government has cut a very droll figure, but on the whole has got out of the scrape very happily. I am not disposed to quarrel with anyone who preserves the peace. It is the only thing in politics worth preserving. And I never was much of a Gladstonian. He showed us what he was worth during our civil war, and I never got over the impression he then made on me. Are you going to visit Cyprus? I suppose there will be a dozen Brightons on it before ten years are out. You should buy an Abbey there and get returned to Parliament by it....

To Charles Milnes Gaskell

Washington, 28 November, 1878.

We broke up our summer establishment a month ago and came here into winter quarters, where we find ourselves on the whole more contented than anywhere else in this miserable little planet. I suppose we are of less significance here than elsewhere. You see in London I can't drop in of an evening to the palace to chat with the Queen, nor will Mr. Disraeli and Mr. Gladstone dine with me whenever I send for them. Here society is primitive as the golden age. We run in at all hours to see everybody. I have a desk in our Foreign Office for my exclusive study, and unlimited access to all papers. We make informal calls on the President, the Cabinet and the Diplomates. Ten days ago I went uninvited to Yoshida's, the Japanese Minister's, and played whist with him and his Japanese wife till midnight, after which I beat him at Go-Bang and he showed me how to play Go; after which we closed with oysters and champagne and *such* a headache the next day. That same day I had called in state on the Chinese Ministers, and was put on a throne and made to drink green tea with the leaves in it. We are bent now on having them to dinner in their national dress, and Secretary Evarts has promised to meet them. Perhaps if I ever go to China, they will return my dinner and impose more green tea-leaves on me. Yoshida, who has since departed for Japan, has already sent me a little blue-and-white Japanese teapot to console me for his absence....

Such a quaint little society, you never saw or imagined. We do not even talk scandal. There is no scandal to talk about. Everybody is virtuous and the highest dissipation is to play whist at guinea points. I don't even indulge in this. We are all of the Darby and Joan type, and attached to our wives. It is the fashion. We are innocently amused by utterly absurd trifles. We are not ennuyés or blasés. We are good-natured. I assure you, it is like a dream of the golden age....

Meanwhile my ponderous work is more than half done, and there remain only a few more folio volumes to get through the press. After hurling the whole batch at the head of an unconscious public, I shall fly the country next year. As no one will ever read the work, I feel but slight anxiety about its success.

It is a curious fact that while you in England seem to be wallowing about in all sorts of troubles, we in America were never so quiet. As nine-tenths of our people, or thereabouts, have passed through bankruptcy in the last five years, we are quite free of debt, and as the operation has been pretty general, every one is about as well off as before. I think on the whole we are fairly prosperous. If your people will wait patiently another year or two, we shall be buying your goods as fast as is good for you or for us....

We have a little dinner tonight, as is not unusual, for we have to entertain all our eminent Boston constituents when they come on. Would you know our company? Behold them! Mr. Sidney Bartlett, aged seventy-nine, head of the Boston Bar, rich, eminent, and considered witty. His son, Frank Bartlett, a contemporary of my own, Mr. Senator Lucius Quintius Curtius Lamar of Mississippi, the most genial and sympathetic of all Senators and universally respected and admired — once a rebel envoy to Russia. Gen. Dick Taylor of Louisiana, brother-in-law of Jefferson Davis, himself one of the best of the rebel Major Generals, a great friend of the Prince of Wales, a first-rate raconteur and whist-player, a son of a former President of the United States. *Ecco!* Six, you observe. We regret that Lady Catherine and you are not here to make eight. We would teach you to eat terrapin.

To Henry Cabot Lodge

WASHINGTON, 29 Jany., 1879.

I have kept your last letter a week since my return from Niagara, waiting until I could get something to say. I have not much now, but such as I have, I send you.

Taylor [1] professes to be deeply mortified at having broken his word. He will not explain why he did so. He says there were circumstances which compelled him to do it. My belief is that he read the paper to some one of his Congressional friends who begged it of him and that it will appear in substance as a Report or Speech. This kind of duress is common enough here, and I imagine that Taylor is peculiarly subject to it from his southern clientéle in Congress. But it may be that Burnside or some other of his army friends who support the bill in the Senate, made a point of friendship of it. I read the paper as he wrote it, and liked it, barring a little Virginianism.

He says that he means, in order to make such atonement as he can, to send you the very best article he can write, for a future number.

Last night Cox dined here, with Godkin and Clarence King. We had much Indian talk. Cox at first was disposed to refuse outright to undertake any work. He can touch nothing until after March 4th for

[1] General Richard Taylor. I was editing the *International Review* with John T. Morse. — H. C. L.

all his time is occupied by cyphers. I finally persuaded him to take the matter into consideration, and you can write to him about it, say next week; but you will have to allow him all the time he wants even if he consents to write at all, which I doubt.[1]

Newcomb is hard at work on his job.[2] I have thought of no one else. I get no time to do anything myself, and shall get none before Congress expires. As for King, he is also dependent on Congress. You want an article on the whole cypher business and should get some young man to do it, who has a reputation to make. If any such is to be found here, I will let you know.

Pray remember me to your wife. Our Niagara journey was very successful and I enjoyed it immensely. I know of nothing very new here. At this season Washington is a monkey-show and I would rather be out of it; but like other monkey-shows it is amusing.

Thanks for the two pamphlets. They are very well done. But why omit the "bulwark of our holy religion," the only thing Strong ever did, which is still remembered.

To Henry Cabot Lodge

WASHINGTON, 1 Feby, 1879.

I would encourage Hayes.[3] He certainly knows China and there is no reason why he should not write a good article. What does he mean by talking about the new editor of the *International* being identical with me? Are you and Morse and I a new Trinity? Please explain to him, when you write, that I am not even an Apostle.

You shall see the sheets of Gallatin when I come back in May, which will be in good time. I have nothing to do with the distribution of copies, though I shall recommend Mr. Gallatin to send a few to the press.

[1] "The Indian Question," in *International Review*, VI, 617.
[2] "The Silver Conference and the Silver Question," in *Ib.*, 309.
[3] Augustus Allen Hayes, Jr. "The Relations between the United States and China" appeared in *Ib.*, 355.

X

EUROPE

1879–1880

To Charles Milnes Gaskell

Even with the lost tribes of literature, London waxes dull and oppressive. My work is finished, at least for the present. A few days more will set me free. We shall probably hide ourselves for a week or two before starting upon our peninsula campaign, and try to recover our nerves after nine months of dinners. Just now I rather look to a week or ten days by the sea-side or among the lakes, and then a plunge into strange wilds.

My work has been very satisfactory in every way, and I have left three months labor for a copyist. Meanwhile I understand that the *Saturday* has been launching thunderbolts at my head for literary sins.[1] I have not seen the reproof, but if there be one subject on which the *Saturday* has always been more idiotic than another, it is America and everything American, so that I can conceive that it may be amusing....

Of London there is little to say. Dinners seem fairly at an end. Parliament will be up soon. No one now seems to expect a dissolution; the talk about it has vanished. Nevertheless, I would not advise you to relax your attention to your future constituency, for if Lord Beaconsfield is calculating on remaining more than another year in active life, he ought to dissolve now. Only his own approaching dissolution will warrant him in meeting this Parliament again. All which does not prevent his own cabinet from avowing that they expect to go on another session.

I have met no one of special interest and except for a few calls and stray dinners have rested in the repose of the Rolls Office. John Green bids fair to become my most intimate guardian and teacher, but poor Green[2] is so awfully fragile that I always fancy I shall never see him again. Henry James haunts the street gloomily....

[1] A review of the *Gallatin*, in the *Saturday Review*, July 26, 1879.
[2] John Richard Green (1837–1883), author of *History of the English People*.

To Henry Cabot Lodge

DIEPPE, 31 August, 1879.

Your letter of the 12th and the accompanying oration came to hand last week, and I read the latter at once with much satisfaction. You have got through this ordeal very happily, and I am sure with an increase of consideration. Indeed you are now sure of your career, an honorable and probably an eminent one, if you are merely patient and persevering.

I am, as you know, a little of a *communard* myself, and I hope your threats of social penalties may not be meant for me, but in any case, I doubt a little whether that kind of diagnosis is always the most successful.

You are quite right in regard to Gallatin. Pruning would improve it. I think fifty pages might come out, to great advantage, and perhaps a hundred could be spared. My only excuse is the great difficulty of judging these things in manuscript. You know how hard it is to decide that any particular letter or episode is *not* possibly important to somebody.

That you and Brooks should like the book is a great pleasure to me, for I suppose you two are my chief audience; at least I know of no one outside of our little set who cares for such things. Tell Morse to pitch in. I do not remember having inspired any part of your review of Hamilton, but that is a trifle. If we are to interest the public, it must be by making a noise. After all, I fancy if I reviewed the book myself, I should hit it harder than Morse will. I know very little, however, about the notices it has had, or how hard it has been hit, or indeed anything on the subject, for I have been out of the way of such things, and too busy to think of the book's fate, especially as I know well what fate is reserved for heavy biographies.

My attack on the English archives has been successful and I am now just beginning an attempt to break into the French papers, with Spain in perspective for November. Our summer in England has been pleasant, although I still confess to thinking America a better place than any on this side, and although we would both pay handsomely to come home for the winter. I don't know that we have made any very fascinating acquaintances. John Green is the brightest and pleasantest of the men in London, to my mind, but I do not find society brilliant there, and it was particularly out of spirits this season on account of the utter ruin of the gentry.

We were much shocked to hear of your brother-in-law's death, your letter being our first knowledge of it. I have some little experience in blows of the kind, and know what a strain it is. Please give our very warmest remembrances to your wife.

Everything with us at home seems to be going on with such unctuous and generous prosperity that I see no excuse for taking any stock in anxious speculations. If you would send us a little sunshine, you would earn our deepest gratitude. Meanwhile keep hard at work, and believe me ever truly yours.

To Henry Cabot Lodge

PARIS, 6 October, 1879.

Andrew Lang, who is in the same house with me here, brought me the September *International* yesterday with your article on Gallatin. I read it with much pleasure. It seems to me the best by far of the reviews I have seen. All sin more or less by adding nothing to the knowledge of the subject; all are taken too much out of the book; they all are deficient on illustration, comparison, in short — criticism in the true sense; all are obnoxious to the complaint they mostly bring against Gallatin, that of being dull, and with no excuse, for there is ample material for a very spicy review. Yours is however much the best, and perhaps as good as you could make it if you are held to what I think the bad habit of following the book.

As for our estimates of Gallatin, I do not see that they materially differ. To my mind the moral of his life lies a little deeper than party politics and I have tried here and there rather to suggest than to assert it. The inevitable isolation and disillusionment of a really strong mind — one that combines force with elevation — is to me the romance and tragedy of statesmanship. The politician who goes to his grave without suspecting his own limitations, is not a picturesque figure; he is only an animal. That old beggar who was an Emperor somewhere, and on his death-bed asked his weeping friends: "Have I not acted my part well?"; that man was picturesque. Gallatin was greater, because he could and did refuse power when he found out what vanity it was, and yet became neither a cynic nor a transcendental philosopher.

One point only of your criticisms which is common to Morse's also, I want to mention. Johnny even goes so far as to accuse me of "glossing over" a "disingenuous report" of Gallatin's by using the word "inadvertence." You call the report "grossly deceptive." Of course I care very little about Gallatin's ingenuousness and he must let his character take care of itself. I only want to call your attention to the fact that my explanation, so far as the "inadvertence" is concerned, is not my invention; the word is Gallatin's; the explanation is his; it is official, contained in a report to Congress immediately afterwards; and it struck me as so obviously true that I did not think of guarding against such a mare's nest, and left the subject without even a note of reference.

I am still dangling about the boulevards, but start for Spain next week. I hope your winter will be pleasant. My wife wishes me to send her friendliest regards to Mrs. Lodge and to you, to which please add mine. Try and write me how politics are going.

To Charles Milnes Gaskell

MADRID, 24 October, 1879.

I had meant to write from Paris to tell you our news, but as there seemed to be little to tell, I thought that on the whole a letter from Spain would be more lively, and a more delicate attention on my part to your refined tastes. We have been a week on the territory of this proud race of Caballeros, and I entirely agree with those who think that a meaner territory may be sought widely and not found. As for Madrid, it is without exception the ugliest and most unredeemable capital I ever saw. If it has one redeeming external feature, I have not seen it. The hotels are bad; the streets vulgar, and the people simply faded Jews. As for the journey, it was most uncomfortable. We slept one night at San Sebastian, which is nothing, and another at Burgos, whose celebrated cathedral does not in my opinion hold comparison with twenty I have seen elsewhere. In short, if I were to draw a just conclusion from my impression, I should say that I think Spain a hole, and that I only want to get out of it. This is the logical result of my statement of facts, and I am mortified to find how little even *my* remarkable wisdom has of logic, for I must own that, in spite of everything, Spain does amuse me. Every day, with perfect regularity, a sky so blue that one can scoop it out with a spoon; a sun so glorious that the shadows are palpably black; a dry, crisp air that tightens all one's muscles and makes life easy; and a good natured, dirty people who are always apologetic if one does not insult them. As for the gallery here, I can't deny that it knocks all my expectations flat. Never did I dream of such Titians. Meanwhile we have nothing on earth to do, and are violently busy. We know about ten words of Spanish, and converse fluently all day. In short, this is a country of non-sequiturs.

Everything is upside down and wrong-end first; but I think it suits an American palate, for the climate is American and as no one pretends to being anything, our American amour-propre has a vacation....

Every morning I take a Spanish lesson, which reminds me of our old days in Rome. This and the gallery, and society, and bric-à-brac, so far represent all I have done, for, in spite of all my diplomacy, I have not yet got the papers I came for. The Foreign Secretary swears I shall have them just as soon as he can find out where they are. The fun is that they belong to his department and to this century. *Cosas de Espagna!* Apparently I have got to go to Simancas, a hole such as only Spain contains....

To Charles Milnes Gaskell

GIBRALTAR, 21 November, 1879.

Perhaps a letter from you is waiting our arrival at Seville. If so I will answer it in advance, for I have just now a little leisure, and my science is not extensive enough to tell me when I shall have any more. My last letter to you was from Madrid, written when Spain was new to me, and when I was still wondering what to expect. Nearly a month has passed, and I feel as though I were a pure Spaniard — or perhaps a Jew, for of late I have been a bit more Jewish than anything else. Chequered is the ocean of life, my dear friend, and I think the part of that ocean in which Spain lies is decidedly more chequered than most. When I wrote to you I was exulting in my first experience of Spanish sun. Hardly three days passed when the skies clouded over, rain began, and for the next ten days we had what the Madrileños were pleased to call their rainy season. At best Madrid is a hole, but in rainy weather it is a place fit only to drown rats in. At the same time the Duke of Tetuan, who is the Foreign Secretary, let me know that there were very few papers to be found, of the class I wanted to see, and the few that existed were too delicate to be shown. Finally, poor Mrs. Lowell,[1] my Minister's wife, seemed to be rapidly sinking, and I was very unwilling to go off and leave Lowell in the utter solitude which weighed on him almost as much as the illness itself. For a whole week we groaned and suffered. Our only bright spot was Lady Bonham who enlivened us now and then. At length we became desperate, and as Mrs. Lowell was rather better than otherwise, we bolted on Monday, the 3d, and, seizing the first express train, we fled southward. Andalusia received us with open arms. The sun came out.

[1] Frances Dunlap.

Cordova was fascinating. The great mosque was glorious. The houses, and especially their hammered iron gates, were adorable. We reached Granada Tuesday evening and stayed there a week with more amusement than I ever supposed my effete existence was now capable of feeling. Everyone has his own standards of taste, and many travellers are bored by Granada. So they are by Rome, Venice and the Nile. To my mind Granada ranks with the *first*-class places, and for beauty stands only second to Naples. While there I made acquaintance with one of the best of the Granadans, Don Leopoldo Equilaz, the local antiquarian, a charming fellow, who took us about, told us stories and showed us curiosities, had us at his house, and led us into temptation, for he inflamed our minds with a wild fancy for following up the Granada fugitives to their final refuge at Tetuan. You would have been delighted if you had seen us at an evening tea in Don Leopoldo's renaissance palace, talking fluid Spanish with the Señora, two padres of the holy inquisition, and two pure Moors of the race of Boabdil; it was life of the fifteenth century with full local color. Among them they persuaded us to visit Tetuan, and so we came down to Gibraltar, crossed to Ceuta, and rode nine hours on donkeys last Sunday to Tetuan, returning on Wednesday, and reaching here yesterday, whence we start on Sunday for Cadiz. The Tetuan journey was hard. Ceuta was awful. The dirt of these eastern cities, like Tetuan, is indescribable. The Hebrew is pervasive and irrepressible. Nevertheless I enjoyed the trip, or parts of it, immensely; the scenery was charming; Tetuan is more eastern than the east, and filthily picturesque beyond anything I ever saw. We brought back a mule-load of rugs and embroideries, and had glorious June weather. But whether my name is now Abd-el-adem, or Ben-shadams, or Don Enrique Adamo, I couldn't take oath, for I have been utterly bewildered to know what has become of my identity, and the Spaniards have been so kind to us that I feel as though I owed them a name....

To Charles Milnes Gaskell

Hôtel du Jardin, Rue de Rivoli,
Paris, 20 Dec., 1879.

. . . .

As for Paris, I hardly know what it is. Except for a short walk after dark, I see nothing of it except manuscripts and books. It is very uncomfortable and cold. The streets are blocked with snow, which has a way of arranging itself in humps, so that cabs can only go at a walk, and rapid movement is out of the question. The fog is always thick, though of course not quite so dense as at times in London. I go to my archives at ten and work till four, with an intermission for breakfast. After that I work at home till bed-time. As yet I have seen no one, and Paris seems far more solitary than Granada or Tetuan. My only wish is to finish with it, and cross the channel.

Cabinet crises pursue us. We left one at Madrid, where the public calmly wait the approaching exit of the little King and Queen. We find one here, and it bothers me in dealing with the Foreign Office. By the time we get to England I suppose we shall find Lord Beaconsfield gone up; and indeed I should think Afghanistan and India would swamp any ministry....

To Henry Cabot Lodge

PARIS, 20 Dec'r, 1879.

Yours of Oct. 19th, that of Oct. 20th, and the accompanying document, followed me to Spain and found me, I think, at Granada. In the rough-and-tumble traveling I have done since then, I have left your letters unanswered.

Your notice of Gallatin is very well done. I think I have before now suggested that you should give your style a little more variety and freedom. The sentences to my ear sound rather too much like each other, and occasionally a mere change of punctuation would relieve the eye, while the ear will often follow the eye and deceive itself; in other cases it is easy to turn a sentence round and begin at the end. The most difficult thing to me is to vary the length of my sentences so as to relieve the attention. In the struggle to do this, I have sometimes found myself doing very clumsy things.

I was very glad to see that you were going to the General Court. As I have always said, you have nothing to do but to go ahead. A few years in the Legislature are a kind of necessity to any man who wants influence. You are near the State House. I suppose our Legislature is not unlike others. Social influence counts for whatever one chooses to make it. If you can make friends of the most influential members, including the Speaker, if you can occasionally bring one home to a family dinner, or to a talk in your library; if you can, in short, make yourself important or agreeable to the leaders, you will next year be in a position to claim a good committee and be a leader yourself. I believe seniority alone gives effective influence over assemblies so you can afford to move slowly.

As for politics, we seem to be in a backwater period. At one time I favored connecting ourselves directly with Sherman, but I doubt it now. Sherman, like Evarts, will hand us over to Grant. On the other side the outlook is rather better, but not much. The Democrats at least are badly frightened and may make a respectable nomination, but as a party, one should keep clear of them. They are more dangerous to their friends than to their enemies. If you have made up your mind what to do, I should like to know what it is, for although I shall hardly be at home much before election day, I am anxious to know what is to happen.

We are excessively sorry to hear bad news about poor Mrs. Parkman.[1] There is no one whom I should miss so much at Beverly; in fact I hardly know what we shall do without her. I can only hope that you will have found some one to take her place, for I know you will miss her as much as we.

I am still hard at work. Manuscripts are clumsy things to read, and there are few slower occupations than taking notes. Probably I shall finish the State Papers here by the middle of January, and go back to London. I leave the results for conversation when we meet. Between now and next July I have got a mountain of papers and books to digest, and shall not have an hour to lose. In fact I shall need all the time I can steal out of the autumn.

We have done some pretty severe traveling since I wrote last, and enjoyed it. I got to feel quite at home in Spain and was sorry to come away, for I long since got over any fancy for Paris. My wife has been very well, and sends her warm regards to yours and to you. So do I.

To Henry Cabot Lodge

22, Queen Anne's Gate, S.W.
22 February, 1880.

Your interesting letter of Jany 10th reached me on arriving here, after six weeks of dull and dismal hibernation in Paris. At the best of times Paris is to me a fraud and a snare; I dislike it, protest against it, despise its stage, condemn its literature, and have only a temperate respect for its cooking; but in December and January Paris is frankly impossible. It has all the discomforts of London without its mildness; all the harshness of New York without its gaiety. Yet I got my papers, which proved to be most interesting. I did a heap of reading which was indispensable and almost as interesting as the papers. I never

---

[1] Catherine Scollay Bigelow, daughter of Dr. Jacob Bigelow.

have had a better-employed six weeks, and have seldom been gladder to finish them. I rejoiced as much to leave Paris, where I got all I wanted and was perfectly well established, as I regretted to leave dirty, hideous, wretched old Spain, where I was refused everything, and swore at every step. Such is the perversity of human nature. We have now been a month in London, where we took a house next door to Westminster Abbey, Buckingham Palace, and Marlborough House, and about equidistant from all three, which I take to be the ideal situation for an American as it is for a Britisher. It is true that there is about as much chance of my frequenting one as the other of these royal abodes. I am too busy. Just now all my days are passed at the British Museum looking over papers — newspapers, I mean — with nothing in them. Pure loss of time, but inevitable. This will take me a month, working from 11 till 4 every day. Then I must return to the Record Office and complete my work there, which will take another month. By that time I hope to get my papers from France and Spain where Lowell is busying himself for me. I must then go to work with my own pen, an article I have not touched since finishing Gallatin. I want to complete the whole foreign work here, so as to be sure there are no gaps to be filled hereafter. This I hope to accomplish by Aug. 1st. Then I must go to Paris again; make a visit or two in England; sail on or about Sept. 15; reach Boston about Oct. 1st; stay a few days to see my family; rush on to Washington to take a house; pass six weeks between Washington, New York and Boston, trying to furnish the house; and get fairly settled to work again about Dec'r 1st.

Such are our plans, which, as you see, are pretty precise. Thus far I have carried out, step by step, the program I made before leaving Washington. If my luck will last to carry me back again, I shall be glad, for, much as I enjoy travelling, and pleasant as London always is, I infinitely prefer home, and I assure you I positively hunger for my Washington life.

So much for myself and our doings. Of you and yours I was glad to get so good an account. Unless you wreck yourself on the rock of the next Presidential election I see no reason why you should not go ahead indefinitely. As for the election, in your place I should have been rather inclined to carry my friends straight to Sherman and to offer him energetic support on the single condition that he would promise not to sell us out to Grant, but to retire, if retire he must, in favor of some other man, or no one. Failing Sherman, I am at a loss to see what can be done, but between ourselves I should think about manœuvring for a renomination of Hayes. What we want is to preserve the present status. Obviously we have not strength to improve it. Therefore — Hayes. But you are on the ground and I am not. Bad as the prospect is from the Republican point of view, it seems to me much worse on the Democratic side. I can see no candidate worth their putting up, and, as I hear nothing of what is doing, I feel as though anything which would result in an undisputed Republican success would be satisfactory to me.

Schurz seems to have got into trouble with his Indian commissioner. This must be a blow to him, but as he has ceased to be anything to us, and so long as he is in the cabinet never can return to his old importance, I don't know that his mischance affects our interests. What interests me far more is to know what our New York independents are doing. They ought to have the names and addresses of ten thousand New York Republicans who will vote against Grant at any cost. With such a list behind them, they ought to dictate both the party nominations. Who is leading them? I see they have issued an address.

We are still mourning for Mrs. Parkman who has carried with her the largest part of our Beverly society. We could have better spared what is left. I only hope you will invent some one to take her place before we return.

I hear very little from anyone. Brooks occasionally writes me a line. Godkin forced himself up to writing once. But except my mother I have no regular correspondent, and she is not political. I think the world writes fewer letters now than ever, perhaps because there is less to write about. Certainly London has not the material for a letter. It is Sunday afternoon. Harry James is standing on the hearthrug, with his hands under his coat-tails talking with my wife exactly as though we were in Marlborough Street. I am going out in five minutes to make some calls on perfectly interesting people.

To Henry Cabot Lodge

22, QUEEN ANNE'S GATE, S.W.
13 May, 1880.

Yours of March 21st has been lying a month in my drawer and, grateful as I am for all the news you are the only person to send me, I have so little to say in reply that a letter is hardly writeable. The *Boston Sunday Herald* and the *New York Herald* keep me tolerably well posted about home affairs, and Harry Sturgis tells me much more. You will be amused to hear that your friend Portal is soon to be married to a Miss Glyn, a girl rather in the style of Mrs. Harry Sturgis at eighteen. I have seen so little of the Portals that I hardly know how the match is liked, but on the face of it I should suppose that it was meant for wear rather than for show. The English are very sensible about these things. Portal is to live in the country and will make an excellent country gentleman, shaming us poor cockneys by his devotion to fox-hounds and cold roast beef.

The American colony is rather large here just now, and decidedly respectable. Besides the Sturgises, Morgans, Walter Burns, Harcourts, Playfairs, Smalleys, and Mistress Alice Mason with her callow brood, there is a swarm of swells whom I don't know and who bask in the smiles of royalty. We are very quiet ourselves, go out little, and as the fashionable people come to town our little tallow-dip disappears in the glare. There is nothing very much worth seeing. No new books have come out to create even a ripple, so far as I know. There is not even a new man of any prominence. Yet society lumbers ahead and one manages to get a good deal of amusement out of it without getting any excitement to speak of. We were more startled by George Eliot's marriage to John Cross than by the elections themselves. As Cross is semi-American by his business connection, she is half-way to emigration. I suppose her American admirers will howl over the fall of their idol, but I can't say I care much for the idol business, and I am clear that if she found her isolation intolerable, she was quite right to marry Cross if she could get him. It is not quite so easy to explain why Cross should have been willing to marry her, for most men of thirty or forty prefer youth, beauty, children and such things, to intellect in gray hairs. Some people say it was a pure marriage of convenience on both sides, but I know that the Cross family have a sort of superstitious adoration of her.

My odds and ends are gradually getting into shape. I have finished with the Record Office, completed my search through the newspapers, collected the greater part of my pamphlets, and sounded all the wells of private collections I could find. In Paris and Madrid copyists are at work for me and ought soon to send their copy. I foresee a good history if I have health and leisure the next five years, and if nothing happens to my collections of material. My belief is that I can make something permanent of it, but, as time passes, I get into a habit of working only for the work's sake and disliking the idea of completing and publishing. One should have some stronger motive than now exists for authorship. I don't think I care much even to be read, and any writer in this frame of mind must be dull reading. On the other hand I enjoy immensely the investigation, and making little memoranda of passages here and there. Aridity grows on me. I always felt myself like Casaubon in *Middlemarch*, and now I see the tendency steadily creeping over me.

This makes me all the gladder to see you plunged into active life. I envy you your experience at Chicago, though I cannot for my life see how you can manage to worry through it without getting squeezed. I still stick to Sherman. Edmunds is totally unfit to be President and I should prefer Blaine. Massachusetts ought to throw her whole weight energetically for Sherman in convention; it is the only way to be digni-fied and consistent. If Sherman is withdrawn, then let the State give its vote to the most respectable candidate on the list, but I confess I think it ought in that case, as a mere matter of respect to a most successful administration, to throw one complimentary vote for Hayes.

Many thanks for your Pinkney minutes which I shall be glad to have. He and Monroe made an awful blunder in signing that treaty; they were fairly scared to death. Now that I see the English side, they appear utterly ridiculous, and poor dear old Jefferson too, but our beloved Federalists most of all. Ye Gods, what a rum lot they were!...

Lowell is expected here on the 17th. I fear his wife is still very poorly, but he has not written me the details. He takes a house near Sarah Darwin's in Southampton, and I suppose will come up at in-tervals. Harry James is expected from Italy at about the same time. He gave us his newspaper criticisms to read, but as I've not read his books I couldn't judge of their justice. These little fits of temper soon blow over, however, and if he is good-natured about it he will get straight again soon.

I am much touched by your loyalty to your venerable Professor, and I feel like two Casaubons, rather than one, at the idea of standing in the attitude of a gray-haired Nestor surrounded by you and Young and poor Laughlin. By the way, did you see how elaborately Stubbs refers to us in his new edition? John Green is one of my intimate friends here, but how he objurgates you fellows for your German style. He says my Essay is bad enough, but you others are clean mad. We chaff each other thereupon.

To Henry Cabot Lodge

22, QUEEN ANNE'S GATE, S.W.
LONDON, 9 JULY, 1880.

Your letter of June 19th was very welcome. Of course I had read the newspapers carefully and followed every step in the Conventions' cavortings, but I was very glad to get a nearer view. Now that the Democrats have trotted out their horse too, we can judge better of the quality of yours.

Garfield seems to me a very strong candidate; whether Sherman would have been stronger I don't know, but certainly Garfield will draw out a very strong party vote.

Hancock seems to me not a first-rate choice. Bayard or Randall or Hewitt or even McClellan would to my fancy have done better. I infer that all the New York Democrats and the old Tilden men thought so too. If Dick Taylor had lived, he would have stopped the unutterable nonsense of putting a pure, unadulterated, West Point, corps-commander at the head of the Democratic party. It was due to want of proper organisation in the South, I suppose.

Of course my path is with you. I can see no single object to gain from bringing Hancock in. As my judgment is always wrong, I suppose his election will follow and prove fortunate, but till then I shall vote for Garfield.

Whether Garfield can carry New York and Indiana is, however, the real question, and it is to New York that all your money and work must go. I hope our friends will do their utmost, not because I care particularly which man is elected, but because it is most important that the election this time should be beyond a doubt.

For you the nomination is of course a most lucky matter. You have as usual nothing to do but to go ahead. As for the "opening" that my [brother] Brooks sees for you, I am glad he sees it, but I doubt whether it is worth your while to strike for openings. You know my way of thinking. I got it from my father, and so I suppose it is merely a piece of hereditary imbecility which I ought to distrust; but at any rate I hold that to be happy in life is possible, so far as depends on oneself, only by being always busily occupied upon objects that seem worth doing. It is the occupation, not the objects, which makes happiness. So I say, go ahead! Make yourself as useful and as busy as you can. If a seat in Congress comes in your way, take it! Don't come abroad! Have always on your hands more than you can do! But as for "openings," they lead as a rule to Hell. Blaine and Ben Butler are the ideal of men who go for openings.

This, however, is only written to argue the other side. Probably if Brooks took my view, I should feel obliged to take his.

So much for politics and philosophical statesmanship. Meanwhile since my last letter the world has run on until I am now within a few weeks of closing my London house and starting to see whether we can pick up a little strength in Scotland before going on board the "Gallia." My work is done, at least so far as it ever will be done. I have made a careful study of English politics from 1801 to 1815, and have got my authorities in order. My Spanish papers have mostly arrived. The French documents are, I hope, coming, although I am still nervous about them. My material is enormous, and I now fear that the task of compression will be painful. Burr alone is good for a volume. Canning and Perceval are figures that can't be put in a nut-shell, and Napoleon is vast. I have got to contemplate six volumes for the sixteen years as inevitable. If it proves a dull story, I will con-dense, but it's wildly interesting, at least to me — which is not quite the same thing as interesting the public.

We are very weary of our London season, which has now lasted six months, but luckily the weather is cool and wet. I suppose we shall stay in Scotland till near September, and reach New York in the "Gallia" on October 5th or thereabouts, whence we must go directly to Washington to furnish our new house. We have taken Corcoran's White House, next his own, on President's Square, and I fear there is a great deal to be done to it before we can get in. When things are set going there, we shall come to Boston for a while. I rather hope to be there for the election, to vote. Then back to Washington for the winter, and I look forward placidly to recurring winters and summers in Washington and Beverly, until a cheery tomb shall provide us with a permanent abode for all seasons.

Of news on this side I have little or none except that America is all here and makes it impossible to believe in a hereafter. Unless we can annex another planet, travelling is a lost art, and home an unknown joy. Mrs. Sturgis is beginning to wonder whether Julian will not be "unsettled" by America, but I don't quite see how you can unsettle anything that never had equilibrium. Julian was always a dancing satyr. Of books there are none on this side. As for society, it is as dingy and solemn as ever. In the last six months I believe we have averaged a dinner every other day, and you can imagine that, as my wife says, we are pretty well dinnered out. Except John Green and Lecky,[1] however, I have met no one who adds greatly to my score. Of fashion and the peerage I know less than ever. Lowell and Mrs. Ronalds monopolise the royal family. Pretty near all England is emi-grating to America, and, in my uniformly untrustworthy opinion, this old shebang will come to grief. Europe has got to do some more heavy revoluting in the next twenty years, and America has a long start.

[1] William Edward Hartpole Lecky (1838–1903).

Anyway, however, we philosophers in this ocean of life have to keep our eyes fixed on the horizon-line or a star, if we don't mean to be seasick. My hobby now is to live until I see custom-houses abolished. Damn 'em! Think of my condition of mind with that custom-house before me until October. That is my platform for our party of the Zukunft.

Give our unanimous love to your wife. Also to the babbies. Julian Sturgis delighted me by writing to his mother an account of Nahant and its beauties!! Your eldest will one day tell you the same perhaps. My brother Charles says he finds middle-age commonplace, but he won't when those twins teach him a thing or two.

XI

WASHINGTON

1880–1886

To Henry Cabot Lodge

WASHINGTON, 30 October, 1880.

Your kind letter was handed to me by my wife in the middle of my struggles with the complications of many kinds at Boston, when I had not a moment to spare for writing. Now that I have got again a breathing-spell, my first thought is to acknowledge it, and to say how sorry I am not to have been able to get at you. When I was not running about Boston, I had to be at Quincy, and all the while I ought to have been here. This must be my excuse for not having made use of your various kind invitations.

Of course I shall feel much flattered by your proposed dedication and I only wish my name counted for more in the public estimation. As it is, you must give it the credit it wants.

We have now been for three months driving about the world, without a minute's repose. It will be at least another month before I shall be able to settle again to my work and to have a roof of my own. When shall you come on here? I suppose your brother-in-law [1] will expect you to stay with him, but my house, when I get into it, will be at your orders. Meanwhile I am at the genial Wormley's watching carpenters, plumbers, painters, paperers, and gas-fitters.

Of politics I can tell you not a thing. Although content to see a Republican triumph, I am not eager to take a hand in it, and I have too much to condone in the acts of that party and its nominee to make me care to proclaim the condonation. My brother Charles has done it for me, and I would rather that he should do it than I. This reconciles me to losing my vote. The pleasure of endorsing De Golyer and the Louisiana Returning Board would not be increased by the effort to decide between the merits of Leopold Morse [2] and R. B. Hayes. If my vote were to be decisive, I should throw it, but even then I should prefer to do it in silence and secrecy.

Nothing can equal the blunder of the Democrats. In throwing over Tilden, it is clear that they threw over all the brains they had. I can

---

[1] Charles Henry Davis (1845–1921).

[2] Leopold Morse (1831–1892), member from Massachusetts.

see no single reason for voting with them, although I can see ample cause for not voting with the Republicans. Meanwhile your course is clear enough and I hope it will be smooth. As for me, I am best off as an outsider.

Things will begin to get lively here in about a month. We are heartily glad to get back, and rather enjoy house-furnishing. I hope you will approve our taste. You know the house. We have taken it for six years and hope not to be disturbed then. You will have time to become well acquainted with it.

To Charles Milnes Gaskell

WASHINGTON, 1 January, 1881.

. . . .

Marvelous quiet and prosperity reign here. I am the only living American who has this year spent more than his income. We hear vague echoes of European troubles, of Ireland and France and Turkey, but we don't know anything about them. My only surprise is that you don't all emigrate to get rid of the Irish. I have read George Trevelyan's book, which is charming. If it only told something about Fox, it would be hardly open to criticism. I have read *Endymion*, with stares and gasps. There is but one excuse for it; the author must be in a terrible want of money; his tenants have paid him nothing, and Mr. Gladstone has docked his pension. If he has not, he should. *Endymion* is a disgrace to the government, the House of Lords, the Commons, and the Jews....

To Henry Cabot Lodge

1607 H STREET
SUNDAY. 21 May, 1881.

The book [1] is an excellent one. I should like to find fault with it, but really do not know how. It seems to be thoroughly good and satisfactory in all respects so that I almost wish it had a few faults to pick upon. If fault is to be found, I am inclined, in going over the same ground a little later, to put it on the extreme monotony of the subject, and I have pretty much made up my mind not to attempt giving interest to the society of America in itself, but to try for it by way of contrast with the artificial society of Europe, as one might contrast a stripped prize-fighter with a life-guardsman in helmet and breast-

[1] *Short History of the English Colonies in America.* — H. C. L.

plate, jack-boots and a big black horse. The contrast may be made dramatic, but not the thing. This is to be, however, the acid test of my own composition, and I am afraid that I shall not succeed so well as you. Luckily I am not in a hurry to fail. You have already created for yourself more interests than I ever had, and can afford to use some of them up. I nurse my one lamb.

I had thought of waiting till I saw you, rather than of writing, but as I doubted when we should meet, I thought best to write. We leave here on Tuesday and reach Boston on Friday or thereabout. I hope to be settled at Beverly the following week. Perhaps one of these days I will ride over to Nahant for a chat, if you can give my horse and me a lodging for the night. Of course there is much to talk about, especially in the political doings of the last three months. Our fight is now pretty well won. Grantism, which drove us to rebellion, is dead. Not a vestige of it is left. One after another every finger of that octopus has been lopped off. The government is now running on a new track, not much better to be sure, but free from organised corruption. There will be rotten places here, as there were with Hayes — more and worse, I fear — but, as with him, on the whole we may rest and be thankful.

To Justin Winsor

BEVERLY FARMS, 27 September, 1881.

I return today the box of newspapers for a new load. It is astonishing how very little information is to be found in them. I want to learn all I can about the social and economical condition of the country in 1800. Can you send me a few books on the subject in the return box with the newspaper volumes? I want the Memoirs of Lindley Murray by himself. New York. 1827. John Fitch's Biography by Westcott, Phil. 1867. Colden's Life of Fulton, 1817. There is, I believe, a History or Memoir about the Middlesex Canal which I want to see; and I want to find out how much banking capital there was in the U.S. in 1800, and how it was managed. I want a strictly accurate account of the state of education and of the practise of medicine. I want a *good* sermon of that date, if such a thing existed, for I cannot find one which seems to me even tolerable, from a literary or logical point of view. If you in your historical work have come across any facts or authorities which would aid me, I should like to beg them of you, especially if they tend to correct me. Thus far my impression is that America in 1800 was not far from the condition of England under Alfred the Great; that the conservative spirit was intensely strong in the respectable classes, and that there was not only indifference but actual aggressive repression towards innovation; the mental attitude of good society looks to me surprisingly mediæval. I should wish to correct this impression. Did Harvard or Yale show anything to the contrary *before* 1800? I can see that Philadelphia was reasonably liberal and active-minded; was any other part of the country equally so? Was there a steam-engine in the United States?...

To Henry Cabot Lodge

1607 H STREET,
29 October, 1881.

Down to the last moment of our stay in Beverly we still hoped to get over to see you and Mrs. Lodge. I had projected a drive to Nahant on our last Sunday. It is my greatest disappointment of the summer that we broke down in this scheme. The fact is, I have worked very steadily and have felt for the first time a sort of nervous fear of losing time. My conscience reproves me for neglecting not only my friends but my family; yet life is slipping away so fast that I grudge every day which does not show progress in my work. I have but one off-spring, and am nearly forty-four while it is nothing but an embryo. After fifty I mean to devote myself to frivolity and friends.

We arrived here the night before last and are again established in winter quarters although the weather is warm and the trees green. Naturally I know as yet nothing of anything. All my cabinet representatives have run off. A new crowd is in the house opposite. No one is much more learned than I am, and no one seems to care much more than I do. Whoever comes in, it is not likely that they will be friends of mine. Luckily it will be hard for Arthur to begin worse than Garfield did, although he can but try.

I have a sort of an idea that Davis told me he was going to China for a year or two. If so, and his house is no longer open to you, I hope you will light here in case you fly so far this winter. We shall be glad to see you again. Perhaps in time the odor of political unorthodoxy will become less strong on our garments, and your constituents will pardon the contamination. It is not likely that I can be of any use to you, but I can always go on with lectures in history.

To Henry Cabot Lodge

1607 H Street,
Tuesday, 15 Novr, 1881.

News travels slow between Lynn and Washington. The *Evening Post* said you had been beaten,[1] but I have not yet heard particulars, and I write merely to inquire about it.

This is one of the draw-backs to politics as a pursuit. I suppose every man who has looked on at the game has been struck by the remarkable way in which politics deteriorate the moral tone of everyone who mixes in them. The deterioration is far more marked than in any other occupation I know except the turf, stock-jobbing, and gambling. I imagine the reason in each case to be the same. It is the curse of politics that what one man gains, another man loses. On such conditions you can create not even an average morality. Politicians as a class must be as mean as card-sharpers, turf-men, or Wall Street curbstone operators. There is no respectable industry in existence which will not average a higher morality.

Whether you have slipped up on this mud-bank, or only have been upset by accident, I do not know, but in any case the moment is one for you to stop and think about it. I have never known a young man go into politics who was not the worse for it. I could give a list as long as the Athenæum Catalogue, from my two brothers, John and Brooks, down to Willy Astor,[2] Ham Fish,[3] and Robert Ray Hamilton. They all try to be honest, and then are tripped up by the dishonest; or they try to be dishonest (i.e., practical politicians) and degrade their own natures. In the first case they become disappointed and bitter; in the other they lose self-respect. My conclusion is that no man should be in politics unless he would honestly rather not be there. Public service should be a *corvée*; a disagreeable necessity. The satisfaction should consist in getting out of it.

So much for your mishap, which I hope will still at last strengthen you even politically. I wish I could send you pleasanter news from here, but it is much worse than your affair. Our friend MacVeagh,[4] after an heroic and desperate as well as prolonged struggle to drag President Arthur into the assertion of reform principles, has utterly and hopelessly failed. The new administration will be the centre for every element of corruption, south and north. The outlook is very discouraging.

[1] For the State Senate. — H. C. L. [2] William Waldorf Astor (1848–1919).
[3] Hamilton Fish (1849–1893). [4] Wayne MacVeagh (1833–1917).

To Henry Cabot Lodge

1607 H STREET,
21 Novr, 1881.

Thanks for your letter which is curious and interesting to me beyond most, as an illustration of political methods. Your enemies treated you exactly as I supposed. The case was only a little more gross than usual. Don't imagine that I suspected *you* of being the dishonest party; if you had been so, the result might have been different. Meanwhile you can count to a certain extent on a reaction in your favor. All I pray for is that, should you find the struggle at last not worth the object, you may fall back on other occupations without regret. In your place I could not. I hope you can.

Life is passing too fast for me to bother much about anything, and as the course of politics can hardly affect me or my occupations otherwise than socially, I do not greatly care what turns up. Probably this is a better time than any other for a political chaos. A few months will show. I think you might find a little visit here useful presently. If so, you will always have this house at your disposal. Come and see how things are. You certainly will not find many reformers; all that swarm have vanished like smoke, and even I have ceased to lisp the word; but you will find a swarm of a different kind which will interest you just as much, perhaps more. Meanwhile I am so glad to get rid of Blaine, that I am content to put up with almost anything, and, like all the rest of the world, am throwing up my cap for Mr. Arthur whose social charms we now understand to be most extraordinary, although only last spring we were assured by the same people that he was a vulgar and a dull animal. To be in the fashion is the first law of nature. My mouth is shut on reform politics for at least two years to come; I have not the physical strength to cry like St. John in the wilderness.

I am afraid that Brooks is poorly, and have written advising him to come on here. Please back up my advice, if you have a chance.

To Charles Milnes Gaskell

WASHINGTON, 29 January, 1882.

I did not see the *XIX Century* article and was in hopes to get it from you, for here I am so absorbed in my own pursuits that I see nothing else. Palgrave did not send me his volume of historico-poetic verses, and therefore I have not seen it. I have not seen Green's new volume, but Woolner sent us "Pygmalion." As I write for five hours every day, and ride two, and do society for the remainder, the opportunity for literature is not a vast one.

Henry James has been in Washington for a month, very homesick for London and for all the soft embraces of the old world. He returns to your hemisphere in May next. I frankly own that I broke down on *The Portrait of a Lady*, but some of my friends, of whose judgment I think highly, admire it warmly, and find it deeply interesting. I hope you may be of their opinion.

I have not read the Life of Cobden or that of Lyell, and it strikes me with a little wonder to think that I should have known both of these men well. It is only not the *fugaces annos*, but the *fugaces continentes* that bewilder me with a sense of leading several lives. Just at present, however, life seems as real and enjoyable as ever. Indeed, if I felt a perfect confidence that my history would be what I would like to make it, this part of life — from forty to fifty — would be all I want. There is a summer-like repose about it; a self-contained, irresponsible, devil-may-care indifference to the future as it looks to younger eyes; a feeling that one's bed is made, and one can rest on it till it becomes necessary to go to bed for ever; in short, an *editio princeps* quality to it, with a first class French binding, which only a Duke, or a very rich Earl of ancient foundation, could feel at twenty-five.

You know my life here, for I have described it to you many times. Poor Henry James thinks it revolting in respect to the politics and the intrigues that surround it. To me its only objection is its over-excitement. Socially speaking, we are very near most of the powerful people, either as enemies or as friends. Among others our pet enmity is Mr. Blaine, whose conduct towards your government has perhaps not endeared him to you. His overthrow has been a matter of deep concern to us, both politically and personally, for we have always refused him even social recognition on account of his previous scandals, and I assure you that to stand alone in a small society like this, and to cut the Secretary of State for Foreign Affairs, without doing it offensively or with ill-breeding, requires not only some courage but some skill. We have gone through this ordeal for many months until at length there has come relief, and I trust that Mr. Blaine is blown up for ever, although it is costing us the worst scandal we ever had in our foreign politics. Today there are plenty of people who would like very well to have made as strong a protest. At the same time I am curiously without political friends, and know not a single man in public life who agrees with me. All my friends have been swept away in the changes of the past year, and I am more despondent about this new administration than about any other of late years. It is wretchedly feeble and characterless. We shall however, I think, make no more outrageous foreign indecencies....

The other day we went out to dine, and to my horror I came face to face with your ursine and ursa-maximine countryman, Edward A. Freeman. I say "to my horror" because I had reviewed very sharply two of his books when I edited the *North American,* and he knew it. He made himself as offensive as usual at the dinner. At the end he attacked me as I knew he would, and told me he had replied to my charges, as I would see in the Preface to the first volume of his third edition of the *Norman Conquest.* I feel not the slightest curiosity to see the reply, and should not know what to think of it, but if you wish to see the *disjecta membra* of your old friend scattered among the other bones in this "Zummerzetshire" bear cave, you can some day glance at the Preface in question and shed a tear over my untimely fate....

To Henry Cabot Lodge

1607 H STREET,
31 January, 1882.

We shall duly expect you next Monday. I should have written about your coming, but have been in great doubt whether we could take Mrs. Lodge in, owing to the uncertainty of other visitors, including Brooks. As you come alone, although of course you will not be *so* welcome, you will more easily find a corner to sleep in. I have not yet heard whether Brooks is to stop here, or how long. I believe otherwise you will find us alone.

History moves on apace. I am getting to Chase's impeachment and the close of my first four years, the easiest quarter of my time. Heaven only knows whether the result is readable. As yet I have not even put it together so as to be read, but I keep hammering ahead, day by day, without looking backwards.

I presume you know more about politics than I do, so I leave that subject untouched. It is not a very clean one just now.

My wife sends her love to yours. We dine at seven, so be sure to take the Limited, if not an earlier train. MacVeagh was here last Sunday, so he is likely to be at home the next.

To John Hay

[WASHINGTON,] Sunday, 30 April, '82.

Your letter from N.Y. was a good deed in a naughty world. We had hoped for a line without expecting it. On the whole, if you will only behave yourself, live in the open air and seek a tolerable climate, I see no reason why you may not live to pronounce a parting address over the graves of all the other hearts,[1] and my only regret is that I cannot engage you in advance to oust the clergyman at my own funeral. Prayer I won't have, but I want a little speech or two, as: "Fellows, this departed heart first discovered the true meaning of sac and soc; he liked sack and claret; he invented Jefferson, Gallatin and Burr; he laughed at King's puns and Hay's jokes; also at Emily Beale's;[2] and any man who could do all that, deserves all he will get when he gets there."

Your suggestions as to the dear Hamilton shall be followed. To me the man is noxious, not because of the family quarrel, for he was punished sufficiently on that account, but because he combined all the elements of a Scotch prig in a nasty form. For that reason I prefer not to touch him if I can help it, and shall follow your advice by cutting out all I can cut, in regard to him, and emasculating the rest....

I have a funny dinner today which I wish you could help me with. Hal Richardson, the architect, O. C. Marsh, Edmund Hudson, of the *Boston Herald*, old George Bancroft, my brother Brooks. What do you suppose they can talk about?

To Charles Milnes Gaskell

1607 H Street, 30 April, 1882.

．　　　．　　　．　　　．　　　．　　　．　　　．

History advances slowly but fairly well. I write and ride and dine and chatter all I can with all who care to waste their eternal souls in that frivolity. Nothing surprises me more, as time goes on, than to find how little the world seems to object to me, or indeed to interfere in any way with my concerns. I have actually taken to the mad effort of trying to conciliate society, so far as this can be done without

[1] A name adopted by the two families. Note paper with the five of hearts stamped in the upper left-hand corner was used, indicating that there were five in the combination. Nothing in these letters indicate the identity of the fifth member, but it is generally thought to be Clarence King.

[2] Daughter of General Edward Fitzgerald Beale and later Mrs. John Roll McLean.

trouble, and on the whole I can't see but that society is willing enough to be conciliated, provided there is nothing to pay for it. Indeed I suspect I might perhaps have an office, if I did not show that I wanted it. At least I might be told that I could be minister to Cochin China or the Feejee Islands, provided I did not take the place. Possibly you may understand from your own experience that the world is ready enough to give one whatever one does not want and would not take. The only thing I want is that they should read my books, but against this there is a rooted opposition which amounts to conspiracy.

2 May. Yours of 12th April comes just as I am closing this. Thanks for your bunch of gossip, which is of more value to me here than to you there, as it gives me in conversation a certain air of knowledge, superficial and offensive, but convenient. I wish I could send you a return, but our world here, though amusing to us, is unknown even to New York and Philadelphia. To do it justice, it is a moral little world enough, and has no Lonsdales or wickedness, except occasional jobbery and political intrigue of a rather common type. I cannot say that I am an admirer of our new President, who is to my fancy a low character, but he tries to conciliate what is supposed to be good society, and somewhat to my horror, I find myself bidden to the White House, although I have been six months across the way without as yet having so much as left the tribute of a card there....

To John Hay

WASHINGTON, June 8, 1882.

DEAR PIKE COUNTY HEART, — I am glad the secret is at last coming out. I was always confident that you wrote that book,[1] or at any rate that you knew who did. The fair Harriet[2] and I shared this dear illusion, and it is quite impossible for you to escape the authorship except by going to England and saying it was Sandy Bliss.[3] I have reason to think that our aunt Tappan has numerous acquaintances in

[1] *Democracy.*

"In the spring of 1879 Henry Adams sent me the manuscript of that work [Democracy], with a view to its publication and with the most strenuous injunctions regarding secrecy of its authorship.... Adams' reasons for keeping the authorship secret were not so much that he feared knowledge of it might visit unpopularity on him; for he cared as little for that as any man I ever knew; but because some of his characters were carefully drawn from prominent living persons who were his friends, and some of these he touched humorously and ironically." — Henry Holt in *Democracy* (ed. 1925). The principal characters represented were Mrs. Bigelow Lawrence and her sister, Miss Fanny Chapman, Miss Emily Beale, James Lowndes, and James G. Blaine.

[2] Harriet Blaine, daughter of James G. Blaine and later Mrs. Walter Damrosch.

[3] Alexander Bliss, step-son of George Bancroft.

England, for I receive no end of messages and letters from there asking whether my wife wrote this work of the Devil. Hitherto I have
replied with indignation that my wife never wrote for publication in
her life and could not write if she tried; but now I will send this newspaper paragraph which will serve my object better. I will write to
King to have your name put on the title-page of an English edition,
with Jim Bludso and little Breeches in a neat appendix. Well, well!
I am really glad you have acknowledged it. Did you and Sandy and
Harriet write it together, or did you do the politics, Harriet the libels,
and Sandy the tenderness?...

Dios guarde, etc. Perhaps Loubat [1] means to challenge you for
writing *Democracy*. Don't you think it would serve you right?

To John Hay

BEVERLY FARMS, 25 June, 1882.

Thanks for your sympathetic interest in my ideal scamp. He was
never a safe scoundrel to deal with, and may well run away and cheat
the world again; but I tote about a hundred-weight of manuscript far
more valuable than his, and he must bide his time. In truth I rather
grudge the public my immortal writings. I neither want notoriety nor
neglect, and one of the two must be imagined by every author to be
his reward. My ideal of authorship would be to have a famous *double*
with another name, to wear what honors I could win. How I should
enjoy upsetting him at last by publishing a low and shameless essay
with woodcuts in his name!...

To John Hay

BEVERLY FARMS, 3 Sept'r, 1882.

I was greatly pleased the other day to receive an English copy of
Democracy by mail, addressed in your hand, for I said at once to my
wife: "This means that the dear Hay has at last acknowledged the
book, and sends us a copy of his English edition." At the same time I
was puzzled at hearing that George William Curtis had told John Field
that the authorship was no longer a secret, that it was now acknowledged, and that your friend Miss Mary Loring was the criminal. Said
I to myself, "Is it then possible that Hay and Miss Loring wrote this
disgusting book together; and all those criticisms of — and by — the

[1] Joseph Florimond Loubat.

sweet Harriet were a mere blind to throw dust in the eyes of the world?" *Je m'y perds!* I give it up, and all the more because this last week I received your letter from Tillypronie which again resorts to the stale device of casting your joint work upon me. That my English friends, like Mrs. Humphry Ward, should do this sort of thing is natural, for, knowing no other American, they are bound to pitch on the only one they ever saw, but that you should do so is shocking. I will bear half the expense if you will write and print a story as "By the author," etc., but in any case I give you the fullest authority and a power of attorney on my behalf to repudiate for me and for my wife all share or parcel in the authorship of that work, which we regard with loathing, as must be the case with every truly honest citizen. Only yesterday my wife learned that even your good and pure Senator George H. Pendleton resented it. When things have got to this point, there is no longer room to hesitate. Every virtuous citizen must join in trampling on these revolting libels. For your sake I regret it, but you must confess that you and Miss Loring and Harriet have drawn it on your own heads....

If you meet Henry James, you will find him a real addition to your pleasure in London, and if you can possibly come upon John Green, the Short Historian, and the pleasantest of Englishmen, unhappily prostrated by consumption, don't fail to see what you can of him.

To turn to our own news, I have only to say that summer is happily passed. I am bored to death by correcting the proofs of a very dull book about John Randolph, the fault of which is in the enforced obligation to take that lunatic monkey *au sérieux*. I want to print some of his letters and those of his friends, and, in order to do so, was obliged to treat him as though he were respectable. For that matter, however, I am under much the same difficulty with regard to T. Jefferson, who, between ourselves, is a character of comedy. John Adams is a droll figure, and good for Sheridan's school; but T. J. is a case for Beaumarchais; he needs the lightest of touches, and my hand is as heavy as his own sprightliness....

Our summer guests have all broken down. Aristarchi, Miss Lucy Frelinghuysen and all the rest have failed us. I know nothing of politics. I care nothing for Conkling, Cameron or Cornell.[1] We are immersed in the ignorance which characterises Beacon Street and Harvard College....

If England agrees with you, as it does with many, I expect to see you a lion in English society, a runner in at Marlborough House, and

[1] Alonzo B. Cornell (1832–1904).

your portrait by Burne Jones in the Grosvenor Gallery, with *Democracy* under your arm.

To Charles Milnes Gaskell

BEVERLY FARMS, 24 September, 1882.

Your *Nineteenth Century* article arrived safely. There are some difficulties in the path of all pessimistic reasoning which makes its conclusions doubtful, and for some centuries yet may seem to confute its truth. Man is still going fast upward. For example, beef has within two years risen here in price, notwithstanding the immense supply, until we can hardly afford to eat it. The reason is that the *people* have learned to prefer fresh meat to salt, and will no longer bring up families on salt pork. The scale of the millions rises steadily with their means, and I have caused an article to be written by the census people to show how steadily their means have risen and are rising. I will send you the article.

With such forces at work, even English farming has a great future. Wheat is a bad crop, but roots, hay and stock will certainly pay. All you have to do is to raise wages, and subdivide capital. Your workingmen, as a class, are still too poor....

To Henry Cabot Lodge

BEVERLY FARMS, MASS.,
Wednesday, 4 Oct., 1882.

MY DEAR LODGE, — Believe me, I am very sorry. Yours truly.[1]

To John Hay

BEVERLY FARMS, 8 Oct., 1882.

MY DEAR HAY-OH, — Your name naturally prolongs itself into a sigh as I think what fun I should have had if I had been with you in England. Why could not you and King have come over in 1880 when we were living there? Then we would have scaled Heaven and gone down into Hell, but now, look-ye, I am a mud-turtle, and for four months I have burrowed here in the ground without sight of sun or stars. Thank the eternal furies, a fortnight from today we shall be again wallowing in human depravity, at New York, and for the next

[1] Pencil notation — Defeat for nom[ination] for Congress. — H. C. L.

eight months I think we shall have the better of you. Florence and Nice are frankly *bête* beside Washington.

Long letters from Sir John and Sir Robert, the brace of baronets, singing your praises, and I am really pleased to think that you like them. Robert Cunliffe is one of my few swans; I am very fond of him, and have always found him a gentleman to the core, which is *muchissimo* dear. The universe hitherto has existed in order to produce a dozen people to amuse the five of hearts. Among us, we know all mankind. We or our friends have canvassed creation, and there are but a dozen or two companions in it; — men and women, I mean, whom you like to have about you, and whose society is an active pleasure. To me, Robert Cunliffe is one of these, not on account of his wit or knowledge, but because he is what a gentleman ought to be....

If you follow your scheme, and write a story "by the author," etc., I hope you will take the new *motif* under your eyes. Describe the sufferings of the anonymous author on hearing his book discussed in a foreign country, and how it gradually led him to murder and self-destruction. Although my brain is much disturbed by the whirl of authors known to have written your book, and the vision of you and King and James listening to revelations on the subject is almost too much for me, still I cannot but feel that, had I such a load on my conscience, the listening to British clack would drive me insane. How you have stood it, I tremble to think. Much as I disapprove the *spirit* of your book (resp. Miss Loring's, King's or De Forest's) I can see that in English reflection it must become more terrible to its creator than to any one else. I can imagine you cowering and crushed under the ignominious popularity you have tumbled into. The situation is tragi-comic in an exceptional degree, and quite new to literature. You can make some atonement for your offence, by explaining the terrors of your atonement. This new crucifixion is unique in history, and should have a great success. After all, to write for people who can't read, as the Frenchman said, may be a severe trial, but the least you can do is to teach them their letters.

I see that the political libel for which you (or De Forest) are popularly supposed to be responsible is to be brought out here in a cheap edition. This, I confess, strikes me as doubtful taste, considering all the circumstances, but perhaps you know best. I am sure you will have been greatly pleased by Folger's nomination in New York, which, to the superficial observer, might seem to lend some color to libels like *Democracy*, etc., but which in truth is evidence that we are improving. I am told that the whole Union Club has kicked over the traces and this time there will be fun. You will deplore Republican defeat, but you will be glad to see Willy Walter's [1] success and especially his energetic support of the tariff. Like him, I stand up for the tariff as long as that duty on copper is kept up, but if Congress shall be rash enough to touch that key-stone of the system and of our liberties, I go in for free trade pure and simple. On this copper — or iron as the case may be — let Willy Walter, and you and I, take a bold stand.

Gilman [2] of Johns Hopkins gives me a very hopeful account of your new University at Cleveland. I hope to see you Professor of Theology and Ethics, President and Corporation, all at once, some day, and perhaps, when copper is free, you will take me in too, and give me something to do. I don't know any history, but I know a little of everything else worth knowing, and can teach just as well without any knowledge at all.

My John Randolph is just coming into the world. Do you know, a book to me always seems a part of myself, a kind of intellectual brat or segment, and I never bring one into the world without a sense of shame. They are naked, helpless and beggarly, yet the poor wretches must live forever and curse their father for their silent tomb. This particular brat is the first I ever detested. He is the only one I never wish to see again; but I know he will live to dance, in the obituaries, over my cold grave. Don't read him, should you by chance meet him. Kick him gently, and let him go.

Houghton declines to print Aaron Burr because Aaron wasn't a "statesman." Not bad that for a damned bookseller! He should live a while at Washington and know our *real* statesmen. I am glad to get out of Houghton's hands, for I want to try Harper or Appleton. Which recommendest thou? I incline towards Harper....

To Henry Cabot Lodge

1607 H STREET.
31 October, 1882.

Many thanks for your kind note. I shall have your luck in one way. The Virginians are red-hot at my introductory chapter. Your South Carolinians are cool in comparison. Luckily for me, the book is but a feeler for my history and I want the mud it stirs.

I wish I could read American history "at one sitting" as you do, but I broke down hopelessly in the middle of Sumner's *Jackson*, and

[1] William Walter Phelps (1839–1894), member of Congress from New Jersey.
[2] Daniel Coit Gilman (1831–1908).

much as I want to read your *Hamilton*, the subject repels me more than my regard for you attracts. To say that I detest my own books is a mild expression, and I should be very sorry to feel so towards my friends' writing. I *cannot* read Bancroft's two volumes, though the Appendices are very entertaining. Sometimes I seriously think my disgust for history will grow on me till it overpowers my perseverance. I say this to explain why I am so cold about other people's books when they are so kind about mine. If they only knew how much more I dislike my own than I do other people's, they would make allowances.

It's hardly worth while to save the party in Massachusetts, so far as Congressmen are concerned. The débacle in New York and Pennsylvania is overwhelming. In Pennsylvania they hope to save Congressmen, but in New York all goes. Grant himself (don't quote it) concedes 80,000 majority. I now look for new combinations, but the Lord knows what.

To John Hay

WASHINGTON, 26 Novr., 1882.

We have been here a month, quite alone, without society, in a cold uncomfortable autumn. I do not know why I should be perfectly happy under such circumstances, but I am. My heart bounds as I tear myself from family, friends, the familiar streets and boyhood associations of the best of all cities, and I rush to clasp in my arms this corrupt and corrupting tombstone of our liberties. Don't tell my secret!

We have been here a month — I repeat myself and *radote*, but in Europe all do so — and have seen no one. I have no gossip to tell you, for I am not now intimate with the powerful. In your ancient throne sits Johnny Davis,[1] but I see him not, nor yet his wife. Miss Lucy is *my* friend, for she reads my books — my poor little black-eyed Susan J. Randolph — and she reads your books too, for the night before last when we were all dining at the Lewenhaupts'[2] — the Sackville Wests; Roustan;[3] Dalla Valle[4] the Eyetalian Charged; Willamov[5] and his new sister Mme. Catalano, whose Italian dragoon-husband ran away and left her with three children and *cent livres de rente* for poor Willamov to take care of, which he is doing; De Bildt[6] and a sous-lieutenant

[1] John Davis married a daughter of Theodore Frelinghuysen.
[2] Count Carl Lewenhaupt, minister from Sweden and Norway.
[3] Théodore Roustan, minister from France.   [4] Marquis A. Dalla Valle.
[5] Grégoire de Willamov, secretary of the Russian legation.
[6] C. de Bildt, secretary of the legation of Sweden and Norway.

de hussars named Feejam, which is some relation to Boojum, being legitimist French for the Comte de Fitz James, as I am told, and much addicted to games of chance; and besides these great people, Miss Beale, Miss Lucy Frelinghuysen and ourselves — amid this gay scene, I say, Miss Lucy remarked in a sweetly meditative manner that she wondered you had not been credited with that much discussed story called *Democracy*, and I hastened to assure her that the newspapers had done you that honor, nor had you, I believe, thought it necessary, any more than my wife, to deny it. As, at the same moment, my wife, unheard by me, was denying it at the other end of the room under the Argus eyes of Lewenhaupt and West, I hope we did all we could to maintain your reputation. By the bye, we are told that the work is being translated into French. For the love of fun, send me a copy. It must be droller than a Palais Royal vaudeville on the English. You seem to think I am going to make myself ridiculous by denying its authorship, but, oh, my poet of the people, I have printed volume after volume which no one would read, and if now the public choose to advertise me by reading as mine Shakespeare, Milton, Junius, Don Quixote and the Arabian Nights, shall I say them nay? Not so, by Hercules! I will let them give me Little Breeches, Castilian Days and the Report of the 40th parallel rather than lose a single possible advertisement for *Anglo-Saxon Law* and *New England Federalism*....

Of Mr. Arthur I can tell you nothing. The Republican party being now a burst bladder, I am going back to it to give it respectability, since I can give it nothing else. The worst of it is that it contains not a single man fit to run for the Presidency. The stalwarts are nominating Edmunds, which shows sense and desperation, but if Blaine and his rivalries reappear, the party will just disappear. I see the whole tragedy in Garfield's blunder about resuscitating Blaine. ... Nevertheless, if he and Conkling and the wretched crew about Arthur will disappear, and if a decent man can be nominated, I believe we can elect him against an indecent Democrat. My own expectation is that the Democrats too will go to pieces in trying to nominate, but if they succeed and do not disgust the country, I see no way of beating them except such as are worse than their success. All my particular friends have come out of the election with great success thus far, and some of them are sure to be on top of the heap anyhow, which consoles me; but after all, it is the unexpected we must now expect....

To Henry Cabot Lodge

1607 H STREET. 26 Dec., 1882.

Many thanks for your kind letter, and still kinder notice. Of the justice of your estimate of the Randolph, I have of course nothing to say. I hope the book deserves your compliments, and though it does not please me, I shall be glad if it pleases anyone else. As for the Sumner,[1] although I agree that it is not a readable book, that its style is that of a twelve-year-old school boy, and its matter three fourths out of place, still there is a good deal in it which was new to me and will affect future historians more than it does the average reader. In this sense it is a serious contribution to history, and makes a positive addition to our knowledge, which is more than can be said of most books. I could not finish it, as a reader, but some day I shall as a student.

I did not put your *Hamilton* on the same level as the *Jackson* because I had not even begun it, having postponed the pleasure till I should come to the subject in preparing Burr for the press. As I have not yet decided what to do with Burr, I do not know when I shall take up Hamilton. My hands are so full that I put things off.

Lounsberry's *Cooper*[2] strikes me as excellent. He falls into one curious error as an artist, which is so common to Cooper himself that I wonder his biographer was not on his guard. He airs his own opinions a little too much. His abuse of England is less effective than if it were in better temper, and his lectures on copyright, &c., are unnecessary. If we could only be impersonal, our books would be better than they are, but I am too much of a sinner myself to blame him. On the whole the English still do better work than we. Morison's *Macaulay* is an instance.[3]

So far as I can see, you are about the only man who is to be congratulated on the result of the Massachusetts election. You have lost nothing, and saved your chances for 1884. As for the Democrats, their troubles are still before them. They think they now have a sure thing of it. I doubt it. They have nothing to stand on, and party principles do not exist. Under such circumstances no party is safe for a week ahead.

Give our best love to your wife. I saw Sam Warren lately. He is to be married on the 25th. I hope the transplanted flower will flourish.[4]

There is no news here, nor any new people.

[1] William Graham Sumner's *Andrew Jackson*, in American Statesmen.
[2] Thomas Raynesford Lounsbury's *James Fenimore Cooper*, in American Men of Letters.
[3] James Cotter Morison, whose *Macaulay* appeared in 1882 in the English Men of Letters.
[4] He married a daughter of Thomas Francis Bayard, of Delaware.

To John Hay

[WASHINGTON,] 7 January, 1883.

. . . .

Of politics I know nothing. The average Congressman, like your dear friend Perry,[1] is now chiefly occupied in swearing at professional reformers and voting for their bills. After the excoriating booting these gentle Congressmen got at the last election, I do not blame them for looking upon us poor reformers with only moderate regard, but I confess to having been immensely pleased to tumble over Kasson[2] the other evening in a very bad temper. "Well, the House has passed your *Boston* bill," said he savagely. He added that Bostonians were "grasping," and other compliments. I could not conceive what he meant till the next morning when I read the House proceedings on the Civil Service Bill, and just howled with delight at Kasson's temper. The gentle Hale,[3] I fancy, is equally pleased to please us. You and your friend Perry and all the half-breeds, stalwarts and jelly-fish should set up a party founded on the glorious principle of contempt for reformers. They are all green with disgust because, having kicked out all the reformers that ever were in office or in Congress, they can no longer find a victim to punish. I believe that I have no longer a political friend in Washington, and so far as I know, am not likely to have one, which saves anxiety now that my work is so well done by those who loathe me. But you should see Don Cameron's smile! He loves us like a father....

Of literature I know but little. Aaron Burr is not to be printed at present. He is to wait a few years. I hate publishing, and do not want reputation. There are not more than a score of people in America whose praise I want, and the number will grow with time. So Aaron will stay in his drawer and appear only as the outrider for my first two volumes of history, about a year before they appear, which may give Aaron three or four more years of privacy. I understand that there are some new novels, but I never read novels — nor write them. I understand from my sister-in-law, Ellen Gurney, that Hon. J. G. Blaine at a dinner party in New York said that Mrs. H. A. "acknowledges" to have written *Democracy*. You know how I have always admired Mr. Blaine's powers of invention! The *Republican* in a list of reputed authors puts J. G. B.'s name first, with Gail as collaborateur.

[1] Perry Belmont (1851–   ), of New York.
[2] John Adam Kasson (1822–1910).
[3] Eugene Hale (1836–1918).

You of course figure in it, and "Miss Hatty Loring," and "Mrs. Adam" (of the British Legation).

To John Hay

[WASHINGTON,] 8 January, 1883.

Thanks for your sympathy about the attacks on my *Bread Winners*.[1] I admit that every now and then, in life, my critics have succeeded in making me feel very sea-sick for a day or two. I am a sensitive cuss and a coward. When I get a real whipping, I feel kind of low about it. I never fight except with the intent to kill; and you can't kill a critic. My consolation has been to take no notice of them; this annoys them much more than any other retaliation; for the life of a critic is too short to recover from neglect. Reply is like scratching their match for them. I have been one, and I know.

To Charles Milnes Gaskell

1607 H STREET, 21 January, 1883.

Your letter announcing Frank Doyle's death grieved me sadly. Death gets to be such a daily matter as one advances in the world, that now I hardly know who of my friends are dead and who are living. They are all equally alive to me at this distance, for I remember everything as it was, and a few changes in such a trifle as life make no impression on the mind....

In the middle of confused politicians and idiotic society, I go on grinding out history with more or less steadiness. I hope to get out two volumes in 1885, and I mean them to be readable. By the by, can you find out for me who is a man named Morison, who has written a very clever sketch of Macaulay? So good a piece of criticism ought to come from some one who is known, but I know not Morison and therefore fear myself unknown.

Five daily hours of work, a little society, a friend or two sometimes to dinner, and more rarely a dinner out, but never an evening, make my quiet life in the days of snow and ice when riding is cut off. The world is too busy at this season to think of anything but its own affairs, and we are quieter now, when others are busy, than when society is asleep. We hear of Europe only through newspapers, and see no reason in them for wanting to go there....

[1] John Hay's novel of the name appeared anonymously in the *Century Magazine*, in 1883.

To John Hay

Washington, 23 January, 1883.

Would that you were now here. Things are getting mixed. The pot boils. If you have a candidate for the Presidency, set him up! I've none, but your friend Miss Beale has got my promise for Logan [1] of Peoria.

Please tell me of something to read. At this season my wife and I stay at home every evening, and our literature is low. Trollope has amused me for two evenings. I am clear that you should write autobiography. I mean to do mine. After seeing how coolly and neatly a man like Trollope can destroy the last vestige of heroism in his own life, I object to allowing mine to be murdered by any one except myself. Every church mouse will write autobiography in another generation in order to prove that it never believed in religion.

To John Hay

Washington, 28 January, 1883.

Whatever you do in this unreasonable world, my dear son of Ohio, never lose your temper! Why should you fly into such frightful paroxysms of rage, and use such horrid language, just because I forgot what had been done with my own arithmetic! If it had been yours, I grant you — but my own! I will never abandon my right to treat my own with neglect....

I gather that McDonald [2] will be the man. Unless I deceive myself, I shall have again to lean towards the Republicans. Your friend Payne [3] is too much for me, and his election just now turns the scale the other way.

Yet I am payned to add that I cannot see how the Republicans are to do any better. The machine will be irresistible if it is allowed to run much longer without check. The blackies will send up solid delegations for Arthur, and New York will be fixed.

Poor King! I suppose he must have got naturalised as a British subject, and married an Irish peeress.

[1] John Alexander Logan (1826–1886).
[2] Joseph Ewing McDonald (1819–1891), of Indiana.
[3] Henry B. Payne (1810–1896), of Ohio.

To John Hay

WASHINGTON, 4 March, 1883.

Two letters of yours are in my drawer. As my wife wrote lately, I postponed doing so; not because I was without material for a letter — far from it; but that you might have your little amusements at intervals. Your letters are very well except in saying nothing of your health. This is an anxious subject with us, because the winter has hit right and left at everyone, and we would gladly know that you at least have escaped. Be not mad at my calling King mad, for mad he certainly is. In the particular case of the Shaw affair, his madness consisted as I understood it, in its usual form of not writing a word for months. Alex. Agassiz inquired of me where he was, as he had not for months communicated with his business associates. Basta! I hope he is all right. He is sure to be forgiven. Your copy of *Democratie* arrived yesterday through the custom house with ten cents duty. It is curious and wonderful. So is your report about the Prince of Wales. Now that Arthur Sedgwick,[1] we are told, acknowledges the book, I can say what I did not care to say to you so long as you were the author, that the book is one of the least sufficient, for its subject, I ever read. Since it came out we have had half a dozen dramas here that might reasonably convulse the world. Thackeray and Balzac never invented anything so lurid as Garfield, Guiteau and Blaine, but even they are surpassed by Brady and Dorsey, and Arthur is a creature for whose skin the romancist ought to go with a carving-knife.... Society is a conspiracy for self-protection against just such attacks as these Star Route people are now making. I find no fault with them... Power is omnipotent in Washington society. I do not go to the White House because I see and hear things I don't like, but I am quite alone, and in a few years more I shall either have to go there or go to prison. At the rate we travel, it is time to bend the knee to Beelzebub or any other President.

Therefore I repeat that your novel, if it was yours, is a failure because it undertook to describe the workings of power in this city, and spoiled a great tragic subject such as Æschylus might have made what it should be, but what it never in our time will be. The tragic element, if accepted as real, is bigger here than ever on this earth before. I hate to see it mangled *à la* Daudet in a tame-cat way. Men don't know tragedy when they see it. What a play of passion we have seen here within two years this day!...

As for politics, this last session is just foul; nothing was ever so

[1] Arthur George Sedgwick (1844–1915).

rotten. I look out now for earthquakes, and a lively shaking up next year. The worst Democratic administration would not be quite so revolting as this....

To Charles Milnes Gaskell

1607 H Street, 25 March, 1883.

News seems rather scarce, for I notice that our friends and visitors have very little to talk about. I am always at work, and make a sort of progress which is neither steady nor fast, but it amuses me and is worth quite as much as the work I see of other people. There is no use in fashing oneself about success. I see very little success going about the world that seems to me successful, and live too near politics not to keep out of it. I expect every day to hear that George Trevelyan has been murdered, and really wish you would give the Irish independence or else clean out the whole island.

So far as I can see, we are all right here. The country is at last filled out; railways all round and through it, and everyone satisfied. I confess to thinking it the only country now worth working for, or pleasant to work in; for until Europe has settled her various disputes, there is no sense of getting on in it; but our ways of life are hateful to the well-regulated, for we do not really care a button what becomes of the human race, if it is not to do something new....

To Carl Schurz

Washington, 30 March, 1883.

You have seen that Aristarchi is recalled.

I have reason to think that he does not want to go home. His ambition is to utilise his experience and abilities on the press. He would like to take such a position as that of Blowitz on the London *Times*, and of course there is no man either in America or in Europe better fitted for such work.

The place he would like would no doubt be on a great morning paper like the *Herald* or *Times*, and in addition a correspondence for the London *Times* and the *Indépendance Belge*, but he is not in a condition to pick and choose. I think at this moment a good offer from any respectable source that would make him feel safe for a year or two, would secure him.

As a correspondent, with the right to support his letters editorially, he would be a power here and everywhere. Of course his field is our foreign relations but there he is easily first. The State Department would cower at your feet. You would have a monopoly, for no other paper has a correspondent who knows more of foreign affairs than John Davis tells them. Aristarchi alone can keep the run of our Mexican and South American affairs; he would do something to correct the overpowering Germanism and Englishism of you and Godkin, and would represent French and Spanish ideas with accuracy which is more than any one else can do.

I should not suggest this idea if I were not persuaded that it would strengthen the paper. Try him with a $3000 offer for a year, and see what he says. Ever truly yours.

To John Hay

WASHINGTON, 8 April, 1883.

.   .   .   .

I never met Lord Acton,[1] a personage of whom I have read much, as in an English novel, somewhat tinged with Neo-Platonism after the style of Mr. Thingamy — Singleton — Sinsomething — whose long dulness I waded through last year. Tell my Lord to come over here and live for the future, not for the middle-ages. As for Henry Bright, he is literary *petit-maître* to his toes, and America would assassinate him. I liked him, but he would die untimely here...

As for us, you will feel the vexation we all feel after long absence, at finding nothing changed. There is bad manners in such stolid indifference to presence and absence, but what can we do? Shall I burn the house to welcome you, or cook the new puppy?

To John Hay

WASHINGTON, 20 April, 1883.

Once more before you return to these primitive forests I write a line, not so much to wish you a pleasant voyage or to ask you to bring me a collection of elephants in your trunks as wearing apparel for me through the custom-house, as to tell you that I have been using your name in a manner which you will no doubt enjoy as much as I do.

Several times within the last fortnight I have been told a story that you and King (sometimes one, sometimes both,) had heard the manuscript of *Democracy* read in a house in Washington, had been asked to write a chapter, and so on with variations (such as that King had

[1] Sir John Emerich Edward Dalberg Acton (1834–1902).

written the account of Worth's clothes in that veracious work), and finally, what was more important, that you both said the house in question was mine.

In each case this story seems to have come from Tom Appleton. I have in all cases, emphatically, and in your names, denounced it as one of Tom Appleton's lies, and offered to stake my existence on the fact that neither you nor King had ever said anything of the sort. I had no hesitation in doing so, because I knew that the part of the story which concerned me was untrue, and as that was the point of it, I was safe in denying for you the whole.

To Carl Schurz

Sunday, 20 May 1883.

I write this line to warn you that Aristarchi goes from here next Wednesday on his way to Europe. He means to see you, and I suspect he will call at the office. He will no doubt talk with you of his plans, and perhaps ask you for letters to Germany, though I think he has got these in other quarters. What is more to the point, I believe he would like an invitation to write as a special correspondent from Europe. As I have already written you all I have to say on the matter, I leave you to make up your own mind whether to utilise him or not.

You seem to be wabbling as painfully as the rest of us on the subject of the next election. Of course the *Evening Post* must above all things be conservative, but I know no reason why you or I should be so, and as I think conservatism in these days a sign of weak intelligence or advancing years, I prefer radicalism. Therefore I want to know what the Free Trade organisation means to do if the Democratic party goes back on it, as it has done in Kentucky. If it falls in your way to get into the councils of the north-western free-traders, I wish you would find out whether we have the means of punishing the Democrats for this kind of conduct. For my own part I would gladly help to organise a free trade party, and if we had the strength to contest a single State, make an independent nomination for the Presidency. Ever truly yours.

To Charles Milnes Gaskell

1607 H Street, 10 June, 1883.

Your letters are a necrology. I feel as though I had also passed over to the next world, and you were notifying me of the latest departures.

If I can judge from life here, it matters very little who goes on or who stays; no one is of consequence enough to raise a ripple, least of all in Washington, where we are always jostling the people who govern the odd millions of our country, and yet we do not care enough about them to make their acquaintance. In a year or two, this batch will be gone and another come. No one cares....

Your account of Harcourt and Swinburne is most interesting. Harcourt suave must be more strange than Swinburne quiet. I admire Swinburne's poetic faculty immensely. No other of my contemporaries has approached him — I mean among men of my age or under — but I long since made up my mind not to seek the acquaintance of poets; it spoils their poetry. I knew Swinburne twenty years ago and have needed twenty years to get over it....

To Henry Cabot Lodge

1607 H STREET, 10 June, 1883.

I have read the *Daniel Webster*. As I never have yet read the *Hamilton* I cannot compare the two books, and as I am not a lawyer, I cannot pretend to judge of your treatment of Webster in that character, but I think the book excellent so far as I can judge. You have convinced me that my grandfather's early estimate of Webster's character was not as harsh as I thought, and you have done it with tact and literary skill. Your Webster should have been an actor like Kemble or Cooke. He would have been sublime. To me there is a visible effort in your elaborate excuses and apologies for him, but I doubt whether readers in general will feel it. I think, too, that you might have condensed a little here and there; but I am a little *toqué* about condensation, and am thought crude and hard in consequence. On the whole I have no doubt that this book, which is one of the most difficult to do, is in many ways the best of the series. I have noticed no errors of fact, but, as I am not very familiar with the period, I will not pretend to be an authority about it. With all my care, my own books swarm with errors, and so, I suppose, do others.

I have but one prime test for a popular book. Is it interesting? I did not think von Holst [1] or Sumner readable, still less Gilman. [2] I did not expect Webster to be so, for all Whigs were bores. On reading it, I found myself mistaken; it reads well.

[1] Hermann Eduard von Holst's *John C. Calhoun*, in American Statesmen.
[2] Gilman's *James Monroe*, in American Statesmen.

To John Hay

BEVERLY FARMS, 10 August, 1883.

. . . .

I am glad to hear that you are publishing another novel. I was so frank in telling you my unfavorable opinion of *Democracy*, that I will try to read the new one in hopes that I may be able to speak well of it. Is it not a little risky for your anonymity to lay the scene at Cleveland after laying the scene of *Democracy* at Washington? Two such straws must be fatal.

I have an idea of visiting Cleveland in October. I want to go down to Blennerhassett's island....

To John Hay

BEVERLY FARMS, 29 August, 1883.

Positively I blush! I am not used to such language.... I am used to cuffs, not compliments, and my poor style has been hardened into unnatural rigidity by the blows of criticism. You will make it soft and gushing if you are gentle with it. Never do it again....

The first number of the "Bread-winners" I swore was yours. Certain tricks of expression and handling left me hardly a doubt. The second shook my faith — I hardly know why. Perhaps because the undertone of humor is less marked. I shall continue to watch it. Of Mrs. Dahlgren [1] I have had enough in newspaper extracts. I toil and moil, painfully and wearily, forward and back, over my little den of history, and am too dry-beat to read novels. I would I were on a mule in the Rockies with you and King, but at forty-five every hour is golden and will not return. I painfully coin it into printers' ink, and shall have a big volume of seven hundred pages to show *you* next winter. As it gets into type I cower before it in hope and fear, for it is all I shall make of this droll toy called life....

To John Hay

BEVERLY FARMS, 24 September, 1883.

While waiting anxiously to hear of your welfare in those wild regions which you inhabit, I write a line of interest in the present literary problem of our day.

I am glad you did not write the "Bread-winners." It is a real joy to

[1] Madeleine Vinton Dahlgren (Mrs. John Adolph Dahlgren).

me to feel that there are two men west of the Alleghanies who are capable of doing first rate literary work, and who join humor with style. Should I ever come to Cleveland, I hope you will introduce me to the author. Meanwhile I would like to read his other books, for, of course, all of us, who try to write, know only too well that such skill is only acquired by long and painful effort. As a work of art, I should not hesitate to put the "Bread-winners" so far as the story has gone, quite at the head of our Howells'-and-James' epoch for certain technical qualities, such as skill in construction, vivacity in narration, and breadth of *motif*. It has also one curious and surprising quality, least to be expected from an unknown western writer. Howells cannot deal with gentlemen or ladies; he always slips up. James knows almost nothing of women but the mere outside; he never had a wife. This new writer not only knows women, but knows *ladies;* the rarest of literary gifts. I suppose he has an eastern wife? Under ordinary circumstances, there might be a doubt as to the sex of the author, but here none is possible, for he also knows men and even gentlemen. His sense of humor, too, is so markedly masculine as to take away all doubt on the matter.

If I had a criticism to make it would be that he is a little hard on reformers; he shows prejudice against his own characters. George Eliot used to do this. For my part, I always thought that if I tried to write a novel, I would make it overflow with kindness and see nothing but virtues in the human race.

If the author wrote *Democracy* as is said, he has made a great stride in every way, especially in humor, which is rather conspicuously wanting in that over-ambitious and hard-featured book....

To John Hay

WASHINGTON, 31 October, 1883.

I devoted an hour on the train to the November instalment of the Cleveland novel, which seemed to me to sustain itself, but which I read with the fear of Mrs. Mather on my mind. I am really distressed that she should think my previous remarks on the subject so wanting in perception. In consequence of what she said, I have revised my opinion. I am prepared to make concessions. Please tell her that, if she will concede my points, I will concede hers.

My point is that every book ought to be judged by its strength, not by its weakness. I make it a rule to disregard small blemishes which a little proof-reading would cut out in five minutes, when the composition, style and general handling are excellent.

To illustrate. If I remember right, Mrs. Mather objected that the hero, in youth, travelled in Europe, or did something else, with his *grand-father*. I admit that this is a false note, but see how slight it is. If I were the author, I should correct it. I should boldly say, *grand-mother*. This slight alteration removes the fault. Every American would object that it is untrue to nature to have a grand-father, but I never heard anyone object to a grand-mother.

Again! Mrs. Mather criticised, I think, a *pearl* stud. I agree with her. Yet see again how trifling a change corrects the slip! I will insert in the proof, before it appears in book-form, "mother of" before "pearl." Mrs. Mather will agree that "mother of pearl" is quite harmless.

There is more difficulty in regard to the butler. True, a simple western man ought not to have a butler, but a female help; yet, as he is a widower, this would be highly improper. I am at a loss to meet this difficulty. I fear that even "Buttons" would be undemocratic. Perhaps an old nurse to open the door would answer, and the hero might do his own stretching.

Mrs. Mather also objects that too much accent is laid on the hero's bravery. I agree again. He twice knocks the pistol out of some one's hand. The repetition jars; it is never safe to repeat a *ficelle* of any kind. I will strike out the passage in the proof. How would it do to insert that he turned a double-back-somerset over somebody's head?

There are no doubt other points of objection which I should accept at once. I make it a rule to strike out ruthlessly in my writings whatever my wife criticises, on the theory that she is the average reader, and that her decisions are, in fact if not in reason, absolute. What I mean to point out to Mrs. Mather, in my own defence, is that trifles, which require only a stroke of the pen to correct them, and which are mere matters of proof-reading, ought not to blind us to the larger literary merits of books which do not depend on trifles for their strength. Shakespeare frequently shocks me! In fact, I can see clearly that Shakespeare was a snob. Thackeray's snobbishness was often revolting. Nevertheless, I venture to say, openly and confidently, that in my opinion both Shakespeare and Thackeray wrote as well as Harry James or Mrs. Dahlgren. I venture to think that Desdemona was *felt* by a genius of considerable purity, though to my own mind her conduct was such as I can never approve. Shakespeare evidently did not feel my objections.

The kiss in the green-house is the *pons asinorum* of the book. This is pure masculine work, and I cannot strike it out even to please Mrs. Mather. I must stand or fall by this kiss. Let us hope that women, like the heroine, will end by forgiving it....

To John Hay

WASHINGTON, November 23, 1883.

Your bit of logic after the historico-genealogico-politico-Wendell-Phillipico school is good, but I liked still better that of the New York correspondent of the *Evening Star* not long since, who informed us that Miss Maud Howe [1] had certainly written "The Newport Aquarelle," and *therefore* was no doubt the author of another anonymous story now appearing in the "Century."

To Carl Schurz

WASHINGTON, 12 Decr., '83.

MY DEAR FRIEND, — I was extremely sorry to see the announcement yesterday of your withdrawal from the *Evening Post*. I had heard nothing whatever, from anyone whom I supposed to be well-informed, that led me to expect or to understand any difficulty; and, if it had not been for persistent rumors since my return here, I should have been taken quite by surprise. You will easily believe that I regret extremely the separation. In such cases one does not stop to ask the cause of the trouble.[2] I neither know nor care what it was; but I have perfect confidence that it was nothing which would affect my regard for you. I am quite content to leave it there.

Should you come on here this winter, you will find your old quarters ready for you up-stairs. Perhaps a little visit here would amuse you. We expect Agatha at her usual time.

To Charles Milnes Gaskell

1607 H STREET, 3 February, 1884.

Yesterday I received a bound copy of the first volume of my History. I have had six copies privately printed as a first edition for my own use.

[1] Daughter of Julia Ward Howe.

[2] Mr. Schurz differed in opinion with his colleagues of the *Post*, Edwin L. Godkin and Horace White, on the manner of dealing with the telegraphers' strike.

When I am ready, I shall reprint and publish two volumes at once. Perhaps I may reach this point in the year '86. I admit to thinking the book readable, but to you it would be sadly dull reading. You see I am writing for a continent of a hundred million people fifty years hence; and I can't stop to think what England will read....

Your politics look queerly distorted from this distance, and I have given up the effort to follow them, knowing that we shall all be told quickly enough if anything of consequence happens. Our own politics, for the first time in a hundred years, are almost absolutely indifferent to the people. In a few months we must elect a new President, and no human being can so much as guess who is to wear the crown. No one seems much to want it. For my own part, though I try to be well informed, and am more or less intimate with some of the leaders, I have not the remotest idea whom I would like to see in the Presidency; and none of my old associates have any clear wishes except to keep certain men out. The truth is, our affairs were never in so good a condition; public opinion was never healthier; and barring a few doubtful jobs, no government was ever so economically and sensibly conducted. We have got to the point where our protective duties must be lowered, and in another ten years we shall push Europe hard in manufactures. There is a tremendous amount of activity in every direction; and another generation will see the result. I consider ours to have already done its work, and on the whole it is the biggest on record.

I was rather shocked to see a sort of popular vote taken by some literary authority in England on the ten best writers, and to find that all the candidates except Swinburne were old. Why does not a new batch turn up? Can Lord Houghton have carried off the art of finding new men? When I was at Frystone in '61, I met there Stirling Maxwell, Laurence Oliphant and Algernon Swinburne. Maxwell's posthumous work; and Oliphant's *Altiora Peto*, which I can't read; and Swinburne's last poem, seem to represent still about the best English work in their lines....

To Charles Milnes Gaskell

Washington, 18 May, 1884.

. . . .

My immediate interest is in a house which I am about to build. John Hay and I have bought a swell piece of land which looks across a little square,[1] something like Portman Square, to the White House, where our Presidents live. Hay is the capitalist and takes the corner,

[1] Lafayette, late President's, Square.

while I have forty-four feet of front facing southward. We have arranged our plans; our architect has finished them; they will go immediately to the contractors for estimates; and I hope in about a month to know that work has begun....

My second interest is politics. We have a Presidential election coming on, and I am in opposition, fairly and squarely, on the free-trade issue. We shall probably be beaten, but it makes little difference to me. Revenue reform is bound to come, unless something wild turns up. In our present state of affairs, anything may happen. Parties are going to pieces, and new issues are rising. The world is getting restless. Generally such a state of things ends in blood-letting or revolution. We have seen so much of both in our time that we can afford to let our juniors try their hands at it.

You have noticed that we have had another general liquidation, which the newspapers call a financial crisis. So far as I can see, it results chiefly from want of honesty and want of judgment. The country is richer than ever, but the public distrusts its financiers. A crowd of men have been caught in thieving and swindling; and the knaves have hurt the fools, besides doing a good deal of harm to some good people. No one can say how long the depression will last, but meanwhile we shall probably work harder and better for cleaning out the decay. Economy is going to be a practical science....

Socially I have little to say. With a steady stream of society, I have crowds of acquaintances and what we call friends, but no intimates, nor have I discovered any new Birds of Paradise. You are about my only correspondent. I have no one among the thousands of Europe-seekers this year for whom I should care to take oath that he or she would amuse you. No new literary light has turned its rays towards me, nor any wit or humorist....

To John Hay

Washington, 27 May, 1884.

．　．　．　．　．　．　．　．　．　．　．　．

Politics are meaner than ever. Arthur has lowered both parties to his moral standard. Carlyle[1] and Morrison[2] are a joint failure. Neither party shows a ray of capacity. I am told that Blaine has a sure thing at Chicago; and, if he fails, Arthur must succeed. One or the other is inevitable. Tilden will get the other nomination. I mean to

[1] John Griffin Carlisle (1835–1910), Speaker of the House of Representatives.
[2] William Ralls Morrison (1825–1909), member from Illinois.

vote for Ben Butler. Of the lot, I prefer him; at least he has the qualities of his defects. I know what I shall get.

Dry-rot is the present situation. I look for a big political crash like the Wall Street one, which will squeeze both parties till the rottenness bursts out. My friend MacVeagh has alone told God's own truth, and of course is howled at; the *Evening Post* is just imbecile; the only wise man is Willy Wally,[1] and wisdom has cost him $250,000 for the reformer Eno, besides whatever the Blaine campaign thus far has come to. W. W. P. is to be our next Secretary of State; and you — dear heart — shall be Secretary of the Navy, vice Bill Chandler, and take us on picnics to Quantico.

I meant to go to Chicago, but the prospect was too black. I hoped to vote the Democratic ticket, but even this refuge is vanishing. You had better come home, and go in for office, to help us out of political bankruptcy; for our side of the five of hearts is in a bad way.

To John Hay

BEVERLY FARMS, 3 July, 1884.

. . . .

Of politics I hear not a word. Down hereabouts people look vague, and ask who are to be candidates, and when the election takes place. The bolters privately talk of twenty thousand votes; publicly of twice that number; but my own estimate is about ten thousand, which would turn the State Democratic, except that the Butler and Blaine men will certainly trade votes. On the whole, Mr. Blaine may, I think, count on Massachusetts as probably his, and if his managers here are shrewd enough to sell out the Republican State and Congressional tickets, they can hardly fail to win. Without a trade, I should say the chances were the other way.

I speak not as a bolter, for I am not one, but as a Democrat, who wants to defeat Butler, and can't do it. As the prospect now stands, Massachusetts will vote both for Butler *and* Blaine. Taxes will rise, I guess.

To John Hay

BEVERLY FARMS, 3 August, [1884.]

. . . .

I know no more than Robinson [Crusoe] what is doing in the world, and care but little. Politics at this stage of an election are duller to

[1] William Walter Phelps.

me than at any other time. The mid-summer waiting for the average idiot to make up his mind, is like the stopping in mid-ocean to repack the steam-chest; it makes me sick. As a good Democrat, I hope that if you are going to elect Mr. Blaine you will do it quickly and thoroughly; for I am tired of my independent friends, who are too good to vote for Blaine, and never, no, never, would vote with the wicked Democrats. The amount I hear of this tom-foolery is calculated to make a tortoise-shell cat turn green. One would suppose that this country had never till now elected any president except G. Washington. Dear, dear, dear! How their grandfathers did squeal about T. Jefferson!...

To Charles Milnes Gaskell

BEVERLY FARMS, 21 September, 1884.

. . . .

We are here plunged in politics funnier than words can express. Very great issues are involved. Especially everyone knows that a step towards free trade is inevitable if the Democrats come in. For the first time in twenty-eight years, a Democratic administration is almost inevitable. The public is angry and abusive. Every one takes part. We are all doing our best, and swearing at each other like demons. But the amusing thing is that no one talks about real interests. By common consent they agree to let these alone. We are afraid to discuss them. Instead of this, the press is engaged in a most amusing dispute whether Mr. Cleveland had an illegitimate child, and did or did not live with more than one mistress; whether Mr. Blaine got paid in railway bonds for services as Speaker; and whether Mrs. Blaine had a baby three months after her marriage. Nothing funnier than some of these subjects has been treated in my time. I have laughed myself red with amusement over the letters, affidavits, leading articles and speeches which are flying through the air. Society is torn to pieces. Parties are wrecked from top to bottom. A great political revolution seems impending. Yet, when I am not angry, I can do nothing but laugh.

I am a free-trade Democrat and support Mr. Cleveland. I believe he will come in, and in that case my friends will have to reduce our protective duties. The result of this course, if we persevere in it, will be serious to the world· but about ten years more will be needed to effect it....

Financially we grub along and talk poor, but as no one here need spend money unless he likes, the loss of thousands of millions has little outward effect. No improvement need be expected until things have got settled to a new economic bottom. Most of us are really better off when the great properties shrink. I am sorry for your Wabash, but conservative people here avoid Mr. Jay Gould and expect him to take their money if he can get it. John Hay plays with that edge-tool, but I don't....

To John Hay

WASHINGTON, 26 October, 1884.

I owe you infinite amusement. Ten times a day I drop my work and rush out to see the men lay bricks or stone in your house. Mine is still where it was when you were here; but yours is getting on. The dining room wall is up to the next floor; the parlor and whole front is up to the sills of the parlor windows. At this rate, your next floor will soon go in. The brick-work is beautiful. I am now devoured by interest in your door-arch which must soon be begun.

Richardson put back into my contract every extravagance I had struck out, and then made me sign it. After this piece of work he went off to seek other victims. He is an ogre. He devours men crude, and shows the effects of inevitable indigestion in his size. If Anderson would only give me that five thousand dollars, I would be unhappy. By the way, I was much amused by my brother John who was here last Wednesday, and who has just built a house in Boston. We took him over Anderson's house, and his disgust for his own became alarming. He swore horribly that Anderson's house was the cheapest thing he had ever heard of, and far handsomer than that of Fred Ames which cost a million or two.

Judge Gray has bought the opposite corner to Paine's lot; my old family house; 1601 I Street....

To John Hay

WASHINGTON, 16 November, 1884.

. . . .

The town is mighty lively. What with one thing and another, I find it like an old English country-gentleman's park without the humane notice of man-traps and spring-guns. Everyone wants something, and everyone else wants to prevent anyone from having anything. How to keep one's toes from being trodden on is the sole preoccupation of a wise man's mind.

To Charles Milnes Gaskell

1607 H STREET, 8 February, 1885.

We are on the verge of a change of administration, and though the country takes easily enough to it, we are by no means free from anxieties of the milder sort. After a year of very great depression and business trouble, we hardly know whether things are to be worse or better. The chances seem to be about even, but we are not beyond the possibility of a panic and a squeeze of credit that might send things to the dogs. What with your nervous situation between Egypt and Ireland, and what with the state of industry all over the world, and what with our silver coinage and change of administration, I wish we may get through the year without some ugly crash.

The change of administration affects me very little. My history will go on, I hope, as quietly under Mr. Cleveland as under Mr. Arthur; and as a rule, one's opponents are more obliging than one's friends. Several of my most intimate allies here are likely to be high in power and favor, but the higher they are, the harder they are worked, and the less I see of them. The Foreign Department is the only one with which I have to be intimate, and I am waiting with curiosity to see who is to take charge of it. With Bayard, Pendleton or Lamar, I shall be well satisfied, and these are now most talked about. President Cleveland is a very honest, hard-working man, with plenty of courage and common-sense, but he has little experience and is sure to make mistakes. The party behind him is ragged, timid and stupid.

Fortunately government with us is a secondary matter and follows strictly the current of public opinion. On the whole, though never well directed, we get on successfully, and are as contented as possible....

I suppose the Khartoum and Congo affairs prove that Africa is the great European question of the future. On the whole it is worth some trouble, and England will find it worth her while to take it in hand. We Anglo-Saxon-Americans always make a wild howl about our conquests, wars and excitements, but we always make them pay. England is sure to profit by whatever is done in Africa....

To John Hay

WASHINGTON, 7 [March, 1885.]

. . . .

I pass my time in avoiding the new officials; so you can expect no news from me. New York has come here to swallow us with the most fatuous expression I ever imagined on its face. Five thousand Grover Clevelands swarm the streets. The Ohio face has vanished, and only John McLean holds up his head.

To John Hay

WASHINGTON, 20 April, 1885.

. . . .

I saw Richardson in Boston and lectured him with my usual severity. So far as I could see, I met with my usual success. He seemed much delighted by an equally severe letter from you, and showed me ravishing designs for your fireplaces which economy itself could not resist. Indeed I have given up resistance either on your behalf or my own. You don't back me up, and I don't support myself loyally. I shall get out of it by telling lies to Nick Anderson. When I saw the houses building in Boston, ours seemed like cottages, and I became ashamed of them. As cottages they are thoroughly satisfactory, but as houses they make no kind of show except in an out of the way place like this.

Poor Dr. Hooper [1] died a week ago of heart-disease, and we buried him on Thursday. My wife was with him for the last month.

To John Hay

BEVERLY FARMS, 19 September, 1885.

I thought you had forgotten me, so long is it since my last letter was written; but if you have set up an island, I admit the excuse. Please appoint me governor. I will be as wise as my predecessor and model, Sancho, and will do you credit. You will need it if you mean to start a principality. Even Don Quijote, Sr., did not build houses or buy islands.

My hands have been so full this summer that I have had no time to look about me, and our little trip to Saratoga in search of history had a tragical ending since it cost us your visit. The man-mountain Richardson (I suppose you include him among your purchased mountains)

[1] Robert William Hooper died April 13, 1885, aged seventy-five years.

told us of your sudden appearance and disappearance after our return.

Richardson told me too some tedious tale about our houses being done. I know nothing to the contrary except its impossibility — besides which it is on its face a Richelaisian jest. Big as he is, he turned pale and trembled when he told me he was going on to see what he had done; and should take the next train to the west if —! You can imagine, if the thought of seeing my house-front makes his brazen front blanch, what my delicate sensibilities are suffering. What will you give me for my night-mare as it stands?...

To John Hay

Washington, 4 November, 1885.

Your house is calm as the Pyramids, but your hall ceiling is up, and very handsome. Evans is still at work on the columns. My hall fireplace is finished. I feel sure it is yours, and that Klaber gave it to me to quiet me, and is making another for you; but I can't prove it. Klaber's man is constructing an awful onyx tomb-stone in my library.

Evarts came here this morning to ask about my house. As he has lost the election, I gave him a democratic answer. You can imagine how confidently I could promise to vacate my only shelter with winter coming on....

To George Bancroft

Washington, 11 Feb., 1886.

I have read the Plea,[1] and am exceedingly grateful to you for saying, with dignity and weight such as no one else can command, what history requires should be said.

Although we are quite aware that the path of "sovereignty" — which our grandfathers called tyranny — cannot be longer blocked or impeded, we are bound to record, as the government moves, the distance it has gone, and the shorter stage that remains before it.

Our *Peau de Chagrin* — once called Liberty — has shrunk uncommonly fast; but the future will doubtless find compensation. Ever truly yours.

[1] *Plea for the Constitution of the United States, wounded in the House of its Guardians* — on the legal tender decision of the Supreme Court.

XII

JAPAN

1886

To John Hay

My ship is in the bay, all ready at the quay, but before I wend my way, good-bye to thee John Hay; or words to that effect, for I have not my usual facility at verse today. San Francisco looks dusty, wintry and seedy, as I look over it at 8.30 P.M., from the fourth story of the Palace Hotel. Sea-sickness lies before, and the alkali desert behind this town. I have no choice between the two; but I find the town an unhappy medium.

Our journey was a glorious success. As I got into my train at Boston on Thursday the 3rd, to start for New York, my brother Charles came down to tell me that his directors' car had unexpectedly arrived at Boston that morning, and would return to Omaha the next day. So I went to New York rejoicing; passed a delightful day with King, St. Gaudens, etc., and at six P.M. dragged poor La Farge, in a dishevelled and desperate, but still determined mind, on board the Albany express. Never listen to the man who says that corporations have no souls! At Albany I tumbled into the U. P. car at eleven o'clock at night, and from that moment till we reached here yesterday, we had nothing to think about except to amuse ourselves. The U. P. fed, clothed and carried us, as affectionately as though we had money to lend; and landed us at last, not at Omaha, but in the court of this palace, just like two little Aladdins from school.

La Farge's delight with the landscape was the pleasantest thing on the journey. While I read Buddhism and slept, he tried to sketch from the moving car. His results were a sort of purple conglomerate, but the process amused him. On the Humboldt river our thermometer stood at 98° inside the car; but I am the creature of habit, and you will not be surprised that, even under these circumstances, I had Mme. Modjeska and her husband [1] to twelve-o'clock breakfast. *C'est plus fort que moi!* Clearly I am a breakfasting animal.

Adventures we discard, for we are old and no longer vain; but La Farge makes a delicate humor glimmer about our path. Among other

[1] Helen Modjeska (1844–1909), married Charles Bozenta Chlapowski.

people whom he left in New York, likely to tear their hair on hearing of his departure, was the agent of Cassell, for he is illustrating Shelley's Sky Lark. To this unhappy man, La Farge telegraphed from Poughkeepsie: "The purple evening melts around my flight." I know not how meek the spirit of that man may be, but the evening of most men, under such conditions, would have been purple with oaths. At Omaha a young reporter got the better of us; for when in reply to his inquiry as to our purpose in visiting Japan, La Farge beamed through his spectacles the answer that we were in search of Nirvana, the youth looked up like a meteor, and rejoined: "It's out of season!" [1]

We were yesterday afternoon to see our steamer. So far as we could learn, we were the only passengers. We were given the two best staterooms, with the promise of as many more as we might ask for. If you and King were with us, we would capture the ship, turn pirate, and run off to a cocoa-nut island. As it is, we shall be sea-sick without crime. If La Farge sees anything he wants, I will buy it for you, as it will probably be good. If not, I will spend it for myself, and send you whatever you don't want....

To John Hay

YOKOHAMA, 9 July, 1886.

We have been here a week. Between the wish that you were here with us, and the conviction that you would probably by this time be broken up if you had come, I am distraught. Amusing it certainly is — beyond an idea — but comfortable or easy it is not by any means; and I can honestly say that one works for what one gets.

We have devoted the week to Tokio, and you can judge what sort of a place it is from the fact that there is neither hotel nor house in it where we can be so nearly comfortable as we are in a third-rate hotel at Yokohama, twenty miles away. Here we have rooms directly on the bay, with air as fresh as the Japs make it; and here we return every evening to sleep. Sturgis Bigelow acts as our courier and master of ceremonies, but La Farge has mastered Mandarin Chinese, and

[1] The letters that John La Farge wrote during this journey were published in 1897 as *An Artist's Letters from Japan*. The volume is dedicated to Henry Adams and reads in part: "If anything worth repeating has been said by me in these letters, it has probably come from you, or has been suggested by being with you — perhaps even in the way of contradiction. And you may be amused by the lighter talk of the artist that merely describes appearances, or covers them with a tissue of dreams. And you alone will know how much has been withheld that might have been indiscreetly said.

"If only we had found Nirvana — but he was right who warned us that we were late in this season of the world."

hopes soon to be a fluent talker of Daimio Japanese. As for me, I admire.

Fenollosa and Bigelow are stern with us. Fenollosa is a tyrant who says we shall not like any work done under the Tokugawa Shoguns. As these gentlemen lived two hundred and fifty years or thereabouts, to 1860, and as there is nothing at Tokio except their work, La Farge and I are at a loss to understand why we came; but it seems we are to be taken to Nikko shortly and permitted to admire some temples there. On secret search in Murray, I ascertain that the temples at Nikko are the work of Tokugawa Shoguns. I have not yet dared to ask about this apparent inconsistency for fear of rousing a fresh anathema.

The temples and Tokugawas are, I admit, a trifle baroque. For sticking a decisive bit of infamous taste into the middle of a seriously planned, and minutely elaborated mass of refined magnificence, I have seen no people — except perhaps our own — to compare with the Japs. We have the future before us to prove our capacity, but they now stand far ahead. Some of the temples are worse than others, but I am inclined to let Fenollosa have his way with them, if he will only let me be amused by the humor. Positively everything in Japan laughs. The jinrickshaw men laugh while running at full speed five miles with a sun that visibly sizzles their drenched clothes. The women all laugh, but they are obviously wooden dolls, badly made, and can only cackle, clatter in pattens over asphalt pavements in railway stations, and hop or slide in heelless straw sandals across floors. I have not yet seen a woman with any better mechanism than that of a five-dollar wax doll; but the amount of oil used in fixing and oiling and arranging their hair is worth the money alone. They can all laugh, so far. The shop-keepers laugh to excess when you say that their goods are forgeries and worthless. I believe the Mikado laughs when his ministers have a cabinet council. The gilt dragon-heads on the temples are in a broad grin. Everything laughs, until I expect to see even the severe bronze doors of the tombs, the finest serious work I know, open themselves with the same eternal and meaningless laughter, as though death were the pleasantest jest of all.

In one respect Japan has caused me a sensation of deep relief. In America I had troubled myself much because my sense of smell was gone. I thought I never should again be conscious that the rose or the new-mown hay had odor. How it may be about the rose or the hay I know not; but since my arrival here I perceive that I am not wholly without a nose. La Farge agrees with me that Japan possesses one pervasive, universal, substantive smell — an oily, sickish, slightly fetid odor — which underlies all things, and though infinitely varied, is always the same. The smell has a corresponding taste. The bread, the fruit, the tea, the women, and the water, the air and the gods, all smell or taste alike. This is monotonous but reassuring. I have reasoned much and tried many experiments to ascertain the cause of this phenomenon, but it seems to be a condition of existence, and the accompaniment of Japanese civilisation. Without the smell, Japan would fall into dissolution.

I am trying to spend your money. It is hard work, but I will do it, or succumb. Kaki-monos are not to be got. Porcelain worth buying is rare. Lacquer is the best and cheapest article. Bronzes are good and cheap. I want to bring back a dozen big bronze vases to put on the grass before our houses in summer, for palms or big plants, so as to give our houses the look of a cross between curio shops and florists. Tokio contains hardly anything worth getting except bronzes. A man at Osaka has sent up some two hundred and fifty dollars worth of lacquers, sword-hilts, inlaid work, and such stuff. As he has the best shop in Japan we took the whole lot, and have sent for more. Inros are from ten to fifteen dollars. I shall get a dozen for presents. Good cloisonné, either Chinese or Japanese, is most rare. Fine old porcelain is rare and dear. Embroideries are absolutely introuvable. Even books seem scarce. Japan has been cleaned out. My big bronze vases will cost from fifty to two hundred dollars apiece, but these will be good....

I have not presented my Japanese letters of introduction, as I found it would imply a course of entertainments which I would rather avoid. Tokio is an impossible sort of place for seeing anyone. It is a bunch of towns, and the Europeans live all over it, so that one goes five miles or so to make a call or to see one's dearest friend for five minutes. The thermometer today is anywhere between 90° and 200° in the streets, and calling on formal ministers of state under such conditions is not amusing....

I shall go to Osaka and Kioto in September, unless the country is absolutely closed by cholera. Indeed I should do many other things if I were not anxious to spare La Farge the risk of illness. He continues to be the most agreeable of companions, always cheerful, equable, sweet-tempered, and quite insensible to ideas of time, space, money or railway trains. To see him flying through the streets of Tokio on a jinrickshaw is a most genial vision. He peers out through his spectacles as though he felt the absurdity as well as the necessity of looking at the show as though it were real, but he enjoys it enormously, especially the smell, which quite fascinates him. He keeps me in perpetual good humor.... I am lost in wonder how he ever does work; but he can be energetic, and his charm is that whether energetic or lazy he has the neatest humor, the nicest observation, and the evenest temper you can imagine. When he loses the trains, I rather enjoy it. After all, who cares?

Of startling or wonderful experience we have had none. The only moral of Japan is that the children's story-books were good history. This is a child's country. Men, women and children are taken out of the fairy books. The whole show is of the nursery. Nothing is serious; nothing is taken seriously. All is toy; sometimes, as with the women, badly made and repulsive; sometimes laughable, as with the houses, gardens and children; but always taken from what La Farge declares to have been the papboats of his babyhood. I have wandered, so to express it, in all the soup-plates of forty-eight years' experience, during the last week, and have found them as natural as Alice found the Mock Turtle. Life is a dream, and in Japan one dreams of the nursery.

To John Hay

NIKKO, 24 July, 1886.

Do you happen to know where Nikko is? If not, I cannot tell you. All I know is that it is in a valley among some green mountains in the insides of Japan; that it is pretty; that the hour is 8 A.M., of a sweet morning; that I am lying, in a Jap kimono on the upper verandah of the smallest doll house your children ever saw; that La Farge is below, in the bath-room, painting our toy garden, with its waterfall and miniature mountains; and that at nine o'clock we are to step down to the Fenollosas to breakfast.

Since Monday, July 12, we have been here, and here we are likely to stay. The shortest possible experience of Japanese travel in its most favorable form satisfied me that pleasure lay not there. We had but six or eight hours between Tokio and this place. Four hours were by rail, rather pleasant though hot. I enjoyed looking out at the ridiculous landscape, though it was mostly a rice field, where numerous Japs with immense round hats, and little else, paddled about, up to their knees and elbows in black dirt which I compliment in calling mud. Here and there were groves about temples, or bamboo thickets about cabins. As night came on, bonfires smoked, to keep away mosquitoes, and, by the shade of Yeyas, they were not built without reason; for, although I saw no other four-footed animal, except three pack-horses and three dogs, in fifty miles, the skeets restored a liberal average for beasts of prey. We reached at 9 P.M. a town called Utso-nomiya. So I was credibly informed, at least, and I believe it; for I know that we got into a wagon, and were driven two miles, at a full run, through a street thronged with infant children and paper lanterns. I know not how many we immolated; I soon wearied of counting; but I do know that our driver shouted, at intervals of flogging his brutes; that a devil at his side blew a penny trumpet; that another devil ran ahead and yelled; and that at last we were dropped not at a door, but, as usual, at a counter, and were told to take off our shoes. We were then led across a miniature court, past several open privies (which smelt), and an open bath-house where naked men and women were splashing, up a ladder staircase, to three rooms which were open to each other, and to the air and moon. We were pleased. La Farge and I gamboled in the sprightliness of our youth and spirits. The rooms were clean and adorned with kakimonos and bronzes. We lay on the floor and watched our neighbors below, while Bigelow concocted food out of a can of Mulligatawny soup and boiled rice. After eating this compound and smoking a cigar I would have wished to sleep a little, and in truth our beds and mosquito nets were built. At midnight I wooed slumber; but first the *amidos* or sliding shutters of the whole house below had to be slammed, for twenty minutes; then all the slammers had to take a last bath, with usual splashing and unutterable noises with their mouth and throat, which Bigelow assured us to be only their way of brushing their teeth. I have never known at what hour these noises ceased, but they ended at last, and we all fell asleep.

Presently I was waked by a curious noise in the court. It was a man, moving about, and stopping every few steps to rap two bits of wood together — clack-clack — like castanets. He interested me for twenty minutes. I understand he was the watchman on pattens, and that he thus notifies thieves to be on their guard. During this part of the entertainment I became aware that all was not well with myself; in short that I had an attack of cholera of the worst sort; a pain internal, passing into desperate nausea; then into drenching perspiration, and lastly into a violent diarrhoea. With these afflictions I struggled for an hour or two, and at last crept back to bed, weak as the moonlight which illuminated my sufferings, and hoping only for an hour of forgetfulness; when, long before daylight, the *amidos* began to slam again, the bath began to splash, the bathers choked and coughed, and chaos came.

Towards nine o'clock we consulted. Then it seemed that La Farge was suffering just as I did. Both of us were in a miserable state of weakness, trusting only that the end of our mortal career might arrive soon to bring repose. I was reduced to laughing at La Farge's comments to a point where exhaustion became humorous. Bigelow brewed for us some of my Chinese tea, for Japanese tea was nauseous. We managed to dress; and at half past eleven we were stuffed into a cart and rattled off over roads that we remember. That wagon understood jouncing. We hung on to any handy rail, and, when we could, we fell in the wagon rather than in the rice-fields. Ten miles of these gaieties brought us into a road between rows of huge cryptomerias, which seem to be a kind of giant pine; and when our horses struck this region, the ways being heavy with mud and mending, they refused to go at all. For ten miles they balked every hundred yards, and if an ascent intervened, they balked there besides. Changing horses made the matter worse; the fresher the horse, the more vigorously he balked; while our two drivers beat them over the head and withers with a heavy club. On experiment I found that I could stand — when not laughing — and I thought walking less fatiguing than sitting to see the brutes beaten. I crawled up the hills, and perspired freely with a temperature of 90°, but in course of the day I had four cups of tea, and walked about as many miles. At six o'clock we reached Nikko; I climbed up a long stone stair to our small house; and went energetically to bed.

We have never found out what upset us, nor has Bigelow found out what poisoned his arm and laid him up for a week at the same time. All we know is that our drive to Nikko did us no harm, and in a few days we were all right again, with a fancy for staying quiet and not immediately indulging in the luxuries of Japanese hotels. Our small palace of two rooms, with paper windows and two hospitable shaven priests who say only *Ohio*, satisfy our yearnings. I have had cholera enough for the present. I admit that Mrs. Fenollosa's table had a share in our Sybaritism. The fact that, if we travel, we have nowhere to go where there is anything to see, except to Kioto and the south, is also an element. Kioto and Osaka are hotter than the future life; they are overrun with cholera; so is Yokohama where we had it common, and it has now extended to Tokio. No one seems ever to travel in the north and west, or to go to Kui-sui[1] even for Satsuma ware. Nikko is the prettiest part of Japan; here are the great temples of Yeyas (Iye-yasu) and Iye-mitsu, the first and third Shoguns; here, if it were not for show waterfalls, I can be content, and La Farge can sketch.

In truth the place is worth coming to see. Japan is not the last word of humanity, and Japanese art has a well-developed genius for annoy-

[1] Kiyosumi?

ing my prejudices; but Nikko is, after all, one of the sights of the world. I am not sure where it stands in order of rank, but after the pyramids, Rome, Mme. Tussaud's wax-works, and 800 16th Street, I am sure Nikko deserves a place. Without forgetting the fact that the temples are here and there rather cheap grotesque, the general result of temple and tomb, architecture, ornament, landscape and foliage, is very effective indeed. When you reflect that the old Shoguns spent twelve or fourteen millions of dollars on this remote mountain valley, you can understand that Louis Quatorze and Versailles are not much of a show compared with Nikko.

Photographers give no idea of the scale. They show here a gate and there a temple, but they cannot show twenty acres of ground, all ingeniously used to make a single composition. They give no idea of a mountain-flank, with its evergreens a hundred feet high, modelled into a royal, posthumous residence and deified abode. I admit to thinking it a bigger work than I should have thought possible for Japs. It is a sort of Egypt in lacquer and greenth....

27 *July*. Yesterday arrived from Osaka a large lot of kakimonos, sent up by the great curio-dealer, Yamanaka. I gleaned about two dozen out of the lot. They are cheap enough, but I fear that Fenollosa, who is in Tokio, will say they are Tokugawa rot, and will bully me into letting them go. He is now trying to prevent my having a collection of Hokusai's books. He is a kind of St. Dominic, and holds himself responsible for the dissemination of useless knowledge by others. My historical indifference to everything but facts, and my delight at studying what is hopefully debased and degraded, shock his moral sense. I wish you were here to help us trample on him. He has joined a Buddhist sect; I was myself a Buddhist when I left America, but he has converted me to Calvinism with leanings towards the Methodists.

To Elizabeth Cameron

NIKKO, 13 August, 1886.

Thanks for your kind little note which gave me real pleasure in my Japanese retreat. In return I can only tell you that Japan is a long way from America, but that it is not far enough to prevent my thinking too much about home matters. I have heard but once from there, since I sailed, and luckily all my news was pleasant. In six weeks more I shall be starting for home....

La Farge and I have found shelter in the mountains from the heat and hotels of Japan. We have a little box of a Japanese house, where we look out on a Japanese temple-garden, and on Japanese mountains, all like the pictures that one sees on plates. We are princely in our style. The dealers in *curios* send us, from far and wide, whatever they can find that we like, and our rooms are full of such rubbish. La Farge sketches. I waste time as I can, sometimes walking, or going over the hills on rats of pack-horses; sometimes photographing in the temple grounds; sometimes sitting cross-legged, and looking at bales of stuffs or lacquers; sometimes at tea-houses, watching the sun when it kindly sets behind the big mountain Nan-tai-zan, and leaves us in a less perspiring condition than we are by day. The scenery is very pretty; not unlike that of the Virginia Springs; and the temperature much the same though very moist. Of interesting people I see nothing. I doubt whether there are any such. The Japanese women seem to me impossible. After careful inquiry I can hear of no specimen of your sex, in any class of society, whom I ought to look upon as other than a *curio*. They are all badly made, awkward in movement, and suggestive of monkeys. The children are rather pretty and quite amusing, but the mammas are the reverse; and one is well able to judge at least the types of popular beauty, seeing that there is little clothing to hide it, and that little is apt to be forgotten.

This branch of my historical inquiries has not proved rich; but, though the people are not a success in regard to personal attractions, they are very amusing indeed, and have given us infinite varieties of laughter ever since we saw our first fishing-boat. I do not advise you to allow yourself three months' leisure in order to get used to various pervasive smells, and to forget all your previous education in the matter of food, houses, drains, and vehicles. If you can live on boiled rice or stewed eels, or bad, oily, fresh tea; or in houses without partitions or walls except of paper; or in cities absolutely undrained, and with only surface wells for drinking water; or if you can sit on your heels all through five hours at the theatre, and can touch the floor with your forehead when I call upon you; and say *Hei* and *Ha* at stated intervals, you will do very well in Japan. I do all these things with less success than is to be desired, for I cannot sit on my heels at all, and I suffer to the extent of anguish even in sitting cross-legged; Japanese food makes me sea-sick, and the smell of Tokio seems to get into food, drink, and dreams; but I have not yet had my three months' education, and have even evaded it by flying to the mountains and by getting myself fed and protected after the American manner. After ten days of modified Japanese experiments I was content with what I had learned. Nothing but necessity would induce me to try another Japanese article of food or to pass another night in a Japanese inn, for the first experiment proved nearly fatal; and although I did not fear death, I shrank from dying of Japanese soup in a Japanese inn, with Japanese women to look at as my last association with earth. This weakness on my part shows the sad effects of too long life. One ought to enjoy poisonous mushrooms fried in bad oil, and to delight in looking at wooden women without any figures, waddling on wooden pattens.

Our faculty for laughing has been greatly increased, but we try in vain to acquire the courteous language of the country. No European can learn to track out the intricate holes and burrows in which Japanese courtesy hides itself. I wish I could master, in order to teach you, the ceremony of the *Ocha-no-yu*, or honorable five-o'clock tea. I declined to buy a book which contained paintings showing fifty arrangements of the charcoal to boil the kettle on this occasion; and as many more of the ways in which a single flower might be set in a porcelain stand. My friend Bigelow bought the pictures and is professor of the art. Simpler tasks satisfy me. Seeing the woman who has charge of our horses eating hard green plums, I requested Bigelow to tell her with my compliments that she would suffer from stomach-ache. Her reply, profoundly serious, was to the effect that my remark had truth; her stomach did respectfully ache. I learned much from this attitude of respect which even the digestive apparatus of a Japanese peasant woman assumes towards a stranger.

I have bought *curios* enough to fill a house, but nothing that I like, or want for myself. The stuffs are cheap and beautiful, but I have found no really fine embroidery. The lacquer is relatively cheap, but I do not care for it. I can find no good porcelain or bronze, and very few wall-pictures. Metal work is easy to get, and very choice, but what can one do with sword-guards and knife handles? I am puzzled to know what to bring home to please myself. If I knew what would please you, I would load the steamer with it....

To John Hay

NIKKO, 22 August, 1886.

I have still to report that purchases for you are going on, but more and more slowly, for I believe we have burst up all the pawn-brokers' shops in Japan. Even the cholera has shaken out the little that is worth getting. Bigelow and Fenollosa cling like misers to their miserable hoards. Not a kakimono is to be found, though plenty are

brought. Every day new bales of rubbish come up from Tokio or elsewhere; mounds of books; tons of bad bronze; holocausts of lacquer; I
buy literally everything that is merely possible; and yet I have got not
a hundred dollars' worth of things I want for myself. You shall have
some good small bits of lacquer, and any quantity of *duds* to encumber
your tables and mantles, but nothing creditable to our joint genius.
As for myself, I have only one *Yokomono* — or kakimono broader
than it is long — and one small bronze, that I care to keep as the fruit
of my summer's perspiration.

For Japan is the place to perspire. No one knows an ideal dogday
who has not tried Japan in August. From noon to five o'clock I wilt.
As for travelling, I would see the rice-fields dry first. I have often
wondered what King would have done, had he come with us. I've no
doubt he would have seen wonderful sights, but I should have paid his
return passage on a corpse. For days together I make no attempt at
an effort, while poor La Farge sketches madly and aimlessly.

By the bye, a curious coincidence happened. Bigelow announced
one morning that King and Hay were coming from Tokio with loads
of curios for us. La Farge and I stared and inquired. Then it appeared that Bigelow and Fenollosa employ two men — Kin, pronounced
King, and Hei, pronounced Hay — to hunt curios for them, and had
sent them word to bring up whatever they could find. I thought this
one of the happiest accidents I ever heard, and I only wish that
Messrs. King and Hay had brought better things, as their American
namesakes expected. They meant well, but they lacked means.
Nevertheless they brought a few nice bits, to sustain the credit of
their names.

Fairly bored by sweltering in this moistness, I stirred up Mrs.
Fenollosa to a little expedition last Tuesday. Fenollosa is unwell; La
Farge is hard at work; but Mrs. Fenollosa, Bigelow and I, started to
visit Yumoto, the Saratoga, or White Sulphur, of Japan. Yumoto lies
just fourteen miles above us among the mountains, and with one of
my saddle horses I could easily go there and return on the same day;
but such a journey in Japan is serious. Only pedestrians, coolies, or
Englishmen work hard. Mrs. Fenollosa summoned five pack-horses.
All Japanese horses known to me are rats, and resemble their pictures,
which I had supposed to be bad drawing; but these pack-horses are
rats led by a man, or more often by a woman, at a very slow walk.
Mrs. Fenollosa mounted one; Bigelow another; I ascended a third; a
servant and baggage followed on a fourth; the fifth carried beds,
blankets, linen, silver, eatables, and drinks. At half past eight the

caravan started, and at half past ten it arrived at the foot of Chiu-zen-ji pass, where one climbs a more or less perpendicular mountain side for an hour. I preferred my own legs to the rat's, and walked up. So we arrived at Lake Chiu-zen-ji, a pretty sheet of water about seven miles long, at the foot of the sacred mountain Nan-tai-zan. On the shore of this lake is a temple, where pilgrims begin the ascent of the mountain, sacred to Sho-do Sho-nin, who devoted fifteen years of his valuable existence, in the eighth century, to the astounding feat of climbing it. As it is very accessible, and only eight thousand feet above the sea, Sho-do Sho-nin is a very popular and greatly admired saint, and some five thousand pilgrims come every August to follow his sainted steps. Next the temple are some inns, but not a farm or a human dwelling exists on the lake or among the mountains; for if the Japanese like one thing more than another it is filthy rice-fields, and if they care less for one thing than another, it is mountains. All this lovely country, from here to the sea of Japan, is practically a dense wilderness of monkeys, as naked as itself; but the monkeys never seem out of place as a variety, though I have not met them in society, and speak only from association. We stopped at an inn, and while lunch was making ready, Bigelow and I went out in a kind of frigate for a swim in the lake. After lunch, sending our beasts ahead, we sailed to the next starting-point, just the length of a cigar. Another two miles of rise brought us to a moor for all the world like Estes Park and the Rocky Mountains. Crossing this, we climbed another ascent, and came out on an exquisite little green lake with woody mountains reflected on its waters. Nothing could be prettier than the path along this shore, but it was not half so amusing to me as our entrance into the village of Yumoto, with its dozen inns and no villagers; for, by the roadside, at the very entrance, I saw at last the true Japan of my dreams, and broke out into carols of joy. In a wooden hut, open to all the winds, and public as the road, men, women and children, naked as the mother that bore them, were sitting, standing, soaking and drying themselves, as their ancestors had done a thousand years ago.

I had begun to fear that Japan was spoiled by Europe. At Tokio even the coolies wear something resembling a garment, and the sexes are obliged to bathe apart. As I came into the country I noticed first that the children were naked; that the men wore only a breech-clout; and that the women were apt to be stripped to the waist; but I had begun to disbelieve that this disregard of appearances went further. I was wrong. No sooner had we dismounted than we hurried off to visit the baths; and Mrs. Fenollosa will bear me witness that for ten minutes we stood at the entrance of the largest bath-house, and looked on at a dozen people of all ages, sexes and varieties of ugliness, who paid not the smallest regard to our presence. I should except one pretty girl of sixteen, with quite a round figure and white skin. I did notice that for the most part, while drying herself, she stood with her back to us.

When this exceptionally pleasing virgin walked away, I took no further interest in the proceedings, though I still regard them as primitive. Of the habits and manners of the Japanese in regard to the sexes, I see little, for I cannot conquer a feeling that Japs are monkeys, and the women very badly made monkeys; but from others I hear much on the subject, and what I hear is very far from appetising. In such an atmosphere one talks freely. I was a bit aghast when one young woman called my attention to a temple as a remains of phallic worship; but what can one do? Phallic worship is as universal here as that of trees, stones and the sun. I come across shrines of phallic symbols in my walks, as though I were an ancient Greek. One cannot quite ignore the foundations of society.

23 *August.* My poor boy, how very strong you do draw your vintage for my melancholy little *Esther.* Your letter of July 18 has just reached me, and I hardly knew what I was reading about. Perhaps I made a mistake even to tell King about it; but having told him, I could not leave you out. Now, let it die! To admit the public to it would be almost unendurable to me. I will not pretend that the book is not precious to me, but its value has nothing to do with the public who could never understand that such a book might be written in one's heart's blood. Do not even imagine that I scorn the public, as you say. Twenty years ago, I would have been glad to please it. Today, and for more than a year past, I have been and am living with not a thought but from minute to minute; and the public is as far away from me as the celebrated Kung-fu-tse, who once said something on the subject which I forget, but which had probably a meaning to him, as my observation has to me. Yet I do feel pleased that the book has found one friend.

25 *August.* I can't say, "let's return to our sheep," for there are no sheep in Japan, and I have eaten nothing but bad beef since landing. As for returning to my remarks on Yumoto as connected with the sexes, I decline to do it. In spite of King, I affirm that sex does not exist in Japan, except as a scientific classification. I would not affirm that there are no exceptions to my law; but the law itself I affirm as the foundation of archaic society. Sex begins with the Aryan race. I have seen a Japanese beauty, which has a husband, *Nabeshame,* if I hear

right — a live Japanese Marquis, late Daimio of Hizo, or some other place; but though he owns potteries, he has, I am sure, no more successful bit of bric-à-brac than his wife is; but as for being a woman, she is hardly the best Satsuma....

To John Hay

KIOTO, 9 September, 1886.

Kioto at last! La Farge and I made an impressive entry at nine o'clock last night, with our suite, by moonlight, and this morning — at half past six o'clock — we are sitting on our verandah, looking out over the big city, he sketching, and both of us incessantly wishing that you and King were with us, for there is no kind of doubt that Japan is *omoshirvi*, a word we pronounce *amushrvi*, which means amusing, and is always in use. Kioto is *omoshirvi* as we look over it; a sort of Japanese Granada. For two months we have heard and talked of nothing but Kioto, and here we are! Think of it, dissolute man! It is being in the new Jerusalem with a special variety of Jews. You see at once why La Farge and I are up and active at six A.M....

La Farge and I, after six days of boiled and furious activity at Yokohama, trying to get things done, which is something the Japanese never do, gave it up; but I would have given you a present if you could have seen us on our expedition last Friday to what the old books called the *Dye boots*.[1] This remnant of the vanished splendor of Kamakura is about twenty miles from Yokohama, and next to Kioto and Narra, we have damned it persistently for two months because of the heat. I bought — for you or others — various specimens of so-called Kamakura lacquer, the only instance in human history where *nacre* has been used with success; and every time I saw the stuff, I cursed it because I had not had energy to see the Dai Butsu. Last Friday we saw it, and as La Farge says, it is the most successful colossal figure in the world; he sketched it, and I, seizing the little priest's camera, mounted to the roof of his porch, and, standing on my head at an angle of impossibility, perpetrated a number of libels on Buddha and Buddhism without shame at the mild contempt of his blessed little moustache, which is ächt Japanesisch of today. This is not my story. I mention it in passing Kamakura, for we saw no more of the city which is no longer existing or visible; but having lunched at a teahouse, and watched a heavy shower make the roads hopeless, we were persuaded by the Ho — Houro, Japanese phœnix, an acute disease

[1] Daibutsu, or Great Buddha.

known as a travelling servant whose death in torture is a matter only of hours — to return by way of the beach of Enoshima. Although we knew that all view of Fuji — the only object of such a trip — was hopeless, we let ourselves in for what proved to be an hour's walk over a soft sand-beach in a steam-bath. In half the distance La Farge fell into his jinrickshaw exhausted, and I tumbled into the Pacific ocean and swam or waded to the next village. When I tried to come out of the water, the surf covered me with black sand; my clothes were so wet that I could not get them on, and my boots were full of water. So I put on my coat, tied a yellow oil-paper rain-cover round my waist, and seating myself in my kurama, stuck my naked legs over the foot-board, and was whirled through the village like a wild Indian. The curious part of the matter was that in a mile of transit to the nearest tea-house, not even a child raised an eyelid of surprise, whereas La Farge, who followed later, in complete European costume, was received with enthusiasm. Evidently my outfit is the one expected from Americans in this country. We drove back to Yokohama afterwards in the dark, and I could not wonder at the calmness with which my legs had been received. As we drove through mile after mile of village without front walls, every house offered a dimly lighted study of legs in every attitude. My eyes still whirl with the wild succession of men's legs, and of women's breasts, in every stage of development and decomposition, which danced through that obscurity.

On Sunday we took a French steamer for Kobe.... Kobe is only the European settlement for Osaka and Kioto, a kind of waiting-room, to Yamanaka's, towards whose shop I am leading you.... Only one lesson was impressed more deeply than ever on my heart; which was that if I want good things, I must buy Chinese. In porcelain there is no comparison; in embroidery, none; in kakimonos, not much. The best Chinese is always out of sight ahead, as in cloisonné, and, I think, even in bronze, though bronze is *the* Japanese metal. Only in gold lacquer and small metal work, like sword-guards, or perhaps small ivories, like netsukes, where Japanese humor and lightness have the field to themselves, the Japanese excel. They are quite aware of their own inferiority, and the prices they pay for good Chinese or Corean work are out of all proportion to their own....

My trouble is in the temptation to buy masses of indifferent work, which is the best I can get.... None of the things are large. Except for temples or gardens the Japs make few large things for themselves. Their small houses and low rooms are not suited to big ornament. Everything you see of that sort, especially tall bronzes, porcelains and lacquers, unless it comes from temples or gardens, is made for export and is not true Japanese. Things like *Inros*, lacquer boxes a few inches long; *netsukes* of ivory or wood; *fukusas*, or embroidered and woven stuffs like my eagle-and-ocean screen; swords; small kaki-monos; tea-jars from two to twelve inches high; flower vases, porcelain or bronze, from ten inches to eighteen in height; in short, anything that will go on a table, or is easily handled, is Japanese domestic de-coration. The big vases, especially the big grotesque bird-flower-and-dragon vases, are *never* seen out of the shops in Yokohama. No Jap-anese ever dreamed of such decoration, except perhaps for a temple or some public place. All his best, choicest and Jap-sneeziest work is in little things to be worn, or to be shown to guests at his Cha-no-yu, or Tea-party, in a bare little room, about ten feet square, with walls of Chinese simplicity; white plaster and wood unplaned....

Sunday, 12 *Septr*. This travelling is taking hold of my system. We cannot stand the pace. At our age occasional repose is a benefit. La Farge and I have jounced in kurumas, rattled through temples; asked questions, and talked Japanese, or listened to it, till we cower in fear before every new suggestion. We are nauseated by curios; I de-test temples; he is persecuted by letters of introduction, and I, who have delivered only one of mine, pass all my time trying to escape hospitality. At last I understand the duties of life. Never be hospi-table to a traveller. He is only happy in freedom. Damn him, and let him go.

One Japanese interior is highly amusing, but the joke is not rich enough for two. I find myself here with La Farge, T. Walsh, of Walsh, Hall & Co., two interpreters; a travelling servant; the Governor of Kioto's secretary; three Kioto merchants; and madness! The temples are ordered to produce their treasures for us; the houses drag out all their ancestral properties, and very curious they are; the artists in porcelain, the dealers in curios, and even the schools we are expected to inspect as connoisseurs. Today we had three hours at the house of Kassiobawara San, an elderly merchant here, who happens to live in the oldest house in the city; then at noon we started in kurumas, with a stewing heat, for a river twelve miles off; then we shot what the *Ho* calls "rabbits" for an hour, in a boat; we got through the rapids only to jounce for another hour or two in kurumas back to Kioto, where two makers of porcelain and a big curio dealer were sitting at the door of my room, and a Japanese gentleman was waiting to call on La Farge. The Japanese gentleman sat till half past eleven, thereby driving us to wish ourselves in bed or somewhere.

All the same, since leaving Nikko we have just piled in the impressions. If we do not soon become masters of the Japanese science, we shall at least learn something of our own to take its place. We will turn out a new Japan of our own. La Farge has bought materials enough — vast mounds of rubbish — to construct a world of decoration, paint forests of pictures, and exhaust the windows of Christianity. I have learned so many new facts of which I am ignorant, that I could fill winter evenings with my want of knowledge. The only branch we have not yet exhausted is that of the dances, and we intend to begin today on this sphere of usefulness. Geishas are ordered for this evening. If they please me as little as most of their Japanese sisters, I shall not want further acquaintance. I am in hot pursuit of the Butterfly Dance, and have started a chase through the temples in search of it. On the whole, Osaka and Kioto pan out well.

Wednesday morning, 15 *Septr.* I close this despatch by reporting that we had our Geisha ball, in all the forms, last night. No words can give you an idea of the drollness. I am lost in astonishment at this flower of eastern culture. I cannot quite say that it is like an imaginary theatre in a nursery of seven-year-old girls, or that it is absolutely and disgustingly proper, because all my Japanese friends got drunk on saki, and some of the singing women were highly trained; but for an exhibition of mechanical childishness I have seen nothing to equal it except a Japanese garden, or a batch of Japanese dolls. Absolutely the women's joints clacked audibly, and their voices were metallic.

I will tell you all about it when we meet; but La Farge is so much more amusing about it than I can be, that you had better wait till our book comes out, in which he will write the story, and I draw the pictures.

XIII
WASHINGTON AND QUINCY
WITH TRIPS WEST AND SOUTH
1886–1889
To Charles Milnes Gaskell

1603 H Street, 12 December, 1886.

My father's death [1] came at last as quietly as his long decline had come gently. I had been back from Japan about a fortnight, and had at once gone to see him. I thought him failing so slowly that he might well survive the winter; but he was liable at any moment to give out and the end could not be far....

My journey to Japan had at least the advantage of consuming five months, and of doing it in a very amusing way. I suppose I may call myself rather an old traveller; but I never made any journey half so entertaining. My sense of humor developed itself so rapidly that I was in a broad laugh from the time I landed at Yokohama, and can't help laughing whenever I think of the droll island and people. I took with me a well-known New York artist, John La Farge, an old acquaintance, and a very unusual man, who stands far away at the head of American art, but who interests me more as a companion than as a painter, for he kept me always amused and active. We were three months on shore, and became quite Japanned. If it were not that the country and people are now as familiar to everybody as though they were a part of Clapham, I should be half tempted to tell you something about them; but the traveller has at last learned his own rank in boredom, and has the sense to hold his tongue. The only practical result of the trip has been to make me earnest to close up everything here, finish history, cut society, foreswear strong drink and politics, and start in about three years for China, never to return. China is the great unknown country of the world. Sooner or later, if health holds out, I shall drift there; and once there, I shall not soon drift back. You may find me there with a false pig-tail, and a button on the top of my head as a mandarin of a new class....

I am trying to boil up my old interest in history enough to finish my book, but the fuel is getting scarce. I think the chances about even whether it will ever be published or not. Society is getting new tastes,

[1] Charles Francis Adams died November 21, 1886.

and history of the old school has not many years to live. I am willing enough to write history for a new school; but new men will doubtless do it better, or at least make it more to the public taste.

To John Hay

Washington, 1 May, 1887.

. . . .

I see that Eli Thayer has gone for Nicolay. I have gone for your poem in the *Century* of today. If this is fruit of your mature wine, I think you are happy in preserving the flavor of your vine-yard. 'Tis pretty, Nay, 'tis much! Perhaps the conclusion is a little weak; but I would not care to strengthen it. King says we ought to publish our joint works under the title of "The Impasse Series," because they all ask questions which have no answers; but nothing has any real answer, and when one walks deliberately into these blind alleys where Impasse is stuck up at every step, one cannot, without a certain ridicule, knock one's head very violently against the brick wall at the end. Victor Hugo did this, to the delight of Frenchmen; but, for our timider natures, let us go on, as before, and, when we see the brick wall, take off our hats to it with the good manners we most affect, and say in our choicest English: *Monseigneur, j'attendrai.* You have done it charmingly. Please say it some more.

Yes, Angell was my scholar, but I prefer his visits....

To Charles Milnes Gaskell

1603 H Street, 8 May, 1887.

. . . .

An intelligent and agreeable fellow has turned up here at your legation; about the last place one looks for such. His name is Spring Rice,[1] and he has creditable wits. Mad, of course, but not more mad than an Englishman should be. Unluckily he is here only for a short time, and goes back to the Foreign Office in the autumn. He drops in at times on me for meals, and pays in a certain dry humor, not without suggestions of Monckton Milnes's breakfasts five and twenty years ago. Other Englishmen twain or more have been here, and, for some unintelligible or unremembered object, have sat at my table; but I forget me as to their names or looks — except the Yates Thompsons, who were scourging the land with a *wilde, verwegene Jagd.* The statistician does not improve with age and newspapering....

[1] Sir Cecil Arthur Spring Rice (1859–1918), later British ambassador at Washington.

To Elizabeth Cameron

WASHINGTON, Friday morning, [1887.]

Your note reached me as I was going to dine with the venerable historian [1] at six o'clock. After dinner I called again to see you, but once more failed.

Your invitation is seductive to a cookless wanderer on what Mr. Longfellow was pleased to call life's solemn main, meaning probably that the voyage was always serious when the wanderer was unfed. My trouble, however, is not so much one of food as of a sentimental wish to see you again, and hear of your welfare, you being more or less the only friend whose meeting I have not dreaded for fear of hearing ill tidings. I hope my harvest of thorns is now gathered in, and I can enjoy the few flowers there are....

To John Hay

[QUINCY,] 28 June, 1887.

•   •   •   •   •   •   •   •   •

My gaiety has been exhausting and continuous. I have called on two old ladies of eighty or more, and have frequented various invalids and persons in bad condition. Dr. William Everett has called upon me. I have returned the civility. I have given rifles to my two twin nephews, with which they are as certain as possible to kill each other, or some one else; but I don't care, because they have a big new sailboat which will drown them if they escape shooting. They are twelve years old. My nieces all prefer jack-knives, an amiable taste, showing refinement and literary propensities.

In the entire horizon that bounds my cell, I see nothing that would bear shipment to London.... Sturgis Bigelow has come home to nurse his father [2] who is either dying or pretending to die; I think the former, though the doctors have hinted the latter, because H. J. B. is so bent on his own way that they can never tell what else ails him. I write history as though it were serious, five hours a day; and when my hand and head get tired, I step out into the rose-beds and watch my favorite roses. For lack of thought, I have taken to learning roses, and talk of them as though I had the slightest acquaintance with the subject.

In short, the summer is just what I expected, with a few details better and a few worse....

[1] George Bancroft.
[2] Henry Jacob Bigelow (1818–1890). He died October 30, 1890.

To Elizabeth Cameron

QUINCY, Sept. 12, 1887.

Tell Martha that I know all about it, and distinctly remember my sufferings at her early age. Perhaps she won't believe it, but you must assure her that I never hesitate to tell a lie....

My brother Brooks will be back from Europe on Octo. 1, and on that day I shall fly to Washington, and perhaps further. Frosts are excellent for babies, but I prefer other milk for men.... Perhaps you would like to go to Mexico. If King will take us with him, we can have a republican time. I must explode into space somewhere, after this summer of galley-slave toil. My comfort is to think that the public shall suffer for it, and any number of defunct statesmen will howl, in the midst of their flames, at the skinning they are getting this season, owing to my feeling cross.

To John Hay

QUINCY, 13 Sept., 1887.

I shall be in New York on October 1, or soon afterwards, and thence to Washington direct, where I am to wait for King. He will tell you what we mean to do, for I shall be guided by him. You would do well to join us. You will have to make a good many jokes to brighten up the last half dozen centuries, and you should lay in a supply in Mexico.

I too have been working, like a Buffalo Bill, all summer, and I carry back to Washington a whole new volume prepared for the printer since June 15. At last I have bowed to the caligrapher, and weeping I dictate. With this vile modern innovation I shall spoil my work, but I shall either be in my pleasant grave on this day two years, or my history will be done and out. I have notified the Japanese government to begin operations in China at that date....

To Elizabeth Cameron

WASHINGTON, 23 Oct., 1887.

My first cook comes tomorrow, an Irish lady who has worked for the whole diplomatic corps, including the Gerolts, Schlözer,[1] Thornton, and Aristarchi.[2] I suppose she drinks, or has fits; but I liked her voice.

[1] Kurd von Schlözer.   [2] Grégoire Aristarchi Bey.

Will you come and dine with the Chinese Minister,[1] who will be my only dignitaried guest this winter? He has some rare porcelain, and I want him to divide it between us. Tomorrow we are to have a storm and I am going to Mt. Vernon with the Endicotts and Herschels. This is the alternative to dinners. If this melancholy procession does not finish me, I shall try to survive till you come.

I know of nothing that I want in the way of shopping, unless you happen to see a chimney that doesn't smoke. If so, buy it for me if not too dear, as James Lowther said of the tooth-brush. If you are going to get dresses in New York, I shall not expect you before Thanksgiving, which is the worse for me as I shall never see the dresses. Your diplomatic flock is scattering. I suppose you will see Jenisch [2] in New York on his way to the journey I did not make,...

To Charles Milnes Gaskell

Washington, 30 October, 1887.

If I have not written since your last letter three months ago, my reason was that I had nothing to say. I passed the whole summer at Quincy taking care of my mother; and during those four months I never left the place for a night. On leaving Quincy four weeks ago, I meant to make a trip to Mexico; but at the last moment was stopped by telegrams which announced floods, fever and broken roads, so that Clarence King, who was to be my companion, would not go. Of the world I see and hear nothing; but I have worked very hard, and have completed a third volume; so that only one more volume remains to be done, and I hope in two years to close up my life as far as literature and so-called usefulness go. I have got to the point where they bore me.

Winter is beginning again. To make a little fresh interest I have bought a green-house, and have taken to forcing roses and things. The amusement is rather more expensive than a good-sized yacht, but it is an aristocratic occupation, and I am singular in following it, for in this city no other gentleman cultivates flowers or fruits. As long as I have roses to give away, no one will comment on my gray hair or bald head, or the crows-feet that are deep as wells under my eyes. The women at least will see nothing but ambrosial curls. As I never dine out or go into society, I cannot introduce the fashion of wearing garlands, but I can look at them, which must be pleasanter. My table is loaded with flowers, and I have to buy Chinese vases, at God knows what cost, to

[1] Chang Yen Hoon.　　[2] Mr. Rücker Jenisch, attaché of the German Legation.

show them. Flowers and bric-à-brac are refined tastes, but, when combined with history, would ruin Ferdinand Rothschild....

To Charles Milnes Gaskell

Los Baños de S. Diego,
8 March, 1888.

In the course of aimless wandering I have drifted for a day to this Spanish hole in the middle of Cuba, and bethink myself that I owe you a letter. An evening with nothing to do at a Cuban sulphur-bath tends to recall one's friends to one's mind. While the chattering Cubans are playing loto at the next table, I will try to write a few pages to bore you.

I forget where or when my last letter was written. I can only remember that I had a more than usually unsatisfactory winter at Washington. I have got into a bad way of never leaving my house except to see one or two intimates, like John Hay. Society scares and bores me, and I have wholly dropped it. During the cold weather I pass an hour every afternoon at my greenhouse and watch my roses. If it were not that friends are very good natured, and come in unasked to breakfast and dinner, I should be a hermit. One of my most valuable allies is a young fellow of your Legation, whose name I have already mentioned to you — Spring Rice — who not only comes two or three times a week to dinner, and keeps me posted about the world's doings, whether I care for them or not, but also brings Englishmen with him, if he thinks them worth knowing. Among others he brought Mr. Chamberlain,[1] who took kindly to my habits, and asked himself several times to dinner without other company than ourselves. Chamberlain amused and interested me. He talked much and well, very openly, and with a certain naïveté that I hardly expected. He was a success in society, and was received with an amount of attention that seemed to puzzle him, considering how little favor he got from newspapers and politicians.... On the whole he made a decided mark, and held more than his own against all comers. His opinion of America is not a high one, and he took little trouble to disguise it; but as he studied it only on the political side, he did not disturb our complacency. His chief objection was that we cared little for statesmen and orators....

I have been particularly well all winter, but the disease of restlessness is quite as trying as most fevers. Clarence King was ordered by

[1] Joseph Chamberlain (1836–1914), who was in the United States to negotiate a treaty on North American fisheries.

his physicians to take these absurd baths for rheumatism. I made every arrangement to come with him. John Hay, who has some chronic inflammation of the vocal cords, agreed to be of the party. At the last moment King's physicians would not let him go; but I was bound to go somewhere, so I took my companion, Theodore Dwight, and started with him and Hay for Florida three weeks ago. Hay left us after a fortnight, to return home, but Dwight and I rambled on, crossed from Florida to Havana, and have been a week in Cuba. I like summer, and palms, Spain and garlic; I do not much object to dirt or smells; and this time I thought my stomach so strong that I went even to a bull-fight, which was declared to be the most splendid ever seen in Havana. Splendid it certainly was, but one bull settled my stomach so effectually that I left the other five to the mercies of the rest of their admirers. Havana is a gay ruin, but after being kept awake five nights by the noise and smell, I thought that country air would do us good, so we came about a hundred miles into the western end of the island. Next Wednesday I expect to start back in order to reach Washington on the 18th.

Meanwhile history has made little progress. I want to go to the Fiji Islands next summer, a five months affair; but am in doubt whether I can fairly get away. The object of such long expeditions about the Pacific is to tire myself out till home becomes rest. If I can do this within two years, things will be simplified. Otherwise, there is no help but to start then for good, and go till I drop. You can have no idea of the insanity of restlessness. Reason is helpless to control it....

To Elizabeth Cameron

QUINCY, 10 June, 1888.

When I bade you good-bye and climbed your Vestibule Train, with a mind which, as you may have observed, was for once quite bird-like for cheerfulness and anticipation of pleasure, I could not help a slight depression at finding that astonishing creation of man's genius and luxury to be entirely intended and used for the conveyance of Chicago German Jews. Why did Matthew Arnold see nothing to interest him in our civilisation? I saw, between Harrisburg and New York enough in a single Vestibule Train to interest the remainder of my life in answering a single conundrum — why the German Jew should be the aim and end of our greatest triumphs in science and civilisation.... I arrived at the Brunswick and took a solitary dinner, after which I found myself

fairly desperate in a ghastly solitude. Under more favorable conditions I could have taken, like my friend whose name I have forgotten
in Musset's *Caprices de Marianne*, to a bottle of wine, and tobacco, till
stupefaction should bring back content; but after June 1 I drink no
wine till October, so this reserve was barred, and at half past nine I
took to solitaire. Degrading as the confession is, I had nothing better
to do, and I wasted immortal time trying to think how cards should be
put one on another. Five years ago, I should have treated with proud
consciousness of superiority the suggestion of such a fall; but I was
glad, last Thursday night, to shuffle cards and wish for October when
wine would be allowed. Yet in the midst of my most interesting combination, a knock came at my door, and Clarence King appeared.
Soon afterwards La Farge came in. They taught me all the nothing-
ness of art, science and society till after midnight, and I was with them
all the next day and evening, when King and La Farge became so exhausted by the prolonged mental effort that both went to sleep, one on
the bed, the other on the sofa, where I left them at King's room, while
I resumed solitaire. So it is that, as civilisation ends in the Chicago
Jew, the society of our most amusing friends leads back to shuffling of
cards. Yet you wonder that I long for the Cannibal Islands....

To John Hay

QUINCY, 8 July, 1888.

I would give a ream of ruled law cap, written full of history, to be
going with you to Colorado; but yet awhile I must abide here, and, to
admit the truth, the frenzy of finishing the big book has seized me,
until, as the end comes nigh, I hurry off the chapters as though they
were letters to you. I think that five more chapters will pretty much
finish the story. A concluding Chapter or Book must be still written on
topics and tendencies, but I shall begin printing next autumn.

I am glad to see your hand again on the Lincoln. Criticism is not
needed, but I have now gathered about me an epidermis of nerves
sensitive at peculiar and arbitrary points. I know that my sensitive
points are no more properly sensitive than a million others, but I trust
to the devil to be good enough to spare me more, or I shall never get
through a proof-sheet at all. My last axiom, invented within three
months, is that the present tense must never be employed in historical
writing, and can never under any circumstances be so good as the past
tense; while the word *now* should be ruthlessly struck out wherever it
occurs, no matter under what apparent necessity it is used. I com-

municate this satanic idea to you on Mark Twain's theory of getting rid of it. Perhaps if you take it up, I may forget it. Anyway it is sure to make you uneasy, which is always good for a middle-aged and indolent protectionist....

To Elizabeth Cameron

QUINCY, 15 July, 1888.

. . . .

She [Martha][1] ought to come here and be my secretary, and relieve Dwight, who is now a sort of literary factotum, and will soon be in general charge of the establishment, from the kitchen to the barn. I don't know how he can manage a farm, but I do know that neither my brothers nor I can do any better, so you may see him milking a cow, and reading an old MS. at the same time. We none of us know our whole genius till we've been tried....

Midsummer has come, the strawberries and roses have dropped and faded, my last half-dozen chapters are begun, and my nephew Charley has beaten everything with his new cutter the Babboon; I am as cold as usual in a Boston summer, and my brothers are taking their families to the Glades in order to be colder; Stanford White has sent me a salmon from Ristigouche, and John Hay has gone to Colorado; my mother is still eighty years old or more, and Miss Baxter is in New York; I see or hear dimly that some new political jackanapes is set up for President, and that Congress is likely to be in session for two months yet....

To John Hay

QUINCY, 22 July, 1888.

. . . .

My fury about the historical present was a long-penned but always forgotten volume of irritation at your collaborator's extravagant and exuberant indulgence in that obscene habit. I am not aware that you sinned. Yet I object even to saying in my favorite phrase: "The greatest of all philosophers, the wise and polite Kung-fu-tse, observes." The assertion is ridiculous on its face, for Kung died more than two thousand years ago....

Deep am I in the peace of Ghent. I am haunted by the idea that no general historian has given a detailed account of a negotiation. Ban-

[1] Martha Cameron.

croft slurs the treaty of 1783. I know no model for such a narrative, yet it interests me more than war. Is a foreign ideal on record?...

To Elizabeth Cameron
QUINCY, 19 August, 1888.

. . . .

Did you, or did you not, leave any plants in my greenhouse? The question is one which I would gladly have answered in the negative, for, ten days ago, I received a series of telegrams and letters from Washington, from which, among a mass of incoherent details about contractors, storms, plants and Mrs. Durkin's bonnet, we eliminated the central idea that, in the process of rebuilding the greenhouse, the contractor had removed the sides while he loaded the top, and one morning, while Mrs. Durkin was putting on her bonnet, he had come in to announce that the whole greenhouse roof was flat on the ground, with the plants and Durkin under it. Durkin must have got out, for he wrote me the same day a letter in which the i's and h's played hide and seek in the least expected corners, but except to inform me that the contractor was Bosh, and that I must rebuild the whole place on a new plan, he furnished no information even about his own sense of wrong. I telegraphed to Ward Thoron to stop building, wind up the concern, sell the plants, and convert the place for the time into a summer garden. So there is an end of the greenhouse; but I hope you had nothing in it, or that whatever you had has not been crushed or sold. For the present a garden will remain there, but only for spring and autumn purposes.

I admit to being greatly pleased with this catastrophe, for I wanted to have liberty for some newer folly, and the garden was beginning to be a bore....

To John Hay
QUINCY, 9 Sept., 1888.

. . . .

I sit at my desk six hours every day, and spin my web with the industry of Anthony Trollope. I can hardly believe my own ears when I say that tomorrow my narrative will be finished; all my wicked villains will be duly rewarded with Presidencies and the plunder of the innocent; all my models of usefulness and intelligence will be fitly punished, and deprived of office and honors; all my stupid people, including my readers, will be put to sleep for a thousand years; and when they wake up, they will find their beards grown to their waists, and will rub their eyes, and ask: "Do the crows still fly over Washington?"...

To Elizabeth Cameron

QUINCY, 16 Sept., 1888.

By October 1, I shall begin to start the caravan for Washington again, and probably open house on the 15th, if the lady who works for the crowned heads of Europe condescends to save you the trouble of finding me another cook. I carry back the last volume of my history, finished; and I begin at once to print the whole affair. China looms in the distance. I believe your husband and the other gentlemen who haunt the Capitol, have been trying to pick a quarrel with China so as to get me shut out, or massacred when in; but it won't matter. If shut out I shall set up an empire of my own on an island by itself, and if massacred I shall go straight to Heaven or somewhere else with the missionaries. The Senate means well, but it is too well-intentioned for its supply of human weaknesses....

To John Hay

QUINCY, 23 Sept., 1888.

I have composed the last page of my history, and the weather is so wet that for a week I've been in vain trying to do Gibbon and walk up and down my garden. I wish Gibbon had been subjected to twelve inches of rain in six weeks, in which case he would not have waited to hear the bare-footed monks sing in the Temple of Jupiter, and would have avoided arbors as he would rheumatics. I am sodden with cold and damp, and hunger for a change....

To Elizabeth Cameron

U. P. CAR 010. ON THE PLATTE RIVER.
17 October, 1888.

Here I am again, in your old quarters, still warned that God hates a liar, and that Truth is mighty. This time I am taking my baronet [1]

[1] Sir Robert Cunliffe.

where the sunset beckons. Beyond the night, beyond the day, that happy baronet follows me — the most delighted and astonished baronet that ever was, because the old car happened to be returning empty from Boston, and picked us up at Chicago to carry us over the U.P. territory. No Duke ever felt so grand as my modest Sir Robert in his own particular car.

We shall go up to Portland by the Short Line, and then down to San Francisco by the new Shasta route. There we shall become mortals again, and knock about California for three weeks, before returning by way of New Orleans and St. Augustine to Washington, about November 27....

The weather is, even here, cloudy, cold and raw, the plains dull and brown, and the wind rough. We shall grumble if the sun fails us to-morrow, for we have pursued it as though we were still as young lovers as when we pursued the British maidens whose age is now as doubtful as that of the geologic reptilians, whose bones Marsh digs from these weary plains. As yet our mistress, the sun, has shone but two days since we left the coast. I suppose it is because we are growing old. Anyway I object. No amount of physical comfort atones for such neglect.

At Chicago Frank McVeagh devoted himself to us, and Mrs. McVeagh threw open her exquisite house, to which mine is a cheap log-cabin, and asked charming young persons to dine, who made the venerable British lion curl his mane and purr with pleasure. I asked each of the fascinators to share our ear and hearts, such as they were; but as usual they trampled on us, and we were obliged to wander on alone, like the last buffalo....

To Charles Milnes Gaskell

Union Club, San Francisco, 28 October, 1888.

Robert's arrival broke the long stillness of the summer, and started me off, on the 13th, to take him wherever he wanted to go. Since then we have wandered steadily westward, four thousand miles, through all sorts of scenery and people; stopping at Salt Lake; visiting the Shoshone Falls, which tourists have hardly yet discovered in the lava deserts of Idaho; descending the Columbia River in Oregon; and turning south seven hundred miles down the Pacific coast till we arrived here yesterday morning. I took Robert out to see the sun, setting in a hazy summer light over the Pacific; and I offered to take him on, still westward, as far as the sun went; but he showed at last the effect of age and travel; he refused to go further, and turned his face eastward. Apparently we are at the end.

I think he has enjoyed the trip, though the work is certainly hard, and the fatigue more steadily exhausting than one at first suspects. As for me, I am always contented when in motion, and ask no better than to wander on. Tomorrow we start for the Yosemite; and when we are done with this part of California we shall go south to the Mexican border, and home to Washington by way of New Orleans. We expect to reach Washington about Nov. 25, and Robert sails December 12 for Liverpool. Robert is the same pleasant travelling companion that he was twenty years ago, and takes life as gaily and with as much appreciation as ever. I am heartily glad to have this outing with him, for the chance is small that we should ever renew our youth in any other way. We sometimes speculate whether you would enjoy our adventures, such as they are; and whether you would be intolerably bored by suffocating dust and jouncing carts; vast sand deserts, and barren sage-brush plains, over which one has to travel, day and night, without much sleep, till one's ideas of the world become altogether upset, and even the solidest Yorkshire valet gets tired of wondering where the country-seats are. Fortunately Robert brought no valet, and we carry our own dust, inch deep, with a green reflêt, in patience, without being obliged to dust a servant too. I expect to find Robert quite ground away, as by a sand-blast, before I get him across the great American plains....

At this distance I think even Ireland seems a less overpowering element in the cosmos than it seems nearer home; and one finds the Chinaman take the place of the ubiquitous Irishman, politics and all. Both are rather a bore; but the Chinaman bores one in a new way, as Dr. Johnson said of the poet Gray....

To Elizabeth Cameron

YOSEMITE VALLEY
Sunday, 4 Nov., 1888.

With the deepest contrition for having disobeyed and offended you, I must still confess that here we are in the Yosemite Valley, and, unlike the ambitious youth Rasselas, we are anything but eager to leave it. Last night a little rain fell — the first since April — and today all the hills are white, and the pines powdered with snow. I have just returned from a long day in the mountains, where the fresh snow was about us, and where I felt myself a modified, though deteriorated, black bear, with strong prejudices against civilisation. In this spirit, inflamed by an atmosphere of third-rate Britishers created by a party of belated globe-trotters who have drifted here to our perdition, I am trying to reconcile myself with my fellow-man by writing to you, who are the chief reconciling element. For the moment the Yosemite is a good enough Gobi for me; but, though I feel ashamed to say so to you, it is true that the other day, arriving at San Francisco, I took my baronet out to the Cliff House, where the Pacific was rolling in its long surf in the light of a green and yellow sunset; and there I pointed to the Golden Gate and challenged the baronet to go on with me. Ignominiously he turned his back on all that glory, and set his face eastward for his dear fogs; and I, too, for the time, submitted; but the longing was as strong as ever....

My baronet has enjoyed his journey, which has indeed been a succession of rapid and fantastic changes such as even I, who have travelled in America occasionally could hardly take in. When I wrote to you from the Platte Valley we were already well shaken up to new sensations. We had — or he had — seen Tuxedo, Chicago, and U.P. Car 010 which was the loftiest emotion of all; but the next day he learned what sagebrush was; the third, he saw Salt Lake and passed an afternoon wandering along its shores; next he had a sensation watching the Utah Mountains for a whole day, which ended by bringing us to Shoshone. You should have seen us two animated dust-heaps driving across twenty-five miles of fluid dust and solid lava to see Shoshone Falls, and clambering down and up that pleasing ravine, much as though we slid down from Table Rock by a rope. My legs ached for a week, and my very hat stood on end with terror, but this was a trifle compared to its condition when the mainspring of our wagon broke, on the way back, and the baronet and I were bumped for twelve miles of solid lava blocks in a solider dust, till we regained our car. Then we struck a furious storm on the summit of the Oregon mountains, and ran twenty miles down-hill over trees corduroying the track; but I preferred this to running over cows, as in Idaho, though the cows are perhaps a softer road-bed. We went down the Dalles by steamer, with a rain-accompaniment, and saw Portland through a water-fall heavier than the Shoshone. The day passed in running by Mt. Shasta in northern California was another sensation worth having; but we found San Francisco dull in spite of its swell club-house; and we lost our glory when we left our car.

Last Monday night we started for the Sierras and arrived here Wednesday afternoon. Since then we have passed a year or two in the amusement of climbing the face of cliffs three thousand feet high, and standing on their edge afterwards. This sensation certainly takes away one's breath, if that is its object, and at last I have struck on the edge business, leaving it to the baronet on the principle that his son may just as well succeed now as later to the baronetcy. I prefer to break my own neck short of three thousand feet, not requiring so much time as the Britisher for reflection in the air. Tomorrow we go after the big trees, another sensation. Then we go back to San Francisco; thence to Monterey, Santa Barbara and New Orleans, and finally to Washington on or about the 25th....

My baronet is a charming companion, and I am but an indifferent one whose only virtue is a willingness to go anywhere and stay as long or as short a time as he likes, and whose chief vice is to discuss geology by the hour without understanding the first principle of it. If I bore him, he does not bore me, but is appreciative, and quite hostile to all useful information. Even the lurid figure of Mr. Gladstone has been temporarily overshadowed in his mind by the cliffs and forests of the Yosemite, and we shall cast our votes on Tuesday among the big trees, indifferent to what political party they belong. I do not believe them to be republican, democratic or Gladstonian, but if they are either, more's the pity, and they may yet live to forget it....

To Elizabeth Cameron

CHARLESTON CLUB, 23 February, 1889.

I am very doubtful whether I can ever return to Washington. My decline in morals and manners, owing to the evil influences of Tom Lee and Willy Phillips has been so rapid as to leave little hope of ultimate recovery. I am afraid to look Martha in the face, and dare not meet you until I am purified by the moral atmosphere of the new administration. My two companions have led me into wild excesses. We succeeded in getting, with much difficulty, to a light-house where Tom Lee was to shoot ducks, and Phillips was to enjoy perpetual summer. The summer began by landing in an open boat, after breaking a quarter of a mile of ice with oars, and then wading through a mile of half frozen swamp. Tom's shooting consisted in chasing ducks over ponds; and, as ducks fly rather faster than lightning, we had nothing but cold boiled pork and potato to eat. Getting tired of this sport, we tried to escape from North Carolina, but escape was impossible. After long imprisonment we seized an open boat, and made a perilous voyage in Arctic cold, to Roanoke island. There we were detained a week or two, searching for the lost colony of Sir Walter Raleigh. A steamer at last passed near, and we hailed her at midnight from the shore. She took us aboard and carried us to Little Washington, a sweet tranquil spot, but one from which no man was ever known to come away. By this time — which was just a week ago — we were reduced to extreme despair, and my two companions could only sustain themselves by obliging me to learn euchre and poker, by means of which they took away all my money, leaving me no resource but to follow them as long as they would pay my expenses. They dragged me on board a small steamer at three o'clock one morning, and carried me fifty or sixty miles up the Tar River. There, at a spot called Tarbow, they landed, and after another night of anguish, owing to Tom Lee's aversion to drummers, we caught the first train that came by. It happened to be bound south on the Atlantic Coast Line, and I found myself at Charleston the next morning, in a drenching rain, cold as Archangel, and dirty as an Esquimau.

Tomorrow these savage men are to take me to Savannah. From there I know not what to expect. I have overheard Tom Lee talking of a ball, with which your name was coupled, and which seemed to be expected for the week after next. Perhaps I may be carried back to Washington, if he wants to go to the ball; or perhaps I may be sent to some spot still more dreadful than North Carolina, if there is one. I am at their mercy, and shall continue to play euchre and eat shad as long as life holds out....

To Charles Milnes Gaskell

WASHINGTON, 21 April, 1889.

.   .   .   .

Robert and I ceased our wanderings only in December, and I started again in six weeks to pass the month of February knocking about an unknown region called the North Carolina Sounds, a vast wilderness of sand, mud and forest, populated by wild ducks and a genial fish called the shad. When March began, I had to return, for the printers could no longer be neglected, and I have made my contract for publishing the eternal history which has been the bore of my friends and myself for ten years. The first two volumes are pretty nearly ready, and will appear, I suppose, either in the summer or autumn, to be followed by the rest as fast as the publisher pleases. The printing and preparing tie me down quite tight, so that I shall not run away again till all is finished....

We have had a change of administration here which has interested many people, but makes little difference to the world or society. I know not a man in the new lot, high or low, and for the first time in thirty years, have not an acquaintance in the cabinet. Acquaintances grow somewhat scarce, at best, as one becomes more exacting with age. The dread of a bore grows to horror. John Hay remains my only companion, but he too starts for England in three weeks....

Our new minister to London, who is known familiarly here as Bob Lincoln, will, I hope, be liked. He is a good fellow, rather heavy, but pleasant and sufficiently intelligent. I have known him slightly for some years. Hay has known him since childhood, and is very intimate with him. Unless Hay himself were to have the place, Lincoln was as good a man as was likely to be sent....

To Elizabeth Cameron

WASHINGTON, 19 May, 1889.

· · · · · · · · · · · · · · · ·

Theodore Roosevelt was at Lodge's. You know the poor wretch has consented to be Civil Service Commissioner and is to be with us in Washington next winter with his sympathetic little wife. He is searching for a house. I told him he could have this if he wanted it; but nobody wants my houses though I offer them freely for nothing. I went to talk Central Asia with Rosen the other day, and Rosen complained of the rents charged at Beverly. I told him I had two houses there, either of which he might have for nothing; but he will go on, just the same, scolding about rents. Luckily he offers no objection to our Asiatic Mystery, and I expect to make a sort of Marco Polo caravan. History bids fair to get quickly out of the way. By next January I hope it will be finished....

To Elizabeth Cameron

WASHINGTON, 2 June, 1889.

In half an hour I must start for New York and Boston, and I intend to amuse myself for the last half hour by writing a word to you. The town is at an end. Everyone except Justice Gray[1] and Secretary Bayard[2] has got married or gone, and those two Arcadians are to get married and go next week. By way of celebration we have had rains —

[1] Horace Gray (1828–1902) married, June 4, 1889, Jane Matthews.
[2] Thomas Francis Bayard married, May 7, 1889, Mary W. Clymer.

oh, but real rains that you read about. At the first glimpse of sunshine yesterday I started off on Daisy to see what was left of the universe. I found all the old bridges gone on Rock Creek, and had to come down to our new bridge to cross, where Martha's little waterfall quite roared. Rock Creek tumbled like the rapids at Niagara. I came across, and down to the Potomac about half way to the Chain Bridge. The whole thing was running loose. The canal was busted and running like an insane mule. The river was quite superb. I raced with casks and beams, but they beat me, though Daisy was going an easy seven miles. This morning, Pennsylvania Avenue is flooded and the trains and steamers can't run. I am going to try the B. & O. train at noon, for I must meet King and La Farge at dinner at seven, but I doubt whether even the B. & O. will get me through....

Quincy, 9 June. On arriving here last Tuesday evening I found my mother already unconscious and rapidly sinking. She died Thursday night, without recovering consciousness or speech. The decline was so rapid that I knew nothing of it till I arrived, although we were aware that it was likely to happen at any time....

Apparently I am to be the last of the family to occupy this house which has been our retreat in all times of trouble for just one hundred years. I suppose if two Presidents could come back here to eat out their hearts in disappointment and disgust, one of their unknown descendants can bore himself for a single season to close up the family den. None of us want it, or will take it. We have too many houses already, and no love for this....

To Anna Cabot Mills Lodge

Quincy, 18 June, 1889.

Dear Mrs. Lodge,

Many thanks for your kind letter.

I return brother Sturgis's remarks, which were evidently meant for feminine sympathies rather than for criticism. Of course I sympathize, but can't tell him so. Our conclusions are too far apart. Sturgis is, like everyone else, bound to find Paradise in this world, and seems to be in dead earnest. Thousands and millions of men have taken his road before, with more or less satisfaction, but the mass of mankind have settled to the conviction that the only Paradise possible in this world is concentrated in the three little words which the ewig man says to the ewige woman. Sturgis calls this the Fireside, and thinks he knows better. He looks for his Paradise in absorption in the Infinite.

Probably the result will be the same. Sooner or later, fate commonly gets bored by the restless man who requires Paradise, and sets its foot on him with so much energy that he curls up and never wriggles again. When Sturgis can't squirm any longer, and suddenly realizes that Paradise is a dream, and the dream over, I fear that he is too sensitive a nature to stand the shock, and perhaps it wouldn't be worth his while to try.

I am very hard at work for the summer, and still looking for that Japanese box which comes not though it should. Thanks for your kind invitation. If I go anywhere I shall certainly come to you. Tell Constance I am in despair about her dress.   Ever truly yours.

To Elizabeth Cameron

QUINCY, 27 June, 1889.

Your letter from Raith, written at the news of my mother's death, reached me yesterday, and today I see the announcement of your father-in-law's death....[1]

I know that Mr. Cameron's death must be an event of very serious consequences to your husband and his family, but I know too little what consequences to expect, to be able to say anything about it. I have been through all these experiences recently, and know only that nothing is to be said.

A million thanks for your kind sympathy with me. The world has some slight compensations for its occasional cruelties. I suppose, for instance, that in gradually deadening the senses it cuts away the unpleasant as well as the pleasant. As I walk in the garden and the fields I recall distinctly the acuteness of odors when I was a child, and I remember how greatly they added to the impression made by scenes and places. Now I catch only a sort of suggestion of the child's smells and lose all the pleasure, but at least do not get the disgusts. Life is not worth much when the senses are cut down to a kind of dull consciousness, but it is at least painless. As for me, waste no sympathy. My capacity for suffering is gone....

To John Hay

QUINCY, 21 July, 1889.

.   .   .   .

By this time you are on the Eiffel Tower or Mont Blanc or some such treiffel, enjoying the change of climate, and the *cotelettes à la*

[1] Simon Cameron died June 26, 1889.

Boulangère. I can not follow you. My range of vision does not extend beyond Nahant. My excitement is going to Baseball matches with my nephews and nieces. We saw your Cleveland heroes beat our Boston swells, and Chicago get a severe rebuke from us. Unfortunately I have not seen John L. Sullivan, though I would go far to do so, nor have I read the report of his famous battle, nor heard a word of Clarence King, nor been to stay with Mrs. Cabot Lodge, though I see that both Cabot and Teddy Roosevelt are on the shop-counters in apparent self-satisfaction, which makes me as sick as Possum[1] to reflect that I too can no longer avoid that disgusting and drivelling exhibition of fatuous condescension. All books should be posthumous except those which should be buried before death, and they should stay buried....

To Charles Milnes Gaskell

Washington, 24 November, 1889.

I have lost count of our letters, and remember only that I have heard nothing from you for a very long time. Luckily time no longer affects me. I have become as indifferent as the Egyptian Sphinx to the passage of centuries, and my friends always remain young because I don't see them. You can't imagine how pleasantly I remember England, and how very much alive you all are, though you have been dead or quarrelled these many years.

I am as dead as a mummy myself, but don't mind it. As a ghost I am rather a success in a small way, not to the world, but to my own fancy, which I presume to be a ghost's world, as it is mine. Things run by with spectre-like silence and quickness. As I never leave my house, and never see a newspaper, and never remember what I am told, the devil might get loose and wander about the world for months before I should meet him, and then I should not know who he was. You can have no idea how still and reposeful, and altogether gentlemanly a place the world is, till you leave it.

Spring Rice has come back again with a dozen or so of admirals whom he is personally conducting about the dangers of youth and ocean. Occasionally he shelters them with me for a while, to rest a bit and doze over my dinner-table. They seem a temperate set, and I don't fear their dozing under it. The town is filled with all sorts of foreigners on all sorts of conferences about the most ridiculous trifles, such as trade with Patagonia, and fog-horns. Spring Rice runs the

[1] His dog.

fog-horns, and so I hear them. He has broken down Admiral Mure Molyneux and one tough old sea-captain by dissipation, and has packed them off to sea to get well. In another fortnight he will have worn out the lot, and will be the only admiral left....

I have thrown upon the cold world two children in the shape of volumes, the first of eight or ten of which I am to be delivered. As they lost all interest for me long ago, I cannot believe that they would interest my friends, so I have sent no copies about. If any American should ask if I sent them to you, say Yes, — and that you have read them with much pleasure. The conversation will not go further, and both of us will have made a proper appearance before posterity....

XIV

HONOLULU AND THE SOUTH SEAS

1890

To Charles Milnes Gaskell

WASHINGTON, 13 April, 1890.

. . . .

I have not sent you my history for the reason that I do not think it a pleasant book for English reading, and do not care to send my old friends anything that would annoy them. In case you should hear it spoken ill of, you can always plead ignorance, and if you hear it spoken well of, you can smile acquiescence. Half of it is now out. The rest will follow in the autumn.

By that time I expect to be a pirate in the South Seas. In thus imitating Robert Louis Stevenson I am inspired by no wish for fame or future literary or political notoriety, or even by motives of health, but merely by a longing to try something new and different. Civilisation becomes an intolerable bore at moments, and I never could abide an eternity of hares and rabbits, Ireland or protective duties. As the English speaking world seems content to busy itself with these practical pursuits, I mean to take a vacation; but I know not where or how long. Anything may happen — even my reappearance in Europe.

To Charles Milnes Gaskell

WASHINGTON, 4 July, 1890.

. . . .

The summer waxes and still I hang on here, detained by the last sheet of Index, and by hopes of taking John La Farge with me again — this time to the South Seas. Hay also remains here, held by the last sheets of his great work, and we bask in the tropical heat of this empty city, alone in our houses. Hay gets north next week. My own movements are uncertain, but I am liable any day to start for San Francisco and Samoa. I shall need no preparation, for every last order is given, my trunks are ready for packing, and my wardrobe is ready also. I have fitted myself out for two years in the South Seas; but the length of my absence will depend wholly on my feelings. I may return in two months, if I find myself more bored there than here. I may be gone for twenty years if I find myself more bored here than there. I may turn up in England for a change, and you need not be surprised any fine day in April or May to see me walk into your breakfast room. Time is nothing to me, and health is the only unknown element of travel. Barring illness or accident I may go anywhere and do anything.

My disease is ennui, probably the result of prolonged labor on one work, and of nervous strain. The reaction of having nothing to do after steady labor without change for so many years, is severe. Probably it will rapidly disappear with travel. It has hitherto always done so....

To Elizabeth Cameron

NEW YORK, 16 August, 1890.

I arrived here at half past twelve last night, and now that I have finished packing, paid for my tickets and stateroom, bought my last little pair of shoes (I have now a dozen, I think,) and nothing more to do but look after La Farge who is struggling with the whole Inferno, I find your note of yesterday, and take a rest in answering it, or at least in acknowledging it. As I wrote you a line from the Lodges', yours is already answered.

I never felt the sensation before of hurrying about with a hundred things on my mind, and only one thing in it. The prepossession made me forget even my last proof-sheets, which must now go to Dwight. I am also a stranger of late years to the choking sensation of departure, and hardly know whether to be glad or sorry at feeling it once more. Until now I never fairly realised that life has become mainly a series of farewells.

So be it, since it can be nothing else.... La Farge I saw at nine o'clock. He had then three pictures to paint, two windows to lead, and his packing to do, but promised to be ready at four o'clock. He was very gay and impecunious as ever, and is going to take his Japanese boy with him. To my constant amusement he always ends with the same grave serenity that he shall do this at his own expense.[1]...

(*In pencil.*) 6.45. Here we are en route, without delay, running along the Hudson. La Farge is in high spirits, and already flattering himself with the appointment of court painter to the King of the Sandwich Islands....

[1] The artist also wrote letters descriptive of scenes and impressions which were published in 1912 as *Reminiscences of the South Sea*, illustrated by a number of his studies in colors.

To Elizabeth Cameron

"ZEALANDIA," TUESDAY, 26 August, 1890.

. . . .

As usual, the sea off California was up-and-down, swash and roll, trying as possible to a landsman, but it moderated a little yesterday, and we got on our legs again. We do not go to meals, but this is chiefly because the boat is full, and our seats offer no attractions. Our state-rooms are pleasant, on deck, airy and private, and there we live, reading, sleeping, and now writing. Presently I shall get out my water-colors, and try to set La Farge to painting. The sky is thick and we have had little sun, but occasionally the sea is intensely blue. On the whole I see nothing peculiar about it. In fact I am disappointed. I thought that half way to the Islands I should feel the charm of tropical seas; but it is very like the Atlantic at the same season, and just now the sky is gray and the water almost muddy in color....

Thursday, 28th. If one must go to sea, these are certainly the seas to go to. Day after day we roll lazily along, the north-east trades blowing us gently ahead and never a change in their force or direction. The air is exquisitely soft; the sky always cloudy with broken masses of warm grey water-clouds, and now and then the sun comes out on a patch of blue sky, and shows us an ocean so intensely blue that the eye wonders whether the color is not really black. The ship is well enough if not good; of the passengers I know nothing. La Farge remains as always the pleasantest of companions. It is now seven o'clock in the morning, and I am now taking my cup of early tea. Then I will read an hour on deck. I shall pass several hours trying to sketch the water and sky, with queer results, and I shall swear at my own stupidity for an hour or two more. The evening will be given to indolence and drowsiness over cigars on deck in the dusk, watching the water and struggling moon. Then bed at ten, and so in forty-eight hours we sight Molokai.

Friday, 29th. The flying-fish are usually my only variety of sight, and they amuse me perpetually, for they really fly long distances — fifty or a hundred yards — and look like exaggerated dragon-flies, sometimes as large as a mackerel; but yesterday we had a sunset that roused us all. Such softness of greys, violets, purples, reds and blues you will never see, for you will never venture into these deserts. Afterwards came a full moon, with light clouds, and it seemed to set every-one to singing and spooning. When I went to bed, I undressed by light of the moon's reflection on an intensely blue sea — at ten o'clock at night — a strange, tropical effect.

Saturday, 30*th.* 7 A.M. Molokai is in sight on our left, a dim bank in fog, and Oahu ahead, a higher range of hills behind which is our port, Honolulu. The air is still soft as the clouds, which are always a delicate violet that makes sunset and moonrise equally refined. At ten o'clock we shall arrive, and already the Sandwiches seem companions of one's youth, familiar as La Fayette Square.

Honolulu, Sunday, Aug. 31. We arrived yesterday morning at ten o'clock, and having established ourselves at the hotel, breakfasted and got up our enormous baggage-train, we started out at two to find Mr. W. O. Smith, my friend Hartwell's brother-in-law, to whom I brought a letter. We discovered him at his office, expecting us, and, after a very short preamble, he drove us up to Hartwell's house. The drive of about two miles was amusing as a comedy, and full of "Look at that!" and "What is that?" and "What good eyes she has!" and so on, but I can't stop to speak of Kanakas or palms or banyans or reds or purples or flowers or night-gown costumes or old-gold women with splashes of color, but must hurry to our house which we reached at last over a turf avenue between rows of palms. We were half an hour in getting into it, for it was closed, and John, the keeper, was missing; but we had enough to do in looking about. The place is at the mouth of a broad mountain-valley opening out behind Honolulu, and overlooking the town and harbor, to the long line of white surf some three miles away, and then over the purple ocean indefinitely southward. The sense of space, light and color, in front, is superb, and the greater from the contrast behind, where the eye rests on a Scotch mountain-valley, ending in clouds and mist, and green mountain-sides absolutely velvety with the liquid softness of its lights and shadows. Showers and mist perpetually swept down the valley and moistened the grass, but about us, and to the southward, the sky was always blue and the sun shining. The day was hot in the town, and the air like a greenhouse, but up here the north-east trade-wind blew deliciously. As for the grounds, they were a mass of palms, ferns, roses, many-colored flowers, creepers interspersed with the yellow fruit of the limes, and unknown trees and shrubs of vaguely tropical suggestions, all a little neglected, and as though waiting for us. The house when we got into it was large, for Hartwell has seven or eight children, and there was an ample supply of all ordinary things. Both La Farge and I were eager to move in at once. Mr. Smith drove us back to the town at five o'clock, and helped us to order our house-keeping necessaries; and I never but once saw La Farge so much amused and delighted with everything he saw, as in this afternoon's excitement where all was new and full of life and color. We dined at the hotel, and at eight o'clock reached our house again, and installed ourselves. While our rooms were made ready we sat on the verandah and smoked. The full moon rose behind us and threw a wonderful light as far as the ocean-horizon. On the terrace were twin palm trees, about fifty feet high, glistening in the moonlight, and their long leaves waving, and, as Stoddard [1] says, "beckoning" and rustling in the strong gusts, with the human suggestion of distress which the palm alone among trees conveys to me. La Farge never understood or felt the palm-tree, and I am a bit conceited at thinking that last night I brought him to a true way of thinking. Then we took some supper, and I eat my first mango, which, rather to my surprise, I found delicious, a little acid, and smooth as oil to the tongue. Therewith, after a sleepy, palmy, moon-light, tropical pipe, we went to bed, with doubts of centipedes and quadrupeds, but with the consciousness of a day full of boyish fun and frolic....

Tuesday, Sept. 2.... We are established as quietly as we should be at Beverly. As yet we have not even taken a drive, and our only visit to the town was last evening at sunset to buy Apollinaris and soap. Our cook is expected to-day. We have not even left our letters of introduction or made a call, and not a word has been said about going off to the other islands, or our trip to the volcano.... Although this is only our third day of Kanaka paradise, we are as lazy as though it were our third year. Yet La Farge has been out with his paint-box every day, and brings home, or rather brings in, wild daubs of brown and purple which faintly suggest hills and our great storm-cloud that we keep, so to speak, in our stable-yard, for it seems always to hang there. My own water-color diversions are not so amusing, but look like young ladies' embroidery of the last generation. If I could learn to paint like Martha, I should do wonders, but I cannot reach so far into high art, and only try to do like Turner or Rembrandt, or something easy and simple, which ends in my drawing a very bad copy of my own ignorance; but it has the charm that I felt as a boy about going fishing: I recognise that I am catching no fish on this particular day, but I feel always as though I might get a bite tomorrow. As far as I can see, La Farge gets no more, and is equally disappointed with every new attempt. I mean to photograph everything so that you may see it all, but photography is no longer an amusement now that it is all mechanical, and you have fifty pictures in half an hour....

[1] Charles Warren Stoddard.

Sept. 5. We are lazy and dread more ocean, but we have been to breakfast with Judge Dole and to dinner with Mr. Dillingham, and Mr. Bishop has shown me his kihalis, and his new Museum, and I have ridden on the ambling rocking-horse of the island, and I have driven La Farge up the Nuuanu valley, where we live, to the great divide or pass, Pali, five or six miles up, where the lava cliff suddenly drops down to the sea-level, and one looks northward over green valleys and brown headlands to where the ocean, two or three miles distant, is breaking in curves and curls along the coast. The view is one of the finest I ever saw, and quite smashed La Farge. Yet I am amused to think what my original idea was of what the island would be like. I conceived it as a forest-clad cluster of volcanoes, with fringing beaches where natives were always swimming, and I imagined that when I should leave the beach I should be led by steep paths through dense forests to green glades where native girls said *Aloha* and threw garlands round your neck, and where you would find straw huts of unparallelled cleanliness always in terraces looking over a distant ocean a thousand feet below. The reality, though beautiful, is quite different. The mountains are like Scotch moors, without woods, presenting an appearance of total bareness. One drives everywhere over hard roads, and can go to most places about Honolulu by horse-car or railroad. On the other islands, travel is more on horseback, but the stories of cockroaches and centipedes, not to mention scorpions, make one's teeth chatter; and the mosquitoes, at night, are as bad as at Beverly. The absence of tropical sensation is curious. One would come here to escape summer. The weather is divine, but the heat never rises above 84°, and at night the thermometer always stands at 75° with a strong breeze — too strong to sit in. After our July in Washington I feel as though I had run away to a cool climate, although the sense of a constant temperature is a constant surprise....

To Elizabeth Cameron

STEAMER "W. G. HALL." 13 Sept., 1890.

At sea again, or rather in port, for just now, at seven o'clock in the morning, we are leaving the little village of Kailua, and running along the south coast of the island of Hawaii. We tore ourselves yesterday morning from our comforts at Honolulu, and after a day and night of seasick discomfort on a local steamer, filled with natives, we are now in sight of Mauna Loa, and at evening shall land at Punaluu on the extreme south-eastern end of the island. As I detest mountains, abominate volcanoes, and execrate the sea, the effort is a tremendous one; but I make it from a sense of duty to the savages who killed Captain Cook just about here a century ago. One good turn deserves another. Perhaps they will kill me. I never saw a place where killing was less like murder. The ocean is calm and blue; the air so warm that I turned out of my sleepless berth at the first light of dawn. The huge flat bulk of Mauna Loa stretches down an interminable slope ahead of us, with the strange voluptuous charm peculiar to volcanic slopes, which always seem to invite you to lie down on them and caress them; the shores are rocky and lined with palms; the mountain-sides are green, and packed with dark tufts of forest; the place is — an island paradise, made of lava; and the native boats — queer long coffins with an outrigger on one side resting in the water — are now coming out at some new landing-place, bringing mangoes, pine-apples, melons and alligator-pears, all which I am somewhat too nauseated to eat. Our steamer is filled with plaintive-looking native women — the old-gold variety — who vary in expression between the ferocious look of the warriors who worshipped Captain Cook and then killed him, and the melancholy of a generation obliged to be educated by missionaries. They have a charm in this extraordinary scope of expressions which run from tenderness to ferocity in a single play of feature, but I prefer the children, who are plaintive and sea-sick in stacks about the decks, and lie perfectly still, with their pathetic dark eyes expressing all sorts of vague sensations evidently more or less out of gear with the cosmos. The least sympathetic character is the occasional white man. Third-rate places seldom attract even third-rate men, but rather ninth-rate samples, and these are commonly the white men of tropical islands. I prefer the savages who were — at least the high chiefs — great swells and very much gentlemen and killed Captain Cook.... We have been ashore to see where Captain Cook was killed, a hot little lava oven where the cliffs rise sharp over deep water — some old crater-hole — of all sorts of intense blue.[1] Only a hut was there, donkeys and mules, a few natives and a swarm of crabs jumping over the red rocks by the black-blue water. Mauna Loa slopes back for forty miles....

KILAUEA VOLCANO HOUSE, *Monday*, Sept. 15. 7 A.M. Our pilgrimage is effected at last. I am looking, from the porch of the inn, down on the black floor of the crater, and its steaming and smoking lake, now chilled over, some two or three miles away, at the crater's further end. More impressive to my fancy is the broad sloping mass of Mauna

[1] Kaawaloa, in La Farge, 38.

Loa which rises beyond, ten thousand feet above us, a mass of rugged red lava, scored by deeper red or black streaks down its side, but looking softer than babies' flesh in this lovely morning sunlight, and tinged above its red with the faintest violet vapor. I adore mountains — from below. Like other deities, they should not be trodden upon. As La Farge remarked yesterday when I said that the ocean *looked* quiet enough: "It *is* quiet if you don't fool with it. How would *you* like to be sailed upon?" The natives still come up here and sit on the water's edge to look down at the residence of their great Goddess, but they never go down into it. They say they're not rich enough. The presents cost too much. Mrs. Dominus, the king's sister, and queen-expectant, came up here in the year 1885, and brought a black pig, two roosters, champagne, red handkerchiefs, and a whole basket of presents, which were all thrown on the lava lake. The pig, having his legs tied, squealed half an hour before he was thoroughly roasted, and one of the roosters escaped to an adjoining rock, but was recaught and immersed. Only princesses are rich enough to do the thing suitably, and as Mrs. Dominus is a Sunday-school Christian, she knows how to treat true deities. As for me, I prefer the bigger and handsomer Mauna Loa, and I routed La Farge out at six o'clock — or was it five — to sketch it with its top red with the first rays of the sun.... We had a lovely day's drive yesterday up here, over grassy mountain-sides, and through lava beds sprinkled with hot-house shrubs and ferns. The air is delicious, and the temperature, when the clouds veil the sun, is perfect either for driving or walking. If we can only escape the steamer on the windward side! but that implies sixty miles of horseback, partly in deluges of rain.

HILO, *Sept.* 18. If you do not know where Hilo is don't look for it on the map. One's imagination is the best map for travellers. You may remember Hilo best because it is the place where Clarence King's waterfall of old-gold girls was situated. The waterfall is still here, just behind the Severance house where we are staying. Mrs. Severance took us down there half an hour ago. She said nothing about the girls, but she did say that the boys used habitually to go over the fall as their after-school amusement; but of late they have given it up, and must be paid for doing it. The last man who jumped off the neighboring high rock required fifteen dollars. Mrs. Severance told this sadly, mourning over the decline of the arts and of surf-bathing. A Bostonian named Brigham took a clever photograph of a boy, just half way down, the fall being perhaps twelve or fifteen feet. So passes the glory of Hawaii, and of the old-gold girl — woe is me!

As La Farge aptly quoted yesterday from some wise traveller's advice to another, à propos of volcanoes: "You will be sorry if you go there, and you will be sorry if you don't go there, so I advise you to go." We went. The evening before last we tramped for two hours across rough blocks and layers of black glass; then tumbled down more broken blocks sixty or eighty feet into another hole; then scrambled half way down another crater — three in succession, one inside the other — and sat down to look at a steaming black floor below us, which ought to have been red-hot and liquid, spouting fountains of fire, but was more like an engine house at night with two or three engines letting off steam and showing head-lights. The scene had a certain vague grandeur as night came on, and the spots of fire glowed below while the new moon looked over the cliff above; but I do not care to go there again, nor did I care even to go down the odd thirty or forty feet to the surface of the famous lake of liquid fire. It was more effective, I am sure, the less hard one hit one's nose on it. We tramped back in the dark; our lanterns went out, and we were more than three hours to the hotel....

Tomorrow we start, through mud and gulches of torrents, on a five days' ride to Kawaihae, eighty miles to the westward, where we take steamer again. If you will believe it, I do this to avoid a day's seasickness.

STEAMER "KINAU," *Tuesday, 23 Sept.* I take it all back. Hawaii is fascinating, and I could dream away months here. Yet dreaming has not been my standard amusement of late. Never have I done such hard and continuous travelling as during the last ten days, since leaving Honolulu. I have told you how we reached Hilo. Friday morning early we left Hilo, according to our plan, with a circus of horses, to ride eighty miles, divided into four days. Rain was falling as we drove out the first eight miles to take horse at the end of the road, but we started off like Pantagruel, and in an hour arrived at a lovely cove or ravine called Onomea, where La Farge sketched till noon; one of the sweetest spots on earth where the land and ocean meet like lovers, and the natives still look almost natural. That afternoon we rode eight miles further. The sky cleared; the sun shone; the breeze blew; the road was awful, in deep holes of mud, with rocky cañons to climb down and up at every half mile; but I never enjoyed anything in travel more thoroughly than I did this. Every ravine was more beautiful than the last, and each was a true Paul and Virginia idyll, wildly lovely in ways that made one forget life. The intensely blue ocean foamed into the mouths of still inlets, saturated with the tropical green of ferns and dense woods, and a waterfall always made a background, with its sound of running water above the surf. The afternoon repaid all my five thousand miles of weariness, even though we had to pass the night at one of Spreckles' sugar plantations where saturnine Scotchmen and a gentle-spoken Gloucestershire housekeeper entertained us till seven o'clock Saturday morning; when we started off again over the same mud-holes and through more cañons, which disturbed La Farge because the horses were not noble animals and warranted little confidence; but to me the enjoyment was perfect. At noon we lunched at another plantation where a rather pretty little German-American woman, of the bride class, entertained us very sweetly, and closed our enjoyment by playing to us Weber's last waltz, while we looked out under vines to the deep blue ocean as one does from the Newport cottages. That was at Laupahoehoe plantation, and that afternoon we passed Laupahoehoe and rode hard till half-past five, when I dismounted before a country-house, and, before I realised it, tumbled up steps into an open hall where three ladies in white dresses were seated. I had to explain that we had invited ourselves to pass the night, and they had to acquiesce. The family was named Horner, and were Americans running several plantations and ranches on the island. We passed the night of Sunday at the plantation of another son, or brother, of the same family, at Kukuihaele, and strolled down to see the Waipio valley, which is one of the Hawaiian sights. Yesterday we rode twelve miles up the hills, stopping to lunch at the house of one Jarrett who manages a great cattle ranch. Jarrett was not there, but two young women were, and though they were in language and manners as much like other young women as might be, they had enough of the old-gold quality and blood to make them very amusing to me. They made me eat raw fish and squid, as well as of course the eternal *poi* to which I am now accustomed, then after lunch, while La Farge and I smoked or dozed and looked across the grass plains to the wonderful slopes of Mauna Loa and Mauna Kea, the two girls sat on mats under the trees and made garlands of roses and geranium which they fastened round our necks — or rather round my neck and La Farge's hat. I was tremendously pleased by this, my first *lei* — I believe they spell the word so, pronouncing it *lay* — and wore it down the long, dusty ride to Kawaihae where we were to meet the steamer, and where we arrived just at dark in an afterglow like Egypt. The girls also drove down, one of them returning to Honolulu by the same steamer. Kawaihae seemed a terrible spot, baked by the southern sun against a mountain of brown lava without a drop of fresh water for miles. When I dismounted and entered the dirty little restaurant, I found our two young ladies eating supper at a dusky table. They had ordered for me a perfectly raw fresh fish, and the old-goldest of the two showed me how to eat it, looking delightfully savage as she held the dripping fish in her hands and tore its flesh with her teeth. Jarrett was there, and took us under his care, so that an evening which threatened to be so awful in heat and dirt, turned out delightful. They took us to a native house near by, where a large platform thatched with palm-leaves looked under scrubby trees across the moonlit ocean which just lapped and purred on the beach a few yards away. Then they made the mistress of the house — an old schoolmate, but a native and speaking little English — bring her guitar and sing the Hawaiian songs. They were curiously plaintive, perhaps owing to the way of singing, but only one — Kamehameha's war-dance — was really interesting and sounded as though it were real. A large mat was brought out, and those of us who liked lay down and listened or slept. The moon was half full, and shone exquisitely and Venus sank with a trail like the sun's.

From this queer little episode, the only touch of half-native life we have felt, we were roused by the appearance of the steamer at ten o'clock, and in due time were taken into the boat and set on board. I dropped my faded and tattered *lei* into the water as we were rowed out, and now while the "Kinau" lies at Mahukana, doing nothing, I write to tell you that our journey has been fascinating, in spite of prosaic sugar plantations, and that I am yearning to get back to Waimea, where I might stay a month at Samuel Parker's great ranch, and ride his horses about the slopes of Mauna Kea, while indefinite girls of the old-gold variety should hang indefinite garlands round my bronze neck.

Sept. 24. Honolulu again.... Now that I look back on our Hawaiian journey of the last ten days, it seems really a considerable experience, and one new to common travellers in gaiters. If you feel enough curiosity to know what others think of the same scenes, read Miss Bird's travels in the Sandwich Islands.[1] I have carefully avoided looking at her remarks, for I know that she always dilates with a correct emotion, and I yearn only for the incorrect ones; but you will surely see Islands of the soundest principles — travellers' principles, I mean — if you read Miss Bird, who will tell you all that I ought to have seen and felt, and for whom the volcano behaved so well, and performed its correct motions so properly that it becomes a joy to

[1] Isabella Lucy (Bird) Bishop, *The Hawaiian Archipelago*, 1875.

follow her. To us the volcano was positively flat, and I sympathised actively with an Englishman, who, we were told, after a single glance at it, turned away and gazed only at the planets and the Southern Cross. To irritate me still more, we are now assured that the lake of fire by which we sat unmoved, became very active within four-and-twenty hours afterwards. These are our lucks. I never see the world as the world ought to be.

In revenge I have enjoyed much that is not to be set down in literary composition, unless by a writer like Fromentin or a spectacled and animated prism like La Farge. He has taught me to feel the subtleness and endless variety of charm in the color and light of every hour in the tropical island's day and night. I get gently intoxicated on the soft violets and strong blues, the masses of purple and the broad bands of orange and green in the sunsets, as I used to *griser* myself on absinthe on the summer evenings in the Palais Royal before dining at Véfour's, thirty years ago. The outlines of the great mountains, their reddish purple glow, the infinite variety of greens and the perfectly intemperate shifting blues of the ocean, are a new world to me. To be sure, man is pretty vile, but perhaps woman might partly compensate for him, if one only knew where to find her. As she canters about the roads, a-straddle on horseback, with wreaths of faded yellow flowers, and clothed in a blue or red or yellow night-gown, she is rather a riddle than a satisfaction....

To Elizabeth Cameron

HONOLULU, Sept. 27, 1890.

Our steamer is lying at the wharf; our trunks are on board; four o'clock in the afternoon has come; we have yet to dine, before driving down in the moonlight to take possession of our staterooms. At midnight, or soon afterwards, the "Alameda" sails, carrying us two thousand miles further....

La Farge and I had our audience of the King yesterday. We went to the little palace at half-past nine in the morning, and Kalakaua received us informally in his ugly drawing-room. His Majesty is half Hawaiian, half negro; talks quite admirable English in a charming voice; has admirable manners; and — forgive me just this once more — seems to me a somewhat superior Chester A. Arthur; a type surprisingly common among the natives. To be sure His Majesty is not wise, and he has — or is said to have — vices, such as whiskey and — others; but he is the only interesting figure in the government, and is

really what the Japs call omusurvi — amushroi — amusing. I have
listened by the hour to the accounts of his varied weaknesses and
especially to his sympathies with ancient Hawaii and archaic faiths,
such as black pigs and necromancy; but yesterday he sat up straight
and talked of Hawaiian archeology and arts as well as though he had
been a professor. He was quite agreeable, though not, like our own
chief magistrate, an example of the Christian virtues. I would not be
thought to prefer Kalakaua to Benjamin Harrison, but I own to finding him a more amusing subject.

Socially this seems a queer place. I cheerfully forgive society for
ignoring us, for I have caught glimpses enough of it to imagine worse
than Washington horrors; but I find it strange that no one ever suggests our doing anything social, or tells us of anything to be done, or
desirable to do. I make my own inferences, but without much real
knowledge. After a month, I know little or nothing of Honolulu. We
know everybody of much account, but we have not even been put up
at the club. Almost no one has called on us. As for dinners or parties,
we have as yet cost Honolulu not a bottle of wine. Apparently in order
to see the interior of a white man's house here, one must invite oneself
into it, as we did on our journey last week. I should suppose we had
given offence, except that no one seems to do more than we do, or to
have more social vogue.

To Elizabeth Cameron

Apia, October 9, 1890.

Well we are here, and I am sitting in the early morning on the verandah of a rough cottage, in a grove of cocoa-nut palms, with native
huts all about me, and across the grass, fifty yards away, I can see and
hear the sea with its distant line of surf on the coral reef beyond. Natives clothed mostly in a waist-cloth, but sometimes their toilet completed by a hybiscus or other flower in their hair, pass every moment
or two before my cabin, often handsome as Greek gods. I am the guest
of Consul Sewall,[1] whose consulate is within the same grove, near the
beach....

Sunday morning at nine o'clock or thereabouts, the "Alameda"
turned a corner of Tutuila, and I saw the little schooner knocking
about in the open sea beyond. The day was overcast, threatening rain.
From the shore, half a dozen large boats, filled with naked savages,
were paddling down with the wind, singing a curiously wild chant to

[1] Harold Marsh Sewall (1860–1924).

their paddles. La Farge and I felt that we were to be captured and probably eaten, but the cruise of sixty miles in a forty-ton schooner, beating to windward in tropical squalls, was worse than being eaten. We dropt into the boat among scores of naked Samoans, half of them swimming, or clambering over our backs, with war clubs to sell, and when we reached our schooner, we stood in the rain and watched the "Alameda" steam away. That was our first joy. Whatever fate was in store, we had escaped from the steamer, and might die before another would come.

The cutter was commanded by Captain Peter, a huge captain, but little skilled in the languages with which I am more or less acquainted. His six sailors were as little fluent in English as though they had studied at Harvard. Captain Peter talked what he supposed to be English with excessive energy, but we could catch only the three words "now and again," repeated with frequency but in no apparent connection. "Now and again" something was to happen; meanwhile he beat up under the shore into quieter water, and presently, in a downpour of rain, we cast anchor in a bay, with mountains above, but a sand-beach within the coral reef, and native huts half hidden among the cocoanut palms. I insisted on going ashore straightway without respect for H. M.'s mail, and Captain Peter seemed not unwilling. A splendid naked savage carried La Farge, in an india-rubber water-proof, mildly kicking, from the boat to the shore, and returned for me. I embraced his neck with effusive gratitude, and so landed on the island of Tutuila, which does not resemble the picture on the Oceanic Steamship Company's colored advertisement. I found it densely covered with tropical mountains and vegetation, but glad as I was to set foot on mountains and see vegetation, I was soon more interested in the refined hospitality of the cultured inhabitants. We entered the nearest hut, and put on our best manners, which were none too good, for the natives had manners that made me feel withered prematurely in association with the occupants of pig-sties. Grave, courteous, with quiet voices and a sort of benevolence beyond the utmost expressiveness of Benjamin Franklin, they received us and made us at home. The cabin was charming when one looked about it. Nearly circular, with a diameter of some forty feet, its thatched roof, beautifully built up, came within about five feet of the ground, ending there on posts, and leaving the whole house open to the air. Within, mats covered a floor of white corals, smooth and almost soft like coarse sand. Fire was made in the middle of the hut. Only women and children were there. One was staining a tapa-cloth; another was lying down unwell; others were sitting about, and one or two naked children, wonderfully silent and well-behaved, sat and stared at us. We dropped our umbrellas and water-proofs and sat down on the mats to wait for Captain Peter to sail; but presently a proud young woman entered and seated herself in silence after shaking hands. Captain Peter succeeded in making us understand that this was the chief's daughter. Other young women dropped in, shook hands and sat down. Soon we seemed to have a *matinée*. As no one could say more than a word or two in the other's language, communication was as hard as at a Washington party, but it was more successful. In a very short time we were all intimate. La Farge began to draw the Princess, as we called her, and Wakea — for that was her name — was pleased to drop her dress-skirt, and sit for him in her native undress, with a dignity and gravity quite indescribable. The other girls were less imposing, but very amusing. One, Sivà, a younger sister of the Princess, was fascinating. Of course I soon devoted my attention to talking, and, as I could understand nothing, talk was moderately easy; but through Captain Peter we learned a little, and some of the touches of savagery were perfect. I asked Sivà her name — mine was Hen-li — and her age. She did not know her age; even her father, an old man, could not say how many years old she was. I guessed fourteen, equivalent to our eighteen. All her motions were splendid, and she threw a plate on the floor, as Martha Braggiotti would say, like a race-horse. Her lines were all antique, and in face she recalled a little my niece Lulu, Molly's sister. Presently she brought a curious pan-shaped wooden dish, standing on eight legs, all of one block; and sitting down behind it, began to grate a dry root, like flag-root but larger, on a grater, over the dish. This was rather hard work, and took some time. Then another girl brought some cocoa-nuts full of water, and she poured the water on the grated root. Then she took a bundle of clean cocoa-nut fibre, and seemed to wash her hands in the water which was already muddy and dirty with the grated root. We divined that she really strained out the grated particles, which were caught on the fibre, and wrung out by another girl. When all the grains were strained off, the drink was ready, and we realised that we had got to swallow it, for this was the *kawa*, and we were grateful that in our first experience the root was grated, not chewed, as it ought to be, by the girls. Please read Kingsley's account of it in the "Earl and the Doctor,"[1] a book you will probably be able to borrow from Herbert, as it was done for or by his brother Pembroke. A cocoa-nut half

[1] *South Sea Bubbles, by the Earl and the Doctor* — George Robert Charles Herbert, Earl of Pembroke, and George Henry Kingsley.

full of it was handed to us, and as usual La Farge, who had kicked at the idea more than I did, took to it at once, and drank it rather freely. I found it "not nice, papa, but funny"; a queer lingering, varying, aromatic, arumatic, Polynesian, old-gold flavor, that clings to the palate like creosote or coal-oil. I drank the milk of a green cocoa-nut to wash it off, but all the green cocoa-nuts in the ocean could not wash out that little taste. After the *kawa* we became still more intimate. Besides Wakea and her sister Sivà, we made the acquaintance of Tuvale, Amerika, Sitoa, and Faaiuro, which is no other than Fayaway, I imagine. We showed them our writing, and found that they could write very well, as they proved by writing us letters on the spot, in choice Samoan, which we tried to translate, with the usual result. So evening came on; we had some supper; a kerosene lamp was lit; and La Farge and I began to cry out for the *Siva*.

The *Siva*, we had learned to know at Hawaii, is the Samoan dance, and the girl, Sivà, had already been unable to resist giving us snatches of the songs and motions. Sivà was fascinating. She danced all over, and seemed more Greek in every new motion. I could not understand what orders were given by the elders, but, once they were assured that we were not missionaries, all seemed right. The girls disappeared; and after some delay, while I was rather discouraged, thinking that the Siva was not to be, suddenly out of the dark, five girls came into the light, with a dramatic effect that really I never felt before. Naked to the waist, their rich skins glistened with cocoa-nut oil. Around their heads and necks they wore garlands of green leaves in strips, like seaweeds, and these too glistened with oil, as though the girls had come out of the sea. Around their waists, to the knee, they wore leaf-clothes, or *lavalavas*, also of fresh leaves, green and red. Their faces and figures varied in looks, some shading the negro too closely; but Sivà was divine, and you can imagine that we found our attention absorbed in watching her. The mysterious depths of darkness behind, against which the skins and dresses of the dancers mingled rather than contrasted; the sense of remoteness and of genuineness in the stage-management; the conviction that at last the kingdom of old-gold was ours, and that we were as good Polynesiacs as our neighbors — the whole scene and association gave so much freshness to our fancy that no future experience, short of being eaten, will ever make us feel so new again. La Farge's spectacles quivered with emotion and gasped for sheer inability to note everything at once. To me the dominant idea was that the girls, with their dripping grasses and leaves, and their glistening breasts and arms, had actually come out of the sea a

few steps away. They entered in file, and sat down opposite us. Then
the so-called Siva dance began. The girls sat cross-legged, and the
dance was as much song as motion, although the motion was incessant.
As the song or chant, a rhythmical and rather pleasant, quick movement, began, the dancers swayed about; clapped their hands, shoulders, legs; stretched out their arms in every direction and with every
possible action, always in harmony, and seldom repeating the same
figure. We had dozens of these different motives until I thought the
poor girls would be exhausted, for they made so much muscular effort,
feet, thighs, hips and even ribs working as energetically as the arms,
that they panted at the close of each figure; but they were evidently
enjoying it as much as we, and kept it up with glances at us and laughter among themselves. All through this part of the performance, our
Princess did not dance but sat before us on the mats, and beat time
with a stick. At last she too got up, and after ten minutes' absence,
reappeared, costumed like the rest, but taller and more splendid.
La Farge exploded with enthusiasm for her, and expressed boundless
contempt for Carmencita. You can imagine the best female figure you
ever saw, on about a six foot scale, neck, breast, back, arms and legs,
all absolutely Greek in modelling and action, with such freedom of
muscle and motion as the Greeks themselves hardly knew, and you can
appreciate La Farge's excitement. When she came in the other
dancers rose, and then began what I supposed to be a war or sword
dance, the Princess brandishing a stick and evidently destroying her
enemies, one of whom was a comic character and expressed abject
cowardice. With this performance the dance ended; Sivà got out the
kawa dish; Wakea and the others went for our tobacco, and soon we
were all sprawling over the mats, smoking, laughing, trying to talk,
with a sense of shoulders, arms, legs, cocoa-nut oil, and general nude-
ness most strangely mixed with a sense of propriety. Anyone would
naturally suppose such a scene to be an orgy of savage license. I don't
pretend to know what it was, but I give you my affidavit that we could
see nothing in the songs or dances that suggested impropriety, and that
not a word or a sign during our whole stay could have brought a blush
to the cheek of Senator H—— himself. Unusual as the experience is
of half dressed or undressed women lying about the floor, in all sorts of
attitudes, and as likely as not throwing their arms or their shoulders
across one as one lies or sits near them, as far as we could see the girls
were perfectly good, and except occasionally for hinting that they
would like a present of a handkerchief, or for giving us perhaps a ring,
there was no approach to familiarity with us. Indeed at last we were

extinguished by dropping a big mosquito netting over us, so that we were enclosed in a private room; the girls went off to their houses; our household sank into perfect quiet, and we slept in our clothes on the floor as comfortably as we knew how, while the kerosene lamp burned all night in the centre of the floor.

The next morning we very unwillingly tumbled into our boat, after a surf bath, and then, for the next four or five hours, we were pitching about, in a head wind and sea, trying to round the western point of Tutuila. Nothing could be more lovely than the day, the blue sea, and the green island stretching away in different planes of color, till lost in the distance. At two o'clock that afternoon we rounded our point, and our boat went ashore to fetch off Consul Sewall and Lieut. Parker on their return from Pango Pango, where they had gone to settle on the new naval station. They came instantly on board, and we four Americans then lay on the deck of that cutter from two o'clock Monday afternoon, till two o'clock Wednesday morning, thirty-six hours, going sixty miles, in a calm, with a vertical sun overhead, and three of the four seasick. You can conceive that we were glad to reach Apia on any terms, and tumbled ashore, in a leaky boat, in the dead of night, only too glad to get shelter about the consulate. Our only excitement at sea was a huge shark that looked like a whale. Once ashore, supper and bed were paradise; but my brain and stomach went on turning somersaults, and I was not wholly happy.

October 12. Sunday here, when it should be Saturday, but Samoa is above astronomy. Time has already made us familiar with our surroundings. I find myself now and then regaining consciousness that I was once an American supposing himself real. The Samoan is so different from all my preconceived ideas, that my own identity becomes hazy, and yours alone remains tolerably clear. I took one day of entire rest, after arriving, and passed it in looking at the sea, and rejoicing to have escaped it. The second day we performed our visits of ceremony. First, we called on King Malietoa, and I assure you that I was not in the least inclined to joke about him. He is not *opéra bouffe*, or Kalakaua. The ceremony was simple as though we were in a democratic republic. We began by keeping his Majesty waiting half an hour while we lounged over our cigars after breakfast. When we arrived at the audience-house, we found Malietoa gone, but he was sent for, and came to receive us. The house was the ordinary native house, such as we were in at Tutuila. We sat on the floor. Malietoa was alone, without officers or attendants, and was dressed as usual with chiefs on state occasions, in an ordinary white linen jacket and trousers. He is an

elderly man, with the usual rather pathetic expression of these islanders, and with the charming voice and manner which seem to belong to
high chiefs. He talked slowly, with a little effort, but with a dignity
and seriousness that quite overawed me. As the interpreter translated,
I caught only the drift of his words, which were at first formal; then
became warm in expressions of regard for Americans; and at last
turned to an interesting and rather important discussion of the political dangers and uneasiness in these islands. He said nothing of his
own sufferings or troubles, but seemed anxious for fear of disturbance
here, and evidently dreads some outbreak against his own authority
unless the three foreign powers execute their treaty promptly, which
the three foreign powers seem, for reasons of their own, determined not
to do. If you want a lecture on Samoan politics, I am in a fair way to
be able to give you one; for though I loathe the very word, and of all
kinds of politics detest most those of islands, I am just soaked with the
stuff here, where the natives are children, full of little jealousies and
intrigues, and the foreigners are rather worse than the natives. The
three foreign powers have made a mess, and the natives are in it.
Even in case they fight, I do not much expect to be massacred, as
Americans are very popular indeed; but I am a great *ali* — nobleman —
because all the natives knew the frigate "Adams,"and I am the first
American who has ever visited the country merely for pleasure; so I
feel bound to look grave and let Sewall do the talking. Malietoa was
sad and despondent; Mata-afa, the intermediary king, who led the
fighting after Malietoa's deportation, and was deposed by the treaty
of Berlin, seemed also depressed, but was even more earnest in his expressions of gratitude to America. We made also a ceremonial call
on Mata-afa, after we had seen Malietoa, and while we were going
through the unavoidable *kawa*, which becomes a serious swallow after
many repetitions, Mata-afa talked of his gratitude to America. I
won't bore you by explaining why he is grateful. I don't much care
myself; and was much more interested in watching the dignity of his
face, the modulation of his voice, the extraordinary restraint and refinement of his rhetoric, and the exquisite art of the slight choking in
his voice as he told us that his only hope was in Christ and in America.
I felt more interest in the art of his civilisation, you understand, than
I did in the detail that Bayard and Sewall had saved the islanders
from being killed or enslaved. As rhetoricians and men of manners,
the great Samoan chiefs, and, for that matter, the little ones too, make
me feel as though I were the son of a camel-driver degraded to the
position of stable-boy in Spokane West Centre. Aristocracy can go no

further, and any ordinary aristocracy is vulgar by the side of the
Samoan. For centuries these people have thought of nothing else. They
have no other arts worth mentioning. Some day I will tell you of their
straw mats, their chief artistic pride; their houses, too, are artistic in
their way, and their taste in colors is splendidly bold; but their real
art is social, and they have done what in theory every scientific society
would like to do — they have bred themselves systematically. Love
marriages are unknown. The old chiefs select the wives for the young
chiefs, and choose for strength and form rather than beauty of face.
Each village elects a girl to be the village maiden, a sort of candidate
for ambitious marriage, and she is the tallest and best made girl of the
good society of the place. She is bound to behave herself, and marry a
handsome young chief. The consequence is that the chiefs are the
handsomest men you can imagine, physically Apollos, and the women
can all carry me in their arms as though I was a baby.

The chief of Apia is Seumano, the hero of the hurricane, who took his
boat through the surf and saved the shipwrecked crews. Our government sent him a present of a fancy whaleboat, very handsome though
a little like a man-of-war, requiring about fifty men to move it. Seumano is a giant in strength; his wife, Fatolea, is quite a *grande dame*,
and their adopted daughter, Fanua, is the village maiden, or Taupo, of
Apia. Sewall got Seumano, who is as warmly American as all the rest,
to give us a big Siva dance that we might see the thing properly, and
the occasion was evidently one of general interest. In general the scene
was the same as at Nua in Tutuila, but instead of an improvised affair,
Seumano gave us a regular party, with the whole village taking part or
looking on. Fanua was the centre girl, and had nine or ten companions. Fanua wore an immensely high and heavy headdress that belongs to the village maiden. The others were dressed in the Siva costume, but spoiled their effect by wearing banana leaves round their
breasts, in deference to missionary prejudices. The figure is everything in the native dance, and the color counts almost as much as
dress with you creatures of civilisation. The banana leaves were as
little objectionable as such symbols of a corrupt taste could be, but
they reminded one of the world and the devil. Our impromptu at Nua
was better, for though some of the girls were more or less grotesque,
the handsome ones, with fine figures, were tremendously effective.
You can imagine what would be the effect of applying such a test to a
New York ball-room, and how unpopular the banana leaf would be
with girls whose figures were better than their faces. Nevertheless the
Siva was a good one, especially in the singing and the drill. The older

women sat in the dark behind the girls, and acted as chorus. Sewall, his vice Consul Blacklock, La Farge and I sat in front, opposite the dancers. Towards the end, when the dancers got up and began their last figure, which grows more and more vivacious to the end, Fanua, who had mischief in her eyes, pranced up before me, and bending over, put her arms round my neck and kissed me. The kissing felt quite natural and was loudly applauded with much laughter, but I have been redolent of cocoa-nut oil ever since, and the more because Fanua afterwards gave me her wreaths, and put one over my neck, the other round my waist, dripping with cocoa-nut oil.

October 14. I am hazy on dates. This may be any day of the week or month. I only know time by its passage. The weather has been warm, about 88° at noon-day, though cool enough except from eleven till four. Yesterday morning I took my boat out fishing on the reef. By the bye, I have set up a boat, as one sets up a carriage. The Consulate had none, and I thought I could repay Sewall's civility no better than by giving him a boat; so we have a swell man-of-war's boat with five fine natives to row us, and an awning and a consular flag, fine as Fiji. These luxuries are not inexpensive. A boat here costs as much or more than a carriage at home; but here I must be a great *ali* or bust. So, as I had nothing for my boat to do, I took it out to see how the natives fished. My stroke oar, or coxswain, did the fishing, and succeeded in catching a squid, or octopus, about twelve or eighteen inches span in the tentacles. The process was curious, but the fun came afterwards. Sewall sent the squid to Mele Samsoni — in English, Mary Hamilton — a native woman, married to an elderly American, who lives near by — and asked her to make some squid soup for us. So at noon we had a lunch in Samsoni's hut in the banana grove hard by. There was old Hamilton — once a whaleman and pilot — his wife Mele or Mary — three girls who live with them, Sewall, Blacklock, La Farge and I, sitting on the mats with the lunch spread on banana leaves before us. The squid soup was first distributed, and I found it delicious; rather rich, but not so strong as either clams or oysters. The squid is cut up and boiled in cocoa-nut milk. I am certain that in French hands it could be made a great success. To my horror I was then given a large dish of the squid itself. I had seen it for sale, dried, as an article of food in Japan, and had even tried to eat it in Honolulu where our American friends regarded it as they do oysters or truffles; but this was my first meeting with it face to face, and I attacked it with the shudder of desperate courage. In the end I eat nearly the whole beast, refused to eat anything else, and afterwards sucked half a dozen oranges, drank a green cocoa-nut, smoked a cigar and dropped off asleep, while Mele Samsoni fanned the flies from me with a banana leaf.

October 16. Yesterday I moved into my native house. We sleep and eat at the Consulate, but I have set up a native house as a studio and reception room. It is a large, handsome hut, commonly used as the guest-house of the village. The native church stands between it and the sea which is fifty yards away. Mata-afa's house is a few rods to the right, across the village green. Native houses are scattered round the green. Bread-fruit trees and cocoa-nut palms surround us. Just now half a dozen girls in costumes varying between the ordinary missionary nightgowns and the native waist-cloth, are chattering about the place, doing so-called work for us. Yesterday Mata-afa sent us a chief with a big green turtle as a gift, which is a present only made to great people. We are engaged for no end of feasts and dances, and I fear that the missionaries are deeply disgusted because we have caused their best parishioners to violate church discipline by our grand Siva at Seumano's, which turns out to have been a political event and demonstration of Samoan nationality. As we avow without disguise our preference for old Samoan customs over the European innovations, we must expect to give offence; but a just fear of ridicule restrains me from the only truly comfortable step of adopting the native want of costume. Possibly the mosquitoes and fleas have something to do with the ridicule too. Yesterday afternoon we took the boat to town, which is a mile or more away, and a heavy rain drove us to shelter in Seumano's where we were entertained with a pineapple and the infernal *kawa* which I swallow only by compulsion. I asked Seumano to show us his fine mats, so the women took down the bundle from the cross-beams where their valuables are stored, and untied it, producing half a dozen mats, about the texture of the finest Panama straw, some five or six feet square. These are the Samoan jewels and heirlooms, which give distinction and power to their owner, and are the dowry of the women. The gift of a fine mat will pay for a life, and the last war was caused by an attempt to confiscate mats. If possible I will buy one and send it to you, but you can do nothing with it, for it is too rare for use, and not showy enough for ornament. You will have to put it into a coarser mat, tie it with cords in a bundle, and put it up in the attic, if you wish to be appreciative and Samoan. Fine mats are rarely made now; the whole number of them in existence is small and diminishing; they are more highly prized than ever by the chiefs, and I am almost ashamed to take any out of the country. Just as I am writing, a woman has come in from a neighboring village with four fine mats for sale, and I have bought the oldest and most worn, but the best, for a little more than thirty dollars. If I send it to you, it must go to Martha as a dowry to secure her a handsome young chief for a husband. Three or four such would secure her the swellest match in Samoa.

October 17. Yesterday afternoon Sewall took La Farge and me to call on Robert Louis Stevenson. We mounted some gawky horses and rode up the hills about an hour on the native road or path which leads across the island. The forest is not especially exciting; not nearly so beautiful as that above Hilo in Hawaii, but every now and again, as Captain Peter, or Pito, used to say, we came on some little touch of tropical effect that had charm, especially a party of three girls in their dress of green leaves, or *titi*, which La Farge became glowing about. The afternoon was lowering, with drops of rain, and misty in the distance. At last we came out on a clearing dotted with burned stumps exactly like a clearing in our backwoods. In the middle stood a two-story Irish shanty with steps outside to the upper floor, and a galvanised iron roof. A pervasive atmosphere of dirt seemed to hang around it, and the squalor like a railroad navvy's board hut. As we reached the steps a figure came out that I cannot do justice to. Imagine a man so thin and emaciated that he looked like a bundle of sticks in a bag, with a head and eyes morbidly intelligent and restless. He was costumed in a dirty striped cotton pyjamas, the baggy legs tucked into coarse knit woollen stockings, one of which was bright brown in color, the other a purplish dark tone. With him was a woman who retired for a moment into the house to reappear a moment afterwards, probably in some change of costume, but, as far as I could see, the change could have consisted only in putting shoes on her bare feet. She wore the usual missionary nightgown which was no cleaner than her husband's shirt and drawers, but she omitted the stockings. Her complexion and eyes were dark and strong, like a half-breed Mexican. They received us cordially enough, and as soon as Stevenson heard La Farge's name and learned who he was, they became very friendly, while I sat by, nervously conscious that my eyes could not help glaring at Stevenson's stockings, and wondering, as La Farge said, which color he would have chosen if he had been obliged to wear a pair that matched. We sat an hour or more, perched on his verandah, looking down over his field of black stumps, and the forest beyond, to the misty line of distant ocean to the northward. He has bought a hundred acres or more of mountain and forest so dense that he says it costs him a dollar for every foot he walks in it. To me the place seemed oppressively shut in by forest and mountain, but the weather may have caused that impression. When conversation fairly began, though I could not forget the dirt and discomfort, I found Stevenson extremely entertaining. He has the nervous restlessness of his disease, and, although he said he was unusually well, I half expected to see him drop with a hemorrhage at any moment, for he cannot be quiet, but sits down, jumps up, darts off and flies back, at every sentence he utters, and his eyes and features gleam with a hectic glow. He seems weak, and complains that the ride of an hour up to his place costs him a day's work; but, as he describes his travels and life in the South Seas, he has been through what would have broken me into a miserable rag. For months he has sailed about the islands in wretched trading schooners and stray steamers almost worse than sailing vessels, with such food as he could get, or lived on coral atolls eating bread-fruit and yams, all the time working hard with his pen, and of course always dirty, uncomfortable and poorly served, not to speak of being ill-clothed, which matters little in these parts. He has seen more of the island than any literary or scientific man ever did before, and knows all he has seen. His talk is most entertaining, and of course interested us peculiarly. He says that the Tahitians are by far finer men than the Samoans, and that he does not regard the Samoans as an especially fine race, or the islands here as specially beautiful. I am not surprised at the last opinion, for I do not think this island of Upolo very beautiful as these islands go; certainly not so beautiful as the Hilo district of Hawaii; but I shall wait for our own judgment about the men and women. Tahiti and Nukuheva are his ideals, which encourages us with something to look forward to. He had much to say about his experiences, and about atolls, French *gens d'armes*, beach-combers, natives and Chinamen; about the island of Flatterers where the natives surrounded him and stroked him down, saying "Alofa," "love," and "You handsome man," "You all same as my father"; and about islands where the girls took away all his plug tobacco and picked his pocket of his match-box, and then with the utmost dignity gave him one match to light his cigarette. But the natives, he says, are always respectable, while some of the whites are degraded beyond description. Pembroke, in his "South Sea Bubbles" has scandalised all Polynesia by libelling the chieftainess of one island where he was very hospitably treated, and is said to have behaved very ill. I can easily understand getting very mixed up about Polynesian morals, for I feel that the subject is a deep one, and the best informed whites seem perplexed about it; but I remember how much poor Okakura was perplexed by the same subject in America, and how frankly La Farge and I avowed our own ignorance even among our own people. Stevenson is about to build a house, and says he shall never leave the island again, and cannot understand how any man who is able to live in the South Seas, should consent to live elsewhere.

October 22. Time runs on, bringing no great variety, but every day a little novelty to amuse us. I have taken to my water-colors again, because I find that La Farge will not paint unless I make-believe to do so. We sit in our native house, receiving visits; watching what goes on among the natives of the village; firing off our Kodaks at everything worth taking; and sketching the most commonplace object we can find, because the objects worth sketching are unsketchable. Every day I pick up more queer knowledge of the people about me — knowledge that would have made a great Professor of me twenty years ago, but now has no other value than to amuse me for the moment, and perhaps to amuse you some day when my wanderings end. Our great neighbor Mata-afa comes over to see us often, and sends us many fruits and eatables; but the most entertaining of his attentions is the *tafalo* which he sends every day. Usually at eleven o'clock we hear shouts from the further side of the village green, and instantly two splendid young men, dressed only in their waist-cloths — lavalavas — of green leaves, with garlands of green leaves round their heads, come running and jumping and shouting across the green towards our house. As they come near we see that their faces are blackened; sometimes one whole side is black, sometimes only a square or wedge-shaped patch at the corner of the mouth; and their look is ferocity itself; but they arrive in a broad laugh, and one of them carries a wooden trough, full of baked bread-fruit kneaded with cocoa-nut milk and generally a little salt-water, which he sets on the ground under our eaves, and then ladles out with his hands into large bread-fruit leaves, after which they bound away again. I can do no more than taste it, for it is a rich, pasty stuff, like corn-starch or batter; but the natives consider it a great treat; and yesterday Mele Samsoni and Fangalo and various other guests came to share Mata-afa's generosity. La Farge and I photographed the two men as they ladled out their *tafalo*; but I fear it will be a long time before I know how my photograph succeeded.... Remember that the photograph takes all the color, life and charm out of the tropics, and leaves nothing but a conventional hardness that might as well be Scotch or Yankee for all the truth it has. The women especially suffer, for they pose stiffly, and lose the freedom of movement and the play of feature that most attract us. The bare back of a Samoan woman, when she is in motion, is a joy forever. I never tire of watching the swing of their arms, and the play of light over the great round curves of their bodies. At this moment two of them are sitting on the mats by my side, Tagata — or Kanaka, as she calls it — is a giantess who lives with Mata-afa, either as his daughter or niece or wife, I cannot decide which; for Mata-afa is believed to have had so many wives that the world never knows which is the last. Tagata is as jolly as she is big, and talks a little English. Today her hair is powdered with lime to give it a proper red tone for a picnic we all attend tomorrow; she looks like a *marquise*, but instead of jewels in her hair, she has tied round her head a single reddish-purple ti-leaf, as classical as any Greek coin. Her face is not classic, but broad, good-natured and in its way rather fine. I have photographed her half a dozen times. On the whole the jolliest girl is Fangalo whose photograph I send to Hay. Fangalo and the two other girls at Samsoni's supply our house with flowers every morning, and generally the whole foreign population — English or American — is to be seen lounging on Samsoni's porch, or sprawling on mats in his enclosure, laughing with Mrs. Samsoni or Fangalo or the others.... Fanua is not handsome, but the photograph is peculiarly hard on her. When excited she is not without effectiveness, witness her Siva....

Day after tomorrow we start on a boat-journey along the coast to visit the chief towns. Seumano, our chief at Apia, escorts us in his boat, and is certain to make a great affair of it. He has already written ahead to prepare for our reception. We shall have *kawa*, roast pig, *tafalo*, Sivas and gifts wherever we go. Consul-General Sewall goes with us. Tonight we dine with the German Consul Stuebel. Tomorrow a big feast *chez* Papalii, the Samoan native chief justice.

To Anne Cabot Mills Lodge

SAMOA, October 21, 1890.

Two months have passed since I left your door, and I have been at least two years absent, if I can measure the time from the long months I have passed in seasickness and repining. Occasionally I get on shore for a week or two, and then I am quite happy except for dreading more sea. We arrived here a fortnight ago, and a fortnight hence we leave for Tahiti. Then we sail for the Marquesas. By that time I expect to be finished, and I shall probably decline to sail again anywhere, so you had better arrange to visit me in the Typee valley next summer, and bring Constance and the boys. I have discovered that the equator is the very place for cool summer weather, and I am unable to contemplate the terrors of returning to a warm climate.

Just now we have settled into a haven of rest under the wing of Consul-General Sewall, at whose table we make a joint household, while for our studio and state apartment we have a native house, shaped like a turtle, nearly forty feet long, and open all round, unless we choose to drop the mats. The floor is of coral stones covered with mats. We have introduced tables covered with tapa-cloth, and even the barbarous chair of your civilization. Bananas and oranges hang on the centre posts, cocoa-nut bottles and cups decorate our shelves. We are surrounded by other native houses and the native church, the sea laps the shore a few rods away, and the green is shaded by large breadfruit trees and cocoa-nut palms. Banana groves extend outside our village, and beyond the bananas is a forest more or less dense to the mountains. La Farge is sketching the sea, just behind him a big native woman, who has just walked in, adorned with a brilliant purple shirt and tapa waist-cloth, has seated herself and is watching him. We have just had a long morning visit from Mata-afa, the king whom the Germans set aside, and who lives in the house opposite us, about twenty yards off, in the middle of the village green. Natives in groups, usually without other clothes than their blue or red or yellow waist-cloths, pass continually along the path or road which skirts the beach, and their chocolate skins glow in the sun, against the surf-line of the coral reef outside. The whole thing is obviously a stage decoration, and I constantly expect to see the prima-donna, in green garlands and a girdle of ti-leaves, step out of Mata-afa's house, and begin to invoke the cuttle-fish or the shark, with a Wagnerian chorus of native maidens.

La Farge and I are school-boys on a lark. We have been as amused as though we were supernumeraries at the opera. Every day brings us some new variety of childhood's fables. Samoa is very little changed from what it was in pagan times. The Christianity is native, and differs little from the native paganism except that more customs are kept secret. I am not sure but that if we stayed here a few months anywhere except in Apia, we should be obliged, in order to maintain our dignity as chiefs of America, to take wives and contract alliances with neighboring chiefs. The relation need not be permanent, and our partners at our departure would be regarded with great respect and would probably marry native missionaries instead of pining for us. As far as the women are concerned I am confident the alliance would be eagerly welcomed, and, as far as I am concerned, I admit that I have seen a fair number of women who would by no means discredit the situation. Of course our high standard of morals and the approaching arrival of our steamer will prevent us from entering into arrangements justly repugnant to the habits of American society, but as high chiefs, and guests of chiefs, we ought to do it, according to Samoan standards, if only as a testimony of sympathy with the people. Every married woman here, after a few years residence with her husband, returns to her father with half the children, and lives as she likes. I think the custom will commend itself at once to New York society, not to mention that of Washington.

We have plunged deep into Polynesian customs, in conversation at least. Once a day I pump all the information out of at least one Samoan chief, and it is great fun. Owing to their familiarity with our frigate, the "Adams," the natives caught on to me at once as a great man, and Sewall has cultivated the illusion. We are the first Americans who ever travelled here for pleasure, without a business object, and this singularity confirms the simple native in his view of us. I am rejoiced to find, for the first time in my life, that my name is worth something to me, but the natives are solid aristocrats to a man, and they evidently know a swell when they see one. The credit is theirs, not that of my respectable ancestors, who would think me a worse savage than the Polynesian.

Our European rival, Robert Louis Stevenson, lives in the hills and forest, where he cannot rival us in social gaiety. We have been to see him, and found him, as he declared, very well. I should need to be extremely well to live the life he has led and is still leading, but a Scotchman with consumption can defy every fatigue and danger. His place is, as he says, "full of Rousseaus," meaning picturesque landscapes. I saw no Rousseaus, the day being unfavorable, but I saw a very dirty board cabin, with a still dirtier man and woman in it, in the middle of several hundred burned tree-stumps. Both the man and woman were lively, and in their respective ways, amusing, but they did not seem passionately eager for constant association with us, and poor Stevenson can't talk and write too. He naturally prefers writing.

Please do not let my remarks get beyond the family. The Polynesians are like all other maniacs. Every remark about them comes back and makes trouble. In these vast ocean spaces a whisper echoes like W. W. Phelps's voice, and causes earthquakes. As we have already offended every white man within sight of our track since leaving New York, we would not further rouse a spirit of revenge. Let it be enough that we have become Samoans in spirit and only abstain from adopting their dress and habits out of pure moral conviction that the Congregational Church is the only safe guide in those matters. I do not doubt that Stevenson is like ourselves, only more Presbyterian.

I mean to enclose some photographs if I can get them, to show what is the matter with us; but remember that the photograph takes all the fun out of the tropics. Especially it vulgarises the women, whose charm is chiefly in their size and proportions, their lines, the freedom of their movements, the color of their skin, and their good-natured smile. Sometimes though rarely they have also straight noses and fine faces, but generally the face is thought of less consequence than the form and scale. The young men are superb, and in their leaf garlands look like fauns. The scenery is also spoiled by photographing. The softness of lights and colors, the motion of the palms, the delicacy and tenderness of the mornings and evenings, the moisture of the atmosphere, and all the other qualities which charm one here, are not to be put into a photograph, which simply gives one conventional character to New England and Samoa alike. Now New England is not alike.

I am not quite so sure about Tahiti after all. La Farge threatens to stay here if his letters permit. I ask no better. In that case we shall not reach Tahiti much before January. Still you had better write to me to the care of the American Consul at Tahiti. You will not get this letter before December, and your reply cannot reach Tahiti before February. I cannot at the earliest leave Tahiti before that time. Probably I may be there or at the Marquesas an indefinite time, for the seasick mariner does not easily find conveyances in those regions and time is the most common of all commodities there. I do not yet allow myself to look ahead, but the further I go, the more I am appalled by the horrors of the journey back, and its increasing length.

We start in three days on a malanga, or coasting trip along the islands. Seumano, the chief of Apia, escorts us with his swell boat, the gift of our Government. We are to have feasts and dances at all the chief villages, and shall receive gifts.

My love to Constance[1] and all yours. Tell Constance that the native girls here are rather in her style. Ever yours.

[1] Daughter of Henry Cabot Lodge and later Mrs. Augustus Peabody Gardner (1865–1918).

To Elizabeth Cameron

IVA IN SAVAII, 26 October, 1890.

If you consult my Stieler's atlas, you may — or may not — find
the island of Savaii at the west end of the Samoan group. Iva can
hardly be more than twenty miles in a direct line from Apia; but it is,
or should be, about five hundred in time. Our adventures have not
been startling, but varied.

We left Apia at two o'clock Friday afternoon, October 24. Do not
be bothered by Friday not being the 24th; it's a way we have here.
Our outfit was royal. We took our own boat with five men for our
traps and extraordinary needs, while Sewall, La Farge and I, with
Awoki and our boy-interpreter, Charley, a half white, embarked with
Seumano on his beautiful American boat, the gift of our government,
and rowed out with a crew of ten men, and the flag of Samoa. When
we caught the trade wind, we hoisted our sails, and for the next three
hours ran along the shore of Upolo, the middle island, in smooth water, the fringing coral reef on our right, half a mile away, and on our
left the beautiful mountains of Upolo. The afternoon was exquisite,
and the colors divine; we had no cares, except that La Farge complains much of feeling seasick and weak; and Seumano reclined his
huge bulk in the stern of the boat, with an inimitable air of unconsciousness that time, space or thought exists.... The crew sings all
kinds of songs, chiefly historical and local, and I am becoming quite
attached to Samoan songs. They have sometimes a certain amount
of melody and lilt which, except at two o'clock in the morning, I can
hear with some enjoyment.

At about four o'clock we landed, supposing we were to pass the
night, but we had only a banana-leaf spread, after the somewhat
cocoa-nut oily cooking of the natives. I make frightful efforts to eat
the food, and do rather better at it than either Sewall or La Farge, for
the food itself is excellent; but Papalii's big feast of Thursday rather
upset me, especially two hundred and forty-seven cold roast pigs of
every possible size, which were brought in, greasy and black, in the
arms, or on the shoulders, of half-naked natives, and piled in a huge
mass on the grass in the rain. After that my appetite for native cooking was slow to recover, but I made heroic efforts to play-pretend, and
tried one thing after another to please our hosts. We broke up the
feast early to call on the Père Gavet, a French missionary priest, whose
church, or what remains of it after the hurricane, stood hard by. The
Père received us with evident pleasure, and La Farge did the talking.

Then we took boat again, and rowed three miles further, to a town called Satapuala. Just at dusk we drew up to the long white beach, and as we landed our baggage the darkness came on, and the moon began to glow. We bathed in the warm ocean, with its floor of white sand, as charmingly as though we were not afraid of all sorts of sharp animals supposed to be hastening to seize our toes. Then we stepped across a fringe of palms and creepers, and found ourselves on a sandy green, or greeny sand, with several native houses, of the usual turtle-back shape, scattered about. One of these was brightly lighted, and as we entered it, we found that it had been charmingly decorated with palm leaves and flowers, for our reception. A gigantic young chief received us. An equally gigantic young woman, the chief's sister, also received us, she being the *taupo*, or village maiden. They were of very high family, children of a former king. His name was Saipaia; hers was Leolofi. They received us with the same grave dignity which we meet everywhere, and immediately the long banana leaves were spread on the floor, and the invariable bread-fruit, taro, chickens, pigeons and combinations of cocoa-nut, with mullet and smaller fish, all cold, and cooked, I believe, in oil, when roasted in their furnaces of hot stones, were set before us, with the usual apology for poverty, and excuses about "befo' the war." We sat down, cross-legged if possible, and eat, or pretended to eat; and when eating was decently performed, we chiefs drew back and smoked, while the village dignitaries took their turn, and the lower people with the children looked in from outside.

October 27.... The feast at Satapuala having been disposed of, the floor was cleared, and the Siva began. It differed little from Seumano's Siva in Apia, as far as the scene was concerned, but in other ways the difference was great. Except Leolofi, no woman danced. All the dancers were men, and, among them, Saipaia took the chief's part. I tried hard to admire his performances, but without much success. Some of the figures were interesting, and in some cases the dance became actual acting, and in its way amusing, but it is hard to keep up a mere historical interest in jumping and making faces. Leolofi was splendid — something like a Titanic cow, such as Zeus had a fancy for — but her style was rather that of calm indifference than of action, and as a dancer her motions and poses were rather languid, a bar or so behind time. They kept it up till midnight, and we might have gone on all night, in which case we should have had the wilder and more undress performances that are no longer given in missionary circles; but we were tired, and so were the dancers, and we broke it up at twelve o'clock. The moon was superb, and La Farge and I strolled on the beach, watching the wonderful combination of clouds, calm sea, and white beach, all running into each other, as though a water-color artist of unlimited capacity had painted the scene with careful exclusion of all apparent difficulties. La Farge is fond of describing the peculiarity of the Polynesian world in this way. Sky, sea and land are all judicious water-colors, toned with one general purplish wash with the most exquisitely delicate gradations, but never running into violent contrasts. Even the whites have an infinite gradation of violets, when contrasted with the dead white of a ship or a house.

Saturday morning, after a swim in the ocean, we bade farewell to our host and hostess, to whom I made my usual present of ten dollars; and then, taking boat, we rowed along passing the end of our Upolo island, and crossing a strait a mile wide to the little island of Manono where we landed at a village called Faleu, on the southernmost point. The spot was so picturesque that, as soon as we were established in our house, we got our water-colors out to paint the opposite shore of Upolo with its extinct crater-mountain, and the marvellous green water of the strait between. A heavy rain soon wiped out our greens, and we tried to paint the greys. The village gathered about and watched us, and I tried to draw the children. Naturally all my painting was childish, but I hope I induced La Farge to catch something worth keeping. Suddenly we were interrupted by a delegation from the neighboring villages bringing food in palm baskets. At their head came two huge young men, with clubs, crowned with garlands, and girt with green leaves. At almost twenty paces distance they stopped and performed a fantastic comic dance to the great amusement of the village, throwing their clubs in the air, and catching them, and acting a mock fight. When they finished, the orator, or *tulafale*, came forward: an old man leaning on a staff, who looked bewilderingly Homeric, and made a long speech, enumerating a number of things unintelligible to us. All this little scene was classic to a point quite beyond belief. I could imagine Seumano to be Ajax, and we his companions. He sat lazily, with his huge bulk, by my side, repeating in a low voice what the orator was going to say, and at the end merely thanking them in one word. Then they all disappeared and the day went on, with intervals of *kava*, food, and a walk half way round the island. In the evening the villagers gave us a Siva which I thought extremely good. The island is very remote from white men, and is famous for its success in war. The dance-songs were all local and mostly war-like. The girls were good-looking, well-made, and extremely well-dressed in leaves and flowers; they wore only their old, native, Siva dress, bare to the waist, with

strings of red, coral-like berries hanging to their necks and half covering their breasts. The *taupo*, or village maiden, was a very young girl,
quite small, who was evidently not up to her position, and her married
sister, the ex-taupo, did the real work. When the girls were tired, they
came over and sat among us, and the young men danced. They did it
extremely well, but we were exhausted with want of sleep, and could
not keep our eyes open. At ten o'clock we stopped the dance, I fear
rather discourteously. La Farge and I strolled in the wonderful moonlight along the sandy road, in the black shadow of the palms, with the
native houses glimmering in the moonlight, and the surf rolling over
the coral reef half a mile away. The natives passed us with an *alofa* or
a *tofà*, or stopped to try to say a word of English; and a splendid young
chief, who had danced for us as grotesquely as a village clown, came
by, with a silver-headed cane marking rank I suppose, and stopped to
receive our thanks with the same grave and rather sad dignity which
seems to mark most of the greatest chiefs. In all this I was most
struck by the absence of anything suggesting impropriety. I rather
expected drunken orgies. I find that *kava* is about as intoxicating as
lager-beer, and as for the women, I might marry any of them, and divorce them as easily as in America; but they are the most valuable of
the village possessions; I must have a long courtship through third-
parties; I must pay two or three hundred dollars; and I must be the
prey of all my wife's family as long as I live. As for common women, I
do not doubt that a common man could have as many of them as he
wanted; but we are great chiefs, and we can't even approach a common woman. We must sustain our rank. We could marry and send
away a dozen wives in succession, if we liked, without loss of character
to them or to us, and any *taupo* in Samoa would be glad to marry us on
these terms; but we could not possibly get such a girl on any other
terms without committing what is regarded as the worst possible theft
on the whole village and clan. We should be obliged to make repara-
tion, not to the girl but to the village. So far from the girls being loose
livers, all the best are not only well behaved but are carefully watched
and guarded. You may imagine that our respectability is safer here
than anywhere in civilised lands.

   Our severest day thus far was yesterday. We left Manono at seven
o'clock in a native boat, paddled by a native crew, while our own boats
escorted us. We were to visit the little island of Apollima, which is
nothing but a volcano's crater, sticking up in the ocean a mile west of
Manono. The volcano was long since extinct, but one side of the crater
is open to the sea through a narrow break in the coral, and the heavy

ocean swell rushes and foams in and out of the little harbor through this passage just broad enough to admit a boat with paddles. To get there, we had to leave the protection of the great coral reef within which we had sailed till then all the way from Apia, and to trust ourselves in a light whaleboat to the full sweep of the trade wind. Luckily a mile is not more than infinity. Just as I was becoming uncomfortable with the tossing of the boat on the big waves, we reached the dark cliffs of lava and turned into the channel. For two minutes I forgot to be seasick. We were swept on the foaming and roaring surf directly on the coral rock till we fended off with poles, and then, paddling hard, the crew forced the boat round a corner and into a cove where we were soon dragged and swept into quiet water. The men carried us ashore on their backs, and I felt as though I would never like to get away faster than I came, for the idea of being shut up there a week or two by a sudden storm, was dispiriting. The old crater was occupied by a dozen native houses of the poorer class, whose only wealth seemed to be a few cocoa-nut trees. Sewall climbed to the top of the island. As I have seen ocean enough, I sat in the missionary's hut and drank a cocoa-nut till I was tired, and returned to the beach. We stayed only an hour or so, and then put out again. The exit looked more difficult than the entrance, but I was surprised to find that after a moment of rush through foaming surf, we were again tossing outside without sign of violent exertion. We had far more trouble in getting on board Seumano's boat, but we tumbled in at last, without tumbling overboard, and spread our sails for Iva in Savaii, four miles to the westward. We were three quarters of an hour only before getting within the fringing reef into calm water, and we were comparatively free from seasickness, but I do not like open boats in the middle of the Pacific, with the trade wind blowing fresh, and a good deal of sea. We escaped with a drenching and some amusement. Drenching in warm water and warm air matters little; but we were glad to land at last, among friends, and I sat all day cross-legged, receiving village chiefs, making speeches and drinking *kava*, glad to watch dreamily the children playing, the old men talking, and the palms rustling above.

October 28. Yesterday was a great day for the American *ali*; especially for the *ali* Atamu, who is not a little surprised to find that Seumano has attributed to him the distinction of this great *malanga* or boat excursion. We seized the morning to rest, for we were all used up, dyspeptic and sleepy. Our repose was broken after lunch. At about two o'clock our host, the *ali* Selu, who is a rather European or missionary Samoan and talks English, took us to a house on the village green, and seated us there, cross-legged, to receive the chiefs. The day was fine, all the women and children, and some men, were scattered about, to see the show, which was like the reception of the Prince of Wales when I was young and serious. Such affairs are rare here, and the people enjoy the fun. There we sat for two or three hours, till my back and legs ached as much as my head did. Whatever we came to Samoa for, we got it this time. Everything was shown us. First, we had a military review and sham fight. The whole military strength of the village, about two hundred men, dressed in their most barbaric leaves, feathers and flowers led by their *taupo*, or village maiden, and all armed with clubs, big bush-knives, and Snyder rifles which they fired at frequent intervals, showed us a battle in which the shouting, leaping, running, and confusion proved how incompetent the Parisian stage managers must be. For a fantastic exhibition of Polynesian savagery or barbaric fun, I want to see nothing better. Then all sat down, and the *tulafale*, or orator, rising in the centre, about sixty yards from us, made a speech, leaning on his long staff, with arms crossed. Our chief, Selu, then replied for us. Then the gifts were collected which had been thrown; yams, *taro*, and several small pigs which squeaked and kicked Homerically. Then the dance began: first, the girls, then the men, and lastly four very small girls, who went through it all with the precocity commonly attributed to American children. Neither men, women nor children showed the smallest idea of a distinction between what was beautiful and what was not. Like the Japanese they gave exquisite charm of posture, song and movement alternately with clownish grimacing and jumping, and the one seemed as natural to them as the other. I saw very little grossness and no indecency, though the costumes were simple enough, and neither men nor women were likely to be shocked. Probably the missionaries are responsible for the propriety, for Iva is rather a missionary stronghold, and I never saw a more curious contrast than at suppertime, when each hut was brightly lighted by its fire, and from every hut came the singing of an evening hymn, which sounded to me very like a Siva song. During the show, I toiled over my Kodak, and took thirty or forty views, none of which I expect to find successful, but which, even if only one turns out well, may help La Farge to paint a Siva picture. After two or three hours of this display we had an interval for supper. The sun set with an afterglow like extravagant painting; the moon rose with a full flood of violet light; and we started in for a new Siva at eight o'clock with only the light of the fire, fed by dry palm leaves, to show the dancers. The firelight is most picturesque, but a bit warm for the tropics. My head ached, and my back ached worse. I was sleepy and weary of savagery for the moment. Yet the sitting dance of the girls charmed me as much as ever, and I think I find it more beautiful now than I did when I first saw it with such delight at our little haven in Tutuila. La Farge still avers that Sivà was more charming than any other girl we have met, but we have met so many that a law is risky that excludes competition so much at large. We had four *taupo*, past and present, sitting with us last night, and they gave us rings and *tapa* mats. We were all kissed, or had our noses rubbed in the afternoon dance....

October 29. The next morning, as soon as the wind rose, we bade good-bye to Iva, and walked about three miles, along the shore to Papalii, the home of the Malietoas. We were received with the usual form by eight or ten chiefs who were mere imitations of Ajax and Odysseus, and who sat round the guest-house exchanging solemn speeches with us, until my eyes could not keep open. Luckily Malietoa's niece, Aenga, "the first lady of the land," was there, and, as was her duty, devoted herself to entertain us. Aenga is a big, good-natured girl, a little too negresque, but bright in her way and extremely sympathetic. Nothing could be more touching than the way in which she rolls up her cigarettes and smokes them, occasionally spitting with great neatness and accuracy; but she does not care for my pipe. On this occasion she sat in the chief's place and presided, while another girl made the *kava*, and a third, by hereditary right, passed round the cup. We went through our speeches, and a rather palatable cup of sago, I think, and swallowed our *kava*, but cut the feast, and stretched ourselves on the floor of our house where Aenga entertained us while we napped. In the afternoon we had another *talofo*, or military reception, with Malietoa's black assassins in the place of distinction....

October 30. We left Aenga on her hillside, looking over a stage-blue sea, and drinking cocoa-nuts or sucking oranges or smoking cigarettes, to reflect on the fortune which had caused her grandmother to be noosed by one of the old Malietoas who had hidden himself in the top of a tree to waylay beautiful *taupo* passing along the path beneath — whence came Aenga as well as Melietoa Laupepa, the king now recognised by our various governments. Our path was equally strewn with *taupo*. After another walk of an hour through a long succession of native houses scattered under the cocoa-nut trees close by the waterside, we came to Safotulafai, the town of the great chief Lauati. Here we had another grand reception, a dozen chiefs sitting about the large guest-house, which was charmingly decorated with green vines and hybiscus flowers. Two stout, good-natured *taupo* were present, and sat with us on chairs at one end of the house, and led us to the feast afterwards, spread out on banana leaves under an awning outside. Lauati himself looks like Herbert Wadsworth. He is a great orator and a man of the highest social and political influence. Evidently he laid himself out to make our reception impressive, although I do not think the afternoon military display, big as it was, quite equalled that at Iva.... Seumano then brought us back to the guest-house where we found the *taupo* Fa-auli, Lauati's daughter, and while she prepared sugar-cane for us to chew, we lay about her on the mats and babbled. Suddenly someone remarked that Fa-auli was going to make an evening prayer, and she began with a long impromptu missionary address, very prettily delivered, alluding, as I could make out, to us and our *malanga*, and closing by the Lord's prayer and a long hymn. The next moment the dancers, in full barbaric nakedness, came in — four men — and sat down on the mats. The evening Siva then began by the light of the burning palm leaves, which in the strong breeze, threw out flames and flying embers across the house, and made my sleepy eyes smart with smoke. I was too drowsy to care much for the dancing until Fa-auli appeared, but I really wish you could have seen her. She danced for some two hours, more or less, and I came gradually to the opinion that she lay a good bit over any dancer I had seen. She wore a dress rather more scanty than usual; indeed she had only a black cloth about ten inches wide, ornamented, I think, with beads or color of some kind, and showing the outline of the hip on one side, like a Parisian opera dancer except that this was the real thing, and made our ballets seem preposterous. Fa-auli's figure was splendidly full, round and firm, though her legs were large. Glistening with cocoa-nut oil, she stood out against the rich brown of the background like an ivory image of Benvenuto's. Her movements were large and free, full of strength; sometimes agile as a cat's, as when she imitated a rat and swung on the cross-beam; sometimes divinely graceful, as when she imitated ball-playing, or splashed imitation water over companions in bathing, or waved her hands about in the thousand movements of the regular sitting Siva. I never had fully understood how little mere beauty of face had to do with beauty itself until I saw what a houri Fa-auli became the moment she showed her form; and the contrast was all the more startling when presently she and her companion *taupo*, tired, came over, and sitting down by us, said quietly that they were no longer in the church.[1] To amuse us, they, like Aenga, had sacrificed themselves....

[1] The missionaries excommunicated members who should participate in forbidden dances.

To Elizabeth Cameron

·VAIALE (SAMOA), 8 November, 1890

·   ·   ·   ·   ·   ·   ·   ·   ·   ·   ·   ·   ·   ·   ·

Stevenson returned our call the other day, and passed several hours with us. He was cleaner, and his wife was not with him, for which reasons perhaps he seemed less like W——E——. He talked very well, as usual, but said nothing that stuck very hard. He will tell his experiences in the form of Travels, and I was rather surprised to find that his range of study included pretty much everything: geology, sociology, laws, politics and ethnology. We like him, but he would be, I think, an impossible companion. His face has a certain beauty, especially the eyes, but it is the beauty of disease. He is a strange compound of callousness and susceptibility, and his susceptibility is sometimes more amusing than his callousness. We were highly delighted with one trait which he showed in absolute unconsciousness of its simplicity. The standard of domestic morality here is not what is commonly regarded as rigid. Most of the traders and residents have native wives, to whom they are married after the native custom: that is, during pleasure. A clerk in the employ of an American trader named Moors was discovered in too close relations with the native wife of a lawyer named Carruthers. The offence was condoned once, and this lenity seemed very proper to Stevenson, who declared that he had no difficulty in forgiving his wife once, but not a second time. Recently the scandal was renewed, and caused great tribulation. Stevenson was deeply outraged, and declared that he would no longer dine with Moors for fear of meeting the clerk. Moors, who has had various wives to say nothing of incidental feminine resources, was also scandalized, and dismissed the clerk, though the clerk was indispensable to his business. Carruthers was painfully saddened. The woman's father, an old native, was worst of all. I have not yet learned the views of Mrs. Stevenson; but we are curious to know why, in the light of their own experience, they could not have suggested the easy device of advising Carruthers to let his wife go, and allowing the clerk to marry her. The unfortunate clerk is the victim of outraged Samoan morality, and is to be sent back to San Francisco where the standard is, I presume, less exalted. This part of Stevenson's talk was altogether the most humorous, and as grotesque as the New Arabian Nights; but Stevenson was not in the least conscious of our entertainment.

Samoa becomes more curious, in this sort of grotesqueness, the more one sees of it. The sexual arrangements are queer enough, and the stories of old Samsoni, or Hamilton, formerly pilot, harbor-master, American Vice Consul, and what not, amuse me beyond description, though they are rarely capable of record. In my last letter, somewhere, I may have mentioned Taele, a native woman who keeps a supervision of our native house. Taele is still young; hardly more than twenty; and unusually pretty. Her prettiness so attracted a recent British Consul, that he married her, after Samoan custom, and she was known as his wife. They had a child, a handsome boy, now five or six years old, who lives with our old village chief To-fai, close by our sleeping-quarters, and is inseparable from the old man. A couple of years ago or thereabouts, the Consul was ordered elsewhere, and went, leaving Taele with a small pension and the hope of his return. Taele waited for him dutifully until she despaired of his return, and then she married a native carpenter who had been a missionary teacher. Very recently I learned from Mele Samsoni that the second husband had gone off to another province and had taken another wife. Taele quietly remains here, much respected and very interesting in the melancholy style of some Samoan beauty; but she is scared into the forest because I want her to serve as a model to draw from. She cannot endure the idea of being painted, even in full dress, covered up to the ears, and is in deadly terror because I wanted her to wear the *lavalava*, or waist-cloth, which every native habitually carries. Yet I have no doubt that Taele will have another husband soon.

In other ways the natives are more inscrutable. Chiefly for want of something to talk about during the interminable visits of native chiefs, I ask questions about the old customs, families and religion. Three times out of four, when I reach any interesting point, I am blocked by the reply that what I ask is a secret. At first I thought that this was only a way of disguising ignorance, but was assured that it was not so. I am pretty well convinced that all matters involving their old superstitions, priesthood, and family history, are really secret, and that their Christianity covers a pretty complete paganism with priests and superstitions as strong as ever. Indeed, To-fai made no bones of telling me, at great length, the whole story, and on his information I have in several cases surprised other chiefs into admissions that they did not intend to make; but I am still convinced that the Samoans have an entire intellectual world of their own, and never admit outsiders into it. I feel sure that they have a secret priesthood more powerful than the political chiefs, with supernatural powers, invocations, prophecy, charms, and the whole paraphernalia of paganism. I care too little about these matters to make any searching inquiry, so they may keep their secrets for anything I shall do; but I never imagined a race so docile and gentle, yet so obstinately secret. They never killed a missionary, but they are just masters in playing the missionaries off. The chiefs especially detest the missionary teachers, who are all common people of no social rank, and who have mostly chosen to become teachers in order to get a position of any kind, which can be done only by undermining the power of the chiefs....

Our lunch today was only remarkable for my having at last tasted *pollolo*, a Samoan delicacy of the repulsive order. The *pollolo* is a curious salt-water worm, or long thin creature like a very slim earthworm; it appears only once a year, just at dawn, at a certain place on the coral reef opposite our Consulate. As the day happened about ten days ago, we all went out to see the show, starting at four o'clock with the first light of dawn. As we bumped and hauled over the coral, we could gradually see a dozen or more boats, mostly the narrow native dug-outs, about a distant spot near the outer, or barrier reef. When we came up, we joined them, and, peering into the water, with the growing light, we could at last see one or two long, thin, thread-like creatures swimming near the surface. They had some sense akin to sight, for when I tried to catch them with my hand, they swam away. At last I caught one, and as I looked at him in the hollow of my hand, the little wretch kicked himself in pieces, and I had half a dozen little kicking earwigs in my hand. The same thing happened in the water. As the day dawned, the creatures became thicker, but each soon divided into inch- or half-inch sections, and the top of the water soon swarmed with things, which the boat-people caught with fine hand-nets, or sieves, and turned into pails. Nothing seems to be known of the creature, or why he should come on one particular day of the year, at certain, far distant spots, for an hour before dawn, and should disappear at sunrise. The water was but two or three feet deep on the coral rock, and the creature has ample motive power to come out or go in as he likes, but he comes and goes only by the calendar. The natives eat them raw; but to keep the luxury longer, they cook it with cocoa-nut meat, pounded, and Fatuleia brought some of it for lunch; a greenish, pasty stuff, like fine spinach. I tried it on bread, and thought it rather like *foie-gras*....

November 21. Yesterday Seumano had his great feast for his little daughter, "The Bush sheltering from the Wind." The crowd was immense, some two thousand people, mostly a mass of brown backs, and garlanded heads. Three hundred and fifteen pigs were immolated on the occasion, and Seu's house was like a shop, full of gifts of *tapa*, bottles of beer and drink of various kinds hung from the roof, umbrellas, fine mats, and what not. My present was my usual ten dollars in gold, which I would have made twenty except from the fear of being ostentatious. About a dozen or fifteen *taupo* were there, some from Savaii, some from the opposite end of this island, Upolo, all in a house by themselves, dressed in the *taupo* style, some *fa Samoa* without other covering than their *siapas* or fine mats round their waists, others horribly *fagotées* in paper tinsel and silk or cheap satin bodies. Of course they were dripping with cocoa-nut oil, and my right hand became saturated from handshaking. Some of them were prettily decorated. One had powdered her hair with the small purple and white petals of a flower, which stuck on, either with cocoa-nut oil or gum. They commonly wore necklaces of the red pepper, like coral. Some wore bodies of braided purple *ti* leaves, looking like armored fish. Some were quite handsome, and had fine figures, but none of them seemed to me equal to Leolofi or Fa-auli....

November 22. While I was writing, Fatuleia sent an invite for the afternoon to another dance. She had been disgusted by the crowd of the day before, and wanted us to be better treated. After lunch we went in our boat to Seumano's, and were asked to come into his house. This was a distinction, for, at the time, a curious family meeting was going on there, which we were glad to see. Seumano's relations sat on one side of the house, and Fatuleia's on the other. Between them, a woman was spreading one fine mat after another, yesterday's gifts to Vao, "The Bush" etc. One or two of the mats were very old, and quite in tatters; one or two were very fine; all were jewels in Samoan eyes; and after each was shown, murmurs of "good" rose among the audience. The woman showed all, and announced at the close that thirty fine mats and two thousand *tapa* had been given. Then we were politely dismissed and the family turned to the task of redistributing the fine mats among each other, for a gift in Samoa has always to be returned in equivalent, and the task is one of great delicacy. Naturally every one expects to receive something more than he gave, and, as this is impossible, the less favored betray their displeasure in open complaints. I should have liked to see this part of the affair, but old John Adams, in the most high-bred, aristocratic English, sent us off to see the dances, and we went.... When the dancers were all tired, we were allowed to go, and on our way home we went with Mele Samsoni to call on the *taupo* of Fangaloa, a town at the east end of this island, where we mean to go next week, on another boat excursion. Our call was duly formal. We carried two tins of canned salmon and five loaves of bread, as the regular gift of the occasion. We found the handsome *taupo* receiving. Three good-looking girls were making *kava*, and for the first time in my experience the *kava* was chewed, not grated, which is supposed to improve it. Our present was graciously received, and immediately divided, more than half of it being given, rather to my disgust, to a chief from Savaii who was also making a call. I gave the *taupo* a cigar, which she lighted, and five minutes afterwards I saw my cigar in the mouth of another man, while my girl returned to her cigarette. This is the fate of every gift, except money, and for that reason I prefer to give money, for I do not like seeing my umbrellas, silk scarfs, gowns, cigars, etc., parading about town on strangers; and they are sure to pass through a score of hands, in this communistic society, before they are lost from sight. In return for our present, we received some of the usual eatables in a basket, which Mele Samsoni received for us, and presently politely returned, much to my relief, at learning that I was at liberty to disembarrass myself of these troublesome gifts....

One never, or almost never, sees a tall figure which is thin or weak, or a short figure disproportionately stout. All are evenly developed, and differ chiefly in the tendency to be thick and heavy in details. After sixteen they coarsen rapidly, and lose their firmness of figure. Both Fa-asei and Puipui were taken by me for married women who had children, till I was assured to the contrary. By-the-bye, Samsoni reassures me as to the probable first cost of a *taupo* wife. In pigs and mats, she would come higher, in apparent price, than in coin. Cash-down, in Chilian silver dollars, Samsoni thinks that a hundred dollars would be sufficient. This is about seventy dollars in gold. Dog-cheap, as far as the gift is concerned; but unfortunately the family expects further to share all one's possessions, and the wife often runs away to her father in order to extort a double dowry for her connections. Indeed the tie between father and daughter is stronger, through life, than that between husband and wife. As I expect to sail for Tahiti in three weeks, I will wait and see whether I cannot do better there....

We are already old Polynesians. Probably every chief on the islands knows all about us, and would be glad to have us for guests. Hereabouts we are adopted acquaintances with every man and child. As I stroll to my dinner at seven o'clock, in the dusk, I am greeted by half the dim figures that pass me, with a *Tofà, Atamou*, though I can reply only *Tofà*, for I cannot even see them, much less call them by name. *Tofà* is Good-night; Good-bye, Sleep well, or whatever you please at parting, as *Alofa* is a similar greeting. *Akámou*, or *Akámu*, is *Atámu*,

Adam, for the natives interchange *k* with *t* in all their words, spelling with a *t*, but pronouncing *k*. It is regarded as a vulgarism, but is nearly universal, and very ancient. *Akamu* is my native name, and is becoming more familiar to me than my own. La Farge's native name is La-fa-el-e, which he likes because it happens to be identical with Rafaele, the *l* and *r* being also interchangeable, or rather, the *r* being almost unpronounceable with Samoans.... The old women and the young chiefs rarely come near us. They dislike white men because the girls like them and prefer to marry them. The old chiefs are on the girls' side, and dislike only missionary influence. Even there, they are hostile chiefly to the native teachers, and because native missionaries are hostile to them. The few white missionaries are becoming liberal, and there is almost a breach between them and the mass of native teachers. Seumano's great feast the other day was an æra in this matter, for the leading white missionaries, for the first time, publicly looked on at the *Siva*, which was a formal abandonment of their old attitude. I am relieved at this concession, for it prevents an open quarrel between us white laymen and the white clergy; but it forebodes a desperate struggle with the native teachers, who are a low caste, struggling to retain power.

If we could get rid of the native teachers and substitute trained sanitary inspectors, Samoa would be vastly benefited. The Samoans suffer chiefly from sores, which are very slow to heal in this climate, and their own medical practice is that of the old women. They take cold as we do, and their colds are almost as severe. I am rather surprised to find them complain of head-aches, for they live chiefly on fruits and vegetables or fish. My chief, To-fai, an elderly man of the highest rank, and a redoubtable warrior, has had a very severe cold and head-ache for several days. Yesterday I dosed him with quinine. He was well enough to let me ask him questions for two hours, which implies strength at least, for the Samoans easily weary of any effort, especially intellectual; but I was asking about subjects which are *saa* to the common people, and *vavao*, or forbidden, except among the highest and most courageous chiefs, who can afford to disregard their rules. I asked much, too, about their *a-itu* or spirits, ghosts and devils, of which they have a plenty, though commonplace enough. To-fai is an *esprit fort*, but my coxswain, Sa-mao, who is himself a chief of good rank, was charmingly childlike in his good faith. There is a devil that haunts the road at a river-ford about a mile beyond us, and howls at night, or appears as a large beast of various characters, and I tried hard to get Sa-mao to take me to see him, but Sa-mao admitted he had himself never seen an *a-itu*. Samsoni has a pretty good ghost story of his own, but chiefly for his queer, abrupt way of telling it; and it was evidently a case of native terrorism to drive him out of some property....

To Elizabeth Cameron

5.30 A.M. November 27, 1890.

· · · · · · · · · · · · · · ·

We have seen much of Stevenson these last few days, and I must say no more in ridicule, for he has been extremely obliging, and given me very valuable letters of introduction to Tahiti and the Marquesas. He has amused and interested us, too, and greatly by his conversation. Last evening he came at five o'clock, and brought his wife to dine with us. Their arrival was characteristic. He appeared first, looking like an insane stork, very warm and very restless. I was not present, and the reception fell on little Mrs. Parker, who is as delicate and fragile as Stevenson, but as quiet and gentle as a flower. Presently Mrs. Stevenson in a reddish cotton nightgown, staggered up the steps, and sank into a chair, gasping and unable to speak. Stevenson hurried to explain that she was overcome by the heat and the walk. Might she lie down? Mrs. Parker sacrificed her own bed, and gave her some cognac. Stevenson says that his wife has some disease, I know not what, of a paralytic nature, and suffers greatly from its attacks. I know only that when I arrived soon afterwards, I found her on the piazza chatting with Mrs. Parker, and apparently as well and stalwart as any other Apache squaw. Stevenson then devoted an hour to me, very kindly, and was astonishingly agreeable, dancing about, brandishing his long arms above his head, and looking so attenuated in the thin flannel shirt which is his constant wear, that I expected to see him break in sections, like the *pollolo*. He has an infinite experience to draw upon, and to my great relief is not a Presbyterian, but is as little missionary as I am. His sufferings here as a farmer are his latest fund for humor, and he described, with bounds of gesticulation, how he had just bought two huge farm horses, and stabled them in a native house near his; and how at midnight, in a deluge of rain and a gale of wind, he had heard unearthly howls from the stable, and had ventured out with a lantern. As he approached, by the glimmer of the light, he became aware of two phantom excrescences protruding from the stable roof. These were his horses' heads, which, after eating off the roof of the house, were wildly tossing in the storm, while the legs and bodies were inconceivably mixed up, inside. I have stopped to eat a mango, which Stevenson says is a stimulant almost as strong as fluid extract of coco. I hope it is, for I have then a reason for liking them....

Enough of Stevenson. His stories are not for me to tell, and towards eleven o'clock, we summoned our boat crew, and sent him back by water, in the moonlight to Apia. We may never see him again, for he talks of going to Auckland next week, and some day I suppose we too shall go away somewhere. Our parting last night, on the beach, in the Samoan moonlight, was appropriate, and my last distinct vision of his wife was her archaic figure in the arms of my coxswain, trying to get her legs — or feet — over the side of my boat....

LE-PA, *December* 4. The most interesting part of our experience at Aleipata was the old chief who entertained us royally, and made us rich gifts. As usual I felt like Odysseus, and had to diminish my supply of gifts considerably, and double my usual present at parting. The old man gave me a fine mat, the first I have ever received in the character of guest, although I now possess half a dozen from one source or another. Sagapolutele looks like an old Arab sheik such as pilots one's boat down the Nile cataract. He talks very freely about old Samoan customs, and said he had Fiji blood. He has turned to the church in his old age, and with Arab simplicity explained that he was once the best dancer in Samoa, but since he had grown weak he had become missionary, or preacher, and could no longer dance, nor was there anyone left who knew how to dance. Our boatman, Maua, who talks English, explained to us that the chief had been "the baddest man in all Samoa," but Seumano denies it, and says he only had "plenty wives." Sagapolutele talked freely of Samoan superstitions. He is a sweet pagan, and has an *a-itu* or spirit of his own — the ghost of his son, killed in the last war — who is always about the place, and came, in likeness of an owl, to announce our arrival, or *malanga*, before it was known otherwise. His village *a-itu* is the cuttle-fish; the spirit of the kingdom is the rainbow — aatua is the province or kingdom, and the spirit is Atúa. We talked long about spirits and local customs; but his brother, the Tulafale, developed a real historical genius; wrote out for me their oldest poem about Pili and Siga, a new thing to me; and promised me a quantity of poems or songs, and traditions. I shall hand them over to Stevenson.

Yesterday we sailed a mile or two out to sea, and visited an island — Nuutele — an old crater, like Apollima, with one side open to the north-east. I wanted to geologise, for I am growing amused by the geological problems hereabouts. You know from Darwin's *Voyage of the Beagle* about the amount of geology yet settled or unsettled in regard to the South Seas. Most of the islands — thousands in number — have the wonderful peculiarity of being just flush with the surface of a very deep ocean. Of course this precise level must be due to some equalising cause, acting at the surface. Darwin made a great reputation by suggesting that the Pacific Ocean was a field of exhausted or expiring volcanoes, and that as volcanic activity ceased, the volcanic islands subsided; as the tops went slowly under water, the coral polyps took possession, and built as the volcanoes sank. The theory is lovely, and I adore it. After visiting Hawaii, I can believe anything, and deny nothing; but just for fun I like to make theories of my own, and have manufactured six or eight that delighted me. All are equally reasonable and untenable. So I stick to Darwin and subsidence; and I visited Nuutele today to satisfy myself that it was the top of a lava crater that had subsided ten thousand feet, and, with five hundred feet more subsidence, would become a coral atoll. What I found was a mud volcano, absolutely without lava, except that its *stratified* sandstone cliffs were full of sharp-edged pieces of lava, as well as of fine-grained sand and shell. To prove something or other, I knocked a small piece of shell out of the cliff at sea-level. I suspect it to be a recent shell, and if so I have proved that Nuutele, and probably all Samoa, was no lower than it now is, when the crater-sides were raised. That is to say, the only thing I have proved is that one Pacific island was first a sea-beach, and then was elevated about five hundred feet, and since very ancient times — say ten thousand years, perhaps — has not subsided at all. Indeed a very recent coral bed shows eight or ten feet of elevation. Naturally I feel rather floored about subsidence, but will go at it again with sublime defiance of facts. Darwin must be sustained or the Pacific will never be calm.... I have walked a couple of miles along the shore geologising, only to find evidence of upheaval — only about eight feet, but uniform over the whole island, at least at the east end....

December 5. The gift business is a severer burden than the taupo duty. My boat is half filled with mats, *tapa*, wooden bowls and other presents, which become a bigger load every day, and require rather large returns. I am now giving some twenty dollars a day in return-gifts, and this is on a very moderate estimate of the money-value of their presents. I want to check them, and can do it only by adopting a rule, and letting them know beforehand that my present is fixed. The chiefs bring, or give me, commonly, several pigs — sometimes half a dozen — a dozen or more chickens, large fish, any quantity of taro, and all the supplies for twenty men; and besides this, they think it right to give me mats, bowls, and other things precious to them, and now becoming costly in Apia. If I increase my presents, they double theirs. They are ruinously extravagant in such matters, and of course expect the same style from me. I give gold, because they commonly get much of that, but would have to divide all other presents, like canned provisions, biscuits or clothing, on the spot, with their village who bring the eatables for us. In short, travelling *en prince* has almost as many difficulties here as in other places, and costs even in this primitive world, about fifty dollars a day, yet it is necessarily harder on the host than on the guest. Pretty much every chief is a poor man because he is obliged to share all he has in the world. They sell land, or mortgage it, and are always hard up. Communism always victimises the strong. Property victimises the weak. I am no philanthropist, and care not a *real* (the coin used here) whether communism or property is the sounder system; but La Farge is conservative and insists on preserving what is established. I defer to La Farge's sound views, especially as last night he sat out a Siva till midnight, and fairly used up dancers, crews, taupos and me, always threatening to be strong when he gets well....

Apia, *Decr.* 11. We arrived safely at home — or our Consulate — at four o'clock yesterday afternoon, with the usual effect of picnics fresh in our minds. In short, I was glad to get back. As the devil arranges these matters, there is always some flatness in one's second glass of champagne. I am getting to know my Polynesian too well, and to feel the opéra bouffe side of him. When I know him better, I shall get back on the serious side; but La Farge is a terrible creature to see fine comedy, and, about a week after he has caught a new point of view, I am sure to catch on to it. He is now filled with delight at the moralities of the simple savage, and with disgust at his somewhat vague ideas of cleanliness. Yet, to my vast relief, our twelve days of rather trying travel, which has cost me a hard strain, has done him good, and he has come back in better health, he says, than at any time since we started. This is illogical enough to please us both, and as he found little to sketch on our travels, he is the more ready to work now. We have exhausted the islands, and know more about them than any other pleasure-traveller has ever learned.

To Elizabeth Cameron

VAIALE, 15 December, 1890.

We find Stevenson still here. He has not gone to Auckland. Apparently we are to see much more of him, for the steamer "Richmond," which is our only conveyance to Tahiti, will not return here for six weeks....

We are not without distinguished society. Saturday afternoon Mata-afa came over to see us, as he often does; but this time he brought some presents of *tapa* and baskets, explaining that he is now poor and has little to give. The formula is almost a matter of course, but in this case it is probably more than a form, for Mata-afa is an abdicated king, and is struggling with difficulties. I think he would be a marked man anywhere, but he is a long way the most distinguished chief in these islands, and the only one we have met who carries his superiority about him so decidedly as to set him at once apart. He brought me on Saturday, some old songs I had asked for, and which he had good-naturedly caused to be written out. Two of his oldest followers were with him, and sat at the end of our native house, while Mata-afa himself, in the regulation official white jacket, sat on a chair between us. I had much to ask him about the legendary songs, and he, with a deprecatory smile as though I were a spoiled child, told me at great length the story, or a part of the mass of stories, about Pili, "the Lizard," which seems to be the principal material of Samoan verse. It was not very amusing, and he was aware of it, but I asked him to go on, and he must have toiled an hour, giving sentence after sentence for translation by our boy Charley. I shall not bore you with the doings of Pili, either the father or the son. You can read volumes of such childlike stuff by getting from the Congressional Library either Fornandez' great book about Hawaii, or Sir George Grey's Maori Legends about New Zealand,[1] or Turner's volume on Samoa,[2] or half a dozen other books on the South Seas. Polynesians are not imaginative, but eminently practical, with childish ideas as to what is humorous or imposing. My object is only to find out what they have done; so I listened with gravity to Mata-afa, who labored on, until at length Stevenson dropped in, and we turned to discussing the latest appearance of a certain interesting spirit or female enchantress who recently killed a young chief, in whose father's house we stayed at Vao-vai. I thought then that we were rather an interesting company, as the

[1] *Polynesian Mythology and Traditionary History of the New Zealand Race*, 1855.
[2] George Turner, *Samoa a Hundred Years Ago and Long Before*, 1884.

world goes. Mata-afa may fairly rank as one of the heroic figures of our times. Stevenson is a person sufficiently known to fame; and La Farge will probably not be less well known a hundred years hence than now. The group struck me as rather a peculiar one, considering that we were a good many thousand miles from places where people usually hunt lions, and I felt encouraged to think that even here I was not in an atmosphere of hopeless mental stagnation. Stevenson stayed to dine with us, and was quite on his manners, but as usual had to borrow Sewall's clothes. La Farge and I promised to come up to his place next morning (Sunday), and to send our breakfast before us.[1] I cannot conceive why they should ever be without food in the house, but apparently their normal condition is foodless, and they not only consented but advised my making sure of my own breakfast. Stevenson himself seems to eat little or nothing, and lives on cheap French *vin ordinaire* when he can get it. I do not know how this régime affects his complaint, for I do not know what his complaint is. I supposed it to be phthisis, or tubercular consumption; but am assured here that his lungs are not affected. The German physician here says that the complaint is asthma; but I am too weak in knowledge to explain how asthma should get relief from a saturated climate like this, where constant exposure leads also to severe colds, not easily thrown off. Asthma or whatever you please, he and his wife, according to their account, rarely have enough to eat in the house, so I sent off a native, at seven o'clock in the morning, with a basket of food, while I started on foot at half past ten, and La Farge followed at eleven on horseback. This was my first experiment at walking hereabouts. The climate is not stimulating to legs. Since we arrived, the season has changed; the blessed trade-wind has died out, and the apparent heat is much greater. I walked very slowly, under an umbrella, but was soon in a state of saturation, and, as the path is not interesting, I found pedestrianism a bore, but arrived just at noon, letting La Farge precede me a few minutes. We found Stevenson and his wife just as they

[1] "We have had enlightened society: La Farge the painter, and your friend Henry Adams: a great privilege — would it might endure. I would go oftener to see them, but the place is awkward to reach on horseback. I had to swim my horse the last time I went to dinner; and as I have not yet returned the clothes I had to borrow, I dare not return in the same plight: it seems inevitable — as soon as the wash comes in, I plump straight into the American's shirt or trousers! They, I believe, would come oftener to see me but for the horrid doubt that weighs upon our commissariat department; we have often almost nothing to eat; a guest would simply break the bank; my wife and I have dined on one avocado pear; I have several times dined on hard bread and onions. What would you do with a guest at such narrow seasons? — eat him? or serve up a labour boy fricasseed?" — Stevenson to Henry James, December 29, 1890. *Letters of Stevenson*, II, 255.

had appeared at our first call, except that Mrs. Stevenson did not think herself obliged to put on slippers, and her night-gown costume had apparently not been washed since our visit. Stevenson himself wore still a brown knit woollen sock on one foot, and a greyish purple sock on the other, much wanting in heels, so that I speculated half my time whether it was the same old socks, or the corresponding alternates, and concluded that he must have worn them ever since we first saw him. They were evidently his slippers for home wear. He wore also, doubtless out of deference to us, a pair of trousers, and a thin flannel shirt; but, by way of protest, he rolled up the sleeves above his shoulders, displaying a pair of the thinnest white arms I ever beheld, which he brandished in the air habitually as though he wanted to throw them away. To La Farge and me, this attitude expressed incredible strength, and heroic defiance of destiny, for his house swarmed with mosquitoes which drove us wild, though only our heads and hands were exposed. Of course it was none of our business, and both Stevenson and his wife were very friendly, and gave us a good breakfast — or got it themselves — and kept up a rapid talk for four hours, at the end of which I was very tired, but Stevenson seemed only refreshed. Both La Farge and I came round to a sort of liking for Mrs. Stevenson, who is more human than her husband. Stevenson is an *a-itu* — uncanny. His fragility passes description, but his endurance passes his fragility. I cannot conceive how such a bundle of bones, unable to work on his writing without often taking to his bed as his working place, should have gone through the months of exposure, confinement and bad nourishment which he has enjoyed. Their travels have broken his wife up; she is a victim to rheumatism which is becoming paralysis, and, I suspect, to dyspepsia; she says that their voyages have caused it; but Stevenson gloats over discomforts and thinks that every traveller should sail for months in small cutters rancid with cocoa-nut oil and mouldy with constant rain, and should live on coral atolls with nothing but cocoa-nuts and poisonous fish to eat. Their mode of existence here is far less human than that of the natives, and compared with their shanty a native house is a palace; but this squalor must be somehow due to his education. All through him, the education shows. His early associates were all second-rate; he never seems by any chance to have come in contact with first-rate people, either men, women or artists. He does not know the difference between people, and mixes them up in a fashion as grotesque as if they were characters in his New Arabian Nights. Of course he must have found me out at once, for my Bostonianism, and finikin clinging to what I think the best, must rub him raw all over, all the more because I try not to express it; but I suspect he does not know quite enough even to hate me for it; and I am sure that he would never have the fineness to penetrate La Farge, though, compared with La Farge, I am a sort of Stevenson for coarseness. He is extremely civil, and gives me things of his own to read, and which have not been published, and he would not trust to strangers; he gives us letters to Tahiti, and shows a strong wish for our society; but I dare not see him often for fear of his hating me as a Philistine and a disgrace to humanity, because I care not a copper for what interests him. On the other hand he is perfectly safe with La Farge, and La Farge is still safer with him. After all the extreme intimacy of my long acquaintance with La Farge, I am always more and more astonished at the accuracy of his judgment. I knew how fine it was, and how keen, but the infernal triumph of the man is his correctness. I never have managed to catch him in an error. His judgment of men and women is as unfailing as his judgment of a picture, and he understands a Polynesian quite as well as he does a New Yorker. He sees all round a character like Stevenson's, and comments on it as if it were a painting, while Stevenson could never get within reach of him if they were alone on an atoll. The two characters in contact are rather amusing as contrasts; the oriental delicacy of La Farge seems to be doubled by the Scotch eccentricities and barbarisms of Stevenson who is as one-sided as a crab, and flies off at angles, no matter what rocks stand in his way.

December 18.... Two more personages of interest to us have come to dinner. One is named Atwater; [1] he was formerly our consul at Tahiti; a Yankee who married into the chief native family, and, through his wife, got large interests in cocoa-nut plantations and pearl islands. He suffers from asthma and cannot live in Tahiti now, but is on his way there, to attend to some business. For taking the fun out of everything, a Yankee matches a Scotchman, and Mr. Atwater has perhaps been long enough in the South Seas to reach the universal lava-foundation of commonplace. Even the natives are not exempt, and I found, on our last tour round the island, that the happy and indolent islander is extremely bored by his ideal existence. I was slow to believe it, but the *taupo* were frank on the subject, and the young men were devoured by the wish for something new. I believe that ennui is the chief cause of their wars; but at a large village called Saangapu, in the district of Safatu, I met an example of restlessness that beat even my own or Atwater's. In the dusk of evening, as I returned

[1] Dorence Atwater.

to our hut after a stroll along the beach, I was surprised to find a native talking English with La Farge. He turned out to be our host, Angápu, the chief of the village, and a nephew of our own chief, Seumano tafa, our companion and escort. Angápu is a dignified, middle-aged man, and speaks English with the same high-bred beauty of tone and accent that struck us so much in old John Adams at Apia. He has been a great traveller as a common Kanaka seaman, and has been to San Francisco, New Orleans, New York, Liverpool, Glasgow, Hamburg, as well as to Australia, China, Japan, and all over the Pacific. I asked him whether he was satisfied to stay at home now, and he replied that he would like to go off again; but Seumano, who, as head of the family, can control his movements, would not consent. Angápu was bored by the smallness of Samoan interests and the restrictions of society, yet he is a considerable chief, belonging to a powerful family; his position is one of power and his duties and responsibilities must be constant enough to give him steady occupation. His village was one of the largest and richest we saw. With all this, he was unhappy because he could not go off as a common sailor before the mast, to knock about the ocean in cold climates which were his horror. In his presence I felt myself an ideal representative of stay-at-home, immovable fixity and repose. Atwater is another example of restlessness. Evidently Tahiti bores him, and he finds San Francisco a relief. He calls himself a bad sailor, yet he wanders from San Francisco to Sydney, and back again, as though the ocean were a French play. He told us much about his pearl-fishing, which seems to have amused him most, but he says that in New York or Paris he can buy pearls cheaper than he can fish them, and in infinitely larger quantities and of better quality. He says that he can buy pearls at San Francisco and sell them at a profit in Tahiti, and that the pearl industry is but an adjunct to that of mother-of-pearl; a sort of accidental margin for the business.

Atwater was very friendly and promised to prepare the way for us at Tahiti, especially with his brother-in-law, Tati Salmon, the head of the greatest native family on the island, to whom Stevenson had already given us a letter. Tati Salmon is half London Jew; half hereditary high chief of the Tevas or Tefas; and looks down on the Pomares with lofty contempt, as parvenus. We shall probably put ourselves at once under his protection, and fly from Papeete where Pomare and Frenchmen have sway.

Our other distinguished visitor is named Shirley Baker, and dined with us last evening. In these parts of the world, three persons seem to be pre-eminent among the English. One is old Sir George Grey [1] of New Zealand, about whom you can read much in Mr. Froude's dull book called *Oceanica*. I shall probably never meet Sir George Grey, for I have no letters to Auckland. The second is Sir John Thurston at Fiji, whose guest I expect to be. The third is Shirley Baker,[2] who ruled despotically the Tonga group of islands, called Friendly on the maps, several hundred miles south of Samoa. Thurston at Fiji did not approve of Baker's doings at Tonga, and at last, just before we left home, took the strong step of sending a war-vessel to deport Baker, and practically to annex Tonga to his own government. I have taken care not to know anything about the subject, that I might have no prejudices about the men, but the affair has made a great noise in these hollow oceans. Baker was naturally angry, and I imagine that he wants revenge and reinstatement. He has lately come here from Auckland, perhaps with the idea of going to Washington and seeking aid from you and sister Anne. Last evening he dined with us, a London-aldermanic looking person, doubtful on his aspirates, but singularly quiet, restrained and intelligent. His talk was very interesting to us, for he is a converted missionary who has been thirty years at Tonga, and knows more than anyone else of Tongan history and affairs. You are happily ignorant that Tonga was the missionary stronghold where they played pranks such as uncontrolled priesthoods commonly indulge in. Tonga too is or was a stronghold of the Polynesian race, and a central point of its distribution. Probably New Zealand got its Maoris from Tonga, for the Tongans were great navigators, while the Samoans never ventured far to sea, or attempted foreign conquests. Baker had a great deal to say on these subjects, and said it well; but I suspect he is writing a book, for he seemed cautious about telling all he thought; and on the Polynesian battleground where everyone has an exclusive and extravagant theory to argue — the source of the Polynesian race — he would go no further than suggest that the race and the pig came together, and must be traced back to Asia together. This strikes me as inadequate treatment, but perhaps I do not sufficiently respect the pig; and I have an opposite hobby, that the race came necessarily with the trade-winds — not against them — which Baker rejects, riding too confidently on his pigs against the wind....

December 30. The obstinately wicked get their reward. Here is an outcast who fled from his own country to escape the interminable bore

---

[1] Sir George Grey (1812–1898), late Prime Minister of New Zealand.
[2] Shirley Waldemar Baker (1835–1903).

of its nickel-plated politics and politicians; yet when he seeks refuge in an inaccessible island of the South Seas, ten thousand miles from an Irishman, he finds politics running round like roosters without heads. Politics are commonly more or less *bouffe*, but here the whole thing is pure Offenbach. The bloody villain is Stuebel, the German Consul. If Stuebel says it rains, he means mischief. If he says it doesn't rain, he lies. If he says nothing, he is deep in conspiracy. War is to break out in Savaii at once; Manono is coming to seize Malietoa; Stuebel has written to Tamasese to be ready; the "Sperber" is going to Tutuila; the "Leipzig" is going to fetch the new Chief Justice; Malietoa is to be deposed, and the Germans are to seize the islands. Stuebel is at the bottom of it all. Every day these stories come to us. Old Samsoni waddles up, almost insane with native rumors, and predicts civil war within twenty-four hours. Mata-afa always has some absurd native story which he tells us with his grave, quiet smile, as though he were sorry to amuse us with his people's folly. You can imagine me in this poultry yard. After several times expressing myself in my usual offensive and dogmatic manner on the character of this small beer, I have sunk into silence more or less sullen, and let the talk go on as it will. As far as I can see, it is all the play of these brown-skinned children, who are bored for want of excitement, and are quite capable of getting up a fight about nothing, but meanwhile we are standing along the shore, glasses in hand, watching for the smoke of the "Iroquois" which is supposed to be bringing our Swedish Chief Justice from Tutuila. The Chief Justice is to settle everything, it appears; but what is to happen if the unfortunate man should prove to be a tool of the wicked Stuebel?...

XV

THE SOUTH SEAS

1891

To Elizabeth Cameron

Samoa, January 2, 1891.

. . . .

Then the long financial drama has had a many-sided personal interest still stronger than the purely artistic perfection of Parnell and Grandpapa Gladstone. I have read through it from October to December 16 with more excitement than I ever expected to feel again in such subjects. The first mysterious squeezing of the market; the slow yielding of stocks; the howls and groans of the unfortunates whom the bears hugged; the awful crash of the Barings, and my own narrow escape from being stranded penniless here; the collapse day by day, and the gradual taking form of the mysterious power that was to profit by it all; the looming up of Jay Gould in the background, and his gentle, innocent-minded comments day by day on the situation; the seizure of Pacific Mail; the seizure of Union Pacific; and the unrelaxing severity of the grip that is to restore order by creating chaos — all this would be a delight if I were twenty years younger, for, if you happen on my new volume of Essays which ought soon to be published, you will see that I wrote the first chapter of this story in an article called the "Gold Conspiracy." The second chapter has been my brother's administration of Union Pacific, and its foredoomed failure. The last chapter — in my lifetime — has still to come, but is close at hand. I do not know the climax, but am devoured by curiosity. According to my diagnosis, Jay Gould too is foredoomed to failure; his scheme is still more impracticable than my brother's, and he has personal and political enmities infinitely more serious. If I am right, and if Gould must fall, I see the most splendid possibilities of a climax. Will he subside quietly? Will he break down? Will he be hung on a lamp-post? Will government and society stand under the shock?

My brother Charles will doubtless live to write the story and the epitaph of Jay Gould, who is certainly a great man, worth writing about. If I thought I should be alive twenty-five years hence, with my full powers of mind and body, I should prepare to continue my history, and show where American democracy was coming out. We shall know all about it by that time. As yet we can but guess, and Jay Gould has much to tell us. Unfortunately I am cursed with the misfortune of thinking that I know beforehand what the result must be, and of feeling sure that it is one which I do not care to pursue; one with which I have little or no sympathy, except in a coldly scientific way; and a man cannot with decency or chance of success take a part in a stage-play when he cannot help showing the audience that he thinks the whole thing a devilish poor piece of work.

You find my last two volumes more critical — deliberately fault finding? — than the earlier ones. They were written chiefly within the last five or six years, and in a very different frame of mind from that in which the work was begun. I found it hard to pretend either sympathy or interest in my subject. If you compare the tone of my first volume — even toned down, as it is, from the original — with that of the ninth when it appears, you will feel that the light has gone out. I am not to blame. As long as I could make life work, I stood by it, and swore by it as though it was my God, as indeed it was....

January 9. I am interested to find that even the Samoan child, which should have no nerves, living in a climate like a hothouse, and always in the open air, still has tantrums of hysterics, and yells like a demon, half an hour at a time, rolling on the ground and kicking, apparently without cause, and at any hour of the day or night, greatly to the disturbance of my sleep, as they can be heard half a mile away. One of the English missionary ladies informs me that their parents are too indulgent, which sounds like New England.

Great events have occurred here during the last ten days. Our Swedish Chief Justice has arrived, and the islands have begun their new career as an independent power under the Berlin treaty. The Chief Justice is a young man named Cederkranz, who looks honest and fairly intelligent, but has one eye that seems to be fixed, and glares perversely into space. He arrived in the midst of our confusion caused by the Parkers' departure, Fanua's wedding, and the departure or arrival of various war-vessels and mail steamers. Fanua was married at the British Consulate, her husband, Gurr, being a British colonial here, and taking her as a wife after our law. We breakfasted that day with Stuebel, the German Consul, and after breakfast took the Chief Justice to Fanua's wedding reception. You will observe that since our travels have ceased, you hear no more of the old-gold girl. The *taupo* stays at home, and so do we. Poor Aenga, it seems, is in a manner banished at Sa-papalii in Savaii, where we saw her. I learned that she incurred displeasure by a *tendresse* for Seumano's son, probably because he has a wife already, and Malietoa or Seumano or he himself thought divorce unadvisable. At all events we have heard nothing from her or from Taa-uli or Fa-asaei or any of our other *taupo* loves, and have had no more Sivas or cocoanut oil. Fanua was married without assistance from *taupo* colleagues, though she wore a very becoming wedding-dress of fine mats. She had a ball, too, but La Farge and I do not go to balls; not even to that in honor of the Chief Justice. To atone for this want of respect, I stimulated Consul Sewall to give the Chief Justice a dinner, regardless of expense, to throw all previous Samoan entertainments into outer darkness. For four days Sewall has devoted all his energies and thoughts to this dinner. We are very short of ladies here, but the wife of the British Consul, Cusack-Smith, arrived just in time. She is a young blonde of the modern British type, rather pretty and painted-silky in costume. Mrs. Clarke and Mrs. Claxton, the British missionary wives, filled up. Mrs. Claxton is pretty and not over missionaried. The native wife of Blacklock, a consular official, made a fourth; and Sewall asked Mrs. Stevenson, who sent a letter in reply, so characteristic that I begged it of Sewall, and intend to inclose it to you as the most amusing product of Samoa I have met. Stevenson himself has sailed for Sydney after an affectionate parting with us; and Mrs. Stevenson did not appear at the dinner. ... These were all the ladies eligible. The men were Cederkranz himself; Cusack-Smith, of the good-natured polo type; Stuebel; Captain Bishop and a small ships-crew of lieutenants and doctors from the "Iroquois"; and half a dozen subordinate German, Swedish and American consular, official or missionary parties. Twenty persons sat down at table under a forest of palms and ferns. You know too well my weaknesses to need my giving you a detailed account of my sufferings. Sewall kept his word, and the dinner was three hours long. I was placed next to Stuebel as the only intelligent person in the company, and managed to have some pleasant talk. On my left was one Ulfsparre, a young and interestingly muddle-headed Swede. La Farge sat between Clarke, the missionary, and Henneberger, the doctor of the "Iroquois," who was supposed to be the charmer of the navy and devoted his powers of fascination to ungrateful Mrs. Cusack-Smith on his left. Of Cederkranz I could see and hear nothing, as he sat three places from me on my right. I earnestly hope that this great entertainment strengthened and extended Secretary Blaine's purposes and influence in the South Seas; but I admit to having felt prodigious comfort when the ladies and their husbands departed under umbrellas at eleven o'clock, and I slipped off to finish my cigar in the soothing darkness of the verandah of my own sleeping cabin, whence I heard a louder and louder uproar of conviviality at the Consulate long after I was in bed, and needed not the later information of La Farge to acquaint me that most of the young men were drunk, and that Captain Bishop, who, like ourselves, drank nothing, being a reformed inebriate, was waving a lantern patiently for an hour or two, on the verandah, as a signal to his lambs in the dining-room to collect about him and go aboard ship.

We learn today that, after all, Mrs. Stevenson came down last evening, arriving late; that her horse refused to ford the stream between Apia and here; that she could not get a boat, and was not strong enough to walk; so she had to pass her evening at the missionary house, the missionaries being here. More traits! What with her shoes, her horse, and herself, she is charming.

APIA, *January* 14.... I have even refused to go with Consul Sewall, on the "Iroquois" to Pango-Pango, though he urged me strongly and wanted me much; for he was going on a job that I had in a manner driven him into. A murder of a very curious kind was committed at Pango-Pango on the night of December 20. The victim was one of the "Iroquois" crew; a seaman named Power, coxswain of the Captain's gig; a good fellow, popular with everyone on board, and without a known enemy on shore. Captain Bishop and the officers of the "Iroquois" showed incompetence or indifference, or both, in investigating the crime; and in the want of amusement, I took it up, and induced Sewall to begin an investigation. The first result was a quarrel with Captain Bishop, in which he showed himself an ass, and quickly backed down. The second result was that Sewall had to go to Pango-Pango, and I refused to go with him. My true reason is that I will not consent to appear, without official authority, as a meddler in official business; but my interest in the case is great, and I am sorry not to be at hand to help Sewall as amateur detective.

How would the story do for a Samoan melodrama? The murdered man, Power, had been in Samoa before, as one of the crew of the "Adams," two or three years ago. He came back in the "Iroquois" which arrived about December 1, or soon afterwards, while I was circumnavigating this island. When I got back to Apia, December 10, the "Iroquois" was in the harbor, and my boat passed under her stern as I steered across to the Consulate. The next day she sailed to Pango-Pango, our coaling station in Tutuila. Power did not go ashore till Sunday, December 20, when he, with his closest intimate and chum, a seaman named Brennan, and three or four other men, went ashore on leave, and passed the day playing poker inside the bar of a drinking saloon, kept by an American named Pike. Power won a few dollars, coming out a little ahead. He left the card table four or five times, for two or three minutes at a time, but never went further than the immediate front of the house, and was not seen to speak with any-one but his party. At sunset — six o'clock — all returned to the ship. Very soon afterwards, towards eight o'clock, he suggested to Brennan to swim ashore, and have some more poker. Brennan agreed, and understood that they were to send out a canoe from shore, to the ship, secretly, in the dark, to fetch off two or three other men, who could not, or would not swim. These men, when cross-questioned by Sewall, say that Power did ask them to swim ashore, but the weather was threatening, the swim was long, and they not only refused to go, but thought it strange that Power, who, as Captain's coxswain could al-ways get leave, should want to do it. This took place between eight and half past eight, and ten or fifteen minutes later, Power and Bren-nan crawled out through an open space in the bow, and dropped from the chains into the water. They had agreed to swim to a point, some four hundred yards away, but the wind rose, with rain, the current was strong, they wore their clothes as they stood, and Brennan, being the weaker swimmer, could make no headway to the point, and at last, nearly exhausted, turned on his back to rest. He heard Power hail "Hallo, Shortie!" — Brennan's nickname — and the voice came from the direction they had intended to go, as though Power were well on his way to the point. Brennan was carried further into the harbor, and made out to reach the pier, near Pike's saloon. As soon as he got ashore, he walked along the beach to the point, expecting to meet Power. Failing to find him, Brennan called out: "Power, Power!" so loud that he was heard on the ship. Still Power did not answer, and Brennan walked back to Pike's, meeting natives who spoke to him. As the saloon was closed, he paid a native a dollar to take him to Pike's house, some distance beyond. He found Pike; they returned to the saloon; drank one bottle of whiskey; and Brennan, taking another, went on board ship in a canoe at twelve o'clock. He waked two of his mates and took them up to the forecastle, where they drank the whiskey, and discussed what had become of Power.

The next morning, at quarters, Power's absence was reported. The same afternoon one of the ship's boats, between the pier and the anchorage, about a hundred yards from the ship, came on a body, floating in the water. The head was gone; both arms were cut off at the shoulder; one leg was gone; the other was cut to the bone; and the body was recognised by its tattooing, a part of a trouser leg, and a shoe. The autopsy showed no sign of drowning, but clear evidence of hacking with a knife or cleaver.

Brennan gave himself up at once, and was put in irons as charged with murder. Sewall sent for him, the "Iroquois" having returned here, and I heard Brennan tell his story, which was perfectly straight. He is, I believe, as ignorant as I am. Who, then, committed the murder, and why? You will probably say, offhand: "He met some native, as he came out of the water, and the native knocked him on the head to rob him." That would be the natural European explanation, but it is the last to occur to us. Natives never commit European murders. They very rarely indeed commit murder at all, and when they do so they kill each other, not for money but for revenge. No common Samoan would dare to murder a white man, for he is naturally timid, and dislikes violence, and knows he would certainly be hung. We put the probability of such an explanation last of all possible clues, and yet we have literally no evidence to warrant another, except the speaking fact that Power should have wanted to go ashore at all, that night; should have deceived Brennan into accompanying him; and should have behaved throughout in the way we would expect if he had some secret inducement powerful enough to overcome every obstacle. Who was she? This is the conundrum that interests us, and you see what a sweet melodrama it suggests. Had Power old relations with some woman? Had he made an agreement to meet her? The point of this suspicion is very Samoan. The woman must be an unusual person if her husband — or anyone else — commits murder out of jealousy. Few Samoan women are murdered, yet not many are Penelopes. Very few Samoan men would dare murder a white for such a cause — perhaps no one would dare it, unless he were a half-caste or a chief. Even then he must be a conspicuous personage. Who is he?...

January 18. In the evening Consul Sewall arrived from Pango-Pango, after a week of discomfort, heat, seasickness and vexation, and total failure to discover his murderer. He has gone over the whole place with a comb, so to speak, and put everyone through the teeth of it, only to find that no clue leads to a result. The mystery remains mysterious and more melodramatic than ever. I am rather glad for the sake of art. The *mise-en-scène* becomes the more effective, and the instantaneous disappearance of a strong man, at a spot within call of several hundred people, on shipboard and ashore, without trace of struggle or suggestion of cause, is a lovely motive for a South Sea drama, while the surroundings are among the most beautiful in all

Polynesia. My prosaic mind is now paralysed by the commonplace idea of sharks; for the astonishing incompetence of the ship's officers in their original investigation leads me to doubt whether the beautiful Dr. Henneberger took the trouble to make certain that sharks could not cut heads and legs off, as well as tear arms from the shoulders; but I struggle against this suggestion as fatal to my drama, which needs a dusky savage with a cleaver and some strange archaic motive. Luckily the mystery abides, and leaves one free to imagine whatever one prefers....

To Elizabeth Cameron

PAPEETE, 6 February, 1891.

Tahiti! does the word mean anything to you? To me it has a perfume of its own, made up of utterly inconsequent associations; essence of the South Seas mixed with imaginations of at least forty years ago; Herman Melville and Captain Cook head and heels with the French opera and Pierre Loti. Of course I expected something different from what I find, yet the reality fits in, after a fashion. Here is what I find, or at least here is where I am. A cottage of three or four rooms and a verandah. In front, a little garden twenty feet deep, with flowers and vines. Then a paling; then the road; then the sea, or rather the harbor, with small waves flopping on the beach, twenty yards from me as I write on the verandah; then a broad stretch of blue water until, ten miles away, the horizon ends with the soft outline of the mountains of Moorea, another island, which reminds me of Capri, as the water does of the Bay of Naples. La Farge and I have just finished our first breakfast in our new establishment, and I feel highly pleased because it was quite Parisian. Our new cook is a Frenchman, bearing the name of Peraudot. I pay him fifty dollars a month in Chilian money, or about thirty-five dollars in gold; and if you were only here, you would find my new breakfast-table better than at Washington. In an hour we are to go to see the King.

We have been here but two days.... Early one morning we entered the harbor of Papeete, and hauled up close to the shore. Atwater, our former Consul, and young Doty,[1] a Georgetown youth, our actual Consul, came on board to receive us, and I asked to what hotel I had best send our trunks. "Well! there is no hotel in Papeete," the two gentlemen rather awkwardly replied. I was a bit staggered, and asked where then I could go. They suggested that I had better take a cot-

[1] Jacob L. Doty.

tage. Could I find one furnished? "Well! no! probably not. But there were one or two to be had, and I might soon buy or hire furniture." Then and there we stepped on shore and went house-hunting. We shortly learned that there was but one available cottage, and that we must vacate it on the 15th. I wish you could have seen its condition. Fortunately we had no choice, so Doty took us to breakfast, and by miraculous efforts of Awoki we slept in our cottage that night.

So here we are. *J'y suis, mais je n'y reste pas.* Next week we must put our new cooking-stove and our pots and pans in a whale-boat, and move elsewhere. As we never meant to remain in Papeete, we are not annoyed, but rather pleased, and meanwhile have begun a vigorous social campaign, necessarily short, but still to us formidable. Papeete is the strangest little corner of earth you ever invented to amuse Martha. Here is a native King, Pomare, with no functions whatever except to drink. His divorced Queen is of course a Teva, since the Tevas are the true princes of Tahiti, and equally of course she is a Brander by connection. Please consult Miss Gordon-Cumming's [1] book on these family matters. Then comes the French Governor who is a Martinique negro. I am gratified to learn that some governments are stupider than our own. The French actually send here a full corps of West India negroes to govern a people almost as high-blooded as Greeks. Society now consists, as far as I can learn, of the Branders and their connection. These are four or five sisters, daughters of a deceased London Jew named Salmon, who married the Teva heiress and created a princely house of Salmon. As my letters are likely to be filled with Salmons or Salmonidae, please grapple at the outset with the following consanguinity:

One of Salmon's daughters married King Pomare, and a few years ago got a divorce. She now lives in a house behind the Consulate.

Another daughter married Atwater, our Consul, and lives a little way behind the town.

Another daughter married Brander, a Scotchman of good family, and had nine children. Brander died of softening of the brain, and some years later she married another Scotchman named Darsie, and has had three more children. She now lives in the country, two or three miles behind here.

I won't bother you with the other sisters, who can wait. So can the brothers, Taati and Narii Salmon, gentlemen of the first importance here, of whom I shall probably have much to say hereafter. As yet we have called only on the Queen that was; Mrs. Darsie, and Mrs.

[1] Constance Frederica Gordon-Cumming, *Fire Fountains.*

Atwater; and found only Mrs. Darsie and Mrs. Atwater at home. They are both women of a certain age, decidedly Polynesian, rather handsome. We liked them. They talk excellent English, and are familiar with America and Europe.

If there were a Court, these would be it. Pomare's sale of his royal rights to the French, and his pleasant vice of royal drunkenness, have left Tahiti courtless. The nicest royalty was said to be the Princess Moe, wife of Tamatua, another brother, once king of the neighboring island of Raiotea, but expelled for potting his subjects with a rifle when drunk. You have read of the Princess Moe in the Earl and the Doctor, where "that unutterable cad, Pembroke," according to Stevenson, gave an account of her that exasperated everybody in these regions, and quite broke up poor Moe, who, in consequence, never would visit Europe. Miss Gordon-Cumming, too, had much to say of her. Stevenson adored her, and gave us a letter of introduction to her; but our first news on arrival was of Moe's death, which happened a month ago. Her husband Tamatua died before her. So that chapter we found closed.

Now then! Of all the female Salmonidae, Mrs. Brander-Darsie and her twelve children are naturally the most pervasive. Everything social in Papeete is Brander. The nine Brander children are now grown. Five of them are handsome young men; and they are chiefly to be found about our Consulate, where we tumbled headlong among them, howling for houses, beds, cooks, laundresses, social instruction and general advice. The howls were very obligingly responded to; and from Doty we learned much of the private history of these youths. It is rather interesting. Their father, Brander, was the great merchant of these seas. His plantations produced cocoa-nuts by the million; his pearl-fisheries sent tons of shell to Europe; his ships carried all the trade of the islands; his income was very great, and his wealth estimated by millions. He sent all his sons to Europe to be educated as royalties, and the boys duly coronetted their handkerchiefs and their Gladstone bags, and bore themselves so as to do credit to their uncle-cousin, the King of Tahiti. They were English subjects, and were Scotch gentlemen, so they went to Universities, and I've no doubt were howling swells, as all bloods-royal should be. Then their father died, and his estate, when settled, shrank to the modest amount of a million dollars. The widow took half, leaving half a million to be divided among nine children equally. The boys who were educated on the scale of a million apiece, were reduced practically to nothing, or just enough for a modest bachelor's establishment in Papeete. Here they are, very gentlemanly young Englishmen. They want careers, and they find our Consulate convenient.

Socially speaking, I have now described Papeete. No one else exists here except the occasional French naval officer, who is not specially at home among the Salmonidae. The Martinique governor and his adjuncts are still less favored. Apparently La Farge and I are welcomed, but you can judge of the number of travellers from the fact that literally Papeete has no hotel. Even Apia, small as it is, had more than one tolerable hotel, but Papeete has no accommodation of any kind for travellers. Yet the shops are fairly good — much better than in Apia, and European customs are very long fixed. I get an excellent French cuisinier at European wages, but I cannot get a cottage with a sitting room. The same queer contradictions run through the whole place. The little town, with its suspicion of French provincial queerness, and its streets running under shade-trees along the water-wall, is sweetly pretty. Neat schooners, in two or threes, are hauled up, stem and stern, against the sea-wall. There is no perceptible tide. Occasionally a man walks by. Sometimes he drives a pony in a chaise or cart. Quiet reigns except when broken by the frigate's regular calls. The air is like that of Naples. In the evening nothing stirs; by ten o'clock the silence is tremendous. There is a little club, and my first act was to sit down on the verandah and play dominoes; it seemed so obviously the correct thing to do; and at other tables half a dozen Frenchmen also played dominoes. To me the atmosphere is more than tinged by a South Sea melancholy, a little sense of hopelessness and premature decay. The natives are not the gay, big, animal creatures of Samoa who sang and danced because their whole natures were overstocked with life; they are still, silent, rather sad in expression, like the Hawaiians, and they are fearfully few in number. I catch myself always wondering what their towns will be like; but their towns, at least hereabouts, are thin and uncared for, and their houses seem never to belong where they stand. Even within ten years, life has fast drained away. There is far less sense of activity, less society and less gaiety, than ten years ago. Probably I like it better, but then it is not what I expected. Melancholy in such air and with blues so very ultramarine, has charm, and if La Farge could catch it in color, he would do something uncommon delicate; but behind the melancholy there is disease, and the old Hawaiian horror crops up here to make one sick with disgust. Except in the remoter places, the poor natives are all more or less diseased. They are allowed all the rum they want, and they drink wildly. They are forbidden to dance or to keep any of

their old warlike habits. They have no amusements, and they have
gens d'armes....

Tahiti is very — very old; seamed and scarred by deep valleys, with
mountain ridges sharp as knife edges, and not forest-covered, like
Samoa, but showing great stretches of red earth or jungle-like grass-
land. It is bordered by the same broad coral reef as in Samoa, with a
broad edge of surf. As in Samoa, the low shores are covered with
cocoa-nut palms, but the phylloxera has been introduced, and has
turned its attention so vigorously to the palms that they are all yellow,
diseased and dying. Mango trees grow everywhere, and we are re-
velling again in their turpentiny lusciousness. You can see from all
this that we have found nothing very new or startling to us; only a
sort of half-way house between Hawaii and Samoa....

Tuesday, February 12. I never saw a people that seemed so hopelessly bored as the Tahitians. The foreign residents here avow it with
unnecessary energy, and the natives express it in every look and attitude. Rum is the only amusement which civilisation and religion
have left them, and they drink-drink-drink, more and more every year,
while cultivation declines, the plantations go to ruin, and disease
undermines the race. The melancholy of it quite oppresses me, though
La Farge, being at last very well, seems unconscious of it. Last Sunday
afternoon at five o'clock we strolled up to hear the native band play,
in the little square before the unfinished building meant for a royal
palace. All the books talk of this band-playing, from Charley Stoddard's to the last newspaper correspondent's letters in the New Zealand Daily Polynesian, if there is one. I expected a gay little crowd
with some French vivacity, but I found only a dozen men walking up
and down by threes and fours, and about twice as many native or
half-caste women in the usual cotton night-gowns, sitting on benches
or on the wet ground, and appearing as little amused as myself. A few
vehicles were drawn up by the side of the street, and the ex-Queen
Marau with her sister Manihini drove up and down the road in a somewhat dilapidated pony-wagon.... From Papara I propose driving on,
across the isthmus of Taravao, as far as the district of Tautira. There
Stevenson staid, as the guest of the chiefs Ori and Arié, and was
adopted as a brother by Ori, and "given a name," as you can see in the
dedication of his new South Sea poem: "The Song of Rahéro."[1]
"Giving a name" is a serious matter here, like giving a title of nobility
in Europe, only more so, because a real name, or title, is here a fixed
thing, and goes with certain lands. In fact, to "give a name" is a

[1] In vol. XVI of the complete edition of Stevenson's writings.

regular feudal enfeofment; and Mrs. Salmon, as head chiefess, was by no means pleased with Ori for giving Stevenson a serious distinction of the kind....

February 13. La Farge has settled down to painting, varied by his usual mania for collecting photographs. I call it a mania because with me it has become a phobia; and he is almost afraid of telling me about his photographs because I detest them so much. Not that I blame him; for in my own line of manuscripts I did the same thing, and had to collect ten times what I could ever make useful; but I hate photographs abstractly, because they have given me more ideas perversely and immoveably wrong, than I ever should get by imagination. They are almost as bad as an ordinary book of travels....

I was delighted to see that some one was attacking my Vols. v and vi, in the *Tribune,* not that I wanted to know what he had to say in the way of attack, for I like abuse as little as other men do; but that I felt sure at last that I had one unknown reader. Till then I doubted greatly whether a hundred copies of the book had been sold. I still doubt, but am a little more hopeful. Really I think I do not much care, for I feel that the history is not what I care now to write, or want to say, if I say anything. It belongs to the *me* of 1870; a strangely different being from the *me* of 1890. There are not nine pages in the nine volumes that now express anything of my interests or feelings; unless perhaps some of my disillusionments. So you must not blame me if I feel, or seem to feel, morbid on the subject of the history. I care more for one chapter, or any dozen pages of *Esther* than for the whole history, including maps and indexes; so much more, indeed, that I would not let anyone read the story for fear the reader should profane it....

To Elizabeth Cameron

PAPEETE, February 23, 1891.

At last we are about to leave Papeete where we shall have staid near three weeks instead of one, as I had expected. The only result of staying the extra time is to make us more glad to go. Papeete is one of those ideal spots which have no fault except that of being insupportable. Stevenson warned us of its character, yet I am not sure but that, at some future day, when the halo of its distance again surrounds it, we may look back on our stay here with wonder that it bored us. The sun and moon leave nothing to desire. The mountains and the sea are fit for all the Gods of a Deological Cyclopædia. The town is different from anything I ever saw in the long catalogue of towns I have met, and has an expression of lost beatitude quite symbolic of Paradise, apart from its inhabitants. As for its inhabitants, I cannot imagine why I should be so worried by them, but I am; and yet they are more amusing than we had a right to expect. My chief trouble is the pervasive half-castitude that permeates everything; a sickly whitey-brown, or dirty-white complexion that suggests weakness, disease, and a combination of the least respectable qualities, both white and red. To be cooped up among two or three thousand such people, in a dirty shanty, with similar so-called cottages within ten feet on either side, makes one forget how exquisitely the morning sun filters through our vines and lights up our breakfast table, and how blue the sea is, before our gate, to say nothing of the tones of the mountains of Moorea, in the distance. Yet even when I forget the half-breeds and the cottages, and go swimming, so to speak, in the blue and purple light, I never lose consciousness of a sort of restless melancholy that will not explain why it should want to haunt a spot that by rights ought to be as gay as a comic opera. If Samoa were not a proof to the contrary, I should think that the fault was mine, but Samoa was never melancholy, though it was sometimes tiresome. Tahiti, or at least Papeete, is distinctly sad…. My favorite stroll is back to the saluting battery, which stands on a shoulder of the central mountains, several hundred feet above the town. After Tahitian fashion, the battery is there, with the paraphernalia of a fort, but without other sign of life. I can lie down on the decaying parapet, and watch the sunset without society; and what strikes me more and more, with every visit, is the invariable tone of pathos in the scenery. Upon my word, even the French tricolor looks softly purplish and shockingly out of place. Lovely as it is, it gets on my nerves at last — this eternal charm of middle-aged melancholy. If I could only paint it, or express it in poetry or prose, or do anything with it, or even shake it out of its exasperating repose, the feeling would be a pleasant one, and I should fall in love with the very wrinkles of my venerable and spiritual Tahitian grandmother; but when one has nothing else to look at, one rebels at being forever smiled upon by a grandmother whose complexion is absolutely divine, and whose attitude indicates the highest breeding, while she suggests no end of charm of conversation, yet refuses to do anything but smile in a sort of sad way that may mean much or mean nothing. Either she or I come near to being a fool….

PAPARA, 26 *February*. We escaped from Papeete two days ago…. Unlike Samoa, Tahiti has a road. The French built it, and it is not bad, at least on this side of the island. If you can stand another dose of geology, you will understand better why the road is good; why the drive was pretty, and why Mr. Darwin and Mr. Dana are the eyes and lungs and liver of science and geology, for they have made an immortal name by discovering that all this part of the Pacific has sunk, is sinking, and is morally bound to sink, in order to explain how the coral polyp can, at the rate of an inch a year, more or less, keep the eighty coral atolls of the neighboring Paumotu archipelago just flush with the surface of the ocean. This is clear as the sun, isn't it? You see the whole mystery as plain as you see me, sitting here on Tati Salmon's broad porch, at seven o'clock in the morning, with the velvet-green mountains, streaked by long white threads of waterfalls, looking down on me as though they wanted to know when they are to sink and disappear under water, to leave only a coral atoll above them, as I can certify that they are morally obliged to do, in order to be scientific. Bear me out now, and never let on that I question the truth of the universe. If Darwin and Dana choose to sing this song of McGinty, and insist that Tahiti must have sunk to the bottom of the sea, I, who swear by them, have no scruple in adopting and believing their faith — only the road from Papeete here runs the whole distance along the foot of an old line of sea-cliffs, carved and modelled in charming variety by water-action, and evidently extremely ancient. At the foot of these old sea-cliffs is a strip of flat ground, evidently the old coral reef, sometimes a few yards wide, sometimes half a mile or more, and elevated barely ten feet above the sea-level. Out at sea, sometimes near, but never very far away, is the more modern barrier reef with its surf as usual. So, here as in Samoa, instead of subsiding, the wretched island has certainly — at least on this side — risen ten feet in its last geological movement, after having remained stationary for many ages; and neither above nor below, in the water or out of it, can I see the faintest trace of a sign that anything ever was different; which is the reason why the road is level and good; the scenery charming, and Darwin always right.

At eleven o'clock we arrived at Papara, and were set down at Tati's door. Door is not the right word, for one is not very conscious of doors hereabouts; but Tati's house is an old French affair, and though not very different from a Mexican adobe house, is planned with some regard to exits and entrances. From the first moment, I felt contented — and I assure you, the sensation was both pleasant and unaccustomed, for some months have passed since I have felt disposed to say to the passing moment — Stay! The house stands flat on the sea-shore, and as I shook hands with Tati, and his old mother, and his sister, I caught glimpses of an intense blue sea, through the open doors and windows behind; a sea that came close up to the grass, and had three lines of surf rolling in, through an opening in the reef, and rolling close up till they sent small waves into the entrance of the little river that flows close by the house. We sat down to breakfast on the inner verandah, that looks up to the hills, and we had at last the delight of feeling the cool mountain air again, coming down just to oblige us. Tati is charming as a host, and his resemblance to Richardson is more and more striking. He is intelligent, well-informed, full of interest, especially in all matters that concern his tribe and island, and a grand seigneur such as can seldom be seen in these days; for the eight Teva districts of the island have no will but his, and his influence is greater than that of the French government, the Pomares and the church together. Tati is a young man still, thirty-eight years old, and his wife is not here. I never like to ask about wives in the South Seas, so I have not yet disturbed this part of the family. The present lady of the house, *ad interim*, is Tati's sister, a young lady lately returned from Hamburg, with health affected by a German climate, and with no small amount both of intelligence and beauty of the Miriam type. In her, Miriam is stronger than the old mother, who is pure native, and delightful; almost untouched by Europe as my Samoan matrons were. Old Mrs. Salmon will not sit at table with us; she sits on the floor, like a lady, and takes her food when she wants it. When she is inclined to talk, she tells us about pagan Tahiti; old songs, superstitions and customs. We know almost all of it, for we have been over the ground in Samoa, and we recognise here the wreck of what was alive there; but here the women wear clothes and no longer dance or swim on the reef. Long ago, each district had its professional beauties who were carried about on *malangas* and matched with the professional beauties of other districts. The great swells made songs for themselves, to be sung when they went out to show their figures by riding their planks on the surf. No more beauties exist. Neither Tati nor any other chief can shew me a handsome woman of pure blood. Instead of fifty or sixty thousand natives, five or six thousand are scattered in straggling houses round the island, without social life except in the church. Tati summoned his people to give us a *himene*, all that is left of the old song and dance. The very name — hymn — shows why this fragment has survived. The singing was almost identical with the Samoan, but more finished and elaborate. Some of the songs were old, and some were Teva war songs; but the life was gone....

TAUTIRA, *March* 1. The old chiefess kept us till twelve o'clock of

Thursday night telling the legend of a young chief of marvelous power, whose process of selecting a wife involved such difficulties of translation as kept Miss Pree and Master Winny much wider awake than I was. We all lay on mats on the verandah, in the moonlight, while the surf roared softly near by. Only La Farge and I had remained. Tati had gone to Papeete; a place he hates, and calls a nasty hole. Winny Brander stayed to take us to Tautira. We were quite happy so. The old chiefess was fascinating; and her daughter whose nickname is Pree, short for Beretania — Britain — has great charm, both of face and manner. I think you would enjoy the manner if not the face, but you will never see her. She is twenty-four, I believe. At Hamburg, while studying music, she broke down; her lungs were affected, and the doctors ordered her home. She came — by way of Cape Horn, Valparaiso and Easter Island — but she saved only her life, not her lungs. She coughs incessantly, and is bored besides. One may survive either of these afflictions, but not both.

Friday morning we bade goodbye to Papara. For once I was heartily sorry to leave a place, and would gladly have lingered; but no solid excuse seemed to offer itself, and as both our hostesses were soon to go to Papeete to bid Mrs. Darsie goodbye, we felt a little in the way. So off we went, taking Winny Brander with us, and sending our luggage on, in another wagon. Certainly Tahiti is lovely beyond common words. I seemed almost to feel again the freshness of my first travels, when the sun had not grown so stupid and prosaic as it is now. Of course Tahiti is not so grand in scale, or so varied in landscape as Hawaii, but it is exquisitely graceful in outline, and radiant in light and color. I have seen more brilliant blues and greens in Samoa, but never so enchanting a variety of light and shade, or of vegetation. We drove always on the level strip at the foot of old sea-bluffs, but, as we advanced, the vegetation became richer; the orange trees and bread-fruit gave a deeper green to the roadside; the ferns grew thick on the dripping banks, and the sea actually glowed blue through a lace-work of the long pandanus and cocoanut leaves. We stopped for two hours at a very dirty Chinaman's eating-place to lunch. This was on the isthmus of Taravoa. There the road crosses from the west to the east side of the island; and from there we entered the peninsula of Taiárapu. Plunging through mountain streams which were luckily low, we rattled along till about five o'clock when we performed what resembled a double somerset into the river at Tautira. We struggled through the stream and beyond the valley, half a mile further, till we came to our house in the village of Tautira, looking out over the reef,

for all the world exactly like our quarters at Apia. Awoki and
Peraudot had everything ready for us. Our host, Ori, Stevenson's
friend and brother, beamed on us. We called at once on Arié, the
chief, a conventional official, with a round face, who speaks French,
and has been to Paris. You can judge of our remoteness by two details.
Here we are at the end of the inhabited island; the road stops, and
there are no villages beyond. Here, too, we can find no interpreter.
Except Arié and the French priest; a Scotchman, deaf as a block, and
bearing, if you please, the name of Donald Cameron, boat-maker; and
a waif long ago wafted from England, named Parker, who lives on the
road to Taravoa, no one here speaks or understands a foreign language. Winny Brander stayed a day to start us, but could find no
interpreter for us. I sent at once for Donald Cameron, who was an old
man at whom I howled wildly orders to make tables and stands.
With Ori we try to hold converse by dictionary. Stevenson stayed
here for two months in the same situation, but we do not willingly put
up with deprivations that Stevenson thrives on. In other ways we are
better off. The house is comparatively large and has a good big room
in the centre, for living in. We can get neither milk nor meat, but
Peraudot manages to feed us in one way or another. My only griev-
ance is that they won't let me swim in the sea, for fear of some
poisonous fish or coral, I know not what; while the river is full half a
mile away. Then, too, as in Apia, one's walking ground is confined by
streams that cross the road at short intervals and have no bridges....

Every evening La Farge and I stroll to about the point from which
the enclosed photograph is taken, and there we wait for the after-glow,
which lasts about half an hour, and gives a succession of lights that
defy imitation or description. La Farge is trying to suggest them in
water-color, and some day you may see what he makes of it; but glass
is the only possible medium for such tones, and even glass could not
render all. Should you go to New York, you stop at his studio, and
ask to see the sketches he has sent home. They would certainly amuse
you, after reading my letters about the same things. Only I fear you
would be ashamed of me for venturing to touch a brush when he was
near. He has a wonderful faculty for getting light into his color. I
study in vain to find out how he does it, though I see all his processes.
I mix my colors by the dozens, and lay one deep wash over another;
but the result is always feeble and timid. He splashes in deep purples
on deep greens till the paper is soaked with a shapeless daub, yet the
next day, with a few touches it comes out a brilliant mass of color and
light. Of course it is not an exact rendering of the actual things he

paints, though often it is near enough to surprise me by its faithfulness; but whether exact or not, it always suggests the emotion of the moment.

Our days are quiet beyond anything you ever knew. As the chief Arié told us at our arrival, nothing ever happens here. The people have but one social amusement. Nearly every evening they sing in a sort of concert which they call a *himene*, and which is in fact a curious survival of the old dance music such as we knew so well at Samoa, but appropriated as hymn-music for church purposes. It is pretty and well done; better than the Samoan, and more developed; but it is monotonous and to me it wants the accompaniment of the dance movements for which it was made. The dance degenerated here so low that it had to be abolished. La Farge hopes to find means of seeing it, but I cannot believe that the women I see here could possibly dance well, or that the men are well enough trained to make an effective show. The people have lost the habit, as they have lost that of kava-drinking, human sacrifices, and other harmless and simple pagan practices. People who wear clothes can't dance. So they sit on the ground and sing....

March 8. Apparently we are destined to play seconds to Stevenson. For myself I don't care, and am willing to play second to anyone who goes first — Stevenson or Goward or even James G. Blaine or Benjamin Harrison — but it is hard on the immortal Scotchman. If you have read his ballad of Rahéro just out, you will see it is dedicated to Ori, and the dedication is rather the prettiest part of it. Ori exchanged names "in the island mode" with Stevenson, giving him the name Teriitera, and Stevenson takes it *au sérieux*, as the ballads show. Much was said on the subject, and Stevenson's native name here is always Teriitera. I dreaded a repetition of this baptism, and tried to show total indifference to the native custom; but last evening when we were taking our absinthe before dinner, Ori informed me that I was to take his name, Ori, and then and there I became — and had to become — Ori, and he Atamu. La Farge also had to go through the same process. Although Ori is, I think, only a nickname, and probably not an island title like Teriitera, it happens to be the name used by Stevenson in dedicating his poem. I presume that Stevenson — or Teriitera — and I are brothers of the Teva clan, and that his poem bears my name. The situation is just a half-tone too yellow-green. I fear that Stevenson will fail to enjoy the jest, and I am myself not altogether clear about it, for without the express approval of Tati and his mother, I do not care for such adoption....

To Elizabeth Cameron

Tautira, Sunday, March 16, '91.

A week ago today we made up a large bundle of letters, and a box of La Farge's water-colors. As the "City of Papeete" was to sail for San Francisco on the 12th, we made Ori hunt up a wagon for us, and at two o'clock on Sunday afternoon we started for Taravao, to hand our letters and box to the *gen d'arme* or resident or mail agent or Chinaman or whoever might be the proper person. Our first adventure was one which occurs here with much regularity. In plunging into the river, at its deepest part, which is luckily only a hole of about three feet just now, the horses balked, and left us planted. To get us out of the water, and up the opposite bank, was a matter of half an hour, for the horses had to be taken out and La Farge and I had to be taken out too; and then the wagon had to be hauled out by hand. After this delay we rattled along over green grass and under foliage of Paradise, and through small streams that set traps for us in the road, until our harness broke and we nearly upset. Another half hour started us off again over more grass, under more huge wild-orange trees, breadfruits, cocoanuts, mangoes, and wonderful big leaved, glossy trees that look like the magnolia grandiflora run mad; and all the way the blue sea — theatrically blue and arranged in harmonies — gave little love-slaps on the sand a few yards away, where the trees leaned over the water to keep it cool. Two hours of this jaunt brought us to the Chinaman's at Taravao, where we found the *gen d'arme*, and the *resident*, and the mail agent, sitting under the palm-leaf shed or rain-shelter, playing dominoes — of course — and drinking vermouth. After all, we were not so far from the Bois de Vincennes and the Barrière de — Tahiti; *coelum non dominum*, or dominoes; we too sat down and shared the vermouth, while La Farge in his very best French explained our object. Then we drove back to Tautira successfully; and after a week we learn that our last Sunday's effort was perfectly unnecessary; that the "City of Papeete" has not yet sailed, and that our drive was the only advantage of our otherwise wasted energy....

I am bored — oh great Taaroa, known in Samoa as Tangaloa, how I am bored! Never have I known what it was to be so bored before, even in the worst wilds of Beacon Street or at the dreariest dinner-tables of Belgravia. My mind has given way. I have horrors. No human being ever saw life more lovely than here, and I actually sit, hour after hour, doing nothing but look out at the sky and sea, because it is exquisitely lovely and makes me so desperately homesick; and I cannot understand either why it is so beautiful or why it makes me so frantic to escape. We have seen not a human being except villagers whom we cannot talk with. In desperation at sitting still, I try to paint, and the painting seems more futile than the sitting still. We have read all the works in Tahiti, and as for me, I am so tired of reading about the virtues and vices of the Tahitians that I wish I could see some. As for the Tahitians that have come within my acquaintance, except when they happened to be Jews, they have been the most commonplace, dreary, spiritless people I have yet seen. If they have amusements or pleasures, they conceal them. Neither dance nor game have I seen or heard of; nor surf-swimming nor ball-playing nor anything but the stupid mechanical *himene*. They do not even move with spirit. If I were not afraid of extravagance I should say that they were more melancholy than Hawaiians.

As the devil will always have it, the governor sent word that neither of the French war-vessels could go to the Marquesas, at the very moment when I was becoming eager to go. As I am honestly too miserable at sea to risk a month in a small schooner, I saw myself obliged to abandon the Marquesas at the same time when I realised the true inwardness of Tahiti. Add to these causes of seriousness that our cook Peraudot broke down with headache, and went back to Papeete, and that La Farge and I were reduced by some mysterious article of diet to the decided opinion that life was not worth living when it depended on the liver. On the whole, the past week on this crumpety-tree has been far from gay to this pair of kwangle-wangle-kwee. As the poet truly said, very few people come this way....

I ought surely to enjoy a month of quiet beauty here. Alack, it is disease! I had a vague hope that somewhere in the round world, merely on the chances of the cards, I should sooner or later happen on some spot where a combination of attractions or amusements would detain me and give me interest or occupation; but the hope has almost vanished. The Polynesian is thin. The Melanesian is thick. The Mongolian irritates me with his invariable air of cheeky superiority — just, but ungenerous. Motion alone amuses, and I see only the desert of Gobi that offers room for even a moderate exercise of the horse.

Sunday, March 23. The last week has gone better, thanks to an improvement in the conditions of Mr. Mallet's [1] (is that his name?) problem, and to a visit from Tati, who came here to load the Richmond with oranges, and brought with him a Los Angeles man named

[1] William Hurrell Mallock's *Is Life Worth Living?*

Meserve, who is getting orange trees for California. Tati is like a northwest wind at home; he brings freshness and gaiety wherever he goes. He not only made things lively here, and started the people off in schemes to amuse us, but he laid out our own plans....

With Tati and Meserve, we went on the reef one afternoon.... The reef is an excessively curious coral wall, standing some two feet above the level of the lagoon, and averaging forty or fifty feet wide, like a superb boulevard, with a shining surface, absolutely unbroken by the smallest stone or inequality for miles. The outside surf constantly washes over it, and the surges of boiling foam every few minutes swamp one up to the knees, and often take one unexpectedly in a way that disturbs one's scientific reflections.... La Farge was luckier. He was delighted with the picturesqueness of the reef, with the water always rushing in little cataracts over its inner walls, and dashing in blue and green masses, dissolving into what Shelley calls star-showers, on the outer plane. Apart from a little nervousness as to the particular kind of poisonous coral, or slimy mass of tentacles, or purple or red animated bladders with indefinite worm-like arms, on which one walks, one is not reasonably nervous, for a big wave would knock one clear into the lagoon where one would be perfectly safe in three feet of water. The natives who go outside in canoes to fish, are sometimes, in heavy weather, obliged to jump the reef on a big wave, and do it generally all right. Tati told us of one native who was chased by a shark, and had just time to drop himself, canoe and all, on the reef. He split up his boat on the spot, threw his fishing-tackle into the surf, and bade goodbye to the ocean then and there, scared out of his life. A big shark, twenty or thirty or forty feet long, is an appeal to our finest instincts as I know, for one gave us his society on our sail from Tutuila to Apia. The shark is a great family God among the natives. Our chief Arié has him. One of them carefully escorted the body of the member of the family who was last brought here by boat to be buried.

March 29. My own calm has not been much disturbed of late, and I go on, trying every day to make pictures, and every day learning, as one does in a new language, a word or two more, just to show that the thing is laughable. Still, I have learned enough, from La Farge's instruction, to make me look at painting rather from the inside, and see a good many things about a picture that I only felt before. Perhaps this is worth while. Perhaps it isn't. I don't know, and think I don't care. La Farge is not much better off, for although he knows and cares intensely, he satisfies himself rather less than I do, and has been for a week as blue as his own ultramarine, the favorite subject of despondency being dissatisfaction with his work. I really think that at times his impressionable nature tries to turn itself out of its shell like a crab. Still, when we come to blues, I tell him truthfully that I can go him better every time, and beat his head off on color in that line of art if in no other; which seems rather to encourage him....

PAPARA, *April* 4. Back again at Tati's. The festivity is on account of the opening of a bridge, which took place yesterday.... There was Hinari, our old grandmother, sitting on her mats surrounded by small grandchildren; her daughter Marau — the Queen, you remember; Miss Pree, more handsome, and I thought more delicate than a month ago; Manihini, or Chica, or familiarly Cheeky, a handsome girl of twenty or so; the three Brander boys, Norman, Arthur and Winny; a big daughter of Tati's and another of Marau's that look like pictures from Gulliver's travels; no end of smaller children, dogs, chickens, occasional pigs, horses and domestics; and beyond, hardly a stone's-throw away, the surf rolling in miles of foam straight up to our hands. Tati, surrounded by all his duties and household cares, seemed to take us in at a gulp, as easily as if we had been more children. Hinari, Marau and the two sisters were cordial as possible, and we sat down to dinner feeling a little as though we had returned to the world.

In its way, which is a queer enough little way, Tahiti does represent a sort of world. The fête of the bridge-opening was the sort of thing that one naturally puts in a novel. At nine o'clock, the Governor punctually appeared at Tati's, the *chéferie*; and of course we were all in white suits to meet him. Monsieur de la Cascade was, I believe, a banker at Martinique or Guadeloupe, and I should say he was a quadroon, but a *mourir de rire*. La Farge and I, on comparing notes, found that he was a wonderful combination of August Belmont and the typical stock-broker of the Gymnase and vaudeville, who will turn out either to be the victim or the villain, but villain twice out of three times. He was very affable, and gave us all sorts of invitations which we could not accept, jerking out his conversation with a sort of Japanese mixture of deference, patronage and suspiciousness. His staff was modest, and hardly worth describing. We had to be formal for near two hours with this little man in a tall silk hat, frock coat, and tri-color sash, until I sighed for our old Samoan receptions and the speeches of the *tulafales*. Then we went ahead to the bridge, Marau and Manihini and the Branders in charge of us; but the bridge was dull. One or two hundred natives in bright dresses, and faces sometimes pleasant and sometimes plain but never beautiful, lined the road, but did not sing or dance or show more animation than so many

European peasantry would have done. The actual formalities were stupid beyond the proper limits of French officialdom. Then we had a lunch which was better, and to my mind quite prettily done. The Governor was host, and sat on one side of a long table with a big bouquet of leaves in front of him as though he wished to blot out his majesty King Pomare who sat opposite in his goggles. At that hour in the morning, Pomare was not obviously drunk, and made no noise. Almost back to back with him, at a parallel table, was Marau with her sister Manihini. Tati and I sat opposite to the Governor again, looking at the King's back. The rest of the company, mostly French officials or trades-people, did not interest me to the extent of their numbers, which was perhaps a hundred. We eat our dishes, drank our Bordeaux, and had a toast to the ladies, and there an end.

In the afternoon we had an entertainment of a different sort, which Tati and I witnessed alone, for the others were all scattered elsewhere. A division of the district, say a hundred or more people, came to Tati's for the division of a present of salt pork and other food, made by the government to the laborers on the bridge. Tati was asked to see to the division to prevent a row, and he had an idea that perhaps they might get dancing and be amusing. Once more I was disappointed. The natives were, as Tati said, far too drunk for making a dance. I do not understand the thing. They could have drunk very little, yet indubitably drunk they were, Tati said with excitement chiefly. They were sober enough not to permit actual fighting, and the women and children were apparently not at all worried by the drinking and the drunkards, but they seemed to me a rather more drunken crowd than I ever saw abroad. They were noisy but not funny. Tati, used to his own people as he is, had to stand over them all the time to prevent a row, and was evidently much pleased to get it over.

PAPARA, 8 *April*. Very unwillingly we shall probably leave Tati's hospitality tomorrow. Our visit here has been one of the bright spots of our travels. If I struck such episodes often, I think I should travel indefinitely, yet I hardly know what it is that we find so pleasant. As long as the women were here, we had society, for they would be interesting persons in any countryhouse. The old lady, Hinari or Grandmother, is a very fine type indeed; quite a royal person in her island way. Naturally I have treated her for what she is; that is, next to Mata-afa, altogether the most interesting native figure in the whole Pacific. Apparently she felt that I meant what I said, for she was very goodnatured and open with us. She told us freely her oldest legends and traditions, and took a motherly interest in us. My adoption into the Teva clan by Ori was rather a joke. Indeed I had sent word to the old Chiefess through Tati, a month ago, that I should not think of accepting such a relationship without her formal and express approval. I supposed she would have given it on our arrival here, but she did not; nor did she ever call me Ori, as she should naturally have done if she approved, so that I rather inferred that she did not like the adoption, as she was said to have been displeased by that of Stevenson. I was quite upset, last Monday morning, just before they all went away, when the old lady with a certain dignity of manner, drawing a chair near mine, sat down and made me a little formal speech in native words, which of course I did not understand, and which Marau, who was in the secret, instantly translated. The speech was, I believe, the proper, traditional and formal act of investiture, and conferred on me the hereditary family name of Taura-atua, with the lands, rights and privileges attached to it. The compliment from such a source was so great as to be awkward. To be sure, the lands attached to the name of Taura-atua are only about a hundred feet square, a few miles from here; but the name is a very real thing, and was borne by Tati's ancestors, and is actually borne now by his second son. To give it to me was a sort of adoption. Of course, I expressed my sense of the honor, and got Marau to speak for me; after which she turned to La Farge and repeated the same form to him, conferring on him another name, also real and hereditary. The whole thing was done simply but quite royally, with a certain condescension as well as kindness of manner. For once, my repose of manner was disturbed beyond concealment. So I am now Taura-atua and Ori-a-ori; a member of both outer and inner Tevas, and a close relation of Tati himself. La Farge also is Teva by double adoption, and I suppose we are both brothers of Mrs. Stevenson. The adoption was the more formal because it was done in the presence of Tati, Marau, and all the family then here, and they had been consulted beforehand. I was glad of this, because I like them all, and especially took interest in Marau, the queen, who is a woman very much out of the common. She is, I imagine, somewhere in the thirties, and her face and figure have grown heavy and somewhat Indian, as is rather the rule with the women here. If she was once handsome, certainly her beauty is not what attracts men now. What she has is a face strongly marked and decidedly intelligent, with a sub-expression of recklessness, or true old-goldishness, that always charms me and Clarence King when it is real. One feels the hundred generations of chiefs who are in her, without one commoner except the late Salmon, her deceased parent. Hebrew and Polynesian mix rather well, when the Hebrew does not get the better; and Marau, like her brother Tati, is more Tahiti than Syria. At all events she is greatly interested in Tahiti history, poetry, legends and traditions, and as for ghost-stories, she tells them by the hour with evident belief in them, and entire confidence in the independent evolution of native ghosts and ghost-seers. As everyone here does in his heart believe in all the old native spiritual faiths; and Christianity is just one more, only successful because Jehovah is biggest and has licked Taaroa and Oro, there is nothing really strange in Marau's frank outspokenness; but it is entertaining all the same. Marau has the same big, Richardsonian ways that her brother Tati has. She always seems to me to be quite capable of doing anything strange, out of abstraction; as she might mistake me for her small child, and sling me on her arm without noticing the difference, such as it is, in size. She is good-natured, I should say; easy, indolent, and yet, like her race, capable of committing any kind of folly, and of going to the devil like a true Polynesian for sentiment or for appetite, for love, jealousy or ennui. Luckily she is now pretty well past her *jeunesse outrageuse*. The next generation is the one now in trouble, and of that I hear much, but see little. Poor Pree has had to go to Papeete to see her doctor again, and I fear her cough is worse. La Farge has made a little drawing for her album, and I have written in it a metrical translation of a dozen lines from the Odyssey. Manini is a true girl, with no formed character. All of them went away on Monday, leaving us alone with Tati and his wife. Tati's wife is shy and avoids us, probably because she speaks none of our languages, and is neither a Pomare nor a chiefess in her own right. Tati does everything. This afternoon he drove us in the farm-wagon a mile or two through the woods to see my duchy, Taura-atua. Apart from the personal interest in my estate of six orange trees and a mango or pandanus, I was interested in the glimpse of history. Some fifteen generations ago, old Taura was a great warrior. I imagine him like Pa-tu in Samoa. He was military chief of the two districts here, and must have led several thousand men, but never owned any land except the hundred feet square on which his house stood. There Tati showed us the stones which limited the low platform or terrace on which the house stood. As Taura-atua I had also a private Marau and the right to order human sacrifices. I took investiture of my duchy in the shape of an orange. On our way back we spied sharply for the cave in the cliff where the heads of Tati's ancestors are hidden, and which Tati himself does not know. The old man, whose hereditary duty was to take up the heads and keep them oiled and fresh, can no longer climb up there, and has no son to succeed him, and is bound by oath to tell the secret to no one else. The family must lose its heads. Tomorrow we bid Tati good-bye. He is a dear fellow.

To Elizabeth Cameron

OPUNOHU, 19 April, 1891.

Tahiti is lovely; the climate is perfect; we have made a sort of home here; and I never shall meet another spot so suitable to die in. The world actually vanishes here. Papeete was silent and sleepy; Tautira was so remote that existence became a dream; but Opunohu is solitude such as neither poetry nor mathematics can express. Now that I have seen this little island — Moorea or Eimea — I see that it was once a big volcano, enormously long ages ago. The crater was on the level of the sea, but its walls rose, like those of Kilauea and Haleakala in the Sandwich Islands, several thousand feet above the floor of the crater. Peaks, sharp as knives and toothpicks, still remain three or four thousand feet high. We are in the old crater, and need imagination to know it, for it is two or three miles long, and instead of being a great pit, like Kilauea, it broke its sides out in two places into the sea. So it now makes an irregular amphitheatre, looking out on the ocean through the Opunohu bay, and the neighboring Cook's Bay, each some two miles long, while the valley behind us, which was the crater, extends back still greater distances till it abuts against walls of lava-rock worn and colored by time. Geology breaks down in measuring time here. Nothing has ever changed. The seasons are all summer; the trade-wind has always blown; the ocean has always been infinite about it. Moorea is the oldest spot of earth I ever saw. Compared with it, Tahiti is a younger brother. I believe it has stood here since time began, and oceans cooled. At all events, I defy geology to prove the contrary; and have my private opinion of Darwin and Dana, as by this time you know. If Tahiti was sad, Moorea is sadder. Man somehow got here, I think about a thousand years ago, and made a society which was on the whole the most successful the world ever saw, because it rested on the solidest possible foundation of no morals at all....

To Elizabeth Cameron

Papeete, Sunday, May 3, 1891.

. . . .

Like Robinson Crusoe and Herman Melville, I have been able to turn my mind to nothing except escape from my island. I wanted so much to carry out my promise of reaching London by September, that after the "Richmond" sailed without us, I persuaded myself to risk my precious health in a sailing vessel, and I instructed Captain Harte to charter for me the best schooner he could find to take us to Fiji. The best schooner he could find was the "Nassau" of thirty-five tons, which means a little boat fifty feet long and twelve feet wide, in which we were to sail two thousand miles as best we could. With full consciousness of the misery I should certainly suffer, I authorised Harte to pay fifteen hundred dollars for this cockboat for the voyage to Fiji. No sooner had I made the offer than the German firm here took up the "Nassau" for a trading cruise, and the captain decided that his interests required him to do what the firm wished. Then I made the same offer general. I applied for any schooner properly built and commanded, and even offered to buy any of them if they could not be chartered. All my offers were refused. No one would either charter or sell, or enter on discussion of terms. Of the dozen schooners about these islands, not one could be had. I have passed a week in useless search, and am now obliged to give it up. As for a larger vessel, I have no hopes. No vessels bound westward come here. Indeed no vessels except the "Courtney Ford" and "Tropic Bird" are to be found within a thousand miles. The chance is very small that any ship will turn up which can go out of its course so far as Fiji for any money whatever. I thought seriously of returning to San Francisco in the "Tropic Bird," and crossing to Europe by way of New York, if my letters offered any excuse for so wild a course; but our letters are innocent of any such matter. So we must wait another month for the "Richmond," and go down to Auckland in midwinter, in order to go on either to Fiji or Sydney, with the certainty of stormy passages in small steamers that are worse than sailing vessels. Meanwhile I have exhausted Tahiti which is a true Crusoe island. Luckily we are not unhappy here. I am not even in low spirits, as I was at Samoa in the last month of my stay there. La Farge is well and apparently happy, and busy painting. Our society is limited enough; but our sisters Beretania and Manihini are next door; Marau comes up and down from Faaa, and is almost energetic. Our grandmother Hinari comes to town occasionally. I tell the women that of all the straight-laced, puritanical, highly moral communities I ever struck, Tahiti is the strictest; for they will not even come to breakfast on our porch, or sit there to watch the sunset; and Marau discourses eloquently on the propensities of Papeete society for scandal, although she knows that I come from Boston and scandal cannot touch a Bostonian. I tell them that all the most highly moral young women in America come to breakfast and dine with me in Washington, but it produces no effect on them....

Sunday, May 10. Another week of exasperated idleness. A schooner called the "Gironde" has come in. It belongs to the German firm, and I have been trying to charter it. The firm uses it to bring cocoanuts and such produce to freight ships with, and although the schooner barely pays its way, the owners refuse even to discuss letting us have her for six weeks. I have got so far as to suggest willingness to pay two thousand dollars net, besides another thousand for the expenses of the vessel, which is five times as much as they ever dreamed of getting for a six weeks use of the wretched craft; but still the old Dutchman will not listen. Naturally I am vexed, for I could get a good yacht for such a price in America; but here I am helpless. Still, I think by dint of perseverance and money, I can drive an idea even into a German head; or if not, I can make noise enough to attract some other vessel; for there are about fifteen such schooners plying from Papeete to the neighboring islands, though none but the "Gironde" are in port....

By way of excitement or something to talk about, I sometime ago told Marau that she ought to write her memoirs, and if she would narrate her life to me, I would take notes and write it out, chapter by chapter. To our surprise, she took up the idea seriously, and we are to begin today, assisted by the old chiefess mother, who will have to start us from Captain Cook's time. If I had begun this job when we first arrived, I might have made something of it; but now at best I can do only a fragment.... The Polynesian woman seems to me too much like the Polynesian man; the difference is not great enough to admit of sentiment, only of physical divergence. The old-gold woman has most of the drawbacks of modern women, except the extreme nervous sensitiveness. She is physically better adapted to her work, but intellectually she suffers the more. The old-gold woman is incapable of resisting any impulse. She yields easily to a stronger will, which is natural enough; but she yields also to any temptation, no matter how slight. She has no habit of resistance. She yields to a lover, which is not surprising, seeing the force of the passion; but, in her, I doubt whether there is a thought of resistance, unless it is fear of being killed by a husband; for jealousy is violent here. If another lover comes along, she yields just as easily to his will. The same weakness runs through every appetite she has, and makes her drink, for example, or do whatever comes into her head that is not absolutely *tabu*. This weakness is the cause of the fearful depopulation of the Pacific Islands, but the poor creatures have still gone gaily to destruction, and only of late years one begins to see the look of sadness which always goes with civilisation, and means that a race has opened its eyes to its cares....

Wednesday, May 13. My life here has ceased to be more than mere waiting for departure; yet I have actually begun on Marau's memoirs, and sketched the introductory chapter after taking a mass of memoranda from her dictation. The work is useful in distracting my thoughts from sheer vacuity, and it teaches me a little more, or at least a little more exact knowledge of the island than I should ever have got from books or conversation. The trouble is that Marau never stays here two days, but dashes off to Faaa, five miles out of town, to look after her children or her farm or whatever she has there; and unless I pursue her to Faaa, I must wait till she comes up again before I can go on. Next Saturday we are to have a native breakfast at Faaa, after the style of our Samoan banana-leaf feasts; no plates or knives or forks; but plenty of breadfruit and pig. We are sure to find it amusing, and in my opinion quite as good as our own style of French cooking, which has become intolerable. Housekeeping is as much of a bore here as everywhere else, and the cook problem quite as insoluble. Our cousins Pree and Cheeky are shocked at the way I let myself be robbed; and indeed I suppose the waste of my establishment would run theirs, though to me the whole expense seems small after the waste of your — I mean my household at Washington. Are you naturally a good economist? I suppose I am not, for I can economise only in scale, not in detail. Here no one spends more than two or three thousand dollars a year, I imagine, or has it to spend. The British Consul is paid £600, I think, with some allowances. Our Consul gets a thousand dollars and a sort of house. My friend Tati, who is the great man here in native estimation, told me all about his life, which has been a hard struggle to make a mere living, and to feed his children. He tells me that his sister Mrs. Darsie, *veuve* Brander, after closing up all her affairs, can hardly be worth more than a hundred and fifty thousand dollars; yet Brander was much the richest merchant hereabouts. There are at least a dozen houses competing here for the business of these scattered islands under French rule — Paumotus, Marquesas, Tahitian and what not, containing barely thirty thousand people, half of whom absolutely refuse to work for wages — and the whole value of exports combined does not exceed $1,500,000 in gold. Naturally men can make no large fortunes on such a business, and if life were not a constant picnic, they could not live here at all....

To Elizabeth Cameron

PAPEETE, Sunday, 17 May, 1891.

Marau gave us a feast yesterday at Faaa.... Marau's feast was very pleasant and simple. The house is a rough sort of cottage in the midst of a great cocoanut plantation, four miles from here, on the sea-shore. The feast was spread on a low table under a palm-leaf trellis ornamented with yellow leaves, and we were all ornamented with wreathes like Greek Gods. We sat cross-legged on the mats, and ate all sorts of tasteless native dishes, much better to my mind than our own greasy French stuff, but rather funny than nice. I drank orange rum, which is only orange juice slightly fermented, a sort of orangeade, which, with ice, I rather like, and which seems harmless. Only Marau, Pree, Manini, Norman and Arthur Brander, two native ladies married to foreigners, and the French *médecin* were the party. After the long breakfast we had much singing, including a *himene*, till five o'clock, when we drove in. Compared with the frank savagery of our Samoan feasts, this was highly civilised and almost Versailles; but the native customs were as much kept up as could be expected where savagery has been so long *tabu* as here. The only genuine native article was the nose-flute, which is rather a pretty accompaniment to their songs....

Sunday, 24 May.... Meanwhile another week has passed in this lazy life, and here is another lovely Sunday morning with the women going to church in their red calico nightgowns, and the blue sea looking as gentle as a peacock. The longer I stay here, the less I am bored. Being now thoroughly adopted into the Teva family, I find myself provided with occupation, for I have at last got them into a condition of wild interest in history. My interest appears to have captured the old lady, who astonished her children by telling me things she would never tell them; and as they had to act as interpreters, they caught the disease one by one, till at length they have all got out their pens and paper, and are hard at work, making out the family genealogy for a thousand years back, and tracing their collateral connections in every direction. The difficulties and complications are very amusing, and as I am always asking questions and forgetting the answers, they never get their minds clear. The old lady's memory is prodigious, but even she often makes mistakes. Marau tells me a story, Moetie (Mrs. Atwater) tells me a different one; the old lady laughs at both, and tells it in a way totally unlike either. Tati is coming from Papara today, and will doubtless join the dance. I have stopped writing the memoirs because I found that, without the genealogy to hang it on, the narrative was always wrong or unintelligible; but every day a crop of new stories, legends or songs, turn up, until a year's work would hardly be enough to put them in shape. If Alexandre Dumas had ever struck this *trouvaille* he would have made a wonderfully amusing book of it. Stevenson could have done it, too, but he never got in with the old lady, and only touched the outside rim of Tahitian history. His Legend of Rahéro is extremely well done, and has only the fault of being done with more care than the importance of the legend deserves. In reading it, one is constantly worried by wondering that he should have worked so hard on so slight a subject. Rahéro was a very subordinate figure in history, and connects with nothing. The legends and poetry of the island can be made interesting only by stringing them on a narrative, and Stevenson could have done it better than any one else, for he has a light hand, when he likes, and can write verse as well as prose. My hand is too heavy for such work, and here I am anyway only a passing traveller trying to find a moment of amusement to vary the wild monotony of island life. You cannot in your loftiest visions imagine the quiet of Tahiti. Even time does not seem to pass here; the seasons do not vary; the years run into one; and geological epochs are unknown. The sun comes and goes, as individuals are born and die, but the rest never changes, or changes too little for notice. Rain falls occasionally, but no storm worth the name comes near us. Generally eternal sunshine falls on eternal cocoanuts. The purple ocean looks vaster about us than it does from shipboard. I gaze over it by the hour, wondering what lies beyond....

Sunday, May 31. Positively I have worked. I am not quite so brazen-faced as to claim to have done real work; but I have been quite as busy as I should be at home. I have untangled two centuries of family history, and got it wound up nicely. I have rewritten two chapters, making a very learned disquisition on Tahitian genealogy, mixed up with legends and love-songs. The thing would be rather pretty if I only knew how to do it, or perhaps it might be better if I were writing it on my own account; but as it is for Marau in the first person, I have to leave out everything risky. All the family have labored in a most unusual spirit of interest, but they are now pretty well exhausted. Energy in Tahiti is very brief affair. I shall not have time to carry the memoirs beyond an introduction, and shall leave it with Marau to finish if she chooses, and send it to me to put in shape for printing privately. If she does it, you shall see it; but I have no faith in the future of any undertaking left in Tahiti to the people. They finish nothing. My papers may perhaps be kept, but generally even papers are scattered and lost. Marau is the only one of the family who carries the interest to the point of enthusiasm, and she finds it hard to work alone. When the old chiefess dies, no one will be left on the island who has any real accurate knowledge of the past. The Pomares never amounted to much, and Hinoi, the last male of the family, is an owl for stupidity....

Monday, June 1. Tahiti is as lovely as ever in bidding us good-bye. Our family is affectionate, and we shall be a little sad at ceasing to be Taura-atua and Terai-tua. Marau is to go on with her memoirs, and send them to Washington. So she says, with her ferocious air of determination, half Tahitian and half Hebrew; and if she keeps her word, I shall have a little occupation at Washington which will amuse you too, for I have begged her to put in all the scandal she can, and the devil knows she can put in plenty. She tells me today that her late lord, King Pomare, is very ill, and supposed to be dying. Apparently I am fatal to Kings. Kalakaua and Pomare march to the grave as I pass. I should be employed by the anarchists.

To Elizabeth Cameron

HITIAA, TAHITI, 4 June, 1891.

Our last day on Tahiti. I breakfasted with my family. The old chiefess never sits at table, she hates such Europeanisms, and she had to go to church to pray for Pomare and the sick; a special prayer-day on account of the epidemic of fever and dysentery which has been ravaging the island ever since we arrived. So Marau presided, with her brother Nari, just from the Paumotus. By the bye, Nari, who is as charming as Tati in his way, showed us, at La Farge's request, a box of pearls which was the total result of fifty tons of pearl-shell. The shell is worth about a hundred dollars a ton, I think — or a thousand — or a hundred thousand — I neither know nor care which, and my love of inaccuracy, and want of memory drive La Farge half mad. He is — don't laugh! — phenomenally accurate and precise. No one will believe me, but I tell what I know, when I say that he is as systematic, exact and conventional as he thinks he is. The world altogether misunderstands us both. He is practical; I am loose minded, and looser still in my management of affairs. He is to be implicitly believed wherever facts are in question; I am invariably mistaken. *Revenons à nos perles!* Nari's box contained half a dozen pearls — or seven — or five, or, in short, a small number. He valued them at an average of about a hundred dollars, gold, apiece; his consignee, the animal Jorss, estimated them at less than half. None were worth buying.... Besides Marau and Pree and Nari, all the Brander boys were at table: Aleck, Norman, Arthur and Winny; and we had a gay breakfast; but I cared much less for the gaiety than I did for the parting with the dear old lady, who kissed me on both cheeks — after all, she is barely seventy, *va!* — and made us a little speech, with such dignity and feeling, that though it was in native, and I did not understand a word of it, I quite broke down. I shall never see her again, but I have learned from her what the archaic woman was. If Marau only completes the memoirs, you will see; and I left Marau dead bent on doing it.

So Taura-atua and Terai-tua y Amo drove away from the home of their nobility, and left forever the scenes where they had been great warriors and splendid lovers. I wrote poetry then. Marae-ura was her name, and she lived at the pae-pae, among the bushes. I had to leave her because *my* family objected; but I immortalised her in verse. That was a century — or two — or three — ago. Time goes so fast! Four months seem now an eternity — just the time I have been here, and must take to get elsewhere, counting from one o'clock yesterday afternoon when we started from Papeete on our drive to Hitiaa. We need not have made the journey, but we wanted to see the east side of the island, which is almost prettier than the west. The road, much of it, is a narrow and rough wagonway cut in the cliff, and not safer than it should be; but it always skirts the big ocean — such a big ocean! — and when it wanders a few rods away, it runs through a grassy avenue of forest — not tropical, as one imagines it, but much as it might be in England, if England produced palms and breadfruit besides oaks and ash.

After rambling four hours or more among this somewhat bumpy but all the more beautiful road, we arrived towards sunset at an ideal Tahitian village — Hitiaa — where I am now writing, on the green turf, or at least grass, before the hut, with the surf close behind me, and the big trees above. It is almost the prettiest spot we have seen. To the southward, twenty miles or so across the bay, we see our old quarters at Tautira, and our little steamer lies three miles down the shore, loading with oranges. The season is mid-winter. The temperature has fallen several degrees, and is now about eighty. The ocean is rough with the trade-wind, and looks as blue as I feel at going again upon it. The people are as friendly and mild as ever, and, for the moment, are not drunk. Tati, who has the oranges to ship, received us with open arms, as big and handsome as ever. I wish you knew him, for he is to me quite fascinating, with the sort of overflow of life that made Richardson so irresistible. If he ever stays with me at Washington, you and I will have him to ourselves, and not let the natives misunderstand him. His wife, a sweet-presenced native woman who speaks no foreign jargon, and ripples out from time to time only with *tiritaratauauteve*, or something like it — for these sounds mean everything — bids us *iorana* which is good-morning, or good-day or goodnight, like the Samoan *alofa*; and then tells the small baby Tita, *haremai*, which means *come*; or, to pacify La Farge I will say *go*; and that is all we know about it. Our native house is perfectly clean, and has a floor, and beds, and the host and hostess think it their duty to watch us undress, and dress in the morning. My bath in the river is a levee. *Aue!* 't will all be over tomorrow.

RAROTONGA, *June* 10. We ran out of Hitiaa into a rough sea which washed our low deck; but we stopped three hours at Papeete and got some dinner, and again bade good-bye to all our family, with tender parting from the old chiefess. At four o'clock on the afternoon of the 5th we were off again, bobbing about in the big swell, and going nine miles an hour southwestward.... Rarotonga is a small replica of Moorea, six hundred miles on our way. The British resident, Mr. Moss, was friendly, and took us to see the Queen, Mokea, to whom Marau had given us a letter. Mokea is big, middle-aged, goodnatured, with a certain breeding, but she is as Polynesianiacally untalkative as most of her race. These little islands are so small — so very small — and so like each other, that they tell nothing. The natives all wear clothes, have stopped their old amusements, and are missionary ridden. Their morals and conversation are supposed to be at least liberal still, but they go to church five times a Sunday. In an hour we are off for Fiji, twelve hundred miles, or a trifle more than five days.

Sunday, 14 *June*.... This is what seamen call Paradise. To me, the South Seas are vile. Three days out of four we have head-seas, or cross-seas, that knock us all about, and feel like the British channel. The trade-wind never blows steadily; but, like any other wind, hauls

round ahead after a day or two; a heavy swell is always coming from the
south or somewhere to roll one out of one's meals; and the sea is dull
in color; the sky is grey and almost cold; even the sunsets and sunrises are spiritless. I have now sailed over this ocean in pretty much
all seasons, and ought to know it from end to end; so I look forward
with abject horror to twelve or fourteen thousand more miles, when
twelve or fourteen hundred have brought me so low.... Well, we are
now in sight of the first outlying islands of the Fiji group. Tonga already lies behind us, just out of sight; and in forty-eight hours we
should be ashore at Suva, under Sir John Thurston's protection. Only
eighteen hundred and fifty miles have we travelled when we get there,
but the Richmond goes barely nine miles an hour, and will take ten
days, with her stoppage at Rarotonga, to cover the distance. By
schooner I should have taken more than three weeks, and how miserable I should have been! That at least is escaped. Of course the Richmond has no other advantage. Passengers enough, including a missionary and his wife, and four ramping children; Frenchmen three or
four; stray mysteries a few; but no one whom I want to exchange a
nod with. I prefer the captain and crew, who are plain English, very
friendly and simple; and as for the crew, pretty seedy in spots....

GOVERNMENT HOUSE, SUVA, FIJI ISLANDS, *June* 16, 1891. Bravo!
Here we are at last, in Sir John Thurston's hands, and only a trace of
inward rolling reminding us of the Richmond and the sea. Our last two
days on board were not so bad, and we turned up well and smiling
to enter Suva harbor yesterday morning. Sir John sent his private
secretary to fetch us ashore, and brought us at once up to the Government House where he is alone, his wife and family being at Sydney.
The house covers half an acre of ground on the hill overlooking the
harbor and sea, with mountains stretching far away; an exquisite
view; but the strangest sensation is the dropping suddenly into civilised life after a year's absence. Suva is a scrap of England dropped into
space. We lounge in a big library among newspapers and magazines.
We dress for dinner. The young men are nice-mannered and play
cricket. The women wear dresses and play lawn-tennis. We talk of
home and are taught botany and politics. Sir John is agreeable, very
intelligent and educated, with very little that suggests British-
English; rather the Australian or Australasian type, which is a kind of
first cousin to the Harvard College American. As yet we have done
nothing but unpack trunks and wash off sea-associations, and look at
a game of cricket. We have not even been down to the little town.
As for the Fijians, we have seen nothing of them except a few choco-

late men, with huge mops of hair sticking out straight, reddened with lime as in Samoa. A lovely sentinel, with a waist-cloth and a hundred weight of hair, and a gun on his shoulder, walks day and night before the house. Our attendants at meals are three gigantic Fijians in barbaric want of costume, and cannibalistic masses of hair, who smile kindly on us since they are deprived of their natural right of eating us. Curiously enough, I have always found the cannibal a most insinuating fellow, remarkable for his open and sympathetic expression. His impression of human nature is evidently favorable. He regards men as I regard snipe. Even the Solomon Islanders, who are still, when at home, cannibals of the most gormandising class, and black as night, look like the jolliest, cheeriest and friendliest of human kind. Once among cannibals, I feel that my heart is with them. They may eat me, but they will do it in pure good-fellowship. Sir John is to take us to the ancients haunts of Fijian civilisation, and I believe he is to begin tomorrow with some expedition. I am delighted to find that he has sound views on savages, and insists on their retaining all the savagery possible, consistent with a cuisine which excludes man-steaks from the *menu*. So we shall go through all the forms again, and I hope we shall have dances and songs worth our trouble....

June 20. Just now, we are trotting with the Fijians, who amuse me mildly, and I feel much as though I had returned to my long-lost archaic home, so familiar are their Samoan faces and songs. Sir John took us, two days ago, on our first excursion. With Captain Grenfell and several officers of the British corvette "Cordelia," we went twenty miles in Sir John's small steam yacht, inside the reef, to the Rewa river, a stream about as large as the Thames at London, and stopped at the chief's place to have a reception. The whole affair was a sort of variation on our Savaii excursion last autumn, but so different in detail as to be rather new. The Rewa district, or province, or kingdom, or whatever it might be, is the delta of the Rewa river, and as like Holland as you please. I never saw a prettier, sunnier, cheerfuller scene than the sluggish stream with its thatched native houses, and its boats of natives coming and going to or from our show. We arrived at about three o'clock, and were taken to the chief's house which was given up to us. I was rather surprised to find the Fijian native house quite the finest I had yet seen. It is much like the Samoan in a way, but the decoration shows taste, and the dignity of it is really something pretty effective. The sides are thatched up to the eaves with leaves; for Fiji is quite a cold place, and the mercury goes as low as 64° at night now. When wind blows, one feels positively shivery.

Fiji houses are lighted by half a dozen doors, closed by a sort of mats if necessary. They are very large, so that when our mosquito nets were all hung up at night, they looked like a camp under a huge roof. We went through our old ceremony of the *kava* first, with much singing but no speeches; many men but no women; and the men differing immensely in type between black African negro and light Polynesian. Rewa is largely Tongan, which is Polynesian. The Tongans came here and conquered part of the island, and still show their blood; but the Rewa chiefs have none of the wonderful general uniformity of beauty which the Samoans had. They seemed to me rather ugly as an average, but more intelligent. They seem to have no fancy for oratory, and none of the love of posing which delighted us so much at Samoa. Nymph and naiad, orator and faun, have no place among the practical Fijians. The poetry has pretty much all gone. When we came to the dances, we saw this still more plainly. The dances were just what I have been unable to find in the other islands, and they were certainly very effective, but they were war-dances and nothing else. A phalanx of men, perhaps a hundred in number, with war-clubs, axes, spears and war-paint of black and vermilion, go through a regular war-dance, beginning with slow, and ending with quick movements. The effect was fine and very savage, and the warriors brandished their clubs and spears as though they still knew how to use them. The women and children and non-dancers in general, sat about, on the grass, perhaps fifteen hundred of them, and I studied their looks carefully, but without much satisfaction. They run from black to red, but are coarser by far than the Samoans, and are a mere brutal mob compared with Tahitians. The brutality shows most in the women, who have evidently been treated as pretty poor creatures, with none of the eminent social advantages that were enjoyed by their neighbors to the eastward. I regret to say that the morals of Fijian society, where women were practically slaves, were very much better than in Samoa, Tahiti and Hawaii, where women were almost equals with men; and what is worse, the women are going to the bad rapidly since polygamy and clubs were prohibited by the missionaries. The children die, and the mothers prefer not to have them. The chiefs debate the causes of the decline in population, and when they are tired, refer it to the Governor General. In the native council, one very old chief who rarely spoke more than a grunt of approval, paralysed the audience by an address which, Sir John says, ran much like this: "I am an old man, and a fool, and know nothing, and what I say is not worth your hearing. When I was young, these things were not so; the children lived; the women took care of them. Now the children die; the women neglect them. I am an old man and a fool. You are young men and know everything. What I say is said by a fool; but I see no good in talking and sending to tell the governor that we leave it all to him and the Queen. When I was young, things were different, and though I am a fool, and you are wiser and young, I think, instead of leaving it all to the governor to ask him to give us back the right of clubbing the women." Painful as it is to admit such a possible moral *impasse*, the best judges here seem to think that the old man's advice was the only practical means of avoiding the destruction of the race. Polygamy and clubbing were the foundations of society, and when they were taken away, society began slowly to perish. I do not commit you to sympathy with views of this nature. Of course, American women, not the men, do the necessary clubbing nowadays, and maintain society by their own energy; but the archaic world is very simple and humorous in its frank way of showing us the blessings of our virtues. Fiji, like Tahiti and Samoa and Hawaii, is a monument to our high moral standard. All is for the best in our best of possible worlds. The virtuous woman flourished with the help of the club at Fiji. The excessively unvirtuous woman flourished like the breadfruit at Tahiti. Both perish in the presence of our enlightenment and religion....

If we were only beginning our travels I should gladly linger here, for Sir John is a charming host, very kind, intelligent and frank; an excellent talker, and full of experience in all matters connected with the Pacific; so that our stay would have been a first-rate education for travel; but now we know as much about the Pacific as most people can boast, and especially the romantic part of it, so that we have no more great experiences to desire except to eat the durian and mangosteen in the Malay archipelago. My chief fear is to find them out of season, which would be an inexpressible disaster since they were my chief object in coming to the tropics at all. Surely I should be obliged sooner or later to return, and ten thousand miles of ocean are a high price for one durian.

To Elizabeth Cameron

FIJI, Sunday, 28 June, 1891.

I am now passing Sunday at Joske's station, at the village of Vuni Ndowa some forty miles up the Rewa river. Mr. Joske is a young Englishman, gentlemanly and well educated, the magistrate of the district, and his station is beautifully situated, on a bluff or hill above the river, and looks south and west towards distant mountains. The day is exquisite. The native house is cool and softly lighted; Sir John has gone to church with the two magistrates, Carew and Joske; Mr. Berry, Sir John's brother-in-law, another official, is reading on the lounge; young Spence, the private secretary is reading in the reclining chair; La Farge is reading in another chair, and all will soon be dozing. Our party consists of these seven men, reckoning myself as one, and we are doing Sunday here, before starting tomorrow morning for the mountains....

The next morning we were up bright and early, and before nine o'clock were away in boats dragged by a steam launch by the same way we travelled before, along the coast, inside the reef, until we reached the mouth of the Rewa; then up the river to the sugar-mills where we arrived soon after noon, but stopped only to get upon a stern-wheel, light-draught steamer of the sugar company, and then passed on. The day was very fine, and as we got higher up, the banks became very pretty, and the groups of people, sometimes Fijians and sometimes Indian coolies, exquisitely picturesque; but I imagined myself in India. The river bank was lined with fields of sugar and bananas; comparatively few cocoanut palms and almost no breadfruit; the people very dark; the landscape flattish; hardly a trace left of our old Polynesian scenery and surroundings. With hundreds of acres of bananas ripening for the Sydney market, none were offered us to eat, or were eaten by the people except cooked green. Not an orange or a lemon or a lime, far less a cocoanut or custard-apple, was brought to the Governor; and as for the garlands of our youth and beauty, we are now far from Samoa and Tahiti, and never shall wear garlands any more, or see the flaming hybiscus in the hair of our fauns and naiads. Fiji is practical and unromantic. Now and then our steamer stopped either to pick up a local magistrate or to receive a native chief, who brought the usual gifts of big baskets of yams, taro, and a pig, which was immediately divided among our escort; but we got nothing, and saw only groups of elderly savages squatting on the bank.

Romance is gone, but prettiness remains, and we had enough to amuse us all day until towards five o'clock we reached the head of steam navigation, and stopped for the night at the native village called Viria. Here as everywhere the houses are large and apparently clean, and the village is neat, but our receptions have none of the fun of Samoa. We sit down cross-legged on the mats, and we take our kava with the due forms, but the ceremony seems to me a little cold and perfunctory. After the kava we are left to ourselves. No *taupo*, in tinsel and cocoanut-oil, smiles on us, or dances for us; indeed we see no women young or old, and few children. Instead of the noisy, playing, singing swarms of young that bothered our lives at Samoa, Fijian villages are quiet and to me rather melancholy. The Tahitians are sad, but they do at least sing their *himenes* as though they were Siva songs. The Fijian evening hymn is a regular slow psalm-tune, more serious than Old Hundred, and when the night has fallen, this lugubrious music is heard all about, near and far, announced by the beating of the wooden drums which resound over the whole country, from every village, at prayer-time morning and evening. We have our supper, and then smoke and chat awhile, and go to bed, having seen as nearly as possible nothing of the natives.

Saturday (*yesterday*). La Farge, Spence and I started again at nine o'clock, in a canoe, roofed over with thatch, so that we could see little and sleep a good deal. Sir John and the others rode or walked the fourteen miles to Joske's. Our canoe was poled by six natives, and we were nearly five hours on the way. The weather was beautiful, and the scenery was pretty. As we go up the river, the stream becomes rapid in places, and our canoe scrapes the gravel, so that one gets ahead slowly. I lay on my side and watched the bank or the boats that passed. The country was hilly and wooded, but no mountains. The prettiest thing is the tree-fern, which grows everywhere, but the trees are not very fine. The landscape is rich, but the richest thing about it is that for the first time since ten months ago, we are not in sight of the sea. We reached Joske's station towards two o'clock, and found ourselves in what I imagine to be like a hill station in India. The houses are native, but the people in it, the books and reviews, the tastes and the conversation are English. Even the house-servant is an Indian who looks like a prince in disguise, and wears bangles and long oiled hair with a red silk skull-cap. The curry is divine, but nothing Fijian is even suggested to eat, unless it is the yam, which here takes the place of the cocoanut, the breadfruit, the wild-plantain and the banana of Polynesia. The landscape is lovely, but it is more like a summer day in the Alleghanies than like an island of the South Seas....

July 2. We have labored steadily up the water-channels of the Rewa till we are now in the centre of the island, shut in by mountains. Not a dozen white men have ever penetrated these regions, and, of these, nearly all were government officers. The journey is very amusing. Sir John travels like Stanley in Africa. We have certainly a hundred and fifty native carriers and attendants, who are strung out in a long line, winding across the river and round the gorges, as picturesque as if they were on the war-path. Our mode of travel has so far been easy. I turn out of bed at seven; put on a jacket, a *sulu*, or *pareu* or *lava-lava* (as you like to call the waist-cloth, here, or in Tahiti or in Samoa), and slippers, and tumble down to the bathing-pool, which is always in the river close by. The sun is just rising above the mountains, the mists lie over the valleys, and the thermometer ranges from 54° to 60° at daybreak. The water is cool and fresh like the air....

Once, at Na Vuna Wai-wai Vula, I think it was, two days ago, Sir John was detained till afternoon to hold a big council, and give a wigging to an unfortunate chief, or Mboule, whom he threatened to hang and shoot and burn if he didn't make his people behave themselves. The chief defended himself with great dignity, and quite won my sympathies; but as a matter of fact the people are still savage, and would be back at their old practices in six months, with their incantations and wars and cannibal feasts, if the foreign government were taken away. All the older men about us have been glorious cannibals within twenty years. As it is, they are ornaments to human nature, especially when painted black and vermilion in stripes down their faces, or with black faces beautifully spotted with vermilion. Our day's journey once begun, we walk, if the path is dry; and, for the river crossings, Mr. Joske, who runs the party, has provided three *chaises-à-porteurs*, in which Sir John, La Farge, and I are carried, while Joske, Carew, and Berry bravely wade. Poor Spence sprained his ankle in wading, and has been sent back by boat. Our boats had to be left behind two days ago; our horses still earlier; and today our road was a river-gorge, perfectly wild, and a mere bed of round rocks. We make short days; four hours' walking is the utmost I have had to do; but it satisfies me, and as the sun is hot, I am more than ready to get into quarters and plunge into the river; but sometimes when we arrive early, we have a big reception, and a *meke-meke*, or dance. The men march up, with spears and clubs, as they did at Rewa, and go through various movements symbolic of all sorts of mischief to their enemies. The women never appear. We bring too many men with us for the peace of the Fijian hearth. By the way, we are now in the land of hearths. The nights are cold, and the big native houses have often half a dozen hearths, with large logs smouldering in them. Our evenings are always quiet; no songs except hymns; no dances; no visitors. We get our dinner at seven; smoke and chat till nine; then go to bed and sleep peacefully in the big, dark houses, till some one stirs at dawn. I lie awake a good deal, but nothing seems to imitate me. Once in a while I hear some night-bird, more or less uncanny, but the silence of the night is rather strange. The whole forest seems to have nothing to say.

Today we have marched two hours through as wild and beautiful a ravine as I want to see, coming out at the mountain village of Na-son-go, which is different from all we have seen; and our house is growing conical until I begin to think myself in Africa, and about to buy a girl for a feast. Yet the scenery is very like the Virginian Alleghanies, if you would throw in a few tree-ferns and palms and long pendent creepers. Occasionally a green parrot squawks about us, but I have seen no parroquets. We find no fruits but wild lemons of which we make lemonade. We get no food except chickens and yams, for the pigs and *taro* go to the army. The people are poor, very African, and yet sometimes not ill-looking; but the villages are extremely pretty, and Sir John Thurston has done more in a dozen years to make the country human than has been done by the French in fifty years at Tahiti. The natives are cutting roads, or paths, with energy that is miraculous, and very grateful to my tender feet. We are now beyond the farthest range of even the European trader; when the natives want anything, they must walk a day to the nearest trader's; these hill tribes are set apart under the absolute authority of the governor, and no white or black nonsense is suffered to interfere with his will; but yesterday we tramped for some two hours along a new road cut through the forest on the sharp side of the mountain, and, except a few steep places, the path was perfect. In another ten years, I've no doubt the whole interior will be intersected by easy paths, which will doubtless make my next visit less alarming to my imaginations. Just now I am lying awake o'nights because our next move is through a forest and over a mountain range by a rough native track.

Besides the novelty of finding at last an unknown country where the simple savage is truly simple, and would gladly eat you if such were the Christian commandment, we have at last reached a region where science has got another tough job to settle with its conscience. For the last two days we have tramped between vast walls of conglomerate and breccia, the wreck of older mountains long ago broken into small bits and carried down probably below the sea to be compressed solid under heavy weights of wash or lava, and then lifted up again at least seven hundred feet. The torrent has cut deep through these beds, and the natives make use of caves in them for burial places. What interests me more is that we have reached a spot where coral rock is said to lie on or in the mountain-side. Tomorrow Sir John is to go for that coral, and will take me with him. If we find it, I shall not have the first gleam of an idiotic suspicion when or how it got there, or what it wanted there anyhow, but it will be rather fun. I have been hunting everywhere for a raised coral bank, not because a raised coral bank has the smallest personal interest to me; but because it is a kind of coral-line conundrum which, as a serious Darwinian, I am morally bound to defy and repudiate. Darwin says that the coral islands have miraculous powers of sinking, while all the coral islands I have seen are perfectly stupid evidences of rising. Till now I have never seen or heard of a clear case of rise more than perhaps two or three hundred feet. Here they claim a thousand or more feet of it. If we can settle this, I give you all the advantages. The next time you meet a geologist you can hit him on the head with my specimens, like Abner Dean of Angels.

July 4. We duly went for the corals yesterday, but the bed of the stream being most evil walking, we went no further than was necessary to select specimens from the loose rocks and boulders in the dry part of the channel. These were quite enough to prove anything under the sun. In pity for you I will only say that all Viti Levu seems to be one big mass of broken volcanic stones in sand-beds, with shells and coral, all solidified into a coarse conglomerate, and proving elevation of at least three thousand feet, while vast amounts of mud, discharged from the volcanoes, made foot-hills and flat alluvial shores. I regret to say that my fourth coral group is still more disgustingly anti-Darwin than any of its predecessors. With this final blow, my battle for subsidence ends, leaving me knocked clean out of the ring at every round. You may breathe more easily, for you will hear no more geology from me. The day turned to rain and became melancholy. La Farge sketched and Sir John and Mr. Berry photographed, in a dismal drizzle. We were driven early into our hut, and so to dinner, our baccy and our beds. The party is quite a cheerful one, and fond of fun in a quiet way. Five of the six are fifty or more years old, so we are not sky-larks, but we keep our dotage fairly green. Even the mornings are not hard. I was up at half past six today, and plunged into the pool in a morning mist which looked a fair sample of rain. We breakfasted hastily, and started at ten minutes before eight. As the river-bed became here a mass of big boulders with constant wading, we left it, and struck straight up the spur of the mountain, by a native wood path, slippery with mud, and often giving no foothold but roots. The creeks and ravines round Washington have sides much like these Fiji valleys, except that we rose a thousand feet in an hour. For about three hours and a half we climbed pretty steadily, until we stood at last twenty-three hundred

feet above sea-level, with a drizzling mist and a temperature of 62°.
La Farge gave in, but the Governor had provided for this well understood probability, and La Farge was promptly reclined in his palanquin, and carried the last mile or two. The rest of us reached the top,
with our army of carriers, or part of it; and there we lunched; and then
and there, to my great disgust and to the lively amusement of the
party, Sir John made me drink Ben Harrison's health, and our guard
fired three rounds of shotted cartridges in honor of the day. I en-
treated them not to tell my friends that they had played so rough a
practical joke on me as to harry me with Benjamin and the Fourth of
July in the middle of the forests of Fiji where no white man had been
before me, but they swore they would print it. I don't think they will
quite descend to this, but La Farge is sure to tell it, so I might as well
tell it myself. Then we began to descend again, by another breakneck
trail. As I had two stalwart Fijians, with mop heads, to pull me up
hill, and to tumble upon whenever I slipped going down, I got along
very well. La Farge, by the grace of his Christian merits, escaped being capsized, and was a most picturesque sight as his bamboo boat was
carried among the tangles of palms, ferns, creepers, and tree-trunks,
now standing apparently on one end, now on the other, and swaying
above a noisy crowd of black wild-men. Sir John led our column, following close on the wood-choppers, and as a path had to be cleared for
the palanquin, we came down slowly, which gave Sir John time to
show me the botany of the forest, and especially the peculiar ferns. I
had a fair taste of the tropical forest. Flowers were rare and not much
worth noticing, but like a true Yankee I consoled myself by reflecting that at every step I trampled on plants worth at least five dollars
apiece in New York or London, and that no emperor tossed so much
possible wealth about, as I did. The forest had a charm of its own, not
of color or of scent or of any of the qualities that we like most in our
woods, but for depth of verdure, richness of parasitic growth, with
lines and masses quite strange to our notions, and a certain waste and
extravagance quite profligate and reprehensible, but not wicked. The
missionaries would stop it if they could, but the rains fall, and the
ferns and creepers still cling high on the tree trunks. The tree-fern is
almost unnaturally graceful and delicate, rather too much like feminine art-decoration, but it is at least wild, as all the forest is. Neither
cocoanut palm nor bread fruit intrudes here. We had an hour of this
lounging among the ferns and orchids; then we reached our creek
again, still the Na-songo, close to its head-waters, under an amphitheatre of mountain, and here we went into camp at half past one. We

are now beyond even the native villages, and are in the least frequented parts of the forest, but we live as usual. Hundreds of people bring up yams and other food. Huts are built for us as we go. Above all, I drop down to the creek and get my dip morning and evening, while La Farge laughs at me for saying that the water has a pleasant chill. He suffers from cold. I expect to suffer also, when we reach three thousand feet tomorrow, and the temperature at night falls to the forties.

July 5. Camp-fires last night, and, later, rain, with thermometer at 62°. I slept not at all, till morning, owing I guess to tea; and the outlook was dismally wet when I clambered down to my bath among the boulders. Our breakfast and meals grow painfully tinned; even a roast yam is a luxury. Today being Sunday, we had native prayers and left camp at nine. Another desperate, slippery, headlong climb up the mountain began our march. La Farge was lashed into his palanquin and dragged up somehow; I did not see him, being much too busy with dragging my own legs. Dense forest surrounded us everywhere, even when we walked along narrow spurs hardly six feet across, with an indefinite drop on either side, where a single big tree blocked the whole road. For three hours and something more we tramped through the soaked woods, slipping and sliding down ravines, and clambering up, until at last we turned the flank of the range, and came on an open grass spot, thirty-one hundred feet above sea-level, and looking far westward over the valley of the Singa-toka. I was heartily glad to escape from the wet Rewa country to the dry central and western region, where patches of grass are scattered about among patches of forest. We lunched at our grass-patch, and then tumbled down to the camp on the Singa-toka river, a little mountain stream, in which I seated myself with the utmost rapidity, weary though I was with five hours of heavy tramping. La Farge too walked the last half. Our camp is still far from villages. We carry a good-sized village with us, but see nothing except wild country. Last night we were sixteen hundred feet above sea-level; tonight we are twenty-three hundred, but the clouds tonight lie on the mountain behind us. I hope our next march will at least have drier foothold, but my feet and legs hold out better than I feared.

July 7. Light rain fell all night, and when we broke up our camp the next morning, yesterday, the rain was still drizzling, and we began our march in a path slippery with trampled mud. As usual we had a narrow valley to cross, and then a steep hill, by a true Fijian trail, straight up, without curve or holding-ground for our boots. Powers alive, how we slipped and swore! A stalwart naked Fijian, whose toes clung to the mud, took me by the hand and lifted me up the hill-side. Two others supported La Farge. Sir John led the march, also drawn up by an aid. About two hundred natives in single file, carried boxes and bags, or followed for their own amusement, carrying nothing. We were happier than usual in having only a short range to climb, and were well over the worst in fifteen minutes, but Carew, who is a heavy man, was badly blown and looked quite blue when we reached the top. Then we tramped on along another of the knife-edges which seem to form the crests of all these mountain-ranges. Slipping and sliding up and down the inequalities of ground, we splashed on among masses of ferns and brush, with splendid *dakua* or kauri-gum trees here and there rising far above us; but our tramp was not long, and we soon tumbled down again into the next valley, coming out, in an hour, on the little village of Mata-kula, with a dozen conical huts, on the long spur of the mountains we had just crossed. This was Sir John's objective point. In this valley where the Singa-toka takes its rise, he hoped to establish a sanitarium, and our journey was for the purpose of exploring the ground, and planning a road. Here we are within fifteen miles of the sea to the westward, and twenty-two hundred feet above sea-level. The valley is the widest in all the mountain region; about two miles long by half a mile wide; but the mountains all round it are so cut up by ravines, and their sides so steep and stony that, if this valley does not answer, there seems to be no chance of getting suited, and Sir John had been sure that we should find here an elevation of three thousand feet. The discovery that we could get no more than twenty-two hundred feet out of it, quite upset his calculations. We went into quarters at once. As the only decent house in the village was the missionary's, which is a box for stowing at most half a dozen beds, Sir John, Mr. Berry, La Farge and I are there, and there we have meals. The others are quartered all about, among the huts or under shelter of palm-ferns for tents. I was satisfied to rest yesterday, for my legs were draggy, so I lay on a fern-bed in front of our hut, and dried my clothes and boots as the clouds disappeared and the air became dry. We are now in a dry country, where I can no longer get my dip in the mountain streams. Water is brought up by the children in bamboos from half a mile away. Towards sunset I strolled down, across a reedy, rank meadow, to the little river which hardly trickles along its bed, deep under a bower of dense trees and ferns. Broad patches of coarse grass are interspersed among the masses of forest. Green parrots and parroquets fly out of the cover. We had a dinner of pigeon-curry which was uncommonly good, and today I have begged Joske to try a parrot-curry and baked bananas. We are still among the poorest mountain tribes, and our supplies are far from splendid; yams and taro are the staple food, and I hanker after neither. Ripe bananas are not to be had; we are beyond the region of fish, and we won't eat pig. Our village seems to be the only one in this valley, and between here and the coast is a rough and sharp descent of more than two thousand feet which cuts us off from luxuries. Today is lovely. We slept as usual on our mats, with ferns underneath, after an evening round a regular old-fashioned camp-fire. I can sleep on fern, but the ridges are still rough, and by seven o'clock I am quite ready to come out and watch the mists roll away, while I toast my legs before the fire and drink a cup of cocoa. One by one the party turns out and inquires the minimum temperature of the night. The range yesterday was from 73° at noon to 54° at dawn this morning. Now, at noon again, it is 80°or very near it, a lovely day, and I am sitting on the ground, under a shelter of ferns which the men have made for me, and trying to write on my knees without breaking my back....

July 12. We left Mata-kula at half past nine o'clock and walked up the valley, through open meadows, into more forest, trampling along as usual, over a path more or less broken by gullies and streams, until in about two hours, we came to the great wall which lines the northern side of the island, and which must be the lip or edge of what was once an enormous crater, the other lip of which is the island of Vanua Levu, sixty or seventy miles across the water. Out of this huge hole the vast mass of broken stone must have been thrown which now makes the mountains of both islands; a bed of pudding-stone or agglomerate at least three thousand feet deep, and tilted so as to incline southward to the coast some sixty or eighty miles away at Suva. So much my travels have taught me, but I doubt whether I can make money out of the investment. You are welcome to all the profits. I did not even make a landscape out of it, although we stood on the crest of a precipice like the Pali at Honolulu which is one of the finest views in the world. The whole valley beneath us was full of clouds and mist which eddied up to us, and looked like an active volcano, but cut off all outlook. I lay an hour on the grassy edge while Sir John climbed further up the hills to fix the site of his sanitarium, for we were all satisfied that this was the proper spot. We were twenty-four hundred feet above the sea, and an extra five hundred feet could easily be got by rising a bit to our right where a stream was tumbling into the mist. When we had lunched and finished prospecting, we began our descent, and slid or stumbled down the sharp hill-side in the clouds, until about five hundred feet below we got beneath them, and could see across a dozen miles of open hills and valleys the ocean to the northward. An hour's work, and a descent of twelve or fifteen hundred feet, brought us to the village of Wai-kumbo-kumbo, another hamlet of the mountain-tribes, where we halted for the night. As usual the villagers were gathered to receive us; the head-man presented the usual whale's tusks, and the people brought the pigs and yams to feed our carriers. Then we took a bath in the mountain stream, and felt happy. The loveliest enjoyment of tramping is the getting to the end of the day's journey. A new village is always amusing and often charming. Wai-kumbo-kumbo was a poor little place, and our house was stuffy, with only one small entrance to creep through, and much suspicion of bugs, centipedes, and mice; but the place was picturesque and lively with a swarm of half-naked blacks, who looked as savage as ex-cannibals should. Under mosquito-nets one feels almost protected from wandering insects, and with a little more light I could have eaten my stewed parrot off my boots without difficulty, for appetite is not one of the missing virtues in mountain tramps. Sleep is harder. Before I have been half an hour asleep, some of our guard tumble in and go to bed, waking me of course. Then a mouse squeaks to her young ones in the thatch by my ear. Then a rat walks across the mats, pat-pat-pat. Then a pig sets up a terrible squealing as he is dragged down to be drowned or otherwise killed at the stream, while I see the light of the fire which is heating the stones in which, wrapped in banana leaves, he is to be baked for breakfast. The natives squat about their fires, drinking kava and smoking, till late at night, and they murmur distantly. A child in a near hut has whooping cough. Still I do get to sleep at last, invariably, and wake at six by daylight or moving about me. Then I lie till seven, thinking of — England; and then I turn out for my toilet among the rocks in the stream. Breakfast comes in time; our carriers take our traps; and soon after nine we are off. This was the last march and went to the sea through a hilly, bare, brown country, under a hot sun, on a splendid day. After the first hour, La Farge was mounted on a horse belonging to the young magistrate of the district, Marriott, who sent him up for the purpose. The rest of us walked. Berry and Joske have left us, to explore the ranges to the east, and we shall not see them for three or four days. Sir John, Carew and I tramped along the road, which was a real road, grassy and springy, and we took it easy. At noon we stopped by a stream and had a cup of tea. Half an hour afterwards we met some men who brought us some green fresh cocoanuts to drink,

and I assure you that the world offers few things more refreshing than
a green cocoanut to a thirsty traveller. The last two hours of our
march seemed hard, for my toes got rubbed and sore from two days'
successive tramp. We gradually left the hills, crossed a plain, and entered a mangrove swamp, walking an hour or so along a dyke just above
the tides. We were probably not more than four hours and a half on
foot, and ten miles at the utmost, but we were uncommonly glad to
reach the village at last, where the "Clyde" was waiting us. The day
was still young; we arrived at half past three, and we had a deal still to
do. Everything was ready for our reception, and the town of Vanua-
kula looked delightfully pretty and cool in the shade of its glossy-
leaved *ifi* or chestnut trees. We had chairs on the grass, and received
our whale's tusks and speech, and then looked on at a *meke-meke*, or
war-dance like that we saw at Rewa and elsewhere. The dancers come
in enveloped in fantastic mountains of white *tapa*, which is wound
round them up to their necks; coils and puffs, making them look like
walking bags, brandishing long spears and clubs. When the dance is
over, they uncoil themselves, and leave the *tapa* in a big heap on the
ground as a gift for the Governor. Then the women, in a long procession, dressed, or rather fagotées, in violent purples, yellows, reds and
every other color to be bought in tinsel-paper or cheap cloth, marched
in, carrying baskets of food, including fish and crabs. The girls, or
virgins, wear no tunics, and have pretty figures. On one side of their
heads the hair is braided in queer little tails; a mark of their marriageable character. This was the first time I got a fair sight of the women,
and on the whole they were not so bad as I expected; but these coast
towns are as much Polynesian as Fijian. The whole affair was pretty
and gay, all the more because we could rest, and take off our shoes,
and drink cocoanuts. Then at sunset we bathed in the river Tavua,
and had some dinner, after which the Governor sent us on board the
"Clyde" for the night. The "Clyde" lay near three miles below, and
we had to be rowed or poled or dragged an hour among the mangroves,
which are weird at best, but by the dim light of a new moon, just setting, are an experience. Once on board, our day was not ended, for the
captain made us a whiskey cocktail, and we were kept awake pretty
much all night by noise, and were turned up at six by Sir John coming
aboard with twenty or thirty followers. At seven we were off, a thoroughly weary and sleepy party, and I, for one, cross as a Yankee
cannibal, but we watched the coast, had some crab-curry for breakfast, and soon after nine o'clock ran into the river Mba, or Ba, and
landed at the first town. This is another large river which drains the

northwestern coast, and has sugar plantations, and a civil magistrate of the first class, a young Englishman named Marriott. We are comparatively civilised here. The native chief is a *Roko*, or Prince, who has Mboules (the B is always pronounced Mb) under him. He gave us a big, clean house, with pretty mats, chairs, a table and even a looking-glass, pleasing to one who had not seen a reflection of his beard for a fortnight. The reception was very correct and formal; the *kava* or *angona* as it is called here, was prepared and drunk with the exactly proper singing. The *meke-meke* or war dance in the afternoon was particularly good, and the *tapa* made a big hill. The Roko looks like an Arab and is soft spoken as such a high-born cannibal should be. The people are not beautiful — far from it — but the scene at the *meke-meke* was extremely pretty, with sitting groups and lively colors. We were very tired and slept much of the day, and the bath was by no means a clear mountain stream; but we are comfortable, which is lucky as we remain three days. Yesterday we were rowed up the river three miles to Marriott's station, where we lunched on real cooked things, and made the acquaintance of Mrs. Marriott, a pretty, sweet, refined London girl, just married and only a few weeks buried in this ultra-remote cane-brake. As La Farge remarked, it was pathetic, and needed only a baby to be tragic; but the solitude, the flies, the mosquitoes and centipedes, and even the natives, are not much more of a bore than at an American or English watering-place. The climate is exquisite and healthy; the distant mountains are beautiful, and there is no want of work. On the whole, once over homesickness, the life is tolerably intolerable. After lunch we crossed the river to the sugar plantation and were received by the manager's wife, another young woman, but from Sydney, and I was interested to watch the contrast. Mrs. Fenner is as American as Mrs. Marriott is English. I do not understand why Australia should be almost typically American, but all the Australians I meet might come from Chicago for any British peculiarities they show. They are quite as well acquainted with America, apparently, as with England, and have as many American faults as we have. Mrs. Fenner received us with the same pie-crust fluency and thinness that we know so well in Washington congress-women, and united the same delicacy of appearance with the same perfect self-possession which make our own social aristocracy preëminent....

July 15. We left Nailanga and the Mba river Monday morning, and steamed back past the coast we had already seen, until we came off the small village of Tonga-vere, and in trying to approach it, ran aground. As we were inside the reef, and on a soft sand, the running aground was no special matter, and we were not troubled with fears of being eaten, as Pembroke and Dr. Kingsley were, who were wrecked a few score miles to windward of us, and cautiously sailed in open boats in full view of all the settled islands, including Tairuni, where Sir John Thurston was then living, and of course eating Earls and Doctors daily with his kava. The joke was too good to be put into South Sea Bubbles, but Pembroke did lose his yacht, while we had only to tramp half a mile through mud at low tide in order to land at Tonga-vere, and establish ourselves in the guest-house among the mud channels of a small stream with no chance of a bath. These little coast villages have nothing but mangrove swamps to recommend them, and our errand there was not calculated to recommend us. This part of the coast is apparently the oldest and classic ground of Fiji where the venerable primitive God Dengue had his residence, and where the old ancestor-worship still clings even to the elders and communicants of the Church. Sir John stopped here to give the back-sliders a terrible wigging, and order a village to remove bodily to another residence where it should be made more civilised. Yesterday morning we walked a couple of miles back to see the wicked village, which was the usual score of huts with a mud ditch round it, and inspired no sympathy. In the mountains we inspected a house in which the old religion had lately been practised. Nothing about it was different from other houses except that from the centre of the roof hung eleven cords of sinnet with a basket at the end. The ancestors have been disgusted at their descendants for becoming Christians, and have left. The first object is to induce them to return, so the priest prays and makes offerings until at last the ancestors return and slide down their string into the basket. As far as this goes, the amusement is harmless, but the next step is to conspiracy, human victims, wars and general confusion; so Sir John puts them all in prison and they go to Suva and work "in the government service," as they say, for prison is an easy residence, and the natives rather like it. We brought several prisoners with us as carriers. The term of one expired last Saturday, but he said he should go along with the Governor still, and so he has. Generally they are in prison for some woman-scrape, for human nature in that respect remains quite independent of civilisation; but sometimes a whole batch gets shut up for heathen practices which are a form of sedition. Everyone knows that the natives are all Christians only in form; they try any sort of God that comes handy, on the idea that it can't do harm and may do good. The officials have to carry on a constant struggle to keep the heathen practices within bounds, and to me the contest seems quite humorous, for the natives are excellent at lying, and have no fixed principles more than a six-year-old child. Having settled that job, and passed a disagreeable night in a suspiciously dirty house, with little to eat and nothing to drink in the way of water, we left Tonga-vere yesterday at eleven with a mob of native Mboules, or chiefs, and their tails, on their return to the villages. We ran about twenty-five miles to the eastward as far as Viti-levu Bay. The coast looks bare, brown and mountainous, like Scotland. I cannot account for the difference between Fiji and the other South Sea Islands. Fiji is never soft or graceful. As La Farge says, it has insides. This northern shore is harsh, and at this season looks cold, for the trade-wind blows half a gale in our teeth, and our little steamer labors hard against it, while the men who are towed behind in open boats are nearly swamped and chattering with cold. We reached Viti Levu Bay at about half past four o'clock, and met there our companions Berry and Joske, who had tramped down through the mountains. We are all quartered in the big native house of Joni Mandraiarivi, John Sourbread, a nephew of old King Thackambau, who hung Joni's father, after the happy native prejudices of too near relationship; but Joni took to education and became a protégé of Sir John, who has raised him to the magistracy so that he is a sort of king. Here we pass a day; then on to Suva and Sydney....

July 25. Here we are at the New Hebrides Islands.... We left Fiji two days ago in the steamer "Rockton," which is a megatherium compared to the "Richmond," and is really a comfortable, tolerably steady ship of some fifteen hundred tons. Our last week in Suva was uneventful. Sir John was always kind and attentive; we were always indolent and dyspeptic — "dull dogs," as President Hayes once correctly described my friend Godkin and me. Lady Thurston did not arrive, as expected, but the day of our departure did, and we came on board the "Rockton" with little regret, for Fiji makes no appeal to sentiment. The Fijians are not sympathetic. They have been, till our time, about the most feelingless, ferocious brutes on earth, and Dahomey was a kind of Paradise compared with it. They look it....

July 31. Sydney at last. We got on shore at noon.

XVI

FROM SYDNEY TO PARIS

1891

To Charles Francis Adams

SYDNEY, 3 August, 1891.

I find on arriving here your kind letter of May 3, on the subject of St. Gaudens' figure.[1] It is natural that St. Gaudens should be nervous about the impression I might get of it, for I was myself so nervous about his success that I refused even to meet him from the moment he began the model, and persisted in the refusal till I left. As my friends are determined that I shall be satisfied with the work, I am at least relieved of a heavy anxiety on their account, though I can't help still looking forward with a little dread to my own first sight of it, not because I doubt that his artistic rendering of an idea must be better than my conception of the idea, but because the two could hardly be the same, and what is his in it might to me seem to mix badly with the image that had been in my mind. No doubt, time and familiarity with the work would set me right, but the first sense of a jar might be nasty...

As for La Farge, I am now dragging him to Liverpool like a truant, to ship him over to his poor son Bancel, who is scared out of his front teeth by the old man's prolonged absence. I had meant to put in another year here, to do the Malay Archipelago and India, before going up to China; but if I were to stay in the Malay Archipelago, La Farge would stay too, and kick square out of all traces; and though I should like no better than to keep on indefinitely as we have been going, I have enough bowels of mercy to wish not quite to ruin his poor sons. I want him, too, to do some more windows before he goes to perdition, and I have besides a comforting conviction that unless I mean to go wholly to pieces, I must get myself a little patched at Paris or New York...

[1] The monument in Rock Creek Cemetery, Washington, D.C.

To Henry Cabot Lodge

SYDNEY, NEW SOUTH WALES.
4 August, 1891.

Your letter of March 23 reached me on my arrival here a few days ago, which was more good-fortune than falls to the lot of some letters, which have never reached me at all, but must be cruising about the Pacific like Wandering Epistles of Hebrews. I hope they do not suffer from seasickness as I do.

Thanks for your summary, political and social. Since leaving America, I have taken again to reading American newspapers, and am wonderfully well posted on current topics. In the middle of the Pacific Ocean all things assume a curiously level grade of interest. The political and social status of a few half-naked Samoans, Tahitians and Fijians, seems just as important as the doings of Australia, the card-play of the Prince of Wales, or the speeches of Benjamin Harrison. I am far from assigning to each of these subjects even a relative standard of importance, but I am struck with the curious perspective which equalises the little with the big. For a year I have been living in communistic societies such as are the ideal of reformers, and such as I used to lecture about so learnedly. Samoa and Fiji are both of them almost pure communisms where private property is either unknown or disregarded. I found the system rather a pleasant one. On the whole, it suited me better than our own. It is intensely aristocratic, and gives enormous influence to the individual; it is indolent and pleasure-seeking; and it is perfectly indifferent to everything except women and war. Australia seeks to rival Polynesia with some success. The antipathy to work, and the love of amusement, are something like Samoa, and follow at a long distance the more perfect arrangements of Fiji; but I do not regard Australia as a success. It is neither one thing nor the other, and the people shirk work without getting real happiness in idleness.

On the whole I have been greatly entertained. The South Seas swarm with laughable satires on everything civilised, and especially on every known standard of morality. They flourished in outrageous defiance of every known moral, economical, social and sanitary law, until morality and economy were taught them, and then they went, promptly and unanimously to the devil. Nine in every ten perished of virtue, among all the islands and races, little and big; and they go on perishing with an unanimity quite conclusive. I do not undertake to draw a moral from their euthanasia. Only the wise draw morals, and I am one of the foolish, who grow foolisher every day, and less able to see six inches before their noses; but I suppose there is a moral somewhere. Evidently the savages needed legislation.

La Farge and I have just finished Fiji. Thanks to Governor Thurston whose guests we were, we saw it in a way new to travellers, and we know it, I think, nearly as well as we know the smaller groups of Tahiti and Samoa. As financial investments, none of the Pacific islands, except the Sandwiches, are worth touching. They are not worth any one of the West Indies, if you lumped them all together. In fact, they are worth less than nothing, for they require large expenditures. Nevertheless Germany, France, Australia, New Zealand, and the Lord knows what other countries and governments, are squabbling for the possession of these wretched little lava-heaps; and such is now the dead-lock that no one dare tell the Solomon Islanders to stop murdering and eating Englishmen.

The European in face of the tropics is a sweet study. He admits himself to be an abject failure there; he can make nothing of it; he can't work; he can't digest; he can't sleep; he gets disease, and he grumbles without ceasing; but he won't let anyone else go there. He bars the Chinaman, hates the negro, and keeps sharp watch on the Indian coolie. He won't let anyone alone. He can't keep his hands off of stray land, even though he can do nothing with it. I find no fault with him; on the contrary, he does only what he must do in the nature of nature; but what the deuce can he make of it?

On the whole, I am satisfied that America has no future in the Pacific. She can turn south, indeed, but after all, the west coast of South America offers very little field. Her best chance is Siberia. Russia will probably go to pieces; she is rotten and decrepit to the core, and must pass through a bankruptcy, political and moral. If it can be delayed another twenty-five years, we could Americanise Siberia, and this is the only possible work that I can see still open on a scale equal to American means.

Australia and New Zealand are not likely to change very much. They can go little further, for they have nowhere to go. Things are already fixed in grooves here, and the grooves are pretty shallow. I think they would do better on the long run, if there were no such thing as steamers or rapid communication. They might then develop character.

La Farge and I are going up to Paris. Not that we are at all tired of rambling, but that La Farge really must go home, and I am not disposed to travel alone. My future movements are uncertain, but my teeth need lots of attention. Give my love to your wife and Constance. Perhaps they will come over to see me, if I can't get to them. I don't suppose they hanker after a Presidential election much more than I do.

To Elizabeth Cameron

August 12, 1891.

Here we are, on the "Jumna"! but if you are an exact individual, and want to know where we are, I'm afraid you must consult a pretty good atlas. I know that the North Queensland coast is about a hundred rods ahead, and we are just slowing up to drop a mail at some small settlement which, on special inquiry of an officer, I learn is called Port Douglas. The captain tells me we are in 17° south latitude. I think we have come about two thousand miles from Sydney, or six thousand from Tahiti, which leaves eleven thousand still to do....

Our stay in Sydney, after my last big despatch was mailed, which is now hurrying to you by the southern route, offered not a particle of interest. Australia and the Australians bore me. They are second-rate United States, when viewed from the tourist's standpoint, and even if they were first-rate, they are not what I came to see. We were not expected. We had not an acquaintance, and were not anxious about making one. I was only eager to be off, and rejoiced hugely when at half past six o'clock on the evening of Thursday the 6th, we scrambled into our sleeping-car and started — Sewall, La Farge and I, with the *impayable* Awoki. Then at last I began to understand how huge Australia is. We travelled all night and all the next day — twenty-eight hours — more than seven hundred miles, through a country very like California, only to reach Brisbane, which, on the map, is next door to Sydney. At Brisbane we slept, and at noon, Saturday the 8th, we went aboard the steamer "Wodonga," and sailed — and sailed — and sailed — three days, until yesterday — Tuesday the 11th — at noon, we came to anchor off Townsville. Never mind what a deuce of a time we had in getting ashore, or how we lost a trunk, or what Townsville was like. Always California or Mexico! We did get ashore, and eat some native oysters, and got aboard a tender, and were carried out five miles to the "Jumna," and started north again at dark. On the whole, none of us have been more disagreeable than nature made us, unless I was a shade more offensive than usual; and, considering that our tempers were severely tried by the bad management of the steamers, this modified praise speaks loud in our favor. In one respect we are greatly pleased. The voyage is like steaming on a river. Not only are we always in smooth water, within the great Australian barrier reef, but we are generally behind islands, and both islands and coast are extremely pretty, especially in the soft sunlight. The weather is again warm, and grows warmer every day. The journey is a real enjoyment, barring the inevitable discomforts of travel. I wonder that I never heard of the charms of this route, but every charm has some blemish, and this particular amusement is tempered by what tempers so many of our best sources of virtuous happiness — its danger. Everyone on board, from the captain to the cook, is thinking of the "Jumna's" companion-ship the "Quettah," which tore out her bottom on a sharp rock in Torres Strait, and went down with all on board, except one woman who swam a week or two, and was saved. Another great steamer of the same line had the same fate before. Torres Strait, which we enter two days hence, is one of the most dangerous navigations in the world, but if the steamers risk it, we can, and since we have seen that Governor le Marquis de la Cascade of Tahiti, was wrecked in the Paumotus in the "Volage" on the trip to the Marquesas which he invited us to make with him, we think we have lost our chance of shipwreck. Anyway we sail merrily on, and as I am an oriental fatalist, I accept whatever is to be. Our fellow passengers are, as on the Atlantic, chiefly Jews. The rest are mostly colonials and uninteresting. One or two offer possibilities of humanity. We shall know more of them, perhaps, and, if not, then we shall do without. The sky is blue; the sea is green; the shore is opaline; and white clothes are a luxury....

Sunday, 16 *August*. We have been ten days travelling, by rail and steamer, and only a few hours ago got clear of Australia. That "Quettah" affair, which did in fact hurry considerably the ultramundane travels of the passengers, has to answer for delaying us twenty-four hours, for, when we approached Torres Strait, we pulled up every evening at dark, and anchored for the night. This was always my ideal of ocean travel, and as far as that sort of comfort is concerned, nothing ever equalled going to sea in Australia; but one's progress is slow. Our captain, who is a young man, commanded the "Quettah," and has spoken to me several times of his wreck. The ship struck and went down in three minutes, before anything could be done, but a boat of more or less naked people, hardly alive, got ashore the next morning, and the captain was among them. We passed the spot, and anchored near it, night before last. Naturally the captain does not hanker after hitting more unknown rocks in the night; and nothing is more possible, for the bottom is seldom more than one or two hundred feet deep, and a good-sized paving-stone on edge would be a danger. We did not clear the Strait until yesterday morning, and then we had to stop at Thursday Island, and pass the day taking pearl-shell on board. Thursday Island — our twothousandandfourhundredandfortyonth island — is the last outlying fragment of Australia. I suppose it is the limit of the Pacific ocean, and that, this side of it, we are perhaps in the Malay archipelago. New Guinea is only a couple of hundred miles to the northward, but as I'm not going there, I cared more about Thursday Island, which is the dreariest of dreary English settlements, on a bare burned shore of sand and granite, for all the world like New England in a July drought. We went ashore for the day. The Australian navy was there — seven gunboats just come out from England, and roaring regattas for the pleasure of the seamen and a score or two of whites who think they live here. "The second richest place in Queensland," said the indignant shop-keeper resenting some remark of Sewall's. Much pearl-oyster is fished up in or about these reefs, and every black scoundrel one sees slips out of his pocket a paper of pearls which he offers you for sale at prices which, for all that I know, may be dirt cheap, but are rarely worth the attention of one who does not know a good pearl from a bad one. La Farge and the females of the ship seemed to think none were good. On the other hand I was half tempted to buy the whole lot at a bargain, and try selling them in Paris. One or two smaller ones were good in shape, but I was told were off color. Generally the color is a little steely and hard; but I know not what color is right, and to my medieval-archaic mind the most ornamental pearls are the irregular ones, which leave something to the imagination. Of course, this taste is not only bad, but ignorant, foolish, extravagant, vicious, wicked and perfectly ridiculous; but I am not maintaining it against you; I do not suggest anyone's wearing barbaric pearls; and only in the recesses of the Malay Archipelago I venture to think that though I prefer women's necks to be round and white, I see no necessity for insisting that their ornaments should match. Anyway I bought no pearls, and was very weary of Thursday Island in a very brief time. Of all the dreary spots I have seen since August last I have seen nothing so depressing as Thursday Island; and all because of the settlement; for the islands at a distance are not bad, and the colors of the water are wonderful. We left there, deeply depressed, the only woman who interested me on our ship; a Mrs. Rowan, of Melbourne, very intelligent with paint and piano, and the nearest approach to refinement we have met among the antipodeans. She had taken a wild fancy for coming up here to meet her brother-in-law, Lord Charles Scott, who is admiral of the fleet; but when she saw the place, she nearly wept, and I think we could have induced her to go away with us to Batavia or anywhere else, had we been in search of adventures.

Friday, August 21. We have stopped for an hour or two at Bali, the island next to Java, and La Farge and Sewall have gone ashore in the boat, to see what they can, and to send a telegram to Batavia if possible. The place is pretty; a broad plain with a range of forest-clad mountains behind it, all seen through opaline haze. To my fancy the small Dutch town looks better from the water than it would probably look in its own light, and as its temperature, under an almost vertical sun, promises to be something cordial, I have preferred shade and the sea breeze. Our voyage has been encouragingly successful. By Sunday we shall have run off four thousand miles since Sydney; eight thousand since Tahiti; and, for the first time, a long voyage has been really pleasant. All the way from Brisbane we have been in calm water, like a river, with land generally in sight; perfect weather; divine moonlight; and, these last two days, grand volcanic mountains to watch as we ran by the long chain of islands on our left. I wonder that no one ever told us of the charm of this route, and I am still more astonished at my own gross ignorance, for until within six weeks or so I was still under the impression that Torres Strait was a path rarely used, and that no traveller ever came that way. Had I been told that it was an impassable labyrinth, I should have believed it. Instead, I find it the regular route of large steamers, and, except for a few awkward places, a perfect Paradise of navigation.... Sewall and La Farge have returned, and we are off again. They brought a peck of mangosteens aboard, and so I have eaten my first mangosteen, and accomplished half my object in going round the world. The other half — the durian — was not to be had here, but we are promised it at Batavia and Singapore. This is grand! Had I returned to America without eating the mangosteen and durian, life would have been unendurianable. I must have come back here to eat the durian and die. As for the mangosteen, it is certainly a good fruit — has admirable points, no doubt — but as yet I do not quite feel its poetic side enough to understand why it should be thought so supremely superior to the mango, our old staff of life. Probably further experience will enlighten my taste.

To Elizabeth Cameron

26 August, 1891.

We landed at the port of Batavia last Sunday (23d) at noon, and were received instantly by the custom house officers with an announcement that cholera had broken out, that it was likely to spread rapidly, and that we had better be careful. Both La Farge and I have run the gauntlet of cholera too often to be much affected by knowing its neighborhood, but I was deeply depressed by the thought of possible quarantines to face at Singapore, Ceylon and Naples or Marseilles. If we are caught in that way, we shall see Paris only in the wild winter. I was tempted to escape by returning on board the "Jumna" and sailing at once for Aden, but La Farge is so eager about Java that he is more likely to fling up all his duties and stay here, than to hurry away. If I were to announce to La Farge my intention of staying for two years in these parts, I am confident he would stay too, and let his affairs go to the dogs. I only wish his feeling for travel were a little more energetic in his own line, so as to leave some artistic record; but I have not seen him touch a brush since we left Tahiti, near three months ago, except for two or three trifling sketches almost worse than none. Luckily I am as conscienceless as he — more so, for he really does at times feel, or thinks he feels, remorse; whereas I long ago satisfied myself that no gratuitous aid to one's fellows results in anything but harm to them, and in supporting La Farge so long I am quite aware that he, not I, is the person at whose expense the journey is really made. In the long run, what costs me only a few thousand dollars, must cost him much that he lived for, and can never recover. Just now my plans happen to accord with his duties, so I shall drag him to Paris and send him home; but he will never forgive me. His delight with Java from the first glimpse of its Dutch marsh at Priok, the port, was much greater than mine. Hot, dusty, windy, we had to drive an hour over a fever-stricken marsh, along a ridiculous Dutch canal which gave one a mental somersault as though it were all a pantomime, and I was morose and gloomy as I am condemned to be, only more so; but La Farge was radiant with delight, and so he has been ever since, never tired, never complaining, and never even warm. Batavia amused him vastly, and it is really a droll place, as though the Hague had been overrun by hordes of Malays and Chinamen in a midsummer drought. I strolled out of our hotel that Sunday afternoon alone, for La Farge had gone out driving with Sewall; and luck led me to tumble into the Sunday afternoon performance of the military band. The scene was enough to compare with a full-dress reception at the Royal Academy in high-art days; and that was the funniest spectacle ever man saw on this small planet. Batavian life is not so queer as that, but the show was decidedly entertaining, especially the Malay coachmen in red liveries, with tall stiff European hats and cockades on top of turbans or powdered hair. The crowd was bright with colors and a sort of hotch-potch of races, but my only acquaintance was the eternal Jew fellow-passenger, a very respectable Cohen pair, with whom I had not exchanged so much as a bow on ship-board, but who were not resentful on that account. The next day, Monday, was almost wholly lost in getting our passages by the Messageries boats to Singapore and Colombo, but I was consoled to find that by schedule-time, we should reach Colombo by Septr. 7, which is well, and promises success. In the evening we all — La Farge, Sewall and I — came up by rail forty miles to Buitenzorg — Sans Souci — the Saratoga of Batavia. As I came round the world, as you have so often heard me say, only to eat two fruits, the durian and mangosteen, I thought it well to lose no time, and got our landlord at Batavia to send out and procure me a durian, which was brought me just before starting; a sort of spiked, pine-apple-shaped thing, slung in leaves. I had to take it with me, and the smell was very decided, though not even La Farge found it at first overpowering. If I ever write a roaring farce, I shall choose for my subject, not like Dumas the *Chasse aux Chastres*, but the *Chasse au Durian*. From the start we were in the worst social odor with the Dutchmen. The conductor informed us that the durian must go in the baggage-wagon, and bore it off with ill-concealed surprise at our tastes. We arrived at the hotel Bellevue at Buitenzorg. The landlord received us at best without enthusiasm, and showed us his rooms as though he would rather kick us than have us enter them, but when he caught sight of the durian among the luggage he burst into fury, and became as offensively Dutch as Limburg cheese, and far more so than the durian. As he talked in Dutch-German, with extreme roughness of voice and manner, and would not listen to any remarks or even apologies, but flatly forbade the durian and ordered it to be removed in state by the Malay servants; and as I make it a rule of never bandying words with — Dutchmen, we lost our durian and our tempers— or, at least mine — but we enjoyed the joke even of our landlord. Buitenzorg in the evening was cold and dreary, and as I felt enough insulted, I agreed with La Farge to come on to Garoet, some two hundred miles in the interior, a long railway journey of ten hours, starting at eight o'clock in the morning and arriving at six at night, or rather, at dusk. Sewall left us to join another friend going to Anjar, but La Farge and I actually came to Garoet yesterday, and probably return tomorrow. The two hundred miles of country was a total surprise to me, as usual. We were promised beautiful scenery, and I imagined something wild, dense and mountainous. Nothing of the sort. More or less distant mountains lined our track on both sides all the way, but they bore no tropical forest; the landscape was bare or slightly wooded, and burned, except in the valley and terraces where every foot of land was given up to rice. China cannot beat Java in cultivation. This island contains twenty-two million people, and down to the last baby they must all have worked on the terracing of these rice-fields. As I never loved a paddy-field, and easily tire of cultivation, I was soon weary. The villages were not much better. I expected signs of old civilisation, but not a bit. Not a temple or a shrine or a trace of thought; no architecture except huts less interesting than the Fijian or Samoan; no nothing. Only rice, and Malays as like as rice-grains; picturesque enough, but monotonous, Java seems to be a big factory of rice and coffee. Somewhere the people must have a life of ideas, traditions, dances, songs or art, and superstition or religion perhaps, but we have no time to seek it. On the outside, the Dutch have wiped out whatever trace ever existed of whatever could interest me. I never before met a people, least of all, Mahomedans like all these, who showed no sign of having even a sacred grove to worship. Java is Japan without everything that makes Japan interesting. La Farge of course wants to get all the photographs, cloths, silks, and costumes, he sees; but on that point, and as far as I know, only on that, his natural balance of judgment is wanting. He covets any rubbish he sees, because some day, as his imagination never fails to suggest, he may have to make a window filled with Javanese peasants hoeing rice-fields — or Japanese bar-maids washing parrots — or what you like. The passion approaches a *tic* with him. He conceals it from me now, because I have not concealed from him my opinion of it; but it has really nothing to do with the interest of the place he is in; it is only the interest of a possible picture in his fancy. I don't think Java would please him long, especially if he could not escape the Dutch. Meanwhile we have sent for durians, and have religiously opened and tasted them. The comedy was not closed by the eating. A somewhat dry, sweet rind round a horse chestnut smelling of bad cheese, is all I can make out of it. If I was not disappointed, I should laugh more than ever, for I cannot believe that what I have eaten is what Wallace described, though the description tallies in all but the supposed quality of the flavor. The mangosteen is delicious; a poem in fruit; a white sonnet of delight, shut in a lovely case of pink Japanese lacquer with a purple exterior like a small pomegranate. Truly the mango is but a coarse and common food compared with the refined and soul-compelling elevation of the mangosteen; but the durian will remain forever a mystery and a doubt.

August 28. We came back from Garoet yesterday to our Batavia hotel, and sail tomorrow morning for Singapore. At Garoet we had but one day, and were frozen at night. We saw the hot baths and the swarming people, and we had a little dance in the evening, when two very small dancing girls went through various meaningless steps to the music of four instruments, with singing that pierced the brain. We see Japan everywhere, but it is Japan without the fun, and the dancing was even more conventional than that of the Kioto Geishas. Luckily for us, we found a young Dutchman at the hotel, who spoke a little English and was civil and helped us. In Batavia we cannot get an interpreter or commissionaire or servant who understands any language, even Dutch, and we are at our wit's end to do anything. My idea of the Dutch is now fixed forever, and who do you think is my typical Dutchman? ———. I meet him everywhere, and he is odious; but yesterday, all through a very hot, dusty day on the railroad, we had the society of women of the Dutch species, and they were another revelation. A very distinguished middle-aged woman, evidently the wife of the Resident at Badong, overwhelmed us, with three daughters; all in one small first-class compartment, the only one on the train. I never understood how flesh could be pitchforked onto girls, till then; and how clothes could be stuck over the flesh. The effect of square corsets was wonderful. The four drank beer and eat hardboiled eggs or other refreshments at rapid intervals all day. They were innocuous, but superb specimens of Batavian grace. On the whole I want to see no more Dutch colonies. While willing to admit that the only ultimate object of our race is to be born, to feed, and incidentally to die, the world so organised fails to interest me, and industry devoted solely to that purpose is distinctly a bore. As our last experiment, we have once more tried the durian, and given it every chance in its favor; but to me the result is sadness, I cannot understand its merits, and it will remain, like the alligator pear, one of my solemn life-mysteries. Nevertheless, the object of my long journey is accomplished. Nothing remains but to return to the simple roses.

September 1. According to schedule, I should have reached Ceylon today; but I have not done badly in reaching Singapore yesterday morning. We had only two days of sea from Batavia, and always the tropic beauty of the Malay waters; no motion; warm weather, growing hot as we passed the equator; indolent days and nights on deck; plenty of room; and, as the steamer was French, a fairly eatable table. Sewall joined us again, and we had chance acquaintances — colonial, English, German and French; no Dutch. The parting from Batavia was not sorrowful; the arrival at Singapore was almost commonplace. A year ago La Farge and I were thrilled by excitement at reaching Honolulu, and now we are so hardened to novelties, that we hardly see a novelty in the most chaotic city in the world. Singapore would have fed our imaginations for a month if we had come here first, for it is a sink of races; a sort of eddy where the east and west whirl about in a wild particolored waltz, and Asia performs all her parts at once, on top of all. If you do not care what Singapore is, you can always utilise it for Martha's education; so tell her some day that if she were with me, she would see a big city beautifully laid out, on the water, with charming drives, and a famous botanical park, and any number of country-houses or cottages, like Beverly; and this fine English city is just crammed with Chinese, Malays, Hindus, and every kind of Asiatic creature, with turbans and without; with shaved heads, or long wild hair; with clothes of every imaginable color and kind, or with no clothes at all; and the streets sparkling with variety of colors, lines and movement, till one's eyes are tired of watching it; especially as the atmosphere is like a vapor bath. The Japanese are also here. The jinrickshaw skitters in every direction; humped cattle, or buffalo, draw the heavy carts and drays; Chinese houses, with their hollow roof-lines, show by contrast how good the Chinese architecture is; and a Gothic, stone church, with one or two bronze statues of English work, show how bad our art is. On the whole, as La Farge remarked on driving up yesterday morning, the chief use of such a place is to make one feel *how* bad artists we are. One always doubts a little in Europe or America, whether a statue, a picture or a building may not, after all, have some one good point that might save it from sweeping damnation; but here one *feels*, without reasoning or wasting time about it — that our art is wholly, in big and in small, artificial, and hopeless. One does not even care to discuss the matter. In a place like this, where one feels all or nothing, discussion is as bad as art. With all Asia dancing up and down before one's eyes, one has not superfluous energy enough to argue about London and Paris. As Sydney Smith said to Venables: by all means consider it damned, and go on with the story. The story is short, for we have less than two days here. Sewall led us into a dinner last evening at our Consul's. Probably you never heard of a youth from Idaho named Wildman,[1] who married a niece of Nevada Stewart named I forget what, but who was educated for the stage, and married Wildman. I had never heard of either party until I was led last evening into their house, and as I have eaten their curry

[1] Rounsevelle Wildman.

I will say nothing against them. Sewall says that Wildman is the damnedest fool living; but perhaps he exaggerates. Mrs. Wildman is not a fool — I guaranty. Perhaps the stage has left rather more trace on her make-up than is thought the best style in England, but the climate of Singapore is fatal to color and complexion, so that no reasonable gentleman can object to counter-agents. She was rather a startling revelation to me here in Singapore, and I watched her with some interest and curiosity; but I was foolish to accept her invitation, for I detest false relations, and any relations at all must be false, between me and Wildman. Yet I enjoyed the dinner; I liked the other guests — two or three gentlemen of the English colony; I laughed much, and talked more; and I drank champagne! Here is a list of half a dozen follies of which I am glad because they are true follies, though so small as to be useless for any sensible good or harm; but the trace of moral headache this morning is distinct, and takes a curious form, which seems to me, as well as I can think it out, to be a little entreaty repeating itself: Please, please, *please*, don't, don't, *don't*, paint your eyes!

Sunday morning, Sepr. 5. Ceylon in sight, and two thousand miles more run off since Batavia; ten thousand since Tahiti. Fairly more than half, at last; for London can hardly be more than six thousand miles ahead.... We left Singapore Tuesday evening on the Messageries steamer "Melbourne" with few passengers, and none, except Rajah Brooke,[1] that we knew. To the Rajah, Sir Julian had given me a letter, and I made his acquaintance at once. He is a quiet, rather shy man of sixty or thereabouts, and is alone. Apparently he has as little knack for acquaintance-making as we have. Our first two days were very fine and perfectly calm; but when we got beyond the protecting shore of Sumatra, and struck across the Indian Ocean, we quickly became acquainted with what is called the Southwest monsoon, which is uncommonly like our Southeast trade-wind in the Pacific, and blows so hard and dead ahead, as to make my life a burden even on this large ship.... Here is Ceylon, wrapped in mist or cloud mostly, and showing as little outline as she can; but still enough to tell me that by night I shall have forgotten the steamer, and shall have made acquaintance with my last island. This is triumph. I feel like a new incarnation of Krishna or somebody, when I think that I have really seen all those islands that I have told you about since this time last year. After this, if I can only return home contentedly, and help Cabot Lodge and Teddy Roosevelt to save the country, what more has life to offer? For

[1] Sir Charles Anthony Johnson Brooke (1829–1917), second rajah of Sarawak.

the soul of Siva, how many islands are necessary for me, if all these are not enough? All the same, oceans are a bore. I have nothing to tell you about the Indian ocean that differs from other oceans, which accounts for my having nothing to tell you at all. Everywhere the same watery blues and grays, and not even a fine sunset to amuse us. We are running just north of the equator, and the sun is directly over our heads, but it's a watery kind of sun, and has no merit but its watery heat. How I wish we had got at last to the Red Sea; there I would reflect on Moses and look out for Sinai; but a dismal ten days of monsoon lies between Ceylon and Aden.

To Elizabeth Cameron

Tuesday, September 8, 1891.

We landed at Colombo at eight o'clock Sunday evening, in a temper and with feelings of the most depraved sort. Although we were the only passengers to Colombo, the Messageries officers, stewards and all, totally neglected us, gave us no notice when, where or how to land, and after causing us to lose two hours of light, deliberately let us go off at last as we could, at our own expense, in a native boat, handling our own luggage, without apology, although our situation was again and again, with the utmost civility made known to them, with the request, not for aid, but only for information. I do not think we do this sort of thing in America, but it has happened twice to us since leaving Brisbane, and is, I think, the rule in the east. Steamers do not land passengers, but forget them. Had I been in my usual form, I should not have cared, but I had a cracking headache and a cold, and could not eat all day, and was exhausted by the moist heat, and generally felt more like a dead beetle than ever before I bade you goodbye. When we got to a hotel, I crept to bed, and tried to find a spot on my pillow where my head would lie without cracking open, and so dozed till morning with the prospect of the long-expected fever at last. In the morning the headache departed, but I was left very weak, and terribly oppressed by the damp heat of Colombo — a rice-field heat — which has made me think that if Bishop Heber had known more of the matter he would have made an improvement in his poetry, and would have altered it to: "What though the ricey breezes, blow damp o'er Ceylon's isle!" Spice, I know not, but Colombo is in a big rice-swamp, and I felt as though I were in a Turkish bath, and could not get out. All this was owing, I am sure, to something eaten on the "Melbourne" — I suspect the Camembert cheese — and to being obliged to pass the nights on deck with little sleep and no comfort. Steamers in the tropics are made just like steamers in Greenland. I have not yet seen one — except the American line to Australia — constructed with any reference to the passengers' comfort, or any means of making them comfortable; and if I could hang a few constructors, I would certainly do it in memory of the suffering I have seen them cause to women and children; but the stupidity of the European man is quite radiant, and no one proclaims it louder than the officers who are condemned to command European ships. Between French cheese and French cabins, my life was not worth taking; but my life is a trifle; and I wanted to take some Frenchman's when I saw what happened to others. A delicate little English girl, about Martha's age, was on board; colorless and thin, like all these tropic birds, but talking broken Malay, and rather interesting. On our last night on board, the heat in the cabin was great, the child was taken very sick, and while her mother was examining her, at the table in the saloon, by the light, the little creature fell flat on her face in a dead faint. She was not seasick, but exhausted; and the mother was not allowed to change cabins, or to have air, or to give the child any relief, though the ship was empty, until in a state of ferocity, she went to the Captain. She was howling furious about it, and I gave her what sympathy my sufferings tended to rouse.

Of course our first act, Monday morning, was to seek the Consulate, which I found at eleven o'clock in charge of a small native girl who was then sweeping it, but who seemed to divine my character, for she pointed to a pigeon-hole where I found letters.... Ceylon is certainly the most interesting and beautiful island we have seen, taking its many-sided interests into account. In one way, Hawaii is grander; in another, Tahiti is more lovely; but Hawaii is a volcano and Tahiti a dream; while Ceylon is what I supposed Java to be, and it was not — a combination of rich nature and varied human interest, a true piece of voluptuous creativeness. We have seen nothing to approach the brilliancy of the greens and the luxury of the vegetation; but we have been even more struck by the great beauty of the few girls we have caught a glimpse of; especially their eyes, which have a large, dark, far-off, beseeching look, that seems to tell of a coming soul — not Polynesian.

September 10. Kandy is pretty — very; and the surrounding country is prettier still, full of hills and valleys, flowers, elephants, palms and snakes. Monkeys are here also, but I have seen none wild. Another Paradise opens its arms to another son of Adam, but the devil of restlessness, who led my ancestor to the loss of his estate, leads me.

I cannot stay three days contented. Socially Kandy seems as impossible as are all these colonial drearinesses, and intellectually man is indubitably vile, as the bishop justly says. In all Ceylon I cannot buy or beg a book on the Ceylon art, literature, religion or history. Of all that has been published on India, not even a stray volume of Max Müller have I seen here, except in the little library of the Sacred Tooth, the Buddhist Temple where the true faith is now alone taught by aid of our master's Tooth, or Tusk — for it is said to be ivory. Of course we visited the famous temple at once, for here is now the last remaining watchfire of our church, except for Boston where Bill Bigelow and Fenollosa fan faint embers. The Temple — Dalada Maligawa, Palace of the Tooth — was a sad disappointment after the Japanese Temples. The art is poor, rather mean, and quite modern, and even the golden shrine of the Tooth had little to recommend it except one or two cat's-eyes. Occasionally a refined piece of stone carving — a door-way or threshold — built into a coarse plaster wall, shows where some older temple has been used for modern ornament, and gives an idea that Ceylon had refinement in the thirteenth century. Hence our tears, or rather our restlessness; for photographs tell us of immense ruined cities in the jungle, a day or two distant; cities as old or older than our æra, where Buddhism flourished like the wicked, more than two thousand years ago. To get there, we must travel day and night in ox-carts; but what of that? We swallow the oxen more willingly than the fevers, snakes, leeches and ticks, with which the deserted cities are said to be now inhabited. So we start tomorrow for Anuradhpura, and, if possible, for Polonnaruwa, and shall return only just in time to take our steamer, the seventeenth....

ANURADHPURA, *Sunday,* 13 *Sepr.* The ox-cart was funny, but not bad, if one must pass nights in these hot regions. We have come about eighty miles from Kandy, and have passed portions of two days inspecting this very sacred city, which is very much out of the world, in a burned jungle, with perfect roads, an excellent government inn, or Rest-house, and a poor native village, much fever-stricken, infested by jackals, with no whites except government officials in the whole district. I wanted to see the island, and this is it, I suppose, or at least the dry part of it, and sufficiently undisturbed by Europeans, of whom only a few travellers ever come here. I have looked through the inn-book, and found not a name known to me, during a record of eight or ten years; but, for that matter, since leaving San Francisco I have come across no one I ever knew before, so I could not count on finding them here. Yet Ceylon is a place where vast numbers of travellers come — or at least pass — and these ruined cities are the chief interest of the island; so they are visited by about one Englishman a month, thank Buddha, and praise to Siva and Vishnu, not even the photograph fiend is here. As for the ruins, they are here beyond question, and we have duly inspected them. Imagine a great plain, covered with woods. Dumped on this dry plain are half a dozen huge domes of solid brick, overgrown with grass and shrubs; artificial mounds that have lost their architectural decorations and their plaster covering, but still rise one or two hundred feet above the trees, and have a certain grandeur. Each of these dagobas represents an old temple which had buildings about it, stone bathing-tanks, and stone statues of Buddha, chapels and paved platforms decorated with carved or brick elephant-heads, humped oxen, lions and horses. When Buddha flourished here, two thousand years ago, vast numbers of pilgrims came to worship the relics supposed to be hidden under the dagobas, but still more to pray at the sacred bo-tree, which is the original shoot brought here more than two thousand years ago from the original bo-tree under which Buddha attained Nirvana. This then, was Anuradhpura; the bo-tree; six dagobas with relics; and one or two temples more or less Brahmanic, that is, rather for Siva or Vishnu than for Buddha, though Buddhism ran here a good deal into Brahmanism. As long as Buddhism flourished, Anuradhpura flourished, and the kings went on building tanks, both for bathing and for irrigation, some of the irrigation tanks being immense lakes, with many miles of embankment. When Buddhism declined, the place went gradually to pieces, and nothing but what was almost indestructible remains. Of course we cared little for the historical or industrial part of the affair, but came here to see the art, which is older than anything in India, and belongs to the earliest and probably purest Buddhist times; for Anuradhpura was the centre of Buddhism even then. I expected — never mind what — all sorts of things — which I have not found. To my surprise and disappointment, all the art seems to me pretty poor and cheap. Compared with Egypt or even with Japan, Ceylon is second rate. The huge brick dagobas were laid out on a large scale, with a sense of proportion that must have been artistic, but the want of knowledge or use of the arch makes the result uninteresting. The details are not rich; the stone carving is not fine; the statues are not numerous or very imposing even in size; and all the stone-work, even to the bathing-tanks, is so poorly and cheaply done, without mortar, rivetting or backing, that it can't hold itself up. I have hunted for something to admire, but except the bigness, I am left cold. Not a piece of work, big or small, have I seen that has a heart to it. The place was a big bazaar of religion, made for show and profit. Any country shrine has more feeling in it than this whole city seems to have shown. I am rather glad the jackals and monkeys own it, for they at least are not religious formalists, and they give a moral and emotion to the empty doorways and broken thresholds. Of course we went at once to the sacred bo-tree, which is now only a sickly shoot or two from the original trunk, and under it I sat for half an hour, hoping to attain Nirvana.... I left the bo-tree without attaining Buddhaship. Towards evening we got an ox-cart; a real cart with two wheels, and two slow, meditative, humped oxen, who are also sacred cattle, and who have the most Buddhistic expression in their humps and horns that ever was reached by God's creatures. The cart was hooped over with thatch, and we put two chairs inside, and were slowly driven by a naked Tamil, as though we were priests or even Hindu deities, through the woods, every now and then clambering out to inspect some stone tank or temple among the trees, and in secret deadly terror of ticks, leeches and cobras, not to speak of centipedes and scorpions. Dusk came on just as a family of monkeys scampered up the trees and jumped across above our heads. I felt no sense of desolation or even of remoteness; sensations have palled on me; but the scene was certainly new, and in a way beautiful, for the evening light was lively, and the ruined dagobas assumed a color that art never gave them. This evening we resume our travelling ox-cart, with the dainty little trotting oxen, more like deer than cattle; and travelling all night, we reach Dambolo in the morning, where we have to look at some rock temples. I have no longer any hope of finding real art in Ceylon; even the oldest looks to me mechanical, as though it were imported, and paid by the superficial area; but we want to be sure we have seen all the styles, and the rock-temple is a style. I would rather travel by night than by day, even when packed tight in a cart, with my boots sticking out behind. The moon is sweet, and the air exquisite, jackals and all.

September 15. Before leaving Anuradhpura, we had a dance, after the traditional style of Ceylon. Four men, ornamented with brass arm-plates, silver bangles, and other decorations belonging to their profession, and making music for themselves by thrumming small hand-drums, danced for us, before the Rest-house. They danced well, their training was good, and the dance itself was in a style quite new to us, with a good deal of violent physical exertion at times; but it did not interest me much, and I could see no trace of meaning in it;

not even the overlaid, solemn elaboration of Chinese or Japanese movements, which no one can any longer explain. We paid what seems here, among these terribly poor people, rather a high price for the show — fifteen rupees, or a little more than a sovereign; but we always encourage native industries. At about eight o'clock in the evening, our mail-cart came for us, and we started on the return journey. I think the night travel amused me more than the ruins did. The night air is pleasantly cool, and the moon was bright. We lay on our backs on a mattress, with just room — and barely — for us two. Our little white oxen, with their mystical straight horns, and their religious sacred humps, tripped along, sometimes trotting and sometimes running, their bells tinkling in the quaintest way; and the two wheeled cart, which luckily had springs, tipped about, as though it enjoyed the fun. I slept a good deal, smoked a little, and watched the moonlight on the road and the jungle. We did twenty-eight miles in seven hours, and reaching a Rest-house at three o'clock in the morning, where we had to change into a less comfortable horse-coach. We knocked up the keeper of the Rest-house, and while he boiled water and made tea, we sat in the dark on the porch, listening to the creak of ox-mills, and to the weird cries of the jackals, which seemed to fill the woods, and which are the uncanniest night-sound I ever heard. We were on the road again long before dawn, but at six o'clock we reached Dambolo, and climbed up to the rock temple, about a mile away. When we got there, the priest and the keys were away, and we had to send back for them, while we sat on the rocks and looked over miles and miles of forest jungle, to distant mountains. The cave temples were an exasperating disappointment, mean outside and stupid within. Not stupid, La Farge insisted, but priestlike; long rows of dirty cotton curtains ran round each temple, carefully hiding the statues, in order, no doubt, to extort money for showing them. The statues or figures have no merit as art, but are only conventional Indian Buddhas, sitting or reclining, and coarsely colored; their only value is as decoration, and of course their effect was not only lost but caricatured by concealing them. I think La Farge was angrier than I; but anyway I should not have cared much for the temples which are mere rough holes, without architecture or form. We hurried back to the Rest-house, and kept H. M.'s mail waiting for us till we had breakfasted; then at eight o'clock were on our way again, and at two in the afternoon were in Kandy, which seems deliciously cool and moist after the dry, hot, weary parchment of the plains. We like Kandy as much as though we were children, and it were assorted. The

walks and drives are charming, and the peace is almost as ideal as that
of Papeete.

The "Parramatta" went off last night, but we did not go in her.
When I try to explain even to myself how it happened that this
steamer, which we had taken every possible trouble to catch and with
which we had apparently nothing to do, except to go aboard, should
have managed to lose us, I am really puzzled. Everyone in the east
would say simply that I should not have tried to go by the P. & O.
which is the most unpopular corporation in the celestial system. Not
a good word have I ever heard man speak for it, and my own experience
fully bears out the prejudice. Yet the P. & O. people must have a certain genius, if they could get rid of passengers so firmly bound as we
were. No victim ever entered their slaughtering-pen more resigned
than we were when we went to the office yesterday. All we asked was
to know whether our cabins were comfortable and where they were to
be. The agent could tell us nothing except that the ship was empty;
eighty-five vacancies to some sixty berths occupied; but he had no idea
what special cabins were vacant; he made a rule not to keep plans of
the ships in the office, and therefore could not show me where the
cabins were, or what were their numbers or their sizes; his office would
close at five o'clock, and the ship would sail in the night. Not disgusted by this cavalier treatment, as soon as the ship arrived, at half
past three o'clock in the afternoon La Farge and I pulled out to her, a
mile down the bay, and went aboard. A less inviting steamer I have
read of, but seldom seen. An atmosphere of Scotch-English-Colonial
middle-class grime pervaded the ship and all its arrangements. Dirt,
clumsiness and stupidity were its only recommendations. All the
same, we got the steward, looked at the rooms, said to be vacant, selected two, and hurried back to the town. La Farge, as usual, was
very busy buying photographs, for which my hatred has now become
a real photo-phobia, and left me to secure the passages. I reached the
office just at five. The agent was closing his desk. I gave him the
numbers of the rooms chosen. He explained that both were otherwise
engaged, but I could have two neighboring ones. He had no ship's plan
to show where these were. I suggested that I could not make a decision
without consulting La Farge which would take ten or fifteen minutes.
He turned his back and went on locking his drawers. I turned my
back, and walked gently down stairs. Such is the tale. I admit only
to have been, after the first shock of surprise, excessively glad to escape from the P. & O. and its ships. This morning we mean to secure
cabins on the Messageries steamer "Djemneh" which sails next,

three days after the "Parramatta," and which will land us at Marseilles October 10. So we have three days more at Colombo, with nothing to do. I have already looked at all the cat's-eyes, and find none worth having at less cost than a thousand dollars, which would, I think, buy as good or better in London. No pearls; moon-stones by the bushel, but little different from *nacre*; and only what are called star-stones, or star-sapphires, rather amusing. I like all the stones that appeal to the imagination, like opals and cat's-eyes; and the Asteria, or star-stones, have to me the additional charm of not being in the fashion. Yet I enjoy looking at most gems, and really delight in buying them, except that the pleasure is too costly for my means.

September 27. Two thousand more miles run off — twelve thousand since Tahiti. I feel as though the journey were done, for we have seen the last of the Indian Ocean, and tonight we reach Aden. The voyage has been very quiet and pleasant, all but yesterday. The nights are hot — about 80 degrees — and I pass them mostly on deck. The steamer is the Messageries "Djemneh," an old boat, like the "Melbourne" but smaller. The passengers are few and usual. Some Dutch swine whom I am condemned to sit next; some Portuguese pecora; some French, as unsocial as myself; some English, rather better than common; and some hybrids. Their chief merit is that they are few and quiet. I read much; sleep much; and enjoy the fine weather and the tropic sea — although for that matter one sea is like another to me except in its good or bad temper. Our last days at Ceylon were rather thrown away. We went out for a night to a hotel on the sea at Mt. Lavinia; pretty and slow. We got a juggler who did tricks. I was very warm. *Voilà tout!*

September 29. I went ashore yesterday at Aden. La Farge and I telegraphed recklessly — ten pounds worth — all round the universe, to divert our minds from the heat. Aden should mean oven. Only the camels seemed baked enough to suit it. The sun hits one like a base ball. On board, my thermometer stood at 92° all night; but I was not in it — not much. I lay on a chair on deck where it was about 86°, with air, and very pleasant. I like the Red Sea today, though it is 91° without rest, and thirteen hundred miles long. The water is smooth, like a canal, which is just my style of ocean wave, and it is not red but blue, with porpoises, and now and then a bit of bare, baked rock, but generally no land in sight. Before dawn this morning the sailors fairly hunted me down below with their deck-washing, so I took a shower-bath in the dark, and, to my alarm, little fire-flies seemed to play all over me; but it was only phosphorus and didn't bite. We are all languid with the heat; but the sun is going to set soon, very soft and saffrony, as though it were gentle and childlike — fraud as it is — and we shall have dinner with champagne and ice and punkahs, and my Dutch hog on one side, and a poor Frenchman on the other, whose child died this morning, I think; for I passed the cabin at the time and caught a glimpse of that white horror which becomes so terribly familiar as life goes on; but on board ship no one is supposed to die. Nothing is said, and I do not venture even to ask. The family came on board only yesterday at Aden, and are not known to us.

Saturday, Oct. 3. We entered the Suez Canal at ten o'clock last night, and this morning at seven were stopped by a steamer aground ahead of us. The delay will cost us a day, I fear, but the weather is beautiful, the temperature charming, (80° in my cabin at two P.M. and 70° last night,) and we are patient, though very dull. If we get through by this evening, we shall still be in Alexandria tomorrow morning. This is our only excitement, and I note it only to bar reflections on my slowness.

Thursday, October 8. We should have reached Marseilles today, but our detention in the Suez Canal lasted twenty hours; we passed the greater part of Sunday at Port Said; reached Alexandria Monday morning at six; sailed again at half past eight, and for the last three days have run steadily ahead, with beautiful weather and a calm sea, until now we are well through another brace of thousand miles from Aden, and have but some nine hundred more to Paris. Last evening, after dark, we came through the straits of Messina which were like a French boulevard between the rows of gas-lights on either side. Tonight we pass between Corsica and Sardinia. Tomorrow afternoon at about five o'clock we should reach Marseilles. The voyage has been charming, though as quiet as a Pacific island. We have found no exciting society and nothing to tell about. I have read a volume a day, and thought abominably about the future, which will not arrange itself or let me alone. For the first time I am beginning to feel that the long journey, which seemed interminable, is really ended, and that all the old perplexities, with plenty of new ones, are going to revive. A whole year of vegetation in lonely corners of the ocean, where no social effort was required, and where I have not met one person whom I ever saw before, is shocking bad training for Paris and London. Poor La Farge has been my only victim, and on his sufferings I could look with a calm countenance, or even with a certain amount of sardonic amusement. Men are certainly the most successful invention the devil ever made, and when they arrive at a certain age, and have to be constantly amused, they are even harder to manage than when they are young, mischievous and tormenting.

MARSEILLES, *9th*. On shore at last. Perhaps I shall see you before you receive this closing despatch.

To Anna Cabot Mills Lodge

LONDON, 25 November, 1891.

Your modesty is at least as great as are your many other virtues, but I trust that all my friends may not imitate you, admirable though their model is, for in that case I should fare ill for correspondence, and should even be myself reduced to the painful inquiry whether anyone, cleverer at the work than myself, were among the envious crowd who compete to hear from you. Yet I'll not reproach you, for you have not yet arrived at the fascinating age. The mark of that period of life is when people become more interesting in pen than in person. Until then we all have the right to shirk letter-writing. Hay and I have arrived there, and must write, but you have much still to learn.

Of course I sympathised fully in your feelings about Constance. The truth is that in all the real trials of love, nothing can be said to any good purpose. One must bear or break, and the marriage of a daughter, even as young as Constance, has got to be borne. I could say nothing to make it easier, but I hope that by this time it hurts less.

You are all so lovely about wishing me back that I shall never dare come for fear of diminishing my popularity. If I were wildly amusing myself by travel, I should feel horribly selfish and heartless, but the single merit of travel is that it offers a variety of ways of boring oneself, whereas at home one is reduced to boring one's friends. I can at a pinch endure my own sufferings, but I cannot bear inflicting them on others. The English, when bored, kill something. I always feel as if I, too, were putting up a grouse or a pheasant when I stalk a friend to inflict my dreariness on him. I am sure that I caused Hay's collapse by this kind of diabolic chase.

If Hay really proves to be seriously ill I shall come home to be with him, but I hope the autumn will restore his strength, and that now, as before, his weakness will turn out to be nervous. Perhaps my hesitation to return is partly due to the fear that I might make him worse rather than better. What I seriously prefer is that all the family should come over here next summer, and take a princely establishment somewhere within reach of London, for which Hay should pay, and which should provide amusement for all the husbands — if Cabot could reconcile himself to anything English beyond reach of presidential elections — while I should be properly and suitably petted and cared for by all the wives. Surely this is a modest want which you will all be glad to gratify, and I have only to suggest it in order to secure an immediate adoption of the idea.

In the meanwhile I am not too excessively bored by London, which seems uncommonly homelike and foggy. At times I admit that everything is intolerable, but at other times I find a certain amount of society, and a few old friends who are not wholly decrepit. Most of them too have become somewhat more pessimistic than I myself, and make me feel hopeful in comparison. They assure me that art, religion, literature, philosophy and poetry are all as dead as Achilles and Agamemnon, and can never revive, in short they are *plus fin de siècle que les plus fins* (*de siècle*), and see nothing before mankind except infinite ennui diversified by vice. As I have found a way out, I listen with patience, for, like Sturgis Bigelow, I have taken to religion. For your life don't betray me to him, he would never quite forgive me; for, finding Buddhism a trifle flat and unsatisfactory, I have become a Brahmin and, like Krishna Mulvany, am going on for a new avatar. We shall come to it some day, and what a pity it is that we cannot make my dear cousin the Bishop our new incarnation of Brahma! He looks it so well.

You will have heard all possible news of me long ago. Since the Camerons went home, nothing has happened. Deserted by them and by La Farge, I exist in a solitude indescribably dreary, brightened at times by flashes of hope. Duty calls me back to Asia, and sooner or later that destiny will accomplish itself, for Brahma waits me, but pleasure calls me home, and what to decide I know not. You happy creatures, who can get the meat and drink of eternal life out of a presidential election — why can't you give it to me? Just elect me member of Congress, and see what credit you will do yourselves! Give me an office! Everyone that has an office is all right, and I feel quite sure that if I had an office I should live happily ever after. Hay and I are both dying for no other reason than that we are not made to go to our office every day, and write letters to people who have not got offices but want them.

Yet I should worry on very happily if I had you and the rest of the family over here to amuse me, and I think you all very selfish not to come. Perhaps you might have some plausible excuse for not going with me to the South Sea Islands, but you can have none for leaving me alone here. If I were myself acting selfishly in staying here, you might have some defence, but I am here solely for your good, for I came all this way in search of a new young man to take the place of Spring Rice now grown up. New young women are always on hand, in thirty years I have never known them to fail, but a new young man is the rarest of game. For near a month I have searched, traveled, inquired, advertised in *Truth* and the *Saturday Review*, to no purpose. I can hear of no new young man, and I am regularly planted, for, without him, life is quite too too utter. I can neither go to Asia nor go home till I have found him; when found, his looks shall be my care; I will brush his clothes and pay his tailors, yet even this does not produce him.

Love to Cabot and Mr. Blaine, as well as to Mr. Reed (whom I am not so intimate with as I am with the other two); also to Constance to whom I sent a little remembrance through Mrs. Cameron, which has probably by this time reached her. I should have sent one to you, but was afraid Cabot would think it the mark of a trifling and negative mind, and would not permit you to receive it. Yet it was pretty nice, all the same, and I was sorry you missed it. London still has some fairly nice things in it, though the supply does not increase.

To Elizabeth Cameron

PARIS, 29 December, 1891.

· · · · · · · · · · · · · · · · ·

To change the atmosphere I went down to the table-d'hôte, which is ghastly but quick; and hurried off to the Opéra Comique to perform an act of piety to the memory of my revered grandfather. Some people might think it a queer place for the purpose, and the association of ideas may not be obvious even to you, but it is simple. A century ago, more or less, Grétry produced his opera, Richard Cœur de Lion. A century ago, more or less, President Washington sent my grandfather, before he was thirty years old, as minister to the Hague, and my grandfather was fond of music to such an extent that, if I remember right, he tried to play the flute. Anyway he was so much attached to Grétry's music that when he was turned out of the Presidency he could think of nothing, for days together, but "*Oh, Richard, oh, mon roy, l'univers t'abandonne*"; and as I had never heard the opera, I thought I would see it now that it has been revived at the Opéra Comique. Nothing more delightfully rococo and simple could well be, than the music of Grétry. To think that it was fin de siècle too — and shows it in the words — and led directly to the French Revolution. I tried to imagine myself as I was then — and you know what an awfully handsome young fellow Copley made me — with full dress and powdered hair, talking to Mme. Chose in the boxes, and stopping to applaud "*Un regard de ma belle*." Unluckily the Opéra Comique, which used to be the cheerfullest theatre in Paris, is now to me the dreariest, and poor Richard howled mournfully as though time had troubled him. Unluckily for me, too, the next piece was the Lakmé by Delibes, modern enough, no doubt; but if I abhor the French more in one genre than in another, and find their fatuity more out of place in any other part of the world than in that where I happen to be, my abomination of them is greatest when they try to escape from themselves, and especially when they become oriental. I forgive them for making me wring my teeth with despair at their Greeks and Romans, their English and Americans; but I cannot stand them when they get south of Marseilles and the Suez Canal. After sitting through a baya-dère dance that ground me into the dust, I came away with the last verse in my ears: "*Dieu protège nos amours!*" As far as I can see, this is all God has to do in Paris anyhow....

4 *January*. Luckily I have exhausted all the Paris I can do single-handed, and can devote myself conscientiously to reading. I call it a poor day when I don't finish at least one volume. Imagine my state of happiness, surrounded by a pile of yellow literature, skimming a volume of Goncourt, swallowing a volume of Maupassant with my roast, and wondering that I feel unwell afterwards. These writers have at least the merit of explaining to me why I dislike the French, and why the French are proper subjects for dislike. Even I, who do not love the French, and who, as you know, have never been able even to swallow my friends' Frenchmen, should hesitate to believe that human nature, except in the Solomon Islands, could be quite so mean and monkey-like in its intellectual cruelty as the naturalists and realists describe their fellow-countrymen to be, unless I read every day in the police-reports the proof that they do not exaggerate. At every interval of years I come back here with a wider experience of men and knowledge of races, and always the impression becomes stronger that, of all people in the world, the French are the most gratuitously wicked. They almost do me good. I feel it a gain to have an object of dislike. At least that is real, and I can kick it. Next to having an object to like, I am duly grateful for having an object to detest....

January 7. In my journey of eighteen months round the world, among the remote and melancholy islands where I have been for four months at a time imprisoned, unable to escape, never have I felt

anything like the effect of nightmare that I have got from four weeks
in Paris. Talk about our American nerves! they are normal and
healthy compared with the nerves of the French, which are more diseased than anything on earth except the simple Norwegian blondes
of Mr. Ibsen. In all Paris — literature, theatre, art, people and
cuisine — I have not yet seen one healthy new thing. Nothing simple,
or simply felt, or healthy; all forced even in its effort to be simple —
like Maupassant, the flower of young France — all tormented, and
all self-conscious....

THE END

anything like the effect of nightmare that I have got from four weeks in Paris. Talk about our American nerves! they are normal and healthy compared with the nerves of the French, which are more diseased than anything on earth except the simple Norwegian blondes of Ibs. Ibsen. In all Paris — literature, theatre, art, people, and cuisine — I have not yet seen one healthy new thing. Nothing simple or simply felt, or healthy, all forced even in its effort to be simple — like Maupassant, the flower of young France — all tormented, and all self-conscious....

THE END

INDEX